The
City of Mexico
in the
Age of Díaz

The
City of Mexico
in the
Age of Díaz

by Michael Johns

UNIVERSITY OF TEXAS PRESS, *Austin*

Library of Congress
Cataloging-in-Publication Data

Johns, Michael, 1958–
    The city of Mexico in the age of Díaz /
by Michael Johns. — 1st ed.
        p.   cm.
    Includes bibliographical references and
index.
    ISBN 0-292-74047-6 (cloth : alk. paper).
— ISBN 0-292-74048-4 (pbk. : alk. paper)
    1. Mexico City (Mexico) — History.
2. Díaz, Porfirio, 1830–1915.   3. City
and town life — Mexico — Mexico City —
History — 19th century.   4. Social
conflict — Mexico — Mexico City —
History — 19th century.   5. Mexico
City (Mexico) — Economic conditions.
I. Title.
F1386.3.J6   1997
972'.530814 — dc21   96-44570

The human, the social question [is] always dogging the steps of the ancient contemplative person and making him, before each scene, wish really to get into the picture, to cross, as it were, the threshold of the frame. It never lifts, verily, this obsession of the story-seeker, however it may flutter its wings, it may bruise its breast, against surfaces either too hard or too blank. "The manners, the manners: where and what are they, and what have they to tell?"—that haunting curiosity, essential to the honor of his office, yet making it much of a burden, fairly buzzes about his head the more pressingly in proportion as the social mystery, the lurking human secret, seems more shy.

—Henry James, *The American Scene*

CONTENTS

The
City of Mexico
in the
Age of Díaz

CHAPTER I

City & Nation

The entire man is, so to speak, to be seen in the cradle of the child.
The growth of nations presents something analogous to this; they all
bear some marks of their origin.
— *Alexis de Tocqueville*, Democracy in America

The Aztecs left fragments of their shattered society, from the corn cakes and adobe huts of the peasants to the death cult that stained the sacrificial temples that rose high above their imperial capital of Tenochtitlan. The Spaniards quickly vanquished that sanguinary empire, immediately imposed a new language and a new religion, and slowly introduced private property and production for profit, modern ways that they themselves were just learning from their more advanced European neighbors. For three centuries colonial rule worked to meld Christian and pagan beliefs into an idol-worshiping Catholicism that still reveres saints, virgins, and bloody crucifixes. It herded peasants onto haciendas that fed the cities and silver mines of New Spain and that now export fruit and vegetables to Texas and California. And it blended Indian and Spanish blood into the mestizo — the "half-breed" who was to become the archetypal Mexican.

Yet the traits of that national type did not coalesce into their modern form until late in the nineteenth century. The best accounts of Mexico City during the 1840s and 1850s — Manuel Payno's *Los bandidos de Río Frío*, Guillermo Prieto's *Memorias de mis tiempos,* and Fanny Calderón de la Barca's *Life in Mexico during a Residence of Two Years in That Country* — depict early forms of Mexico's exaggerated courtesy, describe the mestizo's emergence as a dominant racial and cultural type, regret the presence of wretched Indians and their adoration of the Virgin of Guadalupe, and detect the looming influence of Mexico's northern neighbor.

I

But Payno, Prieto, and Calderón de la Barca, like the novelists of the 1850s and 1860s, who merely translated the mannerisms and mores of French society into a Mexican setting, did not see the traits they described as forming a coherent Mexican character. Neither did Ignacio Altamirano, an important liberal thinker and early promoter of nationalism in Mexican letters, or Lucas Alamán, a leading conservative historian. Each, in fact, lamented his country's lack of a national character at mid-century. To Altamirano, "the cult of the Virgin is the only thing that unites us. If we lose it, we will lose our Mexican nationality" (all translations are mine unless otherwise noted). In his 1852 *Historia de Méjico*, Alamán wrote this about a country that had fought a destructive battle for independence in the 1810s, ruined its economy with thirty years of civil war, and suffered a humiliating defeat by the United States in 1847:

> To think that in just a few years we have lost so much of our land [to America]; that our country is bankrupt and in debt; that our valiant army was crushed and has left us defenseless; and above all that we have lost all sense of public spirit and thus any concept of national character: there are no Mexicans in Mexico, a nation that has leapt from infancy to a state of decrepitude without ever knowing the vigor of youth, a nation that has shown no signs of life other than violent spasms.[1]

The traits that emerged over three centuries of colonial rule, and during the two tumultuous generations that followed independence, were shaped into a national character by the advanced machinery of economy and state that could develop only when Mexico attached its fate to a growing world market driven by the United States and western Europe. Railroads, ports, and markets tied the country together economically and generated the wealth that allowed Porfirio Díaz to rule his country, between 1876 and 1911, under the banner of "Order, Peace and Progress."

The dictator delivered all three. He built a government based on the rule of law — a pliable rule of law, but a marked advance over the legal and political anarchy of the two generations preceding his regime. He brought thirty-five years of peace to a country whose independence had touched off six decades of sporadic civil war interrupted only by an American invasion (in the late 1840s) and a French occupation (in the mid-1860s). And he guaranteed that peaceful order with a mounted guard in the countryside and a huge police force in the city.

Peace and order meant progress: Mexican entrepreneurs and foreign capitalists modernized the communal lands and refurbished the mines that now produced raw materials and foodstuffs for Mexican, American, and European markets; Mexico City's merchants and landowners spent most of the wealth produced in the countryside acquiring the culture that let them pose as Europeans; and the government used the rest to organize the ministries that paved the capital's streets, drained its valley's waters, and erected its public buildings.

Within a decade of Díaz's first administration the fragments of Aztec, Spanish, and early Mexican society were being fused by steady markets and a stable government. "Finally," wrote a city paper in 1883, "the Mexican people are coming out of their state of separation and isolation to prepare a dignified celebration of national independence."[2] The Mexican people, in other words, were acquiring a national character. If the pace was quick, the effect was lasting: basic traits that were then acquired, and existing ones that were then solidified, still make a Mexican a Mexican and not someone else. Go to Mexico today, or read about it in the papers, and you will instantly recognize the ideas, the images, and the behaviors of a century ago.

If the age of Díaz was the critical time in the making of the Mexican character, the capital was the central place. Although Mexico's is a profoundly rural culture, as parts of a national character its country ways were first expressed in the capital city. What the paternal, despotic landowner was to his peons, Díaz was to his people, and during his rule Mexico City became home to two hundred thousand peasants who had lost their lands, but not their country ways. The city also was a mecca for the provincial writers and artists who through their paintings and novels brought images of the hacienda, the peasant, and the Indian hamlet to national attention.

Yet the capital was not a passive recipient of the customs and people of rural Mexico: it helped fashion the countryside it came to embody. Mexico City built the commercial and transport systems that tied distant regions to the center. It appointed political henchmen to run the provinces, and if they were loyal let them profit from the new laws they were sent to enforce. It mounted the *rurales*, the rural police, to patrol the countryside and keep the peace. It spread its official heroes throughout the land, idols like Cuauhtémoc, the valiant Aztec warrior; Miguel Hidalgo, the inspired martyr of independence; and Benito Juárez, the stern founder of the modern state. And it represented Mexico before the world—which meant France, England, and America. The capital's upstart gentry adopted the manners of Europe, and they welcomed the Old World's divas and politicians, thanks to fortunes seized from the mines, valleys, and highlands of their enormous and bountiful country.

National character is not a thing we can point to and say, "There it is." It is not a symbol, a government, or a psychological condition.[3] It is a "design for living" that instructs a people how to work, play, and love; wield power, take offense, and get justice; exercise rights, assume responsibility, and respect rules; see their history, honor their word, and treat the opposite sex.[4] That design shapes the lives of all Mexicans, even if its exact color or material varies according to who or where they are within it, even if much of it was stitched together by a small group of powerful people, and even if pieces slowly fray and need repair and replacement.

The idea of examining a people's character may seem presumptuous in an age that tends to mistake appraisal for injury and is often too quick to brand judgments as racist, sexist, or ethnocentrist. Many will flinch at the idea that a nation has essential features that were acquired at a key moment in its history. But a nation's character, like a person's, endures; and we can better discern the possibilities for progress by acknowledging the tenacity of that character and by identifying parts of it that *can* be altered.

Mexicans are now searching for a new type of what they call *forma*—a formula or template that gives order to their society. Mexican history has been a constant search for *formas:* the civil wars that followed independence were a costly and vain attempt to make a nation; Porfirio Díaz ended the fighting and used his dictatorial powers to give his people a modern state; a revolution defeated his tyranny in the name of democracy, land, and liberty; since then one party, the Partido Revolucionario Institucional (PRI), has run the country in a style known as "collective Porfirism." Opposing parties are now crying for fair elections, just as upper-class insurgent Francisco Madero did in 1910. Light-skinned prophets wearing army fatigues and ski masks have adapted Zapata's revolutionary slogan to demand "liberty, justice, and democracy" for Maya Indians in Chiapas. Intrepid journalists write about the *judiciales,* the judicial police who terrorize today's Mexicans with the same impunity that Díaz's *rurales* did a century ago. And Mexicans still see their past as the deeds of individual men rather than the development of larger themes like democracy, civil rights, or even class struggle. That is because politics today is much like that of a century ago: the power of the man prevails over the force of the law. Mexican history is not simply repeating itself. The national character, I am suggesting, has barely changed since the age of Díaz.

I begin with a tour of Díaz's city. By 1890 the capital had acquired the principal geographic feature that defines it to this day—a division into a rich west and a poor east. Late last century peasants began flocking to the city to live in shacks and tenements on the east side's unpaved and sewerless streets, and the affluent and their government began to spend their rapidly growing wealth on the west side. By 1911, Díaz's last year in power, the near west side housed all of the city's treasures. Reforma Boulevard, Alameda Park, the Palace of Fine Arts, and the new post office each meant to declare Mexico's entry into the league of modern nations, and its aristocracy's admission to the ranks of refined peoples. I describe the rapid economic growth and the divided geography of the city and introduce several themes that appear again in later chapters: the effects of the great distance that separated the upper class from its lower and middle orders; the struggle of the wealthy to develop standards of taste for the European goods they were consuming in large quantities; and the creation, through statues on Reforma, of a convenient history that helped a new ruling class and its government understand themselves and their young country.

The provincialism betrayed by the metropolis, I'll show in chapter 3, was more than a simple result of peasants heaped into vast slums, or of the unseasoned gentry trying to shine with European polish. Educated Mexicans admired Paris, London, and New York. Yet they knew, in their hearts, that Mexico was the capital of a peasant land, and that the character of that land lay in the cornfields, the haciendas, and the hamlets. That character necessarily infused the big city. It was revealed in the awful sanitary conditions of the capital, especially on the east side; in the drinking of *pulque*, the ancient Aztec beverage that was as dear to the masses as it was vile to the upper classes; and in the many tens of thousands of ragged peasant migrants, known as *pelados*, whose mere appearance in the downtown could ruin a rich person's outing to a cafe, boutique, or department store. Could the capital assimilate the *pelados* and become an urbane, integrated, and cohesive city? That question exercised the capital's thinkers, who felt that their country, in contrast to Europe and America, and to Chile, Uruguay, and Argentina as well, was weighed down by a rural culture burdened by centuries of poverty, ignorance, and oppression.

The Aztecs are famous for making human sacrifice their society's chief ritual. The "religious frenzy had to be stopped," wrote Justo Sierra, Díaz's education minister; "blessed were the cross and the sword that finished it."[5] But the savagery was replaced by harsh colonial rule. And the war of independence that ended Spain's authority in the early nineteenth century incited two generations of civil strife. Díaz stopped the fighting, but not the violence, which turned into a smaller-scale, grinding sort of cruelty. In chapter 4 we'll look at the mistrust and the violence, and how they were played up symbolically in many ways, such as a craze for bullfighting, elaborate funeral ceremonies, the burning of Judas effigies during Easter week, and macabre celebrations of the Day of the Dead. Practically, they were expressed in what became the unspoken credo of city life: "For the Mexican," writes Octavio Paz, "life presents the chance to *chingar* or to be *chingado*." Translated roughly, this means "to punish, humiliate, and offend, or suffer the inverse."[6] Perhaps no other city in the Americas combined such high levels of mistrust and violence with a penchant for the images and rituals of blood and death.

The extreme separation of the classes, the crudity of a city whose wealthy sought refinement, the ubiquitous mistrust and the intensity of violence all pushed the Mexican's life into gaps between the spoken word and its actual meaning, between the city's hygienic and criminal codes and the reality of its housing stock and police system, between the pomp and circumstance of state and the raw power of politics. Díaz, for instance, won the presidency in 1876 on the slogan of "no re-election" and then had a servile Congress revise his own amendments to the 1857 Constitution to legalize his seven terms in office. He was a *caudillo* who fought his way into power and ruled despotically. But he was also his country's first real president: he ruled with coercion and force and, like his successors in the PRI, he did so behind a veil of fraudulent elections, pliant congresses, and sham courts. No other Latin American country combined the oppression of dictatorship with such an obsession for the appearance of legality and legitimacy. That fetish, I'll show in the last chapter, was one example of a Mexican penchant for giving the form or the appearance of an institution or a behavior while neglecting its substance.

The chasm between rich and poor, the rustic nature of the city, the rancor and the discord, the stress on appearance over substance — these did not make for a safe, elegant, dispassionate, or well-ordered national character. But there may be a point in Schopenhauer's hyperbole: "National character is only another name for the particular form which the littleness, perversity and baseness of mankind take in every country. If we become disgusted with one, we praise another, until we get disgusted with this too. Every nation mocks at other nations, and all are right."[7]

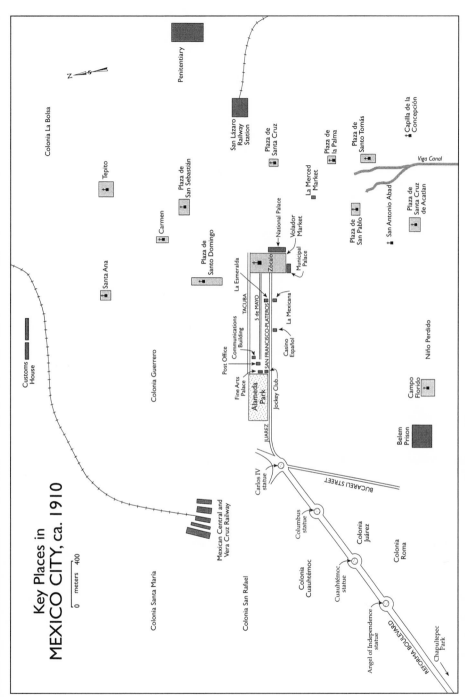

Key places in Mexico City, circa 1910. Courtesy of Cherie Semans

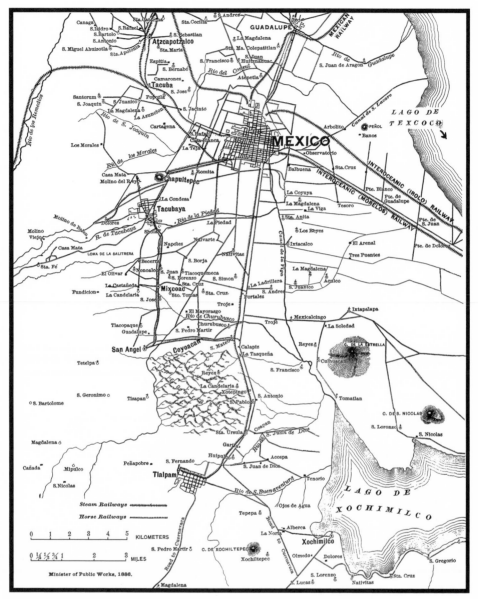

The environs of Mexico City

The west side of the Zócalo.
Courtesy of the Instituto Nacional de Antropología e Historia

Palacio Municipal de MÉXICO

Municipal Palace, circa 1910.
Courtesy of the Archivo General de la Nación

La Mexicana life insurance building.
Courtesy of the Archivo General de
la Nación

La Esmeralda jewelry store.
Courtesy of the Archivo General de
la Nación

The Jockey Club. Courtesy of the Archivo General de la Nación

Colonia Juárez. Courtesy of the Archivo General de la Nación

Independence Day on Plateros Street.
Courtesy of the Instituto Nacional de Antropología e Historia

Porfirio Díaz waving the flag.
Courtesy of the Instituto
Nacional de Antropología e
Historia

El Presidente at the races.
Courtesy of the Instituto
Nacional de Antropología e
Historia

Rurales dispensing justice.
Courtesy of the Instituto Nacional de Antropología e Historia

A toast. Courtesy of the Instituto Nacional de Antropología e Historia

Effigies of Judas waiting to be exploded.
Courtesy of the Instituto Nacional de Antropología e Historia

Pelados and street sellers. Courtesy of the Archivo General de la Nación

A street market. Courtesy of the Instituto Nacional de Antropología e Historia

A flower market. Courtesy of the Archivo General de la Nación

A covered market. Courtesy of the Archivo General de la Nación

An uncovered market. Courtesy of the Archivo General de la Nación

The country in the city.
Courtesy of the Instituto Nacional de Antropología e Historia

Fetching water. Courtesy of the Instituto Nacional de Antropología e Historia

Young beggars in front of the cathedral.
Courtesy of the Instituto Nacional de
Antropología e Historia

A letter writer. Courtesy of the Archivo General de la Nación.

East & West

There is a very marked difference between East and West Mexico.
The former is old, somber, narrow, and often winding and always
dirty, with miserable alleys, deserted and antiquated squares, ruined
bridges, deposits of slimy water, and paltry adobe houses inhabited by
squalid persons. The West is modern and cheerful with open streets
drawn at right angles that are clean, carefully paved and full of shady
parks, gardens, and squares; there is good drainage and the elegant
houses, though at times in the worst architectural styles, are costly,
neat, imposing, and modern.
— *Manuel Torres Torija, "Ciudad de México"*

By the turn of the last century, the Zócalo was the heart of
a city that had become the soul of a nation. The great plaza was enclosed by
buildings that had been raised, remade, and restored throughout three centuries of colonial rule. A wide street sketched a square just inside the four
walls and framed an interior park crowded with trees, fountains, and band
shells. Carts and hacks loaded with goods and people rattled in and out of
the plaza on nine intersecting roads. Empty carriages waited for passengers
in front of a small trolley depot. They parked between the west side street
and the rails that angled into the plaza from each corner and then split off
into several parallel rows that traced smaller squares some twenty feet inside
the quadrangular avenue. Streetcars trundled in and out of the plaza every
minute or so, snatching electricity from a buzzing canopy of poles and
wires. If the scraping and crackling of an approaching car failed to warn a
plodding cart or a dawdling pedestrian, its shrill bell might. Even so, acci-
dents were frequent, especially around the crowded cathedral.

Ragged Indians and poor mestizos wandered in and out of the church in
search of solace, a sign from the Virgin, or handouts from rich believers.

7

Others hawked toys, candy, and pornographic postcards. Pretty girls licensed to sell government lottery tickets might offer to "kiss the ticket for good luck." Prayer books, legends, and images of the disciples were peddled around the cathedral's atrium. But once inside the doleful narthex all commerce, except for pickpocketing and purse snatching, ceased under the watchful eyes of gargoyles, saints, and Jesuses who peered from chapels, confessionals, and their perches atop lavish altars.

As worshipers returned to the plaza through the church's great doorway, the dankness gave way to the fragrances of roses, violets, and carnations. The scents were especially strong in early morning, when dozens of women quitting first mass were lured to the outdoor flower market along the church's western wall. By noon the bouquet of withering blossoms had given way to the cloying smells of cakes, candies, and sugared drinks hawked from neighboring stalls.[1]

No other place concentrated the history, the power, and the peoples of Mexico like the Zócalo. The plaza was, first of all, the symbolic and, in some ways, the literal, repository of Mexican history. After the Aztec capital Tenochtitlan was vanquished, it was destroyed: its causeways were buried, its canals filled in, its temples rebuilt as churches. Interred beneath the great square, in a kind of subterranean museum, were the crumbled palace where Cortés had held Montezuma prisoner, a corner of an Aztec ball court, part of a sacrificial temple, and the sundry accessories of luxury, sport, and death.

Once Tenochtitlan's treasures were looted and most of its people killed by disease, exhaustion, and warfare, the humbled Aztec capital became the headquarters of a new Spanish empire. The conquerors set out to subdue surrounding tribes, rout the ancient Maya, and quarry the northern mines. For three centuries tribute and silver flowed to Madrid through Mexico City, the capital of the Viceroyalty of New Spain, which by the end of the sixteenth century stretched from northern California to Panama. Enough of that wealth remained to make Mexico City the richest metropolis in colonial America, and its huge Plaza Mayor, the Zócalo—with its glorious cathedral and government palaces—the envy of the Spanish New World.

The plaza retained its importance after independence. When the Americans invaded in 1847, and when the French occupied the city in 1864, they hoisted their flags high above the Zócalo. And there, in 1911, after leading his country through a great period of progress, the dictator Porfirio Díaz made his last stand. He mowed down protesters who were chanting "Death to Díaz!" in front of his National Palace.

The Zócalo made so much history because it housed so much power. There was no bigger power in colonial Mexico than the church, and no more impressive structure than the cathedral, which loomed over the plaza from the north side. The builders of eight generations blended baroque, churrigueresque, and classical styles into a structure that compensated for its lack of architectural harmony with an impression of grandeur achieved through sheer mass. Ponderous buttresses divided the white marble and gray sandstone façade into three portals that were covered over the years with elaborate bas-reliefs and sculptures. The twin towers that rise three stories out of a thick basalt and sandstone body and give the structure its lift were finished in 1791, two centuries after the laying of the cornerstone. Each steeple afforded a panoramic view of the city, and a clear look at Popocatepetl and Iztaccihuatl, the snow-capped peaks that rise above the valley some fifty miles to the southeast. And each spire held an enormous bell. The Santa María de Guadalupe, dedicated to the Virgin, weighed ten tons; the smaller Santo Ángel de la Guarda weighed in at three. As they pealed out the noon hour, Mexicans all across the city doffed their hats and made the sign of the cross.

Directly across the square was city hall. The Ayuntamiento, as the Municipal Palace (and its government) was known, stared at the cathedral in a symbolic contest that reflected the tension between the often-sparring religious and secular powers of colonial Mexico. Initially the cathedral won, at least architecturally. Along the ground floor of the whitewashed Municipal Palace ran a colonnade that was opened by a series of wide arches. A small window set directly above each arch had the effect of narrowing the perspective too quickly for a building that stopped so suddenly. Its short corner towers had neither the grace nor the force to offset its squatness. But toward the end of Díaz's reign city hall got a lavish façade, a third story topped by finials, and two renaissance towers.[2] The aesthetic contest was now a draw.

But in the battle for power, both were losers. By the 1860s the church had lost most of its property and much of its influence to the state; by the 1880s the city council took its orders from those in the National Palace. The palace occupied the entire east side of the plaza, extended back for a full city block, and took in light through a dozen internal courtyards. Three imposing entrances pierced its two-story façade, a row of battlements lined its cornice, and a huge clock topped its central doorway. The bell that Father Miguel Hidalgo rang to convene a meeting of independence fighters in Guanajuato on 16 September 1810 was placed just above the second floor's central balcony in 1896. Porfirio Díaz tolled that bell in front of huge crowds at eleven in the evening on 15 September—his own birthday. The dictator then commemorated Hidalgo's famous, and probably mythical, *grito* by leaning out of the balcony and letting loose with a cry of his own: "Viva la Libertad! Viva la Independencia! Viva la República! Viva el Pueblo Mexicano!"[3]

Another kind of power was emerging in the Zócalo—that of money. Markets had been sluggish, investment scarce, and profits scant for most of the nineteenth century. But as the economy surged in the 1880s and 1890s, commerce took its proper place in the plaza. A long commercial arcade ran along the Zócalo's west side. It fronted several distinct but internally connected and freshly renovated colonial office buildings. The southwest corner of the arcade was improved into the neoclassical Commercial Center, home to the city's biggest dry goods store and several import-export firms, mining companies, and law offices. Adjacent two- and three-story buildings housed dozens of fabric stores, tailor shops, and real estate companies.[4]

Petty commerce thrived as well. The arcade's twenty-seven arches were pasted with placards and posters that announced lottery drawings, bullfights, and theater performances. Dozens of stands selling candy, toys, and pinchbeck jewelry filled the colonnade and spilled onto the sidewalk under canvas awnings. Small-time capitalists stamped out visiting cards and engraved initials into metal key-ring discs from tiny stalls crammed into whitewashed corners. Their neighbors told fortunes with the help of canaries, while *rateros*, the petty thieves who prowled the busy arcade, swindled customers in their own way.[5]

Beyond the arched portico, opposite the cathedral's west tower, was the Monte de Piedad, the national pawnshop. It occupied a three-story, eighteenth-century building made of *tezontle*, a pinkish traprock that when mixed with mortar made the bricks that gave unpainted colonial façades their reddish hue. Long series of windows set in stone sills, a cornice topped by a row of finials, and a high-arched doorway lent it the confidence and solidity typical of colonial structures. Hundreds of people came each day to pawn and reclaim items, or bid at auctions on everything from pianos and paintings to saddles and irons.[6]

The Zócalo was central for another reason. It was where different classes of people mingled in a city that was divided into two worlds at the turn of the nineteenth century. Just off the plaza's southeast corner was the Volador Market, named after an Aztec gymnastic game once played there. This fruit, vegetable, and junk market was "a species of bazaar where tawdry and microbic refuse is sold to the credulous and the indigent" and sold back to those who had lost clothes, tools, and jewelry; hence its nickname, "the Thieves' Market." Among other services offered to the illiterate masses were the public scribes seated at tables with paper and pen ready to take dictation. By the late 1880s newspapers, guidebooks, and government reports were lamenting the loss of the Zócalo to the "unkempt," who lived just to the east and worked, shopped, robbed, and loitered in the market, along the arcade, and around the cathedral. Yet businessmen continued to make deals in the Commercial Center, engineers and councilmen wandered in and out of the town hall, and politicians took their orders from the National Palace. Their wives went to an occasional mass in the cathedral, were fitted by seamstresses in small shops above the commercial arcade, and bought flowers along the church's western wall. But the wealthy rarely visited the plaza for enjoyment, except on holidays. They packed the square on the night of 15 September to hear their president's *grito* and to marvel at the "immense Mexican flag" that was draped across the cathedral and lighted up by "green, white and red electric lights." The next day they stood in their carriages to see dozens of floats file into the plaza after their long march down Reforma, past Alameda Park, and along Plateros Street, the main drag through the Zócalo's fashionable west side. Only money, politics, and patriotism, it seemed, could draw the aristocracy to their once-great square, where the military bands now played "for the peon," where Volador Market "offends civilized culture," and where the indigent "scare away decent people."[7]

The story of this chapter is how the Zócalo became the center of a city that divided itself in two as it tripled its size, multiplied its wealth, and augmented its stature. The ruling classes continually moved west during Díaz's thirty-five-year reign. They moved first in the 1870s and 1880s, when they left the Zócalo's near north and east sides for its west side, which by 1880 had become a fashionable district of wealthy lodgings, fancy shops, and business offices. They moved again in the 1890s and 1900s, this time farther out into new suburbs that lined Reforma, a wide avenue that ran southwest for a mile and a half from Alameda Park to Chapultepec Castle. To those who lived there, the west side was not only a separate quarter, but a distinct way of life. The elegant suburbs, the splendid Reforma, the fashionable shopping district that ran along Plateros Street between the Zócalo and Alameda Park—these represented urbane, civilized, and modern Mexico: in a word, Europe. The aristocracy validated its new clothes, houses, and manners by engraving an official version of Mexican history on the public buildings, monuments, and statues that graced their west side.

Just as the west took on the appearance of a modern European or American city, the east assumed the look of a Mexican village magnified a hundred times. It was filled first, in the 1870s and 1880s, by artisans and laborers who had been kicked out of the Zócalo's west side when the upper classes relocated there. These workers moved into tenements that had been made out of the properties abandoned by the wealthy. Then came tens of thousands of peasants, who in the 1880s and 1890s were forced off their fields by railroads, landlords, and mining companies, which linked rural Mexico to the cities of Europe and America. These displaced peasants moved into sprawling warrens of adobe huts, wooden shacks, and one-story brick tenements.

The division of Mexico City into a poor east and a rich west caused what to politician Miguel Macedo was "a profound separation of the classes." This geographical rift reduced the social interaction between the peoples of its respective halves, "who had no contact and no sense of community, to . . . commanding and obeying, . . . being served and serving."[8] This became a defining feature of the capital's character, for the city expressed, by its division, a country whose rulers had acquired the accouterments of modern life, but whose economy was unable to spread even small bits of that civilization among the masses. The result was a poorly integrated society. The upper classes had little sense of noblesse oblige and they did not use their government to create a more culturally cohesive and politically inclusive city. The masses, consequently, had little contact with that urban aristocracy or its state. In the east schools were few, sewers were scarce, and acts of philanthropy were rare. Order was obtained not by machine politics, faith in the law, or belief in the rules of the game. It was enforced by punishing the peasant masses, co-opting the middle classes, and masking a dictatorship with the façade of democracy.

The Economics of a New Geography

The city had come a long way since the 1870s, the decade that ended two generations of civil strife that began with independence and stifled the nation's progress just as western Europe and the United States were launching into industrial capitalism. The Mexican economy stagnated during those sixty years. Trade with Europe, which had been so beneficial to Mexico despite its being monopolized by Spanish merchants, had all but dried up. The northern mines, which had poured money into the capital for three centuries, were ruined, and most of the city's small manufacturers stopped producing altogether.

Mexico's economic chaos was reflected in its politics. Of the seventy-five regimes that ran Mexico in those years, all were corrupt, most were illegal, and many ended violently. The city itself was beset by "great stretches of abandoned terrain, vast mudholes, and swelling trash heaps," and it was at the mercy of marauding rural bands, gangs of common criminals, and thousands of miserable people desperate for food and shelter. Even the upper classes were in disarray. Many aristocratic families lost land, money, and power to generals and cagey lawyers and resorted to securing credit with the family name or speculating in the business of war and chaos.[9]

The first changes began in the 1860s, when some of the city's best families began to move out of their elegant neighborhoods just east and north of the Zócalo. They left behind handsome churches and splendid colonial buildings like the Mint, the Academy of Fine Arts, and San Ildefonso College. And they gave up their eighteenth-century *palacios*, the residential estates that inspired Alexander von Humboldt, in the early 1800s, to crown Mexico the "city of palaces." The move was prompted by Benito Juárez's reformist government, which in its zeal to secularize political power and enrich itself in the process forced the church to sell off its holdings in the late 1850s. At the time the church owned half of the city's buildings. Most were west of the Zócalo, and many were the former houses of merchants, landlords, and mine owners who had lost their fortunes during the first half of the nineteenth century and so forfeited their property to the city's major creditor — the Catholic church. Their one- and two-story houses were divided into apartments and workshops, and let on long-term leases to pious but mostly poor church followers who paid little if any rent.

The mandated auctions of the late 1850s created a privately controlled land market that money could now buy into. And the "Pickax of the Reform," as it was called, proceeded to tear down convents and churches or turn them into flats and offices. Merchants, politicians, and landlords who had been living east and north of the Zócalo were attracted by these changes and lured by new developments in the western part of the city. Alameda Park had been improved and Reforma was laid out during Maximilian's rule (1864–1867). The French-backed emperor seized the Mexican state and was initially supported by the church and its conservative allies, who had been hurt badly by the reforms.[10]

But the move of the upper classes to the west was slowed by the battle to oust Maximilian and his French army in the mid-1860s, and then by internal bickering that lasted into the mid-1870s. The economy remained dormant in these unsettled conditions. To grow, the city needed the huge countryside to make goods for the world; to produce those goods the country needed peace; and to move them it needed sound money and a rail system. "Money," Gibbon wrote presciently, "is the most universal incitement, iron the most powerful instrument, of human industry; and it is very difficult to conceive by what means a people, neither actuated by the one nor seconded by the other, could emerge from the grossest barbarism."[11]

Porfirio Díaz provided the stability that induced foreign capitalists and Mexican landlords and merchants to invest in iron rails and trust in money, and so reverse Mexico's slide into barbarism. "Some will say that this is not republican," conceded an American visitor. "Possibly not, but it is business." The business of exporting silver, copper, rubber, coffee, and henequen (used to make the twine that baled the American Midwest's hay) increased Mexico's foreign trade tenfold between the mid-1870s and 1910.[12] That trade created the wealth that made Mexico City one of Latin America's great cities, and the downtown one of its finest.

By 1880, just four years after Díaz had taken office, the Zócalo was the eastern terminal of an axis of power, wealth, and culture that ran west to Alameda Park. That axis cut a swath eight blocks long and five wide. Its major strip was San Francisco Street, also known as Plateros. (Every block, or at most every two or three, had a street name of its own until 1907, when changes that had been suggested in the 1880s, under the pressure of foreign criticism, finally took hold.[13]) Most of the city's politicians, landlords, and businessmen were residing on or near this axis by the early 1880s. A few held fast to the declining grandeur of the Zócalo's north and east sides. Fewer still had moved west of the Alameda to the new neighborhoods of San Rafael and Santa María.[14]

These early suburbs signaled the start of the aristocracy's second move west, this time to exclusive neighborhoods that began to line Reforma in the 1890s. Until then, the central axis was a zone of mixed uses: handsome residences, swanky shops, and modern department stores competed for space with the offices of import houses, cloth merchants, insurance firms, steamship lines, and mining companies. And it was a zone of diverse styles: colonial mansions, eighteenth-century churches, and new office buildings adorned with beaux arts façades stood side by side on paved streets lit by cast-iron lamps. One visitor was surprised to find San Francisco Street's choicest house crammed "between a large railroad-ticket office and a showy cigar store." Affluent families often lived in flats over shops and bars, or above tiny basement apartments that housed the caretaker, his wife, their children, some chickens, and even a pig or two. When rich lawyers, merchants, and landowners moved out to Reforma in the 1890s and 1900s, the axis became a specialized district of business offices, government ministries, and stores, cafes, and restaurants.[15] Plateros may have lost its moneyed residents, but it gained in prestige by collecting more of their growing patronage.

Plateros was the showcase of this city that had nearly tripled in population between 1870 and 1910, when the entire metropolitan area had over seven hundred thousand residents. The city's economy more than kept pace with its population, judging by indices like the growth in government spending, consumer purchases, and bank loans, much of which was concentrated along the Plateros axis. There was a simple reason for the capital's extraordinary rate of growth: Mexico's economy was susceptible to monopoly — it could be controlled by a few privileged groups, and overseen by one city. As the former capital of a huge colony, Mexico City had advantages that allowed it to dominate other cities, for example, the largest single consumer market in the country, the amassed savings of the wealthiest people, and the spending of the national government. These helped it grab the lion's share of an economy that did not have heavy manufacturing to draw capital out toward resource zones and trade routes, or a rural population with sufficient income to stimulate the growth of small towns and secondary cities.

The countryside was *the* major source of wealth for the city and its ruling class. By the late 1880s, a few thousand families had acquired one third of Mexico's land through a combination of lawful purchase, legal chicanery, and violence. Over half of all Mexicans lived and worked on haciendas whose owners often took their rents and profits to Mexico City.

Like the large landowners, the national government spent most of its money in the metropolis. Mexico City got 80 percent of all national outlays on streets, electricity, and water and sewer systems, and most of the money spent on libraries, schools, and (the mostly subsidized) newspapers. That spending employed two thirds of the city's professionals. The educated, quipped Francisco Bulnes, "used to live from the altar of God," but now, with a decimated church and a robust state, they "resolved to live from the altar of the nation." The country's few large importers worked out of modified colonial palaces and new office buildings to supply the capital with European and American goods brought in through the Gulf ports of Veracruz and Tampico. And they shipped some of those goods, as well as textiles produced in the nearby cities of Veracruz and Puebla, all over the country. Fully one third of Mexico's small class of manufacturers, most of whom used imported machinery to produce light wage goods like textiles, shoes, and cigarettes, operated in the capital.[16]

Mexico City had plenty of other ways to attract business and siphon off the nation's wealth. It was the hub of a rail system that by the mid-1880s had covered most of the country, its downtown banks disbursed three quarters of the nation's credit between 1890 and 1911, and its politicians collected fees for issuing import licences, mining permits, and often the mere permission to do business.[17]

All this business meant jobs and profits for the downtown and property values that by 1900 were seven to eight times higher than those in the city's most exclusive neighborhoods and many times higher than those of any other Mexican city. It also meant shopping. Almost a quarter of the country's retail purchases were made along the axis between the Zócalo and Alameda Park. Much of that money was spent in a dozen or so modern department stores located just off the southwest corner of the great plaza. They had names like the Iron Palace, the Port of Veracruz, and the City of London. After expeditions to these high-rise department stores, the wives of landowners, bankers, and merchants parked their carriages in front of the strip's boutiques and specialty shops. There they ordered cashmere, silk, shoes, and even bibelots, carpets, and furniture, from samples brought out to them. To look at rings, bracelets, and brooches, however, they had to go inside La Esmeralda, the largest of Plateros' many jewelry stores, and certainly the most elegant. Its façade was crammed with as many fluted pilasters, stilted arches, and oval dormers as would fit on its four stories. Those who actually bought jewels at La Esmeralda often took out life insurance at La Mexicana, which stood right across the street and competed with its neighbor for the honor of being the street's flashiest building. La Mexicana's large door was cut at a forty-five-degree angle to the street corner, framed by rusticated columns, and capped with a balustered cornice that ran the length of the first floor. The upper four levels were plastered with escutcheons, modillions, and false iron-rail balconies. Topping it all off was a huge clock framed by a semicircular hood with dentils on its underside and a Greek goddess above it. Like their trades, the façades of these buildings were busy.[18]

Much of the nation's business was conducted in the city, but not by the citizens of Mexico. From their downtown offices in the capital, Americans ran most of the fifteen thousand miles of rail that carried exports to Gulf ports and U.S. border towns and hauled foreign merchandise back to Mexico City. The city-based but British-owned Banco de Londres y México was the country's second-largest creditor. Streets were paved, sewers were laid, and lights were installed by American, Canadian, German, and English firms. And Spanish, German, English, and French businessmen owned the

city's department stores, most of its grocery, clothing, and hardware businesses, and its slaughterhouse and meatpacking plant. Finance Minister José
Yves Limantour meant it when he said "our doors must be open . . . to foreign
capital, or we will never evolve beyond our stagnant and sickly way of life." [19]

The Look of Europe in the Streets of Mexico

The capital also borrowed the culture of Europe and America, which had
created a world economy that beckoned Mexico out of its "stagnant and
sickly way of life." The city's aristocracy liked to display that culture on its
west side strip. The center of it all was Plateros Street. "The love of everything French," recalled poet José Juan Tablada, "encouraged us to call
Plateros, which had no trees, *el boulevard*." When not shopping for Parisian
overcoats and Swiss watches in the boutiques and jewelry stores, the city's
leisure class assumed European airs in the Casa de Plaisant, a café where
men in tailored suits sipped soft drinks and cordials; the Frizac, where the
private secretary of Porfirio Díaz cut deals with his coterie; La Concordia,
whose large glass windows let "the *snobs* eat their truffles and drink their
champagne in plain view of less fortunate passersby"; the elegant Sylvain
Restaurant and its basement bar, the Grill Room; and the more relaxed at-
mospheres of the Café Royal and the pastry shop and coffeehouse El Fénix.
In those days, wrote Tablada, "to say *'Dulcería Francesa'* was to excite everyone. The children thought of edible toys, the women dreamed of bonbons,
and the men smacked their lips at the thought of excellent wines and delicious pastries. All were sold by those delightful downtown stores that were
jammed with the city's best people." [20]

Just off Plateros was the Casino Español, an elaborate neoclassical façade
crammed with escutcheons, friezes, and balustrades. Its garish chandeliers
lit the most exclusive balls of the early twentieth century, including a dance
in honor of Porfirio Díaz on the hundredth anniversary of Mexico's Declaration of Independence. The Jockey Club, the city's most illustrious association, was housed at the west end of Plateros in a converted colonial mansion that was covered in bright tiles and crowned by finials. Here were the
sharp frock coats and shiny top hats of the city's wealthiest men and the
tight-waisted skirts, puffy blouses, and frilly hats of the women, who were
all "quite Parisian in the free use of rouge for lips and cheeks, not forgetting
indigo-blue with which to shade about their dreamy-looking eyes." [21]

Membership in the Jockey Club required a unanimous vote of its associ-
ates. Few dandies made it in, but many did loiter around the "House of

Tiles," as it was called. The fop was known as a *lagartijo*, a little lizard, because his close-fitting suits restricted him to stiff, reptilian movements. The typical dandy wore a double-breasted suit and patent-leather shoes, tucked a marble-handled cane under his arm and stuck a flower in his buttonhole, and covered his dainty fingers with silk gloves he was careful not to stain with his indispensable cigarette.[22]

The action on Plateros picked up in late afternoon, when it was "thronged with handsome women, gay equipages, hurrying messengers [and] dawdling *lagartijos*." All looked out for the "pulque-sodden cabmen [who] drive as recklessly as the more enlightened, but equally heedless, *automovilistas*." Around twilight—"the hour decreed by fashion for its devotees to promenade—the crowd grows denser and the racket increases. Then, a certain class of bedizened and enamelled *mujerzuelas* (disciples of the half-world), who have slept the sweet morning away, make their *début*; the shop windows light up, hundreds of electric signs flash in the growing darkness."[23]

As daylight faded, the city's version of an aristocracy began their drive down *el boulevard*. For two hours Plateros was congested with hundreds of carriages, each lit by a side lantern, and each "creeping along," wrote novelist Federico Gamboa, "as part of an immense, connected, luminous reptile." Modest coaches paled before stately victorias decked with family emblems and initials, drawn by pairs of high-stepping bays docked *a la inglesa*, and driven, somewhat incongruously, by swarthy men wearing tight suits and huge sombreros. Alongside the carriages pranced horsemen outfitted with shiny revolvers, black sombreros, embroidered velvet jackets, and tight leather or cashmere trousers lined with silver buttons on the outer seam. Policemen circulated among the pressing crowd, watching for agile *rateros*, who began "to ply their light-fingered trade" at dusk. By eight the cafés were full, the streets ablaze with electric light, and the sidewalks jammed with strollers. Within an hour the eateries and cafés began to empty out. Most went home; some went to a show.[24]

A block off Plateros were two of the city's three major theaters. The Principal was built in 1753. The Nacional was erected a century later but razed in 1891 to make way for 5 de Mayo Street, which was cut open from the western edge of the Zócalo in the early 1880s and eventually driven through to the new Fine Arts Palace, which was under construction on the eastern edge of Alameda Park by the early 1900s.[25] The Arbeu was built a few blocks south of San Francisco Street in 1875. In these theaters the gentry watched the plays of Racine and Shakespeare and listened to European companies sing Puccini and Verdi.

The city's operatic highlight was certainly the four performances given by Adelina Patti at the Nacional in 1887, when some of the gentry even pawned jewelry to pay the exorbitant prices for seats. A special messenger delivered gifts from the president's wife just as Patti took the stage for her first performance. To make up for what the press had called the audience's tepid response to opening night, Patti was greeted the next evening by long applause. No one but Caruso, it is said, has heard so much since. She then earned it with an apparently stunning rendition of the aria from the first act of *La Traviata*. The Italian soprano finished her third evening with a Spanish song, "La calesera." When she unexpectedly shouted "¡Viva México!" in the midst of it, the crowd roared deliriously, thrilled that their young nation had been cheered by a great lady of old Europe. After her final show, the audience called her back ten times and clapped for another fifteen minutes after her final bow. Díaz himself gave the diva a solid gold crown, ruby-and-diamond earrings, and a golden locket that contained a portrait of herself on one side, and a painting of the Valley of Mexico on the other.[26]

In this arena of heady public display there naturally arose dandified critics who showed off their own culture by criticizing that of the upper classes. Manuel Gutiérrez Nájera was the city's first professional writer, and its chief *flaneur*. Gutiérrez wandered the streets in handsome dress with an umbrella cocked under his arm, a cheroot clenched in his teeth, and his eyes on the world. As the initiator of modernism in Mexican letters, he sought to free his country's writers from the clutches of a decadent Spanish romanticism. Mexicans, he urged, had to learn modern life. The teachers, of course, were the French.[27]

El Duque Job, as Gutiérrez Nájera was known, did take at least one French lesson to heart: the study of city life. His poetry, his short stories, and his criticism—most of which was written in the 1880s and 1890s—were Mexico City's version of Baudelaire's "Paris Spleen." In his famous poem "La Duquesa Job," he describes his "duchess":

My little duchess, the one who adores me,
doesn't have the airs of a great lady:
she's the *grisette* of Paul de Kock.[A]
She doesn't dance the Boston, and doesn't know
the high pleasures of the race
or those of the *five o'clock*.
If she walks on carpet, it isn't in her house,
if she strolls happily down Plateros

and greets Madame Marnat,[B]
it isn't, undoubtedly, because she dresses her;
but because she goes so quickly
to another seamstress's house so early.
My little duchess doesn't have any jewelry,
but she's so pretty, and she's so beautiful,
and her body is so *v'lan*, so *pschutt;*[C]
so that it transcends France
which doesn't equal her in elegance,
not even the clients of Hélène Kossut.[D]
From the doors of the Sorpresa,[E]
to the corner at the Jockey Club,
there's no Spaniard, French or Yankee
quite as pretty, or as naughty
as the duchess of Duque Job.[28]

———

A. Paul de Kock used the *grisette* in his mid-nineteenth-century novels.

B. Owner of a shop on Plateros that sold dresses for the Mexican *grisettes.*

C. French phrases of admiration.

D. Apparently a leading French designer.

E. A clothing store on Plateros.

Gutiérrez Nájera's modernism, like that of the fashionable Mexicans he mocked, came off as a somewhat labored copy of European styles. He expressed "French thoughts in Spanish," wrote education minister Justo Sierra, who might have added "in French and English, too," given the poet's penchant for dropping foreign words—*five o'clock, v'lan, pschutt*—and referring to Parisian characters like "the *grisette* of Paul de Kock" and "the clients of Hélène Kossut." Even his pen name was taken from the title of a Parisian comedy.[29] And what was Mexican about the most famous poem of this promotor of nationalism and modernism in Mexican letters? His duchess, whom he would have chosen over the beauties of Europe and America.

Yet Gutiérrez Nájera did capture the novel aspects of his modernizing city. The busy display on Plateros gave him the setting for his greatest poem, whose protagonist was a seamstress catering to a fashion-conscious aristocracy. In a short story called "La novela del tranvía" ("The Streetcar Novel") he plays the voyeur in the back of a tram. His game is to guess, from the dress, speech, and manners of various passengers, where they reside, how they make a living, and what they might be thinking.[30] And in this stanza from his poem "Las almas huérfanas" ("Orphaned Souls") he sounds the predicament of loneliness and the quandary of namelessness, which were affecting everyone in his growing city:

What a great and beautiful city!
The streets and plazas are crowded with people
Running about, frantically
bumping, hitting, and whacking each other!
The air is blackened
by smoke from belching factories.
What gorgeous palaces, what fabulous lights!
And the buildings, how high they reach!
Yet I'm alone, I don't know anyone;
I hear them speak, but of what I don't know;
If I ask, they shrug—and move on.[31]

The State Tells Its Story

Private citizens sipped their cordials, bought their jewels, and strutted their stuff on Plateros Street. They even wrote verse about it. The state made its mark in a different way. It erected a cluster of fancy buildings, fashioned a beautiful park, and told its version of Mexican history through a series of statues on Reforma. In any given year the federal government spent twice what the municipal administration did on the city. After 1900 the bulk of that spending was on public buildings, many of them designed for the city's 1910 centennial celebration of independence. Guillermo Landa y Escandón, who ran the city as mayor and then as governor between 1900 and 1911, offered prizes for attractive designs. "We must shamefully confess," he wrote in 1901, "that very few buildings of recent construction are handsome enough to merit our capital's title as the City of Palaces."[32] Three of the many impressive buildings that went up were immediately touted as architectural gems. Clustered at the western edge of the axis, near Alameda Park, were the Communications Building, the Fine Arts Palace, and the new post office.

The Communications building was designed by Italian architect Silvio Contri and erected on the former site of the San Andrés Hospital. The first floor of this neoclassical, two-story building was dominated by a series of tall arched windows that eclipsed a modest doorway. The second was lined below and above by balustrades that framed recessed and arched windows divided by columns. Four central finials provided some lift to this heavy building, which was speaking architecturally to the late-eighteenth-century Mining Building, which stood directly across the way. The Mining Building was handsome and symmetrical in the style of Louis XIV, and the craze for things French made it the preferred place for Díaz's state ceremonies. One turn of the century, still Spain's, was talking to another, now Mexico's; yet each was speaking French. Another Italian, Adamo Boari, designed the post office, which replaced the demolished San Hipólito Hospital. The hundred or so arched windows, which were graced by terra-cotta semicircles, gave it a Mediterranean feel. But the imposing doors and square corner towers made that feel one of a florid renaissance armory. The neighboring Fine Arts Palace, also designed by Boari, replaced the razed National Theater. Its construction, begun in 1904, was interrupted first by the Revolution and then by the turmoil of the 1920s. It stood as a mere façade until the interior was finished in 1934. "Every great architect," it has been said, "finds his own antiquity." Boari found too much. This "enormous meringue" was a steel frame supporting a white marble face that was crammed with pediments, porticos, and pilasters and loaded with enough statues to fill a museum.[33]

"That the Americans tear down something ugly and put up a beautiful skyscraper is natural," wrote Tablada. "But that we Mexicans destroy the solid beauty of our colonial architecture for imitations of American buildings is a result of either ignorance or a perverse sense of aesthetics." Architectural historian Luis Salazar agreed. "Today's buildings," he wrote, "lack the solidity, grace, and proportion of the colonial period."[34] They were right. Take the Jesuit college of San Ildefonso, perhaps the best of many splendid eighteenth-century schools, hospitals, and residential palaces. Soft red bricks, detailed stonework around the doorways, perfectly spaced columns highlighted by long horizontal runs of windows and finials — the result is a harmonious blend of the ingredients of great architecture: graceful lines, pleasing proportion, and restrained ornamentation.

Spanish architecture in the capital of New Spain, though at times grandiose, had the poise and balance of a people confident in their purpose. They were a people who dominated the 1500s and spread their way of life into Central and South America for two more centuries.

Mexican architecture, on the other hand, was an expression of a city run by a people who were looking to create their own culture while entirely dependent on the industry and ideas of Europe and America. They copied the places they envied, but those copies betrayed insecurity, anxiety, and inexperience. Boari himself, who once pleaded for a "truly national architecture," admitted that "ornamentation reigns supreme."[35]

Restraint was the key to achieving a harmonious blend of the various styles that made up the easily overdone neoclassical façades of the time. Artistic discretion had yet to emerge in Mexico, where façades were meant to show taste rather than be tasteful, where for the first time in three generations the development of style was free from political instability and economic penury, and where the establishment of aesthetic conventions was hindered by the barrage of imported goods, ideas, and fashions. "It takes an endless amount of history to make even a little tradition," Henry James chided the young Americans, "and an endless amount of tradition to make even a little taste, and an endless amount of taste, by the same token, to make even a little tranquillity."[36] Mexicans knew little of their adopted European tradition, had acquired even less of its taste, and enjoyed none of its tranquillity.

Relief from the glaring excesses of Mexico's modern buildings could be found in the Alameda, a shaded park flanking the west side of the downtown strip. The Alameda was on the city's edge and quite dangerous in the 1860s, when the Empress Carlotta sculpted it into a "darling" but still "neglected garden." The "messy thicket" continued to lose trees to "miscreants living in makeshift lairs" until the early 1880s, when it was finally manicured into a glorious park.[37]

The Alameda was seven hundred feet wide and fifteen hundred long, and thus able to offer plenty of open space amidst its bronze fountains, music stands, aviaries, and hundreds of poplar, eucalyptus, pepper, cypress, and palm trees. Far from the growing slums of the east side and free from the bustle of downtown, the Alameda offered a haven to the middle and upper classes. They treasured Fridays and Saturdays, when they rented shaded seats to listen to police band concerts, the lazy Sundays when the city's 1st Battalion Military Band played Verdi and Bellini before thumping out a schottische and some mazurkas, and the summer evening strolls lighted by the electric lights installed in 1892. But the park was a pleasant place for anyone with the proper temperament and manners. One visitor recognized a young man, who wore a carnation in the buttonhole of his neat suit, as the cashier at a shoe store. And on weekdays servants wheeled carriages past students preparing their morning lessons and by the "tired squad" of older men who sat in the shade to watch sunny afternoons pass by.[38]

At dawn, a few Indians in straw hats, leather sandals, and white cotton pants could be seen sweeping "the Alameda with large, green bushes attached to the end of sticks."[39] Yet the only Indian who truly belonged there was a dead one. The bust of Benito Juárez, who was minister of justice and then president during the tumultuous 1850s and 1860s, is flanked by statues of liberty and freedom and sits atop a twenty-foot pedestal at the base of a long semicircular balustrade of tall fluted columns. The monument was inaugurated with a long paean to this full-blooded Zapotec, who orchestrated the reforms that promised "free speech, equality before the law, and freedom from theocracy." The final flourish of that eulogy read "Hidalgo blesses us, Juárez heartens us, and Díaz supports us with an iron hand."[40]

Declarations like this were part of the state's effort to build a symbolic pantheon of Mexican heroes, an effort every bit as concerted as the material construction of parks and post offices. The dictator attended the inauguration and relished his place among a triumvirate that was officially promoted to incarnate the recent sweep of Mexican history, which it did perfectly. Father Hidalgo was the prophet of independence, the lawyer Juárez was the founder of the state, and General Díaz was master of the nation. The giant monument to Mexico's greatest nineteenth-century Indian was the first chapter in an official history that was being written on the west side at the turn of the century.

The story continued down Reforma. The gentry were at their height when they left the Plateros axis to settle into elegant neighborhoods alongside the avenue, which was opened in the mid-1860s by the Emperor Maximilian, neglected for a decade after his fall, and finally shaped into a handsome boulevard in the mid-1880s. A wide central thoroughfare was flanked on either side by a walkway shaded by a double row of trees. Alongside each pathway was a narrow street that fronted the private mansions and apartment buildings that began to line the upper reaches of the avenue in the early 1890s. An army of orderlies tended trees, swept up trash, and sprinkled water to keep down the winter dust.[41]

Four huge monuments dominated the boulevard. They narrated a history of Mexico that aimed to reconcile the ideas and events of a real past with the ideals and needs of an inexperienced ruling class that was trying to guide a new nation. That story all but ignored Mexico's past as a colony while praising the European world that Spain had introduced it to. It celebrated Mexico's roots in Aztec society, but uncertainly. The Indians, after all, were a subjugated people generally regarded as a drag on progress. And the story honored the men who had fought for independence between 1810 and 1821, and who had battled for a secular state in the 1850s and 1860s. Yet those men were in fact heroes of humiliation, who oversaw economic depression, civil strife, and foreign occupation.

The honor of announcing the boulevard went to Spain's Carlos IV, an inept king who ceded power to his adulterous wife and her corrupt lover. Mexican royalists built an equestrian statue of Carlos in 1803, draping him in a robe, putting a scepter in his hand, and sticking a laurel wreath on his head. This Spanish Claudius was removed from the Zócalo during the war for independence and hidden throughout the tumultuous decades that followed. He reappeared in 1852, this time just west of the Alameda on Bucareli Street, exactly where Reforma would later begin.[42]

This hapless king was the only public testimony to three centuries of colonial rule. The young nation wanted to forget those ignoble and unhappy times and write its own history, one that began with independence. "We Mexicans," proclaimed poet and teacher Ignacio Ramírez, "are descendants neither of the Indian, nor of the Spaniard. We are the children of Hidalgo," the priest whose cry of insurrection launched the fight for sovereignty.[43]

Five blocks down the avenue came Columbus, discoverer of the Americas. He pointed hopefully toward a New World from his spot in the center of a bower surrounded by Beaux Arts palaces, the posh Columbus Café, and the domed Imperial Hotel.[44] Through the image of Columbus, who was tainted neither by the blood of the conquest nor the wrongs of colonial government, Spain could be recognized for having disseminated the culture of western society. "Today we recognize the good works of Spain in America," wrote a city paper, "and no one can deny that the first seed of civilization that was sown in our soil by the Spaniards is now bearing its fruits."[45] That seed, the Mexicans told themselves, may have been sown by Spaniards, but it bore fruit only when tended by the Americans, the French, and the English. Sitting beneath Columbus were Bartolomé de las Casas and Pedro de Gante, the friars who led the spiritual conquest of Mexico. "The apostles," wrote Justo Sierra,

> wrecked temples by the hundreds, burned and broke icons by the thousands, and destroyed every painting or image they thought to be idolatrous. Such zealous men could not have done otherwise in those circumstances. They lost precious information about the life and thought of the aboriginals, losses not compensated for by what the priests did manage to save of their invaluable documents, or what they later found out, wrote

about, or got the Indians themselves to write down. Amends were made, however, by inviting the Indians into the Christian way of life, by abolishing their bloody rituals and beliefs, and by putting them on track to join the civilized world. As history absolves the conquest of its cruelty, so it pardons those who destroyed Indian artifacts. Those men, after all, were not archeologists, they were apostles.[46]

Cortés, on the other hand, was not forgiven. The conquistador was excluded from the Mexican pantheon of heroes. In his place was the Aztec leader Cuauhtémoc, who unsuccessfully defended Tenochtitlan against him and then stoically bore his tortures before dying at the end of a noose tied by the otherwise honorable Spaniard. The Indian warrior stands five blocks beyond Columbus. Bas-reliefs of his torture and imprisonment and carvings of Aztec weapons and amulets adorn the statue's huge pedestal. Cuauhtémoc was the "symbol of heroic valor" wrote the newspapers. It was thus fitting that the statue depict the "courageous prince's . . . eternal bravery, and his scorn for his own torment."[47]

Valor in the face of defeat: here was the sentiment that had become the most cherished quality of this new, battle-scarred nation. Mexicans adored nineteenth-century highwaymen for their brashness and cunning, but what they loved most was the bandit's dauntless stare in the face of the firing squad. The final act in a one-sided war for Mexico's northern territories was the taking of the capital city. American troops raised their flag atop the National Palace and marched to Chapultepec Castle. There a few cadets, soon to be revered as the *niños héroes*, or child heroes, leaped from the ramparts to their deaths. "We admire fortitude in the face of adversity," Nobel laureate Octavio Paz would later write, "more than the most brilliant triumph." Cuauhtémoc, too, incarnated that sentiment. He was thus an Indian whom the Mexicans not only could respect, but glorify. And not just any Indian would do. Two huge Aztecs standing atop black marble pedestals were put near the entrance to the avenue in 1891. No one was sure who they were, or what they were supposed to mean, and they were quickly banished to the eastern part of the city.[48]

Beyond the Indian warrior a lofty column culminates in a bare-breasted angel clutching the proverbial laurel wreath and broken chain. The inscription at its base reads "From the Nation to the Heroes of Independence." On the first tier of a massive pedestal a child walks a giant bronze lion—a people strong in war, gentle in peace—among the allegorical figures of Law and Justice. The chosen heroes of Mexican independence—José María

Morelos, Miguel Hidalgo, Vicente Guerrero, Nicolás Bravo, and Francisco Xavier Mina—occupy the second story. All fought for the revolutionary cause, and all but Bravo were killed by firing squads. The populist priests Hidalgo and Morelos were to independence what Emiliano Zapata and Pancho Villa were to the Mexican Revolution a century later: the leaders of peasants who took up arms against their oppressors. And like their revolutionary successors, Hidalgo and Morelos were first betrayed by the upper classes with whom they had apparently shared the just cause of ending a tyrannical government, and then, once buried safely in the past, they were hailed as heroes by the heirs of their executioners.[49]

Lurking in the shadows of Carlos, Columbus, Cuauhtémoc, and the Heroes of Independence were thirty-six statues of little-known men of uncertain merit. In 1887, the municipal council erected statues to two of the city's "heroes" from the reform years. Complaints about the "common qualities" of those men forced the city to make up with quantity what it lacked in quality. Each of the provinces was invited to send along one or two of its own nineteenth-century champions.[50] Dozens were lined up along Reforma to salute a forty-year struggle between Conservatives and Liberals. The battle over how to build a nation devastated the country for decades and culminated in a crippling civil war between 1858 and 1861. That war enticed the French into the farce of recolonizing what was left of New Spain. But it also secured the reforms that were inscribed in the liberal 1857 Constitution, the document that Díaz was using to make a nation. Those terrible years were thus glorified to honor the present.

The New Neighborhood

Aristocrats took their history lesson each day as they rode along Reforma to and from Chapultepec Park. Maximilian traced out the Avenue as a Champs-Élysées to link the downtown with Chapultepec Castle, an outlying, eighteenth-century palace that became a military college after independence and was later remodeled by the Empress Carlotta to resemble Miramar, the royal couple's castle on the Adriatic Sea. Carriages were pulled along the park's circular road and passed duck and boating ponds, expansive meadows, and stands of ahuehuete and eucalyptus trees. They passed by the castle high up on a knoll to their left, rode past the zoological gardens, and filed back onto Reforma. From benches on the avenue, spectators watched "dashing equestrians exhibiting all the gay paraphernalia of a Mexican horseman; stately vehicles drawn by two snow-white mules; tally-ho coaches conveying merry parties of American or English people; youthful aristocrats bestriding Lilliputian horses, followed by liveried servants." The parade was a daily event by 1890, when the first residential palaces and apartment buildings were filling in the upper portion of the avenue. Twenty years later the procession was marching along a boulevard that was lined with elegant neighborhoods well beyond Cuauhtémoc's statue.[51]

The earliest of these suburbs, San Rafael and Santa María, were built just to the west and northwest of the upper stretch of Reforma in the 1880s and 1890s. They quartered the city's small middle class, made up of the skilled workers, small merchants, and professionals who were above the servants, toilers, and market vendors of the eastern slums, and below the rich land-lords, importers, and politicians who were moving to the avenue by the 1890s. San Rafael and Santa María were two of the city's "least unhealthful" neighborhoods. They were places where people were not afraid of receiving vaccinations from public health workers, and where they benefited from potable water and sewerage.[52] Most residents in these barrios owned modest single-family houses ornamented with a keystone above the wooden door, a slightly decorated lintel over a grilled window, and a plain cornice made by inserting long stone slabs between the upper two rows of bricks. The typical one-story flat was deep and narrow. The front door opened into a vestibule that became a slender patio running along the edge of the house back to the service area at the rear. The *sala*, or parlor, occupied the front room, and behind it followed two bedrooms, the kitchen and dining area, and the bathroom.[53]

The middle classes of Santa María and San Rafael were acquiring the rudiments of the urban civility that the wealthy had mastered and that the masses on the eastern side of the Zócalo had yet to appreciate. Their taste, however, was more Mexican than that of their superiors along Reforma. The foyers and hallways of their houses were filled with flowerpots, bird-cages, and painted water jars; glass cabinets in the dining room displayed a few pieces of china, but the kitchen shelves were full of earthenware cooking pots and clay jars; and a crucifix or a Sacred Heart of Jesus hung over the bed. On Sundays the men put on vests, black jackets, and felt hats, and the women wrapped their shoulders in colorful shawls, known as *rebozos*, and adorned themselves with earrings, brooches, and rings. They went to the Alameda to hear music, occasionally splurged and rented a carriage to ride up and down Reforma, or attended one of the neighborhood house parties, "which often end up in fights, but rarely require the police."[54]

Others went downtown to watch a play. By the 1880s, when drama and opera no longer ruled the stage, the theater was no longer the artistic refuge of the upper crust. The *zarzuela*, a musical and often picaresque comedy that had become popular with small segments of the elite in the 1860s and 1870s, became affordable to the growing middle classes by the mid-1880s. The propriety of the *zarzuelas*, which were performed in one-act shows called *tandas*, declined as their middle-class audience increased. They became bawdy shows that featured short-skirted dancers, spicy language, and satirical portraits of various Mexican types, like beggars, water carriers, or dandified horsemen. The "stupid and obscene *zarzuelas*," complained the newspapers, were "worse than *ópera bouffe*." Gutiérrez Nájera ridiculed the shopkeepers and clerks, who howled "if an actor says something roguish or if an actress lifts her skirt to show her stockings . . . and laugh with the banal chortles of those who attend the theater only when they can get cheap seats." Aristocrats, with their "clean collars and top hats," tended to avoid such crowds of "common hats and cheap *rebozos*."[55]

Yet compared to the poor living east of the Zócalo, the middle class was refined. They ate with knives, spoons, and forks, wiped their faces and hands with napkins, and often hired a maid for laundry service and weekly cleanings. Many drank *pulque*, the alcoholic beverage made from the maguey, but they disdained the rude drunkenness that was so common among the lower classes. Middle-class women were "sincerely religious," wrote criminologist Julio Guerrero, and in a more "advanced" way than those of the lower classes. They were married in church ceremonies not affordable to the masses, and they were not just "superstitious or idolatrous worshipers of religious paintings or parochial saints. They know about the lives of a few biblical saints and several popes, they understand the catechism, and they go to church and have personal and respectful relations with their priests."[56]

Some of the city's wealthy put up small palaces in San Rafael, and others built fancy two-story homes in the southern part of Santa María. But the truly rich waited to build on Bucareli Street, and then along Reforma in the elegant *colonias* (suburbs) of Cuauhtémoc, Juárez, and Roma.[57] Streets in Cuauhtémoc were named Rhine, Danube, and Seine, after the European rivers that Mexican aristrocrats read about. The clean asphalt lanes of Colonia Juárez had names like Berlin, Hamburg, and London — the cities that elite Mexicans dreamed about. Mexico's geography was represented in Colonia Roma's Jalisco, Puebla, and Chiapas Streets — named after places aristocrats were hoping to feel proud about.

These neighborhoods were built by large American companies working with local businessmen and government officials. Mexican entrepreneur Tomás Braniff, for example, who had 20 percent of his capital in urban real estate, owned eight blocks on upper Reforma and sat on the boards of foreign utility and finance companies. The finance minister, José Yves Limantour, owned land along Bucareli and awarded contracts for the provisioning of urban services. And high-ranking officials like Senator Pablo Macedo, president of the Congress Joaquín Casasús, and mayor and city council president Fernando Pimentel y Fagoaga collected handsome fees for linking foreign real estate, paving, and utilities companies to those in charge of licensing subdivisions and disbursing money for water, sewers, and streets. Real estate was a lucrative business. Land prices along Reforma increased sixteenfold between 1880 and 1900, speculators who bought land and sold it two years later often quadrupled their money, and construction firms like the American-owned Mexico City Improvement Company paid out handsome dividends to stockholders.[58]

The suburbs along Reforma, wrote a Spanish visitor, were like "a little corner of Europe that was somehow transposed to Mexico." The tree-lined streets were full of single-family houses, an occasional apartment building, and corner lots occupied by butchers, pharmacies, and grocery stores. Every house was near a streetcar line, enjoyed running water and electricity, and employed a few of the city's sixty-five thousand domestic workers, who in 1910 were 30 percent of the work force and 10 percent of the entire population.[59]

These neighborhoods looked, at first glance, like the residential suburbs of large European cities. But visitors complained that "the styles adopted are many and various, no two houses being alike." A gothic palace of rusticated brick combined dormers with a turret and a gabled roof. Its neighbor was a sprawling three-story mansion with elaborate bay windows and a mansard roof crowned by an iron railing. Across the street a two-story façade was loaded with pediments, pilasters, and friezes and topped off by a steep half-roof with oval dormers. Next door a two-floor Romanesque palace was set well back from the street and protected by a high iron fence. If no two houses were alike, together they spoke to one theme: anarchic grandiosity. But the façades merely warmed one up for the interiors. Ceilings were stuccoed with friezes, lined with dentils, and supported by fluted columns. Heavy drapes covered arched windows and shaded the Steinway. Oriental pillows cushioned Louis XV couches, art nouveau lamps decorated end tables, and glittering chandeliers illuminated numerous wall hangings and bibelots.[60]

The development of taste, as is usually the case, lagged behind the growth of wealth. One reason was a lack of aesthetic conventions in Mexico. Nothing had been built for two generations, and when peace and progress did induce a new round of building, it was not to their former masters that Mexicans looked for inspiration. Spain's architectural creativity was spent, and Mexicans were keen to reject the styles of their former colonizers. They chose, instead, from a wide range of French, English, and American motifs, which were too varied, and came in too fast, to be handled with discernment. Magazines like *El Mundo Ilustrado* and the fashion sections of dailies did try to instruct their readers with photos of "beautiful homes," articles on interior decoration, and examples of proper attire.[61] Yet these journals could only reflect the belief of this insecure aristocracy that busier and bigger meant more beautiful. Few ruling families could boast either impressive lineages or great accomplishments, so they took their cues from their superiors in Europe and America. They hurried to prove their worth to foreign visitors, to the classes beneath them, and, above all, to themselves. Their new houses served just that purpose. And the thousands among the aristocracy with landed estates,[62] like these Morelos sugar barons, were happy to return home after the occasional trip to the hacienda:

> the *hacendados* came down once or twice a year, to an *hacienda* dressed up to receive them. . . . Their coming was an event looked forward to with joy by the laborers and their women. All would be waiting, the children freshly scrubbed, their mothers adorned with pitiful ribbons and ornaments hoarded for the occasion; there would be a *fiesta* with music and dancing and fireworks. The gracious lady, unbelievably beautiful and glamorous, would smile on them and ask the children's names, and distribute a carload of calicoes, shoes, blankets, toys and other things. . . . After a few weeks of country life, however, the *hacendados* would weary of these simple diversions and be off with their train of licenced personal servants to Mexico City.[63]

"At least our peasants," the returning *hacendados* must have thought, "are where they belong."

The Other Side

Those *hacendados* returned to a divided capital. The west was a "city of palaces," where people like themselves lived, the east a "city of dregs," where peasants like their own barely survived. The great divide, we saw earlier, was originally opened in the 1870s, when workers, artisans, and petty merchants were pushed east of the Zócalo into the tenements, warehouses, and shops that had once been colonial schools, monasteries, and residential palaces. Railroads and expanding haciendas threw so many off their lands in the 1880s and 1890s that nearly half of the city's five hundred thousand residents in 1900 were peasants.[64]

These uprooted people moved into slums that were spreading all along the city's bulging eastern rim by the 1880s. "The new, outlying barrios," confessed the mayor in 1884, "lack sewerage and paving, and during the rainy season are virtually impassable." Newspapers noted the emerging contrast between the splendid "central avenues with their luxurious stores . . . and magnificent buildings," and the plight of "the working men who go out to the barrios to live in the muddy pigsties . . . of our sickening tenements, on those open sewers we call streets, that are not so very far from the Zócalo."[65]

Two decades later the east side was worse because it was much more of the same. The inhabited area east of the Zócalo doubled in size between 1880 and 1900, but its population grew many times over. More than one third of the city's people now lived on only 15 percent of its land, in what a journalist described as

> barrios full of squat, dirty, and cracked houses that reek of misery and putrefaction and swarm with motley, disgusting, and shameless people. The pestilent *pulque* taverns are the centers of activity for many women and men of questionable morals and lifestyles. The women are messy and loose, their faded shawls hanging over blouses full of holes that show off too much flesh. The men are filthy, and their long, matted hair hangs down from their sombreros. If one of those many superficial tourists who see only the city's face, that is, the elegant downtown of pleasure and money, were to be taken without their knowing it to one of our barrios and asked where they were, they surely would not know what to say.[66]

The eastern barrios, some with streetnames like Rat's Alley, Dog's Lane, and Pulque Place, were, as one visitor politely put it, "neither harmonious nor attractive." In the 1890s, and again in the 1900s, the Health Department found that most people had to be vaccinated by force, that many tenements, or *vecindades*, packed sixteen to twenty persons to a room, and that over half of all inspected dwellings had cases of typhus. The complete lack of sewers and potable water, the open drainage ditches, and the cramped, poorly ventilated, and shoddy tenements—most in violation of building codes—gave the easternmost districts the highest mortality rates in the city.[67]

Those who were living west of the Alameda saw everything to their east, and to the east of the Zócalo especially, as one vast warren. But in fact the east was made up of at least a dozen distinct barrios, each with its own market, church, and people. There were three kinds of neighborhoods. One was made up of poor communities inhabiting old colonial quarters. These fanned out for seven or eight blocks in a semicircle east of the Zócalo and extended south of the Plateros axis for about eight blocks. Another was built up in the 1870s and 1880s around what were then outlying colonial churches surrounded by small Indian communities. These neighborhoods were on the fringes of the colonial city's long eastern boundary and in a large open space just north of Alameda Park. A third type of barrio evolved in the 1890s and 1900s on empty, outlying swampland to the far north, east, and south.

A good example of the first type of barrio was located several blocks north of the Zócalo, around Santo Domingo Plaza. The square was surrounded by palms and poplars and centered on a statue of La Corregidora, a colonial magistrate who supported the revolutionary cause.[68] The wine-red, eighteenth-century church on the plaza's north side had carved wooden doors to let in the faithful, and a large dome to bathe them in light. But it could no longer call its flock. The bells that once rang out from the campanile had been removed during the secular reforms of the late 1850s. Just east of the church was the School of Medicine. Science had replaced dogma in this former home of the Holy Office of the Inquisition, where doubters were once tortured and occasionally burned on a funeral pyre. Just south of the school, on the east side of the plaza, was the old Customs House, classically colonial with its reddish bricks, narrow windows set deep in stone sills, and thick wooden doors. Medical students often lounged about the plaza, and occasionally a politician or bureaucrat strayed into the square during a break from his sinecure at the nearby Congressional Palace or Supreme Court building.

But the plaza was beyond the downtown's northern fringe of elite respectability, which ended at Tacuba Street. If Santo Domingo was once home to the wealthy, it had been in decline since the 1870s. An arcade on the plaza's west side sheltered the letter writers, who sat at their desks with pens, ink wells, and sheets of variously colored paper. Here one might see a young mother informing her faraway parents about a new baby girl, a recent immigrant telling his betrothed to come to the city, or a carpenter begging the governor for lenience when sentencing his son for disorderly drunkenness. Many of the plaza's surrounding colonial office buildings and residential palaces had been turned into tenements, and many of the city's tiny furniture factories were just off the square. For the first half of the 1880s, when the plaza faced what was still the Customs House, it stored many of the city's rickety carriages and their skinny animals and served as a gathering place for "foul-mouthed drivers with filthy manners." The hack drivers were replaced by clowns in 1885, when the Orrin Brothers Circus started daily shows in the plaza. They lasted for five years, until the city, which had collected handsome fees from the spectacle, yielded to complaints from residents and ordered it out.[69]

The second and most common type of neighborhood began to form in the early 1880s around outlying colonial churches, which until then had been ministering to scattered communities of Indians and poor mestizos. The wealthiest of these barrios was Guerrero. It covered a large area north of the Alameda and was separated from the middle-class suburb of Santa María by tracks leading to the city's major rail station.

Guerrero was designed, in the late 1870s, as a barrio for home-owning artisans and workers. Although craftsmen were then declining as a percentage of the city's work force, and although their guilds were in disarray, they still had enough power to get the government's attention, if not secure its favor. Guerrero ended up housing workers, but not in worker-owned housing. Six wealthy men bought up two thirds of all the plots that were sold on easy two-year terms by the city. They dislodged a few hundred Indians from their hovels around María de los Ángeles Church and built hundreds of tenements. Between 1880 and 1890 Guerrero's population tripled (to thirty-two thousand) while its housing stock grew by only a quarter. Guerrero was not exclusively for workers. A few of the downtown's affluent moved into two-story homes and comfortable apartment buildings in the southwest corner of the neighborhood, some middle-class people managed to build small homes for themselves, and low-level clerks, struggling students, and the pensioned widows of military men lived in decent tenements along the northern edge of the Alameda.[70]

But poor carpenters, bricklayers, and common laborers accounted for over half of Guerrero's residents, and domestic servants, petty merchants, tortilla makers, and hack drivers made up most of the rest. Almost all of them lived in crowded *vecindades* on "wretched streets full of trash and waste," and many of them worked in local warehouses that sold construction materials, hawked goods in the barrio's two open markets, and labored in dozens of small cooper, mason, and metalworker shops. Those who lived near their place of work returned home for lunch; those who did not ate tacos or tortillas and beans served up by local women who cooked on makeshift charcoal stoves on street corners, or they got something from El Baratillo market.[71] In 1899 a reporter had this to say about the market, known for its spoiled meat and unlicensed vendors: "The first time you find yourself in front of El Baratillo, you'll hesitate before entering into the bristling swarm that hovers around the nasty stands. If you do enter you'll be constantly surprised by the degree of ugly poverty in our city. Baratillo is our stock exchange for discarded and stolen goods, it is our den of thieves. Every stand in the market is so original and indescribable that the market looks like a macabre kaleidoscope."[72]

If conditions were rough in Guerrero, they were at least bearable. In other barrios that were erected around outlying churches on the fringes of the old colonial city, life was downright nasty. Industry in these neighborhoods consisted of hundreds of small outfits that made hats, coffins, matches, chairs, glue, and soap. These were not factories, but one-room shops that hired a few workers: "The woman of a bricklayer's helper, the mother of a domestic servant or of a young humble seamstress—they work in a thousand tiny shops, making sweets or toys, mending clothes or cobbling shoddy shoes."[73] Those who did not make goods did the work of cleaning, moving, and selling them. Many of the city's sixty-five thousand servants, most of them women, lived in these communities and made money by scrubbing downtown apartments, doing the laundry of middle-class families, and serving in aristocratic palaces along Reforma. Lots of the city's ambulant merchants, most of its hack drivers, and almost all of its *cargadores*—the human beasts of burden who used tumplines to lug goods around the city—also came from these barrios.

San Sebastián was one such neighborhood. It was located six or seven blocks northeast of Santo Domingo. The church tower rose above recently built, one-story adobe houses whose small doors and shuttered windows faced narrow dirt streets without sidewalks. The barrio had the squat, cramped feeling that typified the east. It was the feeling of confinement that the pretty daughter of a local blacksmith in *La rumba*, a novel about San Sebastián, tried to escape. After she got a job as a seamstress in a downtown boutique, she got hooked on a young philanderer who worked as a clerk in a nearby clothing store. "Remedios felt her dream was coming true. To go from a blacksmith's shop to a downtown store was a big step. To be loved by Cornichón was like being at the gateway to happiness." But soon after they had moved in together, Cornichón abused and then abandoned her. So Remedios returned home, to a barrio "of murderers and thieves that no one dared walk through at night," a barrio that the summer rains turned "into a vast pond of floating dead animals, straw hats, dented pots, staved-in baskets, and laceless shoes," a barrio full of *pulque* taverns that did a brisk afternoon business with local deadbeats and "sweaty policemen seeking refuge from the sun." The main grocery store had few daytime customers apart from "the black swarms of flies that hovered about liquor stains, piles of sugar, and strings of dried sausages hanging next to yellow candles and balls of cheese." But the *pulque* taverns closed at sundown, so when the men finished work they gathered at the store, took their customary tables, and began "to get drunk: a shoemaker lugging about a bunch of soles, a carpenter with his metal braces, and a *cargador* whose mule was waiting outside — all raucously ordered drink after drink." Amidst tobacco smoke and the clamors of drunken men, the women came in to buy tomorrow's coffee, beans, eggs, and oil on credit.[74]

Carmen was just a few blocks northwest of San Sebastián, and like its neighbor was built around a crumbling colonial church. This barrio, wrote a newspaper, was "a disease center." A Mexican chronicler of popular customs described the *vecindades*, which let cheap rooms to "artisans who make shoes on pine benches, seamstresses who stitch clothes around a table, and others doing different kinds of work. The sad inns rent unfurnished rooms by the night and the cheap eateries are dirty, but barbers still seem to have the dignity and importance of centuries past." Dozens of seamstresses walked eight or ten blocks to work in downtown stores that made custom clothing for the upper classes. Like most of the people who lived in the east, they could rarely afford the trams. (Almost three fourths of all streetcar rides, in fact, were taken on first-class tickets.) Neither could they afford rides from the hack, cart, and carriage drivers who lived in Carmen and quartered their animals and guarded their cars in local stables and garages owned by Spaniards. Carmen had lots of young boys who knew the city streets from peddling newspapers and cigarettes and who eventually became drivers. These boys lived behind the whitewashed façades of the tenements and adobe homes that housed the neighborhood's people.[75]

Tepito was northeast of Carmen, almost a mile from the Zócalo. Like its neighbors, Tepito absorbed thousands of rural migrants who poured into the city in the 1880s and 1890s. Some acquired adobe houses, but most rented rooms in *vecindades*. They worked as day laborers, servants, and peddlers. The lucky ones got jobs making bed frames, cardboard boxes, and chairs, or helping out the coppersmiths and ironmongers who shaped metal with anvils and forges in tiny shops. Tepito's two soap factories made it a "neighborhood where soap is made, but apparently never used."[76]

Daily provisions were obtained much as they were in every other barrio. *Lecheros* sold milk door to door from clay vases carried by horses, and leather-capped water vendors poured the liquid from skins and jugs that were strapped over their own shoulders or across the backs of donkeys. The women walked several blocks each day to purchase food in the Santa Ana market, which was well maintained but had a reputation, as many did, for selling stolen merchandise.[77]

To the southeast more barrios grew up around outlying churches. They were named San Lázaro, Santa Cruz, Santo Tomás de la Palma, San Pablo, and San Pedro. These were small communities of bricklayers, *cargadores*, tanners, box makers, candle makers, street cleaners, and pork cookers — "mop-haired men with long fingernails and an extra layer of skin formed from accumulated dirt." The men wore straw hats, white cotton trousers, and leather sandals, and the women covered themselves in dirty skirts, loose cotton blouses, and *rebozos*. Most lived in *vecindades*. Their rooms lined the corridors off the central patio and were furnished with a pine bed, a table, and a rickety chair or two. A picture calendar was stuck to a wall, a large earthenware water jar sat by the door, and one or two pegs in the wall held the family wardrobe. *Vecindades* were run by housekeepers who assigned rooms, collected rents, and controlled access to the main door, which was locked by ten or eleven. Yells followed by the hard rap of a stone hitting a door were heard throughout the night. Although these southeastern barrios were safer in 1910 than they were in 1870, when criminals menaced the streets and the police did not dare enter, they were still places where "knives and pistols wreak a lot of havoc."[78]

La Merced Market was only six long blocks from the Zócalo. According to *El Tiempo*, La Merced was "disgusting beyond belief," much like every other "filthy and repugnant" market that served as the commercial hub of a barrio. The city licensed the vendors of these markets so it could tax them. The money was supposed to keep the markets clean and secure, but La Merced, like most, was simply a bazaar set up on an empty lot without water or sanitation. It was also home to thieves and thugs.[79]

Seen from a nearby roof or church steeple, however, the prospect of these markets was kaleidoscopic. Old women sold chiles and herbs from neat piles arranged on ground cloths. Corn and beans were scooped out of deep woven baskets. Artisans arranged their hand-carved toys and figurines on small wooden stands protected by roofs of canvas or corrugated iron. Shoes and hats were placed in neat rows under a tattered canvas awning. Meat hung from wooden racks, and squash, onions, and tomatoes were piled in neat pyramids atop flimsy stands. Against this backdrop of stalls, aisles, and ground cloths, the wide white brims and the pointy crowns of men's sombreros melded into shifting shapes and colors with the red and blue *rebozos* of black-haired women.

The Viga Canal was the east's pleasure spot. The canal entered the southeastern quarter of the city and eventually flowed east into Lake Texcoco. It was named after the *vigas*, or wooden beams, that once spanned the upper part of its seven-mile course between San Pablo in the north and Lake Xochimilco to the south. Canoes still brought the city flowers and foodstuffs grown nearby on *chinampas*, the raised agricultural beds of the Aztecs. The upper part of the canal, and its adjacent promenade, were the favorite visiting spots of the wealthy when they still lived on the east side of the Zócalo. Fanny Calderón de la Barca described it this way in the 1840s:

> Enter the Viga about five o'clock, when freshly watered, and the soldiers have taken their stand to prevent disturbance, and two long lines of carriages are to be seen going and returning as far as the eye can reach, and hundreds of gay plebeians are assembled on the sidewalks with flowers and fruit and *dulces* for sale, and innumerable equestrians in picturesque dresses, and with spirited horses, fill up the interval between the carriages, and the canoes are covering the canal, the Indians singing and dancing lazily as the boats steal along, and the whole under a blue and cloudless sky, and in that pure clear atmosphere: and could you only shut your eyes to the one disagreeable feature in the picture, the number of *leperos* [beggars] busy in the exercise of their vocation.[80]

Forty years later, few aristocrats were willing to risk their elegant carriages on the unpaved streets, or their delicate sensibilities on the odors and sights of San Pablo for a view of such festivities.[81] And by the 1890s these simple pleasures were completely déclassé. Not for the middle classes, however, who joined the local poor for outings on the canal, especially during the Easter season, when Indians paddled canoes laden with flowers past the musicians and food vendors who jammed the canal's banks. And year round government clerks, small merchants, and department store employees spent their Sunday afternoons with lovers and families on lazy canoe rides to Santa Anita, a little town of thatched houses where they could stroll, buy flowers, and eat tamales and pork tacos.[82]

The final type of settlement was slums built on unoccupied swampland. These communities were located well to the east and northeast of the Zócalo and on the city's southern border. In these zones someone would buy a lot, trace out dirt streets, and put up a dozen brick tenements or a hundred adobe huts. One square block of single-story dwellings might hold eight hundred or a thousand people, without a single privy, or even a drain, among them. "Naturally," a journalist observed, "these poor and dirty people produce lots of waste that remains in the so-called subdivision, poisoning the environment and quickly converting the settlement into a hospital ward."[83]

While the city reimbursed the builders of the western suburbs for providing the water and sewer lines, the sidewalks and street lighting, and the small parks and sidewalk trees that were demanded in detailed and strictly enforced contracts, the contracts issued to builders in the east stated only that someone, at some time, ought to provide services. Or they ordered builders to provide all services in accord with instructions from the Ministry of Public Works, but did not offer to reimburse them. Many landowners started building while their permits were still under consideration; others never even sought them. But it did not matter. Legal or illegal, contract or no contract, the barrios of the east were ignored. "The west gets everything," complained *El Tiempo*, "the east nothing."[84]

La Bolsa was described by a popular guidebook as "sort of a native Ghetto, with dirty and microbic streets, repulsive sights and evil smells; where the inhabitants could never be accused of excess tidiness." The government ignored several petitions for paving, water, and sewers because the settlement, which emerged in the 1900s, was not authorized. La Bolsa was probably the major "crime-spot of the city." Yet frequent petitions for protection brought only sporadic patrols of mounted policemen. A Spaniard and a couple of his friends, one an American, decided to do some slumming in La Bolsa one afternoon. Their story reveals something of the backwardness and isolation of the place. They entered its rutted streets, passed by mean adobe huts and squalid *vecindades*, and saw a people "united in an unhealthy world of filth, dirt, and vice." Almost immediately a pack of "ragged and barefoot boys began to follow us, and the more we penetrated the barrio, the more people there were behind us." Some had seen men dressed in suits downtown, but never in their own neighborhood. The visitors offered to pay one boy as a guide. He took the money and ran, shrieking with laughter. They pressed another into service, this time withholding payment until after the tour. The boy guided them through the streets, accompanied all the while by dozens of ragged kids with names like Bird, Wolf, Nutty, She-Ass,

Sponger, Mean Cat, and Scullion. He pointed out the sites of recent murders, fights, and robberies. They passed by a dead and decaying donkey lying feet up in the street, and came upon a motley crowd screaming outside a *pulque* tavern. The main event was a nasty fight between two women. The men were placing bets on the combatants.[85]

There were more "unhealthy" barrios north of La Bolsa and out around the penitentiary, the one major government structure in the east. Built about the same time as La Bolsa, and similarly unplanned and lacking in services, these barrios were clumped around smoky brick factories, busy rail lines, and crowded freight yards. To some they served as the "breeding grounds for all the vice and misery that is born in this city." It was not uncommon there for small workshops and stores to pay employees with "'money' made of soap, leather, and paper, on which [was] inscribed: 'to such and such, worth so many centavos.'"[86]

Well south of the Plateros axis, between Belem prison and the barrio of San Antonio Abad, was a similarly degraded zone of new barrios. In the 1870s this was a marshland littered with "filthy trash heaps and perfidious robber dens." Twenty years later it was cluttered with adobe tenements, a sanitarium, a slaughterhouse, the warehouses of the Public Works and Water Departments, and several dumps that "men, women, and their children, accompanied by skinny dogs, buzzards, and pigs," picked through for whatever they could eat, wear, or sell. The rainy season, wrote a novelist, turned the streets of this low-lying region into "rivers banked by the walls of buildings — rivers of dirty, greasy, and pestilent water that exposed to all the disgusting innards of the city." In 1884 the governor observed that this area had not yet "felt the civilizing influence of city government." Decades later it still lay beyond the reach of "civilizing" controls, through no fault of its own. In 1899, the Public Works Commission informed the city that the owner of a parcel of land called El Cuartelito, located between the barrios of Niño Perdido and San Antonio Abad, was tracing out plots and looking to sell them. The city distributed fliers warning future residents that it would not provide them with any services.[87]

The Parasitic City

Mexico City is in the middle of an oval basin fifty miles long and forty wide. In 1900, the capital shared that valley with dozens of scattered Indian villages and several nearby towns — San Ángel, Coyoacán, and Tlalpan to the south; Tacubaya to the southwest; and Tacuba and Atzcapotzalco to the northwest. The wealthy had a long tradition of driving their carriages past orchards and maguey fields to spend weekends in these towns, coveted for their flower gardens and tranquillity.[88] That tradition ended in the 1890s, when the aristocracy built homes along Reforma and the resorts began to house the city's new textile, paper, tobacco, and shoe factories. These mills, about fifteen in number, accounted for a third of all Mexican manufacturing in 1910, but employed just 4 percent of the city's work force.

The division of society into industrialist and worker, then the dominant relation in many American and European cities, was ill developed in Mexico. Most workers came from peasant households, and most mill owners were merchants and financiers first, and industrialists second. They were generally foreign-born importers and creditors who knew little about industry, but used their political contacts and credit to fund joint stock companies and factories that routinely enjoyed monopolies met with only rarely in Europe or America. The degree of concentration in textiles, paper, and shoes was similar to that in cigarettes, where two French-owned factories supplied over 50 percent of the Mexican market. These monopolistic plants were large but inefficient. Superior paper, for example, had to be imported, while the nation's biggest tannery could not produce first-class leather for shoe factories, which themselves failed to manufacture high-quality footwear even with imported leather. Even the textile mills, probably the easiest industries to set up quickly and efficiently, employed twice as many workers per machine and had costs 20 percent higher than factories in England or America.[89]

Mexico City's small, outlying, and inefficient industrial sector fit a parasitic upper class bent on looting its own countryside in exchange for the goods, expertise, and taste of American and European cities. That class bought mansions, office buildings, and infrastructure for its city with the money earned on the labor of miners, peasants, and peons working in remote states like Durango, Chihuahua, and the Yucatán. They confiscated that wealth by collecting rents and profits from their rural properties, by receiving fees from American mining companies, by financing and managing part of the trade between the Mexican countryside and the cities of Europe and America, and by taxing the imported goods purchased with the money earned by rural exports.

To the city's wealthy, the masses of the eastern slums were as remote as the peasants who tilled the soil and the peons who worked the mines. But that upper class, which lived by exploiting the countryside, paid for it by having to house its peasants and their rural habits as well.

CHAPTER 3

Peasants & Provincials

*The civilized world evolves, giving rise to new forms of life, art,
and thought, which the Mexican tries to imitate so as to feel equal to
the European; but at bottom the Mexican of today is no different from
what he was a century ago, and his life grinds on inside the seemingly
modern city just like that of the Indian in the countryside: in an
Egyptian immutability.*
— *Samuel Ramos*, El perfil del hombre y la cultura en México

Martín Luis Guzmán was philosophical about the wretched
condition of Ciudad Juárez: "if our faces burned with shame to look at it,
nevertheless, or perhaps for that very reason, it made our hearts dance as we
felt the roots of our being sink into something we had known, possessed,
and loved for centuries, in all its brutishness, in all the filth of body and soul
that pervades its streets. Not for nothing were we Mexicans."[1] Mexico City
was no Juárez, but it knew the same "brutishness" and "filth of body and
soul." Barefoot peasants strayed onto Plateros. The masses drank *pulque*, the
ancient Mexican brew. Large parts of the capital were simply a Mexican village writ large. The great city, after all, could express only the character of
its countryside. Not for nothing was it the capital of Mexico.

Slums, drunks, and beggars were part of every nineteenth-century city, in
Europe and Russia, Latin America and the United States. New York had its
gangs and its lowlifes, Moscow and Saint Petersburg their starving peasants,
Buenos Aires and Rio de Janeiro their immigrants and tenements. But
Mexico City had something more. As a city it concentrated the culture of its
huge, backward, and oppressed countryside — a rural culture that was the
largest and oldest in Latin America. Like no other city in the Americas, the
capital of Mexico mixed the top hat and the sombrero, the mansion and

the hut, the refinements of the aesthete and the squalor of the peasant. The unstable mixture was a result of the pressing weight of the *campo* (country-side) on the capital. It showed a city that was destined to internalize the polarities — of wealth, race, and power — signaled by that great divide.

Hygiene Problems

If the height of a civilization is measured by the depths of its sewer system, as Victor Hugo insisted, then that of Mexico City was shallow indeed. The city not only lacked an adequate system of sewers, it housed tens of thousands in substandard and dangerous dwellings, it had too much floodwater and not enough that was fit to drink, its ruling class was given to neglect and its peasant masses were without the power to object. In 1886 the municipal council confessed that "this cesspool we call a city" needed more lessons in hygiene than any other city in the world. It would spend the next three decades waging a "cruel and incessant battle that was like trying to cover the rags of a beggar with a magnificent cloak." Parts of Mexico City were magnificent enough, but as a whole it went from "one of the most diseased places on earth" in 1887 to "the most unhealthy city in the world" in the 1910s. What may have been hyperbole had its basis in fact. The death rate increased 60 percent between 1878 and 1890, over eight thousand children died each year in the early 1900s, after improvements had been made to the water and sewer systems, and sanitary inspections made in 1904 and 1906 showed the city no better off than it had been two decades earlier. At the end of Díaz's reign, Mexico City's mortality rate (42.3 per 1,000) was higher than all but one of its provinces, more than twice as high as those of Buenos Aires and Rio de Janeiro, and higher even than those of Cairo, Saint Petersburg, and Madras.[2]

The city's geography was against it from the beginning. Mexico sat in the middle of a soggy valley with no natural outlet. Summer rains flooded the three shallow lakes — Texcoco, Chalco, and Xochimilco — that lay just to the east and southeast of the city, and they swelled several streams and canals that cut through the city's northern and southeastern quarters. The Aztecs had accommodated themselves to the valley's wet bottom. They built Tenochtitlan in the middle of a huge lake, constructed causeways and canals, and ingeniously raised beds of muck out of its shallow waters to grow crops year round. The Spaniards rebuilt the city on the valley floor after only partially draining the lakes. Mexico City has since waged a constant, and never quite victorious, battle against the ancestral waters.

The immediate task was to prevent floods. Díaz's first mayor, and his more powerful governor, found the city's few sewer lines clogged, badly in need of repair, and useless when it rained, which it did regularly between May and September. They spent the late 1870s cleaning lines, filling ditches, and repairing sections of the several canals that channeled the city's runoff and waste into nearby Lake Texcoco. New canals checked creeks along the city's northern border and rerouted them into the lake, and the banks of rivulets in the southeast were fortified. The city council congratulated itself in 1880 for having taken the necessary steps to curtail the flooding, but summer rains swamped the city almost every year for the next three decades.[3]

The eastern part of the city, which was lower-lying and poorly serviced anyway, took the brunt of the flooding. But the area just south of the Zócalo and even some of the downtown streets were regularly converted into "black-water lakes that interrupt traffic, stall commerce, and let off horrible smelling and deadly gases that force the people to cover their noses with handkerchiefs to quell the nausea." In October of 1886, when the city was covered by a "veritable lake" that destroyed more than five hundred houses, a daily asked, "Is this city a seaport? It appears so from its streets . . . which are more easily traversed with canoes than with carriages." A newspaper ad solicited a partner for a lifeboat business. The next year an editorial warned that, "if the rains continue, the city, which is now a huge swamp, will become a lake negotiable only by canoes and steamships." Throughout the 1880s the city tried to raise itself above the waters. Streets that were inundated one year were raised the next, subjecting those that had been elevated in earlier years, but were now relatively lower, to more severe flooding. And each time the city raised a street one meter, which it did almost every year, the owners of its buildings raised their sidewalks and patios two. Once-stately colonial palaces took on the appearance, it was said, of "men without legs."[4]

Journalists, downtown merchants, and ordinary citizens complained loudly and often about the flooding and faulted the government for doing nothing about it. By the mid-1880s the city had one thing on its mind: "The drainage project," wrote the papers, "is of the most transcendental importance for the city . . . it is a matter of life or death for residents of the Valley of Mexico." "The government that stops the floods," predicted one critic, "will go down with glory in our history; and the man who heads it will be adorned with an immortal laurel wreath. But where is this government," he asked, "and who is this man?"[5]

Porfirio Díaz made a name for himself, but it was not for stopping the floods. A commission was charged by executive order, in 1886, with draining the valley. It included some of the city's most powerful men, like real estate magnate Francisco Somera, sugar baron Luis García Pimentel, the president's father-in-law, Manuel Romero Rubio, and the future finance minister, José Yves Limantour.[6]

A year later the government borrowed money and in 1889 offered a contract to S. Pearson and Son of London. Pearson proceeded to build a monumental drainage system that had three major components. The first collected runoff and gathered sewage from select parts of the city. The second channeled some of that runoff through canals into Lake Texcoco, which itself was connected via canals to Lakes Xochimilco and Chalco to the south. The most vital component, the Great Canal, took away sewage, drained the swampy area just east and north of the city, and regulated the level of ever-threatening Lake Texcoco. The Great Canal flowed north for thirty miles to a dam that spilled water into a six-mile tunnel that ran beneath the Xalpan Mountains and out of the valley. The entire system was driven by the San Lázaro pumping station, which was built by Mexican engineer Roberto Gayol. The network of canals was finished in 1895, but two years later a giant flood submerged the entire eastern half of the city, and many other quarters as well. The labors of the San Lázaro pumps were then compared to those of Sisyphus. The entire system—canals, pump, dam, and tunnel—was finished and functioning in 1900, at a cost to the national treasury of 15.9 million pesos, a sum equal to half of the entire municipal budget over the thirteen years of construction.[7]

On 17 March 1900, General Díaz, his cabinet, and the entire diplomatic corps listened to fireworks, artillery salvos, and church bells announce the inauguration of the great waterworks. Díaz ordered the canal locks opened and boarded a train to Zumpango, the town at the northern terminus of the works, to see the blackwaters pour out of the valley on their way to the Gulf of Mexico. At a banquet attended by the nation's top politicians, its richest businessmen, and most of its kept writers, Díaz toasted the men in charge of the operations as "heroes of the nation and of humanity." The drainage system, he went on, was his government's greatest accomplishment—"an eternal pedestal to the glory of the nation . . . which will bear witness for future generations that at the end of the nineteenth century Mexico had monuments it could display with pride to the civilized countries of the Old World." *El Imparcial* called these "Roman works," which had moved nearly eleven million cubic meters of earth with three thousand men and five dredging machines, a first of its kind, "not only in America, but in the whole world." To Díaz, the project was "of such supreme importance for our future that it deserves to be ranked in our history on the same level as independence." It was a magnificent project. But the very next year, and for several after that, major areas of the city were flooded. New floodgates and sluices were added in 1908 and 1909, and several riverbeds were dredged. The official press once more proclaimed the end of the floods. Heavy rains in July 1910 submerged neighborhoods along Bucareli Street, large sections of the northeast, and a stretch along the Viga Canal.[8]

If the streets of the city had too much water, its people had too little that was fit to drink. Scarce and dirty water, wrote Antonio Peñafiel, was "a primary source of the capital's permanently unhealthy state." Even the government's subsidized newspapers acknowledged the futility of a sanitary code without an adequate water supply. The common joke was of a policeman who caught a woman giving *pulque* to her infant. "The water," she said, "makes him sick." Except for those living downtown and in the western suburbs, few drank water from a spigot. Most bought it from *aguadores*, who collected water at public fountains and came round to pour it from their leather sacks and clay urns into the earthen jars found in every modest dwelling. The lack of drinking water was worsened by a sewer system that was fully operational only in the new western neighborhoods, patchy in the downtown district, and absent entirely from the large eastern slums. People complained constantly about open and unfinished sections and clogged and overflowing tubes. "Even the sewers on the best downtown streets," griped a daily, "leak refuse openly onto the sidewalks." A more serious problem was "the mixing of potable water with the human waste of the sewers—a major cause of the high mortality rates." Yet another was inadequate flushing. The incidence of disease may have actually declined a little during the rainy seasons, when there was enough water to flush the sewers. The Academy of Medicine blamed the typhus epidemics of 1901 and 1902 on insufficient water for cleansing new sewer lines downtown. The sewers, doctors said, had "caused the recent rise in mortality."[9]

Even worse than poor sewers was none at all. Newspapers, visitors, and government commissions complained throughout the 1880s about pools of waste, piles of refuse, and the consequent stench that wafted over the city. The smell was overpowering, masked only "by the fragrance of flowers in the hands of every passing woman and child." "This city of sewage" wrote one paper, could not be "more neglected, dirty, or full of foul water." Another called Mexico "a City in Danger." There was certainly cause for alarm. But the smart ones knew that "what is needed is patience, because at least for now nothing will be done about the city's public health situation."

Years later newspapers and government commissions were still complaining about open sewers, overflowing pipes, and carts that routinely leaked from their load of night soil.[10] Only the western addition, which had its own water and sewer systems and was beyond the stench of the east, escaped such daily horrors.

After new outbreaks of typhus in 1905 and 1906, the Board of Potable Water was chartered. It was given a large budget and powers of eminent domain to supply the city with drinking water and to ensure that enough water could be flushed at high enough pressure through the sewers to ensure proper cleansing.[11] New pumping stations were installed in the southwest part of the city in 1910, when potable water began to arrive via aqueducts from newly tapped springs in Xochimilco. That water was pumped downtown through an underground gallery that was dug and finally laid with pipes in 1913.[12] Even then, only the central streets, the neighborhoods along Reforma, and sections of Santa María and Guerrero drank tap water and flushed toilets.

But potable water and adequate sewerage could not have offset the city's substandard housing, its people's poor diet, and their unhygienic living conditions. Descriptions of the lack of proper sanitation on the east side come from newspapermen, government workers, and foreigners. They are often sensationalist and unsympathetic, but they all point to one fact: Mexico City was an unwholesome place.

"Architecturally and hygienically speaking," wrote a journalist about the barrios clustered along the city's broad eastern flank in the 1880s, "they aren't any better than the huts of the Hottentots, and they are inferior to the igloos of the Eskimos. Only the worst disease centers of Asia . . . have living quarters as bad as those of our lower classes." Two decades later, some of those *vecindades* sheltered up to eight hundred, many crammed more than a dozen persons to a room, and together they housed well over one hundred thousand of the city's poorest.[13]

"In these gloomy and festering *vecindades* of the walking dead," a reporter wrote in 1896, "there is typically one faulty faucet that leaks green salty water good only for washing a few things, and a privy placed in a dark corner or at the end of a narrow alley. The rooms that line the corridors get no sun, light, or air, and are like dank caves behind whose doors vegetate the families of poor artisans with their women, children and orphans."[14] These dwellings, wrote Julio Guerrero, were full of "nude, skinny, and tobacco-colored children who suffered from distended bellies and were as skittish as Polynesian savages." Those children shared the streets with roving packs of the classic Mexican cur: short-haired dogs that rummaged the filthy markets and picked through huge piles of trash, which often festered for years before the city got around to carting them away.[15]

New migrants, as well as longtime residents without stable quarters, passed the night in *mesones*, the city's cheapest form of transient lodging. They offered little more than "a bare spot to lie down in, a grass mat, company with the vermin that squalor breeds, rest in a sickening room with others — snoring, tossing, groaning brothers and sisters in woe." These *mesones*, which housed about twenty-five thousand each night, were found in dilapidated colonial buildings just north of the downtown, south of the Alameda, and east of the Zócalo. Less fortunate than those who slept in the *mesones* were the five thousand or so who built leaky huts out of planks, cardboard, and canvas in the far eastern part of the city; worse still were the thousand or so who could not afford a *mesón* and had no plot on which to erect temporary shelter. They simply walked a few miles out of town each night to sleep in fields.[16] The one hundred beds of the beggar asylum, built in 1879, and the several hospices erected with money made from the national lotteries in the 1890s and 1900s, could shelter but a few of the most desperate poor.[17]

The tenements, the *mesones*, and the unpaved, insanitary streets were known to spread disease.[18] These conditions were also decried for their part in causing what Calderón de la Barca called the evil of "dirtiness," which she saw as "certainly one of the greatest drawbacks to human felicity in this beautiful country, degrading the noble edifices dedicated to the worship of God, destroying the beautiful works destined for the benefit of his creatures. The streets, the churches, the theatres, the market-place, the people, all are contaminated by this evil." Fifty years later that same dirtiness, according to an American visitor, denied the city "the indefinable quality that makes one either desirous of putting on one's best clothes, or regretful that one has not better clothes to put on." And because it sullied even the few downtown tenements that had electricity, water, and sewerage, the upper classes assumed that the scourge of filth was caused by the "ignorance of the masses."[19]

"In this frightful toll of human life," wrote Health Minister Alberto Pani, "*more than forty per cent. of the total* [deaths] we must recognize surely, besides the physical causes of contagion, of defective feeding, and unhealthful habitation, [as having] this other vital cause of a moral order: *crass ignorance and lack of motherly care.*"[20] Pani pulled his 40 percent out of the hat, but his point that ignorance and derelict parents were major causes of the city's health problems was taken for granted at the time. The following scene from a novel about the medical profession probably happened a hundred times a day and helped the wealthy and the educated middle classes absolve themselves of responsibility for the condition of the masses below them.

"What did your child die of?" the doctor asked the woman whose dead baby's skin was covered with a film of dirt.

"His little hands and face got wet, and then came blood in his stools. I gave him lots of herbs."

"If you had wet his body with soap and water since he was born, he would not be so dirty on the outside, nor would he have needed so much junk on the inside."

The mother might have been hearing Greek.[21]

The upper classes applied soap and water more often than those in the middle classes, who used the public baths a few times a month. For a few centavos these baths—which numbered one for every twelve or fifteen thousand inhabitants in 1900—offered a tiny room with a bathtub, a towel, soap, and a brush. Those living along Reforma, and the middle classes who resided in Santa María or rented rooms in Guerrero or in the best downtown apartment buildings, had the knowledge and facilities to care for themselves properly. Most of the city's population, recent immigrants from country districts, did not. Even if there were affordable public baths, wrote *El Tiempo*, a daily that was sympathetic to the plight of the poor and critical of the city government, "everyone knows that the poor would not want to clean themselves anyway." Another paper agreed that the lower classes "don't even know what personal hygiene is. . . . But without public infrastructure it would not do them much good anyway." The "tens of thousands" of poor people who did want to wash themselves, and their clothes, had no choice but to use "the filthy water of ditches and puddles"—a sight that disconcerted the upper classes, but did little to rouse them to effective action.[22]

Mexicans did have one special hygienic obsession, an incessant sweeping of "the streets or the floors of our homes, rich and poor." The city council was encouraged by the sweeping, but concerned by the warnings of doctors and hygienists that it kicked up "asphyxiating clouds of dust" that spread disease. So the council issued decrees requiring owners to spatter water before sweeping their homes, shops, and sidewalks.[23] The sweeping was perhaps an attempt to offer at least the appearance of cleanliness in a city whose government was such a poor caretaker.

The Drink of Choice

Mexico City was like any number of the thousands of peasant villages it ruled: fouled by nature and lacking the means for proper sanitation. And like some of those they left behind in rural hamlets, many in the big city drowned their sorrows in *pulque*, the immemorial drink of Mexico made from the succulent maguey. This pulpy, acrid, and milky-white drink smelled as bad, at least to the uninitiated, as the city's sewage, yet it accounted for over 90 percent of the alcohol drunk in the capital. *Pulque* was "loved by Mexico City's lower and middle classes," wrote politician Francisco Bulnes, "more than family, more than life, more than country, more than all pleasures licit and illicit." In 1875 forty-one thousand tons of the stuff were brought into the city, one hundred thousand tons were drunk in 1883, and the capital got down three times that in 1910. Per capita intake doubled during Díaz's reign.[24] If Mexico City meant peasants during the Porfiriato, peasants meant *pulque*.

The maguey was cultivated on large haciendas in the nearby towns of Apam, Soltepec, Omestuco, Otumba, Apizaco, and Guadalupe. A mature plant was seven to ten years old and had leaves up to ten feet long, a foot wide, and eight or ten inches thick. If unattended the plant would send up a flower stalk twenty to thirty feet high and die. But just as the plant began to flower the *tlachiquero*, or harvester, sliced it off and scooped out the plant's heart. He left only the outer rind, where the *aguamiel* (honey water), or maguey juice, gathered in a small hollow. Several times daily, for two or three months, he collected the sap by inserting a long narrow tube into the cavity and sucking the juice into a leather sack slung over his shoulder. The sweet liquid was fermented in large vats by adding *madre* — maguey juice that had been allowed to sour. The batch turned to *pulque* within a day. The quickly decaying drink was poured into barrels and loaded every morning onto dozens of railcars that passed right by the haciendas on their way to Mexico City.[25]

The wealthy drank in their private clubs. *Cantinas* (saloons that sold hard liquor as well as wine and beer), *figones* (cheap eateries that served alcohol with food), and *pulquerías* (taverns that poured *pulque*) were for everyone else. Most of the city's 51 *pulquerías* in 1864 were in the plazas. The city had 817 *pulquerías* in 1885 and over 1,200 by 1905. That amounted to one for every three hundred residents, or about one per block in every part of the city east of the western suburbs. *Pulquerías* were independently owned and operated until 1909, when a group of wealthy producers and financiers formed the Pulque Marketing Company and acquired a monopoly on the purchase, transport, and sale of *pulque* with the help of their friend Pablo Macedo, the former president of the Congress. Over several years the company dictated prices, took over taverns, and forced a hundred or so recalcitrant owners out of business.[26]

Pulquerías had two characteristic features: colorful walls and exotic names. Even the humblest corner tavern, a "hole in the wall that can be seen for a block and smelled for two," might be painted pink, bright red, or sky blue. The interior walls were "painted in lurid colors" that depicted "low, bacchanalian scenes" whose central figures were likely to be "frowsy females in diaphanous draperies," a larger-than-life "lady reposing in a green bower," or a "half-veiled Venus." Such spectacles were easily seen by passersby through the open doorway and inspired an unsuccessful campaign by a Catholic newspaper to have them suppressed. The few *pulquerías* that catered to polite people offered innocuous scenes of bullfights or meetings of courteous individuals on a street corner. The names of these taverns fell into several categories. One evoked the sensual pleasures: "The Fountain of Love," "To Delirium," "The Seductress," and "The Love Nest." A second mocked evil and licentiousness with names like "The Tail of the Devil," "The Little Hell," and "The Isle of Sacrifices." A third was vaguely philosophical with pithy names like "Destiny" and "Rebirth," while another appealed to the more melancholy purpose of *pulque* as "The Balm of Sorrow" and "The Remedy of Heartache."[27]

The typical *pulquería* was a one-room saloon on a corner lot. The suggestive power of a bright scene or an exotic name painted on the façade was at times enhanced by a slogan like "Live happily, drink *pulque*." The illiterate learned such maxims from experience. As *pulque* drinkers approached a tavern they typically passed by the cigarette vendor, a few kids taunting a skittish dog, and a couple of men in straw hats, peasant pants, and sandals swearing allegiance to each other. If a man were of more than average height, "a fringe of soiled, vari-colored tissue paper strung across the entrance" from the lintel might brush the top of his head as he stepped up a stone stair to pass through the open doorway. On one side he saw bar stools and tables "thronged with blear-eyed, sodden male and female degenerates."[28] On the other was a long, chest-high bar lined with tall schooner glasses. Behind it were the men who poured out the milky liquid from vividly painted barrels stored beneath the counter. The *pulquero*, wrote a chronicler of the city, was often a "red-faced man who by absorbing the breath of his drunken customers was fortified as if he had been drinking. He had to be jovial and complaisant to withstand his imprudent and annoying customers. And he had to be ready to converse constantly and drink with those who wanted to drink with company. That is why the *pulque* servers are generally fat and jowly."[29] Some bartenders kept tabs with a knotted string or a thin rope strung with shells, a survival, one visitor reckoned, of the Aztec method of counting.[30] Every *pulquero* knew this ditty:

> Do you know that *pulque*
> Is a liquor divine?
> It is drunk by Angels
> Instead of wine.[31]

Drinking *pulque* meant getting drunk, and drunkenness was the social calamity of most concern to the upper classes. Mexicans were apparently four times as likely as Americans to die from alcoholism at the turn of the century. Almost half of these casualties were in the capital. The mystical qualities of the maguey, and the high caloric and moderate alcohol content of *pulque*, led many to believe that the cheap beverage was not only hearty, but healthful. That was a comforting thought for the tens of thousands of lower-class folk who complemented their daily draughts of *pulque* with a meager ration of thirty or forty corn tortillas and a small bowl of cooked beans. *Pulque* crippled livers and it ruined stomachs: the drink was often adulterated with contaminated water, which caused serious intestinal problems and intensified the toxic effects of the alcohol.[32]

Pulque and other popular beverages like *mescal* and *aguardiente* often killed those who drank them excessively; other drinkers became targets of the violence that often accompanied the drinking. Eighty-five percent of those in the city jail at any one time were being held overnight on the charge of "disorderly drunkenness." In 1893 alone, twenty-six thousand were detained for causing trouble while intoxicated, and more than one third of those convicted and sentenced to long terms in prison at the turn of the century were drunk when they committed their crimes. Education minister Justo Sierra branded drinking the "evil of the century." Sierra and many others were disturbed by the apparent connection between drinking and violence.[33]

They were equally concerned about what alcohol did to work habits and energy levels. Artisans took frequent breaks for a drink, and the custom of *hacer la mañana*, or drinking through the night, meant lost days. Workers struck the San Antonio de Abad textile factory when the administration tried to curb their long-standing practice of drinking *pulque* for lunch, and bakers struck violently in 1902 for the right to quaff *pulque* on the job. "The *pulquería* and the *cantina*," bewailed a city paper, "pour out torrents of the venomous liquid each day, converting our men into idiots and sapping the strength of our people."[34]

"A party or celebration is not complete without plenty of *pulque*." But excessive drinking, *El Tiempo* complained, was not confined to the lower classes. The city's writers liked to lubricate their brains with alcohol, and several famous poets and novelists, including Gutiérrez Nájera, died young from poisoned livers. Middle-class men, like the father of professor and politician Ramón Beteta, typically dedicated at least one day of the weekend to getting drunk in a bar, followed by the predictable fights with their wives. The upper classes liked to down aperitifs in the morning and swig "digestives" in the afternoon. Trials were often suspended because lawyers were drunk, and professional exams were frequently given in bars. A primary school text for middle-class children graphically depicted the physical, moral, and emotional aspects of drinking. *Pulque*, the book concluded, was the "great poisoner of our poor masses . . . alcoholic fathers are no better than criminals."[35]

Peasants and Pelados

A visiting Spaniard, Julio Sesto, applauded the press, the government, and the enlightened classes of the capital. He then turned to the city's "black point," its poor masses, who were known colloquially as *léperos* and *pelados*. They went barefoot or wore sandals, were unwashed and often tipsy, capped with straw hats and wrapped in *rebozos*. They often strayed from their eastern slums to lounge around the Zócalo and walk down Plateros, where they managed to get into just about every photo taken of the downtown. The *pelado*, wrote Samuel Ramos in *El perfil del hombre y la cultura en México*, "belongs to the meanest social category. He is the human waste of the great city. Economically less than a proletarian, intellectually he is a primitive."[36] Descriptions of the masses by foreign visitors and Mexican doctors, writers, and politicians were often overwrought and degrading. But they depicted with some accuracy a reality that was much larger and more influential in Mexico's capital than in any other city in the Americas.

To the upper classes who lived along Reforma and the well-off workers and professionals of Santa María, they seemed like an undifferentiated mass of peasants. But Julio Guerrero divided the *pelados* into three groups.[37] The first was made up of the truly wretched. These were *mestizos* who had quit their cornfields and miserable Indians who had lived in the city just long enough to give up their traditional clothing and learn some Spanish. The abrupt transition from a closed rural community to an open city with few economic opportunities for poor migrants encouraged licentiousness without instilling new forms of discipline. These *pelados* tended to be "sexually promiscuous, drink daily, start fights in the *pulquerías* . . . and engage in petty theft." When they earned money they did so as beggars, ragpickers, paperboys, and scullery maids. Some slept in the city's few public dormitories, several thousands in plazas, open lots, and doorways, and tens of thousands on the floors of crowded *mesones*. They washed themselves, and their tattered clothes, when it rained; but even the summer downpours failed to whiten their bare and calloused feet.

A second group was recognizable as "the last line of the Aztecs." The men wore cotton pajama pants, woolen cloaks, and leather sandals; the thin, barefoot women wrapped blue shawls around yellow blouses and braided their long black hair with green string. The men worked as bricklayers, street sweepers, and diggers of sewers and canals. Most of them had lived in the city for some time, and many had grown up in the small Indian hamlets that in the 1870s and 1880s surrounded outlying churches like Tepito and Santa María de los Ángeles in the north, and Santa Cruz Acatlán in the southeast. Others were recent immigrants who had managed, for a time at least, to retain their Indian ways. These more traditional Indians, observed Guerrero, "are less connected to urban society than the *mestizos* and depraved Indians of the first group. They have a higher level of morality, live as couples, and care for their children. The women are loyal and loving to their men in their little shacks and huts."

Those in the third tier tended to have more money than those in the second, but they too were usually illiterate and were perhaps less stable. They were a mix of poor *mestizos* and those Indians who had lived in the city long enough to dress, speak, and act like their comrades of mixed blood. The men and women who sewed, labored in small workshops, and peddled goods in the markets usually rented rooms in *vecindades* and lived with their partners (most couples were not legally married) and their children. The men in the army, however, often went on long stints in the provinces and apparently gave their women too many chances to be led astray. All were victims of economic downturns, during which they and their children were forced to hawk newspapers, shine shoes, beg for money, and even steal food and goods from stalls along the Zócalo's commercial arcade. The unsteady work, the unsanitary tenements, and the high rates of infidelity combined at times to force many of these upper-tier *pelados* into the *ratero*'s life of loitering, drink, and theft.

These *pelados* offended the proprieties of their wealthier compatriots and shocked foreign visitors. Julio Sesto took particular exception to the cotton breeches that "hug the flexible swells of the masculine parts and by tracing outlines, or through holes and tears, expose immodest vulgarities." Others were astonished at the Indians' display of "calm" and "freedom from self-consciousness." One visitor, in 1912, saw "two imperturbable Aztecs in native costume drive a flock of a hundred or more turkeys along San Francisco, the most bustling street of the capital, using a strip of cloth on the end of a stick to direct their feathered charges, and apparently unconscious of the varied world around them. One turkey was holding up an injured and bleeding foot that had been run over by some car." *Cargadores* were hauling crates, suitcases, and birdcages all over the downtown, in and out of the Zócalo, and to and from the rail stations. To the lowly carrier's pleas for work or a larger tip, the proper response was "Dios le pagará" — "God will pay you."[38]

The polite classes were forever complaining about "the dirty and nauseating people" of this "mongrel city." According to them, many among the lower classes relieved themselves in the streets, embraced sexually in the parks, and gave free rein to their children. The city's *pelados*, wrote the Catholic paper *El Tiempo* in 1900,

> constitute one of the most vile underclasses in the world, as dirty as it is insolent. Because these people have done nothing to better their living conditions or civilize themselves over time, it is necessary to keep a strict watch over them, so they do not get out of control and make trouble. Whoever has visited foreign capitals, or even the other cities of Mexico, will agree that the slovenliness of the lower classes in Mexico City, a grubbiness that is a clear indication of their lack of culture, is far worse than anywhere else.[39]

The city was practically given over to the peasantry during the two-week celebration of Jesus' birth, and for the solemn remembrance of his death and resurrection. On each occasion tens of thousands of mostly Indian peasants flocked to the capital. Many lingered around the great cathedral, where they organized themselves into a bazaar in which everyone had something to sell — beads, palms, crucifixes, and, if nothing else, their misfortunes. Lying near the doors of the great church and begging were the halt, the stooped, and the blind, among them "faces so revolting in their disfigurement, and forms so distorted, as to cause one to turn away in sickening horror." Most ended their pilgrimage at the church of the Virgin of Guadalupe, a shrine located on a hill just a few miles north of the city. American journalist James Creelman was interviewing Díaz at Chapultepec Castle in 1908, when he looked out and saw "long processions of Mexican Indians, accompanied by their wives and children, with monstrous hats, bright-colored blankets and bare or sandalled feet, moving continuously from all parts of the valley and from the mountain passes toward Guadalupe." The Indians, wrote another visitor, were arriving at the shrine "from all directions, bivouacking close up against the church. They seemed to have brought not only all their children, but all their furniture in the shape of *petates* [sleeping mats] and earthen bowls, and any incidental live-stock they possessed in the shape of goat or dog. It was quite cold, and in the dusk they seemed like their own ancestors coming over the hills for the worship of the dreaded and dreadful gods." They came to kneel before the statue of Guadalupe. "For a Mexican woman," says Carmen, in Rafael Delgado's novel *Los parientes ricos*, "there is nothing quite like the image of the Virgin." That went double for a Mexican woman who was also Indian. She knelt before Guadalupe, who was Indian like herself, and revealed her sorrows, joys, and hopes. She received, as always, the Virgin's benevolent, caressing gaze. That gaze did not suit the church hierarchy, however, which saw the pilgrimage as a pagan event that mocked their own, apparently more exalted, idea of religious celebration.[40]

Although the upper classes saw in these Indians the ancestors of every Mexican, they let the church perform the acts of contrition. The washing of feet occurred in the cathedral. A dozen old men, who had been selected from among the city's beggars, sat inside the altar railing. An American visitor described the mostly Indian crowd that had gathered as "dense, eager, and perspiring." One priest "was relieved of his outer robe and with a towel on his arm, and accompanied by another priest bearing a small silver basin of water, he passed from the first to the last of the beggars, placing on one foot of each a few drops of water which he immediately wiped away with the towel; after which he stopped and *seemed* to kiss the spot thus washed. He looked glad when it was over."[41]

If the genteel felt bad about the condition of the lower classes, they felt worse when they had to share their main streets with the likes of "a meek, almost naked Indian who goes slithering by, a leprous gang of human live-stock crawling along the pavement, and a beggar in tattered cotton pants hurling insults at passersby." So the city council tried to remove the offensive scenery. An 1897 law against *rateros*—the petty thieves, loiterers, and beggars who plagued the downtown—let the police arrest anyone they deemed suspicious or unsightly. Ten thousand a year were given time in jail to ponder their status. For those who were not in jail, decrees ordered them to put on regular trousers, to replace sombreros with felt hats, or, if they drove hacks or sold newspapers, to wear uniforms. Few complied. When American diplomat Elihu Root visited the capital in 1907, anxious officials handed out five thousand new pairs of pants to cover at least some of the *pelados* whom the statesman might see downtown. Most sold their pants and bought food.[42]

Better efforts were made to hide the masses during the lavish centennial celebration of independence, which was attended by thousands of foreign dignitaries. The newspapers again backed decrees to outfit the poor, arguing that dress codes not only would make them look better, but would deprive them of money for *pulque*. When these legal remedies failed, the police stepped in and kept the illegally dressed from spoiling the festivities that graced Plateros, Reforma, and Chapultepec Park.[43]

Provincials

With their cafés on Plateros, their mansions along Reforma, and their top hats at the Jockey Club, Mexican aristocrats tried to give themselves the aura of Paris, London, and New York. But inside the houses and underneath the jackets was *México profundo*, the inner Mexico found in the poverty and ignorance of the countryside. José López-Portillo y Rojas was typical of his generation of poets and novelists. He wrote about Mexico by describing its rural folk, "the most genuine and direct inspiration of the Mexican people." The clubs, the mansions, and the fancy raiment, he thought, were foreign implants, which in the hands of Mexicans betrayed the untutored sensibilities of those fresh from the countryside. Mexican aristocrats, like provincials everywhere, could observe only one another, not the true cosmopolitans who created the styles and defined the standards. The confidence that braces aesthetic judgment was a quality in short supply among Mexico's ruling class. They relied on the ideas and fashions of their French, English, and American models. They were so anxious, in fact, that foreign merchants, architects, and tailors continually unloaded low-grade and outdated goods, designs, and styles on them.[44]

"We Mexicans," lamented Alfonso Reyes, "were invited to the feast of civilization when the table was already set."[45] It was not that Mexicans got only leftovers; there was enough for those with money, and Mexico's rulers had plenty of that. What they lacked were the proper table manners. They copied their betters, but with a nervous affectation that hindered what one American described as the cultivation of a "pleasantly exacting standard in the amenities of appearance which one must either approximate, or remain an outsider. In the City of Mexico one is nowhere subject to such aspirations or misgivings, in spite of the 'palatial residences,' the superb horses, the weekly display of beauty and fashion. For the place has upon one . . . the effect of something new and indeterminate and mongrel."[46] Mexico City had the effect of something new because the ideas that informed the design of its fancy buildings, the layout of its fine neighborhoods, and the appearance of its wealthy people were all recent imports. It gave the impression of something indeterminate because aristocrats and professionals were choosing fashions and styles without customary guidelines. And it seemed mongrel because Mexico City, like no other capital in Latin America, combined city and country, Spaniard and Indian, and dandy and peasant into an uncertain and volatile mixture.

Mexico City may have been the hybrid capital of a peasant land, but it was still the capital. Newcomers were easily separated from their money, and the city's tall buildings and reckless traffic awed small-town folk. *Chin-chun-chan*, Mexico's most famous *zarzuela*, or musical comedy, mocked a wealthy couple in for a few days of big-city life:

Ladislao: Wanna 'nother ice cream?
Eufrasia: Nah, I'm stuffed, Ladislao.
Ladislao: Well, how 'bout a flavored brandy?
Eufrasia: I'd take some good ol' sweet-sticks and coffee.
Ladislao: Ahhh . . . If those in Chamacuero could only see us now.
Eufrasia: Yah! Their mouths would drop.
Ladislao: Gee, you're lookin' awfully swell tonight.
Eufrasia: And you like a marquis.
Ladislao: You just wait. I'll get real dressed up later in my coat and patent leather shoes, and I'll put on a top hat as shiny as the sun.
Eufrasia: I'll get done up, too. I'll put on my gloves and purple petticoat and a green and red silk scarf.[47]

Such provincials might mistake harlotry for elegance. A group of high-class prostitutes had a box in the National Theater, where they watched *zarzuelas* and scanned for clients. One evening the unsuspecting head of a vacationing rural family bought the empty seats in their box. After seating his wife and daughter, he cordially greeted the lavish ladies, who were obviously of the city's best families. While surveying the marvelous audience during the first intermission, he saw that many among them were staring at his booth. His pride turned to panic when one man shouted obscenities from the floor, before making several lewd gestures that got a chuckle from the crowd. The wounded paterfamilias stood up and yelled back, until a merciful neighbor told him about his companions. He glared at the harlots, puffed out his chest, grabbed his hat and coat, and marched his women out amidst a chorus of sneers and snickers.[48]

The capital may have dazzled regional landowners, but visiting foreigners and those Mexicans who had traveled abroad saw only a crippling provincialism in the nation's first city. That provincialism assumed various guises. One was the questionable taste of an aristocracy whose imprudence permeated the entire architectural and cultural tone of the city. Another was the city's epidemic ennui. Mexico City, as the parasitic capital of a peasant land, lacked the cultural vigor of Europe's great cities, the raw vitality of America's Chicago, New York, and San Francisco, and the sheer ambition of Latin American rivals like Buenos Aires and São Paulo. Mexicans "are extremely industrious," observed a resident American, "and yet, of what we know as 'energy,' I have seen little or nothing." Doña Carmen, a character in Delgado's *Los parientes ricos*, had just returned after a stay of many years in Paris. She came home to see the new western suburbs, the modern department stores, and the charming restaurants that now graced her old city. She found only boredom. The local theater companies were lifeless, the trips up and down Plateros tiresome, the drives along Reforma routine.[49]

And there was, of course, the palpable and widespread rusticity that meant bad sanitation and inadequate shelter and diet among the city's lower two thirds. As the material lives of the masses were debased, so was the aesthetic world of the gentry. Between 1880 and 1910 the city sent railroads, banks, and schools to the provinces. The country returned over two hundred thousand of its people. The big city had not the economic power, the cultural weight, or the political inclusiveness to effectively urbanize that great mass of rural folk.

The City, the Country, and the National Character

Mexico was "anemic." It carried "an impoverished blood in its veins." The symptoms, said Sierra, were skepticism, listlessness, and a stubborn persistence in old ways. José Yves Limantour, the mighty finance minister, balanced Mexico's budgets and created its modern banking system. He also thought he could improve its people: "The Aztec and Latin races will give rise, if we manage the situation properly, to a strong, enlightened, and prosperous race." Managing the situation, Sierra and Limantour agreed, meant fortifying Mexicans for "that terrible law" of the survival of the fittest. The nutrients were "great quantities of iron, supplied in the form of railroads, and large doses of strong blood, supplied in the form of immigration." The Mexican government brought in the railroads, the manufactures, and the foreign capital. It could not get a transfusion of European blood. And when some members of Congress proposed to import Chinese workers, the newspapers claimed that Asians had the wrong blood type. "What can we expect," they asked rhetorically, "from the crossing of an opium smoker with a *pulque* drinker, of a rat eater and a bean eater?" [50]

Díaz enforced the "terrible law" of economic and social competition for thirty-five years. The gains were obvious. The capital got its shops, boulevards, and mansions; innovative governors and skilled engineers contributed to the commonweal; and money replaced race as the prime measure of power and status. Yet at the end of Díaz's reign the city was still suffering from the anemia that Sierra detected at its beginning, the cultural affliction manifest in *pulque, pelados,* and provincialism. The problem, some said, was that government skewed the operation of the law by favoring the fittest for the struggle. Wealth, family ties, and political connections were turned into jobs, business contracts, and special favors, all of which made the efforts of the rich rather rewarding. Direct public spending also favored the wealthy. "We are too worried about beautifying the capital," protested a city paper; "we have electric light and telephone poles that give the great avenues the look of a forest; we open up new streets; we spend our money on the western part of the city; we erect elegant buildings; we pave streets with the most expensive materials." All the while the neglected east was polluting the air with "miasmatic gases that give rise to the epidemics that are so common in the capital city." [51]

The complaints were justified. Neither the municipal nor the national government did anything to promote a sense of public responsibility or inspire individual initiative among the people. Government failed to enforce the housing codes, create a vigilant and fair judicial system, or supply the eastern slums with water, sewers, and schools. Instead, the city's rulers chose to rely on the cheaper patriotism of elaborate celebrations. Mexico's independence, the dramatic suicides of young cadets before advancing American troops at Chapultepec Castle, and the defeat of the French forces at Puebla were so honored. "Let us hope," wrote the governor in 1884, "that some day we will be able to pay homage to our glorious national celebration not only with splendid parades, but with our public works and deeds as well."[52] That day had not arrived, for most of the population, by the hundredth anniversary of the cry for independence.

It has been said that Díaz retarded the cultural progress of his people by adapting his government to their weaknesses, rather than to their better capacities.[53] There is truth in that, but to others the problem was simply that the human stock of Mexico City was too rough for market forces and government ministries to shape into a finished product in just a generation or so. That is certainly what Pinillos, a character in Quevedo y Zubieta's novel *La camada*, was thinking when his friend suggested that the government close the *pulquerías*, educate the poor, and put pants on the *pelados*. "Educate the *pelado?*" screamed Pinillos. "You must be joking! Just leave him alone in his cotton pants with his *pulque* and his knife. He is happy that way. And when he fights, let him be. They'll mangle each other, and another race will take their place!" A character in González Peña's *La fuga de la quimera* had a larger, if equally skeptical, outlook on the possibility of change. Díaz's dictatorship was in its last days, and Don Mañuel was trying to temper his young friend's optimistic forecast of the impending revolution: "Transform an entire people! You think that's easy? Not in thirty years, not in a century. Magic couldn't change us Mexicans, who are always demanding our rights while neglecting our responsibilities."[54]

The slow pace of cultural progress, and confusion about the role of government in that evolution, quickened a discussion that was natural for a young country trying to find its identity in a world dominated by Europe and America. That discussion was about the national character. The first question was "Who are we Mexicans?" Justo Sierra, as usual, had the answer. "We Mexicans," he wrote, "are the sons of two countries and two races. We were born of the Conquest; our roots are in the land where the aborigines lived and in the soil of Spain. This fact rules all of our history; to it we owe our soul."[55]

For more than three centuries that soul inhabited several bodies. Identity in Mexico, until the late 1800s, depended as much on one's rank in a racial caste system — which was designed around the categories of white, mestizo, and Indian, with dozens of possible variations — as it did on distinctions drawn around wealth, property, or work. "A white who rides barefoot on horseback," wrote Alexander von Humboldt in the early 1800s, "thinks he belongs to the nobility of the country. Color establishes even a certain equality among men who, as is universally the case where civilization is either little advanced or in a retrograde state, take a particular pleasure in dwelling on the prerogatives of race and origin. When a common man disputes with one of the titled lords of the country, he is frequently heard to say, 'Do you think me not so white as yourself?' "[56]

Wealthy mestizos often appealed to high court justices for a declaration of whiteness. When the color of their skin was too swarthy for a clear ruling, they were given notice that they might "consider themselves as whites."[57] Those of mixed race were only 20 percent of the population in Humboldt's time. By 1900, when they were well over half of all Mexicans, and even more of those living in the capital city, Sierra could look back and write, "The Mexican nationality was formed out of the nucleus of mestizos, as the colonial viceroys called them — or Mexicans, as we prefer to call them."[58] Yet the Mexican of Sierra's day was still an uneasy mix of Indian and Spaniard.

The Indian was a heroic figure — when placed in the service of Mexican nationalism. The threatened destruction of the *árbol de la noche triste*, the "tree of the sorrowful night," which marked an Aztec victory over Cortés's band in Tenochtitlan, provoked an outcry that saved it as a national monument. Cuauhtémoc's defense of the city earned him a statue on Reforma and placed him in Mexico's pantheon of heroes. The broadside of a political club that had organized against Díaz's 1910 re-election appealed to the patriotism of those who "carry in their veins the blood of Cuauhtémoc, Hidalgo, and Juárez." Each of these heroes had battled foreign intruders, and each exemplified the defining feature of Mexico's nationalism: the defense of the *patria* against outsiders.[59]

Yet if upper-class Mexicans mourned their fallen ancestors, they did not seem to mind that Europeans had taken their place. The conquest was brutal, and the ruin of their native culture made them sad; but they saw that the Catholic host made a more palatable sacrifice than the rites of the Aztecs. "The loss," said Sierra, "was irreparable; the gain immense."[60]

The loss, he also thought, was necessary for the gain. If the duty of colonial priests had been to make obedient Catholics out of the Indians, the task assumed by the secular state was to turn them into responsible citizens. To the Indian lawyer and Mexican president Benito Juárez, that meant switching brands of Christianity. He told a young Sierra that the Indians should be "converted to protestantism; they need a religion that will teach them to read and not to waste their pennies on candles for the saints." To Sierra, and to most of his generation, it meant nothing less than getting them to quit being Indians: "the locomotive will have to whistle in their ears for quite some time, the schools will have to breathe the truth into their souls for two or three generations, before they move."[61]

Moving, of course, was seen as the problem. Samuel Ramos, in *El perfil del hombre y la cultura en México*, saw his country rooted in what he and other observers around the turn of the century called "Egypticism." Like Egypt, modern Mexico was weighed down by its culture. In Mexico it was not the heavy load of a long history, but the more intense imprint of a peasant society that for three centuries had been tied to a backward colonial power and controlled by a system of bureaucratic privilege and racial prerogative. The anchor of that rigid system was the Indian. His grand society had been crushed beneath it, and his dignity robbed by it. He became a slave, a peon, a vassal. In response he hunkered down for the long haul — as serf on the hacienda, as peasant in the village, and as pawn in a spiritual world of incense, candles, and saints. At the turn of the century, says Ramos, the Indian was incompatible with a world "whose supreme law is progress and movement. As if by magic, his 'Egypticism' has infused the character" of Mexicans, even those in the city.[62]

As the dying idioms of the Indians were saved by recording them in manuals, so their decaying cultures were preserved within the body and soul of the mestizo. Oppressed by three centuries of colonial rule and then doormat to a new century of independence, Indians fought back quietly. They imbued the rising race of mestizos, it was said, with their solitude, sluggishness, and suspicion.[63]

CHAPTER 4

Death & Disorder

An absolute refusal to acknowledge that there could be any basis
for the distinction between the ruled and the ruling other than force
and injustice was characteristic of the new society's personality. Here was
the psychological mold of the new Mexican, which gave his mind its
fundamental shape, and made him reject all authority as openly as
he dared.

— *Justo Sierra*, Evolución política del pueblo mexicano

"Death converted into the *calavera*." That is how Diego
Rivera described the work of printmaker José Guadalupe Posada. Rivera
placed Posada, "the interpreter of the pain, the happiness, and the an-
guished aspirations of the Mexican people," in the center of his great mural
Dream of a Sunday Afternoon at the Alameda Park. Posada is giving his arm to
an elegantly dressed figure with ostrich plumes on her hat and a feather boa
around her neck. She is a *calavera* — the image of a human skull.[1]

Posada was born in 1852 in Aguascalientes, moved to León when he was
twenty, and arrived in the capital in 1888. Although he was making Mexico's
best art at the time, he was overlooked by the city's dandies and artists, and
he was buried in a pauper's grave by neighbors, only one of whom could
sign his own name. The city's novelists, wrote José López-Portillo y Rojas,
tried to be "solemn and paradoxical like Hugo, obscene like Zola, and phrase
sweeteners like Flaubert and Goncourt." Its painters fit Mexican life to romantic and classical forms; its architects copied Garnier. But Posada's art,
like Rivera's after him, was Mexican. Many of his fifteen thousand engravings illustrate the Mexican *corridos* — songs, jests, and prayers — that were
composed by nameless bards and sung by minstrels who traveled all over the
country. Others cover broadsides with cockfights, stabbings, and merciful

interventions by the Virgin of Guadalupe, all in garish colors. And some embellish the political criticism of popular periodicals like *El Hijo del Ahuizote*. The snappy captions or witty stories that accompanied his prints were read aloud on street corners, at neighborhood stores, and in *pulquerías*.[2] Honest and hardy, Posada's art appealed to the masses, who were neglected by the city's cultural elite, its politicians, and its civil engineers.

Posada's skulls danced and sang, drank and fought, swept the streets and patted tortillas; they wore the frilly hat of the fashionable lady and the straw sombrero of the lowly *pelado;* they sat in the confessional and rode the streetcars. These *calaveras*, and Posada's vivid depictions of train wrecks, murders, and robberies, turned the constant and awful specter of death into something familiar, even funny. Posada's audience was not squeamish nor did it feel the need to see life, or even romance, apart from the impending reality of death. "Love is the strangest, the most extreme, form of dying," Augustín Yáñez could write in his famous novel of a small village at the turn of the century; "it is the most dangerous and feared form of living death."[3] Posada adorned and lightened his deathly images by drawing on the beauty that Mexicans used, in so many small ways, to soothe and grace the life of their violent capital: the ubiquitous flowers, the colorful *rebozos*, the widespread fondness for music, the geometrical arrangements of fruit in the markets, the poetic use of the diminutive in speech.

Rivera and fellow muralist José Clemente Orozco claimed to have spent time as children in Posada's one-room shop on the ground floor of a crumbling colonial edifice just north of the Zócalo. The floor was strewn with paper and stained with ink, and the walls were plastered with fresh prints of *calaveras* and posters announcing bullfights, circus acts, and the popular one-act plays called *tandas*. Antonio Vanegas Arroyo, the publisher who printed many of Posada's engravings, was forever darting in and out of the tiny shop, which was always packed with "a half-dozen, half-dressed workers who had never used a comb and rarely touched a bar of soap." As young boys, Rivera and Orozco would have seen Posada, a dark-skinned, mustachioed, and portly man in a shirt, tie, and vest, hunched over his table and drawing in reverse on a zinc plate with a special pen in greasy, acid-resistant ink. When finished, he would have dipped the plate, with its edges and back covered in resin, into a bucket of acid. The drawing, protected by the ink, stood out in relief. So too did Mexican life.[4]

The Mexican type that was revealed in Posada's art was "distinguished not by his beauty or culture, or by the refinements of the advanced races."

He was "loyal and long-suffering," wrote Andrés Molina Enríquez, but also "suspicious, fitful, and reckless."[5] These were the qualities that so easily turned into the violence that Posada made beautiful.

Porfirio Díaz was equally artful — in the craft of politics. In Mexico politics often boils down to the management and control of violence, and in this Díaz demonstrated consummate skill. He was able to stop the civil wars and the banditry that had wrecked most of Mexico's nineteenth century, and so maintain a stable government, attract foreign capital, and keep market forces in motion. But if he engineered what was certainly his nation's most remarkable period of economic and political progress, he could not completely extinguish the cruelty and violence. The advances of the 1880s and 1890s, in fact, only seemed to throw into greater relief what Congress deplored as a feast of "crime, malfeasance, calumny, and wickedness."[6]

The sanguinary religion of the Aztecs was met by the rapacity of the Spaniards, and through most of the nineteenth century Mexico was in a state of chronic and dangerous disorder. The political stability and economic growth of the age of Díaz did not end the violence: wealth was too unevenly distributed, poverty was too acute, and government made too little effort to build an inclusive political system. Force was the means used to achieve order. The result was a divided urban culture without faith in either the system or the law.

Pacifying the Country, Policing the City

Díaz's first task was to pacify a countryside that for six decades had been subject to roving bands, forced conscriptions, and the sporadic clashes of chronic civil war. On hand was a corps of mounted rural guardsmen, the *rurales*, that President Benito Juárez had put together in the early 1860s. The *rurales* were toughs who regularly extorted fees from both the robbers they were sent to kill and the citizens they were supposed to defend; in some cases they were themselves former thieves who used their new powers to pursue their old occupations. Díaz needed them. To build a nation he had to control the countryside, a difficult task made harder by his discharging of thousands of soldiers in the late 1870s. This policy saved money and disarmed potential enemies, but it also provided fresh recruits for the desperadoes who were already looting villages, raiding the mail and passenger coaches that ran between Mexico City and its Gulf port of Veracruz, and robbing and even murdering senators right outside the city. The infamous outlaw base at Río Frío, which was just east of the capital and had been cleared out in the early 1870s, again harbored brigands.[7] Congressional leaders clamored for the security that foreign investors demanded before linking Mexico to a growing world market: "If we want to stamp out brigandage, if we want to rid the city of criminals, then we must patrol the city streets and the national roads. If we have to put a man on every corner, then do it; take the troops now useless in the barracks, and surround the city with them; line the roads with *rurales*. And above all, let's give the government the power to punish those who commit crimes."[8]

Here was one congressional directive that Díaz would heed. Between the late 1870s and the early 1880s he further reduced the size and budget of the army while quadrupling funding for the *rurales* and increasing their number from one thousand to seventeen hundred.[9]

The job of humbling rural brigands, Díaz knew, was not for a straitlaced and professional squad, even if he could get one. He fought fire with fire. His ripening talent for luring enemies into his own camp helped him recruit many of the bandits themselves. A popular story told of a subordinate who presented Díaz with a bunch of scarred ruffians as recruits for the *rurales*. The general looked them up and down and had a better idea: "Bring me the ones who beat up these guys."[10]

Díaz meant it, and people believed him. He had a reputation as a ruthless soldier, and was revered for his important role in the famous victory over French forces at Puebla. And in the early years of his presidency, it was Díaz the soldier who often prevailed over Díaz the statesman. The general occasionally tamed a wayward politico with the same tactics his *rurales* used to subdue desperadoes. His then infamous and now proverbial order, "Mátelos en caliente" ("Kill them in cold blood"), was immortalized in a popular folk ballad called "The Martyrs of Veracruz" in which Governor Luis Terán replies to the complaint that the political prisoners he executed on orders telegraphed from Díaz were entitled to a fair trial:

> He ordered whosoever could
> to kill them in cold blood
> and this is the true bent
> of Porfirio our President.[11]

Most of the thirty thousand who served as *rurales* between 1880 and 1910 were illiterate, unmarried men from the countryside. The majority were peasants, but nearly one third were former artisans whose small-town jobs were either eliminated through imports and the products of new Mexican factories, or paid so poorly that joining the guard was an excellent option.

While good pay and harsh punishment prevented defections and double-dealing, these young and rootless men were not known for their discipline. One in four deserted, most in their first year, and another 15 percent were discharged for drunkenness on duty, missed formations, or insubordination. Their unruliness was matched by their flamboyant toughness. Like the Plateados, who were the most notorious of all robber bands, the *rurales* wore gray bolero jackets, felt sombreros, and tight-fitting leather pants studded on the outer seam with silver buttons. This *charro* outfit, as it was called, meant its wearer could "outride, outrope, outshoot, outdrink, and outwomanize any other cowboy." [12] That was the kind of man Díaz wanted on the front line of what he would later remember as a vicious labor of pacification:

> We began by making robbery punishable by death and compelling the execution of offenders within a few hours after they were caught and condemned. We ordered that wherever telegraph wires were cut and the chief officer of the district did not catch the criminal, he should himself suffer; and in case the cutting occurred on a plantation the proprietor who failed to prevent it should be hanged to the nearest telegraph pole. These were military orders, remember. We were harsh. Sometimes we were harsh to the point of cruelty. But it was all necessary then to the life and progress of the nation . . . It was better that a little blood should be shed that much blood should be saved; that blood that was saved was good blood. [13]

By the early 1880s the *rurales* had shed enough bad blood to kill most of the brigands and to cause those who thought about taking their place to think again. Their job of pacification done, they became a rural police force that made sure things went Díaz's way. In exchange for spying, fixing votes, and punishing those who defied the dictator, the *rurales* were allowed to collect protection money and bully the townsfolk. The president, writes the historian of the rural police, rewarded his beloved force with an annual banquet attended by the guardsmen and a legion of diplomats and dignitaries:

> At nine o'clock on the morning of the feast, a corps commander posted elegantly mounted Rurales for three miles along the beautiful Reforma Boulevard . . . The presidential carriage arrived about noon. Then Díaz reviewed the troops from a balcony of the Elysian Tivoli, a magnificent restaurant with sumptuous gardens and a gambling casino, all reserved only for the elite. . . . At the banquet the dictator toasted the Rurales as

guarantors of the safe peace of the people. Not only did the Rurales protect farmers against bandits, but they guarded the innocence of women and children against evildoers. Next, Inspector Ramírez thanked the president for his personal attentiveness to the corps, and then all the company sat down to dinner at a banquet table shaped like a horseshoe and heavily trimmed with floral emblems of state. The menu was absolutely gourmet, usually French, not Mexican: *poulet à l'anglais, filets de boeufs Colbert, pâté de fois gras aspic,* and *salade cresson.* On occasion it was a real Mexican country meal: *mole, carne asada,* and *pulque.* Then — off they went to the gambling tables.[14]

Díaz pacified the countryside, steadied the government, and fired up the economy; yet the capital was more violent than ever. In *La criminalidad en México,* Miguel Macedo noted the capital's murder rate of one per day, or one per thousand inhabitants, and the fact that two thirds of all crimes in Mexico City were of the knifing, shooting, and beating variety: "no comparison can be made between Mexico and the Latin nations of Europe. When looking at the numbers, one gets the impression that Mexico is barbarous, and France, Italy, and Spain are civilized." The barbarism would have seemed greater still had not most violent crimes been committed by and against *pelados* and in the eastern barrios. "Foreigners do not understand," wrote *El Financiero Mexicano,* a newspaper concerned with attracting capital and immigrants, "that almost all the crimes registered in the police reports and the newspapers are committed among the lower classes. There is a world of difference between the educated and cultured class, and the crass and perverted masses."[15]

That world of difference was exploited by the cleverest among those masses. The capital, its newspapers agreed, was suffering from a "plague of *raterismo.*" The number of "*rateros* has increased incredibly," wrote a paper in 1890; "they are in the streets, in the churches, in the parks. One stumbles upon them everywhere." There were even "elegant *rateros*" who robbed the rich around the theaters, in high-class pool parlors, and at train stations. Shoplifters and break-in artists supplied several city markets with stolen merchandise, as did domestics who sold their employers' jewelry, china, and clothing to fences who unloaded the goods at pawnshops and outdoor markets. Domestic *rateros* were so brazen that the press proposed importing more respectful servants from Africa and Asia.[16]

These kinds of complaints by journalists and criminologists may have betrayed the paranoia of the upper classes. But upper-class anxiety was no surprise in a city with lots of violent crime, brazen acts of robbery, and desperately poor people who resented the parade of wealth downtown and got nothing from their government. To deal with what was at least perceived as a grave social danger, a special law against thieves — La Ley contra Rateros — was proclaimed by Governor Rincón Gallardo in 1897. From then on over ten thousand *rateros* were arrested each year. This amounts to about a dozen of every one hundred adult males, but there were probably repeat offenders. The police charged *rateros* with misdemeanor offenses that were judged by an appointee of the governor. Yet almost a fifth of all *rateros* arrested in 1900 had done nothing other than smell bad, beg for money, or appear insolent, all of which raised the suspicion of dishonest living.

But the new policy was meant not just to curb theft, or even rid the streets of undesirables. It also provided workers for hacienda owners. Most of those charged with *raterismo* were given a fine or a short jail sentence. Many were assigned to pick and shovel crews on the city's drainage projects, or ordered to help build the new jail. Yet thousands of these mostly peasant migrants were sent back to the countryside as slave laborers on henequen estates in the Yucatán and as serfs on tobacco farms in Oaxaca's Papaloapan River Valley, which was known as the Valle Nacional (National Valley). "Valle Nacional," wrote a visitor in 1908, "is undoubtedly the worst slave hole in Mexico. Probably it is the worst in the world." Over 90 percent of the workers died within a year. "There are no survivors of Valle Nacional — no real ones," observed a government engineer. "Now and then one gets out of the valley . . . but he never gets back to where he came from. Those people come out of the valley walking corpses, they travel on a little way and then they fall." The press debated the merits of penal colonies and state-run agricultural camps for *rateros,* but neither they nor Congress reported the trainloads of deportees who periodically left the city under armed guard for private haciendas in the far southeast. "The passion for stealing," concluded Francisco Bulnes, a close collaborator and later a critic of Díaz, had become "the master passion of the nation." [17]

If stealing was the master felony, intoxication was the preferred misdemeanor. It was punishable only when accompanied by "scandal," and that was defined by the arresting officer. Drunks who had not committed a "grave" scandal woke up the next morning in a police station and were released. Only about one of every five arrested for drinking were actually sentenced for scandalous drunkenness. That still amounted to 5 percent of the entire male population serving jail time for mixing *pulque* with trouble. In 1902, for example, patrolmen escorted 91,930 to the police stations for drunkenness, but only 18,864 of them had been scandalous enough the night before to warrant punishment. A slight decline in the number of outrageous drinkers in the late 1890s and early 1900s was probably the result of the rounding up of *rateros* that began in 1897. Hundreds of drunken men suffered the same fate as unlucky *rateros:* they were picked up in the streets and the *pulque* shops, put under lock and key, and after the agents of big landowners had paid off the police they were deported to Valle Nacional.[18]

The *rurales* were licensed to track down and shoot bandits. The police had a more difficult charge: they had to find murderers, arrest *rateros,* and jail scandalous drunkards. And they had to do so with restraint, under the watchful eye of the city's polite classes, and without the annual banquets and *charro* outfits that made heroes of the rural guardsmen. Yet the police force was made up of the same sort of peasants who, as *rurales,* were allowed to chase after outlaws, women, and money. "The police," reported the city's governor in 1873, "are recruited from the most ignorant and abject among us, and have no idea of their mission or how to accomplish it. . . . They do little more than hang around taverns or sleep on street corners." Turnover rates of 46 percent a year among the mostly illiterate policemen were typical until the 1880s. And in those early years a cop seldom commanded obedience from his betters, who saw the peasant patrolman more as an object of scorn than as a person worthy of respect. If browbeating failed to cow an enterprising officer, a bribe would settle the matter.[19]

Patrolmen eventually got better training, smarter uniforms, and clubs and revolvers instead of machetes. But drinking, insubordination, and failure to report for duty never ceased to be major problems. And although the police managed to secure the downtown streets and the western neighborhoods, and even send sporadic patrols through most of the eastern barrios, the newspapers were forever clamoring for "policemen who know what they have to do and how to do it, and then go out and do it." Those kinds of cops were rare. Many officers were ignorant men who spent more time fooling with their guns, hanging out in saloons and grocery stores, and sleeping on the beat than they did keeping watch.[20] "The Plastered Patrolman" was published in a city paper. It poked fun at everyone's image of the typically lazy, corrupt, and *pulque*-drinking cop:

He passes philosophically, from one corner to the other, on the cross streets that are his domain. He collects a bountiful and varied tribute from the residents fated to live on his beat. At about nine in the morning he looks around, and if he does not spot the official who oversees his street corners, and of course he hardly ever does, because the officials are never around when they should be, he then ducks into the corner *pulquería* and says, familiarly,

"Hey, what's new?"

"Nothing, Señor Defender; what shall I pour you?"

"Man, it's really early."

"Oh, come on now. Remember, he who washes early has time to dry."

"Well, all right, all right; I'll have one so as not to snub you."

The *pulquero* serves him a drink of *pulque*, and the copper quaffs it down, all at once. He then smacks his lips, lets out a long sigh of satisfaction, pats his stomach and says, "All right, all right. Well, thanks, I'm off because the boss should be passing by soon. And what are you going to serve him, eh?"[21]

Policemen, as this story shows, were stationed at street corners. Gendarmes in Mexico, unlike those in every other city in the world, had specific intersections that they might guard for years. At night they had "little red lanterns, which they set in the middle of the streets and hover near. One sees these lanterns, one at each corner, twinkling down the entire length of the principal streets. There is a system of lantern signals and when one lamp begins to swing the signal is carried along and in a trice every *gendarme* on the streets knows what has happened."[22]

The areas between street corners were not patrolled because the stationary position of the officers made it easier for the roundsmen to keep an eye on them. The government and the police captains were as concerned with watching their own lawmen as they were with catching criminals. This strategy of stationary deployment, and the high levels of crime, explain why Mexico City had far more policemen per capita than any other big city in Europe or the Americas.[23]

What culprits the police did manage to corral were sent to Belem prison, which inhabited a seventeenth-century religious school that was appropriated by the reform government and turned into the city jail in 1866. Each morning hundreds of women swarmed around the entrance. They carried baskets of food for confined relatives and occasionally sat at the tables of letter writers to dictate notes to loved ones. Dozens of undercover police kept a conspicuous watch. While waiting to comfort souls on the inside, a couple of priests consoled those on the outside with words of faith and endurance. Díaz inherited and enforced the reform's antichurch laws of the 1850s, but he quietly allowed priests to say mass and administer the sacraments. Those priests found plenty of customers looking to make their peace with God, because many of those who entered Belem, even for short stays, never left it alive. The prison held 1,017 inmates in 1877, and over 5,000 by 1910. The "conditions in the prison could not get any worse," wrote the city council in 1885, but they did, each and every year. Cholera was rampant, and in 1892 an outbreak of typhus killed over 10 percent of the inmates in just a couple of weeks.[24]

Solitary confinement, at least, was one punishment the damned of Belem did not have to fear. There were only ninety-four single-person cells in 1911, and a dozen inmates were packed into each one of them. It was impossible, under conditions like these, to separate hardened criminals from lesser offenders and those prisoners not yet sentenced. Moldy walls, packed cells, sewage on the floors, and all sorts of sexual transgressions made it "inhuman to put rational beings in there," wrote a police chief, "even if their vices have brought them down to a low, debased state." A new penitentiary was built to alleviate the crowding in Belem. It opened in 1900, on the east side, and was soon overflowing with the city's most dangerous criminals. By the 1910s it was "the most repulsive sore of the capital."[25]

Anarchic Individualism

Murders, thievery, drinking—these were only the most visible forms of the strife that pervaded Mexico. The capital, according to those who lived there, was on a perpetual slow boil. To say that is not to exaggerate the violence, the tension, and the mistrust. Most of the people, most of the time, were not involved in confrontation. But all the evidence we have—crime statistics, newspaper reports, sociological studies, travelers' accounts, and one of the most ferocious revolutions ever—suggests a city whose people were especially divided, suspicious, and quick to take offense.

No amount of legislation, police work, or jail time could blunt the sharp edges of life in the capital. Part of the problem was simply that Mexico City had become a full-fledged metropolis. Like any big city, the capital now had the requisite size, a sufficiently dynamic market economy, and enough different kinds of people to offer the freedom and anonymity of urban life. At the same time, however, the city also weakened the power of kin and community to check a person's behavior, replaced the continuity of generations in the countryside with chronic insecurity, and thereby introduced confusion and estrangement into the lives of city dwellers. These are facts of cities everywhere, but Mexico City offered an additional complication. As the capital of Mexico it could not temper, as did American and European cities, its growing liberties and opportunities with amplified sensibilities of personal control, public responsibility, and respect for the privacy of others.

Just walking around the capital was a strain. The crowded conditions and quick tempo of any large city put walkers on guard. But to Mexicans who had visited the great cities of Europe and America, and to the foreigners in Mexico, the capital was particularly hostile to pedestrians, in spite of its low density and comparatively slow pace. "We are convinced," wrote a city paper, "that the difficulty of walking through our streets is not really because of the number of pedestrians, but because most of them don't know how to walk properly. The number of idiots is infinite. Friends stop right in the middle of the sidewalk for conversations without a thought to those they bother; entire families take up the width of the walkway and force those oncoming into street traffic; dandies walk around in circles sticking people with their canes."[26]

Pedestrians, another daily complained, "stop anywhere and look at anything"— at a woman, at a street vendor, at nothing at all — "and they run after things that don't concern them." This was not the typical ambulance chasing or window shopping of city life. "Mexicans, more than others, have a naïve curiosity aroused by the smallest things." That curiosity ranged from the peasant's ingenuous fascination with street spectacles of any variety — a juggler, an organ grinder, an electric sign in a window — to the aristocrat's ill-mannered stare at a rival's dress, carriage, or company.[27] The guileless curiosity of peasant and gentry alike was symptomatic of a deeper problem: the individual freedoms that came with the railroads, markets, and city streets were not matched by a sense of public responsibility. The habit of adjusting one's behavior to surrounding conditions — for example, by not walking four abreast or stopping for a chat or a look-see in the middle of a sidewalk — was slow to develop.

Inconsiderate strollers made walking the streets an ordeal; peddlers, *cargadores*, and coachmen made it downright dangerous. Vendors would take over sidewalks and obstruct street corners with their piles of goods and then cuss out anyone not interested in buying. *Cargadores* barreling down the way with boxes strapped to their backs scattered pedestrians who already had to dodge the normal hazards of sidewalks in a constant state of disrepair.[28] And the unfortunate person who carelessly stepped into the street to get around a knot of gawkers or out of the path of an oncoming *cargador* might be run down by "insolent coachmen." Their insolence was less a voluntary attitude than a trait necessary in a city where aggression was more useful, and more respected, than politeness and caution. Everyone drove that way on the street, from hacks looking for fares, to the sons of the rich out for a spin, to jacketed coachmen commanding glorious carriages that, to the disquiet of many, brought Plateros to a standstill every afternoon.[29]

To many, Mexico City was "way too noisy," but not with the whiz of traffic and the hum of industry; it was because of colorless fireworks exploded for their simple bang, the regular clang of church bells, staccato cries of peddlers, phonographs wailing all day long, loud conversations conducted between facing balconies and across sidewalks, and the thud of a brick or rock thrown against the locked door of a tenement late at night.[30]

Even when it was quiet, there were the eyes to contend with. Young aristocrats, for example, were not averse to throwing nasty glances in the downtown streets. "They stare at other men," wrote novelist Heriberto Frías, "especially those of the lower classes. They look at them with utter disdain and disgust, and force them, with their scornful gazes, to make way." Those same "Mexican gentlemen manifest their appreciation of feminine beauty by gazing intently at ladies whether in the Alameda or at the theater." And in the guise of chivalry they bowed politely and offered admiring words to the pretty women they passed in the street. The men of the lower classes admired female beauty in less delicate ways.[31]

Hogging the sidewalk, yelling across the street, staring at passersby— these were all true to the Mexican idea of freedom: to do what you want until someone stops you. Everyone's privacy was constantly probed and invaded. And public space, because it belonged to no one in particular, belonged to the first one with enough power to claim a street corner, the right of way, or even a wall, which were almost all illegally painted and placarded with notices and advertisements.[32] The public property of the state, wrote Francisco Bulnes, was not merely pilfered by the unscrupulous, as in New York, Chicago, and London. In Mexico City it was understood that the very purpose of government property was to provide for private gain:

Doing business with the government meant, of course, stealing. It was advised to take everything on contract, from laying fifty thousand kilometers of railroad to removing trash from public offices, all to be manipulated so as to redound to the personal benefit of the contractor. If it were not possible to obtain contracts, the judges ought to sell sentences; the court secretaries, the papers bearing on the case; the clerks, the public trust; the chiefs of the department, the office furnishings, the hospital supplies, the prison food, the arms and ammunition of arsenals; they should rob the troops of their pay; impose fines upon all; sell justice under every form; sell police vigilance, wholesale and retail; steal even the inkstands, pencils, paper, typewriters, and typewriter ribbons — in a word, everything that could be taken ought to be taken, however low and unethical the means to accomplish it might be.[33]

"To live together and share in any human concern," wrote Aristotle, "is hard enough to achieve at the best of times."[34] Times were good during the Porfiriato, but nothing could surmount the anarchic individualism that reigned in Mexico City. One obstacle to reaching a higher level of shared concern in the capital was its two hundred thousand desperately poor peasants. The idea of "civilizing" oneself through the adoption of conventional manners was beyond the means of these folk. They were illiterate, cut off from their traditional ways, and neglected by the upper classes and the government, which made little attempt to elevate them through schooling, charities, or mass political parties.

Another deterrent was the sheer weight of recent history. The law of the land, since independence and until Díaz, had been to take what you could by any means necessary — whether by force of arms, legal chicanery, or state power. That law was tempered by Díaz, but not abandoned. As Mexican capitalism was taking shape in the late nineteenth century under state sponsorship, President Díaz oversaw the formation of a ruling class that relied more on political favor and landlordism than on profits earned through an active and progressive entrepreneurship. The wealthy got that way largely by using the state as a vehicle for their personal enrichment. The government appropriated peasant property for hacienda owners, handed out lucrative public contracts to political insiders, allowed a class of educated men to profit by simply connecting foreign capitalists to Mexican politicians, and gave protected monopolies to businessmen. But that same government did nothing to give the destitute of the eastern slums a reason to develop a sense of respect for their fellow citizens and government.[35]

The growing markets, the geographical mobility, and the density and anonymity of city life created the conditions for urban individualism. That was true everywhere, but in Mexico that individualism became unrestrained, a kind of narcissism, freedom without obligation. Each person, from the politician to the domestic servant, seemed to satisfy his or her own needs without regard for others. Díaz, who understood Mexicans better than anyone because (as we'll see later) he embodied all their contradictions so exquisitely in his own person, observed that "the individual Mexican as a rule

Leave the temple complex by the south side and you can pick up Bus 61 or 62; both go southwest to the Uzumasa Eigamura Movie Village. If, however, you have no interest in stopping off here—a visit will take at least two or three hours—continue on the bus to Koryuji Temple.

🔟 **Uzumasa Eigamura Movie Village** is Japan's equivalent of the United States' Hollywood. Had Kyoto been severely damaged in World War II, this would have been the place to see old Japan. Traditional country villages, ancient temples, and old-fashioned houses make up the stage sets, and if you are lucky, a couple of actors dressed as samurai will be snarling at each other, ready to draw their swords. It is a fine place to bring children. For adults, whether it is worth the time touring the facilities and visiting the museum depends on your interest in Japanese movies. *10 Higashi-Hachigaoka-cho, Uzumasa, tel. 075/881–7716. Admission: ¥1,800. Open 9–5 (9:30–4 in winter). Closed Dec. 21–Jan. 1.*

⓫ **Koryuji Temple** is a short walk south of Uzumasa Eigamura Movie Village. One of Kyoto's oldest temples, it was founded in 622 by Kawakatsu Hata in memory of Prince Shotoku (572–621). Shotoku, known for issuing the Seventeen-Article Constitution, was the first powerful advocate of Buddhism after it was introduced to Japan in 552. In the Hatto (Lecture) Hall of the main temple stand three statues, each a National Treasure. The center of worship is the seated figure of Buddha, flanked by the figures of the Thousand-Handed Kannon and Fukukenjaku-Kannon. In the rear hall (Taishido) is a wood statue of Prince Shotoku, which is thought to have been carved by him personally. Another statue of Shotoku in this hall was probably made when he was 16 years old.

In the temple's Treasure House (Reihoden), you'll find numerous works of art, many of which are National Treasures, including the most famous of all, the Miroku-Bosatsu. The statue has been declared Japan's number one National Treasure. This image of Buddha is the epitome of serene calmness, and of all the Buddhas that you see in Kyoto, this is likely to be the one that will most captivate your heart. No one knows when it was made, but it is thought to be from the 6th or 7th century, perhaps even carved by Shotoku himself. *Hachigaoka-cho, Uzumasa, Ukyo-ku. Admission: ¥500. Open Mar.–Nov., 9–5; Dec.–Feb., 9–4:30.*

From Koryuji, it is easy to head back into downtown Kyoto. Either take the bus (60–64) back past the Movie Village to Hanazono JR Station, where the JR San-in Line will take you into Kyoto Station, or take the privately owned railway, the Keifuku Electric Railway Arashiyama Line, and go east to its last stop at Shijo Omiya. This stop is on Shijo-dori Avenue, where Buses 201 or 203 will take you to Gion, or Bus 26 will take you to Kyoto Station.

However, because we are so close to the area known as Arashiyama, we are going to take the Keifuku Electric Railway Arashiyama Line going west to Tenryuji Temple and the bamboo forests just to the north. This visit is a pleasant end to the day. You may get the chance to watch some cormorant fishing. If you decide to postpone this excursion until tomorrow, use the JR San-in Line from Kyoto Station to Saga Station, or use the Keifuku Electric Railway Arashiyama Station.

Arashiyama

The pleasure of Arashiyama, the westernmost part of Kyoto, is the same as it was a millennium ago. The gentle foothills of the mountains, covered with cherry and maple trees, are splendid, but it is the bamboo forests that really create the atmosphere of untroubled peace. It is no wonder that the aristocracy of feudal Japan liked to come here and leave behind the famine, riots, and political intrigue that plagued Kyoto with the decline of the Ashikaga Shogunate.

⑫ To the south of Arashiyama Station is the Oigawa River and the **Togetsukyo Bridge.** During the evening in July and August you can watch *ukai* (cormorant) fishing from this bridge. Fishermen use cormorants to scoop up small sweetfish, which are attracted to the light from the flaming torches hung over the fisherman's boats. The cormorants would love to swallow the fish, but small rings around their necks prevent their appetites from being assuaged. After about five fish, the cormorant has more than his gullet can hold. Then the fisherman pulls the bird back on a string, makes the bird regurgitate his catch, and sends him back for more. The best way to watch this spectacle is to join one of the charter passenger boats. *Cost: ¥1,500 adults, ¥750 children. Reservations: Arashiyama Tsusen, 14-4 Nakao-shita-cho, Arashiyama, Nishikyo-ku, tel. 075/ 861-0223 or 861-0302. You may also contact the Japan Travel Bureau (075/361-7241) or your hotel information desk.*

The temple to head for is Tenryuji. If you have arrived at Arashiyama Station, walk north; if you have arrived on the JR line at Saga Station, walk west.

⑬ **Tenryuji Temple** is for good reason known as the Temple of the Heavenly Dragon. Emperor Godaigo, who had successfully brought an end to the Kamakura Shogunate, was unable to hold on to his power. He was forced from his throne by Takauji Ashikaga. After Godaigo died, Takauji had twinges of conscience. That is when Priest Muso Kokushi had a dream in which a golden dragon rose from the nearby Oigawa River. He told the shogun about his dream and interpreted it to mean the spirit of Godaigo was not at peace. Worried that this was an ill omen, Takauji built Tenryuji in 1339 on the same spot where Godaigo had his favorite villa. Apparently that appeased the spirit of the late emperor. In the Hatto (Lecture) Hall, where today's monks meditate, a huge "Cloud Dragon" is painted on the ceiling. Now for the bad news. The temple was often ravaged by fire, and the current buildings are as recent as 1900; the painting of the dragon was rendered by 20th-century artist Shonen Suzuki. The garden of Tenryuji dates to the 14th century. It is noted for the arrangement of vertical stones in the large pond and for being one of the first to use "borrowed scenery," incorporating the mountains in the distance into the design of the garden. *68 Susukino-Baba-cho, Saga-Tenryu-ji, Ukyo-ku. Garden admission: ¥500 adults, ¥300 junior-high-school students and younger. (An additional ¥100 is required to enter the temple building). Open Apr.–Oct., 8:30–5:30; Nov.–Mar., 8:30–5.*

One of the best ways to enjoy some contemplative peace is to walk the estate grounds of one of Japan's new elite—Denjiro Okochi, a renowned silent movie actor of samurai films. To reach his estate, you must either walk through the temple gar-

den or leave Tenryuji and walk north on a narrow street
(14) through a **bamboo forest,** one of the best you'll see in the Kyoto
region. Bamboo forests offer a unique composure and tranquil-
(15) lity. The **Okochi Sanso Villa** will soon be in front of you, with its
superb location. The views of Arashiyama and Kyoto are splen-
did, and on the grounds you are offered tea and cake while you
absorb nature's pleasures. *8 Tabuchiyama-cho, Ogurayama,
Saga Ukyo-ku, tel. 075/872–2233. Admission: ¥800. Open 9–5.*

Central Kyoto

*Numbers in the margin correspond to points of interest on the
Central Kyoto map.*

Exploration of central Kyoto follows tours of eastern and western Kyoto, because the sights here are likely to be convenient
to your hotel and you can visit each sight individually rather
than combining them into a single itinerary.

The two major places in this area to see are Nijo Castle and the
Imperial Palace. Let's go to the Imperial Palace first, because
that is one of the sights that requires permission. The easiest
(1) ways to reach the **Imperial Palace** are to take the subway to
Imadegawa or to take the bus to the Karasuma-Imadegawa
stop. You will join the tour at the Seishomon Gate entrance.

The palace was rebuilt on a smaller scale in 1855, and, in fact,
was home to only two emperors, including the young Emperor
Meiji before he moved his Imperial Household to Tokyo. On the
30-minute tour, you will only have a chance for a brief glimpse
of the Shishinden Hall (where the inauguration of emperors
and other important imperial ceremonies take place) and a visit
to the gardens. Though a trip to the Imperial Palace is on most
people's agenda, and despite the space it fills in downtown
Kyoto, it perhaps holds less interest than do some of the older
historic buildings in the city. *Admission free. To visit the Imperial Palace, arrive before 9:40 AM for the 10 AM guided tour in
English. Present yourself, along with your passport, at the office
of the Imperial Household Agency in the palace grounds. For the
2 PM guided tour in English, arrive by 1:40 PM. Sat. afternoon
tours only on 1st and 3rd Sat. of the month; no tours Sun. Imperial Household Agency, Kyoto Gyoen-nai, Kamigyo-ku, Kyoto,
tel. 075/211–1211. Office open 8:45–noon and 1–4 weekdays,
8:45–noon Sat.; no tours 2nd and 4th Sat. of month.*

(2) If you have chosen to visit the Imperial Palace, **Nijojo Castle** is
easily combined on the same trip. Take the bus going west
along Marutamachi-dori Avenue for a couple of stops to
Horikawa-dori Avenue, and then walk two blocks south along
Horikawa-dori Avenue to Nijojo Castle.

Nijojo Castle was the local Kyoto address for the Tokugawa
Shogunate. While it dominates central Kyoto, it is an intrusion, both politically and artistically. The man who built the
castle in 1603, Ieyasu Tokugawa, did so to emphasize that political power had been completely removed from the emperor and
that he alone determined the destiny of Japan. As if to make
that statement stronger, he built and decorated his castle with
blatant ostentation in order to cower the populace with his
wealth and power. Such overt displays were antithetical to the
refined restraint of Kyoto's aristocracy.

Higashi-Honganji
Temple, **7**
Imperial Palace, **1**
Kyoto Costume
Museum, **5**
Nijojo Castle, **2**
Nishi-Honganji
Temple, **6**
Nishijin Textile
Center, **4**
Raku Museum, **3**
Toji Temple, **8**

Central Kyoto

KEY

— JR Trains
— Shinkansen
  (Bullet Train)
╪═╪ Subway
├─┤ Private rail line

0 ___ 440 yards
0 ___ 400 meters

Kuramaguchi

3

Imadegawa-dori Ave.

4

Imadegawa

1

Sembon-dori Ave.

Horikawa-dori Ave.

Karasuma-dori Ave.

Kawaramachi-dori Ave.

Kamogawa River

Marutamachi-dori Ave.

Marutamachi

2

Oike

Oike-dori Ave.

Nijo

Sanjo-dori Ave.

JR SAN-IN MAIN LINE

Hankyu-Omiya

Karasuma

Shijo-dori Ave.

Shijo

Kawaramachi

Shijo-Omiya

Omiya-dori Ave.

Horikawa-dori Ave.

Karasuma-dori Ave.

Kawaramachi-dori Ave.

Takasegawa River

Gojo-dori Ave.

5

Gojo

Tambaguchi

6

7

Kamogawa River

Shichijo-dori Ave.

JR TOKAIDO

MAIN LINE

SHINKANSEN

Hachijo-dori Ave.

Kyoto Station

8

N

Ieyasu Tokugawa had risen to power through skillful politics and treachery. His military might was unassailable, and that is probably why his Kyoto castle had relatively modest exterior defenses. However, as he well knew, defense against treachery is never certain. The interior of the castle was built with that in mind. Each building had concealed rooms where bodyguards could maintain a watchful eye for potential assassins, and the corridors had a built-in squeaking system, so no one could walk in the building without announcing his presence. Rooms were locked only from the inside, so no one from the outer rooms could gain access to the inner rooms without admittance. The outer rooms were kept for visitors of low rank and were adorned with garish paintings that would impress them. The inner rooms were for the important lords, whom the shogun would impress with the refined, tasteful paintings of the Kano school.

The opulence and grandeur of the castle was, in many ways, a snub to the emperor. It relegated the emperor and his palace to insignificance, and the Tokugawa family even appointed a governor to manage the emperor and the imperial family. The Tokugawa shoguns were rarely in Kyoto. Ieyasu stayed in the castle three times, the second shogun twice, including the time in 1626 when the emperor, Emperor Gomizuno-o, was granted an audience. After that, for the next 224 years, no Tokugawa shogun came to Kyoto. The castle started to fall into disrepair and neglect. Only when the Tokugawa Shogunate was under pressure from a failing economy, and international pressure developed to open Japan to trade, did the 14th shogun, Iemochi Tokugawa (1846–1866), come to Kyoto to confer with the emperor. The emperor told the shogun to rid Japan of foreigners, but Iemochi did not have the strength. As the shogun's power continued to wane, the 15th and last shogun, Keiki Tokugawa (1837–1913), spent most of his time in Nijojo Castle. Here he resigned, and the imperial decree was issued that abolished the shogunate after 264 years of rule.

After the Meiji Restoration (1868), Nijojo Castle became the Kyoto Prefectural Office until 1884; during that time, it suffered from acts of vandalism. Since 1939, the castle has belonged to the city of Kyoto, and considerable restoration work has been completed.

Entrance to the castle is through the impressive **Karamon** (Chinese) **Gate.** Notice that one must turn right and left at sharp angles to make this entrance—a common attribute of Japanese castles designed to slow the advance of any attacker. From the Karamon Gate, the carriageway leads to the **Ninomaru** (Second Inner) **Palace.** The five buildings of the palace are divided into many chambers. The outer buildings were for visits by men of lowly rank, the inner ones for higher ranks. The most notable room, the **Ohiroma Hall,** is easy to recognize. In the room, figures in costume reconstruct the occasion when Keiki Tokugawa returned the power of government to the emperor. This spacious hall was where, in the early 17th century, the shogun would sit on a raised throne to greet important visitors seated below him. The sliding screens of this room have magnificent paintings of forest scenes.

As impressive as the Ninomaru Palace is the garden designed by the landscaper Kobori Enshu shortly before Emperor Gomizuno-o's visit in 1626. Notice the crane and tortoise islands flanking the center island (the land of paradise). The symbolic meaning is clear: strength and longevity. The garden was originally designed with no deciduous trees, for the shogun did not wish to be reminded of the transitory nature of life by autumn's falling leaves.

The other major building on the grounds is the **Honmaru Palace,** but, because it is a replacement for the original that burned down in the 18th century, Honmaru holds less interest than Ninomaru. *Horikawa Nishi-iru, Nijo-dori, Nakagyo-ku, tel. 075/841–0096. Admission: ¥500 adults, ¥190 children under 12. Open: 8:45–5 (enter by 4). Closed Dec. 26–Jan. 4.*

If, after the overt opulence and blatant use of wealth demonstrated by Nijojo Castle, you feel in need of some refinement, ❸ make your way to the **Raku Museum.** The museum displays tea bowls made by members of the Raku family, whose roots can be traced back to the 16th century. As a potter's term in the West, *raku* refers to a low-temperature firing technique, but the word originated with this family, who made tea bowls for use in the Shogun's tea ceremonies. *Aburakoji, Nakadachuri agaru, Kamigyo-ku, tel. 075/414–0304. Admission: ¥600 adults, ¥500 students, ¥300 children (additional charge for special exhibitions). Open daily 10–4. Closed Mon., national holidays Aug. 14–17, and Dec. 27–Jan. 5.*

For another change of pace, if you have interest in traditional Japanese silk weaving, visit the Nishijin silk weaving district south from the Raku Museum on Horikawa-dori Avenue at the corner of Imadegawa-dori Avenue. To get to this district, take ❹ the Bus 9. At the **Nishijin Textile Center** here, demonstrations are given of age-old weaving techniques, and fashion shows and special exhibitions are presented. On the mezzanine, you can buy kimonos and gift items, such as *happi* (workmen's) coats, and silk purses. *Horikawa-dori, Imadegawa-minamiiru, Kamigyo-ku, tel. 075/451–9231. Admission free. Open 9–5.*

From the Raku Museum, the Nishijin Textile Center, or Nijojo Castle, use Bus 9 down (south) Horikawa-dori Avenue. Disembark at the Kyoto Tokyu Hotel. Across from the Tokyu Hotel is ❺ the **Kyoto Costume Museum.** It is on the fifth floor of the Izutsu Building, at the intersection of Horikawa and Shinhanayacho. You may want to pop in here to see the range of fashion that starts in the pre-Nara era and works up through the historical eras to the Meiji period. It is one of the best of its kind and, in its own way, gives an account of the history of Japan. Exhibitions change twice a year, with each exhibition highlighting a specific period in Japanese history. *Izutsu Building, Shimogyo-ku, tel. 075/351–6750. Admission: ¥400 adults, ¥300 college and high-school students, ¥200 junior-high and younger. Open 9–5. Closed Sun.*

❻ The last major attractions in central Kyoto are the **Nishi**
❼ **Honganji Temple** and the **Higashi-Honganji Temple.** They were originally just one temple, until the early 17th century. Then Ieyasu Tokugawa took advantage of a rift among the Jodoshinshu sect of Buddhism and, to diminish its power, split them apart into two different factions. The original faction has the west temple, Nishi-Honganji, and the latter faction the eastern temple, Higashi-Honganji. To reach the two temples, walk south on Horikawa-dori Avenue from the Kyoto Costume Mu-

seum Nishi-Honganji will be on the right, and Higashi-Honganji will be a few blocks east (left).

While the rebuilt (1895) structure of Higashi-Honganji is the largest wood structure in Japan, it contains fewer historical objects of interest than does its rival temple, Nishi-Honganji, where many of the buildings were brought from Hideyoshi Toyotomi's Jurakudai Palace in Kyoto and from Fushimijo Castle, which Ieyasu Tokugawa had dismantled outside of Kyoto in an attempt to erase the memory of his predecessor.

Hideyoshi Toyotomi was quite a man. Though most of the work in unifying Japan was accomplished by the warrior Nobunaga Oda (he was ambushed a year after defeating the monks on Mt. Hiei), it was Hideyoshi who completed the job. Not only did he stop civil strife, but he also restored the arts. For a brief period (1582–1598), Japan entered one of the most colorful (and shortest) periods of its history. How Hideyoshi achieved his feats is not exactly known. One legend relates that he was the son of the emperor's concubine. She had been much admired by a man to whom the emperor owed a favor, so the emperor gave the concubine to him. Unknown to either of the men, she was soon with child, namely, Hideyoshi. In fact, Hideyoshi was brought up as a farmer's son. His nickname was Saru-san (Mr. Monkey), because he was small and ugly. Whatever his origins (he changed his names frequently), he brought peace to Japan.

Because much of what was dear to Hideyoshi Toyotomi was destroyed by the Tokugawas, it is only at Nishi-Honganji that one can see the artistic works closely associated with his personal life, including the great Karamon (Chinese) Gate brought from Fushimijo Castle, the Dashoin Hall (also from Fushimijo), and the Noh stage from Jurakudai Palace.

Nishi-Honganji Temple. Visits to some of the buildings are permitted four times a day on application from the temple office. Prior to leaving home, write to the temple (enclosing a self-addressed envelope with an international postage coupon) at Shichijo-Agaru, Horikawa-dori, Shimogyo-ku, Kyoto. Give your name, the number of people in your party, and the day and time you would like to visit. You can also phone for an appointment after you arrive in Kyoto: tel. 075/371–5181; because you'll probably experience language problems, ask your hotel to make the arrangements for you.

Tours of Daishoin Hall (in Japanese) are given occasionally throughout the year. Call for information. Reservations required. Shichijo-agaru, Horikawa-dori, Shimogyo-ku. Admission free. Open Mar., Apr., Sept., Oct, 5:30 AM–5:30 PM; May, June, July, Aug. 5:30 AM–6:00 PM; Nov., Dec., Jan., Feb. 6 AM–5 PM.

Higashi-Honganji Temple: Shichijo-agaru, Karasuma-dori, Shimogyo-ku. Admission free. Open daily 9–4.

From Nishi-Honganji it is a 10-minute walk southeast to Kyoto Station. However, if you have the time, visit the **Toji Temple**, one of Kyoto's oldest temples. Leave Nishi-Honganji by the west exit and take Bus 207 south on Omiya-dori. Get off at the Toji-higashimon-mae bus stop, and Toji Temple will be across the street.

Toji Temple was established by imperial edict in 796. It was called Kyo-o-gokokuji and was built to guard the city. It was one of the two temples that Emperor Kammu permitted to be built in the city. He had had enough of the powerful Buddhists during his days in Nara. The temple was later given to Priest Kukai (Kobo Daishi), who began the Shingon sect of Buddhism; Toji became one of Kyoto's most important temples.

Fires and battles during the 16th century destroyed the temple's buildings, but many were rebuilt, including the Kondo (Main Hall) in 1603. However, the Kodo (Lecture) Hall has managed to survive the ravages of war since it was built in 1491. Inside this hall are 15 original statues of Buddhist gods that were carved in the 8th and 9th centuries. The eye-catching building here is the 180-foot, five-story pagoda, reconstructed in 1695.

An interesting time to visit the temple is on the 21st of each month, when a flea market, known locally as Kobo-san, is held. Antique kimonos, fans, and other memorabilia can sometimes be found at bargain prices, if you know your way around the savvy dealers. Many elderly people flock to the temple on this day to pray to Kobo Daishi, the temple's founder, and to shop. *1 Kujo-cho. Admission (to the main buildings): ¥500 adults, ¥ 400 high-school students, ¥350 children under 15. Open 9–4:30.*

This concludes the exploration of central Kyoto. From Toji Temple, it is about a 10-minute walk east to the central exit of JR Kyoto Station; one can also take the Kinki Nippon Electric train at Toji Station for the one-stop ride to Kyoto Station.

Northern Kyoto

In the northern suburbs of Kyoto are Mt. Hiei and Ohara. Our first destination is Ohara, for several centuries a sleepy Kyoto backwater surrounded by mountains. Although it is now catching up with modernity, it still has a feeling of old Japan, with several temples that deserve visiting. To reach this area, take either the Kyoto Bus 17 or 18 (not city bus) from Kyoto Station and get out at Ohara bus stop. This is a long bus ride, about 90 minutes, that costs ¥480.

From the bus station, the road heading northeast leads to **Sanzen-in Temple,** a small temple of the Tendai sect. It was founded by a renowned priest, Dengyo-Daishi (767–822). The Main Hall was built by Priest Eshin (942–1017), who probably carved the temple's Amida Buddha (though some say it was carved 100 years after Eshin's death). Flanked by the two disciples, Daiseishi and Kannon, the statue is a remarkable piece of work, because rather than being the bountiful Amida, it displays much more the omnipotence of Amida. Although Eshin was not really a master sculptor, this statue possibly reflects Eshin's belief that, contrary to the prevailing belief of the Heian aristocracy that salvation could be achieved through one's own actions, salvation could be achieved only through Amida's limitless mercy. The statue is in the Hondo (Main Hall), itself an ancient building from the 12th century. Unusual for a Buddhist temple, it faces east and not south. Note its ceiling. The painting depicts the descent of Amida accompanied by 25 bodhisattvas to welcome the believer.

Not only is the temple worth visiting, but the grounds are also delightful. Full of maple trees, the gardens are serene in any season. During autumn, the colors are magnificent, and the approach to the temple up a gentle slope enhances the anticipation for the burned gold trees guarding the old, weathered temple. *Raigoin-cho, Ohara, Sakyo-ku. Admission: ¥500 adults, ¥300 senior and junior high school students. Open 8:30–5 (8:30–4 in winter).*

Two hundred yards from Sanzen-in is the small, little-frequented **Jikko-in Temple,** where one can sit, relax, and drink powdered green tea. To enter, ring the gong on the outside of the gate, and then wander through the carefully cultivated garden. *Admission: ¥500. Open 9–5.*

On the other side of Ohara and the Takanogawa River is **Jakko-in,** a temple to touch the heart. To reach it, walk back to the Ohara bus stop and take the road leading to the northwest. In April 1185, the Taira clan met its end in a naval battle against the Minamoto clan. For two years, Yoshitsune Minamoto had been gaining the upper hand in the battles, and this battle was final. The Minamotos slaughtered the clan, making the Inland Sea run red with Taira blood. Recognizing that all was lost, the Taira women drowned themselves, taking with them the young infant Emperor Antoku. His mother, Kenreimonin, too, leapt into the sea, but Minamoto soldiers snagged her hair with a grappling hook and hauled her back on board their ship. She was the sole surviving member of the Taira clan. At 29, she was beautiful.

Taken back to Kyoto, Kenreimonin shaved her beautiful head and became a nun. First, she had a small hut at Chorakuji (*see* Exploring Eastern Kyoto, *above*), and when that collapsed in an earthquake, she was accepted at Jakko-in Temple. She was given a 10-foot-square cell made of brushwood and thatch, and she was left with images of her drowning son and her massacred relatives. Here she lived in solitude and sadness until, 27 years later, death ended her memories and took away the last of the Taira. Her mausoleum is in the temple grounds.

When Kenreimonin came to Jakko-in, it was far removed from Kyoto. Now Kyoto's sprawl reaches this far out, but the temple, hidden in trees, is still a place of solitude and peace, and a sanctuary for nuns. It is easy to relive the experience eight centuries ago, when Kenreimonin walked up the tree-shrouded path to the temple with the autumn drizzle falling and reflecting her tears. *Admission: ¥500. Open 9–5 (10–4:30 in winter).*

The next stop is Mt. Hiei. Take the Kyoto Bus (16, 17, or 18) down the main highway, Route 367, to the Yase-Yuenchi bus stop, next to the Yaseyuen Train Station. You'll see the entrance to the cable car on your left. It departs every 30 minutes, and you can transfer to the ropeway at Hiei for the remaining distance to the top. At the summit is an observatory offering panoramic views of the mountains and of Lake Biwa. *Admission: ¥500 mid-Mar.–Nov., ¥300 Dec.–mid-Mar. Open Oct.–Mar., 9–6; 9–5 (Mid-July–late-Aug., observatory stays open until 9.)*

From the observatory, a serpentine mountain path leads to the **Enryakuji Temple.** It was, and still is, a most important center of Buddhism. At one time, it consisted of 3,000 buildings and had its own standing army. That was its downfall. Enryakuji really began in 788. Emperor Kammu, the founding father of Kyoto, requested Priest Saicho (767–822) to establish a temple on Mt. Hiei to protect the area (including Nagaoka, which was the current capital) from the evil spirits. Demons and evil spirits were thought to come from the northeast, and Mt. Hiei was a natural barrier between the fledgling city and the northeastern Kimmon (Devil's Gate), where devils would pass. The temple's monks were to serve as lookouts and, through their faith, keep evil at bay.

The temple grew, and, because neither women nor police were allowed on its mountaintop sanctuary, criminals also flocked there, ostensibly to seek salvation. By the 11th century, the temple had formed its own army to secure order on its estate. In time, this army grew and became stronger than that of most feudal lords. The power of the Enryakuji threatened Kyoto. No imperial army could manage a war without the support of Enryakuji, and when there was no war, Enryakuji's armies would burn and slaughter monks of rival Buddhist sects. Not until the 16th century was there a force strong enough to assault the temple, though many had tried. With the accusations that the monks had concubines and never read the sutras, Nobunaga Oda (1534–1582), the general who unified Japan by ending the Onin Wars, attacked the monastery in 1571 to rid it of its evil. In the battle, monks were killed, and most of the buildings were destroyed. What structures we see today were built in the 17th century.

Enryakuji is divided into three precincts: the Eastern Precinct, where the main building in the complex, the Konponchudo, stands; the Western Precinct, with the oldest building, the Shakado; and the Yokawa district, a few miles north. The Konponchudo dates to 1642, and its dark, cavernous interior quickly conveys the sense of mysticism for which the esoteric Tendai sect is known. Giant pillars and a coffered ceiling give shelter to the central altar, surrounded with religious images and sacred objects. The ornate lanterns that hang before the altar are said to have been lit by Saicho himself and have never been extinguished throughout the centuries.

The Western precinct is where Saicho founded his temple and where he is buried. An incense burner wafts smoke before his tomb, which lies in a small hollow. The peaceful atmosphere of the cedar trees surrounding the main structures (Jodoin Temple, Ninaido Hall, and Shakado Hall) offers an imitation of the essence of the life of a Tendai Buddhist monk, who has devoted his life to the esoteric. Enryakuji is still an important training ground for Buddhism, on a par with the temples at Koyasan. One comes to visit here because of the feeling of profound religious significance, rather than for the particular buildings. It is experiential, and, though it's only a twentieth of its original size, one is awed by the magnitude of the temple complex and the commitment to esoteric pursuits. *4220 Sakamoto Honhachi, Otsu-shi. Admission: ¥400 adults, ¥250 high-school students, ¥220 junior-high-students, free for younger children. Open Dec.–Feb., 8:30–4:30, 9–4.*

Additional Attractions

Historical Buildings and Sights

The following lists include additional places of interest in Kyoto that were not covered in the preceding exploring tours:

Katsura Detached Villa. Katsura Detached Villa is considered the epitome of cultivated Shoin architecture and garden design. Built in the 17th century for Prince Toshihito, brother of Emperor Goyozei, it is charmingly located on the banks of the Katsuragawa River, with peaceful views of Arashiyama and the Kameyama Hills. Perhaps more than anywhere else in the area, the setting is the most perfect example of Japanese integration of nature and architecture. The villa is fairly remote from other historical sites. You should allow an entire morning for your visit.

Although the villa was built over several decades, beginning in 1620, with new additions over time, the overall architectural effect is one of elegant harmony, thanks to the faultless craftsmanship and the meticulous structural details. The main building includes the Nakashoin, with three apartments containing nature paintings by the Kano family of artists, and the Hall for Imperial Visits, with decorations made from different kinds of rare wood, including sandalwood and ebony.

The garden has several rustic teahouses alongside a central pond. The names of these teahouses—such as the Tower of Moonlit Waves and the Hut of Smiling Thoughts—conjure up the physical control and delicate aesthetics of the tea ceremony.

Katsura Detached Villa requires special permission for a visit. To obtain this permission, applications must be made by mail or in person, preferably at least a week in advance. (In the off-season, Nov.–early Apr., you may be lucky enough to obtain same-day permission.) Indicate which of the tour times listed below you prefer. Application forms are available at JNTO offices throughout the world. You will need to enclose a self-addressed envelope with an international postage coupon. Send the application to the Imperial Household Agency (Kyoto Gyoen Nai, Kamigyo-ku, Kyoto, tel. 075/211–1215). If you go in person, the Imperial Household Agency is open Monday–Friday, 8:45–noon and 1–4. To get there (It's at the Imperial Palace), take the subway to Kitayama Station. Stay in the last car of the subway train; get off at the fifth stop, Imadegawa Station, and use the No. 6 exit. Walk a short distance south on Karasuma Street and go through the Inui Gomon Gate into the Imperial Palace. You will need your passport to pick up your permit, and you must be at least 20 years of age. The time of your tour will be stated, and you must not be late. The tour is in Japanese only, although a videotape introducing various aspects of the garden in English is shown in the waiting room before each tour begins. *Katsura Shimizu-cho, Ukyo-ku, tel. 075/ 381–2029. Admission free. Tours at 10, 11, 2, 3. Closed Sat. (except in May, Oct., and Nov.), Sun., national holidays, Dec. 25–Jan. 25, and when special ceremonies are held (call the Imperial Household Agency to check).*

To reach the villa, take the Hankyu Railway Line from Kyoto's Hankyu Kawara-machi Station to Katsura Station, and then walk 10 minutes to the villa. Or take a taxi from the station for ¥530.

Shugakuin Imperial Villa. Located in northeastern Kyoto, this villa consists of a complex of three palaces. The Upper and Lower Villa were built in the 17th century by the Tokugawa family to entertain the emperor. The Middle Villa was added later as a palace home for Princess Ake, daughter of the emperor. When she decided that a nun's life was her calling, the villa was transformed into a temple. The most pleasant aspects of a visit here are the grounds and the panoramic views from the Upper Villa.

Special permission is required to visit the villa. Follow the same instructions for permission as for the Katsura Detached Villa (*see above.*) *Shugakuin Muromachi, Sakyo-ku. Admission free. Tours (in Japanese only) at 9, 10, 11, 1:30, 3. Closed Sat. (except in May, Oct., and Nov.). Closed Sun., national holidays, and Dec. 25– Jan. 5.*

This villa may be visited on the way back from Mt. Hiei by taking the Eizan Railway from Yase Yuen Station to Shugakuin Station; the villa is a 15-minute walk from the station. If you come from downtown Kyoto, the trip takes an hour on Bus 5 from Kyoto Station, or 20 minutes by Keifuku Eizan train from Demachi-Yanagi station, north of Imadegawa beside the Kamogawa River.

Temples and Shrines

Byodo-in Temple. Located to the south of Kyoto in Uji City, this temple was originally the private villa of a 10th-century "prime minister" who was a member of the influential Fujiwara family. The Amida-do, also known as the Phoenix Hall, was built in the 11th century by the Fujiwaras and is still considered one of Japan's most beautiful religious buildings, where heaven is brought close to earth. There is also a magnificent statue of a seated Buddha by one of Japan's most famous 11th-century sculptors, Jocho. To reach the temple, take the JR train to Uji Station; from there, the temple is a 12-minute walk. Uji is a famous tea-producing district, and the slope up the temple is lined with tea shops where you can sample the finest green tea and perhaps pick up a small package to take home. *Ujirenge, Uji-shi, tel. 0774/21–2861. Admission:¥400 adults, ¥200 children 12–15, ¥150 children 6–12. Open Mar.–Nov., 8:30–5. (9–4 in winter).*

Daigoji Temple. Located in Yamashina, a suburb southeast of Kyoto, Daigoji was founded in 874. Over the succeeding centuries, other buildings were added, and its gardens expanded. Its five-story pagoda, whose origin dates from 951, is reputed to be the oldest existing structure in Kyoto. By the late 16th century, the temple had begun to decline in importance and showed signs of neglect. Then Hideyoshi Toyotomi paid a visit one April, when the temple's famous cherry trees were in blossom. Hideyoshi ordered the temple restored. Be sure also to see the paintings by the Kano school in the smaller Samboin Temple. To reach Daigoji, take the Kyoto City Bus Higashi 9 or the Keihan Bus 12 from Sanjo Keihan, and disembark at the Daigo-Samboin stop. The ride takes about 40 minutes. *22 Higashi Uji-*

So, you're getting away from it all.

Just make sure you can get back.

All The Best Trips Start with Fodor's

Fodor's Affordables
Titles in the series: Caribbean, Europe, Florida, France, Germany, Great Britain, Italy, London, Paris.

"Travelers with champagne tastes and beer budgets will welcome this series from Fodor's." — *Hartford Courant*

"These books succeed admirably; easy to follow and use, full of cost-related information, practical advice, and recommendations...maps are clear and easy to use." — *Travel Books Worldwide*

Fodor's Bed & Breakfast and Country Inn Guides
Titles in the series: California, Canada, England & Wales, Mid-Atlantic, New England, The Pacific Northwest, The South, The Upper Great Lakes Region, The West Coast.

"In addition to information on each establishment, the books add notes on things to see and do in the vicinity. That alone propels these books to the top of the heap."— *San Diego Union-Tribune*

The Berkeley Guides
Titles in the series: California, Central America, Eastern Europe, France, Germany, Great Britain & Ireland, Mexico, The Pacific Northwest, San Francisco.

The best choice for budget travelers, from the Associated Students at the University of California at Berkeley.

"Berkeley's scribes put the funk back in travel." — *Time*

"Hip, blunt and lively." — *Atlanta Journal Constitution*

"Fresh, funny and funky as well as useful." — *The Boston Globe*

Exploring Guides
Titles in the series: Australia, California, Caribbean, Florida, France, Germany, Great Britain, Ireland, Italy, London, New York City, Paris, Rome, Singapore & Malaysia, Spain, Thailand.

"Authoritatively written and superbly presented, and makes worthy reading before, during or after a trip." — *The Philadelphia Inquirer*

"A handsome new series of guides, complete with lots of color photos, geared to the independent traveler." — *The Boston Globe*

Visit your local bookstore or call 1-800-533-6478 24 hours a day.

Fodor's The name that means smart travel.

cho, Fushimi-ku. Admission: ¥*500 adults,* ¥*250 children under 12 years. Open 9–5 (9–4 in winter).*

Fushimi-Inari Taisha Shrine. This is one of Kyoto's oldest and most revered shrines. The Fushimi-Inari is dedicated to the goddesses of agriculture (rice and rice wine) and prosperity. It also serves as the headquarters for all the 40,000 shrines representing Inari. The shrine is noted for its bronze foxes and for some 10,000 small torii arches, donated by the thankful, which stand on the hill behind the structure. To reach the shrine, use the JR train on the Nara Line. If you are coming from Tofukuji, join the JR train at Tofukuji Station and journey for one stop to the south (toward Nara). *68 Fukakusa Yabunouchi-cho, Fushimi-ku. Admission free. Open sunrise–sunset.*

Kamigamo Jinja Shrine. Along with its sister shrine, the Shimogamo Jinja Shrine (farther south on the Kamogawa River), Kamigamo was built by a legendary warrior named Kamo. Such is Kamo's fame that even the river that flows by the shrine and through the center of Kyoto bears his name. However, Kamigamo has always been associated with Wakeikazuchi, a god of thunder, rain, and fertility. Indeed, until 1212, a virgin from the imperial household was always in residence at the shrine. Now the shrine is famous for its Aoi (Hollyhock) Festival, which started in the 6th century when people thought that the Kamigamo deities were angry at being neglected. Now held every May 15, the festival consists of 500 people wearing Heian-period costumes riding on horseback or in ox-drawn carriages from the Imperial Palace to Shimogamo and then to Kamigamo. *339 Motoyama. Admission free. Open 9–4:30.*

Tofukuji Temple. Located southeast of Kyoto Station, this Zen temple of the Rinzai sect was established in 1236. In all, two dozen subtemples and the main temple comprise the temple complex, which ranks as one of the most important Zen temples in Kyoto, along with the Myoshinji and Daitokuji temples. The autumn is an especially fine time for visiting, when the burnished colors of the maple trees add to the pleasure of the gardens. To reach Tofukuji, either take Bus 208 from Kyoto Station to the temple or take either the JR train on the Nara Line or the Keihan train to Tofukuji Station; from either it is a 15-minute walk to the temple. You may want to combine a visit here with the Fushimi-Inari Taisha Shrine situated farther south. *Honmachi, 15-chome, Higashiyama-ku. Admission:* ¥ *300 adults,* ¥*200 junior-high and elementary-school students. Open 9–4.*

Shopping

Temples, shrines, gardens, and the quintessential elements of Japanese culture are all part of Kyoto's attractions, but none of these can be brought home, except in photographs. What can be taken back, however, are mementos (*omiyage*)—tangible gifts for which this city is famous. The ancient craftsmen of Kyoto served the imperial court for more than 1,000 years. In Japan, the prefix *kyo-* before a craft is synonymous with fine craftsmanship. The crafts of Kyoto are known throughout the world for their superb artistry and refinement.

Kyo-ningyo are the exquisite display dolls that have been made in Kyoto since the 9th century. Constructed of wood coated with white shell paste and clothed in elaborate miniature patterned silk brocades, Kyoto dolls are considered the finest in Japan. Kyoto is also known for fine ceramic dolls.

Kyo-sensu are embellished folding fans used as accoutrements in the Noh play, the tea ceremony, and Japanese dance. They also have a practical use—to ward off heat. Unlike other Japanese crafts, which have their origin in Tang Dynasty China, the folding fan originated in Kyoto.

Kyo-shikki refers to Kyoto lacquerware, which also has its roots in the 9th century. The making of lacquerware, adopted from the Chinese, is a delicate process requiring patience and skill. Finished lacquerware products range from furniture to spoons and bowls, which are carved from cypress, cedar, or horse-chestnut wood. These products have a brilliant luster, and some designs are decorated with gold leaf and inlaid mother-of-pearl.

Kyo-yaki is the general term used for ceramics made in local kilns; the most popular ware is from Kyoto's Kiyomizu district. Often colorfully hand-painted in blue, red, and green on white, these elegantly shaped teacups, bowls, and vases are thrown on potters' wheels located in the Kiyomizu district and in Kiyomizu-danchi in Yamashina. Streets leading up to Kiyomizudera Temple—Chawanzaka, Sannenzaka, and Ninnenzaka—are sprinkled with kyo-yaki shops.

Kyo-yuzen is a paste-resistant silk-dyeing technique developed by 17th-century dyer Yuzen Miyazaki. Fantastic designs are created on plain white silk pieces through the process of either *tegaki yuzen* (hand-painting) or *kata yuzen* (stencil).

Nishijin-ori is the weaving of silk. Nishijin refers to a Kyoto district producing the best silk textiles in all of Japan, used to make kimonos. Walk along the narrow back streets of Nishijin and hear the persistently rhythmic sound of looms.

Keep in mind that most shops slide their doors open at 10. Most shopkeepers partake of the morning ritual of sweeping and watering the entrance to welcome the morning's first customers. Shops lock up at 6 or 7 in the evening. Usually, once a week shops remain closed. As Sunday is a big shopping day for the Japanese, most stores remain open on this day.

The traditional greeting of a shopkeeper to a customer is *oideyasu*, voiced in a lilting Kyoto dialect with the required bowing of the head. When a customer makes a purchase, the shopkeeper will respond with *ookini*, a smile, and a bow. Take notice of the careful effort and adroitness with which purchases are wrapped; it is an art in itself. Also, the clicking of the abacus rather than the clanging of a cash register can still be heard in many Kyoto shops.

American Express, MasterCard, and Visa are widely accepted, as are traveler's checks.

The **Kyoto Craft Center** on Shijo in Gion offers two floors of both contemporary and traditional crafts for sale in a modern setting. *Shijo-dori, Gion-machi, Higashiyama-ku, tel. 075/561–9660. Open 10–6. Closed Wed.*

The **Kyoto Handicraft Center** is a seven-story shopping emporium offering everything from tape decks and pearl necklaces to porcelains and lacquerware designed to appeal to tourists. It's a good place to compare prices and grab last-minute souvenirs. *Kumano Jinja Higashi, Sakyo-ku, tel. 075/761–5080. Open 9:30–6 Feb.–Dec., 9:30–5:30 Dec.–Feb. Closed Dec. 31–Jan. 3.*

Shopping Districts

Compared with sprawling Tokyo, Kyoto is compact and relatively easy to find your way around in. Major shops for tourists and natives alike line both sides of **Shijo-dori Avenue,** which runs east–west, and **Kawaramachi-dori Avenue,** running north–south. Concentrate on Shijo-dori, between Yasaka Jinja Shrine and Karasuma Station, and Kawaramachi-dori between Sanjo-dori and Shijo-dori.

Shin-Kyogoku, a covered arcade running parallel to Kawaramachi-dori Avenue, is another general-purpose shopping area with many souvenir shops.

Roads leading to Kiyomizudera Temple are steep inclines, yet the steepness is hardly noticed because of the alluring shops that line the entire way to the temple. Be sure to peek into these shops for unique gifts. Food shops offer sample morsels, and tea shops offer complimentary cups of tea.

Whereas the shopping districts above are traditional in atmosphere, Kyoto's latest shopping "district" is the modern underground arcade, **Porta,** at Kyoto Station. More than 200 shops and restaurants can be found in this sprawling, subterranean arcade.

Gift Ideas

Art and Antiques **Shinmonzen-dori** holds the key to shopping for art and antiques in Kyoto. It is an unpretentious little street of two-story wood buildings that is lined with telephone and electricity poles between Higashioji-dori Avenue and Hanamikoji-dori Avenue, just north of Gion. What gives the street away as a treasure trove are the large credit-card signs jutting out from the shops. There are no fewer than 17 shops specializing in scrolls, *netsuke* (small carved figures attached to Japanese clothing), lacquer, bronze, wood-block prints, paintings, and antiques. Shop with confidence, because shopkeepers are trustworthy and goods are authentic. Pick up a copy of the pamphlet *Shinmonzen Street Shopping Guide* from your hotel or from the Tourist Information Center.

Nawate-dori, between Shijo-dori and Sanjo-dori, is noted for fine antique textiles, ceramics, and paintings.

Teramachi-dori, between Oike-dori and Marutamachi, is known for antiques of all kinds, and tea-ceremony utensils.

Bamboo The Japanese hope for their sons and daughters to be as strong and flexible as bamboo. Around many Japanese homes are small bamboo groves, for the deep-rooted plant has the ability to withstand earthquakes. On the other hand, bamboo is so flexible that it bends into innumerable shapes. The entire city of Kyoto is surrounded by vast bamboo groves. Bamboo is carefully cut and dried for several months before being stripped and woven into baskets and vases.

Kagoshin is a historic shop that has made bamboo baskets since 1862. Only the best varieties of bamboo are used in this fiercely proud little shop. *Ohashi-higashi, Sanjo-dori, Higashiyama-ku, tel. 075/771–0209. Open 9–6. Closed Sun. and holidays.*

Ceramics **Tachikichi,** on Shijo-dori west of Kawaramachi, has four floors of contemporary and traditional ceramics and the best reputation in town. *Shijo-Tominokoji, Nakagyo-ku, tel. 075/211–3143. Open 10–7. Closed Wed.*

Asahi-do, located in the heart of the pottery district near Kiyomizudera Temple, specializes in Kyoto-style hand-painted porcelains, and a variety of other ceramics. *1–280 Kiyomizu, Higashiyama-ku, tel. 075/531–2181. Open 8:30–6 Mon.–Sat., Sun. 9–6.*

Dolls Dolls were first used in Japan in the purification rites associated with the Doll Festival, an annual family oriented event that falls on March 3. Kyoto *ningyo* (dolls) are made with fine detail and embellishment.

Nakanishi Toku Shoten has old museum-quality dolls. The owner, Mr. Nakanishi, turned his extensive doll collection into the shop nearly two decades ago and has since been educating customers with his vast knowledge of the doll trade. *359 Moto-cho, Yamatooji Higashi-iru, Furumonzen-dori, Higashiyama-ku, tel. 075/561–7309. Open 10–5.*

Folk Crafts **Yamato Mingei-ten,** next to Maruzen Book Store downtown, has the best selection of Japanese folk crafts, including ceramics, metal work, paper, lacquerware, and textiles. *Kawaramachi, Takoyakushi-agaru, Nakagyo-ku, tel. 075/221–2641. Open 10 AM–8:30 PM; closed Tues.*

At **Ryushido** you can stock up on your calligraphy and sumie supplies, including writing brushes, ink sticks, ink stones, Japanese paper, paperweights, and water stoppers. *Nijo-agaru, Terramachi-dori (north of Nijo), tel. 075/252–4120. Open 10–7.*

Kuraya Hashimoto has one of the best collections of antique and newly forged swords, as well as reproductions. *Nishihorikawa-dori, Oike-agaru (southeast corner of Nijo Castle), tel. 075/821–2791. Open 10–6; closed Wed.*

Kimonos and Accessories Shimmering new silk kimonos can cost more than U.S. $10,000, while equally stunning old silk kimonos can cost less than U.S. $30. Unless you have a lot of money to spend, it is wiser to look upon new silk kimonos as art objects.

First visit the **Nishijin Textile Center,** in Central Kyoto, for an orientation on silk-weaving techniques. *Horikawa-dori, Imadegawa-minamiiru, Kamigyo-ku, tel. 075/451–9231. Admission free. Open 9–5.*

Then proceed two blocks east on Imadegawa-dori and a block south to **Aizen Kobo,** which specializes in the finest handwoven indigo-dyed textiles. The shop is in a traditional weaving family's home, and the friendly owners will show you a wide variety of dyed and woven goods, including garments designed by Hisako Utsuki, the owner's wife. *Omiya Nishi-iru, Nakasuji-dori, Kamigyo-ku, tel. 075/441–0355. Open 9–5:30.*

Authentic silk kimonos are very heavy; this factor may dissuade some of you from making that special purchase. If smaller objects are your fancy, try a fan or comb. The most famous fan shop in all of Kyoto is **Miyawaki Baisen-an.** The store has been in business since 1823. It delights customers not only with

its fine collection of lacquered, scented, painted, and
but also with the old-world atmosphere that emanat
building that houses the shop. *Tominokoji Nishiiru, Rokkaku-
dori, Nakagyo-ku, tel. 075/221–0181. Open 9–5.*

Umbrellas are used to protect kimonos from the scorching sun
or pelting rain. Head for **Kasagen** to purchase authentic oiled
paper umbrellas. The shop has been in existence since 1861,
and its umbrellas are guaranteed to last years. *284 Gionmachi
Kitagawa, Higashiyama-ku, tel. 075/561–2832. Open 9:30–9.*

Department Stores

Kyoto department stores are small by comparison with their
mammoth counterparts in Tokyo and Osaka. One department
store looks just like the other, as they have similar floor plans.
Scarves, shoes, jewelry, and handbags can be always found on
the ground floor. The basement floor is devoted to foodstuffs,
and the top floor is reserved for pets and pet-care goods, gardening, and restaurants.

Daimaru is the most conveniently located of these one-stop
shopping emporiums. It is along the main Shijo-dori shopping
avenue. *Shijo Karasuma, Shimogyo-ku, tel. 075/211–8111.
Open 10–7; closed Wed.*

Hankyu is directly across from Takashimaya. It has two restaurant floors. Window displays show the type of food served and
prices are clearly marked. *Shijo Kawaramachi, Shimogyo-ku,
tel. 075/223–2288. Open 10–7; closed Thurs.*

Kintetsu is located on the main avenue leading north from
Kyoto Station. *Karasuma-dori, Shimogyo-ku, tel. 075/361–
1111. Open 10–7; closed Thurs.*

Takashimaya has a well-trained English-speaking staff at its
information desk, as well as a convenient money-exchange
counter on its premises. *Shijo Kawaramachi, Shimogyo-ku,
tel. 075/221–8811. Open 10–7; closed Wed.*

Food and Flea Markets

Kyoto has a wonderful food market, **Nishiki-koji**, which
branches off from the Shin-Kyogoku covered arcade. Try to
avoid the market in late afternoon, for this is the time housewives come to do their daily shopping. The market is long and
narrow; when a sizable crowd is present, there is always the
possibility of being pushed into the display of fresh fish.

Two renowned flea markets take place monthly in Kyoto. Reserve the 21st of the month for the famous **Toji Temple market**
and the 25th of the month for the **Kitano Temmangu Shrine
market.** Both are open from dawn to dusk. Among the old kimonos, antiques, and bric-a-brac may be an unusual souvenir.

Unusual Shopping

Shops dedicated to incense, wood tubs and casks, Buddhist objects, and chopsticks indeed offer unusual experiences. But the
prized souvenir of a visit to Kyoto should be the **shuinshu**, a
booklet usually no larger than 4-by-6 inches. It is most often
covered with brocade, and the blank sheets of heavyweight paper inside continuously fold out. The booklet can be purchased

at stationery stores or at temples for as little as ¥1,000 and
serves as a "passport" to collect ink stamps from places visited
while in Japan. Stamps and stamp pads are ubiquitous in Japan;
they may be found at attractions, train stations, and some restaurants. Most ink stamping can be done for free, but at temples you can ask a monk to write calligraphy over the stamp for
a small fee.

Dining

By Diane Durston

*A resident of
Kyoto for over 10
years, Diane
Durston is the
author of* Old
Kyoto: A Guide to
Traditional Shops,
Restaurants, and
Inns *and* Kyoto:
Seven Paths to the
Heart of the City.

"Paris East" is a difficult epithet to live up to, but in many ways
the elegant sister cities do seem to be of the same flesh and
blood—both are the homes of their nation's haute cuisine.

Although Tokyo has been the capital since 1868, Kyoto—which
wore the crown for the 10 centuries before—is still the classic
Japanese city. The traditional arts, crafts, customs, language,
and literature were all born, raised, and refined here. Kyoto
has the matchless villas, the incomparable gardens, the magnificent temples and shrines—2,000 of them. And it is to Kyoto
that you travel for the most artful Japanese cuisine.

The presence of the imperial court was the original inspiration
for Kyoto's exclusive *yusoku ryori*. Once served on lacquered
pedestals to the emperor himself, it is now offered at but one
restaurant in the city, Mankamero.

The dining experience not to be missed in Kyoto, however, is
kaiseki ryori, the elegant full-course meal that was originally
intended to be served with the tea ceremony. All the senses are
involved in this culinary event: the scent and flavor of the freshest ingredients at the peak of season; the visual delight of a continuous procession of porcelain dishes and lacquered bowls
(each a different shape and size) gracefully adorned with an appropriately shaped morsel of fish or vegetable to match; the
textures of foods unknown and exotic, presented in sequence to
banish boredom; the sound of water in a stone basin outside in
the garden; and finally, that other necessity—the atmosphere
of the room itself, complete with a hanging scroll displayed in
the alcove and a flower arrangement, both to evoke the season
and to accent the restrained appointments of the tatami room.
Kaiseki ryori is often costly, yet always unforgettable.

For those seeking initiation (or a reasonably priced sample),
the *kaiseki bento* (box lunch) offered by many *ryotei* (as high-
class Japanese restaurants are known) is a good place to start;
box lunches are so popular in Kyoto that the restaurants that
serve them compete to make their bento unique, exquisite, and
delicious.

Located a two-day journey from the sea, Kyoto is historically
more famous for ingenious ways of serving preserved fish—
dried, salted, or pickled—than for its raw fish dishes (though
with modern transportation, there are now several decent
sushi shops in town). Compared with the style of cooking else-
where in Japan, *Kyo-ryori* (Kyoto cuisine) is lighter and more
delicate than most. The natural flavor of the ingredients is
stressed over the enhancement of heavy sauces and broths.
Pickled vegetables (*tsukemono*) and traditional sweets (*wa-
gashi*) are two other specialties of Kyoto; they make excellent
souvenirs. The food shops are often kept just as they were a
century ago—well worth the trip just to browse.

Kyoto is also the home of *shojin ryori*, the Zen vegetarian-style cooking, best sampled right on the grounds of one of the city's Zen temples. Local delicacies like *fu* (glutinous wheat cakes) and *yuba* (soy milk skimmings) have found their way into the mainstream of Kyoto-style cuisine but were originally devised as protein substitutes in the traditional Buddhist diet.

A few practical notes on dining in Kyoto need to be mentioned. Many of the city's finest traditional restaurants have done business in the old style for generations and do not believe in modern nuisances like credit cards. Though several establishments are changing their ways, it's wise to check in advance. Also, people generally dine early in Kyoto (7–8 PM), so most places (apart from hotel restaurants and drinking places) close relatively early. Make sure to check the listings below before you go. Concerning appropriate attire, the average Japanese businessman wears a suit and tie to dinner—anywhere. Young people, though, tend to dress more informally. Although many Kyoto restaurants do have someone who speaks English, call the Kyoto Tourist Information Center (TIC) at 075/371–5649 if you need assistance in making reservations.

Famous throughout Japan for the best in traditional Japanese cuisine, Kyoto, unfortunately, has never been the place to go for Western food. Recently, however, some fine French, American, Indian, and Chinese restaurants have opened in the city—a welcome surprise to foreign residents (and visitors who've had enough of raw fish and squiggly foods). Apart from the restaurants listed below, Kyoto does have its share of the sort of budget quasi-Western–style chain restaurants found all over Japan, serving things like sandwiches and salads, gratins, curried rice, and spaghetti. These are easy to locate along Kawaramachi-dori downtown, and they usually come complete with plastic models in the window to which you can point if other methods of communication fail.

Kyoto is not without an impressive (depending on how you look at it) array of American fast-food chains, including McDonald's, Kentucky Fried Chicken, Mr. Donut, Tony Roma's, and both Shakey's and Chicago Pizza in case you get homesick. Many have branches in the downtown area, as well as throughout the city. For specific locations, call the TIC. An additional source of information is the *Kyoto Visitors' Guide*, available free at most hotels.

A 3% federal consumer tax is added to all restaurant bills. Another 3% local tax is added to the bill if it exceeds ¥7,500. At more expensive restaurants, a 10%–15% service charge is also added to the bill. Tipping is not necessary.

The most highly recommended restaurants are indicated by a star ★.

Category	Cost*
Very Expensive	over ¥15,000
Expensive	¥7,000–¥15,000
Moderate	¥3,000–¥7,000
Inexpensive	under ¥3,000

*Cost is per person without tax, service, or drinks

Eastern District

Japanese **Ashiya Steak House.** Located a short walk from the Gion district, famous for its teahouses and geisha, there is no better place in Kyoto to enjoy "a good steak . . . a real martini . . . and the essence of traditional Japan," in the words of 30-year-resident and owner, Bob Strickland, and his wife, Tokiko. While you are seated at a *kotatsu* (recessed hearth), your *teppan-yaki* dinner of the finest Omi beefsteak, grilled and sliced in style, will be prepared as you watch. Cocktails, domestic and imported wines, and beer are available, as well as the best Japanese sake. Cocktails can be had in the art gallery upstairs, which has a display of traditional and contemporary arts and crafts. You'll be impressed by the service and the $140 price tag for a 12-ounce steak. *172-13 Yon-chome, Kiyomizu, Higashiyama-ku, tel. 075/541–7961. Reservations required. Dress: informal. AE, DC, V. Open 5:30–11:30 (last order at 10). Closed Mon. and national holidays. Expensive.*

★ **Yagenbori.** North of Shijo-dori in the heart of Kyoto's still-thriving geisha district, this restaurant is in a teahouse just a few steps down a cobbled path from the romantic Shirakawa River in Gion. The *omakase* full-course meal is an elegant sampler of Kyoto's finest kaiseki cuisine, with local delicacies beautifully presented on fine handmade ceramics. The *shabu-shabu* (thinly sliced beef, dipped briefly into hot stock) and *suppon* (turtle dishes) are excellent. Don't miss the *hoba miso* (bean paste with *kinoko* mushrooms and green onions, which are wrapped in a giant oak leaf and grilled at your table over a charcoal hibachi) on the à la carte menu. *Sueyoshi-cho, Kiridoshi-kado, Gion, Higashiyama-ku, tel. 075/551–3331. Reservations advised. Dress: informal. AE, DC, V. Lunch noon–2, dinner 4–11. Moderate–Expensive.*

Rokusei Nishimise. Few restaurants in Kyoto have matched Rokusei Nishimise's magical combination of traditional cuisine served in a contemporary setting. Polished marble floors and manicured interior garden niches offset the popular *te-oke bento* lunch, a collage of flavors and colors presented in a handmade cypress-wood bucket/serving tray. With an 80-year history as caterers of formal kaiseki cuisine, Rokusei also offers an exquisitely different full-course meal each month at reasonable prices. A three-minute walk west of the turn-of-the-century gardens of Heian Shrine, the restaurant itself overlooks a tree-lined canal and is famous for its colorful azaleas in May. *71 Nishitenno-cho, Okazaki, Sakyo-ku, tel. 075/751–6171. Dinner reservations advised. Dress: informal. DC, V. Open 11:30–9. Closed Mon. Moderate.*

Kappa Nawate. Lively (noisy to some ears) and fun, Kappa Nawate has all the boisterous local atmosphere, grilled goodies, and *nama* (draft) beer a dozen people crammed around a counter could possibly ever hope for. The head cook vacillates between edgy and jovial—he has fish to grill and little patience with the indecisive eater. The English menu helps, but the choices are next to limitless: *oden* (vegetables and other foods simmered in broth), yakitori, sashimi, you name it. A favorite after-work watering hole in the middle of the Gion entertainment district, Kappa stays open later than most such grills in Kyoto. *Sueyoshi-cho, Higashi-kita-kado, Nawate-dori, Shoji 2-sujime-agaru, Higashiyama-ku, tel. 075/531–4048. No reservations. Dress: casual. No credit cards. Open 6 PM–2 AM.*

Closed 1st, 2nd, and 3rd Mon. every month; first Mon. and Dec. 24. Inexpensive–Moderate.

Nishimura. You do the cooking at this casual eatery, where the specialty is *okonomiyaki*, a kind of Japanese frittata made with a batter of egg and flour mixed with vegetables and your choice of meat or seafood. It's all smothered with green onions and ginger and topped with a special sauce. You grill it yourself at your table. Nishimura is a stone's throw from Kyoto University, down a path beside the Asahi Shimbun Building, and is surrounded with shrubbery. The food is good, the garden view is wonderful, and the prices are very reasonable. *Hyaku-manben kosaten agaru, Nishiiru, Sakyo-ku, tel. 075/721–5880. No reservations. Dress: casual. No credit cards. Open noon–2 and 5–9. Closed Fri. Inexpensive.*

★ **Omen.** Just south of Ginkakuji (Temple of the Silver Pavilion), this is one of the best places to stop for an inexpensive homestyle lunch before proceeding down the old canal (a walkway beneath the cherry trees known as the Path of Philosophy) on the way to Nanzenji Temple. Omen is not only the name of the shop but also the name of the house specialty: thick white noodles brought to your table in a basket with a bowl of hot broth and a platter of seven different vegetables. The noodles are added to the broth a little at a time, along with the vegetables (spinach, cabbage, green onions, mushrooms, burdock, eggplant, radishes, and others, depending on the season). Sprinkle the top with roasted sesame seeds and you have a dish so popular that you can expect a few minutes' wait before you're seated. Like the food, the restaurant itself is country-style, with a choice of counter stools, tables and chairs, or tatami mat seating. The waiters dress in *happi* (workmen's) coats and headbands; the atmosphere is lively and comfortable. *74 Ishibashi-cho, Jodo-ji, Sakyo-ku, tel. 075/771–8994. No reservations on Sat., Sun, and national holidays. Dress: casual. No credit cards. Open 11–10. Closed Thurs. Inexpensive.*

★ **Rakusho.** Along the path between Maruyama-Koen Park and Kiyomizudera Temple, this tea shop in a former villa is a pleasant place to stop for morning coffee or afternoon tea. A table beside the sliding glass doors looks out on an elaborately landscaped garden that features a pond in which the owner's colorful array of prize-winning *koi* carp, hoping it's feeding time again, lurk just beneath the surface. Flowering plum trees, azaleas, irises, camellias, and maple trees take turns anointing the four seasons while you sip your bowl of *matcha* (frothy teaceremony tea) or freshly brewed coffee. The tea shop is just minutes on foot from Sannenzaka, one of Kyoto's historic preservation districts—a cobblestone path lined with shops on the way to Kiyomizudera Temple. *Kodai-ji Kitamon-mae-dori, Washio-cho, Higashiyama-ku, tel. 075/561–6892. No reservations. Dress: casual. No credit cards. Open daily 9:30–6. Closed 4 times a month (call first). Inexpensive.*

American **Time Paradox.** The Japanese owner-chef here learned most of the great things he knows in California. The tantalizing menu offers homemade *gratins*, thick-crust pizza, spinach omelets, scallops in garlic wine sauce, bread sticks baked fresh while you wait, and crispy spinach, bacon, and avocado salads. Beer and wine are also served. Located a few blocks south of Kyoto University (just north of Heian Jingu Shrine), it is a popular student haunt, heavy on the foreign element. *Yoshida-hondori, Marutamachi-agaru, Sakyo-ku, tel. 075/751–6903.*

*Reservations advised weekends. Dress: casual. MC, V. Open 5
PM–1 AM (last order at midnight). Closed Thurs. Inexpensive.*

Western District

Japanese   **Kitcho.** What Maxim's is to Paris, Kitcho is to Kyoto—classic
cuisine, unparalleled traditional atmosphere, exclusive elegance. Lunches start at ¥45,000, dinners are ¥50,000 and up,
making this perhaps the world's most expensive restaurant.
Although the original restaurant is in Osaka, the Kyoto branch
has the advantage of a stunning location beside the Oi River,
nestled at the foot of the hills of Arashiyama. Here you can experience the full sensory delight of formal kaiseki cuisine. Only
the finest ingredients are used, prepared by master chefs and
served on priceless lacquered trays in exquisite antique porcelain ware—all in an elegant private room sparsely decorated
with a hanging scroll painted by a famous master, whose message sets the seasonal theme for the evening. The ability to
identify the vessels used, an appreciation of the literary allu-
sions made in the combination of objects and foods served, and
knowledge of the arts of Japan all add depth to the experience.
Expect to spend a minimum of two hours. *58 Susuki-no-banba-
cho, Tenryu-ji, Saga, Ukyo-ku, tel. 075/881–1101. Reservations required. Jacket and tie. AE. Lunch 11:30–1, dinner 4–7.
Closed 1st, 3rd Wed. Very Expensive.*

★ **Nishiki.** Tucked inside a rustic bamboo fence, Nishiki sits on an
island in the middle of the Oi River, surrounded by the densely
forested Arashiyama mountains. The *oshukuzen-bento* lunch is
the best sampler of formal, Kyoto-style kaiseki cuisine available at such a reasonable price. Unlike most bento lunches, it is
served in seven courses and is so beautifully presented in a
tiered lacquer box, with meticulous attention to the finest
foods in season, that it rivals meals at three times the price. A
summer lunch might include a course of *kamo-nasu,* the prized
Kyoto eggplant, served *dengaku*-style, smothered in sweet
miso sauce in a silver serving dish the shape of an eggplant itself. The top layer of the lacquered box might be covered with a
miniature bamboo trellis in which are nestled tiny porcelain
cups the shape of morning glories, a favorite summer flower in
Kyoto, each one filled with a different appetizer—a touch of
sea urchin or a few sprigs of spinach in sesame sauce. *Nakanoshima Koen-uchi, Arashiyama, Ukyo-ku, tel. 075/871–8888.
Call for reservations, or expect a 30-min. wait. Dress: informal. DC, MC, V. Open 11–9 (last order at 7). Closed Tues.
Moderate.*

★ **Sagano.** Amid the lush green bamboo forests of the Arashiyama district, this quiet retreat serves one of the finest
yudofu meals (cubes of bean curd simmered in a broth at your
table) in Kyoto. The full course includes such local delicacies as
tempura and *aburage* (deep-fried tofu) with black sesame
seeds and a gingko-nut center garnished with a sprig of *kinome*
leaves from the Japanese pepper tree. Take a seat at the sunk-
en counter, and waitresses in kimonos will prepare the meal in
front of you—with a backdrop of antique wood-block prints on
folding screens, surrounded by walls lined with delicately
hand-painted antique porcelain bowls—or walk out through
the garden to private, Japanese-style rooms in the back. If
weather permits, dine on low tables in the courtyard garden beneath the towering bamboo. It's reasonably priced for this superb combination of atmosphere and good food. Reservations

are a good idea year-round, particularly during the fall tourist season when the maple trees of Arashiyama are at their brilliant-red best. *45 Susuki-no-banba-cho, Saga, Tenryu-ji, Ukyo-ku, tel. 075/861–0277. Dress: informal. No credit cards. Open 11–8. Moderate.*

Spanish **Bodegon.** A white-walled, tile-floored, wrought-iron and blown-glass Spanish restaurant in Arashiyama is about as rare (and as welcome) as decent paella in a neighborhood famous for its tofu. Bodegon sits unobtrusively along the main street that runs through the center of this scenic district, offering guests Spanish wines and Kyoto hospitality. A wildly popular tourist area in daylight, Arashiyama rolls up its sidewalks after dark, so Bodegon is a good place to escape the crowds downtown in the evening. *1 Susuki-no-banba-cho, Tenryu-ji, Saga, tel. 075/ 872–9652. Reservations suggested on weekends. Dress: informal. MC, V. Lunch noon–2, dinner 5–10. Closed Thurs. Moderate.*

Central District

Japanese **Daimonjiya.** One of Kyoto's many famous *ryori-ryokan* (restaurant/inns), Daimonjiya is noted for its superb formal kaiseki cuisine. Located on the Sanjo Arcade in the downtown shopping district, its inconspicuous traditional entrance is easy to miss among the boutiques and record shops that now line the street. A narrow stone path leads down a bamboo-fence corridor to the doorway of this classic 80-year-old inn, a popular haunt of literary men such as the late Eiji Yoshikawa, author of *Musashi.* The evening kaiseki meal is exquisitely presented; the *kaiseki bento* (box lunch) offered at lunchtime is one of Kyoto's finest and is moderately priced. *19 Ishibashi-cho, Sanjo-Teramachi Higashi-iru, Nakagyo-ku, tel. 075/221– 0603. Dinner reservations required. Jacket and tie. AE, DC, V. Lunch 11:30–1, dinner 5–7 (last seating). Very Expensive.*

Ebisugawa-tei. Annexed to the Fujita Hotel, this is the Meiji-period villa of former industrialist Baron Fujita. It contains two excellent steak restaurants, both serving the celebrated, beer-fed, massaged Omi beef. The **Omi** is the more expensive and formal of the two, serving slightly higher quality beef. The **Chidori** is a bit less formal, but also serves superb beef and has a better view of the garden. Stop in at the bar in the basement of the Fujita Hotel for a drink beside the beautiful duck pond and waterfall. *Fujita Hotel, Nijo-dori, Kiyamachi Kado, Nakagyo-ku, tel. 075/222–1511. Reservations advised for both. Dress: (Omi) Jacket and tie; (Chidori) informal. AE, DC, MC, V. Omi open 4–9:30. Expensive. Chidori open noon–9:30. Moderate.*

Mankamero. Established in 1716, Mankamero is the only restaurant in Kyoto that serves formal *yusoku ryori,* the type of cuisine once served to members of the imperial court. The preparation of foods is carried out by a specially appointed imperial chef, using unique utensils made only for the preparation of this type of cuisine. Dressed in ceremonial robes, the chef "dismembers" the fish into elaborately arranged sections brought to the guest on pedestal trays. Prices are also quite elaborate, though in recent years an incomparable *take-kago bento* lunch (served in a bamboo basket) is offered at prices within reach of the rest of us commoners. *Inokuma-dori, Demizu-agaru, Kamigyo-ku, tel. 075/441–5020. Reservations*

*required. Jacket and tie. AE, DC, MC, V. No credit cards for
Takekago Bento at lunch. Open noon–8. Closed once a month.
Moderate–Expensive.*

Mishima-tei. There is really only one choice for sukiyaki in
Kyoto, and that is Mishima-tei. Located conveniently in the
heart of the downtown shopping district, it is also one of the
best restaurants in the area. Kyoto housewives line up out front
to pay premium prices for Mishima-tei's famous high-quality
beef, sold by the 100-gram over the counter at the meat shop
downstairs. Mishima-tei was established in 1904, and climbing
the staircase of this three-story, traditional wood-frame restaurant is like journeying into the past. Down the long, dark
corridors, with polished wood floors, maids in kimonos bustle
about with trays of beef and refills of sake to dozens of private
tatami-mat rooms. Ask for a room that faces the central courtyard garden for the best view, and enjoy your meal in privacy.
Mishima-tei has not yet undergone any extensive remodeling,
so it retains an authentic, turn-of-the-century atmosphere.
*Teramachi, Sanjo-sagaru, Higashi-iru, Nakagyo-ku, tel. 075/
221–0003. Reservations advised. Dress: informal. AE, DC,
MC, V. Open 11:30–10. Closed Wed. Moderate–Expensive.*

Yoshikawa. This quiet, traditional inn with its beautiful landscaped gardens is within walking distance of the downtown
shopping area. The specialty of the house is tempura, either a
full-course kaiseki dinner served in a tatami room or a lunch at
the counter in its cozy "tempura corner," where the chef fries
each vegetable and shrimp in front of you while you wait. Tempura should be light and crisp—best right from the pot—and
for this Yoshikawa is famous. English is spoken. *Tominokoji,
Oike-sagaru, Nakagyo-ku, tel. 075/221–5544 or 075/221–0052.
Reservations advised. Dress: casual at lunch, jacket and tie at
dinner. AE, DC, MC, V. Lunch 11–2, dinner 5–8:30. Closed
Sun. Moderate–Expensive.*

Agatha. This restaurant offers a "mystery" twist on the Japanese *robatayaki* (charcoal grill). The decor is period Agatha
Christie—'40s book covers and movie posters, chic polished
marble walls, potted palms, decent jazz, black-and-white
checkerboard floors, and counter or table seating. Watch the
chef grill interesting variations of traditional Japanese delicacies, such as long-stem white *enoki* mushrooms wrapped in
strips of thinly sliced beef, scallops in bacon, or pork in *shiso* (a
red or green mintlike herb). Both the A-course and the B-
course combine these treats with unadorned standards such as
tebasaki (grilled chicken wings). Salad and appetizers are included, and a wide selection of drinks are available—everything from sake to a gin fizz. Popular with the *juppie* (Japanese
yuppie) crowd, this restaurant has two other branches in
Kyoto, and one each in Osaka, Tokyo, and . . . Boston. *2nd
floor, Yurika Bldg., Kiyamachi-dori, Sanjo-agaru, Nakagyo-
ku, tel. 075/223–2379. Reservations advised weekends. Dress:
informal. AE, DC, MC, V. Open 5–midnight. Moderate.*

Oiwa. At the head of the Takasegawa Canal, south of the Fujita
Hotel, Oiwa serves *kushikatsu*, which are skewered meats and
vegetables battered, deep-fried, and then dipped in a variety
of sauces. The building itself is actually a *kura* (treasure house)
that belongs to a kimono merchant family, and it is one of the
first to have been turned into a restaurant in Kyoto, where res-
torations of this type are still a new idea. The Japanese chef was
trained in one of the finest French restaurants in Tokyo, and his
version of kushikatsu (usually considered a working man's

snack with beer) might be called unpretentiously eleg-
der by the skewer or ask for the *omakase* course. Oiwa is a fine
place to spend a relaxing evening. *Kiyamachi-dori, Nijo-
sagaru, Nakagyo-ku, tel. 075/231–7667. Reservations advised
weekends. Dress: informal. No credit cards. Open 5–10, Sun.
4–10. Closed Wed. Moderate.*

Daikokuya. If you're shopping downtown and want a quick
meal, stop in at Daikokuya for a *soba* (buckwheat) noodle dish
or *donburi*, a bowl of rice with your choice of toppings. The
oyako donburi, rice with egg and chicken, is the best choice
(*oyako* means "parent and child"). The restaurant also serves
sushi in a beautiful Japanese-style setting, with both tatami
and table-and-chair seating. *Kiyamachi, Takoyakushi Nishi-
iru, Nakagyo-ku, tel. 075/221–2818. No reservations. Dress:
casual. No credit cards. Open 11:30–10. Closed Tues. Inexpensive–Moderate.*

Yamatomi. The geisha district that runs along the west bank of
the Kamogawa River is known as Pontocho. Many of the places
along the narrow street are teahouses, and you must be formal-
ly introduced by a regular patron to enter. There are a few reasonably priced restaurants on Pontocho, and Yamatomi is
among the best. The specialty of the house is called *teppin-age*,
a tempura-style meal of battered vegetables, seafood, and
meat that you cook yourself in a small iron kettle at your table.
In the winter, the feature item is *oden*, a combination of vegetables and local specialties simmered in copper vats behind the
counter from which you choose. But it's really the hot, humid
summers that make Kyoto-ites flock to Yamatomi. Summer is
the season when all the restaurants and teahouses along
Pontocho set up temporary verandas out over the river bank so
their guests can enjoy both their meals and the cool river
breeze under the stars. You may catch sight of guests being entertained by geisha on the veranda of the teahouse next door—
paying 10 times the price you'll pay at Yamatomi. *Pontocho,
Shijo-agaru, Nakagyo-ku, tel. 075/221–3268. No Reservations.
Dress: informal. No credit cards. Open noon–11. Closed Tues.
Inexpensive–Moderate.*

Tagoto. One of the best noodle shops in which to stop for lunch
in the downtown area, Tagoto is located on the north side of the
covered Sanjo Arcade, ½ block west of the avenue Kawaramachi-dori. Tagoto has been serving homemade *soba* (buckwheat) noodle soup for over a hundred years in the same
location on a shopping street that is now almost completely
modernized. Tagoto, too, has remodeled, and the result is a
pleasant surprise—modern, yet in traditional Japanese style.
Natural woods, shoji paper windows, tatami mats, and an interior garden combine with slate floors, tables and chairs, and
air-conditioned comfort. Tagoto serves both thin soba and thick
white *udon* noodle dishes with a variety of toppings (such as
shrimp tempura), hot or cold to suit the season. *Sanjo-dori,
Teramachi Higashi-iru, Nakagyo-ku, tel. 075/221–3030. No
reservations. Dress: casual. No credit cards. Open 11–9.
Closed Tues. Inexpensive.*

Coffee Shop **Inoda.** Hidden down a side street in the center of town, this 100-
year-old establishment is one of Kyoto's oldest and best-loved
coffee shops. The turn-of-the-century Western-style brick
buildings along the street Sanjo-dori nearby are part of a historic preservation district, and Inoda's original old shop blends
well with its surroundings. Floor-to-ceiling glass windows

overlook an interior garden; a spacious room seats nearly 100 people. And the coffee is excellent: for breakfast, toast and coffee; for lunch, sandwiches and coffee; for a break from sightseeing, coffee and coffee. It even has some stained-glass windows and a pair of witty parrots. *Sakaimachi-dori, Sanjo-sagaru, Nakagyo-ku, tel. 075/221-0505. No reservations. Dress: casual. No credit cards. Open daily 7-6. Inexpensive.*

Continental **Carnival Times.** Since its opening in 1991, this seafood palace has proved to be one of Kyoto's most popular new restaurants. Located in the 60-year-old Kyoto Electric Co. Building, it has been restored to its original art deco design and then some. When the piano player and saxophonist are on break, a splendid vintage "Symphonion" music box takes over. The food—lobster and four varieties of crab (including Alaskan King)—is marvelous, the wine is Californian, and the service is, if anything, overly attentive. *561-1 Komano-cho, Marutamachi Sagaru, Nakasuji-dori, Kamigyo-ku, Kyoto, tel. 075/223-0606. Dinner reservations advised. Dress: informal. AE, DC. Open 11:30-11:30. Moderate.*

French **Ogawa.** Down a narrow passageway across from the Takasega-★ wa Canal, this is the place to sample the best in Kyoto-style nouvelle cuisine. Finding a seat at the counter of this intimate French restaurant is like getting tickets for opening night at the opera—one you've never seen. With particularly Japanese sensitivity to the best ingredients only in the peak of the season, proprietor Ogawa promises never to bore his guests by serving them the same meal twice. *Ayu* (a popular local river fish) is offered in the summer (or perhaps abalone), salmon in the fall, crab in the winter, shrimp in the spring. Ogawa features marvelous sauces, puddings, and, yes, even fresh papaya sherbet and mango mousse with mint sauce. The full-course meal at lunch and dinner is spectacular, but some prefer to order hors d'oeuvres with wine over which to languish ecstatically for hours. Counter seating is available for only 16. *Kiyamachi Oike-agaru Higashi-iru, Nakagyo-ku, tel. 075/256-2203. Reservations required. Jacket and tie suggested. AE, DC, MC, V. Lunch 11:30-2, dinner 5-10 (last order at 9:30). Closed Tues. Moderate-Expensive.*

★ **Natsuka.** This fine French restaurant overlooks the Kamogawa River. The Japanese couple who manage the place lived and learned their trade in Paris for several years. Natsuka has the most reasonably priced French lunch menu in town (¥1,500 fixed menu). The dessert tray here is sumptuous, with a choice of two freshly baked delights from about eight possibilities. *Pontocho, Shijo-agaru, Higashigawa, Nakagyo-ku, tel. 075/255-2105. Dinner reservations advised. Dress: informal. MC. Lunch 11:30-2, dinner 5-10. Last order at 9 (at 8 on Sun.). Closed Wed. Moderate.*

Indian **Ashoka.** Unlike cosmopolitan Tokyo, Kyoto, with all its fine Japanese restaurants, suffers from a serious lack of international options—particularly when it comes to cuisine. That was true until the owners of Ashoka brought their tandoori chicken (and their wonderful Indian chefs) to town. Marinated for hours and baked on long skewers in a clay oven while you watch, this chicken dish is the closest you'll get to downright spiciness in the capital of the culinary dainty. Ashoka's atmosphere includes red carpets, carved screens, brass lanterns, and tuxedoed waiters, though the dress code for guests ranges from denim to silk. The dazzling *Thali* course dinner offers half a dozen curries in little bowls on a brass tray with rice and tandoori—if you're sure you're that hungry. *Kikusui Bldg., 3rd floor, Teramachi-dori, Shijo-agaru, Nakagyo-ku, tel. 075/ 241–1318. Reservations advised weekends. Dress: informal. AE, DC, MC, V. Lunch 11:30–2:30, dinner 5–9. Closed 2nd Tues. of each month. Inexpensive–Moderate.*

Italian **divo-diva.** Authentic Italian food is prepared by chefs trained in
★ Italy but with a Japanese flair for color and design. The long narrow room has a counter, three small tables, and one elegant long table for parties and large groups. In the short time divo-diva has been in business, it has become one of the most popular restaurants in Kyoto. The contemporary interior has tasteful lighting. The wine list is interesting (and not prohibitively expensive). The pasta and breads are homemade. *Nishikikoji, Takakura-nishi-iru, Nakagyo-ku, tel. 075/256–1326. Reservations advised. Dress: informal. AE, DC, MC, V. Open lunch 11:30–2, dinner 6–10. Closed Wed. and 2nd and 3rd Tues. of each month. Inexpensive–Moderate.*

Mixed Menu **Tinguely.** Located in the same basement as a Chinese restaurant, Mr. Chow's Tinguely overlooks a mini-terrace and has a black interior. This dining spot may be described as ethnic (the menu covers a lot of bases—East and West), eclectic (not the place you'd think the local banking district would frequent—but it does), and kinetic (the flashing, jangling work of artist Jean Tinguely hangs from every rafter). It's a "mysterious space for city adults" in the evening, as the restaurant's slogan says. *Basement of the Karasuma Plaza 21, Karasuma-dori, Rokkaku-sagaru, Nakagyo-ku, tel. 075/255–6810. Reservations advised weekends. Dress: informal. No credit cards. Open daily 11–10. Closed Sun. Inexpensive.*

Northern District

Japanese **Heihachi-Jaya.** A bit off the beaten path in the northeastern
★ corner of Kyoto, along the old road to the Sea of Japan, this roadside inn has offered comfort to many a weary traveler in its 400-year history. Heihachi-Jaya hugs the levee of the Takano River and is surrounded by maple trees in a quiet landscape garden with a stream. Apart from the excellent bento lunch and full-course kaiseki dinner, what makes this restaurant special is its clay sauna, the *kamaburo*, a mound-shaped clay steam bath heated from beneath the floor by a pinewood fire. Have a bath and sauna, change into a cotton kimono if you wish, and retire to the dining room (or to a private room) for a *very* relaxing meal—an experience not to be missed. *8-1 Kawagishi-cho, Yamabana, Sakyo-ku, tel. 075/781–5008. Reservations advised. Dress: informal. DC, MC, V (no credit cards at lunch). Open 11–9. Closed Wed. Moderate–Expensive.*

Izusen. In the garden of Daiji-in, a sub-temple of Daitokuji, a revered center of Zen Buddhism in Japan, this restaurant specializes in *shojin ryori* (Zen vegetarian cuisine). Lunches are presented in sets of red-lacquer bowls of diminishing sizes, each one fitting inside the next when the meal is completed. Two Kyoto specialties, *fu* (glutinous wheat cake) and *yuba* (skimmed from steaming soy milk), are served in a multitude of inventive forms—in soups and sauces that prove vegetarianism to be as exciting a culinary experience as any "carnal" dish can hope to be. Meals are served in tatami-mat rooms, Japanese-style, and in warm weather on low tables outside beneath the trees in the temple garden. *4 Daitoku-ji-cho, Murasakino, Kita-ku, tel. 075/491–6665. Reservations advised in spring and fall. Dress: informal. No credit cards. Open 11–5. Closed Thurs. Moderate.*

★ **Sagenta.** Discovering the town of Kibune is one of the best parts of summer in Kyoto. A short, bump'n'rumble train ride into the mountains north of Kyoto on the nostalgic little Keifuku train lets you off on a mountain path that leads farther up into the forest beside a cool stream. The path is lined on both sides with restaurants that place tables near the stream during the summer months; you can dine beneath a canopy of trees, with the water flowing at your feet. Most of the restaurants along the river are excellent, but some are quite expensive. Sagenta is the last restaurant, at the very top of the slope, serving kaiseki lunches year-round, as well as one-pot *nabe* dishes in fall and winter. It is reasonably priced, particularly for its popular summertime specialty *nagashi-somen*, chilled noodles that flow down a bamboo spout from the kitchen to a boat-shape trough; you catch the noodles from the trough as they float past, dip them in a sauce, and eat them with mushrooms, seasonal green vegetables, and shrimp. *76 Kibune-cho, Kurama, Sakyo-ku, tel. 075/741–2244. Reservations advised in summer. Dress: informal. AE, DC, MC, V. Open 11–10. Closed periodically during winter. Inexpensive–Moderate.*

★ **Azekura.** On the northern outskirts of Kyoto, not far from Kamigamo Shrine, Azekura serves home-style buckwheat noodles under the giant wood beams of a 300-year-old sake warehouse. Originally built in Nara, the warehouse was moved here more than 20 years ago by a kimono merchant named Mikio Ichida, who also maintains a textile exhibition hall, a small museum, and a weavers' workshop within the walls of this former samurai estate. Have lunch on low stools around a small charcoal brazier or on tatami next to a window overlooking the garden and waterwheel outside. The soba noodles at Azekura have a heartier country flavor than you'll find in most of the other noodle shops in town. A perfect place to stop while exploring the *shake-machi* district around the shrine, an area in which shrine priests and farmers have lived for over 10 centuries. *30 Okamoto-cho, Kamigamo, Kita-ku, tel. 075/701–0161. No reservations. Dress: casual. No credit cards. Open 9–5. Closed Mon. Inexpensive.*

American **Knuckle's.** In search of a taste of the Big Apple in the Ancient
★ Capital of Japan? What could be better after a visit to Daitokuji Temple than a Reuben sandwich, some nachos, and a margarita, or the house specialty, Knuckle Sandwich (with homemade Italian sausage), washed down with a cold Corona beer—and don't forget the fresh-baked blueberry cheesecake for dessert. Knuckle's has good espresso and a comfortable atmosphere. The Big Apple without the bite. *Kitaoji-dori, Sembon Higashi-iru, Kita-ku, tel. 075/441–5849. No reservations. Dress: casual. No credit cards. Open noon–10. Closed Mon. Inexpensive.*

Coffee Shop **Honyarado.** Kyoto has always been a university town, and
★ Doshisha University, on the north side of the old Imperial Palace, is one of the oldest and most respected in the city. Honyarado is a "home-away-from-dormitory" for many of its students. During the student movement of the '60s and '70s, Kyoto had its share of "incidents." What's left of the spirit of the peace movement—the environmentalists, the poets, and

the musicians of that era—eat their lunches at Honyarado. The notices on the bulletin are of a less incendiary nature these days (rooms for rent, poetry readings, used stereos for sale), but the sandwiches are still on homemade wheat bread, the stew is still good, and the company still real. Take along a good book (this guide, perhaps?), order lunch, and relax. *Imadegawa-dori, Teramachi Nishi-iru, Kamigyo-ku, tel. 075/222–1574. No reservations. Dress: casual. No credit cards. Open 9:30–9:30. Closed 1st Wed. of each month. Inexpensive.*

Papa Jon's. Just north of Doshisha University is a new American-owned café that serves a light quiche lunch and the finest home-style cakes and espresso in town. Owner-chef Charles Roche features the work of local artists on the walls of his elegant little shop. This, plus the antique European decor and sunlit coziness, provides a welcome place to rest after a visit to the nearby Imperial Palace. *642-2 Shokoku-ji Monzen, Karasuma Kamidachiuri Higashi-iru, Kamigyo-ku, tel. 075/415–2655. No reservations. Dress: informal. No credit cards. Open 11–10. Closed Mon. Inexpensive.*

Lodging

Kyoto is a tourist city, and its hotel rooms are often designed merely as places to rest at night. Most rooms are small by international standards, but they are adequate for relaxing after a busy day of sightseeing. As it is throughout Japan, service in this city is impeccable; the information desks are well stocked with maps and pamphlets about the sights. The assistant manager, concierge, or guest-relations manager is always available in the lobby to respond to guests' needs, although English may or may not be spoken.

Each room in expensively and moderately priced lodgings comes equipped with a hot-water thermos and tea bags or instant coffee. Stocked refrigerators, television featuring English-language CNN news, and radio are standard, as are *yukata* (cotton kimonos), intended for use in the rooms.

Kyoto offers a choice of both Western- and Japanese-style accommodations, including traditional ryokan. If you choose a ryokan, be sure to read the section on lodging in Chapter 1. Not all ryokan offer private toilets and baths, so check in advance if you don't like to share facilities.

Obviously, higher priced inns offer the most personalized service. Be aware that they can be very, very expensive. Prices quoted are usually per person (including two meals) and not per room. Make sure to check carefully, because some ryokan cost as much as U.S. $1,000 per person per night.

Moderately and inexpensively priced inns offer only a fraction of the total ryokan experience. Tubs may be plastic rather than cedarwood. Meals may be served in the dining area rather than elaborately prepared and presented in your room. Rooms may overlook a street rather than a garden. The room, however, will have tatami straw mat floors, futon bedding, and a scroll and/or flower arrangement in its rightful place.

Most accommodations in the Very Expensive, Expensive, and Moderate categories have representation abroad, so ask at the nearest Japan National Tourist Organization (JNTO) office for information on booking. If there is no representation, bookings must be made by writing directly to the establishment. Book at least a month in advance, or as early as three months ahead, if you are traveling during peak spring and autumn seasons or around important Japanese holidays and festivals.

A 3% federal consumer tax is added to all hotel bills. Another 3% local tax is added to the bill if it exceeds ¥15,000. At most hotels, a 10%–15% service charge is added to the total bill. Tipping is not necessary.

Category	Cost*
Very Expensive	over ¥30,000
Expensive	¥20,000–¥30,000
Moderate	¥8,000–¥20,000
Inexpensive	under ¥8,000

Cost is for double room, without tax or service

The most highly recommended accommodations are indicated by a star ★.

Very Expensive

Hiiragiya. Hiiragiya is on par with the Tawaraya (*see below*) as the preferred ryokan among dignitaries and celebrities. The inn was founded in 1818 to accommodate provincial lords and their parties who were visiting the capital. The founder himself was a metal smith whose artful sword guards were commissioned by powerful samurai. Luxurious elegance combined with strength is the pervasive style of this lodging place, which echoes with memories of the samurai visitors during the 19th century. Charlie Chaplin and Yukio Mishima have been among its noted past fans. As the motto of the inn implies: "A guest arrives . . . back home to comfort." Some baths feature stained-glass windows. The cheapest rooms are in the newer annex. *Fuyacho-Oike-kado, Nakagyo-ku, Kyoto, tel. 075/221–1136, fax 075/221–1139. 33 rooms; 28 with bath, 5 without. AE, DC, MC, V.*

Takaragaike Prince Hotel. Kyoto's only deluxe hotel is located on the northern outskirts of the city, across from the International Conference Hall and Takaragaike Pond. Although useful for those attending an event at the conference hall, the hotel is a good 30 minutes from the city center and not convenient for tourists. Nevertheless, its unusual doughnut-shape architectural design provides each room with a view of the surrounding mountains and forests. Corridors along the inside overlook the landscaped inner garden. The fine touches include the huge floral arrangements in the lobby, the impressive chandeliers all around the building, and the original Miró prints, which hang in every suite. The spacious rooms have beds that are probably the largest you'll find in Japan. All rooms are tastefully decorated in pastel colors which complement the natural green of the outside views. This is one of the only hotels in Kyoto with its own authentic teahouse, which overlooks the pond. Demonstrations of the tea ceremony can be arranged upon request. *Takaragaike, Sakyo-ku, Kyoto 606, tel. 075/712–1111, fax 075/712–7677. 322 rooms. Facilities: 6 restaurants (including*

ANA Hotel Kyoto, **6**

Daimonjiya, **17**

Hiiragiya, **8**

Hiraiwa, **21**

Hirota Guest House, **7**

Holiday Inn Kyoto, **2**

Hotel Fujita Kyoto, **10**

Iwanami, **16**

Kyoto Brighton Hotel, **4**

Kyoto Gion Hotel, **18**

Kyoto Grand Hotel, **23**

Kyoto Palaceside Hotel, **5**

Kyoto Tokyu Hotel, **22**

Kyoto Traveler's Inn, **12**

Miyako Hotel, **14**

Myokenji, **3**

New Miyako Hotel, **24**

Pension Higashiyama, **15**

Ryokan Yuhara, **19**

Seikoro, **20**

Takaragaike Prince Hotel, **1**

Tawaraya, **9**

Three Sisters Inn Annex, **11**

Yachiyo, **13**

Kyoto Lodging

*French, Chinese, and Japanese), bars, souvenir shop, meeting
and conference rooms, teahouse. AE, DC, MC, V.*

★ **Tawaraya.** The most famous of Kyoto's inns, this is the abode of
kings and queens, princes and princesses, and presidents and
dictators alike when they visit Kyoto. Tawaraya was founded
more than 300 years ago and is currently run by the 11th generation of the Okazaki family. For all its subdued beauty and
sense of tradition, the inn does have modern comforts such as
heat and air-conditioning, but they are introduced so inconspic-
uously that they hardly detract from the venerable atmosphere
of yesteryear. Rooms feature superb antiques from the Okazaki
family collection. Because the inn is small, the service is first-
rate, while the private gardens provide the beauty and peace
you search for on a visit to Japan. *Fuyacho-Aneyakoji-agaru,
Nakagyo-ku, Kyoto, tel. 075/211–5566, fax 075/211–2204. 18
rooms with bath. AE, DC, V.*

Expensive

ANA Hotel Kyoto. This five-year-old hotel, across from the
Nijojo Castle, is part of the chain that belongs to All Nippon
Airways (ANA), the airline with the largest domestic network
in Japan. Its high-ceilinged lobby looks out to a picturesque
courtyard waterfall. The background koto music that is played
in the lobby is soothing to the senses and reminds you, at once,
even among the ultra-Western decor, that you are in the ancient city of Kyoto. The rooms are long and narrow—rather
small considering the rates. *Nijo-jo-mae, Horikawa-dori,
Nakagyo-ku, Kyoto 604, tel. 075/231–1155, fax 075/231–5333.
303 rooms. Facilities: 7 restaurants (including French, Chinese, and Japanese), bars, shopping arcade, health spa, indoor swimming pool. AE, DC, MC, V.*

Daimonjiya. Just off the busy shopping area of Sanjo-dori Avenue, this tiny inn is as famous for its guest rooms as for the food
served. Each room, with fine wood interiors, overlooks a small
garden. *Kaiseki* (formal Japanese meal with tea ceremony) is
the specialty of the house; the chef was trained at the best
Kyoto culinary establishment. You do not need to be a guest to
use one of the rooms for a meal, but then you would be missing
out on the quintessential ryokan experience. (A branch of the
restaurant Daimonjiya is located in the Tokyo Hilton International Hotel.) *Nishi-iru, Kawaramachi-Sanjo, Nakagyo-ku,
Kyoto, tel. 075/221–0603. 7 rooms. AE, DC.*

★ **Hotel Fujita Kyoto.** This pleasant hotel is situated along the
famed Kamogawa River and is a 15-minute drive from the
Kyoto Station. In the light of a full moon, the waterfall in its
garden sparkles while waterfowl play. The lobby is narrow and
long, with comfortable gray armchairs playing nicely against
deep red carpeting. The Fujita features Japanese and Scandinavian decor throughout, and 18 rooms have Japanese-style
furnishings. *Nishizume, Nijo-Ohashi, Kamogawa, Nakagyo-
ku, Kyoto 604, tel. 075/222–1511, fax 075/256–4561. 195 rooms.
Facilities: 6 bars and restaurants, beauty shop, souvenir shop.
AE, DC, MC, V.*

★ **Kyoto Brighton Hotel.** Opened in 1987, the Brighton is still un-
questionably the city's best hotel in this price range. The
cream-color central atrium is accented with chrome and brass
trim and decorated with sage green furnishings. Hallways circle the atrium, and plants hang from the banisters of every
floor. Glass elevators carry guests up the atrium to their

rooms. On the whole, the Brighton has a simple, clean design that gives it an airy and spacious quality lacking in most Kyoto hotels. Large by Japanese standards, rooms have separate seating areas with a couch and TV, but you can't see the TV from bed. No need to worry about big-city noise: the Brighton is on a quiet side street close to the Imperial Palace (although not within walking distance of most of Kyoto's main attractions). *Nakadachiuri, Shinmachi-dori, Kamigyo-ku, tel. 075/ 441–4411, fax 075/431–2360. 181 rooms, 2 suites. Facilities: 4 banquet rooms, 4 restaurants, 2 bars, outdoor pool, 3 shops, beauty salon. AE, DC, MC, V.*

Kyoto Grand Hotel. The Grand's lobby can sometimes be crowded because the hotel is popular with tour groups. The green concrete building, which is on the drab side, has a circular attachment on the roof—a revolving restaurant. Terrycloth bathrobes, CNN TV, and remote-control toilet gadgetry are all part of the hotel's effort to keep up-to-date. If your room faces the street, make sure to draw the curtains or slide the shoji screens before undressing, because office buildings are right across the way. The Grand is famous for its cheerful and friendly staff. A free bus continuously shuttles guests to and from the Shinkansen central exit of Kyoto Station. The Grand's neighbors include the Nishi Honganji and Toji temples. *Shiokoji-Horikawa, Shimogyo-ku, Kyoto 600, tel. 075/341–2311, fax 075/341–3073. 506 rooms. Walking distance from Kyoto Station. Facilities: 13 restaurants (including Western, Japanese, and Chinese) and bars, indoor pool, sauna, bakery, shopping corner, barber shop, beauty parlor, travel agency. AE, DC, MC, V.*

Kyoto Tokyu Hotel. This seven-story hotel is part of Japan's largest hotel chain. The pillared main entrance, the entrance hall, and lobby are expansive and airy, while the courtyard, with its reflecting pool and waterfall, creates a dramatic atmosphere. The well-appointed rooms, predominantly decorated in off-white tones, are comfortable and spacious. *580 Kakimotocho, Gojo-sagaru, Horikawa-dori, Shimogyo-ku, Kyoto 600, tel. 075/341–2411, fax 075/341–2488. 437 rooms. Facilities: 5 restaurants (including French, Chinese, and Japanese) and bars, meeting and banquet rooms, outdoor pool, wedding hall, beauty parlor, photo studio, souvenir shop, flower shop, travel agency. AE, DC, MC, V.*

★ **Miyako Hotel.** The Miyako, the grand old dame of Kyoto's Western-style hotels, has been around for close to 100 years. It recently completed extensive renovations that left its rooms with a fresh look. The hotel sits dramatically on the western hills of Kyoto, near the temples and shrines of Higashiyama (Eastern Kyoto). Every soundproof guest room offers beautiful panoramic views of the city and the surrounding hills. *Sanjo-keage, Higashiyama-ku, Kyoto 605, tel. 075/771–7111, fax 075/451–2490. 320 rooms, 20 Japanese-style. Facilities: 5 restaurants, coffee shop, lounges, bars, meeting and banquet facilities, shopping arcade, health facilities, outdoor pool. AE, DC, MC, V.*

★ **Seikoro.** This lovely inn is just a stone's throw away from busy Gojo Station, a convenience that makes it popular among both foreigners and Japanese. Established in 1831, the ryokan is managed by a native resident who is fluent in English. Among the interesting decor are Western antiques that mysteriously blend in quite well with the otherwise traditional Japanese setting. When you return to Seikoro after a day of sightseeing, you get the distinct feeling that you are returning to your Japanese home. *Toiyamachi-dori, Gojo-sagaru, Higashiyama-ku, Kyoto, tel. 075/561–0771, fax 075/541–5481. 23 rooms with bath. AE, DC, MC, V.*

★ **Yachiyo.** The special entrance to Yachiyo has low-hanging tiled eaves and woodwork surrounded by carefully shaped bushes, pine trees, and rocks. The sidewalk from the gate to the ryokan curves snakelike into the doorway. Yachiyo is less expensive than its brethren in the deluxe category but nevertheless provides fine, attentive care. You can reduce the cost of staying at this ryokan by choosing not to dine here. Perhaps the biggest draw of Yachiyo is its proximity to Nanzenji, one of the most appealing temples in Kyoto. *34 Nanzenji-fukuchicho, Sakyo-ku, Kyoto, tel. 075/771–4148, fax 075/771–4140. 25 rooms, 20 with bath. AE, DC, MC, V.*

Moderate

Holiday Inn Kyoto. This member of the famous American chain (a 15-min. taxi ride from Kyoto's downtown area) boasts the best sports facilities of any Kyoto hotel, including a bowling alley and ice-skating rink. The hotel is located in a residential area with small, modern houses, occasionally interrupted by large, traditional Japanese estates. Rooms for the handicapped are available. *36 Nishihirakicho, Takano, Sakyo-ku, Kyoto 606, tel. 075/721–3131, fax 075/781–6178. 270 rooms. Facilities: banquet and meeting rooms, 3 restaurants, bar, coffee shop, outdoor pool, indoor pool, gym, and sauna, bowling alley, ice-skating rink, tennis court, driving range, shopping mall. AE, DC, MC, V.*

Iwanami. Amid the antiques shops of Shinmonzen-dori Avenue is this priceless little inn, whose loyal clientele, including many foreigners, would like to keep its existence a secret. The inn has gained such a reputation, in fact, that rooms must be booked well in advance. When booking, be sure to ask for a room with a view of the garden or canal. *Higashioji, Nishi-iru, Shinmonzen-dori, Higashiyama-ku, Kyoto, tel. 075/561–7135. 7 rooms. No credit cards.*

Kyoto Gion Hotel. This hotel sits right in the heart of the Gion geisha district, just west of Yasaka Shrine. It is modest, clean, and the location is excellent—across from the Kyoto Craft Center and a five-minute walk from downtown. *555 Gion machi, Minami-gawa, Higashiyama-ku, Kyoto, tel. 075/551–2111, fax 075/551–2200. Facilities: coffee shop, rooftop beer garden, bar. 130 rooms. AE, DC, MC, V.*

Kyoto Palaceside Hotel. This six-story accommodation is across from the west edge of the Old Imperial Palace, making it easy to slip out of bed for a quick jaunt around the imperial grounds. The white building's spacious and pillared lobby has leather sofas on one side and a souvenir shop on the other. The hotel is recommended for its location and its reasonable prices. *Shimodachiuri-agaru, Karasuma-dori, Kamigyo-ku, Kyoto 602, tel. 075/431–8171, fax 075/414–2018. 120 rooms. Facilities: souvenir shop, French restaurant, banquet rooms, bar. AE, DC, MC, V.*

New Miyako Hotel. This large hotel situated directly in front of Kyoto Station is under the same management as the Miyako Hotel (*see above*); it is used widely by groups and tours. The 10-story white edifice has two protruding wings with landscaping and street lamps reminiscent of a hotel in the United States.

Its location makes it attractive for those planning train trips from the city. *17 Nishi-Kujoincho, Minami-ku, Kyoto 601, tel. 075/661-7111, fax 075/661-7135. 714 rooms, 4 Japanese-style. Facilities: Japanese, Chinese, and Continental restaurants, bar and tea lounge, shopping gallery, barber shop. AE, DC, MC, V.*

★ **Three Sisters Inn Annex** (*Rakutoso Bekkan*). A traditional inn popular with foreign guests for decades, the annex sits on the northeast edge of Heian Shrine, down a trellised path that hides it from the street. This is a quiet and friendly place, and a good introduction to inn customs because the management is accustomed to foreign guests. The hospitality of Kay Yameda is especially welcoming. The annex is nicer than the nearby main branch. *Heian Jingu, Higashi Kita Kado Sakyo-ku, Kyoto, tel. 075/761-6333, fax 075/761-6335. 12 rooms. AE, DC.*

Inexpensive

Hiraiwa. Imagine the ambience of a friendly, Western-style youth hostel with tatami-mat rooms, and you have the Hiraiwa ryokan, a member of the Hospitable and Economical Japanese Inn Group. To be a member, inns must have English-speaking staff and offer clean, comfortable accommodations. Hiraiwa is the most popular of these inns in Kyoto; it's a great place to meet fellow travelers from around the world. Rules and regulations during your stay are posted on the walls. Guests are welcome to eat with the family owners around the dining table in the small kitchen. No private facilities and no baths; only showers are available. *314 Hayao-cho, Kaminoguchiagaru, Ninomiyacho-dori, Shimogyo-ku, tel. 075/351-6748. 21 rooms. AE, MC, V.*

★ **Hirota Guest House.** This hidden treasure of an inn, south of the Imperial Palace, is run by a professional English-speaking guide. A long passageway behind the family's accounting office leads to a lush garden that surrounds a beautifully restored sake storehouse. The Japanese-style rooms have a great view of the secluded, quiet garden. Make reservations well in advance. *665 Nijo-dori, Tominokoji Nishi-iru, Nakagyo-ku, tel. 075/221-2474. 3 rooms, 1 with bath and kitchen. No credit cards.*

Kyoto Traveler's Inn. This no-frills modern inn is located in the perfect spot for sightseeing, with Heian Shrine, Nanzenji Temple, and the museums in Okazaki Park just minutes away on foot. Its 40 Western-style and 38 Japanese-style rooms are plain and small, but clean and practical, all with private bath and toilet. Ask for a room with a view if possible (most don't have one). Because of its location, size, and price, it is often used for group travel as well as for individuals. Head for the coffee shop on the first floor to look out over the river and plot your course for the day. *Heian Jingu Torii-mae, Okazaki, Sakyo-ku, tel. 075/771-0225. 78 rooms with bath. Facilities: coffee shop, meeting and party rooms. AE, MC, V.*

Myokenji. This temple lodging is an alternative accommodation that affords the guest a firsthand look at the activities of monks. Be ready to share a room with several fellow travelers. If you are modest, write ahead for a private room. The reasonable room rate includes breakfast. *Teranouchi, Higashi-iru, Horikawa-dori, Kamigyo-ku, tel. 075/414-0808. 12 rooms. No credit cards.*

Pension Higashiyama. A 10-minute walk from downtown and

the major temples along the eastern foothills, this relatively new, small pension overlooks the lovely Shirakawa canal south of Sanjo-dori. The entire neighborhood fosters a growing family of ducks—just for fun. The pension has created a friendly atmosphere for families on a budget, and is accustomed to foreign guests. *474-23 Umemiya-cho, Shirakawa-suji, Sanjo sagaru, Hihgashiyama-ku. tel. 075/882-1181. 15 rooms; some with toilet, all share bath. Facilities: dining room. AE.*

Ryokan Yuhara. Only a 15-minute walk from the old quarters of Gion and Pontocho, Yuhara is popular among repeat visitors wishing to save a few yen while exploring Kyoto. The friendliness of the staff more than compensates for the spartan amenities. Especially rewarding is a springtime stay when the cherry trees are in full bloom along the Takasegawa River, which the inn overlooks. *188 Kagiya-cho, Shomen-agaru, Kiyamachi-dori, tel. 075/371-9583. 8 rooms. No credit cards.*

The Arts and Nightlife

The Arts

Kyoto is quickly following Tokyo and Osaka as a must stop for both domestic and international artists. Kyoto has played host to the likes of Bruce Springsteen, but it is famous for the traditional arts—Kabuki, Noh, and traditional dances. All dialogue at theaters, however, is in Japanese; the infrequent visitor may find that time is better spent visiting shrines, temples, and gardens.

If you opt to take in a performance, information is available from a number of sources, the most convenient being from your hotel concierge or guest-relations manager. He or she may even have a few tickets on hand, so don't hesitate to ask.

Kyoto boasts a 24-hour recording of the week's tourist events, including festivals, sporting events, and performances. Call 075/361-2911 for a recording in English. Another good source of information is **JNTO's Tourist Information Center (TIC)**, which is located directly across from Kyoto Station. It is strongly suggested that you make a trip to TIC to pick up the latest information on Kyoto's arts scene and other tourist matters. At the TIC office you will find a monthly newspaper for tourists called *Kyoto Visitor's Guide*, which devotes a few pages to "This Month's Theater." If you don't have time to go to TIC, you can call 075/371-5649 for a helpful English-speaking information officer to answer questions.

Gion Corner If there is one performance that should not be missed in Kyoto, it is the quick but comprehensive overview of Kyoto's performing arts at the Gion Corner. The one-hour show features court music and dance, ancient comic plays, Kyoto-style dancing performed by apprentice geisha called *maiko*, and puppet drama. Segments are also offered on the tea ceremony, flower arrangement, and koto music.

To obtain tickets, contact your hotel concierge or call **Gion Corner** (1st floor, Yasaka Hall, Gion, tel. 075/561-1119). The show is quite a bargain at ¥2,500. Two performances nightly are given at 7:40 and 8:40 March 1–November 29. No performances are offered August 16 and December–February.

Before attending the show, walk around the Gion and Pontocho areas. Most likely you will see beautifully adorned geisha and maiko making their way to work. It is permissible to take their picture, but as they have strict appointments, don't delay them.

Seasonal Dances If you are in Kyoto in April, be sure to take in the **Miyako Odori;** or, in May and October, the **Kamogawa Odori.** These dances are performed by geisha and apprentices and pay tribute to the seasonal splendor of spring and fall. The stage setting is spectacular, with festive singing and dancing.

Performances are held at the **Gion Kaburenjo Theater** (Gion Hanamikoji, Higashiyama-ku, tel. 075/561–1115; tickets: ¥1,650, ¥3,300, and ¥3,800) and the **Pontocho Kaburenjo Theater** (Pontocho Sanjo-sagaru, Nakagyo-ku, tel. 075/221–2025; tickets: ¥1,650, ¥3,300, and ¥3,800).

Kabuki Kabuki has found quite a following in the United States due to recent tours by Japan's Kabuki troupes in Washington, D.C., New York, and a few other cities. Kabuki is faster paced than Noh, but a single performance can easily take half a day. Devoted followers pack their box lunches and sit patiently through the entire performance, mesmerized by each movement of the performers.

For a first-timer, however, this all may be too exotic. Unless you are captured by the Kabuki spirit, don't spend more than an hour or two at Kyoto's famed **Minamiza Theater** (Shijo Kamogawa, Higashiyama-ku, tel. 075/561–1155), the oldest theater in Japan. It was recently beautifully renovated and now hosts a variety of performances year-round. December is the month to see Kabuki in Kyoto when the annual *Kaomise* (Face Showing) Kabuki festival takes place. Top Kabuki stars from around the country make guest appearances during this month-long extravaganza. Performance and ticket information can be obtained through the Tourist Information Center (*see* Important Addresses and Numbers, *above*). Tickets range from ¥2,000 to ¥9,000.

Noh Noh is another form of traditional theater, more ritualistic and sophisticated than Kabuki. Some understanding of the plot of each play is necessary to enjoy a performance, which is generally slow-moving and solemnly chanted. The major Noh theaters often provide synopses of the plays in English. The masks used by the main actors are carved to express a whole range of emotions, though the mask itself may appear expressionless until the actor "brings it to life." Particularly memorable are the outdoor performances of Noh, especially **Takigi Noh,** held outdoors by firelight on the nights of June 1–2 in the precincts of the Heian Jingu Shrine.

Performances are given throughout the year at these two theaters: **Kanze Kaikan Noh Theater,** 44 Enshoji-cho, Okazaki, Sakyo-ku, tel. 075/771–6114; and **Kongo Noh Theater,** Muromachi, Shijo-agaru, Nakagyo-ku, tel. 075/221–3049.

Nightlife

Kyoto's nightlife is much more sedate than Tokyo's, but the areas around the old geisha quarters downtown are still thriving with nightclubs and bars. The Kiyamachi area along the small canal near Pontocho is as close to a consolidated nightlife area as you'll get in Kyoto. It is full of small drinking establishments with red lanterns (indicating inexpensive places) or small neon signs in front. It is also fun to walk around the Gion and Pontocho areas to try to catch a glimpse of a geisha or apprentice geisha going to or coming from work.

In the city center, check out the disco scene at **Gaia,** located in the Pleasure Dome Imagium Building (Nishikiyamachi Street north of Shijo, Nakagyo-ku, tel. 075/231–6600). This five-floor "labyrinth," as the owners call it, also has a bar, restaurant, club, and saloon. Another casual evening possibility is the **Pig & Whistle Pub** (across from the Sanjo Keihan Station, in the Shobi Bldg., tel. 075/761–6022). Every weekend the Pig & Whistle is bulging at the seams with U.K. refugees and Japanese, who come for the draft beer, the fish and chips, and the dart board. The music is too loud, but no one seems to mind; the place is open till midnight during the week and 1 AM on weekends. For jazz, blues, and soul, try the Live Spot Rag (5F Kyoto Empire Bldg., Kiyamachi, tel. 075/241–0446), north of Sanjo, which has a reasonable cover charge of about ¥1,200 for its live sessions between 7 and 11 PM. If you're looking for a light dinner or a late-night snack, head for **Kongolo** (Furukawa-cho, Niomon-dori sagaru, Sakyo-ku, tel. 075/751–9276), tucked in a half-basement on a quiet side street south of Heian Shrine. The sleek café/bar serves salads, spaghetti, and fried chicken, along with beer, mixed drinks, and Italian wine. It's open until 2 AM on Saturday and until midnight the rest of the week (closed Tues.).

8 Nara

By Kiko Itasaka

A freelance writer based in Tokyo and New York, Kiko Itasaka *has contributed to* Best of Japan *and* Mainichi Daily News.

The ancient city of Nara was founded in 710 by Emperor Kammu and predated Kyoto as the capital of Japan. Nara was the first capital to remain in one place over a long period of time. Until then, the capital had been established in a new location with each successive ruler. The founding of Nara, then known as Heijo-Kyo, occurred during a period when Japan's politics, arts, architecture, and religion had been heavily influenced by China. Even the Japanese writing system, which was developed at this time, utilized Chinese written characters.

Introduced by China beginning in the 6th century, Buddhism flourished in Nara and enjoyed the official favor of the rulers and aristocracy, as it coexisted with the indigenous religion of Shintoism. Many of Nara's Buddhist temples and monasteries were built by emperors and noble families, while other temples were transferred to Nara from former capitals. At its peak during the 8th century, Nara was said to have had as many as 50 pagodas. Emperor Shomu built the Todaiji, a grand temple complex that was to serve as a central monastery for other Buddhist monasteries constructed in each province of Japan. Todaiji's construction began in 745 and was completed in 752. It was established not only for spiritual purposes but also to serve as a symbol of a united Japan. Emperor Shomu, who emulated Chinese culture, astutely realized that religion could play a strong role in consolidating Japan.

In 784, the capital of Japan was transferred to Kyoto, and Nara was no longer a city of political consequence. As a result, the many buildings of Nara, including the Todaiji, remained essentially untouched by the ravages of war. Kofukuji Temple recalls the power of the Fujiwara clan in the 7th century. Its close connection with Kasuga Taisha Shrine, the Fujiwara family shrine, demonstrates the peaceful coexistence between Buddhism and Shintoism. The Todaiji and Toshodaiji temples both reflect the pervasive influence of Buddhism on the Japanese way of life over the centuries.

For many years, Nara, a small and quiet city, has been a favorite with many travelers in Japan. Apart from many temples and historical sites of interest in Nara, the narrow backstreets of Naramachi, just south of Sarusawa Pond in Nara-Koen Park, have hidden treasures: old wooden shops, merchants' houses, and traditional restaurants. Here you'll find shops selling the crafts for which Nara is famous: handmade brushes (*fude*) and ink sticks (*sumi*) for calligraphy and ink painting, Nara dolls carved in wood, and *Nara-sarashi-jofu*, fine, handwoven, sun-bleached linen (*see* Exploring, *below*).

Most of Nara's sights are within walking distance of the centrally located and picturesque Nara-Koen Park, inhabited by approximately 1,000 very tame (and sometimes aggressive) deer, which roam freely around the various temples and shrines. The deer are considered to be divine messengers; they are particularly friendly when you feed them deer crackers, which can be purchased at stalls in the park. It is a singular pleasure to wander around the lush green park, dotted with numerous ponds, as you stroll from temple to temple.

Most day-trippers tend to visit only Nara-Koen Park, but we recommend skipping some of its sights and taking the time to visit Horyuji, the oldest remaining temple in all of Japan. Horyuji is located in the outskirts of Nara.

It is impossible to see all of the temples and shrines of Nara in one day. The exploring section of this chapter has a two-day itinerary. If you have only one day to spend in Nara, you may prefer to visit Horyuji, and forgo the other temples near it; then you can proceed to explore more of the Nara-Koen Park district.

Essential Information

Arriving and Departing

By Plane   The nearest airport is Osaka International, which is served by frequent flights from Tokyo.

Between the Airport and Center City   There is no direct transportation from the airport to Nara. Bus service is available to central Osaka or Kyoto, from which you can take a train to Nara.

By Train   From Kyoto, the Kinki Nippon (*Kintetsu*) Railway's Limited Express trains take 33 minutes to reach Nara. It leaves every half hour and costs ¥980. Three JR trains from Kyoto make the journey to Nara every hour. The express takes 45 minutes (cost ¥680), while the two locals take 70 minutes.

From Osaka's Kintetsu-Namba Station, Nara is a 30-minute ride on the Kinki Nippon Railway's Limited Express. Trains leave every hour, and the fare is ¥920. The Ordinary Express to Nara takes 40 minutes, leaves every 20 minutes, and costs ¥480. From Osaka, the JR train to Nara takes 50 minutes. The train leaves every 20 minutes and costs ¥760.

From Kobe, take the JR-Tokaido Line rapid train from the Sannomiya Station to Osaka and transfer to one of the trains described above.

Getting Around

By Train   Because Nara's main attractions are concentrated in one area in the western part of the city, you will do much of your sightseeing on foot. However, the JR Kansai Main Line and the Kinki Nippon Railways' Nara Line slice through the city and bring you close to major attractions. Rates depend upon the distance you travel. From downtown to the Horyuji Temple, the ride costs about ¥250.

By Bus   The most economical way to explore Nara is by bus. Two local bus routes circle the main sites (Todaiji, Kasuga Taisha, and Shin-Yakushiji) in the central and eastern parts of the city: Bus 1 runs counterclockwise and Bus 2 runs clockwise. This urban loop line costs ¥150 for a ride of any distance. Both pass by the JR and Kintetsu stations. Bus 52 westward to Horyuji (with stops at Toshodaiji and Yakushiji) takes about 50 minutes and costs ¥640; it can be caught in front of either the Nara Kintetsu Station or the Nara JR Station. Pick up a bus map at the tourist information center (*see below*).

By Taxi   The rate is ¥480 for the first 1.5 kilometers and ¥90 for each additional 360 meters. From Nara Kintetsu Station to Kasuga Taisha by taxi runs about ¥900 one-way; to Horyuji, about ¥5,000 one-way.

By Bicycle Because Nara is a small city with relatively flat roads, it is a good place for cycling. Bicycles can be rented from **Kintetsu Sunflower** (tel. 0742/24–3528), located on Konishi-dori Avenue near the Kintetsu Station (cost: ¥720 for 4 hours; ¥1,030 for 8 hours). Ask the Nara City Tourist Information Office located on the first floor of the Kintetsu Station for further information or directions. Some hotels also rent bicycles.

Important Addresses and Numbers

Tourist Information **Nara City Tourist Information Office** is on the first floor of the Nara Kintetsu Station, tel. 0742/24–4858. Open daily 9–5.

A **City Information Window** (tel. 0742/22–9821) can be found at the JR Nara Station. Open daily 9–5.

Nara City Tourist Center is located at 23-4 Kami-Sanjo-Cho, Nara-Shi, tel. 0742/22–3900. Open 9–9, but the English-language staff is on duty only until 5. This center, a 10-minute walk from both Nara Kintetsu and Nara JR stations, has free maps, information on sightseeing in English, local crafts, a souvenir corner, and a lounge where you can rest and plan your day.

The **Japan Travel-Phone** (tel. 0120/444–800) will give you toll-free English-language tourist information.

Consulates The nearest U.S., Canadian, and British consulates are located in Osaka (*see* Chapter 9).

Emergencies **Police**, tel. 110; **Ambulance**, tel. 119.

English-Language Bookstore **Nanto Shorin Bookstore** (tel. 0742/23–6369) is located on Sanjo-dori Avenue.

Guided Tours

Orientation Tours Tours of Nara in English must be arranged in advance through the Kyoto or Osaka offices of the **Kintetsu Gray Line Bus Company**. Arrangements can also be made at the travel office in the basement of the New Miyako Hotel in Kyoto (tel. 075/691–0903), or by calling 06/313–6868 in Osaka. The fare for the afternoon tour is ¥6,500 adults, ¥4,500 children 6–11, children under 6 free.

Walking Tours The Japan National Tourist Organization (JNTO) publishes the leaflet *Walking Tour Courses in Nara*, which gives brief descriptions of highlights along the way. One two-hour tour includes Nara Park and several nearby temples and shrines; other tours start with a bus ride from the center of the city. Because Nara has no JNTO office, ask for the leaflet at JNTO offices in Tokyo (6-6 Yurakucho 1-chome, Chiyoda-ku, tel. 03/502–1461) or in Kyoto (Kyoto Tower Bldg., Higashi-Shiokojicho, Shimogyo-ku, tel. 075/371–5649).

Personal Guides The **Student Guide Service** (Sarusawa Tourist Information Center, 4 Nobori Oji-cho, north side of Sarusawa Pond, tel. 0742/26–4753) and the **YMCA Guide Service** (at Kasuga Taisha Shrine, tel. 0742/44–2207) are available for free at the JR Nara Station information center, and the Kintetsu Nara Station. Because these services use volunteer guides, it is best to call in advance to determine availability.

American Express offers Travelers Cheques built for two.

American Express® Cheques *for Two*. The first Travelers Cheques that allow either of you to use them because both of you have signed them. And only one of you needs to be present to purchase them.

Cheques *for Two* are accepted anywhere regular American Express Travelers Cheques are, which is just about everywhere. So stop by your bank, AAA* or any American Express Travel Service Office and ask for Cheques *for Two*.

Exploring

Numbers in the margin correspond to points of interest on the Nara map.

At its founding in the 8th century, Nara was planned as a rectangular city with checkerboard streets based on the model of the Chinese city of Ch'ang-an. The city still maintains this highly organized pattern, and it is therefore extremely easy to find your way around, because the streets are mainly at right angles. Many sights are located within or near Nara-Koen Park. Other major temples, such as Horyuji, Yakushiji, and Toshodaiji, are located west and southwest of Nara, and all can be reached by the same bus.

❶ Begin your tour of Nara at the resplendent **Todaiji Temple,** located in Nara-Koen Park. Get there by boarding Bus 2, which departs from the front of the JR and Kintetsu stations, and get off at the Daibutsuden stop. Cross the street and you will be at the path that leads to the Todaiji Temple complex. You can also walk from Kintetsu Station to Todaiji in about 15 minutes. Exit the east end of the station and walk east along Noboriojidori, the avenue that runs parallel with the station building. Walk past the Nara Prefectural Office Building and under Highway 369, continuing east to the next large intersection. Turn left onto the pedestrians-only street that leads to Todaiji Temple. It is lined with souvenir stalls and small restaurants. You may also walk from the JR station but this route is longer and passes through the less attractive modern sections of town. Because you will be doing a lot of walking in Nara, this option seems a waste of time and energy.

As you walk along the path leading to the temple complex, you will pass through the impressive dark wood front gate known as
❷ **Nandaimon** (Great Southern Gate). The original gate was destroyed in a typhoon in 962; it was rebuilt in 1199. The gate is supported by 18 large wood pillars, each 62 feet high and 39 inches in diameter. In the two outer niches on either side of the gate are wood figures of Deva Kings, who guard the great Buddha within. They are the work of master sculptor Unkei, of the Kamakura period (1185–1335). In the inner niches are a pair of stone *koma-inu* (Korean dogs); these creatures are mythical guardians placed beside the gates to ward off evil.

Continue straight along the path leading to the main buildings of the Todaiji complex. In front of you is the entrance of the Daibutsuden Hall, but before entering this building, first go to
❸ the small temple on the left, the **Kaidan-in.** Inside are clay statues of the Four Heavenly Guardians. The images are depicted in full armor, wielding weapons and displaying fierce expressions. *Kaidan* is a Buddhist word for the terrace on which priests are ordained. The Chinese Buddhist priest Ganjin (688–763) ordained many Japanese Buddhist priests here. The original temple was destroyed repeatedly by fire, and the current structure was built in 1731. *Admission: ¥400. Open daily 8–5 (8–4:30 in winter).*

❹ From the Kaidan-in, return to the entrance of the **Daibutsuden** (Hall of the Great Buddha), purportedly the largest wooden structure in the world (157 ft. high and 187 ft. long). The elegant and austere white building, with its wood beams darkened with age, is an impressive sight. Note a pair of gilt ornaments

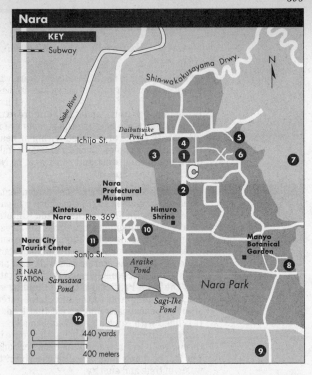

decorating the roof ridge. They are called *kutsugata* (shoe-shape) because they resemble footwear. In ancient times, these kutsugata were not only ornamental; they were believed to ward off fire. They unfortunately did not work, because the hall was repeatedly destroyed by fire. The current Daibutsuden was restored in 1709, at only two-thirds the scale of the original structure. Inside the Daibutsuden is the Daibutsu, a 53-foot bronze statue of Buddha that is perhaps the most famous sight in all of Nara. The Daibutsu was originally commissioned by Emperor Shomu in 743. After numerous unsuccessful castings, the figure was finally made in 749. A statue of this scale had never before been built in Japan, and it was hoped that it would serve as a symbol to unite the country. The statue was dedicated in 752 in a grand ceremony attended by the then-retired Emperor Shomu, the imperial court members, and 10,000 priests and nuns.

Behind the Daibutsu to the right, you'll see a large wooden pillar with a hole at its base. You will also observe many Japanese tourists attempting to crawl through the opening, which is barely large enough for a petite adult. Local superstition has it that those who pass through the opening will eventually go to paradise. Children, in particular, love easing through and watching adults suffer the indignity of barely making it through the opening. In the back of the Daibutsu, to the left, is a model of the original Todaiji Temple. *Admission:* ¥400. *Open daily Jan.–Feb. 8–4:30, Mar. 8–5, Apr.–Sept. 7:30–5:30, Oct. 7:30–5, Nov.–Dec. 8–4:30.*

As you exit the Daibutsuden, turn left and walk up a winding path. Turn right, go up a stone staircase, and then veer left on the slope lined with stone lanterns. On your left, on top of the

❺ slope, you will come to **Nigatsudo** (Second Month Temple), named because of a religious rite that used to be performed here every February. The temple was founded in 752 and houses some important images that are not on display to the public. However, because of the hilltop location, the temple's veranda offers a breathtaking, panoramic view of Nara-Koen Park. *Admission free. Open daily 8–5:30.*

Return along the same incline that led to Nigatsudo and turn

❻ left. The wood structure on your left is **Sangatsudo** (Third Month Temple), named after a rite that was performed annually in March. The entrance is on the right side as you face the building. Founded in 733, this temple is the original structure and the oldest building in the Todaiji Temple complex. As you enter, to your left are some benches covered with tatami straw mats. You can sit and absorb the wealth of 8th-century, National Treasure sculptures that crowd the small room. The principal image is the dry lacquer statue of Fukukenjaku Kannon, the Goddess of Mercy, whose diadem is encrusted with thousands of pearls and gemstones. The two clay statues on either side of her, the Gakko (Moonlight) and the Nikko (Sunlight) bodhisattvas, are considered fine examples of the Nara (or Tempyo) period, the height of classic Japanese sculpture. *Admission: ¥400. Open daily 7:30–5:30 (8–4:30 in winter).*

Leave the entrance of Sangatsudo, and walk straight ahead, following the signs in English for Mt. Wakakusa. You will be leaving the temple grounds and walking along a street. On the

❼ left is the base of **Mt. Wakakusa,** which is actually more a hill covered with grass than a mountain. Once a year, on January 15, 15 priests set the hill's dry grass on fire. The blazes on the entire hill create a grand spectacle. On the right side of the street are many souvenir shops and small restaurants. This area is called Mikasa Sanroku Cho.

Time Out Because there are very few areas to grab a bite in Nara-Koen Park, this is a good place to have a cup of coffee, a snack, or even lunch. Most of the restaurants on the street near Mt. Wakakusa are similar, but a few offer a better selection than the others. **Shiroganeya** (tel. 0742/22–2607) has noodles for ¥650–¥750 and lunches for ¥1,000–¥2,500. **Asahiken** (tel. 0742/22–2384) has a tasty tempura lunch for ¥1,500 and eel for ¥1,200. In both places, you pay when served.

If you continue past all of the restaurants and shops, at the end of the street you will see some stone steps. Go down these and cross a small bridge over a stream, then walk along the path that leads into shady and peaceful woods. At the end of the path, turn left up the staircase before you, and you will be in

❽ front of the **Kasuga Taisha Shrine.** Kasuga was founded in 768 as a tutelary shrine for the Fujiwaras, a prominent feudal family. It is famous for the more than 2,000 stone lanterns that line the major pathways to the shrine, all of which are lit three times a year on special festival days (Feb. 2, Aug. 14–15). For many years after its founding, the shrine was reconstructed, following the original design, exactly every 20 years according to Shinto custom, as is the case with the famous Ise Jingu Shrine in Mie Prefecture. (Kasuga, however, has not been rebuilt in 100 years.) The reason that many Shinto shrines are rebuilt is not only to renew the materials, but also to purify the site. It is said that Kasuga Taisha has been rebuilt over 50 times, the last time being in 1893. After you pass through the torii gate, the first wooden structure you'll see is the Haiden (Offering Hall), and to its left is the Naoraiden (Entertainment Hall). In back of the latter hall are the four Honden (Main Shrines). They are National Treasures, all built in the same Kasuga style, and painted bright vermilion and green—a striking contrast to the dark wooden exterior of most of the temples in Nara. The sacred deer of this shrine are protected, and they roam freely about the grounds. *Admission to Kasuga Shrine Museum: ¥400. Open 9–4. Admission to the shrine's outer courtyard free. For ¥500, you may enter the inner precincts to view the 4 Honden structures and gardens. Open Apr.–Oct. 8:30–5, Nov.–Mar. 9–4:30.*

Leaving Kasuga Taisha Shrine, walk south, down the path lined with stone lanterns and past the Kasuga-Wakamiya Jinja Shrine. Continue down this woody path until you reach a paved road. Cross the road and take the first right, onto a residential street with many traditional Japanese houses. Take the first left and follow it south about 100 yards, till it curves to the right and leads to the entrance of the **Shin-Yakushiji Temple.** This structure was founded in 747 by Empress Komyo (701–760) as a prayer requesting the recovery of her sick husband, Emperor Shomu. Most of the temple buildings were destroyed over the years. Only the Main Hall, which houses many fine objects of the Nara period, still exists. In the center of the hall is a wood statue of Yakushi Nyorai, the Physician of the Soul. Surrounding this statue are 12 clay images of the Twelve Divine Generals who protected Yakushi. Eleven of these figures are originals. The generals stand in threatening poses, bearing spears, swords, and other weapons, and display terrifying expressions. *Admission: ¥400. Open 8:30–sunset.*

Leaving the Shin-Yakushiji Temple, retrace your steps to the residential street you walked down earlier. Turn left down this street and walk to the major intersection at the end of it. Across the street you will see a bus stop, where you can board Bus 1 back to the Daibutsuden stop. If time is limited and you want to skip Shin-Yakushiji Temple, take the path straight down from Kasuga Taisha to the Nara National Museum and Kofukuji Temple. **Nara National Museum** specializes in Buddhist art. The East Wing, built in 1973, has many examples of calligraphy, paintings, and sculpture. The West Wing, built in 1895, features objects of archaeological interest. Each fall during the driest days of November, when the Shosoin Repository, located behind the Todaiji, opens its doors to air its magnificent collection, there is a special collection of part of its ancient treasures on display at the National Museum. For those who are in Nara at this time, it should not be missed. *10-6 Noborioji-cho, tel. 0742/22–7771. Admission: ¥400 adults, ¥130 college and high-school students, ¥70 junior-high and grade-school students (more for special exhibitions). Open 9–4:30 (enter by 4). Closed Mon. (when national holidays fall on Mon., closed on Tues.).*

Leaving the west exit of the East Wing of the Museum, walk west for about five minutes and you will find yourself at the **Kofukuji Temple** complex. This temple was originally founded in 669 in Kyoto by the Fujiwara family; with the establishment of the new capital of Nara, it was transferred to its current location in 710. At its peak in the 8th century, Kofukuji (Happiness Producing Temple) was a powerful temple that had 175 buildings, of which fewer than a dozen remain. The history of this temple reflects the interesting relationship between Buddhism and Shintoism in Japan.

In 937, a Kofukuji monk had a dream in which the Shinto deity of Kasuga appeared in the form of a Buddha, asking to become a protector of the temple; in 947, some Kofukuji monks held a Buddhist ceremony at the Shinto Kasuga Taisha Shrine to mark the merging of the Buddhist temple with the Shinto shrine. Although you can enter many buildings in this temple complex, perhaps the most interesting is the *Kokuhokan* National Treasure House. This unattractive, modern concrete building holds a fabulous collection of National Treasure sculpture and other works of art from the Nara period. *Admission: ¥500 adults, ¥400 high-school and junior-high students, ¥150 grade-school students. Open daily 9–5 (enter by 4:30).*

Also of interest at the Kofukuji Temple complex are the two pagodas. The Five-Story Pagoda, at 164 feet, is the second tallest pagoda in all Japan. The first pagoda at this site was built in 730 by Empress Komyo. Several succeeding pagodas were destroyed by fire, but the current pagoda is an exact replica of the original and was built in 1426. The Three-Story Pagoda was built in 1114 and is renowned for its graceful lines and fine proportions.

There are several fine restaurants within minutes of the Kofukuji Pagoda (*see* Dining, *below*).

Before continuing on to the Western district and Horyuji Temple, take some time out from temple-viewing to walk through **❶❷** **Naramachi**, just south of Sarusawa Pond. This is a maze of narrow residential streets lined with traditional houses and old shops, many of which deal in Nara's renowned arts and crafts. Gangoji Temple lies at the heart of Naramachi, and near it the little town museum known as the Naramachi Shiryokan (Historical Library). Maps to the area are available through the city's tourist information centers and the Shiryokan: A signboard map on the southwest edge of Sarusawa Pond shows the way to all the important shops, museums, and galleries.

Look for **"Yu" Nakagawa** (tel. 0742/22–1322), which specializes in handwoven, sunbleached linen textiles, a Nara specialty known as *sarashi jofu*. From October to April, make an appointment to watch the making of ink sticks at **Kobaien** (tel. 0742/23–2965), for 400 years the makers of fine Nara ink sticks for calligraphy and ink painting. Visit the Silk Road folk-craft shop **Kikuoka** (0742/26–3889) near the Historical Library. On foot or by bicycle, Naramachi can offer a change of pace from ordinary sightseeing, and local residents are friendly and eager to help.

Numbers in the margin correspond to points of interest on the Western Nara Temples map.

From the JR Nara or Kintetsu Nara stations, it is quite simple to visit the four major temples located on the outskirts of Nara. From the Kintetsu and JR stations, take Bus 52, which stops at Toshodaiji Temple, Yakushiji Temple, and Horyuji and Chuguji temples, and returns along the same route. The bus to Horyuji, the farthest temple, takes about 50 minutes and costs ¥640. You can also take the JR train on the Kania Main Line to Yamato-kaizumi station. **Horyuji** is the most interesting of these temples, and it should be visited first. If time allows, go to the other temples as well. Get off the bus at the Horyuji-mae stop and walk down the path leading to the temple complex. Horyuji was founded in 607 by Prince Shotoku (573–621). Some of the temple buildings are among the oldest wood structures in the world. The first gate you pass through at Horyuji is the **Nandaimon,** rebuilt in 1438. The second gate is the **Chumon** (Middle Gate), which is the original gate, built in 607. Unlike most Japanese gates, which are supported by two pillars at the ends, this gate is supported by pillars in the center. Note the unusual shape of the pillars, which are entastic (curved outward in the center), an architectural technique used in ancient Greece that traveled as far as Japan. Entastic pillars in Japan exist only in the 7th-century structures of Nara.

As you pass through the gate you enter the western precincts of the temple. The first building you see on your right is the **Kondo** (Main Hall). On its left is a five-story pagoda. The entire pagoda was disassembled in World War II; after the war, it was reconstructed in its original form, using the same materials that were first used to build it in 607. In back of the pagoda is the **Daikodo** (Lecture Hall), which was destroyed by fire and rebuilt in 990. Inside the hall is an image of Yakushi Nyorai (Physician of the Soul).

From the Daikodo, walk back past the Kondo and Chumon Gate, then turn left and walk past the pond on your right. You will come to two concrete buildings known as the **Daihozoden** (Great Treasure Hall). On display in these buildings are statues, sculptures, ancient Buddhist religious articles, and brocades. Of particular interest is a miniature shrine that belonged to Lady Tachibana, mother of the Empress Komyo. The shrine is only a little over 9 feet in height, and the Buddha image inside is about 20 inches tall.

As you leave the exit of the Daihozoden, turn left, walk a short distance until the path ends, and turn left again. You will be at the **Todaimon** (Great East Gate), which leads to the eastern precincts of the temple complex. The octagonal building is the **Yumedono** (Hall of Dreams), so named because Prince Shotoku used to meditate here. *Admission to all temple buildings: ¥700. Open daily 8–5 (8–4:30 in winter); enter 1 hr. before closing.*

In the rear of the eastern precinct of the Horyuji Temple is an exit that leads to **Chuguji Temple.** As you enter, notice the carefully raked pebbles on which you must walk to approach the entrance. Chuguji was originally the home of Prince Shotoku's mother. After she passed away, it became a temple dedicated to her memory. This quiet nunnery houses a graceful wooden image of the Miroku Bodhisattva, the Buddha of the Future. The famous statue dates to the Asuka period (552–645), and its gentle countenance offers an ageless view of hope for the future. Also of interest is the oldest example of embroidery in Japan, which dates as far back as the Asuka period (552–645). The framed cloth depicts Tenjukoku (Land of Heavenly Longevity). In front of the temple is a carefully tended small pond

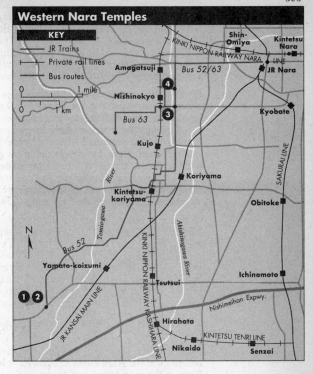

in which rocks are artfully arranged. Although this nunnery is a peaceful and interesting place to visit, it is not worth seeing if you are pressed for time. *Admission: ¥300. Open daily 9–4:30 (9–4 in winter).*

❸ Get back on Bus 52 (going in the direction from which you came) and get off at the Yakushiji-mae stop. **Yakushiji Temple** was originally founded in 680 and was transferred to its current location in 718. As you enter the temple grounds, on your right you will see the **East Tower,** a pagoda that dates back to 1285. The pagoda has an interesting asymetrical shape, so startling that it inspired American scholar Ernest Fenollosa (1853–1908) to remark that it was as beautiful as "frozen music." Although it appears to have six stories, in fact it only has three; it consists of three roofs with smaller ones attached underneath. The **West Tower,** to your left, was built in 1981. The new building in the center is the **Kondo Hall,** which was rebuilt in 1976 and is painted in garish vermilion. These newer buildings are not nearly as attractive as the older structures, and they look out of place in the otherwise attractive temple complex. *Admission: ¥400. Open daily 8:30–5.*

❹ From the rear gate of Yakushiji Temple, it is a 10-minute walk to **Toshodaiji Temple** down the "Path of History," trod by important dignitaries and priests for centuries. The path is lined with clay-walled houses, gardens, and small shops selling antiques, crafts, and *narazuke* (vegetables pickled in sake), a popular local specialty. There are also several good restaurants here (*see* Dining, *below*). Toshodaiji Temple was founded in 751 by Ganjin, a Chinese priest who traveled to Japan at the invitation of Emperor Shomu. At this time, Japanese priests had never received formal instruction from a Buddhist priest. The invitation was extended by two Japanese priests who traveled to China in search of a Buddhist priest willing to undertake the arduous and perilous journey to Japan. Ganjin agreed to go but was unsuccessful in his first attempts to reach Japan.

On his first journey, some of his disciples betrayed him. His second journey resulted in a shipwreck. During the third trip, his ship was blown off course, and on his fourth trip, he was refused permission to leave China by government officials. Before his next attempt, he contracted an eye disease that left him blind. Nevertheless, he persevered in his goal of reaching Japan and finally arrived in 750. Ganjin shared his knowledge of Buddhism with his adopted country and served as a teacher to many Japanese priests as well as Emperor Shomu; he is also remembered for bringing the first sugar to Japan.

In order to enter the temple complex, you pass through the **Nandaimon** (Great South Gate), which is supported by entastic pillars, also seen in the gate of Horyuji. The first building you see is the **Kondo** (Main Hall), which is considered to be one of the finest remaining examples of Nara architecture. Inside the hall is a lacquer statue of Vairocana Buddha, the same incarnation of Buddha that is enshrined at Todaiji Temple. The halo surrounding this figure originally was covered with 1,000 Buddhas, though only 864 remain today. In back of the Kondo is the **Kodo** (Lecture Hall), which was originally an assembly hall of the Nara Imperial Court and was moved to its current location when Toshodaiji was founded. Because all the other buildings of the Nara imperial court have been destroyed, the Kodo is the only remaining example of Nara palace architecture. In the back of the temple grounds is the **Mieido Hall**, in which there is a lacquer statue of Ganjin that dates back to 763. This image is on public display only once a year, on June 6, in commemoration of the birthday of the illustrious priest. *Admission: ¥500. Open daily 8:30–5.*

When you leave Toshodaiji Temple, you can take Bus 63 back to Kintetsu-Nara or JR Nara stations; pick it up right in front of the temple.

Dining

Nara cuisine resembles that of its neighboring city, Kyoto. The specialty of this region is *kaiseki*, carefully prepared and aesthetically pleasing Japanese full-course meals (usually 7–12 courses). Another local specialty is *chagayu*, rice porridge flavored with green tea and served with vegetables in season. Nara boasts the lowest rate of stomach cancer in Japan, and local wisdom attributes this to the healthfulness of chagayu. An unforgettable gourmet experience is your first bite of *narazuke*, tangy vegetables pickled in sake, often served as a side dish with traditional meals in Nara. Most visitors here are daytrippers who do not plan to dine in town, but an elegant Japanese meal in a traditional Nara restaurant is an appropriate and enjoyable way to conclude a day of temple viewing. Those who do not have time for dinner should have a leisurely lunch in one of the restaurants located near a temple. One word of warning: Many Nara restaurants are small and offer limited menus with set courses and no à la carte dishes, so it is a good idea to make reservations in advance. Restaurants tend to close early in Nara, so plan accordingly. Since some places do not have an English-speaking staff or menus in English, it's best to ask someone from your hotel to help make your arrangements. This may seem a lot of trouble for the sake of eating, but the quiet atmosphere and the hospitality of the local residents make Nara a memorable place to enjoy a fine traditional meal.

A 3% federal consumer tax is added to all restaurant bills. Another 3% local tax is added to the bill if it exceeds ¥7,500. At more expensive restaurants, a 10%–15% service charge is added to the bill. Tipping is not necessary.

The most highly recommended restaurants are indicated by a star ★.

Category	Cost*
Very Expensive	over ¥7,000
Expensive	¥5,000–¥7,000
Moderate	¥3,500–¥5,000
Inexpensive	under ¥3,500

Cost is per person without tax, service, or drinks

★ **Onjaku.** Located near the Nara Hotel, this restaurant offers exquisitely presented kaiseki meals in a serene Japanese-style room with gentle lighting. The exterior, with its faded wood walls, is in keeping with the architectural style of Nara. The menu consists only of kaiseki set meals of varying prices. *1043 Kita-tenma-cho, tel. 0742/26–4762. Reservations required. Dress: informal. No credit cards. Lunch 12–1, dinner 5–7:30. Closed Tues. Very Expensive.*

Tsukihitei. A quiet Japanese restaurant set in the hills in back of the Kasuga Taisha Shrine, Tsukihitei serves formal kaiseki Japanese cuisine. Your dining experience begins when you walk up the shaded, wooded path leading to the restaurant. When you make your reservation, ask for a kaiseki set meal. As you dine on delicate morsels of fish, vegetables, and rice, and sip on sweet plum wine, you will look out on the forests surrounding the restaurant. *158 Kasugano-cho, tel. 0742/26–2021. Reservations required. Jacket and tie required. DC, V. Open daily 11:30–7. Very Expensive.*

Bekkan Kikusuiro. For those who want to try kaiseki, but do not want a formal and complicated meal, Bekkan Kikusuiro offers what it calls "mini kaiseki," an abridged version with fewer courses. Unlike standard kaiseki, where each course is served separately, your whole meal will be served on one tray. You can either sit at a table, which is less expensive, or in a Japanese-style room with tatami. *1130 Takahata-cho, tel. 0742/23–2001. Reservations advised. Dress: informal. No credit cards. Open daily 11–8:30. Closed Dec. 31. Expensive.*

Tempura Asuka. Directly south of Sarusawa Pond in Nara-machi, Asuka offers full-course tempura meals and reasonably priced bento or tempura soba noodle lunches. Take a seat at the counter, reserve a tatami room, or sit at a table overlooking the garden. *11 Chonanin-cho, tel. 0742/26–4308. No reservations. Dress: informal. MC, V. Open 11:30–2 and 4:30–9 (last order at 8:30); Sun. and holidays 11:30–9. Closed Tues. Moderate.*

★ **Uma no me.** Kaiseki is not the only Japanese food available in
Nara. Uma no me prides itself on home cooking, featuring roast
fish, tofu, and other home-style Japanese dishes. The atmosphere is friendly and informal, with dark-wood walls decorated
with attractive pottery. This restaurant is within a few minutes' walk of the Nara Hotel. *1158 Takahata-cho, tel. 0742/23–
7784. Reservations required. Dress: informal. No credit cards.
Lunch 11:30–3, dinner 5:30–8:30. Closed Thurs. Moderate.*

Van Kio. Outside the south gate of Yakushiji Temple, this traditional restaurant is famous for its "hot stone steam cookery"
and its exotic meat dishes, including costly Nara venison and
duck. Sushi and vegetarian dishes are also available. The resident landscape gardener, Kawatake-san, sells a selection of
stone lanterns, basins, and other garden ornaments, as well as
a variety of Nara antiques on the premises. *410 Rokujo-cho, tel
0742/33–8942. Reservations advised. Dress: informal. AE,
MC, V. Open 11–10. Closed Mon. Moderate.*

★ **Yanagi-chaya.** Yanagi-chaya specializes in excellent *bento*
meals, served in basic black-lacquer boxes. The food is Nara
style: elegantly simple, with sashimi, stewed vegetables, and
tofu. There are two branches of this revered old teahouse:
(the elder) Yanagi-chaya is on the north bank and overlooks
Sarusawa Pond. *49 Noborioji-cho, tel. 0742/22–7460.* The
younger sister is just east of Kofukuji Temple. *48 Teraoji-cho,
tel. 0742/22–7560. Reservations required. Dress: informal. No
credit cards. Open 11:30–7:30. Noborioji-dori location is
closed Wed., Teraoji-cho branch is closed Mon. Moderate.*

Ginsho. Across from the Nara Shiryokan (Historical Library)
on a tiny side street in Naramachi, this soba noodle shop has a
strikingly contemporary Japanese-style interior in a traditional building that harmonizes with the old neighborhood around
it. Great ten-zaru soba (cold noodles and tempura) or tempura
soba (hot tempura noodle soup) is served. *18 Nishishinya-cho,
tel. 0742/23–1355. No reservations. Dress: informal. No credit
cards. Open 11–2. Closed Mon. Inexpensive.*

Harishin. This quiet little restaurant is located in a restored
traditional Nara home in the heart of Naramachi; you can find it
by looking for its red *noren* (short curtain hanging in the doorway) decorated with a crest of crossed arrows. Open for lunch
only, Harishin serves a Katsumichi bento that comes in a dou-
ble-layer lacquer box and often includes almond fried chicken,
shrimp, seasonal pilaf, vegetables, soup, fruit, and an aperitif
of homemade strawberry wine. It's an excellent bargain. *15
Chushinya-cho, tel. 0742/22–2669. No reservations. Dress: informal. No credit cards. Open 11:30–3:30. Closed Mon. Inexpensive.*

To-no-chaya. One distinctive Nara meal is *chagayu*, a rice porridge flavored with green tea. To-no-chaya offers a light meal
of this special dish, combined with some sashimi and vegetables, plus a few sweetened rice cakes for dessert. From the restaurant you can see the Five-Story Pagoda of Kofukuji Temple.
Appropriately, the name of this restaurant means the "tearoom of the pagoda." *47 Nobori Oji, tel. 0742/22–4348. Reservations required for Chagayu kaiseki. Dress: informal. No
credit cards. Open for Chagayu 11:30–9, for bento 11:30–4.
Closed Wed. and national holidays. Inexpensive.*

Lodging

There is much to see and do in Nara, but surprisingly few people plan to stay overnight. The city has fine accommodations in every style and price range, and because most people think of Nara as a day-trip destination, the streets are deserted at night, allowing those wise enough to tarry a chance to stroll undisturbed beside the ponds and in temple grounds. A 3% federal consumer tax is added to all hotel bills. Another 3% local tax is added if the bill exceeds ¥15,000. At most hotels, a 10%–15% service charge is added to the total bill. Tipping is not necessary. The postal code for Nara is 630.

The most highly recommended accommodations are indicated by a star ★.

Category	Cost*
Very Expensive	over ¥30,000
Expensive	¥20,000–¥30,000
Moderate	¥10,000–¥20,000
Inexpensive	under ¥10,000

Cost is for double room, without tax or service

★ **Edo-San.** A night in this ryokan is an experience of being entirely enveloped by Japanese tradition. The accommodations here consist of small cottages with complete privacy. The cottages, old-fashioned Japanese structures with thatch roofs, are all surrounded by lovely trees, flowers, and other greenery. Deer from Nara-Koen Park occasionally wander onto the grounds of the inn. The excellent food, served in your private cottage, is included in the cost of your stay and consists of a variety of seafood dishes. *1167 Takahatake-cho, tel. 0742/26-2662, fax 0742/26-2663. 11 rooms. AE, DC, V. Expensive.*

Hotel Fujita Nara. This hotel, situated on the main road running from the JR Nara Station to the Nara-Koen Park, offers attractive rooms, simply decorated in beige. The Japanese restaurant serves excellent food. *47-1 Shimo Sanjo-cho, tel. 0742/23-8111, fax 0742/22-0255. 118 rooms. Facilities: Japanese and Western restaurants, coffee shop. AE, DC, MC, V. Expensive.*

★ **Kankaso.** Elegance reigns at this ryokan, located near Todaiji Temple, right in the heart of Nara-Koen Park. The rooms have all been exquisitely decorated with Japanese scrolls, pottery, and other artwork. Great care is taken with the flower arrangements set in the alcove of each room. The communal baths look out on a lovely garden. *10 Kasugano-cho, Nara-shi, tel. 0742/26-1128, fax 0742/26-1301. 10 rooms. V. Expensive.*

Nara Garden Hotel. Located on a hillside above Todaiji Temple, this brand-new hotel is within walking distance of all the sites in central Nara. Rooms here are furnished in light woods with green carpeting and floral bedspreads and curtains. Each has a view of the hillside cherry trees. Although the hotel is small, it does have a restaurant that serves excellent Japanese and French food. *Wakakusa, Sanroku-cho, tel. 0742/27-0555, fax 0742/27-0203. 21 rooms. Facilities: restaurant, banquet rooms, coffee shop. AE, DC, MC, V. Expensive.*

★ **Nara Hotel.** Set right in the heart of Nara Park, this establishment is in fact a site of historical interest. Built in the Meiji period (1868–1912), the architectually delightful Nara Hotel has a graceful Japanese tiled roof and a magnificent lobby with high wood ceilings. Although most rooms have a good view of the surrounding temples, those in the new wing are not as interesting as the turn-of-the-century style rooms in the old wing. *1096 Takabatake-cho, tel. 0742/26–3300, fax 0742/23–5252. 132 rooms. Facilities: Western restaurant, tearoom. AE, DC, MC, V. Expensive.*

Hotel Sun Route Nara. With clean and comfortable rooms, this hotel is a cut above business hotels. Its location near the Kintetsu Nara Station makes it a convenient place to stay. *1110 Takabatake Bodai-cho, tel. 0742/22–5151, fax 0742/27–3759. 95 rooms. Facilities: French restaurant, coffee shop. AE, DC, MC, V. Moderate.*

Japan Pension (Nara Club). Although it's located in Nara, north of the Shoso-in Treasure House, this new family-run pension resembles a small European hotel. Some of its modest-size rooms have skylights, and all are decorated in delicate pink printed fabrics with simple, dark-wood furniture. Each room has a private bath and toilet. The restaurant's dining room overlooks a little garden; Western food is served. You may book a room here with or without meals included. *21 Gomoncho, tel. 0742/22–3450, fax 0742/22–3490. 10 rooms. Facilities: Western restaurant. AE, V. Moderate.*

Kotton Hyakupasento. The name of this pleasant little hotel is a play on words written with Chinese characters that mean 100% Old Capital (rather than 100% Cotton). Popular with young Japanese, it is located on a side street near Sarusawa Pond, a short walk south of Nara Park. *1122–21 Bodaiji-cho, tel. 0742/ 22–7117, fax 0742/26–2771. 14 rooms. No credit cards. Moderate.*

People's Inn Hanakomichi. This attractive, slightly overpriced establishment is located near Kintetsu Nara Station; it is also close to shops and within walking distance of Nara Park. A drawback to its central locale is the street noise, which is especially annoying in the summer when you need to keep your bedroom window open for fresh air. The first and second floors feature boutiques, a gallery, and a café. *23 Konishi-cho, tel. 0742/26–2646, fax 0742/26–2771. 28 rooms: 20 Western-style, 8 Japanese-style. AE, DC, MC, V. Moderate.*

Seikanso. This family-run Japanese-style inn, located in the heart of the old Naramachi district, has a relaxed atmosphere, with most rooms in the wood structure overlooking a central garden. It's a 15-minute walk from the Kintetsu Station and a 25-minute walk from the JR Nara Station to the inn; most of the walk is under arcades. This place is extremely popular with foreigners, so try to make advance reservations. The bath is shared. *29 Higashikitsuji-cho, tel. 0742/22–2670, fax 0742/22– 2670. 13 rooms. AE, MC, V. Inexpensive.*

9 Osaka

Updated by
Nigel Fisher

In terms of industry, commerce, and technology, Osaka is definitely Japan's "Second City," next to Tokyo. It has a long history as a center for trade. Until the Meiji Restoration (1868), the merchant class was at the bottom of the social hierarchy, even though many of this class were financially among the richest people in Japan. Osaka expanded as a trading center at the end of the 16th century. Denied the usual aristocratic cultural pursuits, merchants sought and developed their pleasures in the theater and in dining. Even today, Osaka is known for its Bunraku (puppet theater) and its superb restaurants. Indeed, it is often said that many a successful Osaka businessman has eventually gone bankrupt by spending so much on eating.

In the 4th and 5th centuries, the Osaka-Nara region was the center of the developing Japanese (Yamato) nation. It was through Osaka that knowledge and culture from mainland Asia filtered into the fledgling Japanese society. During the 5th and 6th centuries, several emperors maintained an imperial court in Osaka, but the city lost its political importance after a permanent capital was set up in Nara in 694.

For the next several hundred years, Osaka, then known as Naniwa, was just another backwater port on the Inland Sea. Then, at the end of the 16th century, Hideyoshi Toyotomi (1536–1598), a great warrior and statesman, had one of Japan's most majestic castles built in Osaka as part of his successful unification of Japan. The castle took three years to build and was completed in 1586. Hideyoshi encouraged merchants from around the country to set up their businesses in the city, which soon prospered.

After Hideyoshi died, Ieyasu Tokugawa usurped power from the Toyotomi clan in 1603. However, the Toyotomi clan still maintained Osaka as their base. In 1614, Ieyasu sent his troops from Kyoto to Osaka to oppose rebellious movements in support of the Toyotomis. Ieyasu's army defeated the Toyotomi clan and their followers and destroyed the castle in 1615. Even though the Tokugawa Shogunate rebuilt the castle after they had destroyed it, Osaka was once again apart from Japan's political scene. Nevertheless, the Osakan merchants, left to themselves and far from the shogun's administrative center in Edo (Tokyo), continued to prosper, and they sent products from the hinterland through the city to Kyoto and Edo. During this time of economic growth, some of Japan's business dynasties were founded, whose names we still hear of today— Sumitomo, Marubeni, Sanwa, and Daiwa. Their growing wealth also gave them the means to pursue pleasure, and, by the end of the 17th century (the Genroku Era), Osaka's residents were giving patronage to such literary giants as the dramatist Chikamatsu (1653–1724), often referred to as the Shakespeare of Japan, and the novelist Saikaku Ihara (1642–1693). Chikamatsu's genius as a playwright elevated the Bunraku to a dignified dramatic art. Also at this time, Kabuki was patronized and developed by the Osakan merchants.

With the opening of Japan to Western commerce in 1853 and the end of the Tokugawa Shogunate in 1868, Osaka stepped into the forefront of Japan's commerce. At first Yokohama was the major port for Japan's foreign trade, but when the Great Kanto earthquake leveled that city in 1923, foreigners looked to Kobe and Osaka as alternative gateways for their import and export business. Osaka's merchant heritage placed the city in a good position for industrial growth—iron, steel, fabrics, ships, heavy and light machinery, and chemicals all became part of Osaka's output. Today, the region accounts for 25% of the country's industrial product and 40% of the nation's exports. Since the building of its new harbor facilities, Osaka has become a major port in its own right, as it relies less on the facilities in Kobe.

Osaka is also still a merchant city, with many streets devoted to wholesale business activity. For example, medical and pharmaceutical companies congregate in Doshomachi, and fireworks and toys are found in Matchamachi-suji. The city is also famous for shopping. Head to Umeda, Shinsaibashi, or Namba for the greatest concentration of department stores, movie theaters, and restaurants.

Anyone over 50 in Japan remembers Osaka as an exotic maze of crisscrossing waterways that provided transportation for the booming merchant trade. All but a few of the canals were destroyed, along with most of the traditional wood buildings, during the bombings of World War II. With all the present-day high-rise buildings and broad avenues, it is hard to visualize what the vivacious city must have been like 50 years ago. Today, however, the city is working hard to restore some of the beauty that was lost, with a movement for the greening of Osaka running strong.

Although Osaka may not have many sites of historical interest, it is a good starting point for trips to Nara, Kyoto, and Kobe. As a visitor, you can also participate in one of Osaka's leading pleasures: the pursuit of fine dining. In addition, the city's nightlife is legendary. Be sure to stroll through the Dotonbori district, beside the Dotonbori River, which has more nightclubs and bars per square foot than any other place in town.

Essential Information

Arriving and Departing

By Plane
All domestic and international flights arrive at Osaka International Airport, about 30 minutes from central Osaka. Flights from Tokyo, which operate frequently throughout the day, take 70 minutes. Regular domestic flights from major Japanese cities to Osaka are handled by Japan Airlines (JAL), All Nippon Airways (ANA), and Japan Air System. At press time, Osaka's new Kansai International Airport was scheduled to open in mid-1994. It will be Japan's first 24-hour airport.

Between the Airport and Center City
Airport buses operate at intervals of 15 minutes to one hour, 6 AM–9 PM, and take passengers to seven locations in Osaka: Shin-Osaka Station, Umeda, Namba (near the Nikko and Holiday Inn hotels), Uehonmachi, Abeno, Sakaihigashi, and Osaka Business Park (near the New Otani Hotel). Buses take 25–50 minutes, depending on destination, and cost ¥340–¥680. Schedules, with exact times and fares, are available at the information counter at the airport.

The following hotels operate shuttle bus service to and from Osaka International Airport: Osaka Dai-ichi Hotel, Hanshin Hotel, Nikko Osaka Hotel, New Otani Osaka Hotel, and the Holiday Inn Nankai.

Taxis between the airport and hotels in central Osaka take about 30 minutes and cost approximately ¥5,000.

By Train The Tokaido Shinkansen super express trains from Tokyo to Osaka's Shin-Osaka Station take just under three hours and cost ¥13,480 for reserved seats, or ¥12,980 for nonreserved. The Shin-Osaka Station, which is located on the north side of the Shin-Yodo River, is linked to the center of the city by the JR Kobe Line and the Midosuji Subway Line. The ride, which takes 6–20 minutes, depending on your mid-city destination, costs ¥170–¥200. Train schedule and fare information can be obtained at the Travel Service Centers in the Shin-Osaka Station. A taxi from the Shin-Osaka Station to central Osaka costs ¥1,200–¥2,700.

Getting Around

By Train Osaka's fast, efficient subway system offers the most convenient means of exploring the city, because the complicated bus routes display no signs in English, and taxis, while plentiful, are costly. The six subway lines converge at Osaka Station, at Umeda, where they are linked underground. The main line is the Midosuji, which runs between Shin-Osaka and Umeda in six minutes; Shin-Osaka and Shinsaibashi in 12 minutes; Shin-Osaka and Namba in 14 minutes; and Shin-Osaka and Tennoji in 20 minutes.

Subways run from early morning until nearly midnight at intervals of three to five minutes. Fares begin at ¥160 and are determined by the distance traveled. A one-day pass for unlimited municipal transportation can be obtained at the commuter ticket windows in major subway stations and at the Japan Travel Bureau office in Osaka Station (cost: ¥840 adults, ¥410 children). A subway network map of Osaka is available from the Japan National Tourist Organization and at the Japan Travel Bureau office in Osaka Station.

Adding to the efficiency of the subway system is the JR Kanjo (Loop) Line, which circles the city above ground and intersects all subway lines. Fares range from ¥140 to ¥390, but you can use a JR Rail Pass on this train.

By Bus Economical one-day transportation passes (*see above*) for Osaka are valid on bus lines as well as subway routes, and the service operates throughout the day and evening, but bus travel is a challenge best left to local residents or those fluent in Japanese.

By Taxi You'll have no problem hailing taxis on the street or at specified taxi stands. (A red light in the lower left corner of the windshield indicates availability.) The problem is moving in Osaka's heavy traffic. Fares are metered at ¥540 for the first 2 kilometers, plus ¥80 for each additional 1,500 feet. It is not customary to tip the driver.

Important Addresses and Numbers

Tourist Information **Osaka Tourist Information Center** (tel. 06/305–3311), located on the east side of the main exit of the Japan Railways Shin-Osaka Station, is open daily 8–8; closed December 29–January 3. Another branch (tel. 06/345–2189) at the Midosuji gate of the

JR Osaka Station operates daily 8–8; closed December 31–January 4.

The **Information Center** in the Osakajo Castle (06/941–0546) is open daily 9–5.

Tourist Information Service, Osaka Prefectural Government (tel. 06/941–9200), is located in the lobby of the International Hotel (58 Hashizumecho, Uchihonmachi, Chuo-ku), a five-minute walk from Sakaisuji Hommachi Subway Station (open 9–5 Mon.–Sat.; closed Sun. and national holidays).

Japan Travel-Phone (tel. 0120/444–800) will provide free information service in English 9–5 daily.

Consulates **U.S.,** 2-11-5 Nishitenma, Kita-ku, tel. 06/315–5900.
Canadian, 2-2-3 Nishishinsaibashi, Chuo-ku, tel. 06/212–4910.
U.K., The Hongkong and Shanghai Bank Bldg., 4-45 Awajicho, Chuo-ku, tel. 06/231–3355.

Emergencies **Police,** tel. 110; **ambulance,** tel. 119.

Doctors **Tane General Hospital,** 1-2-31 Sakaigawa, Nishi-ku, tel. 06/581–1071; **Sumitomo Hospital,** 2-2 Nakanoshima, 5-chome, Kita-ku, tel. 06/443–1261; **Yodogawa Christian Hospital,** 9-26 Awaji, 2-chome, Higashi Yodogawa-ku, tel. 06/322–2250; **Osaka University Hospital** (accepts emergency patients by ambulance only), 1-50 Fukushima, 1-chome, Fukushima, tel. 06/451–0051.

English-Language Bookstore **Kinokuniya Book Store Co., Ltd.** (Hankyu Sanban-gai 1-1-3, Shibata, Kita-ku, tel. 06/372–5821) is open 10–9, except for the third Wednesday of the month.

Travel Agencies **Japan Travel Bureau,** Foreign Tourist Division, Sakaisuji Honmachi Center Bldg., 7F, 2-1-6 Honmachi, Chuo-ku, tel. 06/271–6195; **Hankyu Express International,** 8-47 Kakuta-cho, Kita-ku, tel. 06/373–5471; **Tokyu Tourist Corp.,** Kansai Foreign Tourist Center, Wakasugi Osakaekimae Bldg. 10F, 2-3-13, Sonezakishinchi, Kita-ku, tel. 06/344–5488.

Business Assistance Contact **Information Service System Co., Ltd.** (Hotel Nikko Osaka, 1–3–5 Nishi Shinsaibashi, Chuo-ku, tel. 06/245–4015) for business-related assistance, including quick-print business cards and interpreting.

Guided Tours

Orientation Tours The **Municipal Bus System** (tel. 06/311–2995) operates regular sightseeing tours of the city on its double-deck "Rainbow" bus. The tours are in Japanese. The five different tour routes start at the Umeda Sightseeing Information Center. They vary in length from three to four hours and cost from ¥1,970–¥3,680.

The **Aqua Liner** (tel. 06/942–5511) operates a 60-minute tour through Osaka's waterways, departing every hour 10–4 from April through September, there are also evening tours from 6–7 PM on Friday, Saturday, Sunday, and national holidays from three piers at Osakajo, Tenmabashi, and Yodoyabashi. This is the only tour of Osaka conducted in both Japanese and English (cost: ¥1,600 adults, ¥800 children).

Special-Interest Tours Japan's **Home Visit System,** which enables foreign visitors to meet local people in their homes for a few hours and learn more about the Japanese lifestyle, is available in Osaka. Visitors should apply in advance through the **Osaka Tourist Information Center** (tel. 06/305–3311) at the JR Shin-Osaka Station; at the **Osaka Tourist Association** (tel. 06/208–8955) at Sumitomo Seimei Yodoyabashi Bldg.; or at the Osaka **City Tourist Information Office** (tel. 06/345–2189) at the JR Osaka Station.

Excursions **Japan Travel Bureau** (tel. 06/343–0617) operates daily afternoon tours to Kyoto and Nara. Pickup is available at several hotels. **Japan Amenity Travel** (075/222–0121) offers two full-day tours: one to Kyoto only (¥12,000), and one to Kyoto and Nara (¥13,500). They depart from the Osaka Hilton Hotel and include train fare to Kyoto.

Exploring

Numbers in the margin correspond to points of interest on the Osaka map.

Visitors often arrive in Osaka at Shin-Osaka Station, which is the terminal for the Shinkansen super express trains. Located 2 miles north of Osaka's main railway station amid some of Osaka's most modern architecture, it is also close to the Expo Memorial Park. If you should arrive at Shin-Osaka, take either the Mido-suji subway to Umeda or, if you have a Japan Rail Pass, the JR Kobe Line to Osaka Station. Umeda and Osaka stations are right next to each other, on the edge of central Osaka.

Osaka is divided into 26 wards, and, though the official city population is only 2.6 million, if one were to include the suburbs, this number would be around 6 million. Central Osaka is predominantly a business district, but there is shopping and entertainment. This is also the area with hotels and most of the sights that will interest the visitor.

Central Osaka is encircled by the JR Kanjo (Loop) Line. The main railway station, Osaka Station, is at the northern part of this loop. In front of this station and to the east of the Hankyu Umeda Station is the center of the Kita (north) district. While ultramodern skyscrapers soar above the streets, underground is a maze of malls (Umeda Chika Center), crowded with shops that sell the latest fashions, dozens of restaurants, and department stores that offer every modern gadget. This district is one of the two major shopping areas in Osaka. Just to the south of the station are some major hotels, such as the Hilton, the Daiichi, and, farther south, the ANA-Sheraton Osaka.

If you continue south, you come to two rivers, the Dojimagawa and the Tosaborigawa, with Nakanoshima Island separating them. Here is Osaka's oldest park, which is home to many of the city's cultural and administrative institutions, including the Bank of Japan and the Museum of Oriental Ceramics.

Beyond these rivers and south of Nakanoshima Island are the Minami (south) and Shinsaibashi districts. They are very close together and are surrounded by the JR Loop Line. Shinsaibashi is Osaka's expensive shopping street, with stores featuring high-fashion merchandise. The nearby America-Mura, with American-style boutiques, and the Europe-Mura, with Continental fashion shops, appeal to the hip Osaka young. Minami has a wonderful assortment of bars and restaurants, especially on Dotonbori Street. The Bunraku National Theater is also close by, a few blocks to the southeast, near the Nipponbashi Subway Station.

In the eastern part of Osaka, just within the area surrounded by the JR Loop Line, is Osaka's main tourist attraction, Osakajo Castle. Just north of the castle are the futuristic Twin 21 towers of Osaka Business Park. The other major landmark, Shitennoji Temple, is in the southeast corner of the JR Loop Line. The number of tourist attractions in the city are limited and can easily be visited in less than a day.

① The most famed sight in Osaka is **Osakajo Castle** in the eastern part of the city. The easiest way to reach the castle from Osaka Station is to take the Tanimachi Subway Line from Higashi Umeda Station (just to the southeast of Osaka Station) to Tanimachi 4-Chome Station. From there, it is a 15-minute walk up the hill to where Osakajo stands. An alternative route, and one that is slightly easier, is to take the JR Loop Line from Osaka Station to Osakajo Koen-mae Station. You'll still have a walk up the hill from the other side.

Osakajo was one of Hideyoshi Toyotomi's finest buildings. The first stones were laid in 1583, and for the next three years as many as 100,000 workmen labored to build a majestic and impregnable castle. Note the thickness and the height of the walls. In order to demonstrate their loyalty, the feudal lords from the provinces were requested to contribute immense granite rocks. The largest piece of stone is said to have been donated by Hideyoshi's general, Kato Kiyomasa (1562–1611), and brought from Shodo Island. Known as Higo-Ishi, the rock measured a gigantic 19 feet high and 47 feet wide.

Hideyoshi was showing off with this castle. He had united Japan after a period of devastating civil wars, and he wanted to secure his western flanks. He also wanted to establish Osaka as a vibrant merchant town that could distribute the produce from the surrounding wealthy territories. The castle was intended to demonstrate Hideyoshi's power and commitment to Osaka, in order to attract merchants from all over Japan.

Hideyoshi's plan succeeded, but within two years of his death in 1598, Ieyasu Tokugawa, an executor of Hideyoshi's will, took power and got rid of the guardians of Hideyoshi's son. However, it was not until 1614 that Ieyasu sent his armies to defeat the Toyotomi family and their allies. In 1615, the castle was destroyed, and Ieyasu Tokugawa was victorious.

Over a 10-year period, Osakajo was rebuilt according to its original plan by the Tokugawa Shogunate and was completed in 1629. This version remained standing until 1868. The Tokugawa Shogunate's power was at an end. Rather than let the castle fall into the hands of the forces of the Meiji Restoration, the Tokugawa troops burned it. In 1931, the present five-story (8 stories inside) *donjon* (main stronghold) was built in ferroconcrete for the prestige of the city. An exact replica of the original, though marginally smaller in scale, it stands 189 feet high (including 46-foot-high stone walls). At night, when it is illuminated, it becomes a brilliant backdrop to the city.

Inside the castle is a museum with artifacts of the Toyotomi family and historical objects relating to Osaka prior to the Tokugawa Shogunate's reign. Unless you are a Hideyoshi fan, these exhibits have marginal interest. The castle's magnificent

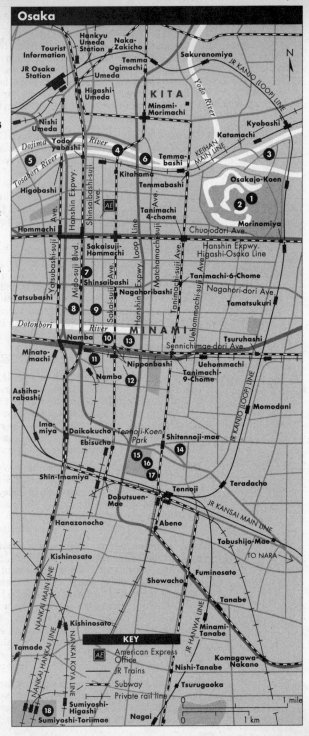

Osaka

exterior and the impressive view from the eighth floor of the donjon are the reasons to see Osakajo. If you are really fortunate, your visit may coincide with cherry-blossom time, when the lovely castle gardens are at their best. *1-1 Osaka-jo, Chuo-ku, Osaka, tel. 06/941–3044. Admission: ¥500 adults, ¥50 children 5–15. Open 9–5 (enter by 4:30), 9–8:30 July 15–Aug. 31 (enter by 8). Closed Dec. 28–Jan. 1.*

② The **Osaka City Museum** is also located on the castle grounds. This museum is a storehouse of municipal memorabilia. On display are books, photographs, and other records of the city's history. *1-1 Osaka-jo, Chuo-ku, Osaka, tel. 06/941–7177. Admission to the permanent collection: ¥300 adults, ¥200 college and high-school students, ¥100 younger students. Admission to special exhibitions varies. Open 9:15–4:45 (enter by 4:15). Closed 2nd and 4th Mon. of each month.*

Leave the castle and, facing north, walk down the hill past Osakajo Hall (a center used for sport competitions and concerts), and cross the overpass near the Aqua Liner (water-bus) pier. On the other side of the Hiranogawa River, you'll come to the New Otani Hotel and, just behind it, the Twin 21 towers of **③** **Osaka Business Park.**

Panasonic Square, on the second floor of one of the Twin 21 structures, the **National Tower Building,** features displays of the Matsushita Electric Group's high-tech developments. Both fun and educational, the exhibits are divided into four zones: Knowing, Learning, Experiencing, and Creating with Electronics. On any given day, you'll see crowds of Japanese schoolchildren absorbed in testing the TV telephone that allows them to see the person they're talking to on a monitor screen, or donning Superman costumes to star and direct in their own mini-TV shows. Other displays allow you to check your golf, baseball, or tennis skills on a video camera at the Swing Check Corner; have your portrait drawn by a robot; and test what you've learned via a computerized question-and-answer session—a computer will even calculate your score. Moderately priced food shops serve sushi and other light fare, and there is also a souvenir shop. *Twin 21, National Tower Bldg., 2nd floor, 1-61 Shiromi 2-chome, Chuo-ku, tel. 06/949–2122. Admission: ¥300 adults and high-school students, ¥200 junior-high and elementary-school students. Open 10–6 (enter by 5:30).*

④
⑤ The **Museum of Oriental Ceramics** is in Nakanoshima Park, on **Nakanoshima Island,** between the Dojimagawa and Tosaborigawa rivers. From Osaka Business Park, take the JR train at Katamichi Station to the Kyobashi stop and transfer to the Keihan Line, which you take to the Yodoyabashi stop. It's a five-minute walk from that station.

The museum opened in 1982 and houses about 1,000 pieces of Chinese and Korean ceramics. The artworks come from the priceless Ataka Collection, which belonged to a wealthy Japanese industrialist, and were donated to the museum by the giant Sumitomo Group conglomerate. The ceramic collection, rated as one of the finest in the world, includes 14 works that have been designated as National Treasures or Important Cultural Properties. *1-1 Nakanoshima, Kita-ku, tel. 06/223–0055. Admission: ¥500 adults, ¥300 college and high-school students, ¥150 junior-high and elementary-school students. Admission to special exhibitions varies. Open Tues.–Sun. 9:30–5 (enter by 4:30). Closed Mon. and the following day if Mon. is a national holiday.*

After your visit to the museum, take some time for a stroll in
⑥ Osaka's oldest park, **Nakanoshima-Koen,** which opened in 1891
and is located at the eastern end of Nakanoshima Island. Also
on the island are **Osaka University** and **Osaka Festival Hall,**
which is considered the city's best concert hall. Major Japanese
and international musicians regularly appear here. The **Royal
Hotel** is at the far end of the island. If you linger till after dark,
you'll be able to enjoy the illuminated view of **Osaka City Hall,**
near the ceramics museum, and of the bridges that link the island with the mainland.

Take the Midosuji Subway Line from Yodoyabashi to Shin-
⑦ saibashi Station. When you emerge, you'll be on **Midosuji Boulevard.** Shinsaibashi and Ebisubashi, which run parallel to
Midosuji, are two of Osaka's best shopping and entertainment
⑧ streets. West of Midosuji Boulevard, you'll find **America-Mura**
(American Village), a group of streets that feature stores with
youth-oriented American clothes. Bright neon signs with the
Japanese version of American names hang over the shop doors
as the sound of rock music booms from inside. The stores carry
an assortment of U.S.-made jeans and sportswear, and they
are tended by Japanese youth who wear punk hairstyles.

⑨ East of Midosuji Boulevard is **Europe Mura** (European Village), with its boutiques of fashionable clothes from European
capitals. The sidewalks in this area, which are made of cobblestones, attempt to re-create the feeling of a traditional
Continental city. Located here are Parco, Sogo, and Daimaru
department stores, some of Japan's top chain stores.

⑩ If you continue walking south on Midosuji Boulevard and cross
the river, you'll come to **Dotonbori,** a broad cross street that
runs alongside the river of the same name. The street and the
area around it are filled with a cornucopia of restaurants and
nightclubs.

A virtual feast for neon connoisseurs, this is the place to stroll
in the evening for a glimpse of nightlife, Osaka-style. Locate
the giant, undulating Kani Doraku crab sign, a local landmark,
walk in any direction, and prepare yourself for a unique sensory
experience.

⑪ Two blocks south of Dotonbori Street is the **Nijinomachi (Rainbow Town)** underground shopping mall, which extends six
blocks east-west. About two blocks from Rainbow Town is **Nan
Nan Town,** another underground mall, which runs eight blocks
south from the southern end of Midosuji Boulevard. Both malls
offer a good selection of clothes, appliances, and unpretentious
restaurants. At the far southern end of Midosuji Boulevard are
the Kabukiza Theater and the Takashimaya department store.
⑫ East of the southern terminus of Namba Station is **Den Den
Town,** where, amid its nearly 300 specialty shops, you can purchase discounted electrical appliances. About a block south of
Nankai Namba Station is **Osaka Stadium,** where the local baseball teams square off.

From Namba Station (the subway station, not the Nankai rail
station), if you take the Sennichi-mae Subway Line, it is just
⑬ one stop east to the Nipponbashi Station and the **National
Bunraku Theater.** Take Exit 7, and you will be right outside the

theater. Osaka is known for Bunraku, and, if you are in the city at the right time, this is an opportunity you shouldn't miss. Osakans have helped make it a sophisticated art form. This puppet form of drama began during the Heian period (794–1192), but it was not until the late-17th and early 18th century that the genius of playwright Chikamatsu elevated Bunraku to a dignified dramatic art. A typical Bunraku play deals with themes of tragic love or stories based on historical events. The story is chanted in song by a *joruri* singer who is accompanied by ballad music played on a three-stringed *shamisen*. Although you may not understand the words, the tone of the music certainly sets a mood of pathos.

Bunraku's actors are puppets, about two-thirds human size. Elaborately dressed in period costume, each puppet is made up of interchangeable parts—a head, shoulder piece, trunk, legs, and arms. For example, various puppet heads are used for roles of different sex, age, and character, and a certain hairstyle will indicate a puppet's position in life. Each puppet is operated by three puppeteers, who must act in complete unison. The *omozukai* controls the expression on the puppet's face and its right arm and hand. The *hidarizukai* controls the puppet's left arm and hand, and any props that it is carrying. The *ashizukai* moves the puppet's legs. This last task is the easiest. The most difficult task belongs to the omozukai. It takes about 30 years to become an accomplished expert. A puppeteer must spend 10 years as ashizukai, a further 10 as hidarizukai, and then 10 years as omozukai.

These master puppeteers not only skillfully manipulate the puppets' arms and legs, but also roll the eyes and move the lips so that the puppets express fear, joy, and sadness in a most lifelike manner. Although they are puppets, their expressions of happiness and anguish are not difficult to understand. *12-10 Nipponbashi 1-chome, Chuo-ku, Osaka, tel. 06/212–2531. Admission: ¥3,800 and ¥4,900. Bunraku performances are scheduled 6 times a year (Jan., Mar., Apr., June, July, Aug., Nov.). Each run starts on the 3rd of the month and lasts about 3 weeks.*

After you leave the Bunraku Theater, walk east for about 10 minutes to the Tanimachi-9-Chome Subway Station. If you take the Tanimachi Subway Line going south, it is only one stop to the Shitennojimae Station and from there only a few minutes' walk to Shitennoji Temple. If you wish to come directly here from Osakajo Castle, take the JR Loop Line from Osakajo-Koen Station or Kyobashi Station going south. If you exit at Tennoji Station, you'll see the street going north up to Shitennoji Temple; Tennoji-Koen Park will be on the left.

14 **Shitennoji Temple,** popularly known as Tennoji, is one of the most important historical sights in Osaka. Architecturally, the temple has suffered. The ravages of fire have destroyed it many times. Maintaining the original design and adhering to the traditional mathematical alignment, the last reconstruction of the Kondo (Main Hall), Kodo Taishiden Hall, and the five-story pagoda was after World War II, in 1965. What has managed to survive is the stone *torii* (arch) gate that was built in 1294 and stands at the main entrance. One does not often see a torii gate at a Buddhist temple. Shitennoji Temple claims that it is the oldest Buddhist temple in Japan. Outdating the Horyuji Temple in Nara (607), Shitennoji Temple was founded by Prince Shotoku in 593.

Umayado no Mikoto (573–621), who is posthumously known as Prince Shotoku or Shotoku Taishi, was one of early Japan's most enlightened rulers. He was made regent over his aunt, Suiko, and set about instituting reforms and establishing Buddhism as the state religion. Buddhism had been introduced to Japan from China and Korea in the early 500s, but it had been seen as a threat to the aristocracy, who claimed prestige and power based upon their godlike ancestry. Prince Shotoku recognized both the power of Buddhism and how it could be used as a tool for the state. His swords and a copy of his Hokkekyo Lotus Sutra, made during the Heian period (897–1192), were stored at Shitennoji, though today they are kept in the National Museum of Tokyo. On the 21st of every month, the temple has a flea market that sells antiques and baubles; it shouldn't be missed if you're in town at this time. *1-11-18 Shitennoji, Tennoji-ku, Osaka, tel. 06/771–0066. Admission: ¥200 adults, ¥120 children. Apr.–Sept., 8:30–4:30; in winter, 8:30–4.*

(15)
(16) To the southwest of Shitennoji Temple is **Tennoji-Koen Park,** where the **Municipal Museum of Fine Art** is located. This museum is best known for its collection of classical art from the 12th to the 14th century. An exception to this are the special exhibitions that feature the works of an Edo period artist, Ogata Korin. Some modern art is also included in its permanent collection (though this seems to appeal more to the Japanese than to foreigners), as well as a collection of Chinese paintings and archaeological artifacts. *1-82 Chausuyama-cho, Tennoji-ku, tel. 06/771–4874. Admission to the permanent collection: ¥300 adults, ¥200 college and high-school students, ¥100 younger students. Admission for special exhibitions varies. Open 9:30–5 (enter by 4:30). Closed Mon.*

(17) Adjacent to the Municipal Museum is **Keitakuen Garden,** with flowers, trees, and a pond. The garden, originally constructed in 1908, was given to the city by the late Baron Sumitomo. An example of the Japanese circular garden, its cherry trees and azaleas are lovely to behold when in bloom. The garden offers a welcome respite from the rest of the city. *Admission: ¥150 adults, free for children under 12. Open 9:30–4:30 (enter by 4). Closed Mon.*

The park also contains the **Tennoji Botanical Gardens** (open 9:30–5). If you are traveling with children, next to the Keitakuen Garden is the **Municipal Zoological Gardens.** The zoo is one of the largest in Japan and has some 22,000 animals caged. *6-74 Chausuyama-cho, Tennoji-ku, tel. 06/771–8401. Admission: ¥500 adults, free for senior citizens and children under 16. Open 9:30–4:30 (enter by 4). Closed Mon., national holidays, and Dec. 29–Jan. 1.*

Before you leave Tennoji-Koen Park you may also notice **Chausuyama Hill,** a prehistoric burial mound and the site of Ieyasu Tokugawa's camp during the siege of Osakajo Castle in 1614–1615.

(18) The final site on this exploring tour is the **Sumiyoshi Grand Shrine.** Most of the Shinto shrines in Japan today were built after the 8th century and were heavily influenced by Buddhist architecture. The three shrines that were built prior to the arrival of Buddhism in Japan are the Ise Jingu (Grand Shrines) at Ise, the Izumo Taisha Shrine near Matsue, and the Sumiyoshi Shrine in Osaka. To reach this latter shrine, take the 20-minute ride on the Nankai Main Line to the southern suburbs of Osaka.

Sumiyoshi Grand Shrine is dedicated to the goddess of sea voyages, Sumiyoshi, and, according to legend, was founded by Empress Jingu in 211 to express her gratitude for her safe return from a sea voyage to Korea. In those days, the shrine faced the sea rather than the concrete urban sprawl that now surrounds it. On the shrine's grounds are many stone lanterns donated by sailors and shipowners as dedications to Sumiyoshi and other Shinto deities that also guard the voyages of seafarers. Note the arched bridge on the grounds, said to have been given by Yodogimi, the consort of Hideyoshi Toyotomi who bore him a son. Of the three ancient shrines (Ise Jingu, Izumo Taisha, and Sumiyoshi), only Sumiyoshi has a Japanese cypress structure that is painted vermilion; the other two are left unpainted with their natural wood showing. According to the Shinto custom, shrines were torn down and rebuilt periodically to the exact specifications of the original. Sumiyoshi, which, incidentally, is also the name given to the style of architecture of this shrine, was last replaced in 1810. Sumiyoshi Matsuri, one of the city's largest and liveliest festivals, is held on July 30 and August 1. A crowd of rowdy young men carries a two-ton portable shrine from the Sumiyoshi Shrine to the Yamato River and back; this event is followed by an all-night street bazaar. *2-9-89 Sumiyoshi, Sumiyoshi-ku, tel. 06/672–0753. Admission free. Open daily Apr.–Oct., daily 6–5; Nov.–Mar., daily 6:30–5. Apr.–Oct., 6:30–5 Nov.–Mar.*

Additional Attractions

The following lists include additional places of interest that were not covered in the preceding exploring tour:

Historical Buildings and Sights

Nintoku Mausoleum. The 4th-century mausoleum of Emperor Nintoku is in Sakai City. Archaeologists calculate that the central mound of this site is 1.3 million square feet; the mausoleum was built on an even larger scale than that of the pyramids of Egypt. Its construction took more than 20 years and required a total work force of about 800,000 laborers. Surrounding the emperor's burial place are three moats and pine, cedar, and cypress trees. Visitors may walk around the outer moat to get an idea of the size of the mausoleum and the grounds. However, entry into the mausoleum is not allowed. To get to the mausoleum, take the JR train from Tennoji Station to Mozu Station (a ½-hr. ride). From there, the sight is a five-minute walk away. *7 Daisen-cho, Sakai-shi, tel. 0722/41–0002.*

Temples and Shrines

Fujiidera Temple. A 1,000-handed seated statue of Kannon, the Goddess of Mercy, made in the 8th century, is the main object of worship here. The statue, a National Treasure, is the oldest Buddhist sculpture of its type. To reach the temple, get on the Midosuji Subway Line from Umeda Station to Tennoji Station, then transfer to the Kintetsu Minami–Osaka Line and take it to

Fujiidera Station. The temple is a few minutes' walk from the station. *1-16-21 Fujiidera, Fujiidera-shi, tel. 0729/38-0005. The statue is on view the 18th of each month, 9-5.*

Temmangu Shrine. A short walk from the Minami Morimachi Station on the Tanimachi line, this 10th-century shrine is the main site of the annual **Tenjin Festival,** held July 24-25, one of the three biggest and most enthusiastically celebrated festivals in Japan. During the festival, dozens of floats are paraded through the streets, and more than 100 vessels, lighted by lanterns, sail along the canals amid a dazzling display of fireworks. A renowned scholar of the 9th century, Michizane Sugawara, is enshrined at Temmangu; he is now considered the God of Academics. *2-1-8 Tenjinbashi, Kita-ku, tel. 06/353-0025. Admission free. Open Apr.-Sept., daily 5:30 AM-sunset, Oct.-Mar., 6 AM-sunset.*

Museums and Galleries

Japan Folk Art Museum. Located in Expo Park, the museum contains outstanding examples of traditional regional handicrafts. On view are ceramics, textiles, wood crafts, bamboo ware, and other items. To get to the museum, see directions to Expo Park, below *10-5 Banpaku-koen, Senri, Suita-shi, tel. 06/877-1971. Admission: ¥360 adults, ¥310 college and high-school students, ¥100 junior-high and elementary-school students. Admission to special exhibitions varies. Open 10-5 (enter by 4:30). Closed Wed.*

Mint Museum. This money museum displays about 16,000 examples of Japanese and foreign currencies. It also exhibits Olympic medals, prehistoric currency, and ancient Japanese gold coins. Near the museum is the Mint Garden, part of which is open to the public for a short period during the cherry-blossom season (usually April); a visitor can stroll on a pathway, shaded by blossoms, along the Yodogawa River. The museum is a 15-minute walk from Minami Morimachi or Temmabashi Station on the Tanimachi Subway Line. *1-1-79 Temma, Kita-ku, tel. 06/351-8509. Admission free. Open 9-4 (enter by 3:30). Closed Sun., holidays, and 2nd and 4th Sat. of each month.*

National Museum of Ethnology. This building, also in Expo Park, offers a range of exhibits on comparative cultures of the world, with displays arranged according to regions. Automatic audiovisual equipment, called Videotheque, provides close-up views of the customs of the peoples of the world. To reach the museum, *see* directions to Expo Park, *below. Senri Expo Park, Senri, Suita-shi, tel. 06/876-2151. Admission: ¥400 adults, ¥250 high-school and college students, ¥110 junior-high and elementary-school students. Open 10-5 (enter by 4:30). Closed Wed. and Dec. 28-Jan. 4.*

Parks and Gardens

Expo Park. On the former site of Expo '70, this 647-acre park houses the two museums listed above, an amusement park called Expo Land (admission: ¥1,000; closed Wed.), sports facilities, and several gardens, including a Japanese garden with two teahouses. To reach the park, take the Midosuji Subway Line to Senri-Chuo Station (30 mins. from Umeda Station), then take the Expoland bus to Nihontei-en-mae Station (30 mins.) or monorail to Banpaku-koen-mae (20 mins.). *Senri Expo Park, Senri, Suita-shi. Admission to park ¥100, but the individual facilities within the park impose separate entrance fees, which vary. Open daily 9–5. Closed Wed. and Dec. 28– Jan. 1.*

Hattori Ryokuchi Park. This recreation park has facilities for horseback riding and tennis, a youth hostel, and a museum of old farmhouses. To reach the park, take the Midosuji Subway Line from Umeda to Esaka stations, then the Kita Osaka Kyuku Line to Ryokuchi Koen Station. The park is a 10-minute walk from the station. *Admission to the park is free. Admission to the Farmhouse Museum: ¥410 adults, ¥300 high-school students. Nonmembers can take a 30-min. riding lesson for ¥5,000. The cost is ¥610–¥710 for 1 hr. of tennis. Have your hotel make a reservation for you a day in advance for horseback riding; no reservation necessary for tennis during the week; if you're going on a weekend, you may need as much as a week's advance reservation. Open Apr.–Oct., 9:30–5 (enter by 4:30), Nov.–Mar., 9:30–4 (enter by 3:30).*

Mino Park. Osakans come here in autumn to admire the dazzling fall foliage, especially the maple trees, whose leaves turn to brilliant crimson. The path along the river leads to the Mino Waterfall. Monkeys reside in a protected habitat. The park is 30 minutes from Hankyu Umeda Station on the Mino Line, north of the Mino Station. *Admission free. Open 24 hrs. year-round.*

Shopping

Osaka's role as a transportation hub for more than 1,500 years has enabled it to prosper first as a merchant town and today as a center of business and commerce. Osakans are known for driving hard bargains, but at the same time, they are practical in their approach to life. Osaka has two main shopping areas: one is centered on Namba Station in the Minami (southern) district, the other on Osaka and Umeda stations in the Kita (northern) district. Minami is the older of the two, but the merchandise sold here is a mixture of traditional and modern goods.

To the northeast of Namba Station are the Ebisubashi Street shopping area and the Nijinomachi (Rainbow Town) underground shopping mall. To the southeast are Namba City and Nan Nan Town underground shopping malls. Farther east from Namba Station, but still within walking distance, is Den Den Town (*see* Electronic Goods, *below*).

Near Osaka and Umeda stations, which connect with underground concourses, are the Umeda Chika Center and the Hankyu Sanbangai and Hankyu Higashidori malls. This complex of stores is the largest underground shopping area in all of Japan and perhaps the world, complete with man-made streams and its own version of the Fountain of Trevi.

Located over Osaka Station is the Acty Osaka Building, a newly opened 27-story shopping and office building. To the west of this complex, near Nishi-Umeda Station on the Yotsubashi Subway Line, are the Dojima and Nakanoshima underground malls.

Osaka's most elegant shopping arcade, however, is Shinsaibashisuji. This covered arcade with marble pavement is located near Shinsaibashi Station on the Midosuji Line, halfway between the Minami and Kita districts. To the east of the arcade is yet another shopping arcade, called Europe Mura (European Village), with trendy, European-influenced clothing. Across Midosuji Boulevard to the west is America Mura (American Village), with clothing styles inspired by U.S. designers, for both the young and old.

Specialized wholesale areas can be found throughout the city. A few retail shops are located in these areas so it is worth a visit. Dobuike is the wholesale area for clothing and accessories (located near Honmachi Station on the Chuo, Tanimachi, and Yotsubashi subway lines, or Sakaisuji-Honmachi Station on the Sakaisuji Subway Line). Matchamachisuji is famous for its rows of toy and doll shops.

Department Stores

All major Japanese department stores are represented in this ultramodern city. Many of them, such as Hankyu, Hanshin, and Kintetsu, are headquartered here. All the department stores are open 10–7 except for Matsuzakaya, which closes at 6:30 (its food hall is open until 7). The following are some of Osaka's leading department stores: **Hankyu,** 8-7 Kakuta-cho, Kita-ku, tel. 06/361–1381, closed Thurs.; **Hanshin,** 1-13-13 Umeda, Kitaku, tel. 06/345–1201, closed Wed.; **Matsuzakaya,** 1-1 Temmabashi Kyomachi, Chuo-ku, tel. 06/943–1111, closed Wed.; **Mitsukoshi,** 7-5 Koraibashi 1-chome, Chuo-ku, tel. 06/203–1331, closed Tues.; **Daimaru,** 1-7-1 Shinsaibashisuji, Chuo-ku, tel. 06/271–1231, closed Wed.; **Sogo,** 1-8-3 Shinsaibashisuji, Chuo-ku, tel. 06/281–3111, closed Tues.; **Takashimaya,** 5-1-5 Namba, Chuo-ku, tel. 06/631–1101, closed Wed.; **Kintetsu,** 1-1-43 Abenosuji, Abeno-ku, tel. 06/624–1111; closed Thurs. There is also a Kintetsu branch at 6-1-55 Uehonmachi, Tennoji-ku, tel. 06/775–1111, closed Thurs.

Gifts

At one time famous for its traditional crafts, particularly its ornately carved *karaki-sashimono* furniture, its fine *Naniwa suzuki* pewter ware, and its Sakai *uchihamono* cutlery, Osaka lost much of its fine traditional industry during World War II. The simplest way to find a wide selection of Osaka crafts is to visit one of the major department stores, many of which carry a selection of locally made crafts.

For folk crafts from all over the country, including ceramics, basketry, paper goods, folk toys, and textiles, visit the **Nihon Kogeikan Mingei Fukyubu,** located near the Umeshin East Hotel in the popular gallery district, within walking distance of the U.S. Consulate. *4-7-15 Nishi-Tenma, Kita-ku, tel. 06/362–9501. Open 10–6. Closed on 2nd Sat. of each month, Sun., and national holidays.*

Electronic Goods   **Den Den Town** has about 300 retail shops that specialize in electrical products (Den Den is a take-off on the word *denki,* which means electricity). It also has stores for cameras and watches. The area is located near Ebisucho Station on the Sakaisuji Subway Line (Exit 1 or 2), and Nipponbashi Station on the

Sakaisuji and Sennichimae subway lines (Exit 5 or 10). Shops are open 10–7 daily. Take your passport, and make your purchases in stores with signs that say "Tax Free."

Dining

Not only are the residents of Osaka known to be passionate about food; they also insist on eating well. Osakans expect the restaurants they frequent to use the freshest ingredients available from the area. This habit developed over the centuries because of the city's proximity to the Inland Sea, which allowed all classes (not just the aristocracy) easy access to fresh seafood. Today Osakans have discriminating palates and demand their money's worth. In fact, Osakans are famous for their gourmet appetites. *"Osaka wa kuidaore,"* the old saying goes—Osaka people squander their money on food.

Osaka cuisine is flavored with soy sauce that is lighter in color, milder in flavor, and saltier than the soy sauce used in Tokyo. One local delicacy is **okonomiyaki,** a pancake which may be filled with cabbage, mountain yam, pork, shrimp, and other ingredients; okonomiyaki is made to order on an iron grill at the table.

Osaka-zushi (Osaka-style sushi), which is made in wood molds, has a distinctive square shape, with pieces of fish or broiled eel placed on top of rice and then pressed together. Another variation of Osaka-zushi is wrapped around an omelet and filled with pickles and other delights. Eel, prepared in several different styles, remains a popular local dish; grilled eels are often eaten during the summer months for quick energy. **Fugu** (blowfish), served boiled or raw, is a gourmet fish that is less expensive in Osaka than in other Japanese cities.

Another Osaka invention is **tako-yaki,** griddle-cooked dumplings with bits of octopus, green onions, and ginger smothered in a delicious sauce. Sold by street vendors in Dotonbori, these tasty snacks and their lively makers are also in evidence at every festival and street market in the Kansai district.

Surrounding Osaka Umeda Station there are a number of "gourmet palaces" with several floors of restaurants of every genre imaginable (and some unimaginable). Exploring them is always fun. Head for restaurants in the Hankyu Grand Building, the Hankyu Sanbangai (in the basement below Hankyu Station), and Acty Osaka (in front of the Osaka JR Station). Most of the big department stores also house scores of good restaurants, notably the Daimaru Department Store in front of the Osaka JR Station.

Osaka's shopping arcades and underground shopping areas abound in affordable restaurants and coffee shops, but when in doubt, head to Dotonbori and Soemoncho, two areas along the Dotonbori River that specialize in restaurants, nightclubs, and bars. If money is not a problem, walk to the northern part of Osaka to Kita Shinchi, the city's most exclusive dining quarter, but be prepared to pay a stiff price for an elegant meal. This area is somewhat similar to Tokyo's Ginza district.

A 3% federal consumer tax is added to all restaurant bills. Another 3% local tax is added to the bill if it exceeds ¥7,500. At more expensive restaurants, a 10%–15% service charge is also added to the bill.

The most highly recommended restaurants are indicated by a star ★.

Category	Cost*
Very Expensive	over ¥6,000
Expensive	¥4,000–¥6,000
Moderate	¥2,500–¥4,000
Inexpensive	under ¥2,500

Cost is per person without tax, service, or drinks

Very Expensive

Benkay. For those who appreciate Japanese-style red snapper (served with stewed plums), Benkay is the place to go. Sea urchin, squid, and prawns are staples on the menu here; tempura and sushi are popular as well. The restaurant utilizes the traditional Japanese decor of blond wood paneling, and there's a sushi bar on one side. *Hotel Nikko Osaka, Nishi Shinsaibashi, 1 chome 3-3, Chuo-ku, tel. 06/244–1111. Reservations advised. Jacket and tie preferred. AE, DC, MC, V. Lunch 11:30–2:30, dinner 5:30–10.*

★ **Chambord.** Named for an elegant French castle in the Loire Valley, the Chambord restaurant is French in every way, from the crystal chandeliers to the chef's innovative cuisine. Specialties served by tuxedoed waiters include tenderloin with chestnuts and mushrooms, boiled lobster with tomato and cream sauce, and roast lamb with green peppers. Situated on the 29th floor of the Royal Hotel, the restaurant treats guests to a panoramic view of Osaka's flickering night lights and river activities. *Royal Hotel, 5-3 Nakanoshima, Kita-ku, tel. 06/448–1121. Reservations usually required. Jacket and tie required at dinner. AE, DC, MC, V. Lunch 11:30–2:30, dinner 5:30–10.*

Le Rendezvous. Located atop the Plaza Hotel, Le Rendezvous offers guests not only an elegant meal but also expansive views of the city. A regal French restaurant with lovely wood paneling and formal place settings, it features French nouvelle cuisine and a fine selection of wines. Chef Paul Bocuse has an established reputation in Japan for presenting eye-pleasing gourmet dishes ranging from beef cuts to choice salmon. *2-2-49 Oyodo-minami, Oyodo-ku, tel. 06/453–1111. Reservations advised. Jacket and tie required. AE, DC, MC, V. No lunch. Dinner 5:30–10.*

Les Célébrites. On the menu at Les Célébrites are French items identified by their association with such painters as Cézanne, Degas, Renoir, and Toulouse-Lautrec. The gourmet selections include such dishes as terrine of eel and spinach, dodine of stuffed wild duck with foie gras, chilled consommé flavored with tomato, and tenderloin steak with morels, as well as French cheeses, green and mixed salads, and, of course, espresso. The two intimate dining rooms (only 33 seats total) are decorated in lavender and pink, and they feature fresh flowers and beautiful chandeliers. You can also come here for breakfast. Les Célébrites is located in the Hotel Nikko, which also has the distinction of hosting another class act: Benkay, a gourmet Japanese restaurant (*see above*). *Hotel Nikko Osaka, Nishi Shinsaibashi, 1-chome 3-3, Chuo-ku, tel. 06/244–1111. Reservations advised. Jacket and tie preferred. AE, DC, MC, V. Lunch 11:30–2:30, dinner 5:30–10.*

Ron. This establishment bills itself as having the best steak in the world; if its bustling business on three floors is any indication, the kudos are not off base. A five-minute walk from Osaka Station, Ron is housed in a five-story brick building. On the menu you'll find fried prawns, fried vegetables, boiled rice, tossed salad, and, of course, prime Kobe-beef steak. The setting is casual and homey with only 13 tables on three floors. Your beef and other delectables will be prepared on the iron grill table around which you sit—the preparation is half the experience. *1-10-2 Sonezaki Shinchi, Kita-ku, tel. 06/344–6664. Reservations advised. Dress: informal. AE, DC, MC, V. Open Mon.–Sat. lunch 11:30–2, dinner 5–10, Sun. and holidays dinner only 4–10.*

★ **Rose Room.** Yet another elegant hotel restaurant, this one is dressed up in green marble and has color-coordinated furnishings. The Rose Room features a formal atmosphere, enhanced by candlelit tables, fresh flowers, and a mirrored ceiling. This intimate establishment seats only 59 guests and serves Continental cuisine. Fish and beef dishes are the specialties, which include grilled sea bass with onion-flavored vinegar, steamed turbot with ravioli, grilled sirloin steak, and Châteaubriand. *ANA Sheraton Hotel, 1-3-1 Dojimahama, Kita-ku, tel. 06/347–1112. Reservations usually required. Jacket and tie required. AE, DC, MC, V. Lunch 11:30–2:30, dinner 5:30–10.*

★ **The Seasons.** This grand, elegant dining room in the Hilton International is located in the bustling restaurant and retail sector around Osaka Station. Subtle colors, lustrous marble, and shining chandeliers blend together in The Seasons to create a lovely, warm ambience. The Continental menu offers selections you'll recognize from home: Maine lobster, fine wines, and the local favorite, Kobe beef. Seating less than 100 guests, the restaurant's formality assures patrons a dining event. Specialties include duckling terrine with goose liver, sliced beef in red wine sauce, and fillet of beef with goose liver in a puff pastry. The quick, lower priced lunch menu is ideal for a sampling of what the Hilton chef has to offer; at night, a pianist entertains. A jacket is required, but a tie is not; management is more lenient in the summer. *Hilton International Osaka, 8-8 Umeda 1-chome, Kita-ku, tel. 06/347–7111. Reservations strongly advised. Jacket required. AE, DC, MC, V. Lunch 11:30–2:30, dinner 5:30–10:30.*

Expensive–Very Expensive

Kobe Misono. This dining spot is a branch of a restaurant in Kobe, and the chefs have managed to transfer the successful Kobe-beef recipe to Osaka. Located close to dozens of other less distinguished restaurants, Kobe Misono stands out for its attentive service and casual ambience. Besides the Kobe beef dinners with all the fixings, the other dishes include a chef salad, scallops, and fried vegetables. One family or couple is seated at each iron grill table; there are only six tables, which seat a maximum of 43 persons. *Near Osaka Station, Star Bldg., 3F, 11-19 Sonezakishinchi, Kita-ku, tel. 06/341–4471. Reservations advised. Dress: informal. AE, DC, MC, V. Open Mon.–Sat. lunch 11:30–2, dinner 5–10; Sun. noon–9.*

Osaka Joe's. First came Miami Joe's, then Tokyo Joe's; now here is the third version of that formidable institution for stone crabs. The obvious specials are the crabs (with melted butter and mustard mayonnaise) flown in from Florida and, for dessert, Key lime pie. Also on the menu are baked prawns, T-bone steak, and lamb chops. The setting is casual, with a distinctive American flair—even the music is from the States. A cozy, rustic bar at the entry seats only eight people; the two dining rooms seat a total of 99. Lunch is served until 3 PM and is relatively inexpensive at about ¥1,200. Dinner can be considerably higher—around ¥6,000 for crab claws. *IM Excellence Bldg., 2nd floor, 1-11-20 Sonezakishinchi, Kita-ku, tel. 06/344-0124. Reservations advised. Dress: casual, but jacket and tie preferred. AE, DC, MC, V. Open 11–11:30 (last order at 10:30).*

Moderate

Fuguhisa. This no-nonsense little restaurant specializes in *fugu ryori,* the blowfish delicacy for which Osaka is famous. Extremely expensive almost everywhere else, Chef Kato's *tessa* (raw blowfish) and *techiri* (one-pot blowfish stew) are the most reasonable and delicious around. What the place lacks in glamour, it makes up for in down-to-earth Osaka-style good food. It's located across from the west exit of Tsuruhashi Station on the JR Osaka Loop Line. *3-14-24 Higashi-ohashi, Higashinari-ku, tel. 06/972-5029. Reservations suggested. Dress: casual. No credit cards. Open noon–10:30 (last order at 9:30). Closed Mon.*

Kani Doraku. The most famous restaurant on Dotonbori, Kani Doraku is noted for its fine crab dishes at reasonable prices. The giant mechanical crab above the door is a local landmark. As you sit at tables or on tatami mats overlooking the Dotonbori Canal, you have a perfect view of the ultramodern Kirin Plaza Building glittering across the water. Full-course crab lunches and dinners are served, as well as a wide selection of crab dishes à la carte. There is an English language menu. *1-6-18 Dotonbori, Chuo-ku, tel. 06/211-8975. Reservations advised weekends. Dress: casual. AE, DC, MC, V. Open 11–11.*

Kanki. *Akachochin,* or red lanterns, are the symbol of inexpensive eating in Japan, but the wonderful combination of Western and Japanese dishes offered at this friendly place makes it different from most *nomiya,* as these inexpensive drinking places are called. Order *"Kyo no osusume,"* the daily special. You might end up with Florentine-style scallops. Table seating is available on the second and third floors. *1-3-11 Shibata-cho Kita-ku (on the northeast end of Hankyu Umeda Station), tel. 06/374-0057. Reservations advised. Dress: casual. No credit cards. Open 6–11. Closed Sun. and national holidays.*

Kirin City. This beer hall is located on the second floor of the fantastic Kirin Plaza Building designed by architect Shin Takamatsu, one of Japan's most controversial new architects. This hypertechno postmodern extravaganza presides over the old Narubashi Bridge on the Dotonbori Canal. Stop here for a cold draft beer and a bite to eat in the Shinsaibashi district. The menu features fried chicken, "city potatoes" (french fries), and chorizo, among many delights. *2F Kirin Plaza Bldg., 7-2 Soemon-cho, Chuo-ku, tel. 06/212-6572. No reservations. Dress: casual. Open weekdays 11:30–1; weekends 11–11. V.*

★ **La Bamba.** You'll find this casual Mexican restaurant and bar hidden down an old-fashioned Osaka shopping arcade near Exit

1 of the Nakazakicho subway station. Nothing on this little street forewarns you that you are about to enter perhaps the only *real* Mexican restaurant in all of Japan. The owner-chef learned his craft in Mexico. The fact that probably everyone from south of the U.S. border who stays for more than a few days in Japan not only finds it—but also signs his name with kudos to the chef on La Bamba's blackboard—should be testimony enough to the superior quality of its tacos, guacamole, burritos, quesadillas, and magnificent pitchers of margaritas. Be careful when ordering here: Although the English menu says "Two enchiladas . . .," the dish comes with only one. You'll be charged double if you order two. *8–2 Kurozaki-cho, Kita-ku, tel. 06/372–4224. Reservations advised weekends. Dress: casual. No credit cards. Open 5–11:30 (last order at 11). Closed Mon. and national holidays.*

Mimiu. *Udon-suki* was born here. The thick, white noodle stew simmered in a pot over a burner at your table—with Chinese cabbage, clams, eel, yams, *shiitake* mushrooms, *mitsuba* greens, and other seasonal ingredients—is an old favorite in Osaka, particularly when served in this traditional restaurant. *6-18, Hiranomachi 4 chome, Chuo-ku (near Honmachi Station on the Dojima-suji Subway Line), tel. 06/231–5770. No reservations. Dress: casual. V. Open 11:30–8:30. Closed Sun.*

★ **Tako-ume.** Take a rest from the glitter of Dotonbori nightlife at this 200-year-old traditional dining spot, which specializes in *oden*, a mixture of vegetables, and things like fish cakes, hard-boiled eggs, and fried tofu, cooked in a broth they say has been simmering here in the same pot for the past 30 years (just add liquid . . .). Sake is poured from pewter jugs, handmade in Osaka. The hot Chinese mustard dip is mixed with sweet miso bean paste, a house recipe. This is one of Osaka's most famous establishments. *1-1-8 Dotonbori, Chuo-ku, tel. 06/211–0321. Reservations advised weekends. Dress: informal. No credit cards. Open 5–11. Closed Wed.*

Inexpensive–Moderate

★ **Kushitaru.** Specializing in dinners served up piping hot on skewers, Kushitaru is an Osaka favorite. Your possible selections include chicken meatballs, celery with sea eel, quail egg with half beak (a Japanese dish), Chinese mushrooms, pineapple with sliced pork, and oysters with bacon. The restaurant is informal and has two dining rooms; the one upstairs is a throwback to the 1970s, with furniture and music of that period—young people love it here. *Located behind the Nikko Hotel, Sander Bldg., 13-5 Nishi Shinsaibashi, 1-chome, Unagidani, Chuo-ku, tel. 06/281–0365. Reservations advised for upstairs, open seating on 1st floor. Dress: informal. AE, DC, MC, V. Lunch 11:30–1:30, dinner 5–11 (last order at 10:30), upstairs opens at 6. Closed national holidays.*

★ **Little Carnival.** Tucked away on the lower level of the Umeda Center Building, you'll find Little Carnival, where singing waiters serve up lobster, salmon, crab, and raw fish. The restaurant's library theme and multiwood paneling combine with dining areas on levels to create a casual, friendly atmosphere that is very popular with young people. Little Carnival also features a big buffet and salad bar, and from 6 to 10 in the evening, a piano player accompanies the singing servers. *Umeda Center Bldg., B1F, 2-4-12 Nakazaki-nishi, Kita-ku, tel. 06/373–9828. No reservations. Dress: casual. AE, DC, MC, V. Open week-*

days 11:45–11:30 (lunch menu 11:45–3); weekends 11:45–11:30.

Yasubei. This small *izakaya* (pub) has both a fun atmosphere and good food. Sit at the counter, where you can watch the chefs at work, or at a table and select from an extensive menu that includes grilled fish, hibachi-grilled chicken, and scallops wrapped in bacon. *Daiichi Blvd., BF2, 1-3 Umeda, Kita-ku (close to Umeda Station), tel. 06/344–4545. No reservations. Dress: informal. No credit cards. Open daily until 10:30 PM.*

Inexpensive

Country Life. The current health boom has at last started to dispel the notion left over from less prosperous days in Japan that brown rice is something only poor people eat. Country Life, with its inexpensive yet gourmet vegetarian meals, has Early American decor; the food (no meat, fish, eggs, or milk) is served buffet-style—all you can eat, and all delicious for very reasonable prices. The restaurant is across the river to the southeast of the Museum of Oriental Ceramics. *3-11 Kyobashi, Chuo-ku, tel. 06/943–9597. No reservations. Dress: casual. No credit cards. Open 11–3. Closed Sat.*

Pig & Whistle. This is a traditional U.K.–style pub, complete with U.K. barflies and dart games. The atmosphere is lively and comfortable, and the food includes fish and chips, fried chicken, and snacks of all kinds. Come here for a draught beer or three after a hard day in the belly of the Osaka beast. Pig & Whistle is a self-service establishment. The bar serves 120 varieties of Scotch and Bourbon. *IS Building, 2F., 1-32 Shinsaibashi-suji, 2-chome, Chuo-ku, tel 06/213–6911. No reservations. Dress: casual. No credit cards. Open daily 4 PM–midnight.*

Lodging

Osaka is known more as a business than as a tourist destination. Although the trend for tourists is still to stay in nearby Kyoto and visit Osaka on a day trip, Osakans would like to see this pattern reversed. Among the city's assets are sparkling new Western-style hotels constructed with comfort and luxury in mind. Osaka bills itself as the premier city of the 21st century; every new building appears to resemble a prototype for future architecture.

Osaka has accommodations for almost every taste, from first-class hotels to more modest business hotels, which unfortunately aren't very distinctive. You may be somewhat disappointed if you expect guest quarters to be along the same lines as the better hotels in the United States. The Japanese hotel designers are often concerned with being efficient and functional rather than elegant and flamboyant. However, discriminating travelers will appreciate the individual attention provided by the solicitous staff at most hotels.

You'll be relieved to discover that a hotel room costs less in Osaka than does one of comparative size in Tokyo. And Osaka has more hotels to choose from than does Kyoto, which is especially important to keep in mind during the peak tourist seasons.

A 3% federal consumer tax is added to all hotel bills. Another 3% local tax is added to the bill if it exceeds ¥15,000. At most hotels, a 10%–15% service charge is added to the total bill. Tipping is not necessary.

Category	Cost*
Very Expensive	over ¥20,000
Expensive	¥15,000–¥20,000
Moderate	¥10,000–¥15,000
Inexpensive	under ¥10,000

Cost is for double room, without tax or service

The most highly recommended accommodations are indicated by a star ★.

Very Expensive

ANA Sheraton Hotel Osaka. One of only a half-dozen Osaka hotels to be classified as deluxe, the ANA Sheraton overlooks the city's picturesque Nakanoshima Island. A handsome 24-story white-tile structure, it has some unusual architectural features, including a six-story rock sculpture behind its main stairway and huge fluted columns in its lobby. There is also an enclosed courtyard with trees. Guest rooms are done in pastel shades and have travertine-marble baths with phone extensions. Each room is furnished with twin or double beds; some rooms have extra sofa beds. The hotel's fine restaurants include the elegant Rose Room (*see Dining, above*). *1-3-1 Dojimahama, Kita-ku, Osaka 530, tel. 06/347–1112, fax 06/ 347–1112. 500 rooms. Facilities: several restaurants (including Chinese, Japanese, and French), coffee shop, indoor pool, sauna, business center, several lounges, underground parking. AE, DC, MC, V.*

★ **Hotel New Otani Osaka.** Osaka's newest hotel, the New Otani is ideally situated next to Osakajo Castle Park on the JR line. Popular with Japanese and Westerners alike, it offers such amenities as indoor and outdoor pools, tennis, superior rooms, and a sparkling marble atrium lobby. The rooms, large by Japanese standards, afford handsome views of Osakajo Castle and the Neyagawa River. The room decor is modern, with twin or double beds, light color schemes, dining tables, lined draperies, and excellent bathrooms with decent counter space. A large selection of bars and restaurants offers enough diversity to suit almost any taste. The New Otani is in Osaka Business Park. If you need to go to midtown Osaka, the Aqua Liner water bus stops right in front of the hotel. *4-1 Shiromi, 1-chome, Chuo-ku, Osaka 540, tel. 06/941–1111, fax 06/941–9769. 559 rooms. Facilities: 18 restaurants and bars, health club with activities. AE, DC, MC, V.*

Hotel Nikko Osaka. An impressive and rather striking white tower in the colorful Shinsaibashi Station area, the Nikko Osaka is within easy reach of Osaka's nightlife. The hotel's atmosphere is lively and even exciting: As you enter, you'll probably be greeted by a doorman in top hat and tails. Some rooms offer contemporary furnishings with Japanese touches and traditional light decor. Higher price rooms have expensive furniture, thick carpets, bedside controls, and cable TV featuring the CNN news station. On the executive floors, the tile baths come complete with hair dryers and phones. The drinking and dining establishments are numerous and varied, and the hotel's management has elevated service to an art. *1-3-3 Nishi Shinsaibashi, Chuo-ku, Osaka 542, tel. 06/244–1111, fax 06/245–2432. 640 rooms. Facilities: 3 bars, including the Jetstream on top floor; French, Japanese, Chinese, and Western restaurants, coffee shop; shopping arcade. AE, DC, MC, V.*

Nankai South Tower Hotel. One of the best features of this three-year-old hotel is its location, right inside the Nankai Namba Station, where travelers can connect with a number of rail lines, including the Nankai train to Koyasan and Wakayama, the subway to Umeda and Shin-Osaka stations, and, eventually, the Nankai train to the new Kansai International Airport (scheduled to open in 1994). This modern tower has 36 floors, but since public spaces are on the lower levels, all of the rooms have views of the city. Rooms are decorated in three color schemes—light shades of blue, brown, and purple—and have low-pile rugs, electronically controlled curtains, and brass fixtures. Suites have kitchenettes and Jacuzzis as well as showers and two toilets. Bathrobes are supplied for those staying on the Executive floors. This is a bright, Western-style hotel, akin to what you'd expect in a Hilton: first-rate comfort but little character. Some will find this a welcome escape from the noise of the city and the challenge of traveling in a foreign land. Be sure to have a drink in the Sky Lounge. *1-60 Namba 5-chome, Chuo-ku, Osaka 542, tel. 06/646–1111, fax 06/648–0331. 548 rooms, including 11 suites and 2 Japanese suites. Facilities: 12 restaurants, 18 ballrooms, 2 private dining rooms; fitness center with indoor pool, hot baths, sauna, shiatsu massage; business center with English-speaking staff; Christian and Shinto chapels.*

★ **Osaka Hilton International.** Glitz and glitter draw both tourists and expense accounters to the Hilton International, Osaka's leading hotel. Located across from Osaka Station in the heart of Osaka's business district, it is a typical Western-style hotel, replete with marble and brass. The high-ceiling lobby is dramatically luxurious, and the hotel's arcade boasts several designer boutiques. Standard rooms are first-rate, with almost all the extras, and the three executive floors offer higher price rooms if you desire even more comfort. The staff is very helpful. *8-8 Umeda 1-chome, Kita-ku, Osaka 530, tel. 06/347–7111, fax 06/347–7001. 526 rooms. Facilities: 4 restaurants, top-floor lounge where lunch is served weekdays, café, coffee shop, fitness center with outdoor tennis, indoor pool, gym, sauna, massage room; business center; designer shops. AE, DC, MC, V.*

Royal Hotel. With a host of restaurants and bars from the basement to the top floor of its tower, the Royal is a self-contained city. The lobby is the perfect spot for people-watching, with crowds going in and coming out of the hotel's many lounges. Guests staying in the VIP tower have access to the swimming club with two sunroofed pools. Standard rooms, either with twin beds or a queen-size bed, are reasonably spacious and have a coffee table, two chairs, and big picture windows (views improve with the higher floors). A shuttle runs from the hotel to the Grand Hotel (nearby) and to the Yodoyabashi subway station. *5-3-68 Nakanoshima, Kita-ku, Osaka 530, tel. 06/448–1121, fax 06/448–4414. 1,167 rooms. Facilities: 15 restaurants; health club with 2 pools, tanning beds, sauna, steam, massage, lounges. AE, DC, MC, V.*

Expensive–Very Expensive

Holiday Inn Nankai Osaka. Although it is located in the midst of the popular restaurant and nightlife neighborhood around Nankai Station, the 14-story Holiday Inn Nankai is actually fairly quiet inside. Americans will recognize the familiar Holiday Inn touches—the rooms are a bit bland, with twin or double beds, modern baths, and a television with standard Japanese stations. The best rooms are found on the 10th floor. Restaurants range from a grill room to a coffee shop with a garden promenade. This is not the best value in the city. *5-15 Shinsaibashisuji, 2-chome, Chuo-ku, Osaka 542, tel. 06/213–8281, fax 06/213–8640. 229 rooms. Facilities: 3 floors of shops, Chinese and Japanese restaurants, pub, coffee shop, grill, outdoor rooftop pool. AE, DC, MC, V.*

★ **Hotel Osaka Grand.** A sister to the superior Royal Hotel, the Grand is a lively first-class commercial hotel with free shuttle service every few minutes to the Royal and to a nearby subway stop. Everything is neat and clean; the staff is large and hardworking. Housekeeping is very good, and the rooms bigger than average for Japan. The decor is somewhat dated but in good repair, and all the food and beverage areas are very popular. A shuttle bus travels every 15 minutes between the hotel and the Yodoyabashi subway station. *2-3-18 Nakanoshima, Kita-ku, Osaka 530, tel. 06/202–1212, fax 06/227–5054. 350 rooms. Facilities: Western and Japanese restaurants, shopping arcade. AE, DC, MC, V.*

Miyako Hotel Osaka. A relatively new, 21-story high rise, the Miyako is filled with expansive public rooms such as the lobby, which rises two stories and is decorated with marble columns and attractive pastel color schemes. The rooms are also pastel; they are modern and inviting, with such extras as bedside television controls, and dining tables. Executive rooms occupy two floors and have plusher appointments. The Miyako is near the Uehonmachi subway stop, and trains for Kyoto on the Kintetsu Line leave from an adjacent building, which makes the hotel convenient for travelers. The National Bunraku Theater is also fairly close. *6-1-55 Uehonmachi, Tennoji-ku, Osaka 543, tel. 06/773–1111, fax 06/773–3322. 608 rooms. Facilities: 6 restaurants, including a roof room, grill, and coffee shop; lower-level shopping arcade, roof lounge, bars, health club with indoor pool and retractable roof, Japanese bath, racquetball courts. AE, DC, MC, V.*

Osaka Terminal Hotel. Across from the Osaka Station (not to be confused with the Shin-Osaka Station, where Shinkansen trains arrive and depart), the Osaka Terminal is housed in a skyscraper and shares floors with offices and shops. It ranks as a minimally first-class hotel but has many restaurants, including a grill and coffee shop. Rooms have minibars, bedside TV controls, and small but modern bathrooms. *3-1-1 Umeda, Kita-ku, Osaka 530, tel. 06/344–1235, fax 06/344–1130. 644 rooms. Facilities: 4 restaurants, 2 lounges, underground shopping access. AE, DC, MC, V.*

Moderate–Expensive

Hotel Do Sports Plaza. Situated in the heart of Osaka's colorful nightlife district, the Do Sports Plaza earned its reputation by catering to sports enthusiasts and athletic teams. Most of the rooms are small, but fairly bright, singles; doubles are not much larger. Located on a commercial block off a sidestreet, the hotel is easily accessible to subway lines. Fitness activities are the main attraction here. The hotel adjoins a members-only sports club that is open to hotel guests for an additional ¥2,500 per person. Facilities at the club include a heated pool, running track, gym, sauna, and aerobics studio. *3-3-17 Minami Semba, Chuo-ku, Osaka 542, tel. 06/245-3311, fax 06/245-5803. 208 rooms. Facilities: restaurant, pub, coffee shop, access to sports club (see above). AE, DC, MC, V.*

Hotel Hanshin. Located near the underground shopping center at Umeda and Osaka stations, the Hotel Hanshin is a pleasant 15-story commercial hotel. Popular mostly with Japanese businessmen, it does manage to attract a few tourists. The moderately priced rooms are found between the 10th and 15th floors. Furnishings are mostly Scandinavian; the tile baths are so small you might say they are claustrophobic. Waterbeds are available. *2-3-30 Umeda, Kita-ku, Osaka 530, tel. 06/344-1661, fax 06/344-9860. 243 rooms. Facilities: Japanese–Western restaurant, coffee shop, 2 bars, sauna, small shopping arcade. AE, DC, MC, V.*

International Hotel Osaka. This massive L-shape hotel may be a bit hard to reach in traffic, but it's a reliable choice. The best rooms are located in an annex where most of the units are situated; if you're on a budget, ask for a room in the back. The color scheme can best be described as reserved and uninspiring. Popular mostly with Japanese clientele, the International's lobby and public areas are often busy with groups coming or going. *2-3-3 Honmachibashi, Chuo-ku, Osaka 540, tel. 06/941-2661, fax 06/941-5362. 393 rooms. Facilities: 1 lounge, 5 restaurants, including Japanese, coffee shop, grill. AE, DC, MC, V.*

Mitsui Urban Hotel. Under renovation for quite some time, the Mitsui Urban now boasts a new lobby, a remodeled bar, and several new guest room furnishings. The decor in the new rooms is the ever-popular pastels; autumn-colored rooms offer coffee makers and other extras. Some of the carpeting in the rooms is new, and the baths are fairly modern, though a bit small. There's also a 17th-floor restaurant. The staff's English is fairly good, considering the hotel receives mostly Japanese guests. The Mitsui Urban is accessible to the Midosuji Subway Line at Nakatsu Station. *18-8 Toyosaki, Oyodo-ku, Osaka 531, tel. 06/374-1111, fax 06/374-1085. 406 rooms. Facilities: lounge, bar, Western–Japanese restaurant. AE, DC, MC, V.*

New Hankyu Hotel and New Hankyu Annex. This busy hotel complex is located in the popular area around Osaka Station, with its restaurants and shopping. The 17-story Annex, a block from the main hotel, houses the newest, largest, and best rooms; it also offers a café, three other eateries, and an indoor pool. The single rooms in the main hotel, however, are about as roomy as telephone booths. Guests are permitted the use of facilities in both buildings. *1-1-35 Shibata, Kita-ku, Osaka 530, tel. 06/372-5101, fax 06/374-6885. 1,249 rooms. Facilities: 5 restaurants in main building, 2 in annex; health club, indoor pool, several bars. AE, DC, MC, V.*

Osaka Airport Hotel. For those with an early flight out of Osaka Airport, this place is located right inside the airport terminal building. These are not the most luxurious rooms for the price, but the location saves time and trouble for the busy traveler. *3F Osaka Airport Building, Toyonaka, Osaka-fu. tel. 06/855-4621, fax 06/855-4620. 105 rooms. Facilities: large variety of*

Japanese and Western restaurants, gift shops, and bars serving the airport and hotel. AE, DC, MC, V.

Osaka Dai Ichi Hotel. As Japan's first cylinder-shape skyscraper, known as the Maru-Biru (Round Building), the Dai Ichi is easy to locate amid the Osaka cityscape. Now somewhat overshadowed by the Hilton, it still receives many groups. The rooms are wedge-shape, and half are small singles that are usually taken on weekdays by Japanese businessmen. The hotel has a coffee shop, which is open around the clock, and an underground shopping arcade. The Dai Ichi is conveniently located across from Osaka Station. *1-9-20 Umeda, Kita-ku, Osaka 530, tel. 06/341–4411, fax 06/341–4930. 478 rooms. Facilities: Chinese, Japanese, and Western restaurants; bar, shopping promenade. AE, DC, MC, V.*

Moderate

Hotel Echo Osaka. This hotel is recommended for those seeking good budget accommodations. Though near the JR station, the Echo Osaka is far from other major parts of the city. The 83 plain rooms offer air-conditioning and routine furnishings, including double or twin beds, uncoordinated carpeting, and small baths. The hotel is neat and clean, if nothing more, and has an accommodating young staff. *1-4-7 Abeno-suji, Abeno-ku, Osaka 545 (near Tennoji Station), tel. 06/633–1141, fax 06/633–3849. 84 rooms. Facilities: Chinese and French restaurants, coffee shop, bar. AE, DC, MC, V.*

Osaka Castle Hotel. This square mid-rise building is unexceptional and receives its name for its location near Osakajo Castle, not for any majestic manner. It boasts a rooftop beer garden in summer and a subway stop in the basement. Rooms are small and not very light; the furniture, which may have been bought from a catalogue, is uninspired. Some rooms in front have good views, but all have dwarf-size baths. You may have to bone up on your Japanese with the front desk. *2-35-7 Kyobashi, Chuo-ku, Osaka 540 (at Temmabashi Station on independent subway line), tel. 06/942–2401, fax 06/946–9043. 120 rooms. Facilities: Japanese, Chinese, and French restaurants; café, beer garden, a handful of shops. AE, DC, MC, V.*

Osaka International Community Center Hotel. The city community center has a hotel with pleasant, well-furnished rooms at reasonable rates. The center hosts lectures and cultural events and offers simultaneous interpreting services. *8-2-6 Kamimoto-cho, Tennoji-ku, Osaka 543. tel. 06/773–8181. 50 rooms with bath. Facilities: library, conference rooms, restaurant, café, bar. AE, DC, MC, V.*

Umeshin East Hotel. In the antiques shop and art gallery neighborhood near the U.S. Consulate, this small brick hotel has an attractive modern design, with a lush green interior garden café, a restaurant, and a bar in its tiled lobby. Rooms are small, but comfortably furnished. *4-11-5 Nishi-Tenma, Kita-ku (a 10-min. walk from Midosuji Subway Line and Umeda Station), tel. 06/364–1151, fax 06/364–1150. 144 rooms. AE, DC, MC, V.*

10 Kobe

By Kiko Itasaka

Kobe has been a prominent harbor city throughout Japanese history. In the 12th century, the Taira family moved the capital from Kyoto to Fukuhara, the western part of modern Kobe, with the hope of increasing Japan's international trade. Fukuhara remained the capital for a mere six months, but its port, known as Hyogo, continued to flourish. Japan opened her ports to foreign trade in 1868 after a long period of isolationism. In order to prevent foreigners from using the profitable and active port of Hyogo, the more remote port of Kobe, located slightly northeast of Hyogo, was opened to international trade. Within a few years, Kobe eclipsed Hyogo in importance as a port.

Now a major industrial city, Kobe has an active port that serves as many as 10,000 ships a year. A century of exposure to international cultures has left its mark on Kobe, a sophisticated and cosmopolitan city. In the hills above the port area is a residential area where foreign merchants and traders have settled over the years. Many Western-style houses built in the late 19th century are still inhabited by Kobe's large foreign population, while others have been open to the public as buildings of historical interest. Many sailors passing through Kobe, beguiled by the charm of this city, have settled here. As a result, Kobe boasts remarkable diversity in its shops and restaurants.

This port city is extremely popular with young Japanese couples and women on vacation, who enjoy the numerous shops, countless restaurants, the active nightlife, and the romantic harbor views. Travelers searching for exotic or traditional Japan will be disappointed by the very modern Kobe, but visitors will be satisfied by the city if they are eager to relax in a cosmopolitan setting with excellent places to shop and a variety of international cuisines to sample.

Essential Information

Arriving and Departing

By Plane The airport for Kobe is Osaka International Airport, approximately 40 minutes away. Frequent service from Tokyo to Osaka is available, as well as direct service from international destinations to Osaka.

Between the Airport and Center City The airport bus to Kobe Sannomiya Station (Kobe's main train station) leaves from the domestic airlines terminal's main entrance and from a stop between the domestic and international terminals approximately every 20 minutes, 7 AM–10 PM. The trip takes about 40 minutes and costs ¥720.

Because public transportation is excellent, a taxi is not a practical alternative for getting into Kobe from the airport.

By Train Japan Railways offers frequent Shinkansen super express service between Tokyo and Shin-Kobe Station. From Tokyo, the trip to Kobe takes about three hours, 30 minutes (cost: ¥14,000). The trip between Osaka Station and Kobe's Sannomiya Station is a 30-minute run on the JR Tokaido Line rapid train, which leaves at 15-minute intervals throughout the day (cost: ¥390). Japan Rail Passes may be used for these trains.

Two other private lines, the Hankyu and Hanshin lines, offer service between Osaka and Kobe for ¥280.

Getting Around

By Train
Within Kobe, Japan Railways and the Hankyu and Hanshin lines run parallel from east to west and are easy to negotiate. Sannomiya and Motomachi are the principal downtown stations. Tickets are purchased from a vending machine and surrendered upon leaving the train. Fares depend upon your destination.

The city's subway system runs from Shin-Kobe Station west to the outskirts of town. Fares start at ¥160 and are determined by destination. A ride between Sannomiya Station and Shin-Kobe Station costs ¥180.

By Bus
The city bus service is frequent and efficient, though it might be somewhat confusing to a first-time visitor. At each bus stop, you will find a pole that displays a route chart of official stops. Enter at the rear or center of the bus; pay your fare as you leave at the front (cost: ¥180 adults; ¥90 children, regardless of the distance). Exact change is needed.

By Taxi
Taxis are plentiful and can be hailed on the street or at taxi stands. The fare starts at ¥540 for the first 2 kilometers and goes up ¥90 for each additional 1,250 feet.

By Portliner
The Portliner is a computerized monorail that services the recently built man-made Port Island, located in the middle of Kobe Harbor. The monorail central station is connected to the JR Sannomiya Station; the ride from the station to Port Island takes about 10 minutes (round-trip cost: ¥440 adults, ¥220 children).

Important Addresses and Numbers

Tourist Information
The **Kobe Tourist Information Center** (078/271–2401), located on the west side of the JR Sannomiya Station, is open daily 9–5:30. Here you can pick up a free detailed map of the city in English. The Tourist Information Center has branches at the JR Kobe Station (tel. 078/341–5277), and Shin-Kobe Station (tel. 078/241–9550), open daily 10–6.

The **Japan Travel-Phone** number for information in English on Kobe and other points in western Japan, tel. 0120/444–800.

Consulates
The closest U.S., U.K., and Canadian consulates are located in Osaka (*see* Chapter 9).

Emergencies
Police, tel. 110; **Ambulance,** tel. 119.

Doctors
Kobe Adventist Hospital (4-1 Arinodai 8-chome, Kita-ku, Kobe, tel. 078/981–0161); **Kobe Kaisei Hospital** (3-11-15 Shinohara-Kitamachi, Nada-ku, tel. 078/871–5201).

Pharmacies
The **Daimaru Department Store** Chuo-ku (40 Akashi-cho, tel. 078/331–8121), located within a three-minute walk of the Motomachi JR Station has a pharmacy department.

English-Language Bookstores
Bunyodo (Kobe Kokusai Kaikan 1st fl., 1-6 Goko-dori 8-chome, Chuo-ku, tel. 078/221–0557); **Maruzen** (1-4-12 Motomachi-dori, Chuo-ku, tel. 078/391–6003).

Travel Agencies
Japan Travel Bureau, Sannomiya JR Station (tel. 078/231–4701).

Guided Tours

Between March 21 and November 30, the City Transport Bureau offers several half-day tours of major attractions in the city and surrounding areas. While the tours are conducted in Japanese, they do give you a satisfactory overview of Kobe. Itineraries vary, depending upon the day of the week. The buses depart from the south side of the Kobe Kotsu Center Building, near Sannomiya Station (cost: ¥2,500–¥3,000 adults, ¥1,200–¥1,500 children). Tickets and information can be obtained at the (Sightseeing Bus Tour Information Office) **Shinai Teiki Kanko Annaisho** on the second floor of the Kobe Kotsu Center Building (tel. 078/391–4755).

A series of sightseeing tours is also offered by authorized taxi services. The tours cover 11 different routes and range in time from two to five hours (cost: ¥7,830–¥19,570). The taxi tours can be reserved at the Kobe Tourist Information Center (tel. 078/271–2401).

Exploring

Numbers in the margin correspond to points of interest on the Kobe map.

The downtown section of Kobe, where most businesses are located, is near the harbor area. The rest of Kobe is built on slopes that extend as far as the base of Mt. Rokko. In the middle of the harbor is the man-made Port Island, which has conference centers, an amusement park, and the Portopia Hotel. The island is linked with the downtown area by a fully computerized monorail that is without a human conductor. The major nightlife area, Ikuta, is just north of the Sannomiya Station.

❶ A good place to start your trip to Kobe is with a visit to the **Kobe City Museum,** where you'll find out about the history of this international port town. Alongside earlier artifacts, the museum has an interesting collection of memorabilia from the heyday of the old foreign settlement, including a scale model of the foreign concession. Three entire rooms from a turn-of-the-century Western house are on display. You'll also discover selections from the museum's famous *namban* collection of prints, screens, and paintings by Japanese artists of the late 16th to 18th century; these artworks depict foreigners in Japanese settings from that period.

To get to the museum, walk south down Flower Road from Sannomiya Station, past the Flower Clock and City Hall to Higashi Yuenchi Park. Walk through the park to the Post Office, across the street on the west side. Walk east on the road in front of the Kobe Minato Post Office toward the Oriental Hotel. Turn left at the corner in front of the hotel and you'll find the City Museum in the old Bank of Tokyo building, at the end of the block. *24 Kyomachi, Chuo-ku, Kobe-shi, tel. 078/391–0035. Admission: ¥200 (more for special exhibitions). Open 10–5. Closed Mon.*

Return to Sannomiya Station, browsing through Nankin Machi (Chinatown) and the Motomachi and Sannomiya shopping arcades *(see* Shopping, *below)* if time permits. Once back at Sannomiya Station, begin your tour of the northern district by crossing the street that runs along the tracks and turning left

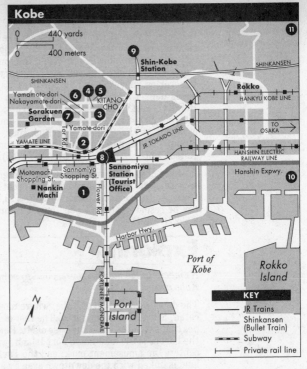

at the first main intersection. You'll see the orange torii gate
❷ of **Ikuta Jinja Shrine.** According to legend, the shrine was
founded by Empress Jingu in the 3rd century.

The road that runs up the right side of the shrine leads up the
slope to Nakayamate-dori Avenue. Cross the avenue and continue up the slope.

Turn right at the corner of Yamamoto-dori. This road is lined
with high-fashion boutiques and restaurants. Turn left at
❸ Kitano-zaka, which leads to **Kitano,** an area where Western
traders and businessmen have been living since the late 19th
century. The district is extremely popular with young Japanese tourists, who enjoy the rare opportunity of seeing old-
fashioned Western houses (referred to in Kobe as *Ijinkan*),
very few of which exist in Japan. Many of the residences are
still inhabited by Westerners, but some have been turned into
museums. More than a dozen Kitano 19th-century residences
are open to the public, and seeing all of them can get repeti-
tious. A few are recommended here for those who are interested. Otherwise, you may simply enjoy a walk around the hills
of this area while you admire the Victorian and Gothic architecture.

For those who want to see the interior of some of the buildings,
continue walking up the slopes from Nakayamate-dori Avenue.
The second intersection crosses Yamamoto-dori Avenue (nick-
named Ijinkan-dori Avenue). At the third intersection, just
past Rin's Gallery (filled with boutiques of Japan's top design-
❹ ers), turn right and walk east to the **Eikoku-kan** (English

House). This structure, inhabited until 1979, is now open to the public. The building was constructed in 1907 by an English architect and was inhabited by another Englishman, J. E. Baker. *2-3-16 Kitano-machi, Chuo-ku, Kobe-shi, tel. 078/241–2338. Admission: ¥600. Open weekdays 9–5, weekends 9–5:15.*

⑤ Three of the Ijinkan in the Kitano area are publicly owned and free of charge. The **Rhein no Yakata** (Rhine House), opposite the English House, has a pleasant German-style coffee shop in-
⑥ side. Near Kitano Tenman Jinja Shrine at the top of the hill is the **Kazami Dori no Yakata** (Weathercock House) made famous on a national TV series some years ago. It is the most elaborate of Kobe's Ijinkan, listed as an Important Cultural Property. Continue back down the slope via Kitano-zaka toward San-
⑦ nomiya Station. One Ijinkan house not to miss is the **Chouéké Yashiki** (Chouéké Mansion), built in 1889. The only house still inhabited, it is filled to the rafters with turn-of-the-century memorabilia from East and West, and Mrs. Chouéké is on hand to show you her treasures and share her vast knowledge of Kobe. Her collection includes a large number of *namban* wood-block prints.

⑧ Return to Sannomiya Station and walk to the **Portliner** plat-form. This automatic monorail leaves every six minutes on its loop line around Port Island, with eight stops along the way. From the Portliner you get a close-up view of Kobe Harbor. Get off at Shimin Hiroba Station. This places you in the heart of this futuristic complex, with parks, hotels, restaurants, and fashion boutiques to explore. (Portliner round-trip fare: ¥440 adults, ¥220 children).

Excursions

Nunobiki Falls

⑨ A quiet side trip from the city is the 20-minute walk up the hill behind Shin-Kobe Station to **Nunobiki Falls,** whose beauty has been referred to in Japanese literature since the 10th century. It is actually a series of four cascades of varying heights, to-gether described as one of the three greatest falls in Japan.

Kikumasamune Shiryokan (Sake Museum)

The district between the Oishi and Uozaki stations on the Hanshin Electric Railway line, once known as Nada, has been a sake-producing region since the Edo period (1603–1868). With pure water from the Rokko Mountains and particularly deli-cious rice available in the area, Nada was an ideal location for sake production. Because of its proximity to the ocean, sake was transported from Nada to Edo (now Tokyo), thus becoming one of the first areas in Japan to distribute its sake to other re-gions. To this day, the 50 sake companies in this brewery dis-trict produce one-third of all the sake in Japan. For the most part, this area is full of huge concrete factories, but some old wood buildings for sake production still continue to operate.

Few tourists visit the brewery district, which is a shame, be-cause the trip can be fascinating. A few breweries have opened
⑩ up small museums. One of these is the **Kikumasamune Shiryo-kan.** As you enter the building, a guide will seat you and show

you a video in English that describes the history of sake production. To enhance your enjoyment of the video, you will be offered a sample of Kikumasamune sake, with an opportunity for refills. After the video, a very enthusiastic guide who speaks a modicum of English will take you to another 330-year-old building, which was originally a sake brewery. This structure was constructed using no nails, and it is in excellent condition. On display inside are sake-producing implements, some of which date back as far as the Edo period (1603–1868). Antique posters and advertisements are also exhibited.

Getting There   To get to Kikumasamune Shiryokan from Kobe, take the local train to Uozaki from the Hanshin Electric Railway Sannomiya Station located under Sogo department store, just south of the JR Sannomiya Station. When you arrive at the Uozaki Station, take the staircase on your left in the station and exit. Walk straight along the road toward the main highway and cross the footbridge on your right. At the end of the footbridge, turn left. Continue along the road before you until you get to the highway. Turn right on the street before the highway, and walk along another small road. On your left you will see a small tunnel that takes you under the highway. Continue walking along this small road for approximately five minutes. On your left, you will see an old brown wood structure, which is the Kikumasamune Shiryokan. *1-9-1 Ozaki Nishimachi, Higashi-nada-ku, Kobe-shi, tel. 078/854–1029. Admission free. Open 10–3. Closed Tues. Apr.–Sept.*

Mt. Rokko

⑪ **Mt. Rokko** is a popular excursion from Kobe. The highest peak of the Rokko Mountains, it offers a magnificent view of the city and the Inland Sea. On top of the mountain are various recreational areas, including the oldest golf course in Japan, built in 1903, and the summer homes of some of Kobe's wealthier residents. The most exciting view is probably from the aerial gondola that runs between the Rokko-sanjo area and the Rokko-sanjo countryside.

Getting There   Take the Hankyu Electric Railway Line from the JR Sannomiya Station to Rokko Station (cost: ¥160). From the latter station, take either a taxi or a bus to Rokko Cableshita Station; a cable car travels from there up the mountain to Rokko-sanjo Station (cost: ¥560).

Shopping

Kobe is a shopper's paradise. Unlike Tokyo, Osaka, and other places in Japan where shops are scattered all over the city, most of the shopping districts in Kobe are in clusters, so you can visit numerous shops with great ease. The historic shopping area of Kobe is known as **Motomachi,** which extends for one mile between Motomachi JR Station and Daimaru department store. Most of the district is under a covered arcade, so even if the weather is inclement, you can wander around from shop to shop. You can purchase nearly anything in Motomachi, ranging from antiques to cameras to electronics goods. One favorite stop for many tourists is the **Maruzen** bookstore, located right at the entrance on the Motomachi Station side of the arcade. This store has an excellent selection of books in English.

At the opposite end of the arcade are two small shops that sell traditional Japanese goods. **Sakaeya** (8-5 Motomachi-dori, 5-chome, Chuo-ku, tel. 078/341–1307) specializes in Japanese dolls. **Naniwaya** (3-8 Motomachi-dori, 4-chome, Chuo-ku, tel. 078/341–6367) has an excellent selection of Japanese lacquerware at reasonable prices. Also try **Harishin** (3-10-3 Motomachi-dori, Chuo-ku, tel. 078/331–2516) on the west end of the arcade for antiques.

Nearly connected to the Motomachi shopping arcade, and extending from the Sogo department store to the Motomachi area for half a mile, is the **Sannomiya Center Gai** shopping arcade. This mall has fewer shops and more restaurants than the neighboring Motomachi. Because of its extremely convenient location right next to the Sannomiya Station, this is a good place to have a quick bite to eat.

The famous pearl company **Tasaki Shinju** (Tasaki Bldg. 6-3-2 Minatojima Nakamachi, Chuo-ku, tel. 078/302–3321) in Center Plaza across from Sannomiya Station has a museum and demonstration hall along with its retail pearl shop.

The new **Sanchika Town** underground shopping mall, which runs for several blocks beneath Flower Road south from Sannomiya Station, has 120 shops and 30 restaurants.

Kobe's trendy crowd tends to shop in the many exclusive shops lining **Tor Road,** which extends from the north to the south of the city on a slope lined with trees. Fashionable boutiques featuring Japanese designers and imported goods alternate with chic cafés and restaurants.

Dining

Kobe beef is considered a delicacy all over Japan. Tender, tasty, and extremely expensive, it is a must for beef lovers. The beef is raised in the nearby Tajima area of Hyogo Prefecture. The cows are fed beer and are massaged to improve the quality of the meat and to give it its marbled texture. As a result, Kobe beef is rather high in fat content, and this may disappoint lean-meat lovers.

Ethnic food fans will also appreciate the many international cuisines available in Kobe. Sailors passing through often stay on in Kobe, and some of them open restaurants that are popular not only with the large foreign community, but also with resident and visiting Japanese. The number of international restaurants is perhaps fewer than in Tokyo, but the quality and authenticity are unsurpassed. Simply walking around north of the Sannomiya Station in the Kitano area, you are bound to come across restaurants representing nearly every cuisine imaginable. From the corner of Hanta-dori and Yamamoto-dori (also known as Ijinkan-dori), there are at least a dozen fine restaurants of every different cuisine imaginable—Italian, German, French, Swiss, Middle Eastern, Thai, American, and, of course, Japanese. Port Island has also begun to gain a reputation for its variety of good restaurants.

A 3% federal consumer tax is added to all restaurant bills. Another 3% local tax is added to the bill if it exceeds ¥7,500. At more expensive restaurants, a 10%–15% service charge is also added to the bill. Tipping is not necessary.

The most highly recommended restaurants are indicated by a star ★.

Category	Cost*
Very Expensive	over ¥10,000
Expensive	¥6,000–¥10,000
Moderate	¥3,500–¥6,000
Inexpensive	under ¥3,500

Cost is per person without tax, service, or drinks

Kobe Beef

★ **Aragawa.** Japan's first steak house is famed for its superb hand-fed Kobe beef. The wood-paneled, chandeliered dining room has an old-country atmosphere. Aragawa's serves melt-in-your-mouth *sumiyaki* (charcoal broiled) steak that is worth its weight in yen—an evening here is the ultimate splurge, but this is considered *the* place for Kobe beef as it should be, at ¥20,000. *2-15-18 Nakayamate-dori, Chuo-ku, tel. 078/221–8547. Reservations advised. Jacket and tie required. AE, DC, MC, V. Open noon–3 and 5–10. Very Expensive.*

Highway. If price is no object, this small and exclusive restaurant has a reputation for serving fine Kobe beef. The quality of the meat is extraordinary. *13–7 Shimoyamate-dori 2-chome, Chuo-ku, tel. 078/331–7622. Reservations advised. Dress: informal. No credit cards. Open 11–9. Closed Mon. Expensive.*

A-1. This is one of the only steak restaurants among many in the neighborhood north of Hankyu Sannomiya Station that serve prime Kobe beef at anywhere near affordable prices. The teppan-style steak is served on a hot grill with a special spice and wine marinade that is as memorable as the voluptuous garlic and crisp fried potatoes. Right across from the Washington Hotel, A-1 has a relaxed and friendly atmosphere. *2-2-9 Shimo-Yamate-dori, Amashi-biru 2F, Chuo-ku, tel. 078/331–8676. Reservations advised. Dress: informal. No credit cards. Open 3–11 PM. Closed Tues. Moderate.*

International

Totenkaku. This establishment has been famous among Kobe residents since 1945 for its Peking duck, flown in fresh from China. The building itself is worth the splurge—built at the turn of the century, it is one of Kobe's Ijinkan (foreigner's residences), the F. Bishop House. You can keep the price down by ordering one of the Chinese noodle specialties. *3-14-18 Yamamoto-dori, Chuo-ku, tel. 078/231–1351. Reservations advised. Dress: informal. DC. V. Open 11:30–9, closed weekdays 2–5. Expensive.*

Gaylord. Just a few minutes' walk from Sannomiya Station, this Indian restaurant, with a flashy decor, is a favorite with Kobe's foreign residents. The curries are on the mild side but are very tasty. *8-3-7 Isogami-dori, Meiji Seimei Bldg. B1, Chuo-ku, tel. 078/251–4359. No reservations. Dress: informal. AE, DC, MC, V. Lunch 11:30–2:30, dinner 5–9:30. Moderate.*

King's Arms. Famous for its excellent platter of roast beef and its traditional atmosphere, the old King's Arms pub has become a Kobe landmark. A portrait of Sir Winston Churchill still presides over the old wooden bar that 38 years ago was the exclusive territory of some of Kobe's thirstiest Englishmen. The clientele have increased in number and kind, but the flavor of the legendary roast beef, the finest Scotch whiskey, and the seriousness of the annual dart tournament haven't changed. *4-2-15 Isobe-dori, Chuo-ku, tel. 078/221-3774. Dinner reservations advised. Dress: informal. AE, DC, MC, V. Open 11:30-9. Moderate.*

Marrakech. Elmaleh Simon, a former sailor and the Moroccan chef/owner of this restaurant, and his wife serve excellent Middle Eastern food. In this cozy little basement dining spot, it is easy to forget that you are in Japan. The couscous and kabobs are particularly delicious, and portions are generous. *Maison de Yamate B1, 1-20-15 Nakayamate-dori, Chuo-ku, Kobe-shi, tel. 078/241-3440. Reservations advised. Dress: informal. AE, V. Open 5-11 (last order at 10:30). Closed Mon. Moderate.*

Rote Rose. A block east of the Kobe Club on the west end of Kitano, this restaurant is owned by a wine importer and is most famous for its wine list, with over 180 selections of fine German wines. To sample them, order the six-glass flight. Although Rote Rose is long known as a family-style German pub, it now serves a range of European dishes, including French sausage and tournedos aux champignon. *9-14 Yon-chome, Kitano-cho, Chuo-ku, tel. 078/222-3200. Dress: informal. AE, V. Reservations advised on weekends. Open 11-2:30 and 5-9:30. Closed Wed. Moderate.*

★ **Salaam.** A light and airy restaurant with potted palms and white walls, Salaam credits itself with being the first Middle Eastern restaurant in Japan. It has a very complete menu with a variety of pickles, desserts, and main courses, such as kebabs, grilled seafood, and lamb. If you find the selection overwhelming, try the special dinners, in which you get a little of everything. Finish off your meal with refreshing hot mint tea and a piece of baklava. *12-21 Yamamoto-dori 2-chome, Chuo-ku, Ijin Plaza Bldg., 2F, tel. 078/222-1780. Reservations advised. Dress: informal. AE, V. Lunch 11:30-2:30 (Sat. and Sun. only), dinner 5-10. Moderate.*

Wakkoku. If you want to try the world-famous Kobe beef without spending a bundle, come to this smart but plain restaurant on the third floor of the shopping plaza adjacent to the Oriental Hotel and across from the Shinkansen station. Don't be distracted by the other restaurants on this floor; Wakkoku is the best choice. Lunchtime prices are lower than dinner—count on ¥3,000 for Kobe beef. *Shinkobe Oriental Park Avenue, Shin-Kobe, tel. 078/262-2838. No reservations. Dress: casual. AE, DC, V. Open 11-11. Moderate.*

Attic. Several years ago, former U.S. baseball player Marty Kuehnert opened this little haven for ballpark refugees and beer lovers of all sorts. Along with the Budweiser, Marty brought pizza, fried chicken, roast beef, and American-style fun to Kobe—complete with juke boxes and peanut shells. *Ijinkan Club Bldg. 3F, 4-1-12 Kitano-cho, Chuo-ku, tel. 078/222-1586 or 222-5368. Reservations for large groups. Dress: casual. AE, DC, MC, V. Open 6-2. Closed Tues. Inexpensive.*

★ **Raja.** A former chef of Gaylord (*see above*) opened this small and unassuming place located near the Motomachi Station. Raja features home-style Indian cooking, with spicy and tasty curries and excellent saffron rice. *Sakaemachi, 2-chome, Sanonatsu Bldg. Bl, Chuo-ku, tel. 078/332-5253. No reserva-*

tions. *Dress: informal. AE, D, V. Lunch 11:30–2:30, dinner 5–9. Inexpensive.*

★ **Wang Thai.** This is one of the few Thai restaurants in the area; it features a menu with hot Thai and slightly less spicy Chinese dishes. *14-22 Yamamoto-dori, 2 chome, Chuo-ku, President Arcade 2F, tel. 078/222–2507. No reservations. Dress: informal. No credit cards. Lunch 11–2:30, dinner 5:30–9:30. Closed Wed. Inexpensive.*

Lodging

Kobe has a wide range of hotels varying in price and quality. Because this is a heavily industrialized city, many businessmen travel here. As a result, the business hotels are conveniently located, and most are quite comfortable.

A 3% federal consumer tax is added to all hotel bills. Another 3% local tax is added to the bill if it exceeds ¥15,000. At most hotels, a 10%–15% service charge is added to the total bill. Tipping is not necessary. Postal code for Kobe is 650.

The most highly recommended accommodations are indicated by a star ★.

Category	Cost*
Very Expensive	over ¥20,000
Expensive	¥15,000–¥20,000
Moderate	¥10,000–¥15,000
Inexpensive	under ¥10,000

Cost is for double room, without tax or service

Very Expensive

★ **Hotel Okura Kobe.** Located in Meriken Park on the wharf, this 35-story hotel is Kobe's finest. Beautifully furnished and fully equipped for the business traveler, the Okura Kobe lives up to the Okura Hotel chain's worldwide reputation for excellence. Room interiors were done by British designer David Hicks, who designs for the Royal Family. The hotel has a well-equipped health club with pool and gym, stunning views of the bay from the Emerald Restaurant, and a hotel shuttle bus to Sannomiya Station. *Meriken Koen, 2-1 Hatobacho, Chuo-ku, tel. 078/333–0111, fax 078/333–6673. 472 rooms. Facilities: 5 restaurants, 2 bars, coffee shop, health club, business center. AE, DC, MC, V.*

Kobe Portopia Hotel. Situated on Port Island, the Portopia is a dazzling modern hotel with every facility imaginable. The spacious rooms look over the port. The restaurants and lounges on the top floors of the hotel have spectacular panoramic views of Mt. Rokko and Osaka Bay. Because of its location, this hotel can only be reached by the Portliner monorail or by taxi. This inconvenience is counterbalanced by the fact that everything from food to clothing is available inside the hotel. *6-10-1 Minatojima Nakamachi, Chuo-ku, Kobe-shi, tel. 078/302–0111, fax 078/302–6877. 761 rooms. Facilities: shopping arcade, beauty salon; indoor and outdoor pools, gym, sauna,* tennis courts; Chinese, Japanese, French, and sushi restaurants, coffee shops. AE, DC, MC, V.

Shin-Kobe Oriental Hotel. The tallest building in western Japan, this luxury hotel is located in front of the JR Shin-Kobe Station, where the Shinkansen arrives. Decor is sleek and modern, with Art Deco motifs in the carpeting and furnishings. The hotel is three minutes from downtown on the subway. *Kitano-cho 1-chome, Chuo-ku, Kobe-shi, tel. 078/291–1121, fax 078/ 291–1154. 600 rooms. Facilities: shopping arcade; indoor pool, sauna, gym; beauty salon; French, Chinese, Japanese, steak, and sushi restaurants. AE, DC, MC, V.*

Expensive

Hotel Monterey. Not far from Sannomiya Station, this little hotel takes you off the busy streets and into old Italy, with its marvelous Mediterranean-style courtyard fountains and European furnishings. Modeled after a monastery in Florence, the Monterey also has modern features that most hotels in Japan lack, such as a fitness room, Jacuzzi, and pool (available to guests at a slight additional charge). While the twin rooms are standard, the duplex (maisonette) rooms with the carpeted bedroom upstairs also have a small lounge area with a tiled floor. Both the Italian and Japanese restaurants on the premises are charming. *2-11-13 Shimo Yamate-dori, Chuo-ku, tel. 078/392–7111. 164 rooms. Facilities: 2 restaurants, bar, gym, and pool. AE, DC, MC, V.*

★ **Oriental Hotel.** A small, distinguished hotel that has been in business for a century, the Oriental is a favorite with those who appreciate old-world hospitality. The rooms are comfortable, and the service is deferential. *25 Kyomachi, Chuo-ku, Kobe-shi, tel. 078/331–8111, fax 078/391–8708. 190 rooms. AE, DC, MC, V.*

★ **Sannomiya Terminal Hotel.** Located in the terminal building above the JR Sannomiya Station, this hotel is extremely convenient, particularly for anyone who has to catch an early train. The rooms are on the small side, but they are clean and pleasant. *8 Kumoi-dori, Chuo-ku, Kobe-shi, tel. 078/291–0001, fax 078/291–0020. 190 rooms. Facilities: French, Japanese, and Chinese restaurants. AE, DC, MC, V.*

Moderate

Arcons. You'll need a taxi to get here from Sannomiya Station, because it's up on the hill in Kitano-cho, in the heart of the Ijinkan district. Many of the immaculate rooms at this little white hotel have a view out over the city to the sea. There's patio dining at the first-floor café when the weather is good. *3-7-1 Kitano-cho, Chuo-ku, tel. 078/231–1538. 22 rooms. Facilities: café. AE, DC, V.*

Kobe Gajoen Hotel. This delightful hotel is a change from the modern impersonal hotels that flourish in Japan. Although it is distinctly Japanese, with delicate cuisine served in a dining room paneled with decorated screens and a staff that bows to guests, the hotel has European furnishings, which come from the time when Kobe was a major port for Western traders. Close to downtown, it is a couple of minutes walk from the west exit of the Hanaku-mae Station on the Hankyu Line. *8-4-23 Shimoyamate-Dori, Chuo-ku, tel. 078/341–0301, fax 078/341–*

0353. 52 Western rooms. Facilities: restaurant. AE, DC, MC, V.

Inexpensive

Union Hotel. A short walk from the Sannomiya Station, the most attractive feature of this business hotel is its low rates. A 24-hour convenience store is located right next door, which comes in handy for midnight snacks. *1-9 Nunobiki-cho, 2-chome, Chuo-ku, Kobe-shi, tel. 078/222–6500. 167 rooms. Facilities: Western restaurant. AE, DC, MC, V.*

11 Western Honshu

By Nigel Fisher

Western Honshu is split through the center by mountains that run east to west. On either side of this split are two distinct regions. The south side of the mountains, facing the Inland Sea, is referred to as the Sanyo region (Mountains in the Sun). The north side of Western Honshu, which faces the Sea of Japan, is called San'in (In the Shadow of the Mountains). From these descriptive names, you might think that Sanyo is the more attractive of the two, but the southern coast, the route that the JR Shinkansen travels from Osaka to Hakata (on Kyushu), is heavily industrialized and visually, if not environmentally, polluted. The San'in coast, on the other hand, has so far escaped the onslaught of fabricated buildings of Japan's economic miracle and retains its identity with traditional Japan.

This chapter sketches an itinerary from Osaka down the Sanyo coast, stopping at Himeji, Okayama, Kurashiki, Hiroshima, and Miyajima before reaching Honshu's westernmost point, Shimonoseki. Then we return to Kyoto (or Osaka) by traveling through San'in. Only a few places are mentioned in San'in, namely, Hagi, Tsuwano, Matsue, Tottori Dunes, and Amanohashidate, but, for the intrepid traveler, much more is left to explore.

Essential Information

Arriving and Departing

By Plane There are domestic airports at Hiroshima, Izumno, Tottori, and Yonago that connect these cities to Tokyo with daily flights. However, Hiroshima is the major airport for this region, with seven daily flights to Tokyo's Haneda airport (1 hr., 15 mins.) as well as direct daily flights to Kagoshima (1 hr., 10 mins.), on Kyushu, and Sapporo (1 hr., 55 mins.), on Hokkaido.

By Train By far the easiest way to travel to Western Honshu and all along its southern shore is by the Shinkansen trains that run from Tokyo and Kyoto through southern Western Honshu to Hakata, on the island of Kyushu. The major stops on the Shinkansen line are Himeji, Okayama, and Hiroshima. It takes four hours and 37 minutes on the Shinkansen to travel to Hiroshima from Tokyo, one hour and 39 minutes from Osaka. To cover the length of southern Western Honshu from Osaka to Shimonoseki (the last city on Honshu before Kyushu) takes only three hours.

JR express trains cover both the southern and northern shores of Western Honshu, making, as it were, an elliptical loop around the shoreline, beginning and ending in Kyoto. Crossing from one coast to the other in Western Honshu requires traveling through the mountains (slow going), but there are several train lines that link the cities on the northern Sea of Japan coast to Okayama, Hiroshima, and Ogori. These are discussed later in the San'in section.

Important Addresses and Numbers

Tourist Information Centers Most major towns or sightseeing destinations have tourist information centers that offer free maps and brochures. They will also help in securing accommodations. The following telephone numbers are for the tourist information centers located at the major tourist destinations in Western Honshu: **Hagi City Information Office,** tel. 08382/5–3145; **Hagi City Tourist Association** at Emukai, tel. 08382/5–1750; **Himeji Tourist Information Office,** tel. 0792/85–3792; **Hiroshima City Tourist Office,** tel. 082/245–2111; **Hiroshima Prefectural Tourist Office,** tel. 082/221–6516; **Hiroshima Tourist Information Office,** tel. 082/249–9329; **Kurashiki Tourist Information Office,** tel. 0864/26–8681; **Matsue Tourist Information Office,** tel. 0852/21–4034; **Miyajima Tourist Association,** tel. 0829/44–2011; **Okayama Prefectural Tourist Office,** tel. 0862/24–2111; **Okayama Tourist Information Office,** tel. 0862/22–2912; **Tsuwano Tourist Association Information Office,** tel. 08567/2–1144.

Japan Travel-Phone The nationwide service for English-language assistance or travel information is available seven days a week, 9–5. Dial toll-free 0120/444–800 for information on western Japan. When using a yellow, blue, or green public phone (do not use the red phones), insert a ¥10 coin, which will be returned.

Emergencies **Police,** tel. 110; **Ambulance,** tel. 119.

Guided Tours

The **Japan Travel Bureau** (JTB) has offices at every JR station in each of the major cities and can assist in local tours, hotel reservations, and ticketing onward travel. Except for JTB's Hiroshima office (tel. 082/261–4131), one should not assume that any English will be spoken beyond the very basic essentials.

Japan Travel Bureau, operating through Sunshine Tours, has one-, two-, and three-day tours from Kyoto and Osaka to Hiroshima. The one-day tour covers Hiroshima and Miyajima (¥49,440 per person). The two-day (¥97,820 per person) tour also includes a hydrofoil trip on the Inland Sea to visit Omishima Island and Ikuchijima Island. The three-day tour (¥142,140 per person) adds a visit to Kurashiki and Okayama.

No guided tours of the San'in region are conducted in English, though the Japan Travel Bureau will arrange your individual travel arrangements.

The Sanyo Region

Though the Sanyo region faces the Seto Inland Sea, only glimpses of water are seen from the train traveling from Osaka to Shimonoseki. Most of the coastal plain is heavily industrialized all the way to Hiroshima. Only from there, until the outskirts of Shimonoseki, does the postwar building diminish and open country begin. Furthermore, because the main Sanyo railway line is away from the coast, to appreciate the beauty of the Inland Sea, you must either make trips to one or more of the islands in the Inland Sea or take a cruise. There are, for example, several day-cruises from Hiroshima, and you can travel the length of the Inland Sea by ferries that ply the waters between Osaka and Beppu on Kyushu. In this chapter, one short trip on the Inland Sea goes to Miyajima, one of the most beautiful (though unfortunately tourist-filled) islands. (In the following chapter, on Shikoku, an excursion is suggested from Takamatsu to Shodo Island, the second largest island in the Inland Sea.)

Getting Around

Except for crossing over to Miyajima island, a 22-minute ferry ride from near Hiroshima, all of the following itineraries through the Sanyo region use JR trains, either the Shinkansen or the local commuter and express trains. Explanations of which trains to take between destinations are given throughout the Exploring section. Essentially, though, the itinerary follows the main trunk railway line along the southern shore of Western Honshu, and it is simply a matter of hopping on and off the trains plying between Osaka and Hakata. Local buses or streetcars are used in the major cities. Driving one's own rented car is not recommended. The roads are congested, and travel by train is faster and less expensive.

Himeji

Numbers in the margin correspond to points of interest on the Western Honshu map.

The first sight of Himeji's castle occurs from the train as it pulls into Himeji Station. Like a magnet, its incredible presence draws you off the train for closer inspection. Himejijo Castle is the grandest and most attractive of the 12 surviving feudal castles. The castle, also known as the Shirasagijo (White Egret Castle), stands on a 150-foot-high bluff and dominates the city. Visually, the castle commands respect.

Arriving and Departing ❶ The city of **Himeji** is on the JR Shinkansen Line, with trains arriving and departing every 15 minutes during the day. The train journey to Himeji is three hours, 52 minutes from Tokyo, 59 minutes from Kyoto, and 42 minutes from Shin-Osaka. The Shinkansen to Okayama (to the west, it is the next destination of this itinerary) arrives and departs every hour during the day. Himeji was severely damaged in World War II and retains little to interest the foreigner. However, the castle miraculously escaped damage, and, because of the frequent train service, it is easy to disembark one train, visit the castle, and reboard another train two hours later.

Exploring From the central exit (north) of the Himeji JR station, the castle is a 15-minute walk or five minutes by bus (fare: ¥140), which leaves from the station plaza, on your left as you exit. There is a Tourist Information Office (tel. 0792/85–3792) to the right of the station's north exit.

The present structure of **Himejijo Castle** took eight years to build and was completed in 1609. Ieyasu Tokugawa had given his son-in-law the surrounding province as a reward for his victory at the Battle of Sekigahara, and this magnificent castle was built to isolate the Osaka *daimyo* (lord) from his friends in the Western provinces. So, the castle was built not only as a military stronghold but also as an expression of Tokugawa power.

The five-story, six-floor main donjon (stronghold) stands 102 feet high and is built into a 50-foot-high stone foundation. Surrounding this main donjon are three lesser donjons. All four donjons are connected by covered passageways. This area was the central compound of the castle complex. There were also other compounds to the south and west. Enemies would therefore have to scale the bluff, cross three moats, breach the outer

Western Honshu

KEY

— JR Trains

═ Shinkansen
   [Bullet Train]

—⊢ Private rail line

Sea of Japan

Miyazu Bay

Maizuru

Amanohashidate **25**

Kinosaki **24**

Kasumi **23**

Kyoto

Osaka

✈ Airport

Osaka Bay

Nishi-
Akashi

Himeji **1**

Kinokawa River

Wakayama

Tottori **22**

Chizu

Shodo
Island

Awaji
Island

Tokushima

Kurayoshi

Tsuyama

Asahi River

Okayama **2**

✈ Airport

Seto Ohashi Bridge

Takamatsu

Yoshino River

Mt. Daisen ▲

Niimi

Soja

Kurashiki **3**

Yonago

Yasugi

Matsue **20**

✈ Airport

Bingo-
Ochiai

Miyoshi

Fukuyama

Seto Inland Sea

Shikoku

Izumoshi

Taisha **21**

✈ Airport

JR SAN'IN MAIN LINE

Shikijiki

Hiroshima **5 – 16**
see detail map

Matsuyama

Gotsu

Gono River

4

Hamada

Tsuwano **19**

✈ Airport

Miyajima

17

Masuda

Susa

Yamaguchi

Nagato

Hagi **18**

Ogori

Toyota

Shimonoseki

Hohoku

N ↙

0 ——— 40 miles
0 ——— 60 km

compounds, and then be raked by fire from the four donjons. The castle existed not only to maintain military control over the Hyogo province but was also meant to impress. Note the aesthetic qualities of the donjon's dormerlike windows, cusped gables, and walls finished with white plaster, displaying a stark power that still inspires awe. From a distance, this white vision gives the effect of a silhouette of an egret, the bird that haunts the rice fields of the surrounding plains. *Admission:* ¥*500. Open 9–5 (grounds open to 6).*

The next stop along the Shinkansen Line is Okayama, a stop for garden lovers. (For anyone anxious to experience the Inland Sea, five ferries a day leave Himeji Port for Sado Island. The one-hour, 40-minute trip costs ¥1,170; however, there are shorter sea crossings to the island from Okayama.)

Okayama

❷ The three most famous gardens in Japan are Kenrokuen in Kanazawa, Kairakuen at Mito, and Korakuen at **Okayama.** Because Okayama is only 35 minutes down the Shinkansen Line from Himeji, and because you will need to change from the Shinkansen to a local train at Okayama in order to travel to Kurashiki, the next destination on our itinerary, it is convenient to visit the gardens and Okayama castle, which you can compare with the one at Himeji. If your time is limited, it is best to skip Okayama and go directly to Kurashika.

Exploring Should you need a map or information on the city, there is a **Tourist Information Office** (tel. 0862/22–2912; open 8:30–8) in the JR station. However, the layout of the city is easy to follow. Just hop on board the streetcar (fare: ¥150) bound for Higashiyama in front of the JR station and go directly north for 10 minutes. Get out at the **Orient Museum.** You'll recognize it by its imitation of Athens' Parthenon. If you have the time, you may want to go inside to see the 2,000 items of Asian art on display. It was one of the first museums in Japan to devote its collection to Asian art and has special exhibits showing how Middle Eastern art reached Japan via the Silk Route. *Admission:* ¥*300. Open 9–5.*

At the Orient Museum, the streetcar turns right. **Korakuen Garden,** however, is straight ahead on the other side of the Asahigawa River (about a 10-min. walk). If you do not want to visit the museum, you may choose to take a bus for ¥150 from Platform 2 in front of the station. This bus goes directly to Korakuen Garden.

Laid out three centuries ago on the banks of the Asahigawa River, Korakuen is a strollers' garden, with rustic tea arbors, extensive lawns, ponds, and artificial hills. The maple trees, apricot trees, and cherry trees give the 28-acre garden a seasonal contrast. Despite the garden's emphasis on the harmony of its elements, it is not astounding in its beauty (and it can get quite crowded). The garden is appreciated for its wide expanse of lawns, a rare commodity in Japan but less of a novelty to Westerners. What is attractive, though, is the garden's setting along the banks of the Asahigawa River, with the backdrop of Okayama Castle, which seems to float above the garden. *Admission:* ¥*300 from the vending machines outside the gate. Open 7:30–6; Oct.–Mar., 8–5.*

It takes less than five minutes to walk from the south exit of Korakuen Garden to **Okayamajo Castle.** Painted black, the four-story castle is known as Ujo (Black Crow), in contrast to Himeji's castle, the White Egret. Okayama's castle was first built in 1573, but, except for the turrets, it fell victim to the bombs of World War II. A ferro-concrete replica was constructed in 1966 and now houses objects of the region's history, including the usual collection of armor and swords. There is also, as behooves its modern construction, an elevator to take you between floors. *Admission: ¥250. Open 9–5.*

Aside from visiting Korakuen, the castle, and, perhaps, the Orient Museum, the other reason for disembarking from the Shinkansen at Okayama is to change to the local JR train for Kurashiki.

Kurashiki

3 **Kurashiki** is a town in which to savor old Japan. During feudal times, the town was the center for merchants shipping rice and cotton from its port to Osaka. No longer a granary or textile town, Kurashiki has become a living museum of the past, surviving on the income produced by some 4 million visitors a year. Miraculously, Kurashiki escaped war damage and the wrecker's ball that has so often preceded Japan's industrial growth.

Arriving and Departing
Commuter trains depart frequently from the Okayama JR station and take approximately 15 minutes to reach Kurashiki Station (not Shin-Kurashiki, where the Shinkansen trains stop). If you are coming directly from Tokyo, Kyoto, or Osaka, you may wish to stay on the Shinkansen until Shin-Kurashiki and take the local train back to the Kurashiki Station. There is a **Tourist Information Office** (tel. 0864/26–8681) opposite the entrance to the train platforms. The main tourist office (Bikan Historical Area, Kurashiki-kan, tel. 0864/22–0542) is located in the center of the old town. Both offices are open daily 9–5. If you telephone the day before, the main office can arrange for a volunteer guide to show you the city. The center of the old town is about 10 minutes on foot from the station and can be reached by walking down the main avenue extending perpendicular from the station; turn left at the street before the Kurashiki Kodusai Hotel.

Exploring
Though one can tour Kurashiki in half a day, the ideal way to enjoy this traditional town is to arrive in the late afternoon and stay the night in a ryokan. Being in Kurashiki on a Monday has an advantage and disadvantage. It is the day that most of the museums close, but for that reason, there are fewer visitors in town.

Amid the industrialized Sanyo coastal plains, Kurashiki is an oasis of the culture of traditional Japan. There are several museums to visit, but, in fact, all of the old town resembles a museum. The curving tiled roofs of the houses, the swaying willows lining the canal, and the stone half-circle bridges from which to watch the white swans float by transport the visitor back in time.

The major museum is the **Ohara Art Museum,** located in the old town. Magosaburo Ohara built this Greek pantheon-type building to house a collection of art that includes works by El Greco, including the Annunciation, Corot, Rodin, Gauguin, Picasso,

Toulouse-Lautrec, and many other Western artists. To counter this preponderance of Western art, an additional wing was constructed in 1961 to house modern Japanese paintings and, more recently, to display Japanese tapestries, wood-block prints, pottery, and antiques. *Admission: ¥800. Open 9–4:30. Closed Mon. and Dec. 28–Jan. 3. When Mon. falls on a public holiday, the museum stays open.*

More Western art, this time Greek and Roman sculpture, may be seen two minutes away at the **Kurashiki Ninagawa Museum** (Kurashiki Bijutsukan; admission ¥600; open 8:30–5). Around the corner from this museum (next to the tourist office) and of more interest to the foreign visitor is the **Kurashiki Folkcraft Museum** (Kurashiki Mingeikan). In four converted granaries, still with their white walls and black-tile roofs of the Edo period, are some 4,000 folk-craft objects ranging from ceramics to rugs and from wooden carvings to bamboo wares from all over the world. This museum is very low-key; the displays are dusty and not very well lit, and the descriptions of objects are in Japanese. Still, the experience of taking off your shoes and walking in slippers on the dark-wood floors puts these folk-craft objects into a context that makes them more real. *Admission: ¥500. Open 9–4. Closed Mon. and Dec. 28–Jan. 3. When Mon. falls on a public holiday, the museum stays open.*

Next door to the Folkcraft Museum is the **Japan Rural Toy Museum** (Nihon Kyodo Gangukan). This museum, one of the two top toy museums in Japan, is a pure delight. It exhibits some 5,000 toys from all regions of the country and has one room devoted to foreign toys. *Admission: ¥310. Open 8–5. Closed Jan. 1.*

Time Out Before leaving this cluster of museums, you may care to drop into the famous **El Greco** coffeehouse (next to the Ohara Art Museum). It has scrumptious ice cream, milk shakes, cakes, and other Western temptations.

All of these museums are clustered together on the north bank of the Kurashiki River. Now cross over the bridge, and in less than five minutes you will reach the **Ivy Square.** This ivy-covered complex used to be a weaving mill. With artful renovation, it now contains a hotel (appropriately named Ivy Hotel), several boutiques, a restaurant, and, in the central courtyard, a summer beer garden. The courtyard and beer garden are popular rendezvous in the early evening, when locals and tourists gather for refreshment. Be sure to browse through the shop that sells Japanese textiles, pottery, and other crafts.

Three museums can be found in the complex. The **Kurabo Memorial Hall** retells the history of spinning and textiles, an industry that, along with the shipping of rice and cotton, was Kurashiki's source of income. In many ways, it is a museum of Japan's industrial revolution, and it includes a video of the factory workshop floor with its scurrying seamstresses and of the dormitory that housed the unmarried female employees (admission: ¥300; open 9–5). The other two museums are the **Torajiro Kajima Memorial Museum,** which has Western and Asian art, and the **Ivy Gakkan,** which is an educational museum using reproductions to explain Western art to the Japanese. *Admission: ¥500 covers all 3 museums, though the only one of*

*any real interest is the Kurabo Memorial Hall. Open 8:30–5.
Closed Mon.*

For many of us, the real pleasure of Kurashiki is not the museums, but rather the ambience of the old town. Even the numerous tourists don't destroy it, but you should try to rise early in the morning to stroll through the old neighborhood and be captivated by the pink glow of the early-morning lights dancing off the buildings, the waterways crossed by arched bridges, and the whispers of the willows lining the streets.

The next stop down the Sanyo Line is Hiroshima, another world away, a world the 20th century first destroyed and then created. Savor Kurashiki while you can.

Hiroshima

❹ Hiroshima will forever be etched in man's conscience as the first place where a nuclear weapon was used to obliterate man. No visitor to the city can fail to be acutely aware of the event, which took place at 8:15 AM, August 6, 1945. On that morning, three B-29s flew toward Hiroshima; two planes were decoys, one flew directly over the city and cut loose a single bomb, codenamed Little Boy. In the center of the city, the bomb exploded at 1,900 feet above the Industrial Promotion Hall. Two hundred thousand people died, including 10,000 Korean prisoners forced to serve the Japanese empire as slave laborers. It was the only bomb to land on Hiroshima during World War II, and it wiped out half the city.

Only one telling reminder remains from the havoc and death that the atomic bomb wrought. Miraculously, the Industrial Promotion Hall did not completely collapse. Its charred structure remains untouched since that fated morning. It has been renamed the A-Bomb Dome and stands surrounded by the new Japan of ferro-concrete buildings.

Arriving and Departing

By Plane. Seven daily flights run between Hiroshima and Tokyo's Haneda airport, and there are flights to Kagoshima, on Kyushu, and Sapporo, on Hokkaido.

By Train. Hiroshima is the major town in Western Honshu and a major terminal for the JR Shinkansen trains; several Shinkansen trains end their run at Hiroshima rather than continue to Hakata on Kyushu. During the day, Shinkansen trains arrive and depart for Okayama, Osaka, Kyoto, and Tokyo approximately every 30 minutes and about every hour for Hakata, on Kyushu. From Tokyo train time is four hours and 37 minutes and, unless you have a Japan Rail Pass, the fare is ¥17,700. The Hiroshima train station also serves as the hub for JR express and local trains traveling along the Sanyo Line. Coming from Kurashiki, the train ride is only an hour if you take the local JR train to Shin-Kurashiki (2 stops) and transfer onto the Shinkansen rather than doubling back to Okayama. There are also two trains a day that link Hiroshima to Matsue on the northern (Sea of Japan Coast) shore of Western Honshu.

By Ferry. Hiroshima is serviced by many ferries. Two important ones are: to and from Matsuyama on Shikoku (16 hydrofoil ferries a day that take 1 hr. at ¥4,950 and 11 regular ferries a day that take 3 hrs. at ¥3,710 for 1st class and ¥1,850 for 2nd class); and to and from Beppu on Kyushu (departs Hiroshima at 10:30 PM to arrive at Beppu at 6 AM and departs Beppu at 4 PM to arrive at Hiroshima at 10 PM at ¥3,600 to ¥10,070.) *Contact the Setonaikai Kisen Co., 12–23, Ujinakaigan 1-chome, Minami-ku, Hiroshima city, tel. 082/255–3344, fax 082/22–4178.*

Getting Around   There are two **Tourist-Information offices** at JR Hiroshima Station: one at the south exit (tel. 082/261–1877), the exit for downtown, and one at the north exit (tel. 082/263–6822), the exit for the Shinkansen. Both provide free maps and brochures as well as help in securing accommodations. There is also the main office, Hiroshima City Tourist Information, in the Peace Memorial Park (tel. 082/247–6738).

The streetcar (tram) is the easiest form of transport in Hiroshima. Enter the tram from its middle door and take a ticket. Pay the driver at the front door when you leave. All fares within the city limits are ¥130. There are seven streetcar lines, and four of them either depart from Hiroshima Station or make it their terminus. Stops are announced by a tape recording, and each stop has its Romaji sign (spelled phonetically in English) posted on the platform. Buses also ply Hiroshima's streets; the basic fare is ¥170.

Taxis are available throughout the city. The initial fare for small taxis is ¥520 for the first mile (¥490 for larger taxis), then ¥70 for every 400 yards. There are also sightseeing taxis. For a three-hour tour, the charge is approximately ¥11,740. Because the taxi driver is not a guide, one may rent a taped recording describing the key sights in English. These special taxis depart from a special depot in front of the Hiroshima Station at the Shinkansen entrance. If you want to arrange for one of these taxis ahead of time, telephone the **Hiroshima Station Tourist Information Center** (tel. 082/261–1877).

Guided Tours   The Hiroshima International Relations has recently established a **Home Visit Program.** To make arrangements, go the day before to the International Center on the ground floor of the International Conference Center in Peace Memorial Park (1-5, Nakajima-cho, Naku-ku, Hiroshima 730, tel. 082/247–8007).

A number of sightseeing tours are available. These include tours of Hiroshima and cruises on the Inland Sea, in particular, to Miyajima Island. A three-hour, 20-minute tour (Japanese-speaking guide only) to the city's major sights costs ¥2,830. A seven-hour tour of both the city and Miyajima costs ¥5,220. These tours are operated by the **Hiroshima Bus Company** (tel. 082/261–7104) and depart from in front of the Hiroshima Station at the Shinkansen entrance.

The **Seto Nakai Kisen Company** (tel. 082/253–1212) operates several cruises on the Inland Sea. Its cruise boat, the *Southern Cross*, operates a 5½-hour trip (9:30–3:10) every Sunday, Monday, Friday, and Saturday, March–November, which includes visits to Etajima, Ondo-no-seto, Kure Bay, and Enoshima (cost: ¥11,250, includes lunch and soft drinks). For a shorter cruise, you can take the boat (10:10 and 12:20) to Miyajima (cost: ¥960 one way, ¥1,810 round-trip). There is also the Sunset Cruise, which leaves Hiroshima Bay at 6:45 PM and returns at 8:40 PM (cost: ¥2,600), with dinner on board as an optional extra, for a total of ¥9,056.

Exploring   *Numbers in the margin correspond to points of interest on the Hiroshima map.*

Entirely rebuilt after World War II, Hiroshima is a modern city. The atomic bomb is its living history. The monuments and ❺ the museum dedicated to "No More Hiroshimas" in the **Peace Memorial Park** are the key sights to visit. To reach the park from the station, take either streetcar #2 or #6 from the Hiroshima Station Plaza to the Genbaku-Domu-mae stop. On disem- ❻ barking from the streetcar, your first sight will be the **A-Bomb Dome.** It is a powerful and poignant symbol. The old Industrial Promotion Hall, with its half-shattered structure, stands in sharp contrast to the vitality and wealth of the new Hiroshima. The A-Bomb Dome is the only structural ruin of the war left erect in Hiroshima, and, for that, its impact is even stronger.

From the Genbaku-Domu-mae bus stop, walk onto Aichi Bridge, the double bridge that crosses the Otagawa (also called Honkawa) and Motoyasugawa rivers. In the middle of the ❼ bridge is the entrance to the Peace Memorial Park. The **Peace Memorial Museum** is at the far end of the park. En route are statues and monuments, but, because you'll probably be re- turning through the park, head straight for the museum, about a 10-minute walk from the bridge. If you require more tourist information, there is a city tourist-information center in the rest house located on the left-hand side of the park near anoth- er bridge crossing the Motoyasugawa River. A less dramatic approach from Hiroshima Station is to take the Hiroshima Bus Company's red-and-white bus #24 to Kokaido-mae, which is only a two-minute walk from the museum, or take streetcar #1 to Chuden-mae for a five-minute walk to the museum.

The Peace Memorial Museum is as disturbing as it is education- al. Through exhibits of models, charred fragments of clothing, melted tiles, and photographs of devastation and contorted bodies, the story of havoc and agonizing death unfolds. Noth- ing can capture the reality of 12,632°F (7,000°C), the surface heat of the atomic fireball, but the remains of the melted statue of Buddha or the imprinted human shadow on granite steps is enough to unnerve our confidence in man's future existence. Most of the exhibits have brief explanations in English. Howev- er, more detailed information is given on tape cassettes, which may be rented for ¥120. *Admission to the museum: ¥50. Open 9–6; Dec.–Apr., 9–5. Closed Dec. 29–Jan. 2.*

❽ On the east side of the museum is the **Peace Memorial Hall,** where documentaries on the effects of the atomic explosion are given in English. (Times are posted at the museum's entrance.) On the west side is the International Conference Center. In ❾ front of the museum on its north side is the **Memorial Cenotaph.** Designed by Japanese architect Kenzo Tange, the cenotaph re- sembles the primitive A-frame houses of Japan's earliest inhab- itants. Buried inside the vaults of the cenotaph is a chest containing the names of those who died in the holocaust. On the exterior of the cenotaph is the inscription (in Japanese), "Re- pose ye in Peace, for the error shall not be repeated." In front of ❿ the cenotaph, the **Peace Flame** burns. The flame will be extin- guished only when all atomic weapons in the world are ban- ished. In the meantime, every August 6, there is a solemn festival in which the citizens of Hiroshima float paper lanterns on the city's rivers for the repose of the souls of the atomic- bomb victims.

⓫ Before you leave the park, pause before the **Statue of the A- Bomb Children.** The figure is of a young girl who died of leuke-

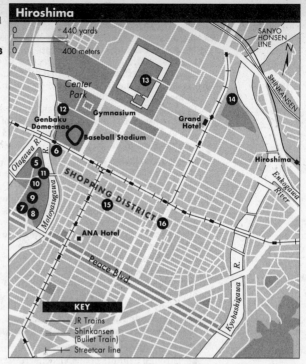

mia caused by the atomic radiation. Her will to live was strong. She believed that if she could fold 1,000 paper cranes (cranes are a symbol of good fortune and long life), her illness would be cured. She died after making her 954th crane.

The Peace Memorial Park is disquieting. It does not engender hope. However, if you cross the Aichi Bridge at the park's northern entrance and walk 200 yards north and east, keeping the river on your left and the baseball stadium where the Hiroshima Carps play on your right, there is the **Hiroshima Science and Cultural Center for Children**. Aside from being a wonderfully laid out hands-on museum, the joy and enthusiasm of the youngsters here dispels some of the depression that the Peace Memorial Park is bound to have caused. Next door is a planetarium, open at the same times as the museum. *Open 9–5. Closed Mon., and the day following public holidays. Admission: free to the Center; ¥410 to the planetarium.*

Ten minutes' walk farther north is the resurrected **Hiroshimajo Castle**. The city of Hiroshima received its name from the castle, Hiroshimajo (Broad Island Castle), when Mori Terumoto built it in 1589. The castle was a Japanese Army headquarters in World War II, and, as was the intent, the atomic bomb destroyed it. In 1958, the five-story donjon (stronghold) was rebuilt to its original specifications. Its interior has been used as a local museum, but since 1989, it has served as Hiroshima's historical museum, with exhibits from Japan's feudal period. *Admission to the castle grounds free; admission to the museum: ¥300. Open 9–6, Oct.–Mar. 9–5.*

BOO.

Sprint's WorldTraveler FŌNCARD. The easy way to call from around the world.

Imagine trying to place a call in another country: You have to deal with foreign currency. Alien operators. And phones that look like they're from another planet.

Talk about frightening.

Now imagine making the same call with a Sprint WorldTraveler FŌNCARD™:

To begin with, you'll reach an English-speaking operator just by dialing one easy, toll-free access code. An access code, by the way, that's right on your calling card.

Not only that, you won't have any trouble remembering your card number. Because it's based on your home phone number.

Now what could be easier than that? So call today and find out how you can get a WorldTraveler FŌNCARD.

Because we may not be able to do anything about the phones you'll have to call from. But at least it won't be a ghastly experience.

Sprint.
1·800·347·8989

All The Best Trips Start with **Fodors**

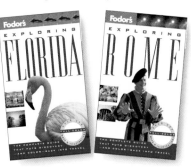

(14) The other place worth visiting in Hiroshima is **Shukkeien Garden.** Situated slightly to the east of the castle on the banks of the Kyobashigawa River, the garden was laid out in 1630 by Lord Nagaakira Asano in a design resembling that of a famed scenic lake in Hangzhou, China. The beauty of the garden stems from the streams and islets winding their way between the sculpted pine trees. Small bridges cross the streams, and, looking down into the waters, you will see exotic colored carp, so praised for their long lives. It is a fitting end for a visit to Hiroshima. You can return to the JR Station by taking Streetcar 9 to the end of the line and then transferring to Streetcar 1, 2, or 6. *Admission: ¥200. Open 9–6, Oct.–Mar. 9–5.*

If you like big cities and want an urban base to explore the Inland Sea, Hiroshima combines international and Japanese urban pleasures with 4,000 bars. In its central district, around (15) **Hondori,** there are the major department stores and masses of smaller shops. The major stores, Fukuya (closed Wed.), Tenmaya (closed Tues.), Mitsukoshi (closed Mon.), and Sogo (closed Thurs.), are open 10–6. Restaurants abound, and oysters are the specialty of the region, best washed down with sake, of which Hiroshima produces some of Japan's finest. There is, of course, a range of modern hotels from which to choose *(see* Dining and Lodging, *below)*, located in the city center to the east of the Peace Memorial Park and around the JR station. To the east of the Hondori Shopping District is (16) **Shintenchi,** an all-important entertainment district.

Miyajima

Numbers in the margin correspond to points of interest on the Western Honshu map.

The most enjoyable part of any visit to Hiroshima is the excur-(17) sion to **Miyajima.** The Japanese have what is known as the "Big Three Scenic Attractions." Matsushima, in Tohoku, is one, Amanohashidate, on the San'in coast, is another, and Miyajima, a small island in the Inland Sea, is the third. Miyajima also has the famous Itsukushima Jinja Shrine, built on wooden supports that extend the buildings into the sea; the shrine is known for its much-photographed torii gate rising out of the waters of the Inland Sea.

The island of Miyajima is only 19 miles in circumference, but its center peaks at 1,740 feet with Mt. Misen. With forested slopes on the mountain and the surrounding Inland Sea, it is a pretty, though touristy, village; Miyajima, with history and tradition everywhere, is delightful either as a day trip or for an overnight stay. Though the religious center of the island is Itsukushima Jinja Shrine, all of the island is sacred. You will note that there are no cemeteries on the island. No one is allowed to die here, or even to be born here. When either time comes, the concerned party must be taken over to the mainland.

Arriving and Departing To reach Miyajima, sightseeing boats leave from Hiroshima *(see* Guided Tours section for Hiroshima, *above)*. However, the easiest, least expensive way is to take the commuter train on the JR Sanyo Line from Hiroshima Station to Miyajima-guchi Station. The train takes about 25 minutes and departs from Hiroshima every 15–20 minutes. The first train departs from Hiroshima at 5:55 AM and, for the return, the last ferry leaves Miyajima at 9:20 PM. From Miyajima-guchi Station, it is a three-minute walk down to the shore and the pier from which the ferries scoot over to Miyajima island. There are two ferry boats. One belongs to JR, and your JR Rail Pass is valid on this boat only. The one-way cost for the train and ferry, without a JR Pass, is ¥560. There are also direct ferries from Hiroshima Ujina Port. They leave seven times a day and take 22 minutes to make the trip (cost: ¥1,250). Allow a minimum of three hours to cover the major sights of Miyajima. More time is needed if you go inland up to the park.

Exploring   From Miyajima's pier, follow the coast to the right (west). This leads to the village, which is crowded with restaurants, hotels, and souvenir shops selling, for the most part, the tackiest of objects to Japanese tourists. At the far end of the village is the park which leads past the **Torii Gate** and on to the **Itsukushima Jinja Shrine.** Expect to be greeted by deer as you walk through the park. The deer are protected, and they take full advantage of their status, demanding edibles and nudging you if you are not forthcoming.

The Torii Gate is located 500 feet from the shore, at an entrance to the cove in which the shrine stands. The gate is huge, rising 53 feet out of the water, making it one of the tallest in Japan. It was built in 1875 and has become a symbol not only of Miyajima but also of Japan. Especially as the sun sets over the Inland Sea, the vermilion structure and its reflection in the rippling water is an unforgetable sight. Past the torii stands the shrine. Poets write of how the shrine's building seems to float on the water. They omit that it "floats" only at high tide. At other times, the shrine stands on wooden stilts above the mud flats.

Itsukushima Jinja Shrine was created in 593 and dedicated to the three daughters of Susano-o-no-Mikoto, the Shinto god of the moon and the oceans. The structure has had to be continually repaired and rebuilt, and the present structure is thought to be a 16th-century copy of the 12th-century buildings. Most of the shrine is closed to the public, but you can walk around its deck, which gives some idea of the size of the building complex as well as a clear view of the Torii Gate. *Admission: ¥300 (or a combined ticket with the Treasure House for ¥500). Open 6:30–6 (6:30–5 in winter).*

Located across from the shrine's exit is the **Treasure House** (Home Tsu-kan). Because every victor of battles that took place on the Inland Sea saw fit to offer their gratitude to the gods by giving gifts to Itsukushima Jinja Shrine, the Treasure House is rich with art objects, 246 of which have been designated as either National Treasures or Important Cultural Properties. *Admission: ¥300 (or a combined ticket with Itsukushima Jinja for ¥500). Open 9–5.*

Adding to this uniquely Japanese scene of the floating Torii Gate and shrine are the **Five-Story Pagoda** and **Senjokaku Hall.** Senjokaku Hall (Hall of One Thousand Mats) was dedicated by Hideyoshi Toyotomi in 1587 and has rice scoops attached to the walls, symbols of the soldiers who died fighting for Japan's expansionism. The Five-Story Pagoda *(Goju-no-to)* dates from 1407. Both are situated on top of a small hill overlooking the shrine. If you climb up the steps to these two buildings for a closer look, a small street on the other side (away from the shrine) serves as a short cut back to the village.

Though many visitors spend only a half a day on the island, those with more time to enjoy its beauty may enter **Momi-jidani-Koen Park,** inland from the shrine. Here in the park is the start of the mile-long gondola that takes you virtually up to the summit of **Mt. Misen.** A short hike at the end of the gondola takes you to the very top. It's worth it; the views of the Inland Sea and Hiroshima beyond are splendid. You may choose to walk back down. *Cost: ¥900 one way, ¥1,500 round trip.*

Miyajima has become a vacation spot for Japanese families; hence, there are many hotels and ryokan in and around the village. One of these ryokan is worth remembering. It is the famous **Iwaso Ryokan** (tel. 08294/4–2233), which has been a host to pilgrims and vacationers for 130 years. Even if you are not staying in town overnight, Iwaso makes an ideal spot for lunch (*see* Dining and Lodging, *below*). Also, be aware that the most exciting, and the most crowded, time to visit Miyajima is in June (lunar calendar) for the annual Kangen-sai Festival, when three stately barges bearing a portable shrine, priests, and musicians cross the bay, flanked by a squadron of festooned boats.

Once back at Hiroshima, the westbound Shinkansen heads for Shimonoseki an hour away, before crossing to Kyushu and terminating in Hakata. Instead of crossing over to Kyushu with the Shinkansen, this itinerary does practically a 180-degree turn to travel east along Western Honshu's northern region, the San'in.

The San'in Region

San'in officially stretches along Western Honshu from Shimo-noseki all the way to Kyoto. However, the special atmosphere of San'in ends on the Sea of Japan coast at Maizuru, just inside the border of Kyoto Prefecture. San'in means "In the Shadow of the Mountains." Whereas the coastline that faces the Inland Sea has the direct light of the sun, San'in has a misty, eerie light that diffuses to cause an ever-changing mood of flirting shadows. Also, San'in has been in the shadow of Japan's economic miracle. The presence of the mountains makes transport expensive between the north and south coasts and has staved off the pollution of sprawling factories and the modern urbanization that have destroyed so much of the Sanyo coast. The influx of tourists, both Japanese and foreigners, has also been less; San'in is off the beaten track, which adds to its appeal.

San'in is different from Sanyo in its lifestyle. Life moves slower. Trains and buses are less frequent. There is an austerity in the architecture, the crafts, and in the attitude of the people, a reflection of the cold winters and the isolation from mainstream Japan. An example of their art may help explain this. To the San'in people, a chipped tea bowl has more aesthetic appeal than the perfected symmetry used by Kyoto's craftspeople. San'in potters will create a crack in a bowl and artfully glaze it. The result is inspiring. The imagination must make the leap to what ultimate perfection could be. This is San'in—inspiring, restrained, forever conceiving perfection but never harnessing it.

Getting Around

By Train Along the Sea of Japan coast, the JR San'in Main Line runs from Shimonoseki to Kyoto. The line is the second longest in Japan, 422 miles, and has the most stations of any line, which means lots of stops and longer traveling times. In addition, the trains are less frequent. Only two limited express trains a day cover the Shimonoseki–Kyoto route in either direction. There are, however, local trains that go back and forth between the major cities along the San'in coast.

At several points along the San'in coast are routes through the mountains to cities on the Inland Sea. A few of the major connecting routes are:

Between Hagi and Ogori: one hour, 30 minutes on the JR or Bocho bus lines. It is advisable to make seat reservations for these buses at JR train stations' seat reservation counters. Despite what some JR booking offices say, the JR bus is covered by the JR Pass.

Between Tsuwano and Ogori: one hour on the JR Yamaguchi Line.

Between Masuda and Ogori: two hours on the JR Yamaguchi Line.

Between Yonago and Okayama: three hours on the JR Hakubi Line.

Between Matsue and Hiroshima: five hours on the JR Geibi and Kitsugi Line (one train a day, departing from Hiroshima at 8:45 AM).

Between Matsue and Okayama: two hours and 25 minutes on the JR Yakumo Limited Express (four Limited Express and five local trains a day). From Kyoto, the train takes six hours. There are also two night trains from Tokyo to Matsue; the trip takes 13 hours.

Unless you do not mind waiting around stations or being stranded overnight, before you set out to explore the San'in, ask any information office at a JR station to list the current times of the trains arriving and departing from the major towns along the San'in. Trains run so infrequently that you will need to plan your time to fit their schedule, unlike many other regions in Japan, where it rarely matters if you miss one train.

Indeed, there are not many trains that set out each day from Shimonoseki to **Hagi,** so plan ahead. The limited express takes two hours; the local takes four hours. Try not to find yourself stranded in Shimonoseki overnight. Shimonoseki is an industrial port town from which ferries leave for various ports on Kyushu, the Inland Sea, and Pusan, across the Sea of Japan in Korea. Even the first hour on the JR train heading for Hagi shows landscape built up with man's factories, but gradually the scenery becomes more natural, and the views of the coastline start setting the tone of San'in and its first major city, Hagi.

Hagi

Although the castle was dismantled in 1874 as a relic of feudalism, **Hagi** retains the atmosphere of a traditional castle town.

Hagi is rich with history, one that is closely linked to the Mori family. Even though the Mori family had opposed the Tokugawa Shogunate and were defeated by Ieyasu Tokugawa in 1600 at the Battle of Sekigahara, the Mori were able to keep their fiefdom for 13 generations. The Tokugawa Shogunate had tried to isolate the Mori as much as possible, but in so doing, the Mori, who had never forgotten their defeat, became the forerunners of the movement to restore power to the emperor. It was the army from Hagi and the surrounding Nagato Province that, on the second attempt, captured Kyoto and turned the tide against the shogunate. Hagi's fame lies not simply in defeating the shogunate but also in supplying the intellectual ideas for the new Japan. Indeed, Japan's first prime minister, Hirobumi Ito (1841–1909), was born and educated in Hagi.

Hagi, too, has another claim to fame: Hagi-yaki. This pottery has been cherished for 375 years for its subtle pastel colors and its milky, translucent glazes. Mind you, the tradition of Hagi-yaki has less than noble beginnings. Returning from Japan's aborted attempt to invade Korea in the late 16th century, a Mori general brought home two Korean potters as "souvenirs." With techniques that were probably used during the Silla Kingdom, these Korean brothers, Yi Sukkweng and Yi Kyung, created Hagi-yaki for their masters. Hagi-yaki has since become second to Raku-yaki as the most praised pottery in Japan. Unfortunately, the two most famous kilns, Rikei's Saka Kiln and Miwa Kiln, do not accept visitors, but several others do. Shizuki Kiln is one; it is conveniently located on the way to the castle grounds.

Arriving and Departing Though the second part of this chapter's itinerary begins at Hagi as if we were coming from Kyushu or Shimonoseki, it is possible to cross over the mountains from the Inland Sea town of Ogori, served by the Hiroshima-Hakata Shinkansen, to Tsuwano by train, and then to Hagi by bus; or you may travel directly to Hagi from Ogori by JR bus, which is the quicker way. Without a JR Pass, the one-way fare is about ¥2,000.

Hagi is surrounded by mountains on three sides and by the Sea of Japan on the fourth. The actual city of Hagi is in the V formed by two rivers, the Matsumotogawa on the east side and the Hashimotogawa on the west side. The major train station for entering the city is Higashi-Hagi (not Hagi), on the eastern side of town. For tourist information at the station try **Hagi Ryokan Kyodo-kumiagi** (tel. 0838/22–7599, fax 0838/22–7517), whose main business is booking accommodations but whose English-speaking owner, Mr. Oki, serves as a helpful adviser to tourists and dispenses official guide maps. The agency is located in the Rainbow Building (the Hotel Royal is at the far right) to the left of the station, in the first office on the left side of the shopping arcade. The **city tourist office** is downtown (tel. 0838/25–3131 and 0838/25–1750).

Getting Around The ideal way to explore Hagi is by bicycle, and there are many outlets where bikes can be rented for approximately ¥1,000. Try the bicycle shop across from the Rainbow Building, left of the station plaza. Alternatively, one can hire a "sightseeing taxi" for about ¥3,900 per hour; it takes about three hours to complete a hurried city tour.

A four-hour sightseeing bus tour (Japanese-speaking guides only) operated by the **Bocho Bus Company** departs from the

Bocho Bus Station, located on the eastern edge of the central city (cost: ¥2,760, plus ¥1,200 for lunch.).

Exploring To get to the Hagi downtown area from the Higashi-Hagi Station, cross the bridge over the Matsumoto River and, bearing right, continue on the street until you reach the Hagi Grand Hotel. Then, take a left, and six blocks up on the right-hand side is the beginning of **Tamachi Mall.** Just on the corner is the **Ishii Chawan Museum.** This small, second-floor museum has a rare collection of antique tea bowls produced in Hagi, including some by the Korean potter whose creations first captured the attention of the Japanese. Also in this prized collection are Korean tea bowls made during the Koryo Dynasty (916–1392). For afficionados this museum is a pleasure, but if you are short of time you may want to skip this to be sure of visiting the Kumaya Art Museum (*see below*). *Admission: ¥350. Open daily 9–5. Closed Dec.–Mar.*

Tamachi Mall is the busiest street in Hagi, with a complement of some 130 shops offering both the latest fashions from Tokyo and the more interesting local products from Yamaguchi Prefecture. You may well wish to return to purchase Hagi-yaki after touring the sights and one of the kilns where the pottery is made. Two stores worth noting are Harada Chojuan and Miwa Seigado. The latter is at the top end of Tamachi, past the San Marco restaurant. Another gallery and store is Saito-an, in which both the masters and "unknown" potters display their works for sale. If you search through the wares, you may be able to find a small sake cup for less than ¥500, or, if you have your gold credit card ready, you may choose a tea bowl by such living master potters as Miwa Kyusetsu for ¥250,000.

At the top of Tamachi Mall, a right turn toward Hagi Bay will lead you through the Teramachi section of town. Numerous temples here cry out for someone to pay heed to them. The locals just take them for granted. Each one of these temples has something to offer and all have a tranquillity rarely transgressed by tourists. There are about 10 from which to choose and explore, from the old wooden temple of **Hofukuji,** with its bibbed Jizo statues, to **Kaichoji,** with its two-story gate and veranda around the Main Hall's second floor.

Instead of walking all the way to Hagi Bay, take a left after the Kaichoji Temple. This street will lead to the **Kumaya Art Museum.** It will be on the left-hand side—look for a big metal gate. The complex was once the home of a wealthy merchant, and the warehouse has been made into a museum, which houses art objects and antiques. Of special note are the scrolls, paintings, a screen of the Kano school, and a collection of ceramics, which includes some of the first Hagi-yaki produced. *Admission: ¥500. Open daily 9–5.*

From the Kumaya Art Museum, take the next left (south and away from the sea) to visit the **Kikuya House.** This was once the home of the chief merchant family to the Mori clan. Though the Kikuya were only merchants, they held a special relationship with the Mori. (After the Mori defeat at Sekigahara, the Kikuya family sent their daimyo money to return to Hagi.) As a result, this house has more extravagance than merchants were normally allowed to display. *Keyaki* (Japanese cypress) was, for example, forbidden to merchants, yet notice its extensive use in this home. This is not your typical family home during the Edo period, but it does indicate the good life of the few. *Admission: ¥370. Open daily 9–5.*

The next stop is **Shizuki-Koen Park,** where the Hagijo Castle once stood and the castle remains are now located. Head west from Kikuya past the NHK broadcasting building, and keep the Sosuien Park on your left. After the next major cross street on the left, you will find the **Shizuki Kiln.** You may want to stop in here and browse over its Hagi-yaki pottery and, if the wallet can bear it, purchase some of the magnificent work. Also, most of the time, you will be welcome to enter the adjoining building where the kilns are fired.

At the next major intersection after Shizuki Kiln, take a left and walk or bicycle along the street between the **Toida Masuda House Walls.** These are the longest mud walls of the Horiuchi samurai section of town, and, for a moment, one is thrust back into feudal times. Follow the walls around and head west to the grand wooden **Fukuhara Gate.** A right turn here leads directly to the **Tomb of Tenjuin,** a memorial to Terumoto Mori, who founded the clan giving rise to 13 generations of Mori rule.

At the memorial, take a left turn and head toward the park grounds. On the left, past the Shizuki Youth Hostel, is the **Mori House,** a long (170 ft.) and wide (17 ft.) building that was once the home to the samurai foot soldiers. *Admission: ¥200. Open daily 8–6:30 (8–4:30 in winter). Admission to the Mori House also covers entrance to Shizuki-Koen Park and the castle grounds.*

The entrance to Shizuki-Koen Park is opposite the Mori House. On the way to the castle you will pass two pottery kilns, **Shogetsu Kiln** and **Hagijo Kiln,** both of which offer the opportunity for browsing, watching the potters at work, and, of course, purchasing the products. Once inside the actual castle grounds, there is the **Shizukiyama Jinja Shrine,** built as recently as 1879; the wood used has weathered to give the shrine a comfortable, reassuring presence. Beyond the shrine is a highly recommended place to visit, the **Hananoe Tea House.** Set in delightful gardens, this thatch teahouse exudes peace and tranquillity. The attendants will make tea for you while you savor the quiet of the gardens. *Admission free, but the tea is ¥400.*

The actual Hagijo Castle is no more. Its demise, though, was unusual. Neither warfare nor fire destroyed it. Instead, the castle was dismantled as a gesture of support for the Meiji Restoration. Also, with the arrival of Western gunboats 15 years before the Meiji Restoration, the castle became vulnerable to attack.

In fact, the Mori family had moved from the castle in 1863 to create a new home and provincial capital at landlocked Yamaguchi. All that remains of the castle are its high walls and wide moats. (It will cost you ¥200 to inspect these ruins.) But the pleasure of Shizuki-Koen Park is its space and setting.

The castle walls and moat are a few steps beyond the Hananoe Tea House. From the top of the walls, there is a panoramic view of Hagi, the bay, and the surrounding mountains inland. However, the best panoramic view is from **Mt. Shizuki,** which rises 470 feet behind the castle. It takes about 20 minutes to hike up the path to the top. On one side of Mt. Shizuki there is a new amusement park (admission: ¥1,000; open: 9 AM–10 PM) that attracts Japanese families but, has little to offer the foreign visitor, except for a monorail that climbs up Mt. Shizuki.

On the way back down Mt. Shizuki, you may want to stop at the **Hagi Shiryokan,** the local history museum. (Admission: ¥300; open 9–5, in winter 9–4.) If your time is limited, forgo a visit to the museum and leave the park to head for Dashoin Temple. It is a lengthy hike, so unless you have a bicycle, in which case it is about a 20-minute pedal, a taxi is advised. To reach the Dashoin, cross over the canal that marks the boundary of Shizuki-Koen Park and follow it south to the Tokiwabashi Bridge. Once over the Hashimotogawa River, take the main road that follows the river upstream. Dashoin Temple is on the right, on the other side of the JR San'in Main Line tracks.

Dashoin Temple is the counterpart to the more frequented Tokoji Temple (covered later). Screened by the surrounding mountains, Dashoin is the final resting place for half of the Mori family. The first two Mori generations are buried at Dashoin. The third generation is buried at Tokoji Temple. Thereafter, even-numbered generations of the Mori generations are buried at Dashoin, and odd-numbered generations are buried at Tokoji. What is unusual about both Dashoin and Tokoji are the lanterns and the placement of the daimyo's wife next to her husband's tomb. Such a close affiliation, or recognition of the wife, in death was not the custom in feudal Japan. The lanterns tell another story.

When Hidehari Mori, the first Mori daimyo to be buried at Dashoin, died, seven of his principal retainers followed, dutifully committing ritual suicide. Extending this custom further, one of the retainers to one of the daimyo's retainers also killed himself. The eight graves are lined up in a row of descending rank. The Tokugawa Shogunate realized that this custom could decimate the aristocracy and decreed that such ritual suicide upon the death of one's lord was illegal. Future generations of retainers gave up their suicidal rights and, instead, donated lanterns. The path leading to the main hall of Dashoin Temple is lined with 603 lanterns. The temple is a special place to visit at any time, but in May the temple grounds burst into a purple haze with the wisteria in full bloom. Another special time to visit is on August 13, when all the lanterns are lit. *Admission: ¥100. Open daily 9–4:30.*

Dashoin Temple is in the southern outskirts of Hagi. We need now to move to the eastern sector of town, the same sector as Higashi-Hagi JR Station. If you are without a bicycle, then walk five minutes to the east of Dashoin Temple, catch the train at Hagi Station to Higashi-Hagi Station, and walk south to Matsumotobashi Bridge. If you are on a bicycle, return to Hashimotogawa River, follow it upstream to Hashimotobashi Bridge, and head into central Hagi. At the Bocho Bus Center, go right and cross over Matsumotobashi Bridge.

Directly east of Matsumotobashi Bridge, the road leads to **Tokoji Temple,** the other cemetery of the Mori family. The temple was founded by the Zen priest Domio in 1691 under the auspicies of Yoshinari Mori, the third lord of Hagi. It is here that he (and every succeeding odd-numbered generation of the Mori family) is buried. You enter the temple grounds through the three-story Sanmon Gate to reach the Main Hall, which contains rather garish images of Buddha. Behind this building are the monuments of the Mori lords and their wives. Needless to say, it is easy to point to the husbands' graves. They are the grandest of all. Surrounding the monuments, amid the pine trees, are 500 lanterns donated by the lords' retainers. On August 15, all of these lanterns are lit: an impressive sight, indeed. *Admission: ¥100. Open daily 8:30–5:30.*

Instead of returning directly to the Matsumotogawa River, keep to the left as you leave the shrine and after a steep climb, you'll reach the **Monument to Shoin Yoshida** (1830–1859). Yoshida was a revolutionary. With the coming of Commodore Perry's Black Ships in 1853, Shoin recognized the need for Japan to step out of feudalism and accept certain Western practices. In his quest to understand the West, he attempted to slip aboard an American ship. He was caught by the shogunate, imprisoned, and later sent home to Hagi to be kept under house arrest. During his arrest, he started expounding a liberal philosophy that suggested both adapting to Western practices and introducing democratic elements into government. In the eyes of the shogunate, these preachings were outright sedition. At age 29, Shoin was executed. His execution inflamed and united the antishogunate elements of Hagi and the Namoto Province (now Yamaguchi Prefecture).

Coming down the hill from Yoshida's monument, take a left turn and you will pass the house of one of Shoin's students, Hirobumi Ito, the first prime minister of Japan. Across the street from the **Ito House** is the **Shoin Jinja Shrine,** with the Shoka-Sonjuku, the private school that Shoin founded to teach his students his revolutionary philosophy. At the shrine's exit, there is a museum, which recounts Shoin's life depicted in three-dimensional scenes with model figures. There are, however, no English explanations of their meaning. *Admission: ¥550. Open daily 8:30–5.*

From the Shoin Jinja Shrine, you can cross the Matsumotobashi Bridge and go straight to Tamachi Mall, or take a right before the bridge and return to the JR Higashi-Hagi Station to journey onward through San'in. The next stop in San'in is Tsuwano, situated inland and nestled in the mountains. En route between Hagi and Masuda is the small fishing village of **Susa.** Besides being located on an attractive bay, few foreigners ever come here, and it has one of Japan's best minshukus (*see* Lodging, *below*). Some might want to stay overnight here rather than at Hagi.

Tsuwano

19 The castle town of **Tsuwano** is a much smaller town than Hagi; because of that, it has an intimate atmosphere. One can quickly feel part of the town and its 700-year history. Indeed, Tsuwano is occasionally referred to as a "little Kyoto" for its genteel qualities, and, like Kyoto, it has a river flowing through town. However, aside from these similarities, Tsuwano is not Kyoto. Tsuwano is a mountain town, small and compact.

Arriving and Departing To reach Tsuwano, you can take the JR train on the San'in Main Line to Masuda, where you must change trains for a 30-minute run up to Tsuwano. You can also take a bus from Hagi's Bocho Bus Center directly to Tsuwano, a trip that takes two hours (fare: ¥1,550). To reach Tsuwano directly from Ogori take the

JR train, which takes one hour. Ogori is 40 minutes on the Shinkansen from Hiroshima.

Getting Around All the sights are within easy walking distance, or one can rent a bicycle (cost: ¥800 for 3 hours, ¥1,050 for a full day). A taxi may also be used at ¥3,950 an hour; it takes about two to three hours to visit the sights. There is a **Tourist Information Office** (tel. 08567/2–1144) at the railway station that has free brochures and will help in securing accommodations.

Exploring Except for the stone walls, nothing is left of the mountaintop castle, but Tsuwano's other attraction, the multicolored carp that fill the waters of the Tsuwanogawa River and the water-filled ditches, is still much in evidence. Indeed, the carp outnumber Tsuwano's residents by 10 to 1. Carp were originally introduced into the river and sewers as a ready source of food should the town ever be under siege. There was no siege, and because the carp live about 60 years, they have had a rather privileged existence. Life is still good for them. If you make your way from the JR station to Tonomachi Street (a 5-min. walk), you can feed these exotic-colored fellows (swimming in the man-made ditches along the street) with "carp snacks" bought at the coffee shop across from the **Catholic Church.** (Gourmands may like to dine on carp at the Yuki Restaurant on Honcho-dori Ave., close to the post office.)

The Catholic Church, though built in 1931, is a reminder of the time when Christianity was outlawed in Japan. In 1865, in an effort to disperse Christian strongholds and cause them extreme hardship, in the hope that they would recant their faith, the Tokugawa Shogunate transported 153 Christians from Nagasaki to Tsuwano. By the time the Meiji government lifted the ban on Christianity, 53 Christians remained in Tsuwano. Thirty-six had been martyred, and the remainder had either recanted or died of natural causes. It's worth stopping at the church: Where but in Japan can one find a Catholic church with floors covered with tatami matting?

A few steps farther up Tonomachi Street, on the left-hand side, is the **Yorakan Museum.** The building was originally a feudal school where the sons of samurai would train in the arts of manhood. Today, in its fencing hall, there is a folk-craft museum. *Admission: ¥150. Open daily 8:30–5:30.*

At the top of Tonomachi Street, the road crosses the Tsuwanogawa River at the Ohashi Bridge. Just on the other side is the **Kyodokan Museum,** with a collection of exhibits that recounts regional history. *Admission: ¥400. Open daily 8:30–5.*

However, you may want to save the time and, instead of crossing the bridge, fork to the right under the *torii* gate, cross the railway tracks of the JR Yamaguchi Line, and follow the river for approximately 250 yards. Indicative of the million visitors who make the pilgrimage each year, the number of souvenir stands and teahouses increases until you reach the **Yasaka Shrine,** where, every July 20 and July 27, the festival of the Heron Dance is held. Behind this shrine is the stepway to the **Taikodani-Inari Jinja Shrine.** The approach resembles a tunnel, because one passes under numerous red torii gates—1,174 of them—to reach the shrine high on the cliffside. (Nowadays, the weak of spirit may reach the shrine by bus along another road.)

From the shrine, you can either hike a hard 20 minutes up to the site of **Tsuwanojo Castle** or take the road down the other side of the shrine to the chair lift, which takes five minutes to reach the base of the castle grounds. To ascend the summit from the top of the chair lift requires a further eight-minute walk. Whichever way you make it to the top, it is worth every effort. The view from where this mountaintop castle once stood sweeps over the tile-roof town of Tsuwano and the valley below. What a marvelous castle it must have been! The original castle was built in the 13th century and took 30 years to build. Its demise took a lot less. Like Hagijo Castle, as a sign of good faith, this castle was dismantled during the Meiji Restoration.

You can walk back down from the castle grounds to the main street or use the chair lift. Because the views from the chair lift are so superb, you may prefer the latter. At the bottom of the chair lift, turn left and then right to cross over the Tsu-wanogawa River. Immediately on crossing the river, take the right-hand street and follow it around to the left, where you will pass by the **Old House of Ogai Mori.** Ogai Mori (1862–1922) was one of the prominent literary figures in the Meiji Restoration. He spent only his first 11 years in Tsuwano (he went to the Yorokan school), but his hometown never forgot him, nor he his hometown. His success as a doctor caused him to travel overseas, and, in so doing, he tried to reconcile the differences between Western and Japanese cultures. His tomb is at the **Yomeiji Temple,** located to the east of Tsuwano's JR station. *Admission to the temple: ¥300. Open daily 8:30–5.*

Next door to the Mori House is **Sekishukan,** a museum displaying Japanese handmade paper *(washi).* Demonstrations of paper-making are given, and there is a display of the Iwami-style paper. On the second floor, there are displays of washi made from other regions of Japan. If you have not seen the process of making handmade paper or wish to compare different regional types, this is a good museum to visit. *Admission free. Open daily 9–5.*

From this museum, continue along the street until the main road and take a left. This will lead you back to town over the Ohashi Bridge. If there is time before your train, and you did not see the exhibition of papermaking at Sekishukan, in front of the station is the **Tsuwano Industry Museum.** Demonstrations are given of the town's traditional industries, and most of the space is given to the craft of papermaking. There is also a section on sake brewing if you have not had the opportunity to witness it before (admission: ¥100; open 8:30–5). Also, five minutes to the east of the JR station and up the hill through the Pass of the Virgin is **St. Maria's Church.** The church was built in 1951 to commemorate the Christian martyrs, and their plight is portrayed in the stained-glass windows. The Pass of the Virgin (in Japanese, Otometoge) is the site of the graveyard where 36 martyrs have their crosses.

The next stop going east along the San'in coast is Matsue, a three-hour, 30-minute ride on the JR limited express. However, you may want to break your journey an hour before Matsue and visit the Izuno Taisha Shrine. If so, disembark from the train at Izumoshi (*see* Izuno Taisha Shrine, *below*).

Matsue

⓴ Of all the towns in the San'in district, the city of **Matsue** is the most well-known as a summer vacation destination. Like the rest of San'in, though, Matsue sees few foreigners, yet it is rich in beauty and heritage. Only scattered archaeological remains exist from the days when the people of "The Eightfold-Towering-Thunderhead Land of Izumo" lived here in the 2nd and 3rd centuries, and only ruins have been left behind of Matsue's early days, when the town became the capital of the Izumo in the 8th century. However, many of today's existing shrines originate from that time, and the more recent past is still visible. Matsue is the only town along the San'in coast with part of its castle intact. In fact, Matsue's castle is one of the dozen castles in Japan that are originals and not ferro-concrete replicas.

Matsue's location is unique. The city is situated inland from the Sea of Japan at the conjunction of two small lagoons. Known as the City of Water, Matsue lies at a point where Nakaumi Lagoon, to the east, connects with Lake Shinji, to the west. This makes Matsue a gourmet heaven, with not only fresh fish taken from the cold waters of the Japan Sea but also the seven delicacies—eel, shrimp, shellfish, carp, sea bass, pond smelt, and whitebait—from Lake Shinji. The narrow isthmus between the Nakaumi Lagoon and Lake Shinji divides the city. However, except for the JR station and the bus terminal, most of Matsue's points of interest are on the northern side of the isthmus.

Getting Around An added delight of Matsue is that even though its population is 140,000, most of its sights are within walking distance of each other; when they are not, Matsue has a comprehensive bus system. For those who would like to be accompanied on their tour of Matsue, the city has a Goodwill Guide Program, which offers an English-speaking volunteer to show you around the city and also escort you to Izumo Taisha Shrine. There is no charge for this, though you should pay your guide's expenses, including lunch. To arrange for a Goodwill Guide, contact the **Matsue Tourist Information Office**, Asahi Machi, Matsue (tel. 0852/27–2598), a day in advance. The office is located in the JR Matsue Station and is open 9:30–6. You can also use this office to collect free maps and brochures.

Exploring The first place to head for is **Matsuejo Castle** and its environs, located diagonally across town from the JR station. Take the bus (cost: ¥170) to Kencho-mae from either stop #1 or stop #2, both located in front of the JR station. (The same buses continue on to Matsue Onsen, should you want to go there first to check into a hotel.) It is about a 10-minute ride, and the Kencho-mae stop is near the Prefectural Government Office. When you leave the bus, walk a little farther to the north; the castle, located in Jozen-Koen Park, is on the left.

Made entirely out of pine, Matsuejo Castle was built in 1611, and, with a partial reconstruction in 1642, it was never ransacked or burned during the Tokugawa Shogunate. Amazingly, soon after the Meiji Restoration, the castle was put on the auction block. Sentimental locals, whose ancestors had been living under its shadow for 345 years, pooled their resources and purchased the castle for posterity.

Built by Yoshiharu Horio, the castle was built for protection. The donjon is, incidentally, the tallest (98 ft.) left in Japan. Camouflaged among the surrounding trees, the castle seems to move with the shadows of San'in's opaque light. Note the overhanging leaves above the top floor, designed to cut down any glare that may prevent the spotting of an attacking force. Inside, the five-story facade contains six levels; the lower floors now exhibit a collection of samurai swords and armor. It is a climb to the uppermost floor, but it is worth it—the view commands the city, Lake Shinji, and the distant mountains. *Admission: ¥400. Open daily 8:30–5.*

In a Western-style building close to the castle is the **Matsue Kyodo-kan** (Matsue Cultural Museum), which displays arts, folk crafts, and implements, including such items as *bento* (box lunch) boxes and hairpins, used during the first three eras after the fall of the Tokugawa Shogunate. *Admission: ¥200. Open daily 8:30–5.*

If you walk out of Jozen-Koen Park at its east exit and follow the moat going north, at the top of the park will be a road leading to the right. A little way up this road, no more than a five-minute walk, is the **Meimei-an Tea House.** Lord Fumai Matsudaira of the Matsue clan built this teahouse in 1779, and it is one of the best preserved teahouses of the period. You must walk up a long flight of stairs to this thatch-roof teahouse, but your effort will be rewarded by both a fine view of Matsuejo Castle and, if you request, tea. *Admission: ¥200; ¥300 for green tea. Open daily 9–5.*

If you return down the side street on which Meimei-an is located to the main road, and take a right (keeping the castle moat on your left), you will reach four historical sights next door to each other. The first is **Buke Yashiki,** a samurai house built in 1730. Samurai at this time lived fairly well, depending on their rank. This house belonged to the Shiomi family, a chief retainer to the daimyo, and you'll notice the separate servant quarters, a shed for the palanquin, and the slats in the walls to allow the cooling breezes to flow through the rooms. *Admission: ¥250. Open daily 8:30–5.*

Next door to the Buke Yashiki is the **Tanabe Art Museum,** dedicated mainly to objects of the tea ceremony and ceramics from the region. The museum also exhibits works of wood-block prints by local artists. *Admission: ¥500 (though it varies according to the exhibition). Open daily 9–4:30. Closed Mon. and Dec. 28–Jan. 3.*

The next house is the **Koizumi Yakumo Residence** (1850–1904), unchanged since he left Matsue in 1891. Koizumi was born of an Irish father and a Greek mother, and was christened Lafcadio Hearn. His early years were spent in Greece, but he left there to study in Britain before traveling to the United States, where he became a journalist. In 1890, he traveled to Japan and soon became a teacher in Matsue. During his tenure he met a samurai's daughter, who nursed him when he fell sick. Recovered, he married her and later became a Japanese citizen, taking the name Yakumo Koizumi. He spent only 15 months in Matsue, but it was here that he became enthralled with Japan, and, in his writings, he helped introduce Japan to the West. He died at the age of 54, while working as a professor at Waseda University in Tokyo. *Admission: ¥200. Open daily 8:30–5.*

Adjacent to Yakumo Koizumi's former home is the **Yakumo Koizumi** (Lafcadio Hearn) **Memorial Hall**. The hall contains a good collection of his manuscripts and other items, including his desk, that reflect his life in Japan. If it is at all possible, you should read his essay "In a Japanese Garden," contained in the volume *Glimpses of Unfamiliar Japan*, in which he writes his impressions of Matsue. You will surely be asked by every local resident whether you are familiar with his work. *Admission: ¥250. Open daily 8:30–5.*

Two minutes from the Memorial Hall is the Hearn Kyukyo bus stop, where you can catch a bus back to Matsue's center and the JR station. The main shopping street is Kyomise Shopping Arcade, located just before the bridge to the JR station. However, you may prefer to shop for crafts at the **Matsue Meisan Center** (open 9–9), located next to the smartest hotel in town, the Ichibata, and on the north shore of Lake Shinji in an area known as Matsue Onsen. At the center, products from all over the Shimane Prefecture are on display and for sale, and, on its fourth floor, performances of folk dances are given four times a day. The Tourist Information Office at the JR station has the current schedule. *Admission to performances: ¥500, but the tourist office will sell them to you for ¥400.*

Should sunset soon be falling, set yourself up for a position to see the sun decline over Lake Shinji. Each sunset is memorable. You can watch one from the Matsue Meisan Center or from the Shinjiko Ohashi, the first bridge over to the south side of Matsue, the same side as the JR station.

The railway station at Matsue Onsen is the most convenient setting-off point for Izumo-Taisha Shrine, the second (after the Grand Shrines at Ise) most venerated shrine in Japan.

Izumo Taisha Shrine

Arriving and Departing To go from Matsue Onsen to **Taisha**, the location of the Izumo-Taisha Shrine, it only takes 55 minutes on the Ichibata Electric Railway (fare: ¥750). You will need to change trains at Kanato Station for the Izumo-Taisha-mae Station. The shrine is just a five-minute walk from there.

You can also arrive there by taking the JR train from Matsue Station back to Izumoshi, then transfer to the JR Taisha Line to Taisha Station, where you can either take a five-minute bus ride to Taisha-mae Station or walk directly to the shrine in about 20 minutes. The only two advantages of using the JR trains are to use the JR Rail Pass and to see the ornate, palace-style JR Taisha Station—it is quite an oddity.

Exploring The **Izumo-Taisha Shrine** has the oldest site for a shrine in Japan, though the contemporary shrine was built in 1874. Entrance to the shrine is under a giant torii arch; then take a 15-minute walk along the path shaded by pine trees. At the end stands the impressive Main Hall, shielded by a double fence so that one can only have glimpses of the architectural style, representative of Japan's oldest shrine construction. The shrine is dedicated to a male god, O-Kuni-Nushi. He is known as the creator of the land. Over time, his role has broadened to include managing fruitful relationships such as marriage and, even more recently, business mergers.

Notice the very steep gabled roof of compressed bark descending from the ridge line, which runs from front to back rather than from side to side. Notice, too, that the ornately carved beams at the roof peak have their ends beveled perpendicular to the ground. This indicates that the shrine is dedicated to a male god. (Shrines dedicated to female gods have their crossed beams beveled parallel to the ground.)

On either side of the compound are two rectangular buildings. These are said to be the home of the Shinto gods, who meet annually at the shrine in October (the lunar month, which often falls in our Nov.). That is why in the rest of Japan, the lunar October is referred to as Kannazuki (Month Without Gods), while in Izumo, October is called Kamiarizuki (Month With Gods).

Despite the shrine's veneration, the buildings are not as worthwhile to see as the experience of the spiritual heritage of the Japanese. Remember, too, that this area predates Nara. It is where Japan was born, where her mythology was founded, and where the invading and successful Yamato and the Izumo peoples accommodated each other's gods during the 2nd and 3rd centuries.

If you would like to go out to Cape Hinomisaki, exit the temple grounds to the west and take the bus (they go every hour) from the Ichibata Bus Terminal for the 25-minute ride (fare: ¥1,150). The seascape contains more of the beauty one sees all along the San'in coast when traveling between Hagi and Matsue. The lighthouse on the cape is open to the public, and one may climb up the 127 feet to the top (remove your shoes first). Built in 1903, **Cape Hinomisaki Lighthouse** is Japan's tallest and beams its light 21 nautical miles out to sea. And for climbing to its top, you will receive a certificate of ascent. *Admission: ¥80. Open daily 8:30–4.*

The next destination up the San'in coast is the Tottori Sand Dunes, two hours by JR train from Matsue. En route you will pass by the town of **Yasugi,** best known for the Adachi Museum of Art (320 Furukawa-cho, Yasugi City, tel. 0854/28–7111), which exhibits the works of both past and contemporary Japanese artists and has an inspiring series of gardens (admission: ¥2,300, half price if you show your passport; open Tues.–Sun. 9–4:30). Yonago is the next major town where buses leave every hour for the 50-minute ride to **Daisen** (fare: ¥590). Mount Daisen, a volcanic cone, which locals liken to Mt. Fuji, is popular with hikers. But only during the autumn is the beauty of the region worth a detour. On the slopes above the town of Daisen is the ancient Tendai sect temple, Daisen-ji. A few subtemples offer lodgings, such as Domyo-n (tel. 0859/52–2038) and Renjo-in (tel. 0859/52–2506), where novelist Shiga Naoya stayed and used the location for the ending of his *A Dark Night's Passing*. These are about ¥6,300 per person with two meals. There are also several overpriced minshukus such as the well-worn and dormitorylike Hakuun-so (25 Daisen, Daisencho, Saihaku-gun, Tottori Pref., tel. 0859/52–2331) for around ¥8,000 per person, including two meals. After Yonago comes **Kurayoshi,** where a 25-minute bus ride takes you to **Misasa Onsen,** a famous 1,000-year-old hot-spring resort claiming the hottest, highest radium waters in the country. Then comes Tottori.

Tottori Dunes

Exploring ㉒ The reason for stepping off the train at **Tottori** is to visit the *hamasaka* (dunes). To reach them, take Bus 20, 24, 25, or 26; they depart from gate 3 at the bus terminal in front of the JR station for a 15-minute ride (fare: ¥250) to the north of Tottori City. The dunes are a unique feature of the San'in coast. They stretch along the shore for 10 miles and are a mile wide. Some of the crests rise up to 300 feet, and they are always in motion. Endlessly, the sands shift and the shadows change. Each dune has wavy rivulets that seem to flow in the wind. The Tottori Dunes are an unexpected phenomenon, and therein lies their interest for the Japanese, though world travelers are likely to be disappointed. The dunes have appealed to the Japanese for making man seem so temporal and insignificant. Literary men would come to be mesmerized by the continually changing patterns of the dunes and the isolation they offered. Now tourists come in droves during the summertime. Camel rides are for hire, and there is a "kiddieland" (playground) to appeal to families. You must walk farther to escape the crowds and find your solitude. Better yet, rent a bicycle from the Cycling Terminal, Kodomo-no-kuni (near the entrance to the dunes), and work your way east to the Uradome Seashore. At the pier near the Iwanoto Bridge, you can board the San'in Matsushima Yuran sightseeing boat for a 50-minute trip along the coast to see the twisted pines and eroded rocks of the many islands that stand offshore (cost: ¥1,100).

Though Tottori is the prefectural capital, it has only marginal points of interest, so rather than stay in Tottori, continue on the JR San'in Main Line up the coast to either Kasumi or Kinosaki. The train parallels the shoreline, offering glimpses of the beautiful seascapes. One particular attraction is **Kasumi Bay,** where, on the east side, the sleepy fishing village of ㉓ **Kasumi** is located. To the left of the harbor is a small headland, **Okami-Koen Park,** which used to be popular for lovers' suicides. Now there is a small restaurant in which to slurp noodles while contemplating the cliffs. Various sightseeing boats also leave from the quay. If you have time while you are in Kasumi, be sure to visit **Daijoji Temple,** located directly inland from the JR Kasumi Station. The temple's origins began in 746, but its fame did not occur until the 18th century, when Okyo Maruyama, a leading artist of the time, came from Kyoto on a field trip with his students. Apparently Maruyama felt inspired, and he designated his students to paint various themes in several rooms of the temple. Some of these themes took a long time to paint, especially the Gilded Peacock. The field trip lasted eight years. *Admission: ¥500. Open daily 8:30–4:30.*

An even more picturesque village is Kundani, two stations farther down the track on the local train from Kusumi (get off at Satsu Station). This small town of 300 people and two bars is a quiet haven on a horseshoe-shaped bay. There is nothing to do here but relax. You can stay at one of the hospitable minshukus.

The alternative to spending the night at Kasumi or Kundani is ㉔ to visit **Kinosaki.** There are a couple of small temples in Kinosaki, **Onsenji** and **Gokurajuji,** to interest the visitor, but the real reason for staying here is the thermal baths. Virtually every inn and hotel has its own springs, but join in the traditional custom of visiting the seven public baths. Don't bother about dressing up. It is perfectly correct simply to wear your yakuta and join the procession from one bath to another. Each of these public baths charges about ¥300 and closes at 11:30 PM (2 close at midnight, the Mandata-yu and the Sato-no-yu). Before taking the baths, you may want to visit the **Mugisen Folkcraft Shop,** at the top of the village's main street, to look at the wickerwork baskets and cases for which the area is known.

Amanohashidate

㉕ The next and final major attraction on the San'in coast is **Amanohashidate.** This is one of the Japanese "Big Three" scenic wonders. Most Westerners are slightly disappointed by it, and, indeed, the younger Japanese are, too. However, in the past, Japanese literati have waxed poetic about Amanohashidate, so you may want to disembark from the train at Amanohashidate Station, rent a bicycle from one of the stores in front of the station, and go and see what all the fuss is about.

Amanohashidate is a 2-mile-long sandbar that stretches across **Miyazu Bay.** Its width varies from 100 to 350 yards, and it is lined with those contorted pine trees that so stir the Japanese imagination. The best vantage point is to take the cable car from the northwest side of **Kasamatsu-Koen Park** (cost: ¥200). To reach there, take the 15-minute bus ride from Amanohashidate Station to Ichinomiya, or the ferry boat from Amanohashidate Pier. (There are also bicycles for rent at the stores in front of the JR station.) When you have finally reached the top of Kasamatsu-Koen Park, don't be surprised to see masses of people standing on stone benches with heads between their legs. This is the "proper" viewing stance to see Amanohashidate. It is even more amusing to watch them take photographs.

The San'in coast continues north as far as Maizuru, and though this chapter ends by reboarding the train at Amanohashidate Station and returning to Kyoto, there are other sights to see. San'in is rich with places to explore, most of which have yet to be inundated with tourists. Any traveler seeking the traditional Japan should leisurely explore the area.

Dining and Lodging

Dining   In most of Japan outside of the large cities, one is usually advised to eat Western-style food in the dining rooms of the larger hotels. However, we strongly recommend that you eat out at local Japanese restaurants. Most reasonably priced Japanese restaurants will have a visual display of the menu in the window. On this basis, you can decide what you want before you enter. If you cannot order in Japanese and no English is spoken, after you secure a table, lead the waiter to the window display and point.

Unless the establishment is a *ryotei* (high-class, traditional Japanese restaurant) reservations are usually not required. Whenever reservations are advised or required at any of the restaurants listed, this is indicated.

A 3% federal consumer tax is added to all restaurant bills. Another 3% local tax is added to the bill if it exceeds ¥7,500. At more expensive restaurants, a 10%–15% service charge is added to the bill. Tipping is not the custom.

Category	Cost*
Very Expensive	over ¥6,000
Expensive	¥4,000–¥6,000
Moderate	¥2,000–¥4,000
Inexpensive	under ¥2,000

Cost is per person without tax, service, or drinks

Lodging Accommodations cover a broad spectrum, from pensions and *minshukus* to large modern resort hotels that have little character but offer all the facilities of an international hotel. All of the large city and resort hotels offer Western as well as Japanese food. During the summer season, hotel reservations are advised.

Outside the cities or major towns, most hotels quote prices on a per-person basis with two meals, exclusive of service and tax. If you do not want dinner at your hotel, it is usually possible to renegotiate the price. Stipulate, too, whether you wish to have Japanese or Western breakfasts, if any. For the purposes here, the categories assigned to all hotels reflect the cost of a double room with private bath but no meals. However, if you make reservations at any of the noncity hotels, you will be expected to take breakfast and dinner at the hotel—that will be the rate quoted to you unless you specify otherwise.

A 3% federal consumer tax is added to all hotel bills. Another 3% local tax is added to the bill if it exceeds ¥15,000. At most hotels, a 10%–15% service charge is added to the total bill. Tipping is not the custom.

Category	Cost*
Very Expensive	over ¥20,000
Expensive	¥15,000–¥20,000
Moderate	¥10,000–¥15,000
Inexpensive	under ¥10,000

Cost is for double room, without tax or service

The most highly recommended restaurants and accommodations in each city are indicated by a star ★.

Hagi

Dining **Higaku-Mangoku.** This small restaurant has the best selection of seasonal seafood in town. *Shimo Goken-machi, Hagi, tel. 0838/ 22–2136. Jacket and tie suggested. Open 11–8. V. Moderate.*
Nakon-mu. This is one of Hagi's better reasonably priced restaurants. The set menu (¥2,500) may include sashimi, baked fish, fish grilled in soy sauce, mountain vegetables, miso soup, and steamed rice. The restaurant has tatami and Western seating available but no English menu (select your food from the window display). *Huru-Hagi, tel. 0838/22–6619. No reservations. Dress: casual. No credit cards. Moderate.*

★ **Fujita-ya.** This is a casual restaurant, full of color, where locals delight in handmade *soba* (buckwheat noodles) and hot tempura served on handmade Japanese cypress trays. *Kumagai-cho, Hagi, tel. 0838/22–1086. Dress: informal. No credit cards. Open 11–7; closed 2nd and 4th Wed. of each month. Inexpensive.*

Lodging

Hokumon Yashiki. This elegant ryokan with luxurious rooms overlooks a garden. The gracious and refined service makes one feel pampered in the style to which the ancient Mori clan were surely accustomed. The location of the inn is in the samurai section, near the castle grounds. *210 Horiuchi, Hagi, Yamaguchi Prefecture 758, tel. and fax 0838/22–7521. 21 Japanese-style rooms. Facilities: Japanese food served in room. AE. Very Expensive.*

Hagi Grand Hotel. Convenience to the Higashi-Hagi JR station makes this the number one choice for an international-style hotel in Hagi. The staff here is helpful and friendly, and the guest rooms are relatively spacious. *25 Furuhagicho, Hagi, Yamaguchi Prefecture 758, tel. 0838/25–1211, fax 0838/25–4422. 190 rooms; half are Western-style. Facilities: Japanese and Western restaurants, shops, travel desk. AE, DC, MC, V. Moderate–Expensive.*

Hotel Royal. Located in the Rainbow Building above Higashi-Hagi JR station, this business hotel is friendly and efficient. The guest rooms are on the small size, but they are clean and comfortable. Businessmen and tourists stay here, and the front desk will arrange bicycle rentals for you. *3000-5 Chinto, Hagi, Yamaguchi Prefecture 758, tel. 0838/25–9595, fax 0838/ 25–8434. MC, V. Moderate.*

Hihumi Ryokan. Although the carpets in the ground floor lounge and along the corridors are stained, the tatami rooms here are clean and well kept. Many have a private bath and a separate alcove with two easy chairs and a table. Ask for a quiet room; those facing the main street suffer from traffic noise. The food, served in your room, is above average but not as interesting as it should be with the Japan Sea so close. The common bath is small and can be congested just before dinner, so time your pleasure accordingly. Located just across the bridge from the JR Higashi-Hagi station, on your right, Hifumi is a mile from the center of Hagi. Bicycles can be rented nearby. *613 Tsuchihara, Hagi 758, tel. 038/22–0123, fax 038/25–3593. 25 Japanese rooms, some with bath. Meals are included in the tariff. No credit cards. Inexpensive–Moderate.*

Fujita Ryokan. Located across the river from downtown and a five-minute walk from JR Higashi-Hagi, this two-story concrete building is the best choice for inexpensive accommodations. The tatami rooms are standard but better kept than the nearby Higashi-Hagi Minshiku, and the common bath is clean. There is a small lounge for relaxing. Try for a room facing the river and with luck you'll see fishermen at work when you wake up. The owners do like their guests to take two meals (Japanese breakfast and dinner) here, but if you stay a night you may be able to persuade them not to enforce this. *Shin-kawa Nishi-ku, Hagi 758, tel. 0838/22–0603, fax 0838/26–1240. 13 Japanese-style rooms. Facilities: dining room. No credit cards. Inexpensive.*

Hiroshima

Dining **Mitakiso Ryokan.** For a kaiseki lunch, or an elaborate kaiseki
★ dinner in a private tatami room, the Mitakiso Ryokan is superb. The inn is one of the most respected ryokan in Hiroshima.
It makes an excellent place to entertain Japanese guests. It is
not necessary to stay at the ryokan in order to enjoy its cuisine.
If do you stay, it is worth splurging and choosing a room with
sliding doors onto the private garden. *1-7 Mitakimachi, Nishi-
ku, Hiroshima 733, tel. 082/237–1402. Reservations required.
Jacket and tie required. AE. Open for lunch and dinner. Expensive.*

★ **Kanawa Restaurant.** Hiroshima is known for its oysters, especially in the winter, when they are fresh and sweet, and
Kanawa is Hiroshima's most famous oyster restaurant. The
restaurant is a barge moored on the Motoyasu River, near the
Peace Memorial Park. Dining is on tatami matting, with river
views. Only oysters are served here, in at least 10 different
ways. *Moored on the river at Heiwa Bridge, Naka-ku, Hiroshima, tel. 082/241–7416. Jacket and tie suggested. AE, V. Open
11–10:30. Closed 1st and 3rd Sun. of each month except Dec.
Moderate.*

Ten Ko. The specialty in this small restaurant is seafood tempura. Part of the secret to good tempura is the continual changing
of the oil (after every 4th or 5th order) so that a delicate crisp-
ness can be achieved. This shop changes the oil frequently
(probably selling the old oil to the lesser tempura shops in the
city). Other dishes are on the menu, but come for the tempura.
*2nd floor, Nakamachi 5-1, tel. 082/247–6088. AE, V. Open 11–
9:30. Moderate.*

Suishin Restaurant. Famous for its sashimi and sushi, this restaurant offers the freshest fish from the Inland Sea—globe-
fish, oysters, and eel, to name but a few. Order à la carte or
from a set selection. If you do not like raw fish, try the rockfish
grilled with soy sauce. Suishin now has an English-language
menu. Ambiance is plain and simple; there's a counter bar and
four tables. *6-7 Tatemachi, Naka-ku, Hiroshima, tel. 082/247–
4411. Dress: informal. AE, DC, V. Open 11–10. Closed national holidays. Moderate.*

Okonomi-mura. In this modern, three-story building there are
two dozen small shops serving *okonomiyaki*, sometimes called
Japanese pizza but more like a Japanese frittata. A bed of noodles is topped with heaps of onions and green and red peppers,
as well as your choice of shrimp, pork, mussels, or chicken. Different areas in Japan have their own style of creating okonomiyaki; in Hiroshima, the ingredients are layered rather than
mixed as is done in Osaka. Seating in these shops is either at a
wide counter in front of a grill or at tables with their own grills.
The chef-waiter prepares the ingredients and starts the grilling; you complete the task. Choosing one shop over the other is
a dilemma, only partially solved by looking at the displays.
Consider trying the Chii-Chau, which is owned by the man who
conceived the idea of creating a mall of okonomiyaki shops. The
complex is close to the Hondori shopping area, just west of
Chuo-dori Avenue. *Okononi-mura Building, Showa-machi,
Naka-ku, tel. 082/241–8758. No credit cards. Open 11–10. Inexpensive.*

Lodging **ANA Hotel Hiroshima.** Opened in 1983, this is Hiroshima's largest international hotel. Located in the business district on

Peace Boulevard, the hotel is within walking distance of the Peace Museum. With glittering chandeliers, the pink-carpeted lobby looks onto a small garden with a waterfall. The tea lounge facing the garden is an excellent place to rest after visiting the Peace Memorial Park. The furnishings of the guest rooms are uninspired, but the rooms have all the extras of a first-class hotel, including English-speaking channels on the television. The Unkai restaurant on the fifth floor has not only good Japanese food but also a view onto a Japanese garden of dwarf trees, rocks, and a pond of colorful carp. Many second-time visitors, as well as the local tourist office, consider the Hiroshima Grand the city's top hotel. *7-20 Nakamachi, Hiroshima 730, tel. 082/ 241–1111, fax 082/241–9123. 431 rooms; all but 4 are Western- style. Facilities: Chinese, Japanese, and Western restaurants, summer rooftop beer garden, free delivery of Japan Times newspaper, indoor pool, sauna, fitness center, shopping ar- cade. AE, DC, MC, V. Expensive.*

★ **Hiroshima Grand Hotel.** The other major hotel in Hiroshima is operated by Japan Airlines. It is slightly more moderate in price than the newer ANA Hotel. Located downtown, four blocks from the Peace Memorial Park and between Hiroshima Castle and Shukkeien Garden, the Grand has established a rep- utation for fine service and comfort. It has less glitter than the ANA Hotel and appeals to the traveler who is looking for quiet refinement. The guest rooms are pleasantly furnished, though the views from their windows onto the street below are unap- pealing. *4-4 Kami-Hatchobori, Naka-ku, Hiroshima 730, tel. 082/227–1313, fax 082/227–6462. 381 rooms, only 6 are Japa- nese style. Facilities: Chinese, Japanese, and Western restau- rants, beauty parlor, post office, shopping arcade. AE, DC, V. Moderate–Expensive.*

Hiroshima Terminal Hotel. This is the smartest and largest ho- tel near the station—located at the back, not the front—and it still has a feeling of newness. An expansive vaulted marble lob- by greets you as you enter. By Japan standards the rooms are spacious. They're furnished in subdued pastels and ochres. The staff is briskly efficient, and many employees speak English. On the penthouse (21st) floor, the Japanese, Chinese, and French restaurants offer panoramic vistas, and there are cafés and a coffee shop on the second floor. Downtown Hiroshima and the Peace Park are only eight minutes away by streetcar. *1-5 Matsubara-cho, Minami-ku, Hiroshima 732, tel. 082/262– 1111, fax 082/262–4050. 440 rooms, mostly Western-style. Fa- cilities: 4 restaurants, coffee lounge, 2 bars, travel desk, flo- rist, modest business center (copier, fax, word processor, business cards, data bank), meeting rooms. AE, DC, V. Mod- erate–Expensive.*

Mikawa Ryokan. This simple ryokan offers the basics—tatami rooms, coin-operated television, air-conditioning, but no rooms with private baths. There are too many guests for the limited toilet facilities—indeed, they can get rather grubby. However, the inn has a good location halfway between downtown and the JR station and is within walking distance of both. Advance res- ervations are requested. *9-6 Kyobashi-cho, Minami-ku, Hiro- shima 730, tel. 082/261–2719. Located 7 minutes on foot south of the JR station; turn right on the street before Aori-dori. 13 Japanese-style rooms. Facilities: breakfast only. AE. Inex- pensive.*

Kenmin-Bunka Center. For a no-nonsense place to stay close to the Peace Memorial Park, this accommodation offers the best value for money in Hiroshima. It is strictly a business hotel, with small rooms and tiny bathrooms, but the decor is cheerful and refreshing, and the bathtubs are deep enough for a good soak. Riyo Kaikan has neither lobby space nor lounges, but it does have an inexpensive cafeteria. Check-in is at 4 PM, and advance reservations are recommended. *1-5-3 Otemachi, Hiroshima 730, tel. 082/245-2322. 200 rooms. Facilities: cafeteria with Western and Japanese food. V. Inexpensive.*

Kasumi

Lodging
★
Marusei Ryokan. Located between the JR station and the harbor, this small, quiet inn in the center of the town is both a place to stay and eat. Hospitality and the owner's English-speaking son, who is also the chef, make this an ideal base for exploring the area. This is the best place in the area to eat *kani-suki* (succulent crab casserole). *Kasumi-cho, Kinosaki-gun 669, tel. 07963/6-0028. 15 Japanese-style rooms, 4 with private bath. Facilities: excellent restaurant. No credit cards. Moderate.*

Kinosaki

Lodging
★
Mikaya Ryokan. This three-story wood inn reflects traditional Japan. It is delightfully old-fashioned, with creaking timbers and spacious tatami rooms. It has its own thermal baths, which look out onto the garden. *Kinosaki-gun, Hyogo Prefecture, tel. 07963/2-2031. 35 Japanese-style rooms. Facilities: Japanese restaurant and thermal baths. AE, DC, V. Expensive.*

Kundani

Lodging
★
Minshuku Genroku Bekkan. This private guest house is a true find. The eight tatami guest rooms are spacious and freshly decorated. None of them, however, have private baths. Excellent Japanese dinners are served. The husband speaks English—his wife tries—and he will likely invite you to the local bar after dinner. The house is in the center of the quiet fishing village, two streets from the sea front. *Kundani Kasumi, Kinosaki-gun, Hyogo Prefecture, tel. 07963/8-0018. (Closest JR station is Satsu. Call on arrival and the owners will collect you at the station.) 8 rooms. Facilities: dinner and breakfast served. No credit cards. Inexpensive.*

Kurashiki

Dining
Hamayoshi. Only three tables (tatami seating with a well for your legs beneath the table) and a counter bar make up this personable restaurant specializing in fish from the Seto Inland Sea. Sushi is just one option; another is sashimi sliced from a live (very ugly-looking) fish! A less adventurous dish is filleted fish lightly grilled. Another delicacy is *shako*, chilled boiled prawns. No English is spoken, but the owner will help you order and instruct you on how to enjoy the chefs' delicacies. Located on the main street leading from the station and just before the Kurashiki Kokusai Hotel. *Chuo-dori, tel. 0864/22-3420. Dress: informal. No credit cards. Open 11-2 and 5-10. Moderate.*
Kiyutei. For the best grilled steak in town, one should come to this attractive restaurant, where chefs work over the fires grilling your steak to order. The entrance to the restaurant is

through the courtyard, just across from the entrance to the Ohara Museum. *1-2-20 Chuo, Kurashiki, tel. 0864/22–5141. Dress: informal. No credit cards. Open 11–9. Closed Mon. Moderate.*

Lodging **Ryokan Kurashiki.** In the atmosphere of the Edo period, this
★ delightful ryokan is made up of a merchant's mansion and three converted rice and sugar storehouses. Close to the Ohara Museum, with the Kurashiki flowing gently before it, this elegant ryokan maintains its serenity, no matter how many visitors are walking the streets in town. The cuisine is famous for its regional dishes, making the most of the oysters in the winter, fish straight from the Inland Sea in spring and autumn, and freshwater fish in the summer. There is a wonderful inner garden on which to gaze while sipping green tea in the afternoons. Here is Japanese hospitality at its best. Even if you are not staying here, you can still experience the ryokan by having lunch (¥10,000 per person) or dinner (¥14,000 per person). *4-1 Honmachi, Kurashiki, Okayama Prefecture 710, tel. 0864/22–0730. 20 rooms, not all with private bath. Facilities: Japanese restaurant and tea-house. AE, DC. Expensive.*

Kurashiki Kokusai Hotel. Owned by Japan Airlines, this is the best Western hotel in town, although it caters mostly to Japanese. The staff doesn't speak much English, and room TVs have no English channel. The lobby has a black tile floor and dramatic woodblock prints by Japanese artist Shiko Munakata. Corridors in the older part of the hotel are dark and somewhat worn, and the rooms in this section are small and in need of redecorating. Ask for a room in the newer annex, which is bright and cheery; those in the back of the building overlook a garden. The location of the Kokusai is ideal—a 10-minute walk on the main road leading from the station and just around the corner from the old town and the Ohara Museum. There is a 24-hour store nearby. The Achi Japanese restaurant serves good seafood from the Seto Inland Sea; tempura is prepared at the table. *1-1-44 Chuo, Kurashiki, Okayama Prefecture 710, tel. 0864/22–5141, fax 0864/22–5192. 106 rooms, 4 Japanese style. Facilities: Western and Japanese restaurants, bar, banquet rooms, beauty parlor, parking facilities. AE, DC, MC, V. Moderate–Expensive.*

Hotel Kurashiki. Above the station, this is an efficient business hotel that is useful if you have an early-morning train to catch. Even after refurbishing it is a little dreary, but at least the bathrooms are custom-made, and not the usual plastic cubicles. Certainly, now with a new coat of paint, this Japan Railways hotel is better than the adjacent Kurashiki Terminal hotel, where the rooms are downright shabby. *1-1-1 Achi, Kurashiki, Okayama Prefecture 710, tel. 0864/26–6111, fax 0684/26–6163. 139 Western-style rooms. Facilities: Japanese/Western restaurant. AE, DC, MC, V. Moderate.*

Kamoi. Located an eight-minute walk from the Ohara Museum, this minshuku is close to Tsurugatayama-Koen Park and the Achi Jinja Shrine. The rooms are simple and tatami-style, but they are very clean. This hostelry is the best bargain in Kurashiki. The food here is very good, too. It should be; the owner is also the owner and chef of Kamoi Restaurant, located across from the Ohara Museum. A visual display in the window shows what is offered, and, inside, the walls are decorated with artifacts such as cast-iron kettles and ancient rifles. *6-21 Hinmachi, Kurashiki, Okayama Prefecture 710, tel. 0864/22–*

4898. 17 Japanese-style rooms, none with bath. Japanese breakfast (Western breakfast on request) and dinner served. No credit cards. Inexpensive.

Matsue

Dining **Ginsen Restaurant.** Close to the Tokyu Inn and not far from the north exit of the Matsue JR station, this restaurant is popular with the locals for its fresh seafood casseroles. The season determines what these are, and with Lake Shinji on hand, the fish is superb and the prices are reasonable. *Asahimachi, Matsue, tel. 0852/21–2381. Dress: informal. No credit cards. Open 11–10. Moderate.*

★ **Kawabata Sushi.** Take sweet, succulent fish from the Sea of Japan, combine them with top-rate sushi chefs, and you have Kawabata. No English is spoken, but the good-loving chefs will make you feel comfortable, and you can point to the fish that take your fancy. The long counter bar is a good place to sit and watch the action, but there are also tables with tatami seating. This sushi bar has more atmosphere than many, with Japanese drums hanging from the walls. The restaurant is located upstairs from a spacious entrance hall—models of the dishes are displayed in a window downstairs—three short blocks from the Matsue Washington Hotel. Walk left from the hotel's entrance to where the street becomes a pedestrian-only mall and then take a right. The restaurant is at the next corner on your right. *Off Kyomise Arcade, tel. 0852/21–0689. No reservations. Dress: informal. No credit cards. Inexpensive/Moderate.*

Hi-daka-toshi-yuki. For fun and socializing with the locals, this yakitori bar with counter service offers a delightful evening's entertainment, good grilled chicken, and flowing sake. *Asahimachi Shimane, Matsue, tel. 0852/31–8308. Located 2 doors from Ginsen restaurant and easily recognized by its red lanterns outside. Dress: informal. No credit cards. Open 11–11. Inexpensive.*

Lodging **Minami-kan.** This is Matsue's most elegant and prestigious
★ ryokan, tastefully furnished and with refined service. It also has the best restaurant in Matsue for kaiseki haute cuisine and *tai-meshi* (sea bream). Even if you do not stay here, make reservations for dinner. *Ohashi, Matsue, Shimane Prefecture 690, tel. 0852/21–5131, fax 0852/26–0351. 27 Japanese-style rooms. Facilities: superb Japanese restaurant. AE. Expensive.*

Hotel Ichibata. Located in the spa section of town, next to Lake Shinji, the Ichibata appeals to those on a restful vacation who want to enjoy the thermal waters. For a long time, the hotel has been the leading place to stay in central San'in and, consequently, shows signs of wear. The guest rooms facing the lake are the nicest but are also the most expensive. Still, if you do not mind the 20-minute walk from the station or downtown, the Ichibata is still Matsue's first choice, if only to watch the sunsets from its vermilion lounge on the penthouse floor. *30 Chidoricho, Matsue, Shimane Prefecture 690, tel. 0852/22–0188, fax 0852/22–0230. 137 rooms, half are Western-style. All of the Japanese-style rooms face the lake; not so with the Western ones. Facilities: Japanese/Western restaurant, thermal baths, summer beer garden. AE, DC, MC, V. Moderate–Expensive.*

Matsue Washington Hotel. The advantage of this upmarket

business hotel is its location in the old downtown section of Matsue, where restaurants abound. There's a pedestrian mall lined with shops nearby; the castle is a ten-minute walk away, and the lake is even closer. The rooms here are modern but very small. Take a more expensive room if you don't want to trip over your suitcase. The coffee lounge on the ground floor serves both as a lounge and a place for light meals. There is also a formal restaurant serving shabu-shabu and other Japanese meals. *Hagashi Honmachi 2-22, Shimane-ken, Matsue, tel. 0852/22–4111, fax 0852/22–4120. 158 rooms. Facilities. Japanese and Western restaurants, coffee lounge. AE, DC, MC, V. Moderate.*

Less expensive (about ¥4,200) accommodations close to the JR station are at the business hotels—the **Green Hotel** (tel. 0852/27–3000) and the **Business Yamamoto** (tel. 0852/21–6121)—or at two small 10-room lodging houses, the **Business Ishiola** (tel. 0852/21–5931) and the popular **Ryokan Terazuya** (tel. 0852/21–3480) which both have only Japanese-style rooms.

Miyajima

Lodging
★ **Iwaso Ryokan.** For tradition and elegance, this is the Japanese inn at which to stay or dine on the island. The inn has a newer wing, but the older rooms have more character. Two cottages on the grounds have Japanese suites that are superbly decorated with antiques. The prices at the inn vary according to the size of the guest room, its view, and the dinner that you select. Be sure, when you make reservations in advance, to specify what you want and fix the price. Breakfast and dinner are usually included in the tariff. *345 Miyajimacho, Hiroshima Prefecture 739, tel. 08294/4–2233. 45 Japanese-style rooms. Facilities: Japanese restaurant, but Western breakfast served on request. AE. Expensive–Very Expensive.*

Jyukeiso Ryokan. For a more modest place to stay, this family ryokan (the owner speaks English) makes a pleasant home. However, it is to the east of the ferry pier (away from the town and shrine), which may not be what you want. Breakfast and dinner are usually included in the tariff. *Miyajimacho, Hiroshima Prefecture 739, tel. 08294/4–0300. 20 Japanese-style rooms, 2 with private bath. Facilities: Japanese restaurant, but Western breakfast served on request. AE. Moderate.*

Shimonoseki

Lodging **Bizenya Ryokan.** Should you have to spend the night in this town waiting for a ferry to Pusan or the morning train up the San'in coast, this small ryokan has clean tatami rooms and offers either Continental or Japanese breakfasts before you leave in the morning. *3-11-7 Kamitanaka-machi, Shimonoseki, Yamaguchi Prefecture 750, tel. 0832/22–6228. To reach the ryokan, take bus at bus stop #2 from the JR station to Nishinohashi bus stop. The ryokan is a 2-min. walk from there. 13 rooms, not all with bath. Facilities: Japanese food served, as well as Continental breakfast. AE, V. Inexpensive.*

Susa

Lodging
★ **Minshuku Susa.** Rooms at this minshuku are huge, at least 10-tatami, and have an alcove for a coffee table and two chairs. The

best look onto the harbor of this picturesque fishing village between Hagi and Masuda on the Japan Sea. The bathroom is
splendid, with an iron Goemon tub (Goemon Ishikawa, a Japanese version of Robin Hood, was boiled alive). Service is more
in the style of a traditional ryokan and such niceties as an orange in the bath to scent the water are not overlooked. No English is spoken, but the staff's friendliness overcomes any
language barrier. Dinner served in a tatami-floor dining room
is an occasion to try the region's delicacies from the sea. *Irie,
Susa-cho, Abu-gun, Yamaguchi Pref., 690, tel. 08387/6–2408.
6 rooms, 2 with private toilet. Facilities: Japanese meals
served in the dining room. No credit cards. Inexpensive–Moderate.*

Tottori

Lodging **New Otani.** This multistory red-concrete building across from
the JR station is the most modern hotel in town. The guest
rooms are compact and are smartly decorated in cream and red.
*Hinmachi 2-153, Tottori-shi 650, tel. 0857/23–1111, fax 0857/
23–0979. 150 rooms. Facilities: Western and Japanese restaurants, meeting rooms. AE, DC, MC, V. Moderate–Expensive.*

Tsuwano

Dining **Yuki.** This restaurant is famous for its carp dishes (such as carp
sashimi and carp miso soup) and mountain vegetables. A small
stream runs through the center of the dining room. *Honcho-
dori, Tsuwano, tel. 0856/2–0162. No credit cards. Open noon–2
and 6–8. Moderate.*

Lodging **Tsuwano Kanko Hotel.** This pleasant establishment is the most
centrally located hotel in town, with fair-size guest rooms and a
friendly staff. The furnishings have become worn and drab,
however, and the Japanese restaurant is only passable.
*Ushiroda, Tsuwano-machi, Kanoashi-gun 699, tel. 08567/2–
0332. 30 Japanese-style rooms. Facilities: Japanese restaurant, but will cook a Western breakfast. AE, V. Moderate.*

★ **Wakasagi-no-Yado.** This is a small minshuku run by a friendly
family who speak very limited English. They are, however, eager to help overseas tourists and will meet guests at Tsuwano
Station. *Mori, Tsuwano-cho, Kanoashi-gun 699-56, tel. 08567/
2–1146. Located 8 mins. on foot from the JR station. 8 rooms,
all without bath. Japanese and Western breakfasts offered. No
credit cards. Inexpensive.*

12 Shikoku

By Nigel Fisher

The smallest of Japan's four major islands, Shikoku is often omitted from tourist plans by both Japanese and foreigners. This is due in part to the fact that, until rather recently, travelers had to take a ferry across the Inland Sea. But with the 1989 opening of the Seto Bridge, which links Shikoku by both road and rail to Honshu at Kojima (south of Okayama), the island is attracting more visitors. Many come to see the 7.6-mile-long bridge that seems to leap from island to island as it arches across the water, high above the ships passing beneath. The bridge is composed of several shorter expanses, making it possible to get off on the small islands between Honshu and Shikoku, with their lookout areas and souvenir shops. Those who make it all the way across the bridge head for Takamatsu to visit the Ritsurin-Koen Garden and then go on to Kotohira and its much revered Kotohiragu Shrine. Far fewer travelers venture beyond Kotohira into the heart of Shikoku and down to its southern shores. This, however, is also likely to change with the Japanese people's growing appreciation of warm days on the beach.

Shikoku's isolation may also be attributed to the rugged mountain ranges that run east to west and divide Shikoku into two halves, each with a different climate. The northern half, which faces the Inland Sea, has a dry climate, with only modest rains in the autumn during the typhoon season. The southern half, which faces the Pacific, is more likely to have ocean storms sweep in, bringing rain throughout the year. With its shores washed by the warm waters of the Kuroshio (Black Current), it has a warmer climate and especially mild winters. The mountain ranges of the interior are formidable, achieving heights up to 6,400 feet, and are cut by wondrous gorges and valleys. Nestled in these valleys are small farming villages that appear unchanged since the Edo period (1603–1868). Shikoku is an island worth exploring, where travelers are greeted more as welcome foreign emissaries than as income-bearing tourists.

Despite the fact that Shikoku has been part of Japan's political and cultural development since the Heian period (794–1192), the island has retained an independence from mainstream Japan. There are some eyesores of factories littering the northern coast, but, to a great extent, Shikoku has been spared the ugliness of Japan's industrialization. The island is still considered by many Japanese as a rural backwater where pilgrims trek to the 88 sacred temples.

The Buddhist saint Kobo Daishi was born on Shikoku in 774, and it was he who founded the Shingon sect of Buddhism that became popular in the shogun eras. (During the reign of the Tokugawa Shogunate, travel was restricted, except for pilgrimages.) Pilgrims visit 88 temples to honor Kobo Daishi, and by doing so, they can be released from having to go through the cycle of rebirth. Many Japanese wait until they have retired to make this pilgrimage, in part because the time is right and in part because it used to take two months on foot to visit all the temples. In modern times, however, most pilgrims now scoot around by bus in 13 days.

Essential Information

Arriving and Departing

By Plane Takamatsu is serviced by seven daily flights from Tokyo and by 10 daily flights from Osaka. Tokushima has five daily flights from Tokyo and 10 daily flights from Osaka. Kochi is serviced by five daily flights from Tokyo and by 23 daily flights from Osaka. Matsuyama has six daily flights from Tokyo and six daily flights from Osaka.

By Train With the 1989 opening of the 7.6-mile long Seto-Ohashi Bridge, Shikoku is now linked by road and rail to Honshu. Instead of the hour-long ferry ride that was once necessary to cross the Inland Sea, the train takes a scant 15 minutes to traverse a series of double-decker suspension bridges, 307 feet above the water.

Shikoku can be reached by taking the JR Shinkansen to Okayama (3 hrs., 50 mins. from Tokyo; 1 hr., 20 mins. from Kyoto), then transferring onto the JR Limited Express bound either for Takamatsu (1 hr.), Matsuyama (3 hrs.), or Kochi (3 hrs.).

Matsuyama can also be reached by taking the JR Shinkansen to Hiroshima (5 hrs., 10 mins. from Tokyo; 2 hrs., 20 mins. from Kyoto). From Hiroshima's Ujina Port, the ferry takes two hours, 45 minutes to cross the Inland Sea to Matsuyama. The hydrofoil takes one hour.

By Ship Takamatsu can also be reached by the Kansai Kisen steamship, which takes five hours, 30 minutes from Osaka's Bentenfuto Pier, and four hours, 30 minutes from Kobe's Naka-Tottei Pier. The boat leaves Osaka at 8:30 AM and 2:20 PM, Kobe at 9:50 AM and 3:40 PM; it arrives at Takamatsu at 2 PM and 8:10 PM. The cost is approximately ¥2,500 and up from Osaka, slightly less from Kobe. Passenger ships travel to Kochi from Osaka (depart at 9:20 PM and arrive in Kochi at 6:40 AM, returning to Osaka with departures at 9:20 PM and arriving in Osaka at 7 AM. Kochi can also be reached from Tokyo by a ship that departs at 7:40 PM, stops in Katsuura, Wakayama Prefecture at 8:50 AM, and arrives in Kochi at 5 AM.

Getting Around

By Train and Bus All the major towns of Shikoku are connected either by JR express and local trains or by bus. Because of the lower population density on Shikoku, transportation is not so frequent as on the southern coast of Honshu. So before you step off a train or bus, find out how long it will be before the next one departs for your next destination.

The main routes are from Takamatsu to Matsuyama by train (2 hrs., 45 mins.); from Takamatsu to Kochi by train (3 hrs.), from Takamatsu to Tokushima (90 mins.); from Matsuyama to Kochi by JR bus (approximately 3 hrs., 15 mins.); from Matsuyama to Uwajima by train (2 hrs.); and from Kochi to Nakamura by train (2 hrs.).

By Car Since traffic is light, the scenery marvelous, and the distances relatively short, Shikoku is one region in Japan where renting a car makes sense. (Remember that an international driving license is required.) **Budget Rent-a-Car** has rental offices in

Maysuyama, Takamatsu, and Kochi, as do other car-rental agencies.

Important Addresses and Numbers

Tourist Information Centers Major tourist information centers are located at each of Shikoku's main cities: **Takamatsu,** tel. 0878/51–2009; **Kochi,** tel. 0888/23–1434; and **Matsuyama,** tel. 0899/31–3914.

Japan Travel-Phone The nationwide service for English-language assistance or travel information is available seven days a week, 9 to 5. Throughout Shikoku, dial toll-free 0120/444–800 for information on western Japan. When using a yellow, blue, or green public phone (do not use the red phones), insert a ¥10 coin, which will be returned.

Emergencies **Police,** tel. 110. **Ambulance,** tel. 119.

Guided Tours

No guided tours covering the island of Shikoku are conducted in English, though the **Japan Travel Bureau** will arrange your individual travel arrangements. The Japan Travel Bureau has offices at every JR station in each of the prefectural capitals and can assist in local tours, hotel reservations, and ticketing onward travel. There are also local city tours, conducted in Japanese, that cover the surrounding areas of each of the four major cities in Shikoku. These may be arranged through your hotel.

Exploring

Numbers in the margin correspond to points of interest on the Shikoku map.

There are three major cities on Shikoku: Takamatsu, Kochi, and Matsuyama. To these three, one may possibly add Tokushima, on the island's east coast. Few overseas visitors travel to Tokushima, but if you can visit there during August 12–15, you will witness one of the liveliest, most humor-filled festivals in Japan. The Awa Odori Dance is an occasion for the Japanese to let all their reserves fall away and act out their fantasies. Prizes are even given to the "Biggest Fool" in the parades, and foreigners are welcome to compete for these awards. Also, near Tokushima are the Naruto Straits, which attract visitors to see the giant whirlpools. At each ebb and flow of the tide, the currents rush through this narrow passage to form hundreds of foaming whirlpools of various sizes.

A short and popular itinerary for the overseas visitor to Shikoku is to arrive at Takamatsu and travel along the north coast to Matsuyama, with one short detour to Kotohiragu Shrine. Such an itinerary could be accomplished in two nights and two days. However, we recommend continuing on from Kotohiragu Shrine, crossing through the mountains to Kochi on the Pacific Coast and traveling around the island's west coast before reaching Matsuyama. From Matsuyama, there is a hydrofoil to Hiroshima.

Traditionally, the major gateway to Shikoku has been Takamatsu. Even with the new Seto Bridge, it has the easiest access to and from Honshu.

Takamatsu

❶ The JR station and the pier at **Takamatsu** share the same location at the north end of Chuo-dori, Takamatsu's main avenue, where most of the large hotels are located. The Takamatsu Information Office (tel. 0878/51–2009) is located in a small office just outside the JR Station. The maps and brochures are limited to Kagawa Prefecture, of which Takamatsu is the capital. If you need information on the entire island, make sure that you visit the Tourist Information Center in Tokyo or Kyoto before you set out for Shikoku.

Three hundred yards down Chuo-dori Avenue, on the left-hand side, the shopping arcades begin. The east–west arcade is intersected by another arcade running north–south (parallel to Chuo-dori). Department stores, shops, and larger restaurants are located in these malls. The small streets off the arcades are crowded with bars, cabarets, and small restaurants.

A bus tour (Japanese-speaking guide only) departs at 8:45 AM from Takamatsu-Chikko Bus Station (near the JR station) and covers Takamatsu's Ritsurin-Koen Park, Kotoshira, and other sights. The tour takes about eight hours, 45 minutes.

The number one attraction in Takamatsu is **Ritsurin-Koen Garden,** once the summer retreat of the Matsudaira clan. The garden is located at the far end of Chuo-dori Avenue. To reach it, take a 10-minute ride (cost: ¥200) on any bus that leaves from in front of the Grand Hotel from stop #2. (The bus makes a short detour from the main avenue to include a bus depot on its route. Don't disembark from the bus until it rejoins the main avenue—Chuo-dori—and travels two more stops.) An alternate route is to take the JR train bound for Takushima and disembark five minutes later at the second stop, Ritsurin-Koen. Ritsurin-Koen was completed in the late 17th century after 100 years of careful planning, landscaping, and cultivation. The garden is actually two gardens. The north garden is more modern and has wide expanses of lawns. The more appealing south garden is traditional, with a design that follows a classical layout. The garden's six ponds and 13 scenic mounds are arranged so that as one walks the intersecting paths, at virtually every step there is a new view or angle to hold the focus of attention. One cannot hurry through this garden. Each rock, each tree shape, each pond rippling with multicolored carp has a fluidity of motion enhanced by the reflections of the water and the shadows of the trees. *Admission: ¥310. Open 5:30 AM–7 PM (5:30–5 in winter).*

Within Ritsurin-Koen's north garden is an **Exhibition Hall,** displaying and selling local products from the Kagawa Prefecture—these include wood carvings, masks, kites, and umbrellas. Another museum exhibits work by local artists, and the **Folk Art House** displays local handcrafts and folk crafts.

However, Ritsurin's gem is in the south garden. It is the teahouse, **Kikugetsutei,** which looks as if it is floating on water. Here, you may enjoy a cup of green tea and muse on the serene harmony of the occasion, just as the lords of Matsudaira did in previous centuries. *Admission: ¥310; tea is an additional ¥310, or you can get a combination ticket for ¥590.*

Ritsurin-Koen is the reason to visit Takamatsu. The bombing of World War II left Takamatsu with few other visible attrac-

484

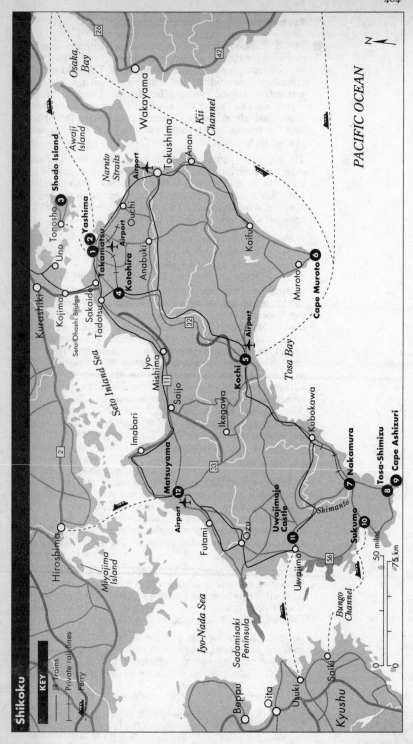

Shikoku

KEY

— JR Trains

— Private rail lines

⛴ Ferry

N

PACIFIC OCEAN

Osaka Bay

Awaji Island

Shodo Island ❸

Naruto Straits

Wakayama

Kii Channel

Tokushima

Anan

Airport

Uno

Tonosho

❶ ❷ Yashima

Takamatsu

Airport

Ouchi

Kurashiki

Kojima

Seto-Ohashi Bridge

Sakaide

❹ Kotohira

Anabuki

Kaifu

Cape Muroto ❻

Muroto

Tadotsu

32

Iyo-Mishima

Airport

Seto Inland Sea

Saijo

❺ Kochi

Tosa Bay

11

Imabari

Ikegawa

Kubokawa

33

Hiroshima

Matsuyama ⓬

Airport

Uwajimajo Castle

Shimanto

Nakamura ❼

Tosa-Shimizu ❽

Cape Ashizuri ❾

Miyajima Island

Futami

Ozu

❶❶

Sukumo ❿

Iyo-Nada Sea

Uwajima

56

50 miles

75 km

Sadamisaki Peninsula

Bango Channel

Beppu

Oita

Usuki

Saiki

Kyushu

2

26

42

tions. However, if you are waiting for a train or ferry, across from the station and behind the Grand Hotel are the castle grounds of Tamamo Park. The **Tamamojo Castle,** built in 1588, had been the home of the Matsudaira clan, who ruled Takamatsu during the Edo period. Now, only a few turrets of the castle are left, but its setting, with the Inland Sea in the background, makes it a pleasant place in which to relax. *Admission: ¥100. Open 8:30–6.*

The reasons to stay overnight in Takamatsu are its modern hotels, the openness of the city, and the opportunity to make excursions to Yashima and Shodo Island.

Yashima

JR trains from Takamatsu Station make the 20-minute run every hour to **Yashima,** or you can take the commuter Kotoden tram from the Chikko terminal (across from the JR station and behind the Grand Hotel). These run 10 times a day; the tourist office can supply a schedule. When you arrive at Yashima Station, simply walk up the hill and that will lead you to the reconstructed village of **Shikoku Mura** and the battle site where, in 1185, the Minamoto clan defeated the Taira family, allowing Yoritomo Minamoto to establish Japan's first shogunate, in Kamakura.

In this open-air museum village, 21 houses have been relocated from around the island of Shikoku to represent what rural life was like during the Edo period. The village may be artificial, but in this age where ferro-concrete has replaced so much of traditional Japan, Shikoku Mura provides an opportunity to see traditional thatch-roof farmhouses, a papermaking workshop, a ceremonial teahouse, a rural Kabuki stage, and other buildings used in the feudal age. Similar to the Hida Village near Takayama, Shikoku Mura presents a picture of what life was like 200 to 300 years ago. *Admission: ¥500. Open 8:30–5; Nov.–Mar., 8:30–4:30.*

Close to Shikoku Mura's entrance is a cable car, which takes five minutes (fare: ¥600 one-way, ¥1,010 round-trip) to travel up to **Yashima Plateau.** Yashima was once an island (it's now connected to Shikoku by a narrow strip of land), and on its summit, nearly 1,000 feet above the Inland Sea, the Minamoto and Taira clans clashed. Relics from the battle are on view in the Treasure House at the Yashimaji Temple (originally constructed in 754, it is the 84th of the 88 sacred temples), but the major reasons for ascending this plateau are the expansive vistas over the Inland Sea and views of Shodo Island.

Shodo Island

A longer excursion from Takamatsu is to **Shodo Island** (*Shodoshima,* in Japanese), the second largest island in the Inland Sea. The ferry (fare: ¥520) takes an hour from Takamatsu Pier to reach Tonosho, the island's major town and port. A hydrofoil also makes the same run, but it does so in 35 minutes (fare: ¥1,100). Tonosho may also be reached by a 40-minute hydrofoil ride from Okayama Pier or on a regular ferry from Himeji Port (1 hr., 40 mins.; fare: ¥1,170). Sightseeing bus tours depart from Tonosho to cover all the island sights, or you can simply use the public buses—they cover the island efficiently and thoroughly. Motor bicycles may also be rented at ¥3,000 a day, including insurance, from Ryobi Rent-a-Bike (tel. 62–6578, open 8:30–5) near Tonsho's pier.

The major attraction on Shodo is **Kankakei Gorge,** an hour's bus ride (fare: ¥610) from Tonosho. The gorge is 3.7 miles long and 2.4 miles wide, hemmed in by a wall of mountainous peaks with weather-eroded rocks. The thick maple and pine forest lining the gorge creates a splash of color in the autumn; in the spring, the profusion of azaleas makes for an equally colorful spectacle. If the grandeur of the gorge is not thrilling enough, you can take an aerial tramway to the summit that travels frighteningly close to the cliffs' walls. Then take a bus back to Tonosho via Kusakabe.

The other principal attractions on Shodo are **Kujukuen** (15 mins. by bus from Tonosho), where 3,000 peacocks roam; **Choshikei Gorge** (25 mins. by bus from Tonosho), which extends along the upper stream of the Denpo River; and the nearby **Monkey Park,** where 700 wild monkeys cavort.

Several minshukus offer accommodation on the island. Try Churchi (tel. 0879/62–3679) with 10 rooms or Maruse (tel. 0879/62–2385) with six rooms, both in Tonosho.

Kotohira

From Takamatsu, the JR train takes 55 minutes to reach **Kotohira** Station, from which it is an eight-minute walk to the steps that lead up to **Kotohiragu Shrine.** (If the JR train is not convenient, you can take the 70-minute tram ride that departs from the other side of the Takamatsu Station plaza.) *Note:* While occasionally there is an open cloakroom to the left of the station, there are no lockers. If you are only visiting for the day, travel light—even small packs become very heavy while you are mounting the 785 stairs to the shrine. This shrine may not rank quite as high in importance as do the Grand Shrines at Ise or the Izumo Taisha Shrine near Matsue, but it is one of Japan's oldest and grandest. It is also one of the most popular shrines in Japan. Four million visitors come to pay their respects each year.

Founded in the 11th century and built on the slopes of Mt. Zozu, the shrine is dedicated to Omono-nushi-no-Mikoto (Kompira, as he is fondly known), the guardian god of the sea and patron of seafarers. Traditionally, fishermen and sailors would come to visit the shrine and solicit godly help for their safe passage at sea. However, their monopoly on seeking the aid of Kompira has ended. His role has expanded to include all travelers, including tourists, though it is uncertain whether messages written in English will be understood.

To reach the main gate of the shrine, you must first mount 365 granite steps. On either side of the steps are souvenir and refreshment stands. However, don't dawdle. There are another 420 steps to the main shrine. Once through the main gate, the souvenir stands are replaced by stone lanterns. The climb becomes more of a solemn, spiritual exercise. Just before the second torii gate is the shrine's **Treasure House** (Homotsu-kan), with an impressive display of sculpture, scrolls, and, despite their Buddhist origins, Noh masks. *Admission: ¥200. Open 9–4.*

Shoin is the next important building. It will be on your right. The building dates from 1659, and its interior is covered in paintings by the famous 18th-century landscape artist Okyo Maruyama. Maruyama (1733–1795) came from a family of farmers and, not surprisingly, looked to the beauty of nature for his paintings. Such was his talent that a new style (the Maruyama school) of painting developed, which may be best termed "Return to Nature."

Onward and forever upward, you'll see the intricate carvings of animals on the facade of **Asahino Yashiro,** and, at the next landing, you'll finally be at the main shrine, a complex of buildings that were rebuilt 100 years ago. Aside from the sense of accomplishment in making the climb, the views over Takamatsu and the Inland Sea to the north and the mountain ranges of Shikoku to the south justify the climb of 785 steps, even more perhaps than a visit to the shrine itself. That is, unless you ask Kompira for good fortune, and, after climbing 785 steps, you may want to.

You should allow a total of an hour from the time you start your ascent up the granite stairs until you return. Just as the feudal lords once did, you may hire a palanquin to porter you up and down (cost: ¥4,500 one way, ¥6,000 round-trip). Riding in a palanquin has a certain appeal, and it most certainly saves the calf muscles, but the motion and narrow confines are not especially comfortable.

It is worth making the time to visit the oldest Kabuki theater in Japan. Located in Kotohira Park, it is only a 10-minute walk from Kotohira Station and is near the first flight of steps leading to the Kotohiragu Shrine. The theater, called **Kompira O-Shibai,** is exceptionally large and was moved from the overcrowded center of Kotohira in 1975. At the same time, the theater was completely restored to its original grandeur. Kabuki plays are now performed only once a year, in April, but throughout the year, the theater is open for viewing. Since the theater was built in 1835, one of the interesting aspects is how the theater managed its special effects without electricity. Eight men in harness, for example, rotate the stage. Within the revolving stage are two trap lifts. The larger one is used for quick changes in stage props, the smaller one for lifting actors up to floor level. Equally fascinating are the sets of sliding shoji screens used to adjust the amount of daylight filtering onto the stage. *Admission: ¥500. Open 9–4. Closed Tues.*

From Kotohira Station, the JR Limited Express train continues on to Kochi, the principal city of Shikoku's southern coast. (Or, you can return to the north coast of Shikoku and travel west to Matsuyama.)

Kochi

5 The views from the train en route from Kotohira to **Kochi** are stunning, though the tunnels through which the train passes sometimes become frustrating. The train goes up the inclines to follow the valleys, cut deep by swift-flowing rivers. The earth is red and rich, and the foliage is lush and verdant. It is an area of scenic beauty that could happily lend itself to exploration by car, though once you are off the main roads, a small knowledge of Japanese will help your navigation.

From Kotohira, the train takes about two hours to reach Kochi. The **Tourist Information Office** (tel. 0888/82–7777) is located to the left of the station's exit. Should you need language assistance while in Kochi, you may telephone the Nichibei School (tel. 0888/23–8118; weekdays 9–5, Sat. noon–5), which has bilingual volunteers who will assist foreigners. The JR bus terminal for direct JR buses to Matsuyama (there is no train line) is on the left wing (as you exit the station) of the station plaza.

The train station is a 20-minute walk from the city center. A taxi ride from the station to downtown is about ¥550. There are also buses.

There are ½-day and full-day sightseeing tours (tel. 0888/82–3561) of Kochi and the surrounding area. These leave from the area around the JR bus terminal at Kochi Station. There are also full-day sightseeing tours (tel. 0880/35–3856) that travel down to Cape Ashizuri. These leave from Nakamura Station and are not available throughout the whole year, so be sure to call ahead.

For residents of Kochi, fishing and agriculture are the mainstays. For the tourist, the major attraction is **Kochijo Castle,** one of the 12 feudal castles to have survived the course of time. The castle is easy to find; its location dominates the center of Kochi.

Kochi's castle is unique in that it is the only one in Japan to have kept both its donjon (stronghold) and its daimyo's residence intact. The donjon, admittedly, was rebuilt in 1753, but it faithfully reflects the original (1601–1603). The stone foundation of the donjon seems to merge into the cliff face of the bluff on which the structure is built. The donjon has the old style of watchtower design, and, by climbing up to its top floor, one can appreciate its purpose. The commanding view is splendid. The daimyo's residence, **Kaitokukan,** is located to the southwest of the donjon and is worth entering to see the formal main room, so elegantly laid out in the Shoin style, a style known for its decorative alcove, staggered shelves, decorative doors, tatami-covered floors, and shoji screens reinforced with wooden lattices. In the castle grounds, beneath the donjon, is Kochi University. It must be inspiring to look up through the library windows to see this feudal structure tower above. *Admission: ¥350. Open 9–5 (enter before 4:30).*

Except for the castle, Kochi is not architecturally the most exciting of towns. However, perhaps because of its warm climate, the people of Kochi are full of humor. Even their local folk songs poke fun at life, such as, "On Harimayabashi, people saw a Buddhist priest buy a hairpin. . . ." Because priests in those days were forbidden to love women, and they shaved their heads, some naughty business was afoot. Kochi is friendly, and fun-loving, and people congregate every evening in the compact downtown area for pleasure. Several streets in the heart of downtown are closed off from traffic to form shopping arcades. Every day of the week seems to be a market day; however, should you be in Kochi on a Sunday morning, be sure to visit the thriving **Sunday Open-Air Market** on Otesuji-dori Avenue, just north of Harimayabashi in downtown Kochi, where farmers bring their produce to sell at some 650 stalls. It is a tradition that has been maintained for 300 years. As an added bonus, you may also see the incredibly long-tailed (more than 20 ft.) roosters for which Kochi is known. The actual village where these roosters are raised is Oshino, though the easiest place to see them is outside of Kochi at the **Long-Tailed Rooster Center** at Shinohara, Nankoku City. *Tel. 0888/64–4931. Admission: ¥300. Open 9–5. Closed Mon.*

During the summer months, residents of Kochi flock to **Katsurahama Beach,** 8 miles southeast of town. Buses depart from the Kochi station plaza and take 35 minutes (fare: ¥530). The beach consists of gravelly white sand, but the swimming is good, and there are pleasing scenic rock formations offshore. There is also the **Tosa Fighting Dog Center** (tel. 0888/42–3315), where the victor of a bout is paraded around the ring dressed in a sumo wrestler's apron, and given the same ranking title as his human counterpart. To get to Katsurahama Beach, either catch the bus from the Kochi station or from the Harimayabashi stop, just before the bridge.

If you prefer to spend an afternoon amid lawns, greenery, and an old temple, take the bus to Mount Godai and **Godaisan-Koen Park.** The 20-minute bus ride departs from the Toden bus stop, next to the Seibu department store on Harimayabashi (fare: ¥300). First visit the **Chikurinji Temple,** which has an impressive five-story pagoda that, despite beliefs to the contrary, is fairly uncommon in Japan. This one can stand up to those of Kyoto; the people from Kochi say it's more magnificent. The temple belongs to the Shingon sect of Buddhism and, founded in 724, is the 31st temple in the sequence of the 88 sacred temples. Down from the temple is the **Makino Botanical Garden,** built to honor the botanist Dr. Tomitaro Makino (1862–1957). The greenhouse has an exotic collection of more than 1,000 plants, and the gardens are full of flowers, which have been planned so that in all seasons something is in bloom. *Admission: ¥300. Open daily 9–5.*

East along the coast from Kochi, the road follows a rugged shoreline, marked by frequent inlets and indentations. Most of the coast consists of a series of 100- to 300-foot terraces. Continuous wave action, generated by the Black Current, has eroded these terraces. The result is a surreal coastline of rocks, surf, and steep precipices. It is about a 2½-hour drive along the coast road out to **Cape Muroto,** a popular sightseeing tour destination to watch the sea crash against the cliffs.

West of Kochi, in the southwestern tip of Kochi Prefecture, is Ashizuri National Park. The JR Dosansen Line goes to Kubokawa Station, where, if you were going straight to Uwajima, you'd change trains. For Nakamura usually there is no change. This last leg of the journey is on the Kuroshio Tetsudo Line, and JR Rail Pass holders will be charged an additional ¥170. At **Nakamura** you continue by JR bus to **Tosa-Shimizu,** where you can catch another bus out to **Cape Ashizuri.** (There are also sightseeing buses that depart from Nakamura JR Station to Cape Ashizuri, tel. 0880/35–3856.) It is wonderfully wild country, with a skyline-drive road running down the center of the cape. At the end of the cape is the lighthouse and the Kongofukuji Temple, the 38th of the 88 sacred temples, whose origins trace back 1,100 years, though what you see was rebuilt 300 years ago.

Returning from Cape Ashizuri, you can reboard the bus at Tosa Shimizu and follow the coastline to **Sukumo** (four ferries a day depart from here for Saiki on Kyushu. Fare: ¥1,650. Sukumo can also be reached directly by an hour's bus ride from Nakamura. Fare: ¥1,100.) With a change of bus, continue north to **Uwajima**, the terminal for JR lines arriving from Matsuyama and Kochi. Ferries depart from Uwajima for Usuki, on Kyushu (Fare: about ¥1,800), which is two stops from Beppu.

Shikoku has three of the surviving 12 feudal castles; one of these is **Uwajimajo Castle,** though the first castle was torn down and replaced with an updated version in 1665. It's a friendly castle, without the usual defensive structures such as a stone drop. This suggests that by the end of the 17th century, war (at least those fought around castles) was a thing of the past. Most people however, do not come to Uwajima to see the castle. They come for the **Togyu Bullfights.** Though there are very similar bouts in the Ogi Islands, Uwajima claims these bullfights are a unique tradition that goes back for 400 years (good for tourism). Tournaments are held five times a year (dates vary, except for the Wareisai Festival on Jul. 23–24, but usually they are Jan. 2, the first Sun. in Mar. and Apr., the third Sun. in May, July 24, Aug. 14, and the first Sun. in Nov.). In these tournaments, two bulls lock horns and, like sumo wrestlers, try to push each other out of the ring. The Togyujo, where the contests are held, is at the foot of Mt. Tenman, about a 30-minute walk from the JR station.

From Uwajima, it is a one-hour 45-minute ride on the JR train to Matsuyama. You can also take a JR bus directly to Matsuyama from Kochi (3 hrs., 50 mins). There is frequent JR train service to Matsuyama from Takamatsu and also a hourly hydrofoil (60 mins. at ¥4,950) and ferry (3 hrs. at ¥3,710 for 1st class and ¥1,850 for 2nd class) service from Hiroshima.

Matsuyama

The two most popular attractions of **Matsuyama** are its castle and the nearby Dogo Onsen.

Matsuyama is Shikoku's largest city, and it bristles with industries ranging from chemicals to wood pulp and from textiles to porcelain. It's a useful town for replenishing supplies—to change traveler's checks, for example—but with the exception of the castle, it lacks character. At the station, you may want to stop in at the **City Tourist Information Office** (tel. 0899/31–3914), located just inside the JR station, for a map and brochures. Downtown Matsuyama, often defined as the Okaido Shopping Center, which is at the foot of the castle grounds, is best reached by taking streetcar #5, which departs from the plaza in front of the train station.

Matsuyamajo Castle is on top of Matsuyama Hill, right in the center of the city. Originally built in 1603, the castle is the third feudal castle in Shikoku to have survived—though barely. It burned down in 1784 but was rebuilt in 1854, with a complex consisting of a major three-story donjon and three lesser donjons. The lesser ones succumbed to fire during this century, but all have been reconstructed. Unlike other postwar reconstructions, these smaller donjons were rebuilt with original materials, not ferro-concrete. The main donjon now serves as a museum for feudal armor and swords owned by the Matsudaira clan, the daimyo family that lorded over Matsuyama (and Takamatsu) during the entire Edo period. The castle is perched high on the hill; unless you are very energetic, take the cable car that shuttles visitors up and down every 10 minutes. *Cost of cable car and admission to the castle: ¥550. Open daily 9–4:30.*

Because Matsuyama has no special character of its own, rather than stay in town, many visitors spend the night at **Dogo Onsen.** It is only 18 minutes away by streetcar, which you can take from the JR Matsuyama Station or catch from downtown—there is a stop before the ANA Hotel. In either case, take streetcar #5. With a history that is said to stretch back for more than two millennia, Dogo Onsen boasts of being one of Japan's oldest spas. It hasn't outlived its popularity, either. There are more than 60 ryokan and hotels, old and new. Most of these now have their own thermal waters, but at the turn of the last century, visitors used to go to the public bathhouses; the grandest of them all was, and still is, the municipal bathhouse (*shinrokaku*), the **Dogo Onsen Honkan.**

Indeed, even if your hotel has the fanciest of baths, to stay at Dogo Onsen or even downtown Matsuyama and not socialize at the shinrokaku is to miss the delight of this spa town. The grand old three-story, castlelike wood building was built in 1894 and, with its sliding panels, tatami floors, and shoji screens, appears as an old-fashioned pleasure palace. It is, in many ways. Two thousand bathers or more come by each day to pay their ¥250 and take the waters. Some of them pay a little more and lounge around after their bath, drinking tea in the communal room. Bathing is a social pastime, and the bath has the added benefit of scalding water that has medicinal qualities, especially for skin diseases.

There are different price levels of enjoyment. A basic bath is ¥250; a bath, a rented *yukata* (cotton robe), and access to the communal tatami lounge is ¥780; access to a smaller lounge and bath area away from hoi polloi is ¥1,000; and a private tatami room is ¥1,300. A separate wing was built in 1899 for imperial soaking. Most of the time it is not used, but for ¥210 visitors are allowed to wander through this royal bathhouse, which is open daily 6 AM–10 PM.

Matsuyama has eight of the 88 sacred temples. The one of note is **Ishiteji Temple,** located 10 minutes on foot from Dogo Onsen Honkan. Representative of the Kamakura-style architecture, the temple has its origins early in the 14th century. It may not be that grand, but its simple three-story pagoda is a pleasant contrast to the public bathhouse. Note the two statues of Deva kings at the gate. One has his mouth open, representing life, and the other has his mouth closed, representing death. Praying at the Ishite Temple is said to cure one's aching legs and crippled feet. The elderly, in fact, hang up their sandals in the temple as an offering of hope.

Dining

The delight of Shikoku is the number of small Japanese restaurants that serve the freshest fish, either caught in the Seto Inland Sea or in the Pacific. Noodle restaurants abound, too. We have not singled out particular restaurants because they rarely differ in terms of ambience or quality of food. You may want to control your adventure in eating by choosing those restaurants that offer visual displays of their menus in the windows. However, if you have been in Japan for a week, you'll probably feel comfortable going into a small restaurant, even without a visual display of the menu in the window, and ordering what the chef recommends. That dish is always the best. Just tell them that you wish to keep the price within certain limits.

In each of the three major cities—Takamatsu, Kochi, and Matsuyama—the entertainment districts have innumerable Japanese restaurants, and the fun of these areas is selecting your own restaurant. However, if you are staying at the Grand Hotel in Takamatsu or are waiting for the train or the next ferry at the JR station and have time enough for a good meal, there are nine excellent Japanese restaurants from which to chose on the second floor of the Grand Hotel's building. All the restaurants have their menus visually displayed in the windows, so you can select the dish and price your meal before you enter. If you are feeling more ambitious, there are dozens of good, small restaurants on and around Nakahonmachi—an arcade that runs parallel to the main boulevard, Chuo-dori. A particularly good restaurant in Takamatsu is Maimai-tei (tel. 0878/33–3360, closed Sun.) which serves excellent Sanuki cuisine at approximately ¥4,700 for two.

In Matsuyama, the Okaido shopping arcade near the ANA Hotel has numerous good restaurants serving Western and Japanese food in all price ranges—the local specialty is *ikezukuri*, a live fish with its meat cut into strips. In Kochi, the entertainment district is crammed with appealing small restaurants and nomiya.

For Western-style cuisine, you are better off eating at the top hotels. The Hankyu, in Kochi, for example, has an excellent French restaurant, as does the ANA Hotel in Matsuyama. If you're on a budget, these hotels have Western-style coffee shops, and the ANA Hotel in Matsuyama also has a delightful rooftop beer garden, open in the summer, where one can also eat well and inexpensively.

Lodging

Accommodations cover a broad spectrum, from pensions and minshukus to large modern, resort hotels that have little character but offer all the facilities of an international hotel. All of the large city and resort hotels offer Western as well as Japanese food. During the summer, reservations are advised.

Outside the cities or major towns, most hotels quote prices on a per-person basis with two meals, exclusive of service and tax. If you do not want dinner at your hotel, it is usually possible to renegotiate the price. Stipulate, too, whether you wish to have Japanese or Western breakfasts, if any. For the purposes here, the categories assigned to all hotels reflect the cost of a double room with private bath and no meals. However, if you make reservations at any of the noncity hotels, you will be expected to take breakfast and dinner at the hotel—that will be the rate quoted to you unless you specify otherwise. A 3% federal consumer tax is added to all hotel bills. Another 3% local tax is added to the bill if it exceeds ¥15,000. At most hotels, a 10%–15% service charge is added to the hotel bill. Tipping is not the custom.

The most highly recommended accommodations in each city are indicated by a star ★.

Category	Cost*
Very Expensive	over ¥20,000
Expensive	¥15,000–¥20,000
Moderate	¥10,000–¥15,000
Inexpensive	under ¥10,000

Cost is for double room, without tax or service

Kochi

★ **Hotel Hankyu.** Located in the center of town, within sight of the Kochijo Castle, the Hankyu opened in late 1985 and is indisputably the best hotel in Kochi. On the ground floor is the modern open-plan lobby, with a lounge away from the reception area and a small cake/tea shop to the side. On the second floor, there are several excellent restaurants. The best omelets on Shikoku are offered at breakfast in this hotel. The spacious guest rooms, decorated with light pastel furnishings, create a sense of well-being, and the staff are extremely helpful to foreign guests. *4-2-50 Honmachi, Kochi-shi, Kochi 780, tel. 0888/ 73–1111, fax 0888/73–1145. 201 rooms, mostly Western style. Facilities: Chinese, Japanese, and French restaurants. AE, DC, MC, V. Expensive.*

Ikawa Ryokan. English is not spoken here, but the genteel hospitality and sophistication of this inn make a stay relaxing and comfortable. Elegant simplicity achieves harmony. Even the few Western guest rooms are simply adorned. Dinner is kaiseki-style and uses the produce of the sea to full advantage. *5-1 Nichu-dai cho, Kochi 780, tel. 0888/22–1317, fax 0888/24– 7401. 40 rooms, mostly Japanese style. Facilities: meals served in one's room, small banquet room, Japanese garden. AE, DC, V. Expensive.*

Washington Hotel. On the street leading to Kochijo Castle and a 20-minute walk from the station, this is a small, friendly business hotel in downtown Kochi. It has a small restaurant, and the rooms are a good size for this kind of lodging. *1-8-25 Otesuji, Kochi-shi, Kochi 780, tel. 0888/23–6111, fax 0888/25– 2737. 62 Western-style rooms. Facilities: Japanese/Western restaurant. AE, V. Moderate.*

Hotel Sunroute Kochi. This business hotel has slightly larger rooms than the average of its kind, but should only be considered if you need to be within walking distance of the station. *1-1-28 Kitahon-cho, Kochi-shi, Kochi 780, tel. 0888/23–1311. 64 rooms. Facilities: breakfast room. AE, DC, V. Inexpensive.*

Matsuyama

★ **ANA Hotel Matsuyama.** This is the best international hotel downtown. It caters to the business executive. The location is excellent, within five minutes on foot to the cable car that travels up to Matsuyamajo Castle. The streetcars that go out to Dogo Onsen pass by the front doors. The hotel has banquet rooms, shopping arcades, and a summer beer garden on its roof. The guest rooms are well maintained, reasonably spacious, and fully equipped, with everything but a hair dryer. *3-2-1 Ichibancho, Matsuyama 790, tel. 0899/33–5511, fax 0899/21–6053. 334 rooms. Facilities: Chinese, Japanese, and Western restaurants; rooftop beer garden open May–Sept. AE, DC, V. Expensive.*

Funaya Ryokan. The best Japanese inn in Dogo Onsen, this is where the imperial family stays when it comes to take the waters. The ryokan has a long history, but the present building was built in 1963. The best rooms look out on the garden. Breakfast and dinner are included in the tariff. *1-33, Godo Yumo-machi, Matsuyama 790, tel. 0899/47–0278, fax 0899/49–2139. 43 rooms; most rooms are Japanese style. Not all rooms have private bath. Facilities: thermal baths. AE, V. Expensive.*

Hotel Sunroute. This business hotel has no particular charm, but its rooms are not too small, and it is just a five-minute walk from the JR station. The best part of the hotel is its rooftop beer garden (open summer only), from which you can catch a glimpse of the castle. *Miyata-cho, Matsuyama 790, tel. 0899/33–2811. 110 Western-style rooms. AE, V. Inexpensive.*

Takamatsu

★ **Kawaroku Ryokan.** This is the best hotel in the center of town amid the shopping arcades, and it offers Western- and Japanese-style rooms, all with private bath. The original Kawaroku was bombed out in World War II. This replacement is unappealing from the outside but is pleasantly furnished on the inside. The rooms have a light, refreshing decor. *1-2 Hyakkencho, Takamatsu, Kagawa Prefecture 760, tel. 0878/21–5666, fax 0878/21–7301. 70 rooms, 21 Western style. Facilities: French restaurant. Japanese food is available in your room. AE, V. Moderate–Expensive.*

Keio Plaza Hotel. The staff is shy but friendly at this efficient hotel, but it is at the far end of Chuo-dori Avenue, near Ritsurin-Koen Park, a good 10 minutes by taxi from the JR station. Guest rooms are reasonably spacious and comfortable, though the rooms facing Chuo-dori do suffer slightly from traffic noise. *11-5 Chuocho, Takamatsu, Kagawa Prefecture 760, tel. 0878/34–5511, fax 0878/34–0800. 180 rooms; 2 Japanese style. Facilities: Japanese and Western restaurants. Moderate–Expensive.*

Takamatsu Grand Hotel. Located on the city's main avenue, Chuo-dori, the Grand is within a five-minute walk from the JR station. The lobby is on the third floor (there are nine independently owned restaurants on the second floor), and the main restaurant is on the seventh floor. Tamamo Park and the Tamamojo Castle are behind the hotel, so the views on that side of the building are quite splendid. All the guest rooms could use refurbishing, but they are clean. *1-5-10 Kotobukicho, Takamatsu, Kagawa Prefecture 760, tel. 0878/51–5757, fax 0878/21–9422. 136 Western-style rooms. Facilities: Western restaurant, Japanese restaurants on 2nd floor. AE, DC, MC, V. Moderate.*

13 Kyushu

By Kiko Itasaka

Updated by
Nigel Fisher

Kyushu, the quiet island southwest of the main island of Honshu, offers a mild climate, lush green countryside, hot springs, and eerie volcanic formations. This island, however peaceful it may be now, was for centuries the most active and international island in all of Japan. To this day, it is considered to be the birthplace of Japanese civilization. The cities of Kyushu are full of sights of historical and cultural significance.

Legend has it that the grandson of Amaterasu, the sun goddess, first ruled Japan from Kyushu. Another tale relates that Jimmu, Japan's first emperor, traveled from Kyushu to Honshu, consolidated Japan, and established the imperial line that exists to this day.

From the 4th century on, Kyushu, as a result of its geographic proximity to Korea and China, was the first area of Japan to be culturally influenced by its more sophisticated neighbors. Through the gateway of Kyushu, Japan was first introduced to pottery techniques, Buddhism, the Chinese writing system, and other aspects of Chinese and Korean culture.

Not all outside influence, however, was welcome. In 1274, Kublai Khan led a fleet of Mongol warriors in an unsuccessful attempt to invade Japan. The Japanese, in preparation for further attacks, built a stone wall along the coast of Kyushu; remnants of it can still be seen today outside Fukuoka. When the Mongols returned in 1281 with a force 100,000 strong, they were repelled by the stone wall and by the fierce fighting of the Kyushu natives; the fighters were aided by a huge storm, known as *kamikaze* (divine wind), which blew the Mongol fleet out to sea. This term may be more familiar in its revived form, used in World War II to describe suicide pilots.

In the mid-16th century, Kyushu was once again the first point of contact with the outside world, when Portuguese ships first landed on the shores of Japan. The arrival of these ships signaled Japan's initial introduction to the West and its knowledge of medicine, firearms, and Christianity. The Portuguese were followed by other European powers, the Dutch and the Spanish. The Tokugawa Shogunate was not entirely pleased with the intrusion of the Westerners and feared political interference. In 1635, the shogunate established a closed-door policy that permitted foreigners to land only on a small island, Dejima, in the harbor of Nagasaki. As a result, until 1859, when Japan opened its doors to the West, the small port town of Nagasaki became the most important center for both trade and Western learning for Kyushu and the entire nation. To this day, the historical influence of Europe is apparent in Nagasaki, with its 19th-century Western-style buildings and the lasting presence of Christianity.

Whether you visit the castle in Kumamoto or the ancient temples of Fukuoka, a visit to Kyushu is a tour of Japan's past. This island is no longer a center of power in Japan, but many cities and their sights have remained untouched and have not been replaced by skyscrapers.

A visit to Kyushu's major attractions requires travel around the island. Fortunately, the journeys between the points of interest in Kyushu afford beautiful views of Kyushu's rich green rice fields, mountains, and the ocean. The starting point of any visit to Kyushu is Fukuoka City, where there is a major airport and a JR Shinkansen train station. Of course, it is possible to travel to the different sights of Kyushu in any order, but in this chapter, a tour that is a circular route is suggested for your convenience; it starts in Fukuoka, proceeds to Nagasaki, Kumamoto, and Mt. Aso, and concludes with a visit to the relaxing hot-spring resort of Beppu (from which you can return to Fukuoka).

Essential Information

Arriving and Departing

By Plane   The only international airport in Kyushu is Fukuoka Airport (*see* Arriving and Departing in Fukuoka, *below*). Nagasaki, Kagoshima, Oita, Miyazaki, and Kita Kyushu all have airports serviced by domestic airlines.

By Train   The JR Shinkansen trains travel only as far as Fukuoka (*see* Arriving and Departing in Fukuoka, *below*). JR trains connect all major destinations in Kyushu.

By Ferry   The Kansai Kisen Line operates ferries connecting the cities of Kobe and Osaka with Beppu (*see* Arriving and Departing in Beppu, *below*) and Kita Kyushu.

Ferries have scheduled runs between the Hakata Pier Ferry Terminal at Fukuoka and Yosu and Pusan, both in Korea. There is also a hydrofoil service to Pusan.

Fukuoka

Numbers in the margin correspond to points of interest on the Kyushu map.

❶ **Fukuoka** is the second-largest city in Kyushu and the starting point for most travel around the island. Many people visiting Kyushu spend at least a day or two here. If you are planning to stop in Fukuoka en route to other cities, you'll discover a few places of particular historical and cultural interest. Although it is the major industrial city of Kyushu, you will immediately sense a slower pace of life compared with that of Japan's other main cities. People in Kyushu are known for their straightforwardness and warmth, and visitors often find this city to be less cosmopolitan but more pleasant than Tokyo or Osaka.

Arriving and Departing

By Plane   Japan Airlines (JAL), All Nippon Airways (ANA), and Japan Air System have 1½-hour flights between Haneda Airport in Tokyo and Fukuoka City. Twenty flights are offered daily. JAL provides service (1 hr. 45 mins.) between Narita International Airport and Fukuoka Airport daily. JAL and ANA also offer a total of eight direct flights between Osaka and Fukuoka (1 hr. 45 mins.) making it convenient for travelers to begin or end their Japan travels in Kyushu.

Between the Airport and Center City   The Fukuoka Airport is located very near the center of the city. A new subway line links the airport with the JR Hakata Station; tickets cost ¥220.

By Train   JR Shinkansen Hikari trains travel between Tokyo and Hakata Station in Fukuoka (time: 6 hrs. 26 mins. to 7 hrs. 24 mins.).

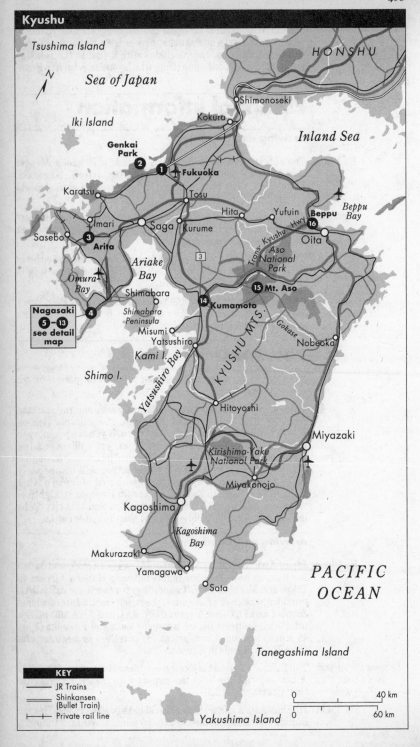

Kyushu

Tsushima Island

Sea of Japan

HONSHU

Iki Island

Shimonoseki

Kokura

Inland Sea

Genkai
Park

2

1 ✈ **Fukuoka**

Karatsu

Tosu

Hita

Yufuin

Beppu

16

Beppu
Bay

Imari

Saga

Kurume

Oita

Sasebo

3

Arita

Ariake
Bay

3

Trans-Kyushu Hwy

Aso
National
Park

Omura
Bay

Shimabara

15 Mt. Aso

Nagasaki

5–**13**
see detail
map

4

Shimabara
Peninsula

14

Kumamoto

Misumi

Yatsushiro

Gokase

Nobeoka

Kami I.

Shimo I.

Yatsushiro Bay

KYUSHU MTS.

Hitoyoshi

Miyazaki

Kirishima-Yaku
National Park

✈

✈

Kagoshima

Miyakonojo

Makurazaki

Kagoshima
Bay

Yamagawa

Sata

PACIFIC
OCEAN

Tanegashima Island

KEY
— JR Trains
═ Shinkansen
(Bullet Train)
╫ Private rail line

0 _____ 40 km
0 _____ 60 km

Yakushima Island

There are 15 daily runs. Shinkansen trains travel between Osaka and Hakata Station, and also between Hiroshima and Hakata. Regular JR express trains travel these routes but take twice as long.

Getting Around

The easiest way to get around Fukuoka is by bus or by one of the two subway lines (the minimum fare is ¥180). The two major transportation centers of Fukuoka are located around Hakata Station and in the downtown area known as Tenjin, the terminal station for both of the subway lines. Buses leave from the Kotsu Bus Center just across the street from the Hakata Station, and from the Fukuoka Bus Center at Tenjin.

Important Addresses and Numbers

Tourist Information The **Fukuoka City Tourist Information Office** (tel. 092/431–3003) is located in Hakata Station. Some of the office staff speak English, and excellent maps of the city and neighboring areas are available. Open daily 9–7. If you plan on staying in Fukuoka for more than a day or two, you may wish to contact The Fukuoka International Association (Rainbow Plaza, IMS 5F, 1-7-11 Tanjin, Chuo–ku, Fukuoka City 810, tel. 092/733–2220, fax 092/733–2215), which serves as an information resource and center for networking.

U.S. Consulate (5-26 Ohori 2-chome, Chuo–ku, tel. 092/751–9331).

Travel Agencies **Japan Travel Bureau** (Daiwa Seimei Kaikan Bldg., 1-14-4 Tenjin, Chuo–ku, tel. 092/771–5211).

Guided Tours

You can take sightseeing bus tours of the major historic sights of Fukuoka City from the **Tenjin Bus Center** (tel. 092/771–2961) or the **Kotsu Bus Center** (tel. 092/431–1171). Not all tours are in English, so it is better to have your hotel call for further information or to ask at the tourist information office.

Exploring

Fukuoka is the commercial, political, and cultural center of Kyushu and the island's largest city. With 1.2 million inhabitants, it is the eighth largest city in Japan. It is small and provincial in comparison to Tokyo, but there is a dynamic quality to Fukuoka whose city council is determined to position the city as Japan's gateway to Asia. Most activities and entertainment events happen around the two city centers, Hakata Station and the downtown Tenjin district. (Use the subway—fare: ¥160—to travel between them.) Most of the places you visit in Fukuoka, whether they are restaurants, shops, or sights, are near these two centers, or can be reached easily from them. The city is divided in two parts by the Nakagawa River. All areas west of the river are known as Fukuoka, and everything east of the river is known as Hakata. Along the Naka and Hakata rivers is Nakasu, the largest nightlife district in Western Japan, with 3,000 bars, restaurants, and street vendors. Fukuoka was originally a castle town founded at the end of the 16th century, and Hakata was the place for commerce. In 1889 the two districts were officially merged as Fukuoka City, but the historical names are still used.

Start your tour of Fukuoka at the **Shofukuji Temple,** which can be reached by a 15-minute walk from Hakata Station, or a five-minute Nishitetsu bus ride from the adjacent Hakata Kotsu Bus Center to the Okunodo stop. This temple was founded in 1195 by Eisai (1141–1215), upon his return to Kyushu after years of study in China. He was one of the first Japanese priests to introduce Buddhism to Japan. Eisai is also said to have brought the first tea seeds from China to Japan. Note in particular the Korean-style bronze bell in the belfry, which is designated an Important Cultural Property by the Japanese government. *Admission free. Open daily 9–5.*

From the Shofukuji Temple, return to Hakata Station and either walk or take a bus from the adjacent Hakata Kotsu Bus Center to Sumiyoshi Station and visit the **Sumiyoshi Jinja Shrine.** This is the oldest Shinto shrine in Kyushu, founded in 1623 and dedicated to the guardian gods of seafarers. An annual festival is held at this shrine October 12–14, complete with sumo wrestling. The temple is located on top of a hill with a lovely view of both the Nakagawa River and the city, and the grounds are dotted with camphor and cedar trees. *Admission free. Open 9–5.*

For a recreational break, take the subway from Hakata Station to Ohori-Koen Park Station, about a 20-minute ride. **Ohori-Koen** is a spacious park, built around a lake that was once part of a moat surrounding Fukuokajo Castle. Bridges connect three small islands in the center of the lake. In early April, the northern portion of the park is graced with the blossoms of 2,600 cherry trees. On weekends you will see many Fukuoka residents taking advantage of this oasis in the middle of an otherwise grim and gray industrial city. Bring a picnic and enjoy a leisurely walk, or boat and fish on the lake.

If you get bored with the pleasures of relaxation in the park, go to the **Fukuokajo Castle** grounds on the outskirts of Ohori-Koen. The castle was originally built in 1607. Little remains here—only a turret, gates, and a small portion of the castle— but the grounds are on a hill with a panoramic view of the city.

Shopping

Fukuoka is famous for two local products—**Hakata dolls** and the **Hakata** *obis* (kimono sashes).

Hakata dolls, popular throughout Japan, are made with fired clay and are hand painted with bright colors and distinctive expressions. These dolls are mostly ornamental and depict such figures as children, women, samurai, and geisha.

Hakata obis are made of an interesting local silk that has a rougher texture than most Japanese silk, which is usually perfectly even and smooth. For local young girls, the purchase of their first Hakata obi is an initiation into adulthood. Other products, such as bags and purses, are made of this Hakata silk.

The main area for shopping is the downtown district of Tenjin, which can be reached by subway from Hakata Station (third stop). Here you will find many boutiques, department stores, and restaurants.

Iwataya Department Store (2-11-1 Tenjin, Chuo-ku, tel. 092/721–1111) carries the most complete selection of merchandise in the area, including Hakata dolls, Hakata silk, and an excellent china department that features some of the distinctive pottery of Kyushu. The store is in the center of the Tenjin shopping area.

Hakusen (Tenjin-2-chome, Shirai, Chuo-ku, tel. 092/712–8900. Open 9–8:30), also located in the Tenjin shopping district, is a specialty shop with an extensive selection of Hakata dolls.

A store that specializes in Hakata silk is **Hakata Ori Kaikan** (Hakataeki Minami, Hakata-ku, tel. 092/472–0761), the best place to get obis and bags. This shop is small, but everything is neatly organized and attractively displayed.

Excursions from Fukuoka

Genkai Park ②
This park extends from Hakata Bay along the coast of Fukuoka and Saga. It has long beaches with white sands and eerie Japanese black pines. The waters of Hakata Bay facing the Genkai Nada Sea are surprisingly clean and relatively uncrowded. You can combine a swim in the bay with a visit to the *boheki*, the ruins of stone walls (next to a beach) that were built in the 13th century to stave off the invasions of the Mongols.

Getting There
By Bus. Take the Nishi-no-ura bus from the Fukuoka Kotsu Center. The trip takes about two hours.

Arita ③
Arita is a small town, south of Fukuoka, that has been a leading pottery center for centuries. In 1616, a Korean potter introduced the art of making white porcelain to Japan through the artisans of Arita. After this, color-decoration techniques were introduced by Chinese artists. The wonders of Arita pottery have long been appreciated in the West. Early Dutch traders first noticed the pottery in Nagasaki early in the 17th century, but it was at the Philadelphia Exhibition of 1876 that Arita ceramics became renowned. The pottery is known for its delicate patterns, which incorporate flowers and birds.

Arita is a small village with one main street that is entirely lined with small pottery shops. These shops all have their own kilns and have been run by the same families for generations. Prices depend on the quality of the ceramic, but you can get a beautiful handmade teacup for around ¥1,000, or a set of five cups and a teapot for ¥5,000. Once a year, at the end of April or early May, there is a large pottery fair, where everything in all the shops goes on sale. At these times, many of the ceramic pieces are priced as low as ¥100.

Getting There
By Train. To get from Fukuoka to Arita, take the Nagasaki Line from the Hakata Station in Fukuoka to the Arita Station. The trip will take approximately 1 hour and 15 minutes.

Nagasaki

❹ Nagasaki, a quiet city of hills with a peaceful harbor, is often called the San Francisco of Japan. The harbor, now serenely dotted with a few fishing boats, was once the most important trading port in all of Japan. In 1639, when Japan decided to close its ports to all foreigners, it appointed the small island of Dejima in Nagasaki Harbor as the one place where foreigners were allowed to land. The only Japanese allowed to have contact with the foreigners were merchants and prostitutes. The Tokugawa Shogunate established this isolationist policy to prevent Western powers from having political influence in Japan. With Nagasaki as the focal point, however, knowledge of the West, particularly in fields such as medicine and weaponry, began to spread throughout Japan. Japan reopened its doors to the West in 1859, thus ending Nagasaki's heyday as the sole international port. Many of the original buildings and churches from the 19th century still stand as testaments to this unique period in Japanese history.

After more than two centuries of prominence, Nagasaki was not the center of world attention until the atomic bomb was dropped on it in 1945. Although the bomb destroyed one-third of the city, enough remained standing so that, to this day, Nagasaki has an atmosphere that mixes both Eastern and Western traditions.

Travelers to Nagasaki will want to pick up a copy of *Harbor Light*, a monthly publication in English that provides detailed information on various activities in the city.

Arriving and Departing

By Plane Omura Airport is approximately one hour by bus or car from Nagasaki. ANA and Japan Air System offer direct flights from Haneda Airport in Tokyo to Omura Airport (1 hr. 45 mins.). There are five daily flights. From Osaka the flights are 1 hour and 10 minutes.

Between the Airport A regular shuttle bus travels between Omura Airport and Na-
and Center City gasaki Station in 55 minutes. The cost is ¥1,100.

By Train Take the JR Nagasaki Line Limited Express train from Fukuoka (2 hrs. 30 mins.). To get to Kumamoto from Nagasaki by train, take the Kamone Line from Nagasaki to Tosu Station (2 hrs.). From Tosu, board the Kagoshima Main Line and get off at Kumamoto (1 hr.).

By Bus The Kyushu Kyuko Bus Company offers bus service between Fukuoka and Nagasaki (3 hrs. 20 mins.; the bus leaves from the Fukuoka Bus Center in the Tenjin downtown district). A bus service also runs between Nagasaki and Kumamoto (4 hrs.).

Getting Around

By Streetcar Streetcars are the most convenient way of getting around Nagasaki. Although they are slow, they appropriately reflect the relaxed atmosphere of Nagasaki and echo another century. The streetcars stop at most of the major sights, and most stops have signs in English. You can purchase a one-day pass for unlimited streetcar travel for ¥550 at the City Tourist Information Center or at major hotels. Otherwise, you pay ¥120 as you get off the streetcar. If you wish to transfer from one streetcar to another, take a transfer ticket (*norikai kippu*) from the driver of the first streetcar as you alight and drop your ¥120 in the box.

By Bus Bus routes exist in Nagasaki, but they are complicated and not very convenient.

Important Addresses and Numbers

Tourist Information The **City Tourist Information Center** (1-88 Onoue-cho, tel. 0958/23–3631) is on the left hand corner (as you leave the station) of the station plaza. There is no sign written in English, so it takes perseverance to find, but the office is useful for maps and directions. Open Monday–Saturday 9–6, closed Sunday. **The Nagasaki Prefecture Tourist Office** (2nd floor, Nagasaki Kotsu Sangyo Bldg., 3–1 Daikoku-machi, tel. 0958/23-4041) is across the street from the JR station one floor above street level in a department store. To reach it from the station, use the pedestrian bridge. The staff is not very helpful, but maps and bus schedules to various areas within the prefecture are available. Open weekdays 9–5:30, Saturday 9–12:45.

Guided Tours

By Boat A 50-minute port cruise of the Nagasaki Harbor departs at 11:40 and 3:15. Fare: ¥900. Take a streetcar to the Ohato Station, then go to Pier No. 1.

By Ricksha Rickshas, though once ubiquitous, are now a rare sight in Japan. Prices vary according to the course you take, but the minimum is ¥2,000 per person. Ask your hotel or the tourist information office to call in Japanese to arrange your tour (tel. 0958/24–4367).

City Tours **Japan Travel Bureau** (tel. 0958/24-3200), offers a few city tours with English-speaking guides. A three-hour tour of the city's major sights costs ¥2,950.

Exploring

Numbers in the margin correspond to points of interest on the Nagasaki map.

Nagasaki is a beautiful harbor city that is small enough to walk around if you have the energy to face some of the steep inclines, which are similar to those in San Francisco. Most of the sights of interest and restaurant and shopping areas are located south of Nagasaki Station.

5 The **Glover Gardens,** with its panoramic view of Nagasaki and the harbor, alongside 19th-century European-style buildings, is a good place to begin your tour of Nagasaki. To get here, board Streetcar 1 from the JR station to the downtown stop, Tsuki-machi, and transfer (don't forget to collect a transfer ticket) to Streetcar 5. Get off at the Oura-Tenshudo-shita stop (the second-to-last stop on the line). Take the side street to the right, cross the bridge over a small canal, and then take the second street on your left up the hill. On your left is the Tokyu Hotel, a place to keep in mind for afternoon tea, and on the right is an array of souvenir shops. Facing you as you turn one corner on the hill will be the Oura Catholic Church. We will return here shortly.

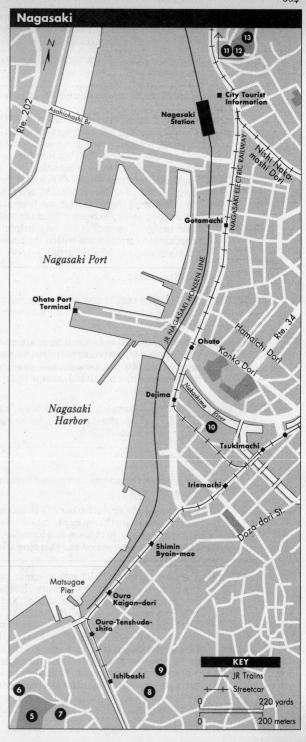

The gardens feature Western-style houses built in the late 19th century. The main attraction is the **Glover Mansion** itself. This house, built in 1863, was the home of Thomas Glover, a British merchant who married a Japanese woman and settled in Nagasaki. Glover introduced the first steam locomotive and established the first mint in Japan. The house remains as it was in Glover's time, and his furniture and possessions are on display. The story for Puccini's opera *Madame Butterfly* is said to have been set here. Escalators going up the slopes toward the Glover Mansion seem out of place, but the grounds are unspoiled, and you get a sense of what Japan was like as it opened up to the West in the 19th century. *Tel. 0958/22–8223. Admission: ¥600. Open Mar.–Nov. 8–6 ; Dec.–Feb. 8:30–5 .*

❻ Located just outside the exit of the Glover Gardens is the **Jurokuban Mansion.** Built in 1860 as accommodations for the American consular staff, it is now a museum that displays Dutch and Portuguese objects related to the history of early trade between these countries and Japan. *Tel. 0958/23–4260. Admission: ¥400. Open Mar.–Nov. 8:30–6; Dec.–Feb. 8:30–5 .*

❼ After you leave the Jurokuban Mansion, continue down the same street past the Glover Mansion for a few minutes. You will come across another 19th-century European-style structure, the **Oura Catholic Church,** which is the oldest Gothic-style building in Japan. The church was constructed in 1865 by a French missionary and was dedicated to the memory of the 26 Christians who were crucified in 1597 after Christianity was outlawed. The church features beautiful stained-glass windows. *Admission: ¥250. Open 8:30–6.*

❽ As you leave the church, walk down the hill, across the canal, and past the Ishibashi streetcar stop. Nearby is the **Tojin-kan Chinese Mansion,** built in 1893 by the Chinese residents of Nagasaki. The hall now houses a gallery of Chinese crafts and souvenir shops. Although this is a favorite with many Japanese tourists, it is probably more popular for its many little shops than for its historic interest. *Admission: ¥515. Open 8:30–5.*

❾ After seeing the interiors of these 19th-century buildings, perhaps you may want to take a stroll. Follow the street to the side of Tojin-kan and after about 100 yards, on your left will be a cobblestone slope known as the **Orandazaka** (Hollander Slope). It is a pleasant walk alongside wood houses built by 19th-century Dutch residents.

❿ The walk along this slope will lead you to the Shimin Byoin Mae streetcar stop, located just in front of Nagasaki View Hospital. Board the streetcar and go to the Tsukimachi stop, where you can see the original site of **Dejima,** the man-made island where the Dutch were allowed to land in the years when Japan maintained its isolationist policy. It is no longer an island, because the area has been land-filled, but there is a miniature reconstruction of the entire village and community of Dejima, as part of the **Dejima Historical Museum.** *Admission free. Open 9–5. Closed Mon.*

⓫ After viewing all of these picturesque sights, Nagasaki may seem to be a quaint port town that time and progress have somehow passed by, but it is important to remember that Nagasaki, along with Hiroshima, was one of the two places where atomic bombs were dropped. In order that the memory of this tragedy will live on, a **Peace Park** was built on the exact site of the epicenter of the August 9, 1945 atomic blast. In a blinding flash, 2.59 square miles were obliterated and 74,884 people were killed, with another 74,909 injured out of an estimated population of 204,000. And it was only a small bomb compared to present-day atomic weapons. To get to this park, return to the Tsukimachi stop and take Streetcar 1 to the Matsuyamachi stop (If you are going to the Peace Park directly from the JR Station, take either Streetcar 1 or 3 to the Matsuyamachi stop, about a 10-min. ride.) At one end of the park is a black pillar, grimly denoting the exact center of the blast. At the other end is a 32-foot statue of a male figure with one arm pointing horizontally, the other pointing toward the sky. The statue is rather ugly, and the message of the positioning of the arms is rather unclear. Every year on August 9 there is an anti–nuclear war demonstration at the Peace Park. *Admission free.*

⑫ Standing on the hill above the Peace Park is the **Nagasaki International Cultural Hall.** To reach it, climb the steps at the southern end of the park, past the Flame of Peace. Inside the hall, which looks like a prefabricated building from early post-war days, are displays of photos and objects demonstrating the devastation caused by the atomic bomb. The museum is far more impressive than the Peace Park itself. Walking through the hall is a sobering experience. Note the tiny corner on the third floor given to the foreign victims of the bomb dropped by the American B29 *Bockstar*. It notes that there were 500 Allied POWs interned in the middle of a factory site, although 200 of them had died of disease, malnutrition, and torture before the bomb was dropped. *Admission:* ¥*50. Open 9–5.*

⑬ One last place to visit in Nagasaki is **Nishizaka Hill,** a short walk from the Nagasaki train station. As you leave the front of the station, turn left and walk along the road next to the train tracks for a few minutes. Turn right on the first major road and you will be at Nishizaka Hill. In the early 16th century, Christian missionaries successfully converted many Japanese to Christianity. Japanese leaders feared the potential influence of Christianity and banned its practice in 1587. In 1597, 20 Japanese and six foreigners were crucified on Nishizaka Hill for refusing to renounce their religious beliefs. A monument was built in 1962 dedicated to the memory of the 26 martyrs, and a small museum documents the history of Christianity in Japan. *Admission:* ¥*250. Open 9–5.*

Off the Beaten Track

An hour by bus to the north of Nagasaki and near Sasebo City is the new **Nagasaki Holland Village Huis Ten Bosch** (1-1, Huis Ten Bosch-Machi, Sasebo City, tel. 0956/27–0001, fax 0956/27–0912). Opened in 1992 at a cost of $1.75 billion, this is Japan's largest theme park (375 acres). The attractions are modeled after 17th-century Holland, with replicas of a Dutch village and the Cathedral of Horn (Dom Horn). Though there are scheduled activities such as horse parades, most of the Japanese tourists spend their time choosing among the many restaurants available and shopping at the numerous souvenir outlets. With an admission cost of ¥3,900, plus additional fees for specific attractions, it can become an expensive day's outing and one that foreign visitors may find only marginally interesting. The complex includes the 330-room Hotel Europa. *Open 9 AM–11 PM.*

Shopping

Hamanomachi, located not far from Dejima, is the major shopping district in the downtown area of Nagasaki. In this area you can find traditional crafts, antiques, and restaurants. Keep in mind that it is illegal to bring tortoiseshell products into the United States.

Gift Ideas **Castella cake.** Based on a Dutch cake, this dessert has long been the most commonly known Nagasaki product. The cake resembles a pound cake, has a moist top, and was popular in Nagasaki when baked goods were still unknown in the rest of Japan. **Fukusaya** is a bakery that has been in business since the beginning of the Meiji period (1868–1912). When you say "castella," most people think of this famous shop with its distinctive yellow packaging of the cake. Tokyoites would never return from a trip to Nagasaki without their Fukusaya castella. *3-1 Funadaikumachi, tel. 0958/21–2938. Open 8:30–8. Closed every 2nd Thurs.*

Glassware. Biidoro Bijutsukan is a museum featuring exhibits documenting the history of Nagasaki glassware, an art that was introduced by the Dutch during the Tokugawa period. Located near the Peace Park, the museum has a small gift shop. The museum annex has a more extensive selection of items for sale. *16-10 Hashiguchimachi, tel. 0958/43–0100; annex: 5-19 Hamanomachi, tel. 0958/27–0100. Open 9–5.*

Kumamoto

Numbers in the margin correspond to points of interest on the Kyushu map.

⑭ In the years of the Tokugawa Shogunate (1603–1868), **Kumamoto** was one of Japan's major centers of power. The main attractions in Kumamoto—the castle and the landscaped gardens of Suizenji-Koen Park—date from this period and are among the most famous in Japan. Kumamoto may no longer be a major political center, but, with its broad avenues lined with countless trees, it is an extremely attractive city and is one of considerable historic interest.

Arriving and Departing

By Plane Five daily flights connect Haneda Airport (Tokyo) with Kumamoto Airport (1 hr. 40 mins.). ANA and Japan Air System (JAS) fly between Tokyo and Kumamoto. From Osaka Airport, ANA has four flights daily (1 hr.).

Between the Airport and Center City A regular bus service connects the airport with the JR Kumamoto Station. The bus takes 55 minutes and costs ¥720.

By Train Japan Railways offers a limited express train from Hakata that stops in Kumamoto (1½ hrs.) en route to Kagoshima. From Nagasaki, take the train to Shimabara, board a one-hour ferry across the Ariake Bay to Misumi, then take the train to Kumamoto. JR Rail Pass holders can save the ferry fare by taking the train to Tosu and changing to the train going to Kumamoto (3 hrs. total).

By Bus From Nagasaki Bus Terminal, you can take a four-hour bus trip to Kumamoto. The bus goes as far as Shimabara, after which you board a ferry across the Ariake Bay for one hour to Misumi, then take the bus directly to Kumamoto Kotsu Center. The cost of this journey, which takes you through some of Kyushu's most beautiful scenery, is ¥2,650 including the ferry ride.

Getting Around

By Streetcar The easiest way to get around Kumamoto is by streetcar. There are two streetcar lines that connect the major areas of the city. When you board the streetcar, take a ticket. When you get off, you will pay a fare that depends on the distance traveled. The chart of the fares is displayed at the front to the left of the driver. A streetcar stop, Kumamoto Eki-mae, is in front of the JR Kumamoto Station, and it is a good 10-minute ride into downtown. Fare: ¥160. One-day travel passes good for use on streetcars and municipal buses are available for ¥500 from the Kumamoto Station Travel Information Bureau (tel. 096/352–3743).

By Bus The main bus terminal is the Kotsu Center, located within a few minutes' walking distance of Kumamoto Castle. Although the buses travel all over the city, the routes are more complicated than those of the streetcars.

Important Addresses and Numbers

Tourist **City Information Office,** 3-15-1 Kasuga, tel. 096/352–3743. This
Information office is in a booth in front of the JR station, next to the streetcar stop. Open 9–5. If it is closed, use the tourist information in the JR station across from the JR seat reservation center.

Exploring

Unlike many other Japanese cities, there is very little activity around the JR station. Shops, restaurants, and hotels cluster downtown under the shadow of the castle. The heart of the town is a broad shopping arcade from which small streets branch off. It comes alive at night with neon lights advertising restaurants and bars.

Kumamotojo Castle, located in the heart of downtown Kumamoto, is where most people begin their tour of Kumamoto City. To get to the castle, board Streetcar 2, get off at the Kumamoto-jo-mae stop and walk up a tree-lined slope toward the castle. Kumamotojo was first built in 1607 under the auspices of Kiyomasa Kato, feudal lord of this region. It is especially famous for its unique and massive concave defensive walls, known as *mushagaeshi*, which made it exceedingly difficult for attackers to scale. It is often referred to as Ginkojo Castle, named after a giant ginko tree that was supposedly planted by Lord Kato. Much of the original castle was destroyed in 1877, after it lay under siege for 57 continuous days by an army from Kagoshima led by Saigo Takamori. It was rebuilt in 1960.

Often, reconstructed buildings are of little interest, but this castle of concrete is an excellent example of reconstruction that manages to evoke the magnificence of the original. By walking around the expansive grounds, you can get a true sense of the grandeur of feudal Japan. Few castles in Japan today, reconstructed or not, can boast of 49 turrets, 18 turret gates, and 29 castle gates. Inside Kumamotojo is a museum for those who are interested in feudal history. It exhibits relics such as samurai armor and palanquins. As you look at the displays, you cannot help but imagine samurai in full regalia, protecting their lord. From the top floor there is an excellent view of Kumamoto. If time permits further exploration of the grounds, go to the Higo Gardens; they are filled with lovely flowers and are a peaceful place to conclude your visit. *Admission: ¥200 (grounds), ¥300 (castle). Open Apr.–Sept. 8:30–5:30; Oct.–Mar. 8:30–4:30.*

To the west of the castle in a modern, redbrick building is the **Kumamoto-keuritsu Bijutsukan** (Prefectural Art Museum) that in the spring and autumn exhibits the famous Hosokawa collection of antiques from the Tokugawa Shogunate era. Be sure to see the full-scale models of the burial chambers with Kumamoto's design of painted geometrical shapes. *Admission: ¥300. Open 9:30–4:30. Closed Mon.*

Going east from the castle, take either Streetcar 2 or 3 to the Suizenji-Koen-mae stop, in front of the **Suizenji-Koen Park,** which features a 300-year-old garden that is a tribute to the art of landscape gardening. The garden was originally created in 1632 by the Hosokawa clan as part of the grounds of their villa. Although the park is often crowded with tour groups and lacks a certain serenity, there are still elements of beauty where the artistry of man has worked with nature. A part of the garden with ponds and small artificial mounds recreates the 53 stations of the Tokkaido (the route between Edo and Kyoto) and its prominent features such as Lake Biwa and Mt. Fuji. *Admission: ¥200. Open 7–6.*

Time Out Take a break in the park at the small, old-fashioned teahouse located by the garden's pond. Here, for a small fee, you can sip green tea as you sit on tatami mats and appreciate the exquisite view. If you get hungry, numerous food stalls in the park offer light snacks. You may very well be in need of refreshment, because a visit to Suizenji-Koen takes at least several hours; it is possible to spend an entire day here.

On the hill to the west of town is Honmyo-ji, a Nichiren temple built by Kato Kiyomasa. It is reached by streetcar from the Kumamoto JR station or by Bus 12 from the Kotsu Center. Kiyomasa is buried here in the tomb at the top of a flight of stairs so that his spirit may look across at eye level to the donjon of his castle, Kumamoto-jo. The temple's museum contains Kiyomasa's personal effects, including the helmet that he wore while campaigning in Korea for his master, Toyotomi Hideyoshi. *Admission to museum: ¥300. Open 9–4:30. Closed Mon.*

Off the Beaten Track

If you have time, you may want to go south from Kumamoto to Kagoshima. The scenic, three-hour train ride to Nishi-Kagoshima passes mountains on the left and the sea on the right. Downtown is a five-minute walk from the JR station. There is a tourist information office to the left as you leave the JR Nishi-Kagoshima Station.

The modern city of **Kagoshima** has few sightseeing attractions. It is usually a jumping-off point to the surrounding country and Okinawa islands, or a stopover on the train ride across to Kyushu's east coast. The **Park Hotel** (15-24 Chuo-machi, Kagoshima 890, tel. 0992/51-1100), two minutes from Nishi-Kagoshima Station, has reasonable rates, clean, efficient rooms, a pleasant coffee lounge, a Japanese restaurant, and a helpful staff. There is also the more expensive (¥14,000 for a twin) and slightly smarter **Kagoshima Tokyu Inn** (Chuo chome 5-1, Kagoshima 590, tel. 0992/56–0109, fax 0992/53–3692), with 182 rooms. In the downtown entertainment district you'll find **Edo-ko Sushi** (Bunka St., 2-16 Sannichi-cho, tel. 0992/25–1890), an excellent sushi bar (counter seating and two tables with tatami seating) with a very hospitable owner. Take the first right off Yubudo (the wide shopping-arcade street), and Edo-ko is the last restaurant on the left. Prices are moderate.

Shopping

One of Kumamoto's most famous products is **higo zogan,** a form of metalwork consisting of black steel inlaid with silver and gold, creating a delicate yet striking pattern. Originally an ornamentation technique for samurai armor, it is now used mostly in jewelry and other accessories. Another popular local product is the **Yamaga doro,** a lantern of gold paper. On August 16, as part of an annual festival, young women carry these gold lanterns through the streets of Kumamoto.

Shimatori Shopping Arcade, located by the Kumamotojo Castle, is a good place to find everything from toothpaste to local crafts. One of the best places to get higo zogan, Yamaga doro, and other local crafts is the **Kumamoto Traditional Crafts Center.** A combination gallery and shop, the center displays crafts from all over Kumamoto Prefecture. It is located next to the Kumamoto Castle Hotel. *3-35 Chiga-jo, tel. 096/324–4930. Open 9–5. Closed Mon.*

Mt. Aso

15 On the way to **Mt. Aso** you pass through Kyushu's radiant green countryside. As you look upon farmers bent over their rice fields, bamboo groves, and other idyllic sights, you have a sense of the peaceful relationship between man and nature. This serene image quickly fades when you arrive at the smoking and rumbling volcano of Mt. Aso; here you become aware of the power of nature and the mortality of man.

Mt. Aso is, in fact, a series of five volcanic peaks, one of which, Mt. Nakadake, is still active. The five peaks, along with lakes and fields at its base, form a beautiful national park. Mt. Aso can be seen either on a day trip from Kumamoto or on a stop on the way from Kumamoto to Beppu. If you are interested in spending more time relaxing in the beautiful national park, you can stay in the many mountain pensions on the other side of Mt. Aso (*see* Lodging, *below*).

Arriving and Departing

By Train   The JR Hohi Line runs between Kumamoto Station and Aso Station (1 hr.). From the Aso Station to Beppu there are three JR express trains daily (2½ hrs.). From the Aso JR Station, you must board a bus (40 min; fare: ¥570) to get to the Aso Nishi Ropeway Station. The ropeway leads you to the top of the crater in four minutes. Fare: ¥820. It is better to begin your trip well before noon, because the last buses for the ropeway station leave mid-afternoon.

By Bus Buses leaving from the Kumamoto Kotsu Bus terminal go directly to the Aso Nishi Ropeway Station (1½ hrs.).

Exploring

Although Mt. Aso National Park is very pleasant, the main reason to come here is to see the one active volcano, Nakadake. From the inside of the largest crater of Mt. Nakadake, which is 1,968 feet across and 525 feet deep, you hear the rumblings of the volcano and see billowing smoke. It is fascinating and yet terrifying to look at this crater and realize that someday Nakadake could erupt. Sometimes the volcano does become overexcited, and visitors can't view it up close, so check at Kumamoto or Beppu before you make this excursion. After viewing the volcano you can descend via the ropeway or walk along a path that leads you back to the ropeway station. If you are up for a hike taking several hours, you can skip the ropeway altogether and follow the path up to Mt. Nakadake and down to the Sensuikyo Gorge. From there you must walk to the Miyaji JR station, the next stop after Aso Station. Because most visitors to the mountain do not choose to take this arduous route, the paths are delightfully uncrowded, and the views of the live crater from afar and of the gorge are awe-inspiring.

Beppu

After all your travels, an enjoyable way to rest your weary body is by soaking in a hot spring. One of the most popular hot-spring resorts in all of Japan, **Beppu** provides over 3,000 sources of hot water not only to the hotels and inns but also to private homes. Beppu is a garish town with neon lights, amusement parks, Pachinko halls by the dozen, and souvenir shops. These ingredients, its location—the sea in the foreground and mountains to its rear—and the variety of hot mineral springs make it a favorite vacation spot for the Japanese. Many tourists come here and do not leave their hotel or inn to see any of the local sights. The leisurely pace of this resort is indicated by the many Japanese tourists walking around the streets in their *yukata* (cotton kimonos), casually strolling and looking as though they have not a care in the world.

The more sophisticated Westerner is likely to find Beppu irritatingly expensive, tawdry, and overcommercialized and might prefer to experience a hot springs resort in more peaceful surroundings, such as Yufuin, situated on a highland plateau, 60 minutes by bus from Beppu (¥940) or 90 minutes by the JR Kyudai line from Oita. Yufuin has one of the country's charming traditional inns, Tamanoyu (tel. 0977/84–2158, Very Expensive) as well as several other ryokan and minshukus (*see* Lodging, *below*).

Arriving and Departing

By Plane The closest airport to Beppu is the Oita Airport, which is served by ANA and JAS domestic flights from the Haneda Airport in Tokyo (1 hr. 40 mins.) and from Osaka Airport (1 hr.).

Between the Airport and Center City — Buses leave regularly from the airport to Beppu City. The one-hour trip costs ¥1,300 and terminates at Kitahama bus stop on the bay side of Beppu's main street.

By Train — The Hohi Main Line travels between Kumamoto and Beppu (3 hrs. 20 mins.). On the way, you can stop at Mt. Aso. The Nichirin Limited Express Train runs between Beppu and Hakata Station in Fukuoka. Over 10 trains travel the route daily (2½ hrs.).

By Bus — Buses travel between Kumamoto and Beppu (3½ hrs.) and between Mt. Aso and Beppu on the Trans-Kyushu Highway (3 hrs.). Sightseeing buses operated by the Kyushu Kokusai Kanko Bus Company travel regularly between Beppu and Kumamoto, stopping at Mt. Aso.

By Boat — Three ferries (two of which make calls at Matsuyama and Imabari or Takamatsu and Sakaide, all on Shikoku), connect Beppu with Osaka and Kobe on the Kansai Kisen Line (in Tokyo, tel. 03/274–4271; in Osaka, tel. 06/572–5181; in Beppu, tel. 0977/22–1311). These overnight ferries leave in the early evening (the direct ferry for Osaka leaves at 7:20 PM and arrives at 8:20 AM. Fare: ¥5,870, 2nd class). Reservations are necessary for first class. A ferry to Hiroshima leaves Beppu at 2 PM and arrives at Hiroshima 7 PM and leaves Hiroshima at 9:30 PM, arriving in Beppu at 6 AM. Fare: ¥3,600–¥5,550.

Getting Around

By Bus — Regular buses travel to most places of interest in Beppu. The main bus terminal, Kitahama Bus Station, is just down the road from the JR Beppu Station.

By Taxi — Because most of the sights in Beppu are relatively close to one another but too far to walk, this is one of the few places in Japan that it may be worthwhile simply to hop in a taxi. Fares range from ¥1,000 to ¥3,000. Hiring a taxi for two hours to visit the major thermal pools would run approximately ¥5,000, after negotiation.

Important Addresses and Numbers

Beppu City Information Office (12-13 Ekimae-cho, tel. 0977/24–2838) is located in Beppu Station and has, so long as you persevere in asking for them, several useful maps and brochures in English. Open 9–5. **Foreign Tourist Information Service** (Furosen 2F, 7–16 Chuomachi, Beppu City, 874 Oita-gun, tel. 0977/23–1119) is located four minutes from the station—use the map posted on the City Information Booth in the JR station. This office has an enthusiastic volunteer staff. Open Monday–Saturday 10–4.

Guided Tours

A regular sightseeing bus service, leaving from Kitahama Bus Station, located just east of the Beppu JR station, covers most of the major sights in the area. The tour lasts about 2½ hours. Although an English-speaking guide is not always available, most of the sights are self-explanatory.

Exploring

Beppu is a resort area; the main attractions are the hot springs. A few sights in Beppu are worth seeing, though many people choose to bypass them, and just recline and relax.

If you are tired of inactivity, visit the **Eight Hells,** the Kannawa section of Beppu, with eight distinctive hot springs. Take Bus 15, 16, 17, 41, or 43 from the stop across from the JR station for the 30-minute trip to Kamenoi Bus Station. (Fare: ¥310.) One of the springs, **Chino-ike Jigoku** (Blood Pond Hell), is a boiling spring with red gurgling water. The vapors from this spring are purported to have curative powers for skin diseases. **Umi Jugoku** (Sea Hell) features not only water the color of the ocean, but also tropical plants. **Oniyama Jigoku** (Devil Mountain Hell) is a place where crocodiles are bred. An entertaining aspect of the Eight Hells are the many vendors nearby who try to sell their wares, such as eggs placed in baskets and boiled in the water. Although it is fascinating to see just how *hot* hot springs can be, keep in mind that this very popular attraction is crowded year-round. Each hot spring charges ¥300 admission, but a combined ticket for ¥1,500 will admit you to all eight. After your tour of the springs, take a bath at Hyotan Onsen, across the road from Kamenoi Bus Terminal. This is one of the more interesting thermal baths. The pool is outdoors, with waterfalls, hot stones, and sand. *Admission: ¥500. Open daily 7 AM–9 PM.*

The other main sight near Beppu is **Takasakiyama Monkey Park,** the home of 1,900 monkeys. To get there, take a bus from Kitahama Bus Station, located just down the road from the Beppu JR station. The bus ride lasts about 10 minutes. These once-wild monkeys were a problem for local farmers, but now they are domesticated. The monkeys are divided into three groups, each carefully guarding their territory. Observation of the hierarchy within each group is fascinating: for example, it is easy to determine which monkey is the leader because he stands on higher ground than his subordinates. This park is particularly fun for children, who are not put off by the striking resemblance in the behavior of monkeys and humans. *Tel. 0975/ 32-5010. Admission: ¥500. Open 8–5.*

All hotels and inns in Beppu will have baths, but if you want to spend a day in a veritable amusement park of hot springs, the **Suginoi Palace** (tel. 0977/24–1141), a part of the Suginoi Hotel, is quite a spectacle. This indoor complex has a variety of hot springs including a sand bath and a saltwater bath. There is also a live cabaret in the evening as well as a vast souvenir-shopping complex, with electronic games—quite ghastly, but a place to visit once. *Admission: ¥2,000 (see* Lodging, *below).* Open 9–11.

Other attractions in Beppu include the **Beppu Ropeway** up to Mount Tsunumi for views over the city and bay (take bus 2, 34, 36, or 37 from Beppu Station and then the 10-min. ropeway to the top. Cost: ¥1,400. Open 9–5) and the **Marine Palace Aquarium** (Admission: ¥1,000. Open daily 8–5). Both have more appeal for Japanese vacationers than for foreign tourists. The small **Take-no Museum** in the center of town exhibits Beppu's celebrated crafts made from bamboo (tel. 0977/25–7776. Admission: ¥500. Open 8:30–6). You can purchase bamboo objects in Kishi-mae, the adjoining shop.

Off the Beaten Track

Those who find the commercialism of Beppu distasteful, often choose the peace and serenity of Yafuin, situated on a plateau an hour's bus ride inland from Beppu (or you can take a 90-min. ride on a JR train from Beppu via Oita). The air here is intoxicatingly fresh, and the pace, slow and leisurely. A helpful tourist office (tel. 0977/84–2446; open 9–7) at the station will supply a map and make hotel reservations for you.

Dining

Until the 20th century, Kyushu was the international center of Japan. Certain Kyushu dishes, not surprisingly, show the influence of China and Europe. Tempura, for example, is often thought of as a standard Japanese dish; in fact, it was introduced by Europeans to Kyushu in the 17th century.

Particularly in Nagasaki, the influence of foreign cuisines is still apparent. In addition to these international dishes, many regions in Kyushu have special dishes that incorporate the food available in that locale.

Beppu is famous for its delicious seafood. Because it is a hot-spring resort town, most people tend to remain in their hotels or inns even for meals. Many of the lodgings available provide fresh, locally caught fish. One particularly popular local dish is **fugu** (blowfish).

Fukuoka, Kyushu's largest city, has a wide range of excellent Japanese and Western restaurants. Many of the best Western restaurants are located in hotels. Fukuoka is well known for its **Hakata ramen,** noodles with a stronger flavored soup than in other parts of Japan. It is also known for its *ikesu* restaurants, places that have a fish tank from which you can select the fish you want to eat, guaranteeing its freshness.

Adventurous eaters will enjoy the challenge of the regional specialty of Kumamoto, **horse meat.** The horse meat is served roasted, fried, and even raw. Another Kumamoto delicacy is called **dengaku,** tofu or fish covered by a strong bean paste and grilled. Dengaku is a good example of Kyushu cuisine with strong flavors, unlike the very delicate taste of food from Kyoto, for example.

Nagasaki is really the place where one gets a sense of the many cuisines that have influenced Kyushu dining. One dish, available only in Nagasaki, and with distinct Chinese, European, and Japanese influences, is **shippoku.** Shippoku is actually a variety of dishes that, when combined, make a full meal. Dinners center on a fish-soup base with European flavorings, to which many foods are added, including stewed chunks of pork cubes prepared Chinese-style, marinated in ginger and soy sauce; rice cakes; and a variety of vegetables. Usually, shippoku is served as one large communal dish, which is unusual in Japan. (In the traditional way of serving and eating Japanese food, individual portions are prepared.) Another distinctive Nagasaki dish is **champon,** heavy Chinese-style noodles in a soup. Not surprisingly, Nagasaki also has some of the best Western restaurants in Kyushu.

A 3% federal consumer tax is added to all restaurant bills. Another 3% local tax is added to the bill if it exceeds ¥7,500. At more expensive restaurants, a 10%–15% service charge is also added to the bill.

The most highly recommended restaurants for each city are indicated by a star ★.

Category	Cost*
Very Expensive	over ¥9,000
Expensive	¥6,000–¥9,000
Moderate	¥3,000–¥6,000
Inexpensive	under ¥3,000

Cost is per person without tax, service, or drinks

Beppu

Fugumatsu. This small, popular restaurant, with a simple, Japanese-style interior, has counters, tables, and private rooms. Its specialty is fugu (blowfish), which is a favorite in the area. Fugu is a potentially poisonous fish that restaurants must be licensed to serve. In the summer a type of *karei* fish that can only be caught in Beppu Bay is served. Fugumatsu has courses starting at ¥5,000. Upon your request you can have less- or more-expensive food; the restaurant will adjust to your budget. It is one block north of the Tokiwa department store and one block from the bay. *3-6-14 Kitahama, tel. 0977/21-1717. Reservations for parties of 10 or more only. Dress: informal. No credit cards. Moderate–Expensive.*

Jin. For an inexpensive evening of beer, sake, and pub-type (*izakaya*) food that includes yakitori and grilled seafood, Jin is popular with Japanese and foreign visitors. Seating is either at the bar counter that looks over displays of fish resting on crushed ice and waiting to be selected by the next diner, or at small wooden tables and chairs. The mood is jovial, and you are sure to start up a conversation with your neighbors. Jin is easy to find: Walk from JR Beppu Station on the right side of Ekimae-dori and towards the bay; it is just before the "T" junction and across from the Tokiwa department store. *422 Ekimae-dori, tel. 0977/21-1768. No reservations. Dress: casual. No credit cards. Inexpensive.*

Fukuoka

Ikesu Kawataro. A large tank full of edible fish sits in the middle of this large establishment, which offers counters, Japanese-style rooms with tatami mats, and regular tables. The tatami section, if you don't mind sitting on the floor for the duration of the meal, is the most pleasant, because the other areas of the restaurant tend to be rather noisy. Try any of the sashimi (raw fish) dishes; they will be remarkably fresh. If you order certain kinds of fish and shrimp, they will still be wriggling on your plate when served. *1-6-6 Nakasu, Hakata-ku, tel. 092/271-2133. Reservations not required. Dress: informal. DC, MC, V. Very Expensive.*

Gyosai. This restaurant has an excellent selection of seafood. Its humble atmosphere belies the quality of the food. Order any of the sashimi dishes or steamed fish. Although the staff do not speak much English, they are very helpful, and gestures and a smile will go a long way. This restaurant has the added advantage of being within walking distance of the Hakata Station. *2-2-12 Ekimae, Hakata-ku, tel. 092/441–9780. No reservations. Dress: informal. No credit cards. Moderate.*

★ **Deko.** A cheerful izakaya just a three-minute walk from the New Otani hotel, this is a delightful place to while away an evening over good food. Seating is Japanese-style at the counter and at shared tables, but there is a well for your legs so you don't have to sit cross-legged. The Western-style seating in the back is outside the fraternity of communal dining. Deko has no English menu, but the staff will do their best to make suggestions. Usually the special of the day is a good choice; it might be an egg roll stuffed with spinach for ¥750. The mackerel lightly grilled in soy sauce and salt is superb. (From the New Otani go diagonally across the intersection, pass the Pachinko parlor on the left-hand side of the street, and you'll come to a tall, new building outside of which there is a big sign that says "Lhasa." Deko is down one flight of stairs.) *1-24-22, Jonan-sen dori, 1 BF, Chuo-ku, tel. 092/526–7070. No reservations. Dress: informal. No credit cards. Inexpensive.*

Ichiki. If you are interested in checking out Japanese nightlife but are not sure where to go, try this bar/restaurant and see how many Japanese spend their recreational evenings. The atmosphere is relaxed and friendly, and as the evening wears on, it is more likely than not that one of your Japanese neighbors will attempt to make your acquaintance. Try the *kushi yaki*, a sort of Japanese shish kebab with fish, meat, and vegetables, fried on a hot flat grill and served on a wood skewer. This is not a restaurant where you just sit down and order your meal, but rather a place where you relax for the evening, have a few beers, and order a few small dishes at a time. The price range for each dish is ¥400–¥1,000. *1-2-10 Maizara, Chuo-ku, tel. 092/751–5591. No reservations. Dress: informal. No credit cards. Inexpensive.*

Kumamoto

Loire. If you are tired of Japanese food and want a good French meal, try this elegant, spacious restaurant located on the 11th floor of the Kumamoto Castle Hotel. Loire has an excellent view of Kumamotojo Castle. The set-course meals, which feature fish or meat dishes, change every month. During some months, special all-you-can-eat buffets are available. The desserts are varied, and are recommended. Those who do not feel like paying so much for the view can instead sample the reasonably priced lunches. *4-2 Jotomachi, tel. 096/326–3311. Reservations advised. Dress: informal. AE, DC, MC, V. Very Expensive.*

★ **Togasaku Honten.** Formal Japanese cuisine is at its best in this restaurant, which serves a set menu. The dinners, served at low, Japanese-style tables, consist of several small courses of fish, meat, tofu, and vegetables, which add up to a very filling meal. The prices are high, but your yen is well spent, because the meals not only are tasty but are presented with exquisite beauty. Togasaku Honten overlooks a peaceful garden, and the staff is formal and polite without being stiff. Ask for a table with a view when you make your reservations. *1-15-3*

Hamazuno, tel. 096/353–4171. Reservations required. Jacket and tie required. DC, MC, V. No lunch. Very Expensive.

A branch of Togasaku Honten with good food at slightly lower prices is located right by the Suizenji-Koen Park. This restaurant is more informal and has Western-style tables. *Togasaku Suizenji-koen, Tsuchiyama Bldg., 2F. 3-4 Suizenji-koen, tel. 096/385–5151. Reservations recommended. Dress: informal. DC, MC, V. No lunch. Expensive.*

Mutsugoro. This casual dining spot, with light-color paper-and-wood walls, is located in the basement of the Green Hotel. Curious, adventurous eaters will note that this restaurant serves horse meat in 40 different ways, including raw horse-meat sashimi and fried horse meat. If you go and decide that these specialties are not to your taste, you can choose from a variety of seafood dishes. As is the case with many informal Japanese restaurants, you order many small dishes. Each dish is about ¥800–¥1,000; for a full meal, you will probably want four or five dishes. *12-11 Hanabata-cho, tel. 096/356–3256. No reservations. Dress: informal. No credit cards. No lunch. Moderate.*

Senri. Couple a visit to the beautiful Suizenji-Koen Park with lunch or dinner at Senri, situated right in the gardens. Senri serves a wide variety of dishes, including seafood, eel, and horse-meat sashimi. Although Western-style tables and chairs are available, the tatami rooms and low tables are really more in keeping with the ambience of the gardens. Even if you do not choose to have a meal here, you can get a light snack or an appetizer. *7-17 Suizenji, tel. 096/384–1824. No reservations. Dress: informal. No credit cards. Moderate.*

Nagasaki

Harbin. This establishment serves Continental cuisine in a dark, romantic setting. The sauces are a bit heavy, and the food is slightly overcooked, but perhaps the chef is only trying to re-create the dishes as they would be served in Europe. It is not hard to imagine the residents of the 19th-century Western-style houses of Nagasaki eating at this restaurant. *2-27 Kozen-machi, tel. 0958/22–7433. Reservations advised. Dress: informal, although most guests wear jackets. AE. Very Expensive.*

Kagetsu. This quiet establishment, set on top of a hill, is Nagasaki's most prestigious restaurant. Dishes are served in the kaiseki manner, but the menu combines Japanese and Chinese cuisine. The building that houses Kagetsu was visited long ago by the Meiji Restoration leader, Ryoma Sakamoto. According to local legend, Sakamoto, while involved in a fight, slashed his sword into a wood pillar and left a gash that is still visible in the restaurant today. *2-1 Maruyama-cho, tel. 0958/22–0191. Reservations advised. Jacket and tie required. AE, DC, MC, V. Very Expensive.*

Fukiro. In this roomy Japanese restaurant with tatami mats and shoji screens, some of the best shippoku in Nagasaki is served. The shippoku combines tasty morsels of Chinese and Japanese food, all presented in an aesthetically pleasing way. To get to Fukiro, you must first walk up a steep set of stone steps. The restaurant is an old Japanese-style building, with a tiled roof and long wooden beams. *146 Kami-nishiyama-machi, tel. 0958/22–0253. Reservations advised. Jacket required. DC. Closed Sun. Expensive.*

★ **Shikairo.** This large restaurant, with its garish decor, is the birthplace of the well-known Nagasaki *champon* noodles, which are the house specialty. With a capacity to seat 1,500 in various sized rooms, Shikairo has an extensive menu. The seafood dishes are particularly good, and the beef with bamboo shoots is recommended; the menu features many excellent Chinese dishes from the Fukien region—a surprise, because most Chinese food in Japan is rather bland. The service is somewhat brusque by Japanese standards but its past reputation still makes the Japanese want to come here. You may not. *4-5 Matsugae-machi, tel. 0958/822–1296. Reservations accepted. Dress: informal. DC. Inexpensive–Moderate.*

Hamakatsu. Fans of the Japanese dish *tonkatsu* (fried pork cutlets) will enjoy the Nagasaki version, which uses ground pork mixed with scallions. Hamakatsu specializes in this local treat. Other dishes are available, but most diners stick with the tonkatsu, especially because it is one of the lower-priced dishes on the menu. *1-14 Kajiya-machi, tel. 0958/23–2316. No reservations. Dress: informal. No credit cards. Inexpensive.*

Kosanko. Within Nagasaki's compact Chinatown district are a dozen or so Chinese restaurants. Most famous of these is Kosanko. Dining is on the second floor, though you'll probably have to wait in the ground floor lobby for a table. Dishes cost approximately ¥800–¥1,000 each and run the gamut from champon noodles to egg rolls and sweet-and-sour pork. Even though its reputation is grander than its cooking, it is a fun, lively restaurant, especially enjoyable if you are with a group. *12-2 Sakura-machi, tel. 0958/21–3735. No reservations. Dress: casual. No credit cards. Inexpensive.*

Lodging

Accommodations in Kyushu are plentiful, and because the number of tourist and business travelers is limited, it is nearly always possible to get reservations. Fukuoka has major hotels with excellent facilities. Nagasaki features grand old hotels and ryokan that, like the city itself, seem to be frozen in the 19th century.

Travelers looking for a more active vacation may choose to spend a few days in the Mt. Aso region at a pension. Pensions are similar to bed-and-breakfasts, with supper served as well. The pensions near Aso are set in the mountains and are located near trails for hiking. Some also have tennis courts.

A 3% federal consumer tax is added to all hotel bills. Another 3% local tax is added to the bill if it exceeds ¥15,000. At most hotels, a 10%–15% service charge is added to the total bill. Tipping is not the custom.

The most highly recommended accommodations for each city are indicated by a star ★.

Category	Cost*
Very Expensive	over ¥20,000
Expensive	¥15,000–¥20,000

Moderate	¥10,000–¥15,000
Inexpensive	under ¥10,000

Cost is for a double room, without tax or service

Beppu

Suginoi Hotel. More than just a hotel, this is a miniresort. Once you arrive and check in, you may not feel any need to go anywhere else. The hotel is situated on a hill with a panoramic view of the city and the ocean. Connected to the hotel is the Suginoi Palace, which features a variety of hot springs, such as the "Dream Public Bath" and the "Flower Public Bath." Once you wash off, you proceed into a room full of plants and trees. You can soak in a standard hot spring, bury yourself in warm sand, or, if you get bored with hot water, move to the swimming pool. Breakfast and dinner are included in the price of the accommodations, and there are both Western- and Japanese-style buffets. Guests tend to wander around the hotel and attend meals in their yukata. The rooms are a welcome break from the opulence of the rest of the hotel—they are rather austere in decoration. If a quiet and refined experience is what you seek, this is not the right choice. It feels a little bit like a Japanese Las Vegas. Nevertheless, this is the most popular hotel in all of Beppu. *Kankaiji-onsen, Beppu 874, tel. 0977/24–1141, fax 0977/21–0010. 600 rooms (80 Western style). Facilities: shopping arcade, conference room, beauty parlor, bowling, restaurant, Japanese banquet hall, pool, children's playground. AE, DC, MC, V. Very Expensive.*

Beppu Kankaiso. This ryokan used to be a hotel with many Japanese-style rooms. It now serves two meals, inclusive in the price of accommodations. The rooms are large and clean. The Japanese rooms can sleep as many as five, which cuts down on the cost per head. Although the baths here are nothing special, the ryokan is close enough to the Suginoi Hotel that it is easy to pay the daily admission of around ¥2,000 and take advantage of their facilities. The food in the Japanese restaurant Orion is excellent. *Kankaiji-onsen, Beppu 874, tel. 0977/23–1221, fax 0977/21–6285. 51 rooms (9 Western style). Facilities: Japanese restaurant. AE, DC, V. Expensive.*

★ **Sakaeya.** Many minshukus are drab concrete buildings that are different from youth hostels only in that they have private rooms. This minshuku is a rare gem in a beautiful old wooden building with surprisingly low rates, which include meals. The meals consist of straightforward Japanese food with fish and rice, but they are prepared in the oven in the backyard, which is heated from the hot springs. Only one public bath is available, but as you relax in it with your fellow guests, you have a sense that this is how the Japanese have been enjoying the wonders of hot springs for centuries. This minshuku is small and is gaining popularity quickly, so make reservations. To reach the inn, take Bus 16, 17, 24, or 25 from Beppu Station. *Idonikumi, Ida, Kannawa, Beppu 874, tel. 0977/66–6234. 10 rooms. No credit cards. Inexpensive.*

If you cannot get in at the Sakaeya, the tourist information Center at Beppu Station has a listing of several other inexpensive minshukus. One to try is **Minshuku Kokage** (8-9, Ekimaecho, Beppu, tel. 0977/23–1753), located just two minutes by foot from the station in the direction of the bay. The three-

story concrete building has 16 rooms, ten of which have private
baths, for approximately ¥7,000 for two people.

Fukuoka

Hotel II Palazzo. Fukuoka's newest lodging is a boutique hotel
created by art director Shigeru Uchida and architect Aldo
Rossi. It's a showpiece of contemporary design and has won an
award from the American Institute of Architects for its innova-
tions. The interior is classically simple, yet dramatic. The glow
of muted lights in the Italian restaurant reflects off the walls,
and the ceiling lights sparkle as if they are stars. The Western-
style guest rooms have simple furnishings, rich, deep-pile carpets, and soft colors. The Japanese rooms are basically traditional, except for semi-partitions that give a feeling of
increased space. *3-13, Haruyoshi, Chuo-ku, Fukuoka 810, tel.
092/716–3333, fax 092/724–3330. 62 (mostly Western) rooms.
Facilities: Italian restaurant, influenced by Japanese presentation, café, 3 bars, nightclub. AE, DC, MC, V. Very Expensive.*

Hotel New Otani Hakata. Located close to central Fukuoka,
seven minutes by taxi from the JR Station, this member of the
New Otani hotel group is typical of modern Japanese comfort—
smart, characterless, and efficient, with sparkling surrounds.
Within those parameters, this is Fukuoka's top hotel. The
rooms are spacious and have a writing table and easy chair;
they're decorated in muted tones. This is one of the few hotels
in all of Kyushu where you can expect most of the staff to speak
English. One very unusual feature is that it offers free baby-
sitting services. The large lobby reception area has a coffee
lounge and adjoins a complex of upmarket boutiques whose
merchandise is the height of fashion and price. *1-1-2 Watanabe-
dori, Chuo-ku, Fukuoka 810, tel. 092/714–1111, fax 092/715–
5658. 423 rooms. Facilities: bars, Chinese, Japanese, and
French restaurants, barber shop, beauty parlor, massage
room, shopping arcade, travel agency, florist, art gallery, tea-
ceremony room, indoor pool. AE, DC, MC, V. Very Expensive.*

Fukuoka Yamanoue Hotel. The name of this hotel means "on a
mountain," and it is on a hill above Fukuoka, with excellent
views of the ocean on one side and the city on the other. The
hotel is a little out of the way—10 minutes from Hakata Station
by taxi or bus (catch the Nishitetsu #56 or #57)—but the spectacular views make the travel time worthwhile. The service is
quietly polite and extremely helpful. The rooms are on the
small side, but not uncomfortably so. *1-1-33 Terakuni, Chuo-
ku, Fukuoka 810, tel. 092/771–2131, fax 092/771–8888. 55
rooms. Facilities: tennis courts, large public bath, Japanese
and Western restaurants. AE, DC, MC, V. Expensive.*

★ **Clio Court Hotel.** This hotel is the best value in Fukuoka. Conveniently located across the street from Hakata Station
(Shinkansen–side), it has remarkably attractive rooms furnished with great care. They are decorated in a variety of
styles, such as art deco and early American. You can request
the type of room decor you prefer when you make your reservations. Request a room with a window—rooms #1202 and #1203
are good choices. One whole floor contains tea-ceremony rooms
modeled on designs by Kamiya Sotan and Hosakawa-Sansai,
both disciples of the founder of the tea ceremony, Sen-no
Rikyu. Another tea-ceremony room is designed with benches

and tables for foreigners. One of the hotel's most pleasant features is the courtyard on the 13th floor, which serves as a beer garden in the summer. One floor higher is the hotel's revolving restaurant serving grilled steak and seafood cooked Western and Japanese style. In 60 minutes, you've seen all of Fukuoka! *5-3, Hakata-eki-chuo-gai, Hakata-ku, Fukuoka 812, tel. 092/ 472–1111, fax 092/474–3222. 194 rooms. Facilities: French, Chinese, and Japanese restaurants; steak house, English-style bar, café bar, sushi bar, florist, art gallery, rooms for the handicapped. AE, DC, MC, V. Moderate.*

Sun Life Hotels. Across the station plaza from the Shinkansen exit there are actually three Sun Life Hotels within 100 yards of each other. All three are business hotels. Rooms at Sun Life 1 are approximately 20% less expensive than those at Sun Life 2 and 3; they are also not as new and spacious. In addition, Sun Life 2 and 3 have Japanese restaurants that are open all day, and computer work-stations for the tireless traveling businessman. *Fukuoka 812 (across from JR Hakata Station on the Shinkansen side), tel. 092/473–7112, fax 092/471–5075. 234 Western rooms. Facilities: Japanese restaurants, coffee shop, computer work-stations. AE, DC, MC, V. Inexpensive–Moderate.*

Suehiro Inn. For inexpensive lodgings, this member of the Japanese Inn Group offers small tatami rooms, three with private bath. Only Japanese food is served in the small dining room, but guests are not required to eat at the inn. The two-story wooden inn, across from Nishitetsu Zasshonokuma Station, is four subway stops from downtown. *2-1-9, Minami-Honmachi, Hakata-ku, Fukuoka City 816, tel. 092/581–0306. 12 rooms (3 with bath). Facilities: Japanese food available. AE, MC, V. Inexpensive.*

Kumamoto

Fujie. On the main street leading directly away from the station, this is a smart business hotel with Western single rooms and attractive Japanese double rooms. The lobby lounge faces a Japanese garden and the restaurant serves well-presented Japanese food. Service is personable and friendly, though the English language in not the staff's strong point. *2-2 Kasuga, Kumamoto 860, tel. 096/353–1101, fax 096/322–2671. 47 rooms. Facilities: restaurant, garden. AE, V. Moderate.*

Kumamoto Castle Hotel. This hotel is conveniently situated near the Kumamotojo Castle and the downtown district. Request a room with a view of the castle, if possible. The Kumamoto Castle is quiet with rooms a cut above those of business hotels. However, not many of the staff speak English. *4-2 Jotomachi, Kumamoto 860, tel. 096/326–3311, fax 096/326–3324. 208 rooms. Facilities: Chinese, Japanese, and French restaurants; coffee shop. AE, DC, V. Moderate.*

New Sky Hotel. Managed by the ANA group, in many ways the New Sky is the best lodging Kumamoto has to offer. In addition to several good restaurants, the hotel maintains a relationship with a health club down the street so that its guests can use the pool for ¥700, or all facilities for ¥1,500. The rooms are small, but they are bright and cheerful. *2 Amidajicho, Kumamoto 860, tel. 096/354–2111, fax 096/354–8973. 358 rooms. Facilities: Chinese, Japanese, and French restaurants; beauty salon, barber shop. AE, DC, MC, V. Moderate.*

Kumamoto Station Hotel. A three-minute walk from the station, this hotel is marginally less expensive than the others listed here and strictly utilitarian. *1-16-14 Kumamoto-shi 860, tel. 096/325–907. 55 rooms. Facilities: small restaurant. AE, DC, V. Inexpensive.*

Mt. Aso

Flower Garden. This small Western-style lodging is surrounded by gardens. The owners also fill the rooms with blossoms of the season. This cheerful place serves bountiful meals and attracts a young crowd. The nearest station is Takamori, and someone from the pension will come and pick you up if you call. *Takamori-machi, Ozu, Takamori 3096-4, tel. 09676/2–3012. 9 rooms, a few with private bath. No credit cards. Moderate.*
Pension Cream House. The rooms at this pension are on the small side, but they are light and airy. The owners do not object to squeezing a group of people into one room, and lowering the costs per head accordingly. As a result, Pension Cream House is a particularly good choice if you go with a group of friends. *Takamori-machi, Ozu, Takamori 3096-1, tel. 0976/2–3090. 9 rooms. No credit cards. Moderate.*

Nagasaki

★ **Hotel New Nagasaki.** Losing its preeminence to the new Prince Hotel, this hotel still has the advantage of being just a two-minute walk from Nagasaki Station. The standard twin guest rooms, the largest in the city, have enough space for a couple of easy chairs and a table. The lobby lounge is sparkling fresh and the French restaurant, Hydrangea, has the airy, light ambience of a conservatory. On the 13th floor is a Chinese restaurant and the Moonlight Lounge for evening drinks; the Steak House serves beef from Goto Island. Many staff members are fluent in English. *14-5 Daikoku-Machi, Nagasaki 850, tel. 0958/26-8000, fax 0958/26–6162. 149 Western-style rooms. Facilities: 5 restaurants, indoor pool, gym, sauna, business center, shopping arcade. AE, DC, MC, V. Very Expensive.*
Nagasaki Prince Hotel. This is the city's newest, grandest, and most expensive hotel. Despite its ugly block tower exterior, the inside is relaxing even if it slightly overdoes the "opulent–look" so popular with new Japanese hotels. The long, rectangular lobby shimmers with glass, marble, and ponds, but the warm red carpet softens the glare. Guest rooms are decorated in the ubiquitous pastels and have natural-colored processed wood furniture. Each room has bedside panels and is equipped with the amenities of a first class hotel. Restaurants run the gamut from the New York Steak and Seafood dining room on the 15th floor to a Japanese sushi bar. One drawback: the Prince is a 10-minute walk from Nagasaki Station but in the opposite direction from downtown, though the streetcar passes by the front entrance and taxis are plentiful. *2–26, Takaramachi, Nagasaki-cho, Nagasaki 850, tel. 0958/21–1111, fax 0958/23–4309. 183 rooms. Facilities: 5 restaurants, room service 7–midnight, beauty salon, florist, parking. AE, DC, MC, V. Very Expensive.*
★ **Sakamoto-ya.** This ryokan, started in 1895, seems to have changed very little from its founding days. Cedar baths are offered in which to soak, and the wood building is a testament to the beauty of the simple lines of Japanese architecture. The restaurant specializes in shippoku food (a meal consisting of

various dishes), and the cost per night includes breakfast and dinner. The inn is very small and has extremely personalized service. The cost of the rooms varies depending on size and location. *2-13 Kanaya-machi, Nagasaki 850, tel. 0958/26–8211, fax 0958/25–5944. 15 rooms. AE. Very Expensive.*

Nagasaki Grand Hotel. This hotel is small and quiet, with a dignified atmosphere. Best of all is the outdoor beer garden. The rooms are compact, but are pleasantly decorated in pastels. *5-3 Manzai-machi, Nagasaki, tel. 0958/23–1234, fax 0958/22–1793. 126 rooms (3 Japanese style). Facilities: French, Japanese, and Western restaurants. AE, DC, MC, V. Expensive.*

Nagasaki View Hotel. This is one notch above a business-category hotel. The large tatami guest rooms, most of which face Nagasaki Bay, also have twin beds in a separate alcove permitting ample space for four guests. The Western-style rooms are half the price, but are modest in size (two twin beds, table and two chairs) and face inland. All rooms have private baths. The large common bath is on the 10th floor with a huge window looking onto Nagasaki Harbor. The location is convenient for sightseeing, shopping, and evening entertainment. *Oura Kaigan-dori, Oura-machi, Nagasaki 850, tel. 0958/24–2211, fax 0958/27–1891. 113 (Western and Japanese) rooms. Facilities: restaurant with Japanese and Western fare, coffee shop, fee parking. AE, DC, MC, V. Moderate–Expensive.*

Yataro. On top of a mountain, about 20 minutes by taxi from the center of Nagasaki, is this ryokan and its annex, which is a hotel. Yataro has an excellent view of all of Nagasaki, and the meals at the ryokan are plentiful and presented with great care. The view from the shared bath is particularly good. You'll probably enjoy staying in the ryokan, where meals are served in your room, more than staying in the hotel annex. Request a room with a view when you make your reservation. The hotel is less expensive than the inn. *2-1 Kazagoshira-machi, Nagasaki 850, tel. 0958/22–8166, fax 0958/28–1122. Ryokan: 56 rooms. Hotel: 169 rooms. Facilities: steak bar and grill. AE, DC, MC, V. Moderate.*

Ajisai Inn One. At this small establishment near the station, opposite the Hotel New Nagasaki, the rooms are small, but they are clean. The staff is friendly, and speaks a few words of English. *11-4 Daikoku, Nagasaki 850, tel. 0958/27–3110. 42 rooms. Facilities: breakfast room. V. Inexpensive.*

Yufuin

Pension Momotaro. The owners of this modern pension go out of their way to make guests feel at home; they'll even take you to the station when you depart. For dinner you can choose from the regional specialty of *gi-tori* (wild chicken), pork, *ayu* (sweet river fish), and shiitake cooked in a pot at the table, or the standard meal, which may be grilled beef over a charcoal brazier and mountain vegetables. Momotaro has three thermal baths, one of which is a *rotemboro* (open air) from which you can soak in 60-degree water and view the inspiring mountains. There are both Western- and Japanese-style rooms in the main building and Japanese-style rooms in the four A-frame chalets. *Yafuin, tel. 0977/85–2187, fax 0977/85–4002. 6 Western rooms, 3 Japanese rooms, and 4 chalets. Facilities: dining room, 3 thermal baths. No credit cards. Inexpensive–Moderate.*

14 Tohoku

By Nigel Fisher

Few foreign tourists make it farther north from Tokyo than Nikko. It is their loss. Tohoku, the name given to the six prefectures of northern Honshu, has country charm, rugged mountains, small villages, its share of temples, and some glorious coastline. For a long time the area was known as Michinoku, which, translated, means the "end of the line" or "backcountry." That image of remote rusticity is still held by many Japanese, and the result has been that Tohoku is one of the areas least visited in Japan. Yet the image does not tell all. Tohoku has some of the country's greatest attractions, not the least of which is its people.

In a land where politeness is paramount, it seems that the people in Tohoku are actually more friendly than their fellow citizens who live in the industrial Tokyo–Osaka corridor. With the exception of Sendai, Tohoku's cities are small, and the fast pace of urban living is foreign to their inhabitants. Also, because of the lack of high-speed trains and the rugged terrain, Tohoku's residents live their lives without many of the urban conveniences that industrialism has brought to the southern two-thirds of Honshu.

The consequence has been that many of the traditional ways and folk arts have been maintained here, as well as an independence of spirit, much like one finds in Hokkaido farther north. Visiting Tohoku gives a glimpse into old Japan. All of the large cities are prefectural capitals (prefectures are similar to states in the United States or counties in Great Britain) and have all the amenities of any international community. However, none of these six cities has particular merit as a tourist attraction, with the possible exception of Sendai.

Tohoku's climate is similar to New England's. The winters are cold; in the mountains, snow blocks off some of the minor roads. However, in Sendai and Matsushima, and along the Pacific coast, snow is rarely seen, and temperatures rarely fall to freezing. Spring and autumn are the most colorful seasons. Summer is refreshingly cool and, consequently, attracts Japanese tourists escaping the summer heat and humidity of Tokyo and points south. August is the month for big festivals in Akita, Aomori, Hirosaki, and Sendai, all of which draw huge crowds.

Tohoku, like all of the island of Honshu, has mountain ranges running along its spine. Most of the island's trains and highways run north–south on either side of the mountains. Hence, when traveling the major roads or railway trunk lines, one tends to miss some of the grandest mountain scenery. This chapter, laid out as an itinerary up the Pacific side of Tohoku's spine and down the Sea of Japan side, embraces the best of Tohoku using the JR trains as much as is possible, but it also takes the traveler to more remote areas.

In brief, the itinerary starts with Tohoku's unofficial capital, Sendai. It then continues on to Matsushima and travels north to Aomori, with detours to Hiraizumi, the Tono Basin, the Pacific Kaigan coast, Morioka, and the Towada-Hachimantai National Park. Those wishing to continue on to Hokkaido from Aomori should jump to the chapter devoted to that island, and then return to this chapter for the journey south. The journey south goes down to Akita and Tsuruoka, where it then turns inland to Yamagata and Fukushima prefectures; from here one

can return to Tokyo, continue south to Nikko, or go west to Niigata and the Japan Alps.

Essential Information

Arriving and Departing

By Plane   Akita has four daily flights from Tokyo's Haneda Airport by
ANA (All Nippon Airways) and two flights from Osaka International Airport by Japan Air System.

Aomori has two daily flights from Tokyo's Haneda Airport by
ANA. Aomori also has flights to Sapporo's Chitose Airport.

Morioka (whose Hanamaki Airport is 50 minutes by bus from
downtown) has two flights from Osaka International Airport
by Japan Air System. Morioka also has flights to Sapporo's
Chitose Airport and to Nagoya Airport.

Sendai has three daily flights from Osaka International Airport by Japan Air System. Sendai also has flights to Sapporo's
Chitose Airport.

Yamagata has four daily flights from Tokyo's Haneda Airport
by ANA and two flights from Osaka International Airport by
Japan Air System.

By Train   The most efficient method to reach Tohoku from Tokyo is on the
Tohoku Shinkansen trains, which run as far north as Morioka.
The Shinkansen makes a total of 71 runs a day between Tokyo
and Sendai (two hours) and Tokyo and Morioka (2 hours and 45
minutes). Some Shinkansen trains stop on route to Sendai at
Fukushima (one hour). North of Morioka, conventional trains
continue on to Aomori (two hours and 35 minutes). To reach
Akita, the limited express from Morioka takes two hours.
Yamagata is now connected to Tokyo by a Shinkansen line that
branches off at Fukushima. Travel time is now only three
hours. Alternatively, Yamagata may be reached by JR limited
express trains from Sendai in one hour, 10 minutes.

On Tohoku's western side (facing the Sea of Japan), the train
from Niigata takes four hours to travel along the Sea of Japan
coast to Akita, and an additional three hours to reach Aomori.
From Niigata inland to Yamagata, the train takes 3½ hours.
(Niigata is connected to Tokyo's Ueno Station by the Joetsu
Shinkansen, which makes the run in two hours.)

Any extensive traveling through Tohoku justifies use of the Japan Rail Pass, which costs ¥27,800 for a week's unlimited travel. For example, the one-way economy fare on the Shinkansen
train from Tokyo to Sendai is ¥10,390; to Morioka, ¥13,570.

By Bus   While the Tohoku Kyuko Express Night Bus from Tokyo to
Sendai is inexpensive (¥5,450), it takes 7 hours and 40 minutes.
It leaves Tokyo Station (Yaesu-guchi side and in front of Tobu
Travel on Yaesu Street) at 10 PM and arrives in Sendai at 5:40 AM.
The bus from Sendai departs at 10 PM and arrives in Tokyo at 5:40
AM.

By Car   The Tohoku Expressway now links Tokyo with Aomori, but the
cost of gas, tolls, and car rental makes driving an expensive
form of travel. It is also considerably slower to drive than to
ride on the Shinkansen. Assuming one can clear metropolitan

Tokyo in two hours, the approximate driving time is five hours to Fukushima, six hours to Sendai, eight hours to Morioka, and 10–11 hours to Aomori.

Getting Around

Transportation in the country areas of Tohoku was, until recently, limited. That is why Tohoku still has been undiscovered by modern progress and tourists. However, that is changing rapidly. Now, using a combination of trains and buses, most of Tohoku's hinterland is easily accessible, except during the heavy winter snows.

By Train Trains are fast and frequent on the north–south runs. They are slower and less frequent (more like every 2 hours rather than every hour during the day) when they cross Tohoku's mountainous spine. Most of the railways are owned by Japan Railways, so Rail Passes are accepted. Be aware that most trains stop running before midnight.

By Bus Buses take over where trains do not run, and, in most instances, they depart from the JR train stations. Though English may not be widely spoken in Tohoku, there is never any difficulty at train stations in finding someone to direct you to the appropriate bus.

During the summer tourist season, there are also scenic bus tours operating from the major tourist areas. The local Japan Travel Bureau at the train station in each area, or the major hotels, will make the arrangements.

By Boat Three sightseeing boats are especially recommended: at Matsushima Bay, near Sendai; at Jodogahama on the Pacific coast, near Miyako; and at Lake Towada. Keep in mind that these boats offer constant commentary in Japanese over the loudspeaker; this can be particularly annoying if you do not understand what's being said. (*See* appropriate Exploring sections for details.)

By Car Once in the locale you wish to explore, a rented car is ideal for getting around. All major towns have car-rental agencies. The Nippon-Hertz agency is the one most frequently represented. Bear in mind, though, that except on the Tohoku Expressway, few road signs are in Romaji (Japanese words rendered in English). However, major roads have route numbers. With a road map in which the towns are spelled in romaji and kanji, it becomes relatively easy to decipher the directional signs. Maps are not provided by car-rental agencies. Be sure to obtain your bilingual maps in Tokyo or Sendai.

Important Addresses and Numbers

Tourist Information Centers Tourist information centers are available at all the train stations at the prefectural capitals. The two largest tourist centers that give information on all of Tohoku and not just the local area are at Sendai's train station (tel. 022/222–3269) and at Morioka's train station (tel. 0196/25–2090). The telephone numbers of each prefectural government tourist department are: Akita, tel. 0188/80–1702; Aomori, tel. 0177/22–1111; Fukushima, tel. 0245/21–1111; Iwate, tel. 0196/51–3111; Miyagi, tel. 0222/21–1864; and Yamagata, tel. 0236/30–2371.

Japan Travel-Phone This nationwide service for English-language assistance or travel information is available seven days a week, 9–5. Dial toll-free 0120/222–800 for information on eastern Japan. When using a yellow, blue, or green public phone (do not use the red phones), insert a ¥10 coin, which will be returned.

Emergencies **Police,** tel. 110. **Ambulance,** tel. 119.

Guided Tours

The Japan Travel Bureau has offices at every JR station in each of the prefectural capitals and can assist in local tours, hotel reservations, and ticketing onward travel. Though one should not assume that any English will be spoken, there is usually someone whose English is sufficient for your basic needs.

The Japan Travel Bureau also arranges a three-day tour of Tohoku out of Tokyo. For ¥225,000, the tour includes Sendai (overnight), Matsushima, Togatta, Mt. Zao, Kaminoyama Spa (overnight), Yonezawa, and Fukushima. Only one breakfast and one dinner are included, and there is a ¥17,000 single supplement. These tours operate daily May 6–October 20.

Sendai

Numbers in the margin correspond to points of interest on the Tohoku map.

❶ With a population of nearly 900,000, **Sendai** is the largest city between Tokyo and Sapporo, on the northern island of Hokkaido. The city is very modern, because American firebombs left virtually nothing unscorched by the end of World War II. The buildings that replaced the old ones are not particularly attractive, but Sendai is an open city with a generous planting of trees that justifies its nickname *mori no miyako* "the city of trees." With 10 colleges and universities, including the prestigious Tohoku University, the city has intentionally developed an international outlook and appeal. This has attracted many foreigners to take up residency. For the visitor, the blend of old customs and modern attitudes makes Sendai a comfortable southern base from which to explore Tohoku.

Sendai is a city in which it is easy to find one's way around. Even the major streets have signs in romaji (Japanese words rendered in Roman script). The downtown area of Sendai is compact, with modern hotels, department stores with the latest international fashions, numerous Japanese and Western restaurants, and hundreds of small specialty shops. Three broad avenues, Aoba-dori, Hirose-dori, and Jozenji-dori, head out from the station area toward Sendai Castle and cut through the heart of downtown, where they are dissected by two wide shopping arcades, Ichiban-cho and Chuo-dori. Between these two malls and extending farther east are narrow streets, packing in the bars, tea shops, and restaurants that make up Sendai's entertainment area.

While it is easy to get one's bearings in Sendai, public transport is not so convenient. There is no useful subway for the tourist, and the bus routes are not easy to follow. Fortunately, the center of the city is within easy walking distance from the train station, and all hotels are between the center and the station.

Tohoku

0 ——— 50 miles
0 ——— 75 km

KEY
——— JR Trains
═══ Shinkansen (Bullet Train)
╫╫╫ Private rail line
- - - Ferry Line

Fukushima

Tsugaru Straits

Miumaya

Tsugaru Peninsula

Mutsu Bay

Shimokita Peninsula

20 Aomori
19 Sukayu Onsen

Mt. Iwaki **18** Hirosaki

Misawa

Hachinohe

15 Lake Towada
17 Yasumiya

Oyu Onsen **16**

Odate **14** Towada-Minami

Noshiro

Yoneshiro River

Kuji

13 Hachimantai

Towada Hachimantai National Park

12 Obuke

Mt. Komaga-take

Oga Peninsula

22 Oga-Onsen
Monzen

21 Akita

Nyuto Onsen **25**

26

11 Morioka

Taro

Jodogahama **9**
Miyako **8**

Tazawako **24**

23 Kakunodate

Omagari

Fujima

10 Take

Sea of Japan

Hanamaki

6 Tono

7 Kamaishi

Omono River

13

Hiraizumi **5**

4 Ichinoseki

Tsuruoka

27

28 Mt. Haguro

Mogami River

Atsumi Onsen

Nobiru

3 Matsushima
2 Hon-Shiogama
1 Sendai

Hojusan Risshakuji Temple **31**
29 Yamagata

30 Mt. Zao

Niigata

Aganō River

49

Lake Hibara
Kitakata

32

34

Inawashiro

33

Aizu-Wakamatsu **35**

Yonezawa

Abukuma River

Fukushima

PACIFIC OCEAN

TO TOKYO

6

N

For sightseeing, taxis are the best means of travel, except for the 10-minute bus ride from the JR station to Sendai's castle.

Like all the urban centers of Tohoku, Sendai has a limited number of sights worth visiting, and these can easily be covered in a morning's tour. The tour is made easier, too, because Sendai's history focuses almost entirely on a fantastic historical figure, Masamune Date (1567–1636). Affectionately called the "one-eyed dragon" for his valor in battle and the loss of an eye from smallpox when he was a child, Masamune Date established a dynasty that maintained its position as one of the three most powerful daimyo (feudal lord) families during the shogun period. But aside from his military skills and progressive administration (he constructed a canal linking two rivers, thus improving the transport of rice), he was also an artist and a scholar who did not close his eye to new ideas.

Exploring

Before starting your city tour, you may want to stop at the tourist information office (tel. 022/222–4069; open daily 8:30–8) on the ground floor of the Sendai railway station. There you can collect useful free maps and brochures about Sendai and the region. While you are waiting for a train, be sure to explore the tempting arrays of prepared foods and numerous restaurants in the underground mall aptly named Restaurant Avenue. You can also dial an English-speaking hotline for visitors' question about Miyagi Prefecture (tel. 0222/24–1919).

Masamune Date's presence is everywhere. His statue dominates the hill, **Aobayama-Koen Park,** on which his mighty castle, Aobajo, stood and served as the Date clan's residence for 270 years. To get to Aobayama, take the bus from platform 9 for the 15-minute ride from Sendai station to the Aoba-goshi bus stop. The hill is easy to spot because it rises 433 feet above the city and is guarded by the high rock walls of the Hirosegawa River to the east and the deep Tatsunokuchi Valley to the south. No wonder Date's castle was considered impregnable when it was built in 1602.

The castle was destroyed during the Meiji Restoration, though the outer gates survived an additional 73 years, until firebombs destroyed them in 1945. Now the **Gokoku Shrine** covers most of the area where the castle stood. The shrine is a rather grandiose building, heavy and cumbersome, but a small rock garden to its right is quite delightful in its simplicity. To the rear of the castle grounds, a 360-foot-long bridge over the deep Tatsunokuchi Valley leads to the **Yagiyama Zoo,** which is not worth visiting.

Near Masamune Date's statue is an observation terrace from which you can look down over the city and plan your next route, a 15-minute walk to Zuihoden Hall, the Date family's mausoleum. On the way there, those who have become fascinated with the history of the Date family, whose rule over the region lasted 270 years, should visit the **Sendai Municipal (City) Museum** (Sendaiishi Hakubutukan), which contains several thousand artifacts connected with the clan, including a collection of armor. The museum is at the foot of Aobayama-Koen Park. *Admission: ¥400. Open 9–4. Closed Mon. and the day following a national holiday.*

To continue on to Zuihoden Hall, cross over the Hirosegawa River, take a right, walk along the river past the sports grounds, cross back over the river and walk up the hill. Zuihoden Hall is to the left. From JR Sendai station, Bus 11 or 12 will take you to the Otamaya-bashi bus stop. The mausoleum is a short walk up the hill.

Zuihoden Hall was also bombed in 1945, but a five-year reconstruction project was begun in 1974. During the excavation, Masamune Date's well-preserved bones were found and are now reinterred in what appears to be a perfect replica of the original hall. Two other mausoleums for the remains of the second (Tadamune Date) and third (Tsunamune Date) lords of Sendai were also reconstructed. These mausoleums cost in excess of ¥800 million to rebuild and are astounding in their craftsmanship and authenticity in the architectural style of the Momoyama period (16th century). Each mausoleum is the size of a small temple, and the exterior is inlaid with figures of people, animals, and flowers in natural colors, which are sheltered by elaborate curving roofs. Gold leaf is used extravagantly on the pillars and in the eaves of the roofs, creating a glinting golden aura. *Admission: ¥515. Open 9–4.*

Next, visit the **Osaki-Hachimangu Shrine,** located in the northwest section of the city, about 10 minutes by taxi, either from downtown or Aobayama. You can also take Bus 10 from JR Sendai station for ¥200. This is the only historic building in Sendai to have survived the war. It was actually built in 1100 by a warrior general of the Minamoto clan. Masamune Date liked it, and, in 1607, had it moved from its original site in Toda-gun to be rebuilt in Sendai. Its free-flowing architectural form has a naturalness similar to the architectural style in Nikko, and its rich, black-lacquered main building more than justifies its designation as a National Treasure. *Admission: ¥500. Open daily sunrise to sunset.*

A 10-minute walk from Osaki-Hachimangu Shrine and to the left (west) of Sendai Station is the **Rinnoji Temple garden.** Use Bus 24 if you are going directly there from the JR Sendai station. Of the several gardens in the neighborhood, this Zen-type garden is the most peaceful. A small stream leads the eye to the lotus-filled pond, the garden's focal point. Flowing around the pond and creating a balance are the waving, undulating hummocks covered with clusters of bamboo. In June the garden is a blaze of color, with irises everywhere, but there are so many visitors that much of the tranquillity is lost. *Admission: ¥300. Open daily 8–5.*

Bustling downtown Sendai is a shopper's paradise. The downtown shopping area is compact, and many of the stores and small shops are in or connected to the two main shopping arcades, **Ichiban-cho** and **Chuo-dori.** Sendai is the unofficial capital of the Tohoku region, and you can find many of the regional crafts made outside of Miyagi Prefecture here. Also along the arcades are many Japanese and Western restaurants; they begin to fill up at around 7 PM as the shops start closing.

Sendai's big festival is **Tanabata** (Aug. 6–8), and, while similar festivals are held throughout Japan (usually on July 7), Sendai's is the largest, swelling the city to three times its normal size with Japanese tourists. The celebration stems from a poignant Chinese legend of a weaver girl and her boyfriend, a herdsman, represented by the stars Vega and Altair. Their excessive love for each other caused them to become idle. The irate king of heaven exiled the two lovers to opposite sides of heaven. However, he permitted them to meet one day a year—that day is now celebrated as Tanabata, highlighted with a theatrical onstage performance of the young lovers' anguish. For the festival, houses and streets are decorated with colorful paper and bamboo streamers fluttering from poles.

If you want a bird's-eye view of the city, the SS 30 Building, 30 stories high, is the tallest building in town since it opened in 1989. The top three floors are reserved for restaurants and viewing galleries. At night, riding up in the outside elevator, with the city lights descending below, is quite a thrill.

Excursions around Tohoku

From Sendai to Matsushima

Matsushima and its bay are the most popular coastal resort destinations in Tohoku and are only 35 minutes by train from Sendai. Hence, one can easily visit Matsushima as a day trip from Sendai or, because there are many hotels and ryokan, stay on the coast rather than return to cosmopolitan Sendai. The Japanese have named three places as their Three Big Scenic Wonders—Amanohashidate on the Sea of Japan in Western Honshu, Miyajima in Hiroshima Bay, and Matsushima Bay. Matsushima made it into the big three because the Japanese are infatuated with oddly shaped rocks, which are featured at Matsushima. Counts differ, but there are about 250 small, pine-clad islands scattered in the bay. Some are mere rocks with barely room for a couple of trees, while others are large enough for a few families to live on them. Each of the islets has a distinctive shape; several have tunnels through them large enough for a rowboat to pass through. It is indeed a beautiful bay and a pleasant day's excursion from Sendai.

Getting There Though one can go directly by train, the prettiest way to arrive
By Train to at Matsushima is by sea. First, however, we suggest you take
Shiogama the JR train (Senseki Line), whose platforms are reached from
2 the Sendai Station basement, for a 30-minute trip to **Hon-Shiogama** Station. (The same train goes on to the Matsushima-Kaigan Station, so this itinerary may be done in reverse.) **Shiogama** is the port city of Sendai and has little appeal, except for one shrine, **Shiogama-jinja,** whose buildings, with bright orange-red exteriors and simple, natural wood interiors, are well worth the climb up the hill before you catch the boat to Matsushima.

To reach Shiogama-jinja Shrine, turn left from the station for about a 10-minute walk. You'll easily spot Shiogama-jinja because it is on a wooded hill overlooking the town. To avoid clambering up the 223 stone steps, don't use the main entrance. Instead, when you see the flashing neon signs of a *pachinko* (Japanese pinball machine) hall in front of you at a "T" junction, go right, and then left down a wide street running along the shrine's grounds. You'll see the entrance and a large gate on your left.

There are actually two shrines, the Shiogama-jinja and the **Shiwahiko-jinja.** The former is the second one you'll reach and is the main building of the complex (admission free). Two other reasons for the climb up to Shiogama-jinja are the view of Shiogama Bay and a 500-year-old Japanese holly tree on the temple grounds. You'll usually be able to recognize it by spotting the Japanese taking photographs of themselves standing before it. Near the Shiwahiko-jinja Shrine is a modern building that houses swords, armor, and religious articles on its first floor and whaling exhibits on its second. *Admission: ¥309. Open Apr.–Nov. 8–5; Dec.–Mar. 8:30–4.*

By Ferry to Matsushima In the summer, sightseeing ferries leave from Shiogama every hour (every 2 hours in the winter) for Matsushima. Whether you catch the gaudy "Chinese dragon" ferry or one that is less ostentatious, the route through the bay will be the same. So will the incessant and distracting loudspeaker naming (in Japanese) the islands. The first 10 minutes of the trip are dismal. Don't fret! Shiogama's ugly port and the oil refinery on the promontory soon give way to the beauty of Matsushima Bay and its islands. *Cost: ¥1,400 one way, second class for the hour-long trip; ¥2,400 for the upper deck in first class. The dock is to the right (seaward side) of the Hon-Shiogama train station.*

Exploring Once you are in **Matsushima,** the key sights are within easy
③ walking distance of each other. Should you need maps and brochures, the tourist office is at the end of the Matsushite-Kaigan pier. The first sight, Godaido Hall, is just to the right as you step off the boat on the pier. Constructed at the behest of Masamune Date in 1600, the temple is on a tiny islet connected to the shore by two small arched bridges. Weathered by the sea and salt air, the small building's paint has peeled off, giving it an intimacy often lacking in other temples. Animals are carved in the timbers beneath the temple roof and among the complex supporting beams. *Admission free.*

Across the street from Godaido Hall is the main temple, **Zuiganji.** Its origins date from 827, but the present structure was built on Masamune Date's orders in 1606. Designated as a National Treasure, Zuiganji Temple is the most representative Zen temple in the Tohoku region. The Main Hall is a large wood structure with ornately carved wood panels and paintings (faded with age) from the 17th century. Surrounding the temple are natural caves filled with Buddhist statues and memorial tablets that novices carved from the rock face as part of their training. The grounds surrounding the temple are full of trees, two of which are plum trees brought back from Korea in 1592 by Masamune Date after an unsuccessful military foray. *Admission: ¥515. Open 7:30–5; shorter hrs. Sept. 15–Mar. 31.*

If you want to know all about how people looked and dressed during Masamune Date's time, a new wax museum, **Ro Ningyo Rekishi Hakubu Thukan,** has opened close to Zuiganji. With life-size figures, the museum displays scenes from the feudal period—battles, tea ceremonies, and processions. *Admission: ¥700. Open daily 8:30–5.*

On the opposite (south) side of the harbor from Godaido Hall is **Kanrantei,** translated as "Water Viewing Pavilion." Originally, the structure was part of Fushimi-Momoyamajo in Kyoto, but when that castle was demolished, Hideyoshi Toyotomi gave it to Masamune Date, who then brought it to Matsushima. Here, the Date family held their tea parties for the next 270 years. Next to Kanrantei is the **Matsushima Museum,** with its full collection of the Date family's armor, swords, pikes, and more genteel items, including an array of lacquerware. *Admission: ¥310 for both Kanrantei and the museum. Open daily 8–5.*

Time Out While in Matsushima, don't pass up the chance to dine at **Ryokan Matsushimajo** (Matsushima Miyagi 981, tel. 022/354–2121), one of the famous old ryokan of Japan. This enchanting building with curved roofs is straight out of the Edo period, and the castlelike structure next door houses some of the guest rooms. Inside there are ancient relics from armor to scrolls and faded paintings. Lunch can be light and simple or more extensive, with a variety of dishes. To make the selection easier, the six options that focus on tempura, sashimi, or veal cutlet are pictured in the menu. The view from the dining room window overlooks Matsushima Bay.

From Matsushima-Kaigan Station it is a 30-minute train ride on the JR line back to Sendai. In the opposite direction from Sendai the train goes to Nobiru, two stops down the line. A 10-minute walk from the station brings you to the beach where, on weekends, the young cruise in their cars trying to attract the attention of the opposite sex. It's a good place to go for youthful company if you know a few words of Japanese. The road follows the shore, and it is a 30-minute hike to Ogatani peninsula for spectacular views of Matsushima.

North of Sendai to Hiraizumi

Another day's excursion from Sendai is north to Hiraizumi. In the 12th century, Hiraizumi came close to mirroring Kyoto as a cultural center. Hiraizumi was the family seat of the Fujiwara clan, who, for three generations, were powerful lords dedicated to promoting peace and the arts. The fourth-generation lord became power hungry, and his ambition wiped out the Fujiwara dynasty. Not too much remains of the great age under the first three generations of the Fujiwara clan, but what does, in particular the Chusonji Temple, is a tribute to Japan's past.

Getting There To reach Hiraizumi, take the JR express train (65 min.) or the Shinkansen (45 min.) on the main Tohoku Line going north to ❹ **Ichinoseki.** At Ichinoseki, there are two options. There is a ❺ local train to **Hiraizumi;** from Hiraizumi Station you can walk to the two major temples. Then a short bus ride is required to reach Gembikei Gorge, southeast of town. After returning to town, another bus is required to get to Geibikei Gorge, east of Hiraizumi. The better and quicker way is to use a taxi and bus combination from Ichinoseki Station, described below.

If your time is short and you wish to limit your sightseeing to Motsuji and Chusonji temples, simply take the local train from Sendai for the 90-minute run to Hiraizumi. You can obtain maps at the tourist office (tel. 0191/46–2110) on the town's main street—take a right from the JR station plaza. To reach Motsuji, walk 1,000 yards up the street leading directly away from the JR station. For Chusonji, you can either walk along a narrow road from Motsuji or return to the JR station and take a short bus ride.

Exploring By taxi from Ichinoseki, it's less than 10 minutes to the first stop, **Gembikei Gorge.** It's a miniature gorge—only a thousand yards long and less than 20 feet deep, but with all the features of the world's best gorges. Once, rushing water carved its path into solid rock; now it is quiet. Because of its miniature scale, you can walk its entire length and appreciate every detail of its web of sculptured patterns; the circular holes (Jacob Wells) scoured into the rock side become personal discoveries.

From Gembikei, either by bus or by taxi, it is a mile to Motsuji Temple. En route is **Takkoku-no-Iwaya,** a cave with a small temple dedicated to Bishamonten, the Buddhist deity of warriors, at its entrance. To the side of the cave and etched into the rock face are faint traces of an imposing image of Dainichi-Nyorai, a pose of Buddha said to have been carved in the 11th century. The temple is a 1961 rendition of the 17th-century temple. *Admission ¥200. Open daily 8:30–5.*

During the 12th-century dynasty of the Fujiwara clan, **Motsuji Temple** was the most venerated temple in northern Honshu. The complex consisted of 40 temples and some 500 lodgings. Eight centuries later, only the foundations remain. The current buildings are of more recent vintage, including the local youth hostel. However, what have survived in good condition are the Heian period Jodo-style (paradise-style) gardens, laid out according to the Buddhist principle some 700 years ago. Off to the side of the gardens is the Hiraizumi Museum, with artifacts of the Fujiwara family. *Admission: ¥515 for the gardens, ¥310 for the museum. Gardens and museum open 8–5.*

Now for the major sight, **Chusonji Temple.** From Motsuji, walk into Hiraizumi and up the main street, stopping at the tourist office for a local map and brochure. The walk to Chusonji is not far, less than a mile up the road from there. Buses make the trip frequently, or you can take a taxi from Motsuji to Chusonji for ¥950.

Set amid thick woods, Chusonji Temple was founded by the Fujiwara family in 1105. At that time, there were more than 40 buildings. War and a tremendous fire in 1337 destroyed all but two halls, **Kyozo** and **Konjikido.** The other buildings in the complex are reconstructions from the Edo period.

Of the two original buildings, Kyozo Hall is the less interesting. It once housed the greatest collection of Buddhist sutras (precepts), but fire destroyed many of them, and the remainder have been removed to the **Sankozo Museum** next door. Konjikido Hall, on the other hand, may be considered one of Japan's most historic temples.

Konjikido (Golden Hall) is small but magnificent. The exterior is black lacquer, and the interior is paneled with mother-of-pearl and gold leaf. In the Naijin (Inner Chamber) are three altars, each with 11 statues of Buddhist deities. Beneath the central altar are the remains of the three rulers of the Fujiwara family—Kiyohira, Motohira, and Hidehira. The power-seeking fourth member's remains are not there. His head was sent to Kyoto so that Shogun Minamoto no Yoritomo could look at his face! *Admission: ¥515 (includes Sankozo Museum). Open daily 8–5.*

The other major attraction of the area is **Geibikei Gorge.** To get to the gorge from Chusonji Temple by rail, you must return to the center of Hiraizumi, take a train back to Ichinoseki, and then change for the train to Rikuchu-Matsukawa. However, the direct route is only about 13 miles, so a taxi (about ¥2,000) is much more convenient.

Geibikei Gorge is Gembikei Gorge's big brother. Flat-bottom boats, poled by two boatmen, ply the river for a 90-minute round-trip through the gorge. The waters are peaceful and slow moving, relentlessly washing their way through silver-streaked cliffs. The high point of the trip is reaching the depths of the gorge, faced with 300-foot cliffs. Coming back downstream would be an anticlimax if it were not for the boatmen, who, with little to do but steer the boat, sing their traditional songs. The boat trip makes a marvelous rest from the temples (cost: ¥1,050).

From Hiraizumi, you can return to Sendai and Tokyo, continue on the train north to Morioka, or, as we do, go east to the Pacific coast before returning inland to reach Morioka.

To the Tono Basin and the Pacific

This itinerary to the Pacific coast requires approximately two days for you to enjoy traditional pastoral Japan and the southern coastline. Tono is rich in traditional ways and folklore, and the coast is an ever-changing landscape of cliffs, rock formations, and small coves.

Getting There From Hiraizumi, take the train north in the direction of Morioka to Hanamaki. If you take the Shinkansen from Ichinoseki, disembark at Shin-Hanamaki. Then take the JR train to Tono for a 70-minute ride. The same train continues to Kamaishi and Miyako. From there, take the train up to Morioka.

Exploring 6 The people of **Tono** like their old ways. The town itself is not particularly remarkable, but in the Tono Basin are old buildings and historical remains that take us back to old Japan and allow the ugliness of modern offices and factories to be temporarily forgotten. The Tono Basin is surrounded by forest-clad mountains, so the setting for this enclave of rusticity is picture-perfect. Along the valley on either side of Tono are several L-shaped *magariya* (thatch-roof Nambu-style farmhouses). Families live in the long side of the L, and animals are off to the side. One of these has been made into a family-run hotel, the Minshuku Magariya (without the animals). To the southeast of Tono is a *suisha* (waterwheel), one of the few working ones left in Japan. In a peaceful, wooded area above the Atago-jinja Shrine are the *gohyaku-rakan* (disciples of Buddha) images carved by a priest on boulders in a shallow ravine. The priest wanted to appease the spirits of the quarter of Tono's inhabitants who starved to death in the two-year famine of 1754–55.

The Tono Basin has much more—temples, including Fukusenji with Japan's tallest wood Kannon (Goddess of Mercy), which was built by priest Yuzen Sasaki to boost morale after World War II; an abundance of shrines; the Tsuzuki Stone, a huge boulder mysteriously balanced on two smaller ones; and a *kappa* pool (kappas are demons that impregnate young girls, who then give birth to demikappas). There is also a redbrick museum and a folk village exhibiting Tono's heritage. All sites are listed on two maps given out by the Tono Tourist Office in the village. *Joint admission: ¥515. Open daily 9–4:30. Closed last day of each month, Sept. 21–30, and Mon. Nov.–Mar.*

Distances between points of interest are too far to walk; unless you have a car, a rented bicycle is necessary. (Many places, including hotels, rent bikes.) Finally, to make the most of the Tono experience, you should read *Tono Monogatari*, translated into English by Robert Morse as the *Legends of Tono*.

(7) *From Tono the train runs down (90 min.) to the Pacific seaport and iron-making town of* **Kamaishi.** Note the 160-foot statue of Buddha (**Karaishi Daikamon**) built in 1970 that stands on Kamazaki Point. To visit the temple take the 15-minute bus ride from JR Kamaishi station. It costs a steep ¥800 to enter and see the 33 small wood statues of Kannon. Then, with a change of trains, the journey turns north to run along the coast **(8)** (another 90 min.) to **Miyako,** a busy, prosperous town that is pleasantly compact and has several reasonable places to stay. **(9)** However, the reason for staying over is to enjoy **Jodogahama,** a 20-minute bus ride (from bus stop 1 at Miyako Station) up the coast. Jodogahama (Paradise Beach) was given its name by a priest who thought it was what the hereafter must look like. The combination of glinting white-quartz beach, the peculiarly shaped rock formations, and the pine trees on the cliffs bending to the wind makes Jodogahama a special place. Two rock formations to spot are **Rosoku Iwa** (Candle Rock) and **Shiofuki Ana** (Salt Spraying Hole).

The best way to appreciate Jodogahama is from the water. Rowboats are for hire, but the easier way to get around is to take a 40-minute cruise around the bay. The boats leave from Jodogahama Pier and are operated by the Iwate Kenhoku Jidosha Company. *Tel. 0193/62–3350. Cost: ¥820. 9 trips a day mid-Mar.–mid-Nov.*

Alternatively, you may want to use Taro as your base (16 min. up the coast from Miyako by the Sanniku Railway. Fare: ¥340). There are several minshukus and hotels offering hospitality in this small fishing village. Walk along the left side of the harbor and you will find a marked, paved nature trail that curves around the jagged, rock-strewn shore. Notice the marks some 100 feet above your head on the side of the cliff at the harbor entrance. These indicate the highest waves recorded. The trail leads to a series of steps that climb to a parking area outside the Sanokuku Hotel. From there it's a downhill walk along the road back to the village.

Further up the Senniku Railway Line is Kuji (fare from Miyako: ¥1,510), where, in the summer, the Ama (women divers) search for oysters. At Kuji the JR line starts again, heading north to Hachinoche, where it connects with the JR Aomori-Morioka route. It is a slow ride up the coast from Miyako to Hachinoche, and much of the beautiful shoreline is missed owing to frequent tunnels.

A Special Detour If you do not go down to the Kaigan coast from Tono, consider **(10)** renting a car or hiring a taxi to get to **Take.** It is especially worth considering if you are traveling at the end of July, when there is a delightful Shinto festival to visit. The road from Tono winds through picturesque hills to reach the village of Take, situated on the slopes of Mt. Hayachine. For centuries Mt. Hayachine has been regarded as a sacred mountain, and every July 31 to August 1 there is the festival of Hayachine-jinja. For two days folkloric stories known collectively as Yamabushi-kagura are acted out in masked dance performances. However, the most colorful part of the festival is on August 1, when a procession of townspeople, wearing lion costumes and wood lion masks, parade through the village en route from the main shrine to a lesser shrine nearby. Because the festival has grown in popularity, it is advisable to telephone the local festival authorities (tel. 0198/48–5864) to secure accommodations.

From Take, the road goes to Fujima, a stop on the Tohoku Line. Morioka is 20 minutes up the line.

Morioka

⑪ **Morioka** is a busy commercial and industrial city ringed by mountains. Because it is at the northernmost end of the Shinkansen Line, it has become a transfer point for destinations to northern Honshu and Hokkaido. However, despite the city's attempt to appeal to visitors, there is little to keep the tourist interested. Once it had a fine castle built by the 26th Lord of Nambu in 1597, but it was destroyed in the Meiji Restoration and all that remains are its ruins. Its site is now the **Iwate-Koen Park,** the focus of town and the place to escape the congestion of traffic and people in downtown Morioka.

Getting There Morioka is the last stop on the Tohoku Shinkansen Line. From here, all trains going north are "regular" JR trains. So while it can take less than one hour to travel between Sendai and Morioka, the same distance to Aomori (north Honshu) takes two hours and 20 minutes. Morioka also has a JR line, via Tazawako, to Akita on the Sea of Japan coast, as well as the line down to the Pacific coast at Miyako.

Exploring The tourist office, Kita-Tohuku Sightseeing Center, in the Travel Stage station lounge on the first floor of the Morioka JR station, has useful maps and other information on Morioka and Iwate prefectures. It can also help arrange accommodations. To reach downtown take Bus 5 or 6 from the terminal in front of the JR station. *Tel. 0196/25–2090. Open daily 8:30–8.*

Should you wish to take a tour of the city, the Iwate Kanko Bus Company offers full-day and ½-day tours with Japanese-speaking guides. *Cost: full-day tour ¥3,600, departs 10:45 Morioka Station, returns 4:45; ½-day tour ¥2,100, departs 9:30 and 1:45 Morioka, returns 3 hrs. later. Tours operate Apr. 20–Nov. 20.*

The major attraction of Morioka is its special craft, *nambutetsu* (ironware). The range of articles, from small wind-bells to elaborate statues, is vast, but the most popular items are the *nambutetsubin* (heavy iron kettles), which come in all shapes, weights, and sizes. Hundreds of shops throughout the city sell nambutetsu, but the main shopping streets are Saien-dori and O-dori, which run by Iwate-Koen Park. Across the river from the park is **Gozaku,** an area of small shops that look much as they did a century ago—a more interesting place in which to browse for nambutetsu. On the other hand, if you are just changing trains at Morioka with little time to spare, the basement floors of the department store under the JR station have a wide selection of nambutetsu.

To reach Gozaku from the park use the Nakano-hashi bridge and take the first main street on the left. A short way down, just past the Hotel Seito, you will find the large Nambu Iron shop and the narrow streets of the Gozaku section on your left.

Beyond Gozaku is another bridge, Yonogi-hashi. At the street corner you'll see a very Western-looking firehouse, built in the 1920s and still in operation. The next bridge, Morioka's pride, is the Kamino-hashi, one of the few decorated bridges in Japan. Eight specially crafted bronze railings were commissioned in 1609 and ten bronze posts added two years later.

If there is time to spare in Morioka, visit the **Hashimoto Museum,** reached by a 35-minute bus ride from the station. (Buses run infrequently, especially during the winter, so verify the time of the return bus before you set out.) Buses 8 and 12 (fare: ¥210) go up to the observation tower on Mt. Iwayama, and the museum is halfway up the small mountain. The museum was created by Yaoji Hashimoto, himself an artist, from a traditional Nambu *magariya* (L-shape thatch-roof farmhouse), rescued from a valley drowned by a dam. The building itself is worth a visit, and the works of Hashimoto and other Iwate artists are an added pleasure, but you could skip the room exhibiting 19th-century paintings by French naturalists of the Barbizon school. There is also one room devoted to ironware and pottery in case you have not had your fill. *Admission:¥700. Open daily 10–5. Closed Dec. 29–Jan. 3.*

Back at the JR station on the Shinkansen platforms, a special *bento* (box lunch) is sold. The content (mostly tuna sushi) is less interesting than the container; it's made of pottery in the shape of a *kokeshi*, the folk-craft doll that is so popular throughout Tohoku.

From Morioka through Towada-Hachimantai Park to Aomori

From Morioka, the main railway line runs northeast to Aomori via Hachinohe. It entirely misses Tohoku's rugged interior, the Hachimantai Plateau. The Towada-Hachimantai National Park is rugged mountains, with gnarled and windswept trees, sweeping panoramas over the gorges and valleys (forming wrinkles in which natives shelter during the region's harsh winters), volcanic mountain cones, and crystal-clear lakes.

Getting There From Morioka, you take the JR Hanawa Line for a 40-minute ride to Obuke. From there, it is best to travel by bus for a distance of about 62 miles to the Hachimantai Plateau. After exploring that area you can rejoin the train at Towada-Minami to travel on to Hirosaki and Aomori. The travel time is less than a day, but you should plan on spending at least one night en route.

Exploring Obuke is at the southern entrance to the Towada-Hachimantai National Park. A bus leaves from Obuke Station for the 50-minute trip to **Higashi Hachimantai,** the resort town where hikers and skiers begin their ascent into the upper reaches of the mountains. A few miles farther on is **Gozaisho Onsen,** a popular spa resort that can be a useful overnight stop. Aside from several large hotels, there is a village complex (Puutaro-mura) of wood cabins with private thermal pools. A huge youth hostel also accommodates skiers in the winter and hikers in the summer.

The left-hand fork leads to **Matsukawa Onsen** (noted for its pure waters), which has a youth hostel and also the Kyoun-so Minshuku (*see* Hachimantai Lodging, *below*). This spa town is on the backside of Mt. Iwate, amid the eerie barrenness left by the volcano's eruption 250 years ago. A faster way of reaching Hachimantai and Matsukawa is to take a bus direct from Morioka (2 hours; fare: ¥1,020). The last stop of this bus is the Hachimantai Kanko Hotel. For Matsukawa, change buses at the stop before in Higashi Hachimantai.

Past Gozaisho is the entrance to the **Aspite Line** toll road, which is a 17-mile scenic road that skirts Mt. Chausu (5,177 feet) and Mt. Hachimantai (5,295 feet). The toll road twists, and with every turn there is another view of evergreen-clad slopes and alpine flowers. From the Hachimantai-chojo (bus stop) it is a 20-minute walk up a path to **Hachiman-numa Pond,** originally a crater lake of a volcano. There is a paved esplanade around the crater, and in July and August the alpine flowers bloom at their best.

The road turning left after Hachimantai-chojo leads to **Toshichi Onsen,** which, at a height of 4,593 feet and located at the foot of Mt. Mokko, is a popular spring skiing resort and a year-round spa town. On the northern side of Toshichi is **Horaikyo,** a natural garden with dwarf pine trees and alpine plants scattered among strange rock formations. In early October, the autumn colors are resplendent.

Just before the end of the Aspite Line toll road is another spa town, **Goshogake Onsen,** noted for its abundance of hot water. This spa and Toshichi are the best spas for overnight stays, especially Goshogake if you want to try Ondoru (Korean-style) steam baths and box-type steam baths. Just outside of Goshogake is a mile-long nature trail highlighting the volcanic phenomena of the area, including *doro-kazan* (muddy volcanoes) and *oyunuma* (hot-water swamps).

After Goshogake Onsen, the toll road joins Route 341. A left turn here leads south to Lake Tazawa, discussed later in this chapter. A right turn at the junction heads north for an hour's ⑬ bus journey to the town of **Hachimantai,** where you can rejoin the JR Hanawa line either to return to Obuke and Morioka or to travel north toward Aomori.

Twenty minutes north of Hachimantai õn the JR Hanawa Line ⑭ is **Towada-Minami.** From here, buses leave to make the 60-⑮ minute trip to **Lake Towada** (fare: ¥980). (If scarcity of time dictates it, you could forgo the Hachimantai Plateau and arrive at Towada-Minami directly from Obuke and Morioka.)

The area around Lake Towada is one of the most popular resorts in northern Tohoku. The main feature is the caldera lake, which fills a volcanic cone with depths of up to 1,096 feet, the third deepest in Japan and which, strangely enough, had no fish in it until Sadayuki Wanoi stocked it with trout in 1903. Since buses frequently travel between Towada-Minami and Towadako (Lake Towada), you may want to get off the bus at ⑯ **Oyu Onsen** and change for a local bus to travel 14 miles to Japan's Stonehenge, **Oyu Iseki**—a circle of stones with another center ring of upright stones, one of them shaped like a sundial. Oyu Iseki was discovered only in the 1930s, but studies have estimated that the ring is 4,000 years old.

After Oyu Onsen, the road snakes over **Hakka-toge Pass**—some of the best views of the lake are from here—and, via a series of switchbacks, descends to circle the lakeshore. Taking a

⑰ right at the lake leads to the village resort of **Yasumiya**, from which pleasure boats depart (from mid-Apr. to early Nov.) every 30 minutes for a run across the lake to **Nenokuchi**. The one-hour trip on the boat (fare: ¥1,130) covers the most scenic parts of the lake, and at Nenokuchi there are bicycles to rent for further exploration. (Rental bicycles are also available in Yasumiya.) From Nenokuchi there is a bus that continues around the lake's northern shore to **Taki-no-zawa**—more superb views of the lake—and then goes on to Hirosaki.

⑱ **Hirosaki** is one of northern Tohoku's friendliest and most attractive cities, said to be the home of Japan's most beautiful women. Its major (and really only) sight is **Hirosakijo** (Hirosaki Castle), but the town has an intimacy that makes it appealing. There is a tourist-information office on the left side of the station (tel. 0172/32–0524. Open 9–5).

Located at the northwestern end of the town in the opposite direction from the JR station and across the river, the castle is an original—a pleasant change from admirable replicas. Built in 1610, it is relatively small but perfectly proportioned, and it is guarded by moats. The gates in the outlying grounds are also original, and when the 6,000 *someiyoshino* (cherry trees) blossom (festival, Apr. 25–May 6) or the maples turn red in autumn (festival, early Oct.–early Nov.), the setting is marvelous. In winter thick snows match the castle's whiteness and give the grounds a sense of stillness and peace (snow festival, early Feb). *Admission: ¥310. Open daily 8:30–5.*

Also, don't miss the five-story pagoda, **Saishoin Temple**, built in 1672. It is located by the river on the southwest edge of town.

At any time, Hirosaki is a pleasant overnight stay, but during the first week of August the city comes even more alive with its famous **Nebuta Festival**. Each night different routes are followed through the town, with floats displaying scenes from Japanese and Chinese mythology represented by huge fanlike paintings that have faces painted on both sides. With lights inside the faces, the streets become an illuminated pantomime.

Hirosaki is a compact little town where you can walk everywhere. In the evening, the small entertainment area is the cluster of narrow streets flanked to its north and east by Hirosaki's two main streets, which cross each other. Near the intersection is a *pachinko* (Japanese pinball machine) center, an easy landmark to spot with its flashing lights, and the next street left leads into the entertainment center. One extremely friendly, inexpensive yakitori restaurant, the **Isehiro**, is the second restaurant on the left after the first cross street. But there are numerous choices for dining, from *izakayas* (small bars) to restaurants with picture menus in their windows, and after dinner there are coffeehouses, *nomiyas* (pubs), and more expensive clubs for further pleasure. Perhaps because of the large resident foreign population in Hirosaki, foreigners are accepted, understood, and welcomed, seemingly more so than in other Tohoku small towns. You'll even find an excellent bookshop, **Kinokuniya** (tel. 0172/36–4511), next door to the Hotel Hokke Club on Hirosaki's main street; the shop stocks a wide selection of English-language books.

The Civic Sightseeing Museum opened in late 1990 to display local industry, crafts, and regional art. *Open 9–4:30. Closed Sun. Admission free.*

From Hirosaki it is a 40-minute local train ride to Aomori.

⑲ If you are heading directly to Aomori from Lake Tazawako (*see below*), rather than spend the night in what is a large, sprawling, unattractive city, choose a Japanese experience by overnighting at **Sukayu Onsen,** near the Hakkoda Ropeway. Buses depart from Towada-Minami, pass by Lake Towada, and stop at Sukayu en route to Aomori. Unfortunately, because of winter snows, the only route to Sukayu Onsen between November 11 and March 31 is an hour-long bus ride from Aomori and the last bus departs at 3:30 PM, but if you can catch it, it's worth it.

It is known that more than 300 years ago a hunter shot and wounded a deer near here. Three days later he saw the deer again, miraculously healed. He realized that the deer had cured himself in the sulphur springs. Since then, people have been coming to Sukayu for the water's curative powers. The inn, and there is nothing but the inn, is a sprawling wooden building with highly polished creaking floors. The main bath, known as Sen Nin Buro (Thousand People Bath), is made of Hiba, a very strong wood. It is not segregated—men and women bathe together. Two big tubs fill the bath house: one pool called Netsu-no-yu is 42° C and feels hotter than the other, Shibu rokubu, which is one degree colder. The other two bathtubs, called Hie–no–yu, are for cooling off by pouring water only on your head so you don't wash the minerals off your body. (*See* Lodging under Hachimantai, *below*.)

Aomori
⑳ **Aomori** is another of Tohoku's prefectural capitals that have more appeal to their residents than to travelers. There is a tourist-information center at the station (tel. 0177/23–2233. Open 9–5, closed Sun.), but most of their brochures are in Japanese. Foreign visitors used to stop here while waiting for the ferry to cross over to Hokkaido. Now, the traveler can transfer to the express train and ride through the Seikan Undersea Tunnel (33.66 miles long, with 14.5 miles of it deep under the Tsugaru Straits) to Hokkaido. The Seikan tunnel is, by the way, the world's longest tunnel under the sea.

Exploring Aomori has only marginal interest unless you can be there for its **Nebuta Festival** (Aug. 3–7). The festival is similar to Hirosaki's (the two festivals are celebrated at the same time). Three-dimensional representations of men and animals parade on floats through the streets at night. Because the figures are illuminated from the inside, the spectacle might be ghostly but for the flaming colors used, which make everything festive.

If you are in Aomori at another time, you can take the JR bus from gate 8 or 9 (cost ¥575; 35 minutes) to **Nebuta-no-Sato** (Nebuta Museum) in the southwest of town, where 10 of the figures used in Aomori's festival are stored and are on display. (The same JR bus continues on from Nebuta-no-Sato to Sukayu Onsen and the Hachimantai Plateau, so if you are coming from that spa, you may wish to get off and visit this museum before continuing into downtown Aomori.) *Nebuta-no-sato. Admission: ¥620. Open 9–8 July–Sept., except during the Nebuta Festival, beginning of Aug.; mid-Apr.–June 30, open 9–5:30; and Oct. 1–Nov. 30, 9–5:30. Closed Dec.–mid-Apr.*

Munakata Shiko Kinenkan is a museum that opened in 1974 in dedication to the locally born artist Shiko Munakata (1903–1975). To reach the Munakata Shiko Kinenkan requires taking a bus from the JR station in the direction of Tsutsui and getting off at Shimin Bunka Senta-mae. Then walk back over the crossing and take a left. You will see the museum on the left. The building is constructed in the attractive azehura-style. Inside, the two-floor gallery displays the prints, paintings, and calligraphy of this internationally known artist. *Admission: ¥300. Open Apr.–Sept. 9:30–4:30; Oct.–Mar. 10–4. Closed on the last day of the month and national holidays.*

You may also wish to visit the **Prefectural Museum** (Kyodo-kan—a five-minute bus ride from the station), which displays folk crafts and archaeological material. *Admission: ¥300. Open Apr.–Sept. 9:30–4:30; Oct.–Mar. 9:30–4. Closed Mon.*

The **Museum of Folk Art** (Keikokan), also five minutes away from the station, has a larger display of local crafts, including fine examples of Tsugaru-nuri lacquerware, which achieves its hardness through 48 coats of lacquer. Dolls representing the Hamento dancing girls of the Nebuta Festival are also on display. *Admission: ¥300. Open 9:30–4:30. Closed Thurs. Nov.–Apr.*

For a quick overview of Aomori there is the ASPAM (Asupamu) Building down by the waterfront, where the ferryboats once docked. The 15-story ultramodern eyesore is easy to recognize by its 249-foot tall pyramid shape. An outside elevator whisks you 13 floors up to an enclosed observation deck. Inside the building are a number of restaurants and exhibits on Aomori's tourist attractions and crafts. *Admission: ¥300. Open 9AM–10PM.*

Aomori ends this excursion north through Tohoku. Now, we go south down Tohoku's Sea of Japan coast. For those of you going first to Hokkaido, either take the train under, or the ferry across, the Tsugaru Straits to Hakodate.

South from Aomori to Akita on the Sea of Japan

So far, our travels have been on the central and Pacific sides of Tohoku. The return journey travels south down the Sea of Japan side to Akita before moving back into Tohoku's mountainous central spine at Tazawako. From there, staying within the mountains, our excursion continues on to Yamagata. Then comes the final leg through the southern Tohoku prefecture of Fukushima.

Exploring Leaving Aomori for Akita (a 3-hour ride), the train goes back through Hirosaki and past **Mt. Iwaki** (5,331 feet high), which dominates the countryside. A bus (40 minutes) from Hirosaki travels to the foot of this mountain. From there, one can take the sightseeing bus up the Iwaki Skyline toll road (open late Apr.–late Oct.) to the eighth station. The final ascent, with the reward of a 360-degree view, is by a seven-minute ropeway, followed by a 30-minute walk to the summit. Back on the train and soon after Mt. Iwaki, the mountains give way to the rice fields and flat plains that surround Akita.

㉑ **Akita,** the prefectural capital (pop. 300,000), is not a particularly appealing place to visit. Indeed, it does not even have a tourist information office at the station except for a small, hard-to-find desk beyond the JR seat-reservation office. Essentially, Akita is a built-up and commercial city whose major attraction for tourists is its famous **Kanto Festival** (Aug. 5–7). In this festival, young men balance a 30-foot-long bamboo pole that supports as many as 50 lit paper lanterns on its eight cross-bars. The area around Akita is said to grow the best rice and have the purest water in Japan, and the combination of these two produces excellent dry sake.

If you have time between trains, **Senshu Park** is a 10-minute walk from the station if you follow the train tracks to the north. It was the site of the now-ruined Kubota Castle, and today it is a pleasant spot of greenery, with cherry blossoms and azaleas adding color in season. Aside from the prefectural art museum, the park includes the **Hirano Masakichi Art Museum,** with a noted collection of paintings by Tsuguji Fujita (1886–1968), as well as works by van Gogh and Cézanne. The building itself is architecturally interesting for its Japanese palace-style roof covered with copper, which slopes down and rolls outside at the edge. *Admission: ¥400. Open 10–5. Closed Mon.*

For regional arts and crafts, make a visit to the **Akita Sangyo Kaikan,** which is a five-minute walk from the park toward the city center. Though this is a museum, there are also crafts for sale (open 10–5; closed Wed.). Two streets to the west of the crafts center is Kawabata Street. This is where everyone comes in the evening to sample the regional hot-pot dishes *shottsuru-nabe* (made with pickled sand fish) and *kiritampo-nabe* (made with rice cakes and chicken), drink the local ji-sake, and be entertained at one of the many bars.

㉒ Only 19 miles to the north and west of Akita is **Oga Peninsula,** a promontory indented by strange rock formations and reefs, mountains clad with Akita cedar, and grassy green hills. Though there are toll roads that trace Oga's coastline, public transport is infrequent. The easiest way to tour the peninsula is by using the services of the Akita Chuo Kotsu bus lines (tel. 0188/23–4411). The tour buses leave from Akita Station, Oga Station, and Oga Onsen. They depart daily late-April–early November. However, the tour is conducted in Japanese.

Instead of continuing south along the Sea of Japan coast from Akita and going directly to Tsuruoka, this excursion detours inland up to **Tazawako,** or Lake Tazawa. After that, the excursion goes south, offering the detour to Tsuruoka en route to Yamagata. (To get directly from Akita to Yamagata take the JR train to Omagari and change onto the Limited Express bound for Yamagata—a two and a half hour journey.)

㉓ On the way to Tazawako, via Omagari, is the small and delight-ful town of **Kakunodate.** Founded in 1620 by the local lord, the town has remained an outpost of traditional Japan that, with cause, boasts of being Tohoku's little Kyoto. Within a 15-minute walk northwest from the station are several 350-year-old samurai houses, all well-preserved and maintained. The most renowned of the samurai houses is Aoyagi, with its sod-turf roof. The cherry tree in Aoyagi's garden is 280 years old. The whole town is full of weeping cherry trees, some 400 in all, which are direct descendants of those imported from Kyoto three centuries ago. *Admission: ¥515. Open 9–4:30 daily in summer. Closed late-Nov.–mid-Apr.*

If there is time before the next train to Tazawako, visit the **Denshoken Hall** located in front of a cluster of samurai houses. The hall serves as a museum and a workshop for cherry-bark handicrafts. *Admission: ¥310. Open 9–5. Closed Thurs. Nov.–Mar.*

Should you wish to overnight in Kakunodate, your choice is limited to one business hotel, four or five ryokan where the owners would like their guests to know some Japanese, and a small minshuku, Huyakusuien, that has been converted from a 19th century warehouse (*see* Lodging, *below*).

From Kakunodate it is a 16-minute ride on the train to **Tazawako.** (The total journey from Akita to Tazawako takes about one hour. The train then continues on to Morioka, another hour away.) You will need to take a 15-minute bus ride (fare: ¥190) from the JR station to Tazawako Kohan on the lake shore, but first drop in at the tourist information office to the left of the JR station for maps and bus schedules. *Tel. 0187/34–0307. Open daily 8:30–5:15.*

Tazawa is Japan's deepest lake (1,394 feet). Its waters are the second most transparent in Japan (after Lake Mashu in Hokkaido). Like most of Japan's lakes, Tazawa is in a volcanic cone, but its shape is a more classic caldera than most. With its clear waters and forested slopes, it captures a mystical quality that appeals so much to the Japanese on vacation. According to legend, the great beauty from Akita, Takko Hime, sleeps in the water's deep as a dragon. Apparently, that is why the lake never freezes over in winter. Takko Hime and her dragon husband churn the water with their passionate lovemaking. Or, perhaps, as scientists say, the water doesn't freeze because of a freshwater source that enters the bottom of the lake.

An excursion boat makes 40-minute cruises on the lake during late April–November (cost: ¥980). There is also regular bus service around the lake (halfway around in winter), and bicycles are available for rent at the Tazawa-kohan bus terminal as an alternative to the cruise boat. If you go by bike, more time can be spent appreciating the beauty of Takko Hime, whose bronze statue is on the western shore.

A 40-minute bus ride (fare: ¥540) from the Tazawako JR station via Tazawa-kohan takes you up to the **Tazawako Kogen Plateau.** Located to the northeast of Lake Tazawa, the journey offers spectacular views of the lake, showing off the full dimensions of its caldera shape. The same bus then continues on for another 10 minutes to **Nyuto Onsen,** a collection of small, unspoiled, mountain hot-spring spas in some of the few traditional spa villages left in Tohoku. Most of these villages have only one inn, so it is advisable to arrange accommodations before you arrive if you wish to stay the night. *(See* Lodging, *below.)*

A few miles east of Lake Tazawa stands **Mt. Komaga-take.** At 5,370 feet, it is the highest mountain in the area, yet it is one of the easiest to climb. A bus from Tazawako Station runs up to the eighth station, from which it takes less than an hour to reach the summit; you'll walk through clusters of alpine flowers if you choose June or July for your hike.

Another old traditional spa town, **Tamagawa Onsen,** is to the north of Tazawako on Route 381. There is frequent bus service between the two towns (90 minutes; fare: ¥1,120). The spa is quaint and delightfully old-fashioned, with wood buildings surrounding the thermal springs. The elderly who come to take the waters are very serious about the curative qualities of the mineral waters. However, think twice before staying here overnight; the inns are a little ramshackle. Beyond Tamagawa Onsen, the road joins the Aspite Line toll road described earlier in the Hachimantai excursion. Since direct JR train service runs between Morioka and Tazawako, an alternative itinerary to the one described in the earlier section is to go first to Tazawako from Morioka and travel up Route 381 to Hachimantai.

Heading south from Tazawako, you can either travel directly down the middle of Tohoku to Yamagata or make a detour to visit Tsuruoka and Mt. Haguro by returning to the Sea of Japan coast. Then turn inland again to Yamagata.

South of Akita and along the Sea of Japan coast toward Niigata are small fishing villages, noteworthy only for the fact that few tourists stop over en route. (There are four trains a day between Akita and Niigata; the trip takes 3 hours and 50 minutes.) The one exception is **Tsuruoka,** the religious center of Shugendo, an esoteric religious sect that combines Buddhism with Shintoism. It's famous for its temple, **Zempoji,** which has a pagoda containing images of Buddha in every pose that could possibly be attributed to him. The city also serves as the gateway for visiting **Mt. Haguro,** the most accessible of the three mountains in the Dewa-san range. All three mountains are sacred to the *yamabushi,* the popular name given to members of the Shugendo sect, but it is the thatch-roof shrine **Haguro-san Jinja,** on the summit of Mt. Haguro, that attracts pilgrims throughout the year.

Nowadays most pilgrims take the easy way up to the summit—a direct bus from Tsuruoka Station along the toll road. The old way, the one that the more devout or foolhardy tourists take, is by train from Tsuruoka to Haguro; from there, they walk up the 2,446 stone steps to the summit. The climb is not for the faint at heart, but the route along avenues of 300-year-old cedar trees—with shafts of sunlight filtering through, the occasional waterfall, the tiny shrines, and the tea shop halfway up—is the reason for reaching the summit. The actual shrine, Haguro-san Jinja, surrounded by souvenir stands, is not so impressive; you'll be glad to get on the bus to return to Tsuruoka, leaving behind on the slopes of Mt. Haguro the numerous small huts used by yamabushi pilgrims engaged in their penance. Once back in Tsuruoka, it is a two-hour train ride to Yamagata.

Should you wish to spend the night in the Tsuruoka area, take the JR train 15 minutes to the south to **Atsumi Onsen,** a spa town where the curative waters are good for your skin as well as your digestive system. Facing the stormy Japan Sea and backed by mountains, the small village lives in isolation. Unfortunately, it lost its old buildings in a fire that swept the valley 40 years ago, so virtually all the buildings are new. One particularly hospitable ryokan is Tachibana-ya (*see* Lodging, *below*). To reach the village use the bus (fare: ¥180) from the JR Atsumi Onsen station; it's a 10-minute journey to town.

Yamagata

Yamagata, with a population of 250,000, is the capital of the prefecture of the same name. For visitors to Japan, Yamagata is more a transportation hub than a destination in itself, but it is a friendly town and anxious to become more of a tourist destination. Pick up free maps and brochures from the tourist information office opposite the ticket turnstiles inside the newly expanded JR railway station. *Tel. 0236/31–7865. Open daily 10–6.*

Getting There To reach Yamagata directly from Tokyo it's best to take the new Shinkansen, which takes just under three hours. There is also direct train service on the JR Senzan Line from Sendai (about 1 hour). To the Sea of Japan coast, a train on the JR Yonesaka Line running between Niigata and Yamagata takes 3½ hours; the train on the JR Rikuu West Line to Tsuruoka, which connects with the JR Uetsu Honsen Line to Akita, takes three hours. Finally, going north, the JR Ou Honsen Line travels up to Tazawako and then over the mountains to Morioka.

Yamagata is also serviced by All Nippon Airways (ANA) flights from Tokyo's Haneda Airport (55 minutes) and by Japan Air System from Osaka (80 minutes). Yamagata's airport is 40 minutes by bus from the city center.

Exploring Yamagata is a small, country town whose major attraction is summer hiking and winter skiing in the nearby mountains. The main event is the August **Hanagasa Festival,** in which some 10,000 dancers from the entire area dance their way through the streets in traditional costume and *hanagasa* hats, so named for the safflowers used to decorate them. For anyone interested in pottery, take a taxi ride (the route is very difficult by bus unless you speak Japanese) to **Hirashimizu** on the outskirts of the city. This small enclave of traditional buildings and farmhouses is a step back in time and a sharp contrast to the modern urban sprawl of Yamagata. About six pottery families live here, each specializing in a particular style. The pottery of Seiryugama is the best known, and, with exhibitions of its wares in America and Europe, its prices are high. Other potteries available are more simple wares, and are more affordable. Seek out the reasonably priced Nanaemon pottery.

30 Most visitors come to Yamagata, though, to make their way to the prefecture's largest draw, **Mt. Zao,** where 1.2 million alpine enthusiasts come December–April to ski its eight slopes. (During the winter, there are direct buses from Tokyo to Zao Onsen.) The mountain's resort town, **Zao Onsen,** is only 12 miles (45 minutes by bus) from Yamagata Station. From Zao Onsen, the first cable car leaves from the base lodge to climb 1,734 feet, and the second one makes the final ascent of an additional 1,839 feet. Even nonskiers make the round trip in order to see the heavy snow on the conifers. The weight of the snow causes the trees to form weird cylindrical shapes, making them look like fairy-tale monsters. In the summer hikers come, though in fewer numbers than the winter skiers, to walk among the colored rocks and visit Zao Okama, a caldera lake with a 900-foot radius.

31 Another attraction, 12 miles outside Yamagata, (30 minutes on the JR Senzan Line toward Sendai) is **Hojusan Risshakuji Temple,** more commonly known as Yamadera Temple. Built 1,100 years ago, Yamadera's complex of temples with steeply pitched slate roofs on the slopes of Mt. Hoju is the largest one of the Tendai sect in northern Japan and attracts some 700,000 pilgrims a year. The small town at the base of the hill has become very touristy with hotels and souvenir shops, but once through the entrance to the temple grounds, a modicum of serenity prevails. Just inside the entrance and to the right is Konponchudo, the temple where the sacred flame has been burning constantly for 1,000 years. The path continues on and up. The ascent is relatively easy, but the path is strewn with fallen rocks, and some of the 1,000 steps are crumbling. On the way to the top is a statue of the Japanese poet Basho Matsuo (1644–1694), who wrote of his wanderings throughout Japan in his 17-syllable poems (haiku). Finally, after a steep ascent, there is the Niomon, the gate leading to Kaisando, where the temple founder is buried.

Into Fukushima Prefecture and out of Tohoku

From Yamagata, there are three possible routes: directly across the mountains by JR trains to Sendai; south and west to Niigata, Sado Island, and the Japan Alps *(see* Chapter 6); or continuing down Tohoku's mountainous spine to the fifth prefecture of the region, Fukushima, from where one can cross over to Nikko *(see* Nikko in Chapter 4).

Fukushima Prefecture is tamer both in scenery and in attitudes than the rest of Tohoku; it was the first region in northern Honshu to become a popular resort area for Japanese families, especially around the Bandai-Kogen Plateau. Mt. Bandai erupted 101 years ago, and in 15 short minutes wiped out over 40 small villages, killing 477 people and resculpturing the landscape. The result was nature's damming of several streams to **32** form hundreds of lakes, the largest of which is **Lake Hibara,** with its crooked shoreline and numerous islets.

Getting There From Yamagata, the Bandai-Kogen Plateau is reached by taking the train to **Yonezawa,** and then taking a two-hour bus ride over the Nishi-Azuma Sky Valley toll road. The whole mountain resort is, in fact, crisscrossed by five scenic toll roads. A direct bus to Bandai-Kogen from Fukushima City departs from near the Shinkansen station and travels over the Bandai-Azuma Skyline drive, offering splendid views of mountains by climbing up through **Jododaira Pass** at 5,214 feet.

All buses from Fukushima City, Inawashiro, Yonezawa, and Aizu-Wakamatsu arrive at **Bandai-Kogen** bus stop, the tourist center on Lake Hibara, where the Japanese vacationers disperse to their campgrounds, bungalows, or modern ryokan.

Exploring While the Bandai-Kogen Plateau area is somewhat spoiled by the hordes of tourists, a particularly pleasant two-hour walk, the Goshikinuma Trail, meanders past the dozen or more tiny little lakes (ponds, really) that are collectively called **Goshikinuma** (five-color lakes), because each throws off a different color. The trail begins across from the Bandai-Kogen bus station and in the opposite direction from Lake Hibara.

A bus that departs from Bandai-Kogen goes straight to Aizu-Wakamatsu, taking 90 minutes. En route, the bus makes a stop **33** at **Inawashiro,** the town on the northern edge of the Lake Inawashiro. The lake is Japan's fourth largest, but, unlike Tohoku's other large lakes, Towada and Tazawa, Inawashiro is not a caldera lake but instead is formed by streams. Hence, its flat surrounding shore is not particularly attractive. The Japanese like the lake, though, for the gaudy sightseeing swan-shape cruise boats that circle on the water. Of more cultural interest (only 10 minutes by bus from Inawashiro Station) is **Hideo Noguchi's** birthplace and a Memorial Museum in honor of his extraordinary life and his research of yellow fever, which eventually killed him in Africa in 1928.

34 An alternative route to Aizu-Wakamatsu is via **Kitakata.** Mud-wall *kura* (storehouses) are to be seen all over Japan, but for some reason Kitakata has over 2,000 of them. They are not only simple places to store rice, miso, soy sauce, and sake, the products of the town however; they are also status symbols of the local merchants. The kura fascination spread in the past so that shops, homes, and inns were built in this architectural style, as each citizen tried to outdo his neighbor. One can quickly use up a couple of rolls of film taking photographs of the many different kura—some are black-and-white plaster, some simply of mud, some with bricks, and some with thatch roofs; still others have tiles.

Aside from the major architectural attractions—**Kai-no-Kura,** an elaborate mansion that took seven years to build, and the **Aizu Lacquer Museum** (both have admission of ¥300 and are open daily 9–5, Apr.–Nov.)—your final goal should be the **Yomatogawa Sake Brewery** (tel. 0241/22–2233). Located in the center of town near the Lacquer Museum, the brewery consists of several kura buildings. One building serves as a small museum to display old methods of sake production. The other buildings are still used for making sake. After a dutiful tour, you are offered the pleasurable reward of tasting different types of sake. *Admission free. Open daily 9–5. Closed July 1–4, Dec. 20–31.*

The tourist office at the local station has a kura walking-tour map for the city, but, if you are short on time, the area northeast of the JR station has a selection of storehouses, including **Kai Shoten,** a black kura storefront of an old miso and soy sauce factory.

35 The train from Kitakata to **Aizu-Wakamatsu** takes 20 minutes. (From Sendai the JR train ride is 60 minutes and from Nikko just over two hours.) The city tourist office is in the center of town (tel. 0242/32–0688), but the JR information and reservation office at the station distributes a free English-language map of the area. The **Tsurugajo castle** in Aizu-Wakamatsu was the most powerful stronghold of the northeast during the shogun period. Because the castle is located on the opposite side—south—of the JR station, take the bus from the station plaza (gate 6 but check with the information booth first) that loops around the city to include the castle and the Byakkotai monuments. The Aizu clan was closely linked to the ruling family in Edo and remained loyal until the end. When the imperial forces of the Meiji Restoration pressed home their successful attack in 1868, that loyalty caused the castle, which had stood for five centuries, to be burned down, along with most of the city's buildings. The five-story castle was rebuilt in 1965 as a museum (admission: ¥310; open 8:30–5) and is said to look like its original, but without the presence it must have had 121 years ago, when 19 teenage warriors committed ritual suicide. Every Japanese knows this story, so it bears telling: These young warriors, known as Byakkotai (White Tigers), had been soundly beaten by pro-Restoration forces in a battle outside the city. The surviving 20 boys retreated to a nearby hillside, Iimoriyama. Then, to their horror, they saw smoke rise from the castle and mistakenly believed the castle to be overrun by the enemy. As good samurai, all 20 boys began a mass suicide ritual. One boy was saved before he bled to death and spent the rest of his life with a livid scar and the shame of having failed to live up to the samurai code. There is now a monument to the 19 on the hill next to their graves. The **Byakkotai monuments,** a small memorial museum, and a strange octagonal Buddhist temple, Sazaedo, are reached by a 15-minute bus ride from the station. You may want to visit Iimoriyama September 22–24, when a special festival is held in memory of the Boshin civil war and the Byakkotai. *Admission: ¥310. Open 9–5, closed Mon. and the day following public holidays.*

To the east of the castle is **Aizu Bukeyashiki,** an excellent reproduction of a wealthy samurai's manor house (open 8:30–5). The 35-room house gives some idea how well one could live during the shogun period. A museum on the grounds displays Aizu craft, culture, and history. Access to Aizu Bukeyashiki is by Higashiyama bus from the JR station. *Admission: ¥700. Open daily 9–5.*

Higashiyama Onsen is a spa town 15 minutes beyond Aizu Bukeyashiki and is, with several modern ryokan, an alternative layover to Aizu-Wakamatsu, especially if one enjoys hot mineral baths. Take the bus from platform 3 or 4 at the JR Aizu-Wakamatsu station for the 10-minute ride (fare: ¥290). The village is in a gorge, and the bus route terminates at the bottom end of the village. Most ryokan will send a car to collect you so that you don't have to hike up the narrow village street. The bus station attendant will telephone the ryokan for you, if you give him the ¥10 for the pay phone. The village's scenic location and its shamble of older houses deserves better than the new and monstrous looking ryokan that have supplanted most of the old. Nevertheless, Hiagashiyama is a Japanese spa town and a pleasant alternative to staying in Aizu-Wakamatsu (*see* Lodging, *below*).

The unfortunate aspect of Aizu-Wakamatsu is that, for our excursions throughout Tohoku, it is the end of the line. Routes south, by train and bus, go to Nikko. Traveling east by train to Koriyama puts you on the Tohoku Shinkansen for Sendai to the north and Tokyo to the south. The train going east leads you to Niigata and the Sea of Japan.

Dining and Lodging

Dining

When traveling in Tohoko, we strongly recommend that you eat out at local Japanese restaurants. Most restaurants that are reasonably priced will have a visual display of their menu in the window. On this basis, you can decide what you want before you enter. If you cannot order in Japanese, and no English is spoken, after you secure a table, lead the waiter to the window display and point.

Unless the establishment is a *ryotei* (high-class, traditional Japanese restaurant), reservations are usually not required except for formal restaurants at a hotel or a ryokan. Whenever reservations are recommended or required at any of the restaurants listed, this is indicated.

Some of the regional Japanese dishes of Tohoku are special, and you should make a point of enjoying them:

Akita is famous for its clean water and its rice, and these two ingredients make good sake. Be sure to try the **kara-kuchi** (dry sake). Akita's **kiritampo** is made from boiled rice, pounded into cakes and molded on sticks of **sugi** (Japanese cedar).

Sendai miso is a red and salty version of fermented soybeans. **Mochi,** found in Sendai, is a tiny rice ball covered with **yuzu** (Japanese citrus) flavored sugar. When put into a cup of hot water, the ball floats and imparts sweetness and fragrance, creating a delicious drink. Sendai's **dagashi** are traditional candies and cakes, usually made with rice, soybean flour, and sugar.

Sansai ryori, from Yamagata Prefecture, refers to a variety of dishes made from mountain vegetables and fish (mostly carp and sweet fish) caught in the streams and rivers.

A 3% federal consumer tax is added to all restaurant bills. Another 3% local tax is added if the bill exceeds ¥7,500. At more expensive restaurants, a 10%–15% service charge is added to the bill. Tipping is not the custom.

Category	Cost*
Very Expensive	over ¥6,000
Expensive	¥ 4,000–¥6,000
Moderate	¥ 2,000–¥4,000
Inexpensive	under ¥2,000

Cost is per person without tax, service, or drinks

Lodging

Tohoku has a broad spectrum of accommodations, from inns and minshukus to modern, large resort hotels. However, because the region has only recently opened itself up to tourists, most of the accommodations are of recent vintage. That means the hotels are utilitarian and functional. The difference between them is that the more expensive the tariff, the larger the lobby area and the guest rooms. Do not expect to find a hotel with character. Moreover, because the Japanese are renowned for their service, politeness, and cleanliness, these characteristics do not differ between hotels. Hence, the hotels listed below are chosen because their locations have certain advantages, their prices are in line for what they offer, and they welcome foreign visitors (some Japanese hotels are timorous of accepting foreign guests because of the differences in language and customs).

All of the large city and resort hotels offer Western and Japanese food. During the summer season, hotel reservations are advised.

Outside the cities or major towns, most hotels quote prices on a per-person basis with two meals, exclusive of service and tax. If you do not want dinner at your hotel, it is usually possible to renegotiate the price. Stipulate, too, whether you wish to have Japanese or Western breakfasts, if any. For the purposes here, the categories assigned to all hotels reflect the cost of a double room, with private bath but no meals. However, if you make reservations at any of the noncity hotels, you will be expected to take breakfast and dinner at the hotel—that will be the rate quoted to you, unless you specify otherwise.

A 3% federal consumer tax is added to all hotel bills. Another 3% local tax is added if the bill exceeds ¥15,000. At most hotels, a 10%–15% service charge is added to the total bill. Tipping is not the custom.

Category	Cost*
Very Expensive	over ¥20,000
Expensive	¥15,000–¥20,000
Moderate	¥10,000–¥15,000
Inexpensive	under ¥10,000

Cost is for double room, without tax or service

The most highly recommended restaurants and accommodations are indicated by a star ★.

Higashiyama Onsen (Near Aizu-Wakamatsu)

Lodging **Hotel Koyo.** Although the Koyo is located in the upper part of this spa village, the buildings across the street block its view of the gorge. A modest hotel with large (10 tatami) Japanese-style rooms, it could use some sprucing up, but the room rate is low. Meals, served in your room and included in the price, are above average. Mountain vegetables, four types of fish, and meat are served. The staff don't speak English, but they are friendly and try to communicate. A driver will pick you up at the bus stop. *Higashiyama Onsen 965, tel. 0242/26–9000, fax 0242/26–9166. 24 Japanese-style rooms. Facilities: mineral baths. AE, DC, MC, V. Moderate.*

Mukaitaki Ryokan. The Mukaitaki is one ryokan in this spa town that retains a traditional ambience, thanks to its plank floors, shoji screens, and screen prints. *200 Kawamukou, Yumoto, Higashiyama-machi, Fukushima-ken 965, tel. 0242/ 27–7501. 25 Japanese-style rooms. Facilities: Japanese dining only, thermal (public) baths. MC. Moderate.*

Akita

Dining **Restaurant Bekkan Hamanoya.** This establishment is the local favorite for *hata-hata* (sand fish), which is a regional specialty and is especially good in the wintertime. *4-2-11 Ōmachi, Akita, tel. 0188/23–7481. Dress: informal. MC, V. Open lunch and dinner. Moderate.*

Lodging **Akita View Hotel.** This hotel has clean, fresh rooms and is the largest of the hotels in Akita. Located on the right side of a Seibu department store and seven minutes by foot from the JR station, it is convenient to shopping but a 10-minute walk from downtown Akita. The staff will give you advice on what to see and do in the city and prefecture. An indoor pool adds to the hotel's appeal. *2-6 Nakadori, Akita 010, tel. 0188/32–1111, fax 0188/33–6957. 115 Western-style rooms. Facilities: Western and Japanese restaurants, coffee shop, 2 bars, indoor pool, health center, shops. AE, DC, MC, V. Expensive.*

★ **Akita Castle Hotel.** With the best location and the most professional service in Akita, the Castle Hotel has well-maintained rooms, but be aware that the larger double rooms (normal American size) fall in the expensive category. The more commodious Japanese-style rooms (only 3 in the hotel) are the same price as the Western-style ones. The bar and the French restaurant offer a park view. *1-3-5 Nakadori, Akita 010 (opposite the moat and a 15-min. walk from the station), tel. 0188/34–1141, fax 0188/34–5588. 206 rooms, mostly Western-style. Facilities: Western, Japanese, and Chinese restaurants. AE, DC, MC, V. Moderate–Expensive.*

Kohama Ryokan. No rooms in this small inn have a private bath; however, it is friendly, homey and priced right. Moreover, it is conveniently located across from the Akita JR station and 100 yards to the right of Mr. Donut. The Japanese-style dinner using local fresh seafood is a bargain at ¥1,500. *6-19-6 Nakadori, Akita 010 (15-min. walk, bearing left from the station, past Mr. Donut), tel. 0188/32–5739. 10 rooms without bath. Facilities: Japanese dining, but Continental breakfast is offered. AE, V. Inexpensive.*

Aomori

Lodging **Aomori Grand Hotel.** Close to the station, this establishment is the best in town for an overnight stay. Its recent refurbishing has made the lobby personable. The lounge for morning coffee has superbly comfortable armchairs, and the Continental Bellevue restaurant on the 12th floor is an enjoyable place to spend an evening. Guest rooms tend to be small. *1-1-23 Shinmachi, Aomori City 030, tel. 0177/23–1011, fax 0177/23–1011. 148 rooms, mostly Western-style. Facilities: Japanese and Continental restaurant. AE, DC, MC, V. Moderate.*

Atsumi Onsen

Lodging **Tachibana-ya.** Many traditional ryokan are reluctant to take reservations from foreigners, especially if they do not speak Japanese. Not so with Tachibana-ya. This resort ryokan in the center of the spa town of Atsumi Onsen welcomes foreign visitors, and its accommodations are excellent. Guest rooms are spacious, with twelve tatami mats and a separate dressing room that is large enough to serve as a second sleeping room, a small kitchen for the maid to prepare meals, a washroom, and a separate toilet with heated seat. Should you wish to bathe privately, there is also a *hinoki* (cedar-wood) bathtub with faucets tapped into the thermal springs. But best of all is a small terrace alcove off the main room with two large leather arm chairs and a table. The sliding glass doors overlook a landscaped garden that surrounds a large pond filled with carp. The best rooms are on the ground floor—room Tokiwa 137 is especially nice. The hotel's buildings are angled so that rooms do not directly face each other, thus ensuring privacy. Service is extremely efficient and friendly. Meals, served in your room are a delight to the eye and palate. The common baths have been splendidly refurbished using natural stone and are filled with steaming water from the thermal springs. *Yatsumi-cho 3, Atsumi-cho 999-72, Yamagata Pref., tel. 0235/43–2211, fax 0235/43–3681. 56 Japanese rooms. Facilities: coffee shop, bar, mineral baths. AE, DC, MC, V. Expensive.*

Hachimantai

Lodging **Sukayu Onsen.** In a vast, rambling wood building in the moun-
★ tains, this traditional Japanese Inn is one of the few left in the
country where men and women are not separated in the main
baths. (There are smaller baths that are segregated.) The sulphur mineral waters have been used for their curative powers
for three centuries. The guest rooms are small and only thinly
partitioned from each other, so light sleepers may find it hard
to fall asleep. A fixed, multi-dish dinner is served in your room.
Japanese breakfasts are served in a large dining room. There is
no village nearby, but ski slopes and hiking trails are close.
*Sukayu Onsen, Hakkoda-Sunchu, Aomori, tel. 0177/38–6400;
fax 0177/38–6677. 134 rooms. Facilities: thermal baths, Japanese food served in one's room. AE, DC, MC, V. Moderate–
Expensive.*

Matsukawa-so. This ryokan is popular for its rustic flair and the
rejuvenating spa waters. It is simple, clean, and traditional, with highly polished wooden floors. Two meals are included,
and all rooms are Japanese style. *Matsukawa Onsen, Matsuo-
mura, Iwate-gun 028-73, tel. 01957/8–2255. 25 rooms. Facilities: dining room, thermal baths. AE. Inexpensive–Moderate.*

Kyoun-so. Just the basic essentials are offered at this little two-
story wooden inn: small tatami rooms and shared bathroom facilities. Meals (optional) are served in a communal room. The
owners are always delighted to have a Westerner stay. Open-
air hot springs are nearby. To reach the inn, you can either take
the 50-minute bus ride from JR Obuke Station or a 110-minute
bus ride from JR Morioka Station. *Matsukawa Onsen, Mat-
suo-mura, Iwate-gun 028-73, tel. 01957/8–2256. 18 rooms. Facilities: dining room. AE, V. Inexpensive.*

Hirosaki

Lodging **Hotel New Castle.** A smart business hotel, on a par with the
Hokke Club (*see below*), the New Castle is fractionally more expensive, though no better. It is, however, a good alternative if
the Hokke is full. The restaurant here offers formal and elegant
Japanese meals. *24-1 Kamisayashi-machi, Hirosaki 036 (located on the castle side of downtown Hirosaki), tel. 0172/36–
1211, fax 0172/36–1210. 59 rooms, mostly Western style. Facilities: Japanese and Continental restaurant. AE, DC, MC, V.
Moderate–Expensive.*

★ **Hokke Club Hotel.** This modern, efficient hotel uses sparkling
marble for its public rooms. These rooms are small, with an
open design giving an illusion of space. Bedrooms tend to be
small, so you may want to upgrade your room. Surrounded by
shops and restaurants, the Hokke Club begins two flights up a
moving escalator. The Kasen Japanese restaurant has excellent formal dining. *126 Dotemachi, Hirosaki 036 (located in the
center of town), tel. 0172/34–3811. 65 rooms, mostly Western
style. Facilities: tearoom, American-style bar (The Jolly Dog),
Finnish sauna. AE, V. Moderate.*

Kakunodate

Lodging **Huyakusuien.** This minshuku is in a 19th-century converted
warehouse, and during the winter months, the drafts constantly remind you of this heritage. Hospitality is limited despite a
brochure that welcomes guests enthusiastically. Meals are

served in a large, cluttered room that holds a small charcoal open fire, a library of old books, and a shrine. Food, included in the price, is average. The tatami rooms are larger than those at some minshukus, but be prepared to hear the coughs and splutters of your neighbors through the thin walls. The bathroom facilities are clean but primitive, and like many residences in rural Japan, they are not connected to a sewage or septic system. The minshuku is in the center of Kakunodate, a 10-minute walk from the JR station and then to the left of the post office. *31 Shimina Kamachi, Kakunodate 014-03, tel. 0187/55–5715, fax 0187/54–3195. 12 rooms without bath. No credit cards. Inexpensive.*

Matsushima

Lodging
★

Ryokan Matsushimajo. This very traditional ryokan is in the center of the town and just up from the shore road. The main building has antique objects of art on its walls, including woodblock prints done by the famous artist Hiroshige. The ryokan, creaking with age, has ancient banisters and polished wood floors. Its sloping tiled roof and adjoining tower make the Matsushimajo look like a castle, but the ryokan is only about 100 years old. Guest rooms have overhead fans, and most of them do not have private baths, but a room overlooking the bay is quite marvelous. Come here for lunch if you are only visiting Matsushima for the day. *Matsushima, Miyagi 981, tel. 022/ 354–2121. 28 Japanese-style rooms. Facilities: Japanese dining room serving lunch and dinner. AE, V. Moderate–Expensive.*

Koganesaneo. The advantage of this minshuku which is in Nobiru, a village situated on the far (north) side of Matsushima Bay, is its location—an easy six-minute-walk from the Nobiru JR station and a block from the beach. Otherwise, the rooms are tiny (six tatami) and the paper-thin walls permit you to hear every guest's footfall. Avoid the room next to the toilet! Food is served in your room in a perfunctory manner, but the fresh Pacific seafood—mussels, crab, oyster, and shrimp—especially in the colder months, is a redeeming feature. *68–46 Aza Minami-yogei, Nobiru, Naruse-machi, Monoo-gun, Miyagi Pref., tel. 0225/88–2183. 12 rooms, none with private bath. Facilities: Japanese food served in one's room. V. Inexpensive.*

Miyako

Lodging

Minshuku Obata. Sixteen minutes on the Senniku Railway from Miyako is Taro, a small village well-located for sightseeing. This large minshuku provides fair-size (eight tatami) rooms, two meals a day, and clean public bath and toilet facilities. The food is adequate, not special, but you will usually have the opportunity to taste the local specialties, scallops and abalone. *60–2 Nokara, Tarocho, Shimohei–gun, Iwate Pref. (15-min. walk from Taro railway station, but owners will collect you by car if you phone them), tel. 0193/87–2631. 16 rooms, none with private bath. Facilities: Japanese breakfast and dinner included. Hosts' son will give guests tour of area. Inexpensive.*

Morioka

For *wanka soba* (buckwheat noodles), there are at least 16 restaurants in the city, some directly across the road from the JR station plaza. Try **Azumaya** (tel. 0196/22–2233) one flight up in a building on Ekimae Kita-dori, right across from the taxi stand on the corner of Ekimae-dori.

Dining   **Restaurant Nambu Robata.** Recognized for its regional specialties cooked over charcoal, the Nambu Robata is like an old country farmhouse with a traditional hearth. Try the grilled fish, which are first filleted and then reassembled. The restaurant is near the Hachiman Firewatch Tower, a five-minute walk from the bus center. Its popularity has grown since we first mentioned it; prices now run close to ¥7,000 per person. *Hachiman-cho, Morioka City, tel. 0196/22–5082. Dress: informal. No credit cards. Open 11:30–9:30. Expensive.*

Restaurant Wakana. This dining spot is within an eight-minute walk from the station—cross the river, fork left and take another left after the Kawatoku Department Store. The Wakana offers good *teppanyaki* (food cooked on a flat grill) and claims the best beef in the city. *1-3-33 Osawakawara, Morioka City, tel. 0196/53–3333. Jacket and tie required. AE, DC, MC, V. Open 11–8. Closed Tues. Moderate.*

Lodging   **Morioka Grand Hotel.** The most personable and smartest modern hotel in town, the Grand is situated on a small hill on the ★ edge of the city, 10 minutes by taxi from the station. Its views are broader, the air is cleaner, and its rooms are slightly larger than most hotels in the area, but this is reflected in the price of the rooms, the most expensive in Morioka. Do not confuse this hotel with the cheaper Morioka Grand Hotel Annex. *1-10 Atagoshita, Morioka, Iwate 020, tel. 0196/25–2111, fax 0196/22–4804. 36 rooms, 21 Western style. Facilities: Japanese and Continental restaurants. AE, DC, MC, V. Expensive.*

Hotel Higashi-Nihon. This is the largest hotel in town and bustles with groups, wedding parties, and banquets. It caters to all and has all the amenities of an international, but impersonal, hotel, including eight restaurants of various international cuisines. The two Japanese-style rooms are slightly larger and no more expensive than the Western-style ones. *3-3-18 Odori, Morioka. Iwate 020, tel. 0196/25–2131, fax 0196/26–9092. 209 rooms, 207 Western-style. Facilities: indoor tennis courts, Japanese and Continental restaurants. AE, DC, MC, V. Moderate.*

Metropolitan Morioka. Located just to the left of the station plaza and one flight up the escalator, this hotel has clean and utilitarian rooms. The combination Chinese/Japanese and Western buffet at breakfast is the best value in town. The staff is extremely helpful, despite the language barrier. Though the hotel has a good Chinese restaurant on the fourth floor, ask the reception clerk to take you across the street and introduce you to Umacho, a tiny *nomiya*, or pub. No English is spoken here, so point to what you want or have the clerk order for you. The Kin Kin, a slowly grilled fish, is delicate and succulent. *1-44 Morioka Ekimae-dori, Morioka, Iwate 020, tel. 0196/25–1211, fax 0196/25–1210. 194 rooms. Facilities: Western, Japanese, and Chinese restaurants. AE, MC. Inexpensive–Moderate.*

Ryokan Kumagai. In a two-story wooden building, this simple hostelry is a member of the inexpensive Japanese Inn Group, offering basic tatami rooms. None of the rooms have a private bath, but there is a small dining area where Japanese and Western breakfasts and Japanese dinners are optional. Located between the station and center city, it is a 10-minute walk from the Morioka JR station—cross the river and walk along Kawinbashi-dori two blocks and turn right (a gas station is on the left and a bank on the right). Cross over one block and the ryokan is on the left. *3-2-5 Oosawakawara, Morioka City, Iwate Pref. 020, tel. 0196/51–3020. 11 rooms, none with private bath. Facilities: breakfast and dinner served. Inexpensive.*

Nyuto Onsen

Lodging Nyuto consists of six small spa villages. The following are the telephone numbers to be called for reservations at each of the villages' inns: **Tsurono Onsen,** *closed in winter, tel. 0187/46–2438.* **Taeno-yu Onsen,** *tel. 0187/46–2740.* **Ohgama Onsen,** *tel. 0187/46–2438.* **Kaniba Onsen,** *tel. 0187/46–2021.* **Magoroku Onsen,** *tel. 0187/46–2224.* **Kuro-yu Onsen,** *closed in winter, tel. 0187/46–2214.*

Sendai

Dining Restaurants abound in Sendai. Many of the Japanese restaurants are along Chuo-dori Avenue, and most of them display their menus in their windows, along with the prices for each dish. The following are just a sampling of the many restaurants from which to choose:

Iwashiya. This restaurant is famous for its fresh sashimi. The specialty is slivers of meat taken from the back of the fish while it is still alive. The slivers and the tail-twitching fish are then presented on a plate before you. Grilled-fish dishes are also available and perfectly done. Service is either at the counter or at tables placed on tatami matting. *4-5-42 Ichiban-cho, tel. 022/222–6645. (Take the alley left just before the Gateaux Boutique on Ichiban-cho, and then the first right. The restaurant is on the right, with a fish tank in the window.) Jacket and tie suggested. No credit cards. Open 5–11. Expensive–Very Expensive.*

Aka-Beko. This small izakaya has an excellent array of foods—sushi, grilled meats on skewers, grilled fish, and tasty soups. There is both a counter and seating on tatami mats. Close to the SS 30 Building and to Ryokan Aisaki, this is one of the friendliest local restaurants in town. *91 Yagamouchi-dori, Sendai, tel. 022/224–2966. Dress: casual. No credit cards. Open 5–11. Moderate.*

Isahachi. On the ground floor the restaurant hums with activity and offers yakitori-style cuisine (grilled skewers of chicken). Downstairs in a slightly quieter ambience, the restaurant offers a range of regional dishes *(kyodo ryori)* as well as beef dishes, including sukiyaki. *4-3-7 Ichiban-cho, tel. 022/222–7080. (Located on Chuo-dori, just north of Hirose-dori; Isahachi has a sign outside and one enters the building through a corridor.) Dress: informal. No credit cards. Lunch 11–2:30, dinner 6–10:30. Inexpensive–Moderate.*

Robata. A fun drinking place, Robata has decorations from traditional folklore. Order the herring *(nisshin)* with your beer—it's a meal in itself. *2-2-2 Kokubucho (next to the Hotel Rich), tel. 022/23–0316. Dress: informal. No credit cards. Inexpensive.*

SS 30 Building. Inside the tallest building in town, the restaurants on the top three floors of the SS 30 do a brisk trade. There are plenty to choose from—**Saboten** (tel. 022/267-4083), on the 28th floor, serves inexpensive fried fish and salads; **Le Monde** (tel. 022/224-2181), also on the 28th floor, serves French food; **Toh-Ter-Koh** (tel. 022/267-0841), on the 30th floor, serves innovative Japanese cuisine with a distinct French influence. Or, if you prefer just a cocktail with your view, drop into **Ermitage** (tel. 022/261-4777), a cozy, Western-style bar.

However, one is really better off for serious French-style cuisine at either **Hotel Sendai Plaza** or **Koyo Grand Hotel.**

Lodging
★

Sendai Kokusai Hotel. The newest of Sendai's hotels (completed in 1990, next to the new SS 30 complex), immediately won attention as the town's leading hotel. The lobby glistens with marble and stainless steel; guest rooms are furnished in light pastels, and larger rooms have stucco arches to exaggerate their size. Fresh flowers add a touch of color. Lighting is subdued—not so good for late-night reading. Competing with the dozen restaurants in the SS 30 Building, the hotel offers French, Chinese, and Japanese fare and two bars. *4-6-1 Chuo, Aoba-ku, Sendai, Miyagi 980, tel. 022/268-1112, fax 022/268-1113. 190 rooms. Facilities: 3 restaurants, sushi bar, 2 bars, coffee shop, children's room, banquet/conference rooms, shopping arcade. AE, DC, MC, V. Expensive–Very Expensive.*

Hotel Metropolitan Sendai. Opened in 1989 under the name Sendai Terminal Hotel and located adjacent to the railway station, this upscale business traveler's hotel has reasonably large guest rooms that are decorated in light colors. The 21st-floor Sky Lounge restaurant offers the best city view—and French food to go with it. Simpler fare at more reasonable prices is found in the coffee shop. *1-1-1 Chuo-dori, Sendai 980, tel. 022/261-2525, fax 022/267-2317. 300 rooms, including 3 suites and 4 Japanese-style rooms. Facilities: restaurants, coffee shop, indoor pool, gym, small business center, banquet rooms. AE, DC, MC, V. Moderate–Expensive.*

Koyo Grand Hotel. The Koyo Grand must be the most weirdly furnished hotel in Japan: It has objects of art from China and Europe mixed with Louis XV reproductions. The total assemblage is a mismatch of statues, mounted deer heads, Regency upholstered furniture, gold painted chandeliers, and ceiling murals. Thankfully, the guest rooms have more simple and standard furniture (though with turn-of-the-century French reproductions); otherwise one might have horrendous nightmares. The hotel has a small but good French restaurant, and also a Chinese restaurant, offering Szechuan and Cantonese cooking. *1-3-2 Hon-cho, Sendai, Miyagi 980, tel. 022/267-5111, fax 022/265-2252. 149 Western-style rooms. Facilities: Japanese, French, and Chinese restaurants. AE, DC, MC, V. Moderate–Expensive.*

Sendai Hotel. Pale colors and cheerful prints make up the decor at this modern hotel, popular with businessmen wishing to stay near the station. Foreign guests enjoy attentive service and get the English-language newspaper the *Japan Times* every morning. *1-10-25 Chuo, Sendai, Miyagi 980 (located 2 min. on foot from the station), tel. 022/225-5171, fax 022/268-9325. 123 rooms, mostly Japanese style. Facilities: Chinese, Japanese, Western, and French restaurants, shopping arcade. AE, V. Moderate–Expensive.*

★ **Ryokan Aisaki.** This inn has been run by the same family since 1868, but the present building is post–World War II. Only two rooms have private bathrooms, but the public bath has the added benefit of a sauna. Still, the hostelry is enjoyable for friendly companionship with other guests, and the owner welcomes foreigners. He speaks fluent English and often will take guests on sightseeing trips. *5-6 Kitame-machi, Sendai, Miyagi 980 (located behind Sendai Central Post Office), tel. 022/264-0700, fax 022/227-6067. 20 rooms, 8 Western style. Facilities: sauna, meals (Japanese) are optional. AE, MC. Inexpensive–Moderate.*

Tazawako

Lodging **Tazawako Prince.** A modern white hotel on the edge of Lake Tazawa, the Tazawako Prince has views of Mt. Komaga-take. Most of the hotel's rooms have balconies. Choose from rooms that are large with a lake view, small with a lake view, or small with a mountain view. Aside from the main dining room, there is a garden room down near the lake. *Katajiri, Saimyoji, Nishiki-mure, Senboku-gun, Akita 014-05, tel. 0187/47-2211, fax 0187/47-2104. Facilities: shops, game room, Japanese and Western dining, boat rentals. AE, DC, MC, V. Moderate.*

Tono

Lodging **Fukuzanso Inn.** Highly polished creaky floors characterize this
★ friendly, old-fashioned ryokan. Rooms have a dressing room/closet area and a small enclosed balcony with table and chairs. Dinner, served in your room, is a marvelous array of a dozen dishes, ranging from sashimi to steamed beef. No English is spoken, but the hospitality is all smiles; the staff lends bikes for sightseeing. *5-30 Chuo-dori, Tono City 028, tel. 01986/2-4120. 25 rooms. Facilities: dinner and breakfast included, Japanese public baths. MC. Moderate.*

Yamagata

Lodging **Hotel Castle.** Conveniently located, the Castle is a modern, utilitarian hotel with small rooms. Guests mill around the lobby area, where there is a coffee/tea lounge (refills on coffee are free). The Chateau Reine French restaurant offers the best dining in town. *2-7 Toka-machi, 4-chome, Yamagata 990 (a 7-minute walk from the railway station), tel. 0236/31-3311, fax 0236/31-3373. 160 Western-style rooms. Facilities: Western, Chinese, and Japanese restaurants, pub. AE, DC, MC, V. Moderate.*

Yamagata Washington Hotel. This new hotel downtown is smart and efficient and has a friendly staff. Reception and the lounge area are one floor above ground level; the coffee shop and Japanese restaurant are on the next floor; and the guest rooms are above that. Rooms are compact, with merely functional furnishings that are at least new. Bathrooms are the typical prefabricated plastic units. *Yamagata 990, tel. 0236/25-1111, fax 0236/24-1512. 156 rooms. Facilities: Japanese and Western restaurants. AE, DC, MC, V. Moderate.*

15 Hokkaido

By Nigel Fisher

Hokkaido is untamed Japan. In the rest of the country it may be said that the cities dominate the countryside—not so in Hokkaido. Its cities and towns are modern outposts of urban man that are surrounded by wild, untamed mountains, virgin forests, crystal-clear lakes, and surf-beaten shores. Hokkaido is Japan's last frontier, and the attitudes of the inhabitants are akin to those of the pioneers of the American West.

Hokkaido was not even mentioned in books until the 7th century; even then, for the next millennium, it was discounted as the place where the "hairy Ainu" lived. The Ainu, the original inhabitants of Japan and probably related to ethnic groups that populated Siberia, were always thought of as the inferior race by the Yamato Japanese, who arrived in Japan from the south (Kyushu) and founded Japan's imperial house. As the Yamato spread and expanded their empire up from Kyushu through Honshu, the peace-loving Ainu retreated north to Hokkaido. There they lived, hunting and fishing in peace, until a hundred years ago.

With the Meiji Restoration in 1868, Japan changed its policy toward Hokkaido and opened it up as the new frontier to be colonized by the Yamato Japanese. The Tokyo government encouraged immigration from the rest of Japan to Hokkaido but made no provision for the Ainu peoples. Indeed, the Ainu were given no choice but to assimilate themselves into the life and culture of the colonizers. Consequently, the Ainu have virtually disappeared as a race. A few elders still speak Ainu, but when they die, so will their language, which has no written form. Long gone are Ainu communities. Only Ainu villages constructed as tourist attractions remain, and they are depressing places.

The Ainu are not the only Japanese aborigines. There was also another race, the Moyoro, which lived before the Ainu, but little is known about these mysterious peoples. Anthropological evidence found on Hokkaido's east coast in the Moyoro Shell Mound, now displayed in the Abashiri Museum, supports the belief that Moyoro civilization ended in the 9th century.

With no visible past and with newly born cities, Hokkaido is a respite from temples, shrines, and castles. For the tourist, Hokkaido is a geographical wonderland. Lava-seared mountains, imposing in their dominance, hide deeply carved ravines. Hot springs, gushers, and steaming mud pools boil out of the ground. Crystal-clear caldera lakes fill the seemingly bottomless cones of volcanoes. Half of Hokkaido is covered in forests. Wild, rugged coastlines hold back the sea, and all around Hokkaido, islands surface offshore. Some are volcanic peaks poking their cones out of the ocean, and others were formed aeons ago by the crunching of the earth's crust. Bears still roam the forests, snagging rabbits and scooping up fish from mountain streams, and deer wander the pastures, stealing fodder from cows. The crane (*tsuru*), which connotes long life and happiness, is often used as Hokkaido's symbol, and Hokkaido's native crane, *tancho*, is especially magnificent, with a red-capped head and white body trimmed with black feathers.

May and early summer bring the blossoming of alpine flowers and lilacs. Also, the cherry trees in Hokkaido are the last to bloom in Japan—in late-April and early May. Summers are drier and cooler than in the rest of Japan, and thus a trip to

Hokkaido allows an escape from the humidity. Hotel space becomes relatively difficult to find, and the scenic areas become crowded with tour groups and Japanese families. September brings autumn, and the turning leaves offer spectacular golden colors, reaching their peak in early October. November and April are the least desirable months; the first falls of snow in November just dirty the roads, and in April the snow melts into a brown mess. The winter makes travel more difficult (some minor roads are closed), and, especially on the east coast, the weather is frigid. Yet it is also a beautiful time of year, with crisp white snow lying everywhere.

One of the delights of traveling through Hokkaido is meeting the people, who are known as the Dosanko. Since virtually all of the Japanese in Hokkaido are "immigrants to a new frontier," there is less emphasis placed on tradition and more on accomplishing the matter at hand. The Dosanko are still very Japanese, sharing the same culture as the rest of Japan, but they are also open to new customs and other cultures.

Hokkaido was born during the Meiji Restoration, a time when the Japanese government turned to the West for new ideas. Hokkaido, especially, sought advice from America and Europe for its development. In the 1870s, some 63 foreign experts came to this island, including an American architect who designed Hokkaido's principal city, Sapporo. Around the same time, agricultural experts from abroad were brought in to introduce dry-farming as a substitute for rice, which could not grow in the severe winter climate. This has left the Dosanko with a peculiar fondness for Europeans. In Sapporo, there is an open warmth displayed to Westerners. In the country, the Dosanko is shy but not timid in coming to the aid of Westerners.

Because Hokkaido consists of more countryside than cities, foreigners appear reluctant to visit the island. Only 23,000 foreigners come each year (16,500 are Westerners), in contrast with the several million Japanese who choose Hokkaido for winter skiing and summer hiking. Since Hokkaido is Japan's northernmost and least developed island, there is a strong sense shared by resident and visitor alike of discovering uncharted territory. It's untrue, of course. Hokkaido has a road and rail network that crisscrosses the island, but the feeling of newness still remains.

Essential Information

Arriving and Departing

For most visitors to Hokkaido, the points of entry are either Sapporo (by plane) or Hakodate (by train).

By Plane Japan Airlines (JAL), Japan Air System, and All Nippon Airways (ANA) link Hokkaido to the island of Honshu by direct flights from Tokyo's Haneda airport to Hakodate, Sapporo, Asahikawa, Mombetsu, and Kushiro. Several other major cities on Honshu (Sendai, Aomori, Akita, Niigata, Nagoya, Osaka, and Hiroshima) have flights to Sapporo. Sapporo's airport is Chitose, 25 miles south of Sapporo. There are frequent trains and buses connecting the city with the airport. *(See Sapporo, below)*. The cost by air from Tokyo to Sapporo is ¥23,850, compared with ¥21,070 by train. Although the policy is subject to change, travelers arriving in Japan on Japan Airlnes from overseas can, with a change of planes at Tokyo, fly at no extra charge to Sapporo.

By Train With the 33.66-mile Seikan Tunnel (opened March 1988) permitting train travel between Hokkaido and Honshu, the train journey from Tokyo to Sapporo is 10 hours, 21 minutes; this trip involves a combination of the Shinkansen train to Morioka, the northernmost point on the Tohoku Shinkansen line, and a change to an express train for the remaining journey. Alternatively, there is the Blue Train (the blue-colored long-distance sleeper) from Tokyo to Sapporo, which takes 16 hours. The Japan Rail Pass covers the train fare in either case, but an additional charge is made for a sleeping compartment (¥13,000) or a bunk (¥6,180) on the Blue Train.

By Ferry The inexpensive form of travel to Hokkaido is by ferry from Honshu. From Tokyo to Kushiro (33 hours), there is the luxury ferryboat *Marimo*, which sails twice weekly and is operated by the Kinkai Yosen Company. (Cost: ¥28,000 first class, ¥14,000 second class.) From Tokyo to Tomakomai (31 hours), another large ferry, the *Shiretoko*, is operated by the Japan Coastal Ferry Company. (Fare: ¥29,660 first class, ¥11,840 second class.) The same company also operates an overnight ferry (15 hours) from Sendai to Tomakomai. The ferry between Aomori and Hakodate (4 hours), which was the way to cross from northern Honshu to Hokkaido before the Seikan Tunnel, plans to stay in operation for those not wishing to take the train through the tunnel.

Getting Around

By Plane The two domestic airlines that connect Sapporo with Hakodate, Kushiro, and Wakkanai are Japan Air System and Nippon Kinkyori Airways. There is also air service from July to October between Wakkanai and both Rebun and Rishiri.

By Train and Bus Japan Railways (JR) has routes connecting most of the major cities. For the most part, the trains travel the unscenic routes and are simply efficient means to reach the areas that you want to explore. Buses cover most of the major routes through the scenic areas, and all the excursions in this chapter may be accomplished by bus.

By Car Cars are easy to rent, and the Nippon-Hertz agency has offices at all major railway stations. An international driving permit, obtainable from any AAA office in the United States, is required for driving in Japan. Driving is on the left-hand side of the road, and speed limits are frustratingly low. For the most part, the Japanese are cautious drivers and obey the rules of the road. International traffic signs are used and are easy to understand. Directional signs are often sufficiently given in romaji (Japanese written in Roman script) to enable non-Japanese readers to navigate, and all major roads have route numbers. Also, the Dosanko are extremely helpful in giving instructions and directions to the Western tourist. The limitation to renting a car is the expense. A day's rental is about ¥11,000, with limited free mileage. Gas and tolls on the few expressways are three times as much as you would find in the United States. The best plan is, wherever possible, to travel long distances by public transport and then rent a car for local trips.

Important Addresses and Numbers

Tourist Information

The Japan National Tourist Organization's **Tourist Information Center (TIC)** in Tokyo (the Kotani Bldg., 1–6–6 Yurakucho, Chiyoda-ku) has free maps and brochures on Hokkaido. Within Hokkaido, the best place for travel information is in Sapporo *(see* Sapporo, *below).*

Other important regional tourist information centers are: **Akan Lake** (tel. 0154/67–2254); **Noboribetsu Onsen** (tel. 0143/84–2068); **Sounkyo Onsen** (tel. 0165/85–5530); **Lake Toya** (tel. 01427/5–2446).

Bus and train travel information centers are available at all the major train stations. The main Hokkaido office of the **Japan Travel Bureau** is in Sapporo; this office is where you are most likely to find English spoken (tel. 011/241–6201).

The Japan Travel-Phone (the nationwide service for English-language assistance or travel information) is available from 9 to 5, seven days a week. Dial toll-free 0120/222–800 for information on eastern Japan. When using a yellow, blue, or green public phone (do not use the red phones), insert a 10-yen coin, which will be returned.

Emergencies

Police, tel. 110; **ambulance,** tel. 119.

Guided Tours

The Japan Travel Bureau (03/3276–7777) operates four-day tours of Hokkaido from Tokyo. For ¥195,700, the tour includes Sapporo (overnight), Nakayama Pass, Lake Toya (overnight), Noboribetsu (overnight), Shiraoi, and back to Chitose. Three breakfasts, one lunch, and two dinners are included, and there is a ¥28,000 single supplement. These tours operate daily from April 15 through October 31.

Hakodate

When traveling by train from Honshu, the first town in Hokkaido to be reached is **Hakodate.** Prior to 1988, crossing over to Hokkaido required taking the four-hour ferry trip from Aomori to Hakodate; now the Seikan Tunnel lets trains make the passage in less than two hours. En route through the tunnel is a railway station 400 feet beneath the sea, where there is a museum dedicated to the construction of the tunnel. You can get off the train here and stretch your legs, take in the museum, and catch the next train 90 minutes later. However, because the first stop in Hokkaido proper is Hakodate with four hours still to go on the train before reaching Sapporo, Hakodate may be a better place to stretch your legs. Stop at the Information Office (tel. 0138/23–5440; open weekdays 9–7, weekends 9–5) just to the right of the Hakodate JR station to collect maps in English. If you arrive in the morning and only want a short stopover, visit the colorful morning fish and vegetable market, **Asa Ichi,** just a three-minute walk south of the station (open every morning, except Sun., from 5 AM to noon, peaking at 8). Recently, it has grown to be more than just a market, with 400 shops selling anything from Kegani crabs to sea urchins, asparagus to cherries. The neighboring **Hakodate Seaport Plaza** is a shopping and restaurant complex that stays open until 7 PM. For those who want a sightseeing tour of the city, the Hokato Kosu Bus Company (tel. 0138/57–7555) runs four-hour trips leaving from JR Hakodate station and covering most of the city sights for ¥4,300. Travel on the streetcars or municipal bus service ranges from ¥180 to ¥220. A one-day bus-and-streetcar pass is available from the tourist office at ¥900.

Exploring

Hakodate's peak was in 1859, when it was one of the three ports in Japan opened to trade with the West. This heritage supplies the attractions for visitors today. Old (sometimes rather decrepit) buildings with definite European- and American-style architecture cluster around the section of town known as **Motomachi.** To get there from the JR station, take the streetcar (3 or 5) to the Suehirocho stop and walk 10 minutes toward **Mt. Hakodate,** the mountain that rises above the city. There is no one particular building that stands out, though a useful spot to start in is the **Orthodox Church of the Resurrection,** founded in 1862 by a Russian prelate and rebuilt in Byzantine style in 1916. A large-scale restoration project was completed here in 1989, and it has become an important tourist attraction for the city. Then head for the **Kyodo-shiryokan** (three minutes away), built in 1880 and now a local museum with artifacts from Hakodate's past. Just to the west of the museum is the building that served as the city's public hall, now referred to as the **Old Hakodate Public Hall,** but with its classical columns and antebellum architecture, it looks as if it should be a manor house in America's Deep South.

In the center of the city is **Goryokaku,** a Western-style fort completed in 1864. You can reach the fort from JR Hakodate station either by bus (7, 12, or 27) from terminal gate 2, to the Gorykaku-Koen-mae bus stop or by streetcar (2, 3, or 5) to the Gorykaku-Koen-mae streetcar stop. From either stop, it is about a 10-minute walk to the fort. The fort's design is unusual for Japan, especially with its five-pointed-star shape, which enabled its defenders to rake any attackers with murderous cross fire. However, the Tokugawa shogunate's defenders were unable to hold out against the forces of the Meiji Restoration, and its walls were breached. Nothing of the interior of the castle remains today, though there is a small museum with relics from the battle. Now the fort area is a park with some 4,000 cherry trees, which, when they bloom in late April, make the stopover in Hakodate worthwhile. There is also an observation tower in the park, but at ¥520 admission, it is not worth the climb for the view. *Open May–Oct., daily 8–8; Nov.–Apr., daily 9–6.*

Behind, as if guarding the city, is Mt. Hakodate, a volcanic hill rising 1,100 feet. The panoramic views of the city from the top are good at any time, but especially at night, with the lights of the buildings and street lamps below. A bus, which takes 20 minutes, goes to the top of Mt. Hakodate from the JR station. For a more interesting trip, take Streetcar 2, 3, or 5 to Jujigai stop and then walk about seven minutes to the cable car for the five-minute ride up the mountain. A restaurant at the top is particularly appealing for its nighttime view. *Cost of cable car: ¥620, one way; ¥1,130, round-trip. Operates daily 9–9 (Mar. 1–Oct. 21); 10–6 (Oct. 22–Feb. 28). The road is closed late-Nov.–late-Apr.*

A number of buildings are being restored around the harbor, close to the Jujigai streetcar stop. One is the **Hakodate Factory** (tel. 0138/22-5656), open every day from 6-8. It's a cross between a fish market, gourmet supermarket, and restaurant. Samples of dried fish are offered, so you can finally get a chance to taste what is in all those packages sold in station kiosks and supermarkets throughout Japan. Also in this area are a number of Western-style bars and cafés with such names as The Very Beast (*sic*), California's Baby, and the Hippy (*sic*) Octopus.

Finally, should you need a bath before leaving Hakodate, take the Streetcar 2 from the JR station for a 15-minute ride followed by a seven-minute walk to Yachigashira Onsen. Here there is a mammoth public bathhouse accommodating 600 people. *Admission: ¥400. Open 6 AM-9:30 PM (Apr.-Oct.); 7 AM-9:30 PM (Nov.-Mar.).*

From Hakodate there are two ways by train to Sapporo. The slow way cuts through the west side of Shikotsu Toya National Park and heads up to the north coast of Hokkaido to Otaru before veering east for Sapporo. The fast way travels along the southern coast before turning north to Sapporo. On this route, one may disembark from the train for visits to Lake Toya and/or Noboribetsu Onsen before continuing on to Sapporo. *(See Toyako Onsen, below.)* For the purposes of this book, both Lake Toya and Noboribetsu Onsen are covered as excursions out of Sapporo.

At the Hakodate train station, you can purchase something to eat. Try the local *eki-ben* (box lunch), the *nishin-migaki-bento*. It consists of *nishin* (herring) boiled in a sweet, spicy sauce until the bones are soft enough to eat. Then, when your appetite returns at Mori station, an hour's distance from Hakodate en route to Sapporo, you can have another well-known eki-ben, *ika-meshi*. This box lunch is made by stuffing a whole *ika* (squid) with rice and cooking it in a sweet, spicy sauce. Each meal includes two or three ika.

Sapporo

Sapporo is not just Hokkaido's capital; it is also the island's premier city. With 1.6 million inhabitants, it is three times larger than the second largest city (Asahikawa) in Hokkaido. It continues to expand, as Hokkaido's unemployed from the economically depressed shipbuilding towns in the southwest and the farms in the central plains migrate to Sapporo for work. The result is that Sapporo, in just over 100 years since its birth, has the benefits of a large city without the street confusion and congestion; however, it also lacks the pre-Meiji historical sights. In 1870, the governor of Hokkaido had visited President Grant in the United States and requested that American advisers come to Hokkaido to help design the capital on the site of an Ainu village. As a result, the city was built on a 100-meter (330-foot) grid system with wide avenues and parks. Sapporo, then, is not the exotic and cultured city one expects to find in Japan. Despite its ever-increasing population, the city has had room to spread. One can walk the sidewalks or underground shopping malls without being swept away in a surge of humanity. Sapporo is architecturally boring, yet it is comfortable; within a couple of hours of walking around, your knowledge of its layout is clear.

By hosting the 1972 Winter Olympics, Sapporo made itself an international city and developed a cosmopolitan attitude. Numerous international-style hotels and restaurants came into being at that time and have stayed. Banks here are used to traveler's checks, and there is always someone on hand to help you out in English. Sapporo readily becomes the base from which to make excursions into the wild, dramatic countryside. The actual time spent exploring Sapporo can be minimal—a day, perhaps two at the most.

Arriving and Departing

By Plane Sapporo's airport, at Chitose, 25 miles south of Sapporo, is Hokkaido's main airport. Since it is new and one of Japan's better ones, attempts are underway to divert some of the air traffic from Narita to Chitose. Japan Airlines (JAL) (tel. 011/231–4411 international; tel. 011/231–0231 domestic), All Nippon Airways (ANA) (tel. 011/726–8800), and Japan Air System (tel. 011/222–8111) use this airport. For information on arrival and departure times, call the individual airlines. For the airport itself (Hokkaido Airport Terminal Co.), dial 0123/23–0111.

Between the Airport and Center City Japan Railways (JR) has frequent train service between the airport terminal (Chitose Airport Station—Chitosekudo—not Chitose City Station) and downtown Sapporo. The trip takes 35 minutes and costs ¥780 for the local and ¥940 for the express (a difference of 10 minutes in travel time). ANA runs a shuttle bus (¥750) that connects with its flights at Chitose and its hotel, the ANA Zenniku, in Sapporo. The Chuo Bus (¥750) runs a shuttle between the airport and Sapporo's Grand Hotel. Taxis are available, but the distance between Sapporo and the airport makes them ridiculously expensive, so they are rarely used.

By Train All JR trains come into the central station, located on the north side of downtown Sapporo. Trains arrive and depart for Honshu about every two hours. Trains to and from Otaru run every hour, as do the trains for Asahikawa, in central Hokkaido.

By Car Sapporo has three expressways: to Chitose and points south and west; to Otaru; and east, halfway to Asahikawa.

Getting Around

Sapporo is a walking city with wide sidewalks; it's easy to find your way around. The **Sapporo Tourist Office** at the Sapporo railway station has a city map, and most hotels have a smaller map marking their hotels and the major points of interest.

By Subway Sapporo's subway is a pleasure. As in Toronto and Moscow, the trains have rubber wheels and run quietly. There are three lines, which makes it easy to use. One (the Nanboku Line) runs from the station south to north past Susukino to Nakajima. A second (the Tozai Line) bisects the city from east to west. They cross at Odori Station. A third subway line (Toho Line) opened in 1989. It parallels the Nanboku Line from Odori Station to the JR station before branching off into the northeastern suburbs. The trains stop running at midnight. The basic fare covering about three stations is ¥180. There is a one-day open ticket at ¥900 that gives unlimited trips on the subway and bus. These tickets are available at the JR Station Underground Commuter's Ticket Office (open Mon.–Sat. 9–6) and at the Odori Station Underground Commuter's Ticket Office (open Mon.–Sat. 9–6).

By Bus Buses follow the grid system; they stop running at midnight.

By Taxi Taxi meters start at ¥470; an average fare, such as from the train station to Susukino, runs about ¥600.

Important Addresses and Numbers

Tourist Information The most helpful and informative places for information on Sapporo and on Hokkaido in general are the **International Information Corner** (Kokusai Joujou Corner, tel. 011/213–5062; open daily 9–5), in the West Paseo of JR Sapporo Station, and the **Sapporo International Communication Plaza's** tourist office, **Plaza i** (ground floor, MN Building, Kita 1, Nishi 3, Chuo-ku, tel. 011/221–2105; open 9–5:30, closed New Year's Day). Other offices that supply information include: **Sapporo City Tourism Dept. Office**, Nishi-2-chome, Kita 2, Chuo-ku, tel. 011/211–2376. Open 9–5; Sat. 9–1; closed Sun. and holidays. **Hokkaido Tourist Association**, Keizai Center Building, Nishi-1-chome, Kita 2, Chuo-ku, tel. 011/231–0941. Open 9–5; Sat. 9–12:30; closed Sun. and holidays. **Sapporo City Tourist Office**, Sapporo Station, tel. 011/213–5062. Open 9–5, except closed on the 2nd and 4th Wed. of every month.

Travel Agencies The Japan Travel Bureau (tel. 011/241–6201).

U.S. Consulate Kita 1, Nishi 28, Chuo-ku, tel. 011/641–1115.

Emergencies **Police** (tel. 110). **Ambulance** (tel. 119).

Doctors **City General Hospital** (tel. 011/261–2281). **Hokkaido University Hospital** (tel. 011/716–1161).

Dentists **The Emergency Dental Clinic** (tel. 011/511–7774); open evenings only, 7–11.

English-Language Bookstores Outside Sapporo, finding English-language books is difficult, so you may want to browse in Sapporo's two largest bookstores with (limited) books in English: **Kinokuniya** (Daini Yuraku Bldg., 2F, S1, W1 tel. 011/231–2131), across from the TV Tower and accessible from Aurora Town, and **Asamiya Bookstore** (Arche Bldg., M3, W4, tel. 011/241–3007), on the east side of Pole Town. The latter is closed on the second and third Thursday of every month.

Road Travel For road-condition information during the winter, call 011/281–6511.

Exploring

The comforting fact about Sapporo is the ease with which one can understand the city's layout. Streets running east to west are called *jo*, and those running north to south are called *chome*. These streets are numbered consecutively, and one block consists of about 100 meters square (approximately 100 yards by 100 yards).

Numbers in the margin correspond to points of interest on the Sapporo map.

Sapporo's few major sites of interest can easily be seen in a day. A good place to start one's visit is at Sapporo's landmark, the ❶ **Clock Tower.** Built in 1878 in the Russian style, with a clock

from Boston added three years later, the Clock Tower is where Japanese tourists take photographs of one another to prove that they were in Sapporo. However, other than being on every Sapporo travel brochure, it is very ordinary to a Westerner's eyes and has little architectural value. Inside the building, a small museum recounts the local history of Sapporo and includes such items as horse-drawn trams, but it lacks information about the Ainu village that preceded present-day Sapporo and from which the city takes its name. (Sapporo is made up from a combination of Ainu words meaning "a long, dry river.") *Admission free. Open 9–4. Closed Mon.*

2 Across the street from the Clock Tower is the **Sapporo International Communication Plaza,** on the third floor of a white office building. The center was recently established to facilitate commercial and cultural relations with the world beyond Japan. It is the best place (far better than the tourist office) for helpful suggestions on travel in Hokkaido and for meeting people who speak English. It is also a useful place to have something translated from Japanese into English. The center has a reading room with books, newspapers, and brochures in English. *Kita 1, Nishi 3, Chuo-ku, tel. 011/221–2105. Open 9–7.* On the ground of the building is **Plaza i,** a new tourist information service for Sapporo that is staffed by volunteers. They are extremely helpful and distribute free brochures, maps, and flyers on current happenings in town, and if they can't help you, they'll send you upstairs. The office will also send and receive faxes for travelers. You may want to browse through its English-language books on Hokkaido and other islands of Japan and take a look at the display of local crafts. *Tel. 011/211–3678, fax 011/219–0020. Open 9–5:30. Closed Mon.*

❸ On the other side of the Clock Tower is the **Hokkaido Tourist Association Office.** Little English is spoken here, and the staff is limited in the amount of useful advice it has to offer, but maps and brochures in English are available. A collection of products, including crafts, made in Hokkaido is for sale. *Keiza; Center Bldg., Nishi-1-chome, Kita 2, Chuo-ku, tel. 011/231–0941. Open weekdays 9–5, Sat. 9–12:30. Closed Sun. and holidays.*

❹ Two blocks south of the Clock Tower is **Odori-Koen Park,** a broad, 345-foot avenue that runs east and west, bisecting the city center. The median of the avenue is the park. Here, in the summer, office workers buy lunch from various food vendors and take in the sun, so long absent during the winter months. For the out-of-towner, it is a place to people watch and to try Hokkaido corn on the cob—an overpriced yet delicious area speciality. It's first boiled, then roasted over charcoal and, just before it is handed to you, given a dash of soy sauce. In February the park displays large and lifelike snow sculptures made for the Sapporo Snow Festival, which has made the city famous. *(See* Nightlife, *below,* and Festivals and Seasonal Events in Chapter 1.)

❺ At the east end of Odori-Koen Park is the **TV Tower,** which stands at 470 feet. It's ugly, but the Sapporo Tourist Association promotes it for the view from its observation platform (open daily 9–8). Don't be persuaded. It costs ¥600 for a view of the city that is better, and free, from any of the high-rise hotels.

Odori-Koen Park is actually at the heart of Sapporo's downtown shopping center, where many of the shops are underground rather than lining the park. The shopping center is located at the intersection where the main avenue heads south from the JR station and where the two subway lines intersect at the Odori Subway Station. Aboveground are large department stores. Two underground shopping malls (especially welcome during the seven-month winters) attract shoppers and diners who come to browse as much as to buy or to eat. Underneath Odori-Koen Park, from the TV tower to Odori Station, is

❻ the **Aurora Town** arcade of shops and restaurants. **Kinokuniya** (tel. 011/231–2131) has opened up a branch here should you wish to browse through a good selection of English-language

❼ books. At Odori Station, Aurora Town turns south to **Pole Town,** a long mall that continues all the way to Susukino.

❽ **Susukino,** Sapporo's entertainment district, is a nighttime reveler's paradise with some 4,200 bars and restaurants offering the Japanese equivalent to bacchanalian delights. *(See* Nightlife, *below.*) Because Susukino is for the night (until 4 AM, if you have the yen and stamina), let's return to the Odori Station and walk up the main street toward the JR station. Along this street are the major banks and airline offices. Here you can change your traveler's checks and confirm plane reservations. Once out of Sapporo, such matters are more difficult to accomplish.

As you walk toward the train station, on your left (west side) will

❾ be the side entrance of the **Sapporo Grand Hotel.** As the name implies, the Grand is built in a traditional European style with substantial pillars and majestic lobbies. Because it appears so out of place in Japan, especially in modern Sapporo, it seems even more of a landmark than the Clock Tower. The hotel has a bustling café looking out to the street, making it a convenient tea or coffee stop. Another good reason for stepping inside is to see the nimble bellgirls scurrying to open doors and heft guests' luggage, which is sometimes nearly the size of the bellgirls themselves.

If you leave the Grand Hotel by its front entrance and go left, you will come to a complex of municipal buildings, on the right. Among them is a large, redbrick building, the grandest structure in Sapporo. It's the **Old Hokkaido Government Building,** built in 1888 and now containing exhibits displaying the early development of Hokkaido. (Open weekdays 9–5, Sat. 9–1, closed Sun.) Beyond this pleasing Western-style building are the **Botanical Gardens,** with some 5,000 plant varieties. This is a cool retreat in the summer, both for its green space and its shade from the sun. *Admission: ¥400, plus ¥110 to visit the greenhouse. Open in the summer 9–4; only the greenhouse is open Nov. 4–Apr. 28, 10–3. Closed Sun.*

Within the gardens, the one museum worth seeing is the **Batchelor Museum.** Dr. John Batchelor, an English missionary in Sapporo during the late-19th century, made it his hobby to collect handicrafts and artifacts used by the Ainu people. Since the Ainu culture was virtually wiped out with Hokkaido's colonization by the Yamato Japanese, this museum takes on more value each year. *Admission: ¥400.*

Farther west is the **Hokkaido Migishi Kotaro Museum** (admission: ¥300), which exhibits the works of a native son, Migishi. This museum was built in 1968 for the sole purpose of housing 220 of the 20th-century artist's paintings. It was designed to reflect the many changes of style that characterize his career. On the next block is the attractive **Hokkaido Museum of Modern Art,** built in 1977, with local and foreign exhibits (admission: ¥250). Both museums, though not holding priceless works of art, enable foreigners to see what in Japanese art is appreciated by the Japanese and, in that sense, are worth visiting. *Both museums open 10–5. Closed Mon. and national holidays.*

Retracing one's steps to the Botanical Gardens and then left (north) for ½ mile, one arrives at the spacious grounds of **Hokkaido University,** Japan's largest campus, with over 12,000 students. The beautifully designed grounds make the campus another summer escape from the concrete to greenery and blossoming flowers. During the warmer months, the numerous green and open spaces connected by wide, lilac-lined avenues make Sapporo a particularly pleasant city.

Cutting back southeast from the university campus, one returns to the downtown area at the **Sapporo JR station.** Underneath the station is another shopping mall with one mouth-watering section devoted to food stalls and restaurants. Recent expansion of the station has created a smart new shopping and restaurant complex known as **Paseo.** The restaurants are good, personable, and reasonably priced while the shops tend to carry expensive designer merchandise. A post office is conveniently located on the West Concourse near the entrance for the train platforms.

About a 15-minute walk east from the station and past the Governor's residence (about a ¥900 taxi ride from downtown) is the

❿ Sapporo Beer Brewery. During the day, free tours around the brewery are offered, but the fun of coming here is the huge beer garden and the cavernous, three-tier beer hall. The beer hall is where most of the action occurs in the evening until closing at 9 PM. It is similar in atmosphere to a German beer hall (it was a German, after all, who, when finding wild hops growing on Hokkaido, taught the local Japanese how to make beer) but instead of bratwurst, *genghis khan* (strips of mutton and vegetables cooked on a hot iron grill) is the favored meal. It's Sapporo's favorite dish, and the beer hall is the perfect place to try it. In the summer, the beer garden is both a day and evening gathering place for locals and visitors. Mugs of beer are downed with gusto amidst exclamations of "Kampai!" In the winter, around February, the beer garden is transformed into a huge **igloo** to become a temporary restaurant. A new addition to the beer factory grounds is a small entertainment complex (open 11–8), which has cafés, a cinema with a 360-degree screen, and groups of actors dressed in traditional Japanese costumes. *Brewery tours 9–3:40 (8:40–4:40 in June, July, Aug.) except for weekends and holidays. Reservations advised. Request a guide who speaks some English. Tel. 011/731–4368. Beer garden and beer halls 11:30–9 (see* Dining, *below).*

⓲ The last place to visit is **Nakajima-Koen Park,** a little less than 2 miles from the railway station. The easiest way to get there is by the Nanboku subway from the JR station to the Nakajima-koen stop; from here it's a couple minutes' walk to the park. Nakajima-Koen Park has a playground with a small lake for boating, a beautiful rose garden, and the Nakajima Sports Center. The park also features two national cultural treasures, one Japanese and one Western. **The Hasso-an Teahouse,** harmoniously surrounded by a Japanese garden, is virtually the only traditional Japanese structure in Hokkaido and is in stark contrast to the new frontier style of architecture on the rest of the island (open 9–4; May–Nov.). The other national treasure is **Hohei-kan,** a Western-style building, originally constructed as an imperial guest house (open 9–5). It is symbolic of an age when Hokkaido was colonized by Japan and the Meiji government looked to the West for the country's modern transformation.

Nightlife

Susukino is Sapporo's entertainment area and the largest of its kind north of Tokyo. Some 4,200 bars, restaurants, and nightclubs, all lit by lanterns and flashing signs, crowd into a compact area. It is mind-boggling and, in itself, justifies an overnight stay in Sapporo. Most of the bars stay open until 4 AM, though the restaurants often close soon after midnight. Just make sure you know the type of bar before you enter. Aside from all kinds of restaurants, from the relatively inexpensive to expensive, there are several kinds of bars: the clubs (the three exclusive ones are **Mino's, Chickary,** and **Saroma**) with many conversational hostesses (¥10,000 and up); the snack bars, with a few conversational hostesses (they don't offer food, as their name suggests, only expensive *auduburus*—bar tidbits); *izakayas,* for different kinds of food and drink; bars with entertainment, either taped video music you can sing along with *(karaoke* bars) or live bands; and "soaplands," which is the new name for Turkish baths or houses of pleasure.

If at all possible, go to the clubs and snack bars with a Japanese acquaintance. For a quiet drink, try the **Prosperity** bar in the Mitsuwa Building (Minamo 5, Nishi 5) on the fifth floor. The owner is friendly, and so is the clientele. For beer, an extensive menu, and hearty companionship, the **Mykirin Beer Entertainment Hall** in the Urban Building (Minamo 5, Nishi 4) has the *Kuma-Daiko* (bearskin drums) beating nightly. Down a small alley (Minamo 7.5, Nishi 4), a wonderful small izakaya bar called **Godai** has an open charcoal hearth for cooking and a bar/counter around it, with a few tables off to the side. No English is spoken, so a few words of Japanese are needed, and most of the food served is grilled fish and seafood. A friendly karaoke bar is **Nakimushi Pierrot,** on the fifth floor of the Japanland Building (Minamo 5, Nishi 5, open to 5 AM), where you can get by on ¥2,500 per person.

Though not nightlife per se, mention should be made here of Sapporo's best-known annual event. In the first week of February, the **Sapporo Snow Festival** is held, and it is the greatest of its kind. Approximately 300 lifelike sculptures, as large as 130 feet high, 50 feet deep, and 80 feet wide, are created each year. The history of the festival began in 1950 with seven statues that were created to entertain the local citizens, depressed by the aftermath of the war and the long winter nights. Now the event is so large that sculptures may be seen in three sections of the city—Odori-Koen Park, Makomanai, and Susukino. The festival attracts some 2 million visitors each year.

Excursions around Hokkaido

Because Sapporo is such a comfortable and reassuring city, albeit architecturally boring, it serves as a convenient base for making excursions into Hokkaido's interior. Following are three which cover the best of Hokkaido:

The first excursion is to Otaru and the Shakotan Peninsula to the northwest of Sapporo; it requires a minimum of a day to complete with a rented car, or two days by public transport.

The second excursion travels southwest of Sapporo through the Shikotsu-Toya National Park and includes crystal-clear caldera lakes surrounded by mountains and hot-spring resorts. To complete the itinerary of this excursion takes a minimum of two days by car, three by public transport, though one can shorten the itinerary to make it a day trip out of Sapporo.

The third and final excursion heads into central Hokkaido through Daisetsuzan National Park, Akan National Park to the east coast, and the Sea of Okhotsk. From there, the itinerary goes along the coast to Hokkaido's northernmost point at Cape Soya and over to the islands of Rebun and Rishiri before returning to Hokkaido. Together, the three excursions take at least six days, but it can be divided, as in this chapter, into three separate trips.

Otaru and the Shakotan Peninsula

This first excursion goes northwest of Sapporo to Otaru on the coast. West of Otaru is the Shakotan Peninsula, which offers a taste of Hokkaido's rugged coastal scenery.

Getting There Otaru is 50 minutes by train from Sapporo. By car on the expressway, Otaru is only 40 kilometers (24 miles) from Sapporo. Less than an hour beyond Otaru, the Shakotan Peninsula begins at Yoichi.

One can take the train as far as Yoichi. From there, buses travel around the peninsula as far as Yobetsu. The road then ends, but ferries travel down the coast to Iwanai, where one can take the train back to Sapporo. In many ways, using a combination of train, bus, and ferry is a better way to tour the Shakotan Peninsula, because part of the western coast has no usable road and a ferry is used. Cars need to backtrack and cross the center of the Shakotan Peninsula via Tomaru Pass.

Numbers in the margin correspond to points of interest on the Hokkaido map.

Exploring **Otaru** is described as "famous for its canals and old Western-style buildings" by the Hokkaido Tourist Office. In truth, Otaru is a commercial city in the shadow of Sapporo. Very few of its 19th-century, wood-frame houses are left standing, and those are sandwiched between modern concrete structures. Instead, what you find is a traffic-congested center city with shops and office buildings, a busy port area from which ferries depart for Niigata to the south and the Rebun and Rishiri islands off Hokkaido's northwest cape, and some ramshackle suburbs.

The major attractions in Otaru are available only in the evening. Otaru has two of Hokkaido's best sashimi restaurants, **Uoisshin** (1-11-1 Hanazono, Otaru-shi, tel. 0134/32–5202) and **Isshintasuke** (1-5-3 Hanazono, Otaru-shi, tel. 0134/34–1790). Connoisseurs of sashimi from Sapporo will make a special trip to these two restaurants, and, because there is frequent train service to and from Sapporo, you can do the same. Your Sapporo hotel will be happy to make reservations at either restaurant; reservations are essential. Should you find yourself with a couple of hours to spare, take a 10-minute walk from the JR Otaru station to the Otaru Canal section of town, which has undergone considerable restoration. Even the gas lanterns are now in working order. The area has numerous restaurants and cafés and many restored turn-of-the century buildings, including the City Museum (admission ¥250; open 9–5, closed Mon.), which is located in a former warehouse. You can first collect a map from the Otaru Tourist Office (tel. 0134/29–1333; open 9–6), secreted away in a small wooden building to the left of the JR Station.

We recommend not dallying in Otaru but continuing west along the coast road leading to **Yoichi** and the Shakotan Peninsula. Before Yoichi are some of Hokkaido's best sandy beaches; once through Yoichi, these beaches soon give way to cliffs rising out of the sea. This is the beginning of the **Shakotan Peninsula.** Two mountain peaks, Yobetsu at 4,019 feet and Shakotan at 4,258 feet, dominate the peninsula's interior. On the north coast are two capes, Shakotan and Kamui, on its eastern and western tips. Sentimental Japanese go to Kamui for the sunsets; the colors fading into the Sea of Japan are romantic.

The Shakotan is a sample of the real Hokkaido. Stalwart cliffs stave off the endless surging sea, while volcanic mountains rise up majestically to dominate the interior. Thick forests blanket the imperial slopes with dark, rich greens, and ravines crease the regal mountainsides. The Shakotan Peninsula is nature in full drama.

The road from Yoichi circles the peninsula, keeping to the coast
③ as much as the cliffs allow. At **Yobetsu,** near Cape Kamui, the corniche road is even more spectacular as it heads south to Iwanai. Unfortunately, soon after Yobetsu the road becomes a track, unsuitable for cars at the time this book goes to print. Unless you can pass this stretch of road, you have to drive back
④ to **Furubira** and cross the peninsula by taking the hairpin road
⑤ through **Tomaru Pass** for a thrilling drive that skirts Mt.
⑥ ⑦ Yobetsu to **Kamoenai** and then goes down to **Iwanai.**

From Iwanai there is a road cutting across the base of the peninsula back to Otaru. There is also the alternative, at Iwanai, to go south and combine this excursion with one through Shikotsu-Toya National Park *(see* the following section on Shikotsu-Toya National Park).

If you make this circular tour of the peninsula by public transport, start by taking the train from Sapporo through Otaru to Yoichi. Then take a bus from Yoichi to Yobetsu. From Yobetsu, a ferry skips down the east coast of the peninsula as far as Iwanai. However, it is best to disembark at Kamoenai and ride the remaining distance to Iwanai on a bus. From Iwanai, trains run back to Yoichi, Otaru, and Sapporo. There is also a bus from Iwanai to Toyako Onsen *(onsen* means "spa"), should you want to go directly to Shikotsu-Toya National Park.

If you have the time and use of a car, instead of returning directly to Sapporo from Otaru, take the picturesque detour that
⑧ climbs **Mt. Tempu** and goes through one of Hokkaido's most sce-
⑨ nic mountain passes before reaching **Jozankei Onsen,** on the outskirts of Sapporo. The detour will add two hours, but the scenery up through the mountains is worthwhile. To make this detour via Jozankei, take Route 3, which branches off Sapporo Road 3 miles after Otaru. The road heads straight into the mountains (the road is closed in the winter) and follows a ravine that winds its way up and around Mt. Tempu before descending to Jozankei. En route, the forests and rock outcroppings make this trip especially beautiful in the late spring, when the patches of white snow are melting into crystal streams. Another good time for this journey is the autumn, when the golden leaves stand out among the dark green of the conifers. It is possible to go from Otaru to Jozankei by bus, but these run infrequently. There are, however, frequent buses between Jozankei and Sapporo.

Jozankei Onsen is a year-round hot-spring resort that attracts skiers from all over Japan during the winter and Hokkaido residents for hiking and weekend camping in the summer. Because Jozankei is virtually an extension of Sapporo's sprawling suburbs, the weekends are crowded with day-trippers. The actual ski area, which is in full swing by the beginning of December (the season lasts through May), is at the **Jozankei Kogen International Skiground,** 25 minutes by bus from the spa. The resort

Hokkaido

36 **Cape Soya**

Rebun Island **38**

Kafuka

Oshidomari

37 **Wakkanai**

Hamatombetsu

Kutsugata

39 **Rishiri Island**

Horondoe

KITAMI MTNS.

Oke

35 **Mombetsu**

Sea of Japan

Tomamae

Nayoro

Mt.Teshio

Rumoi

Mashike

Asahikawa

15 Mt. Asahi

Sounkyo

19

Asahida Onsen

16 **20** Lake Dai

Daisetsuzan National Park

18

Furano

17

21 Lake Shika

Mt. Tokachi

Shirogane Onsen

Mt. Yubari

Ishikari Bay

Yobetsu

3

Furubira

4

Tomaru Pass

5

Yoichi

2

Otaru

1

Kamoenai

6

Mt. Tempu **8**

Sapporo

Iwanai

7

9

Jozankei Onsen

HIDAKA RANGE

Obihiro

Mt. Niseko-annupuri

10

Nakayama Pass

Chitose

Shikotsu-Toya National Park

Mt. Yotei

Toyako Onsen

11

Lake Shikotsu

14

12

13

Shiraoi

Tomakomai

Noboribetsu Onsen

Uchiura Bay

Muroran

Hiroo

Mt. Apoi

Oshima Peninsula

Mt. Kamagatake

5

Hakodate

Fukushima

Tsugaru Straits

N

HONSHU

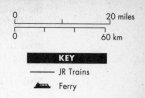

KEY

—— JR Trains

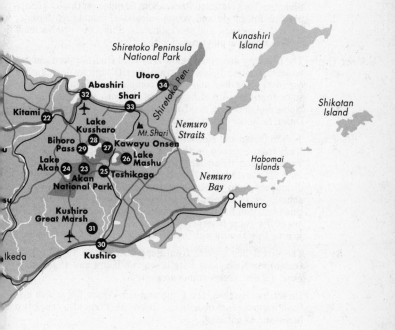

Sea of Okhotsk

Shiretoko Peninsula
National Park

*Kunashiri
Island*

Utoro

Abashiri

34

Shari

32

Kitami

33

22

Shiretoko Pen.

*Shikotan
Island*

**Lake
Kussharo**

*Nemuro
Straits*

**Bihoro
Pass**

28

Mt. Shari

27

Kawayu Onsen

29

26

**Lake
Mashu**

*Habomai
Islands*

**Lake
Akan**

24

23

25

Teshikaga

*Nemuro
Bay*

**Akan
National Park**

Nemuro

**Kushiro
Great Marsh**

31

Ikeda

30

Kushiro

PACIFIC OCEAN

town itself is wedged in a small valley in the foothills beneath the mountains of Shikotsu-Toya National Park. Were it not for the modern, square-block hotels, the village would be beautiful. Unfortunately, while it has all the creature comforts of a resort, plus the hot springs, the hotels' architects have managed to deface nature's beauty. Still, refreshment at a hot spring will be rewarding before heading back to Sapporo.

Shikotsu-Toya National Park

The second excursion loops around the Shikotsu-Toya National Park and includes traveling through Jozankei Onsen, up through Nakayama Pass, down to Lake Toya, and on to the hot-spring spa resorts of Toyako (Lake Toya) Onsen and Noboribetsu Onsen before returning to Sapporo via the Ainu village at Shiraoi and the beauty of Lake Shikotsu. The area of Shikotsu-Toya National Park, about 60 miles southwest of Sapporo, is full of old and young volcanoes, mountains, forests, lakes, hot springs, and several hotels. Shikotsu-Toya National Park is a natural playground with activities for all ages.

Getting There The itinerary described below is by road from Sapporo and can be accomplished by bus and train, even though we describe the car route. Nor does one have to complete all of this excursion, since there are direct buses from Sapporo to Toyako Onsen, Noboribetsu Onsen, and Lake Shikotsu, as well as from Toyako Onsen to Noboribetsu Onsen.

By Train Toyako Onsen and Noboribetsu Onsen are easily accessible by train from Sapporo on the JR Sapporo–Hakodate Line. For Toyako Onsen, disembark from the train at the Toya JR station for a 15-minute bus ride to the lake. For Noboribetsu Onsen, disembark from the train at Noboribetsu and then take the shuttle bus (a 20-minute ride) to Noboribetsu Onsen. Because this excursion lies on the Sapporo–Hakodate train line, if you are either going to or arriving from Honshu by train, consider joining this itinerary at Toyako Onsen or Noboribetsu Onsen.

By Bus The direct bus service from Sapporo to Lake Toya (Toyako Onsen) via Nakayama Pass takes two hours and 45 minutes. *Fare: ¥2,600; reservations necessary.*

Direct bus coaches, the Chuo and the Donan lines, also run from Sapporo to Noboribetsu Onsen; this trip also takes two hours and 45 minutes.

Between Toyako Onsen and Noboribetsu via the Orufure Pass, a one-hour-and-40-minute bus ride operates from June 1 to late-October. *Fare: ¥1,450; 4–6 buses a day; reservations necessary.*

Exploring Leaving Sapporo by car to the first destination, Jozankei, is easy. Take the road running along the west side of the Botanical Gardens; it is a straight run to Jozankei, less than 45 minutes away. All along this itinerary, there are sufficient signs in romaji (Japanese written in Roman script) to give you directional confidence, and the road number is frequently displayed.

Once through Jozankei Onsen (*see above*), the twisting, winding road up through the ravine warns of the high drama of the mountains ahead. The final ascent to 2,742 feet is through a tunnel that opens out at **Nakayama Pass,** where the traveler discovers wide, sweeping panoramas of lonely mountains and peopled plains. In the distance, beyond the surrounding mountain peaks, stands **Mt. Yotei,** rising out of the plains. Mt. Yotei's near-perfect conical shape leads to automatic comparisons to Mt. Fuji, but any native worth his salt would say his Mt. Yotei has no competition.

There is a lodge restaurant (Nakayama Lounge) to the side of the road at Nakayama Pass that serves food (of inferior quality) and refreshments to help you get your breath back after the drive up and before the descent.

Lake Toya The road descends from the pass to Kimobetsu and Rusutsu, where soon after a flat stretch **Lake Toya** suddenly appears. The lake is almost circular and is contained in a collapsed volcanic cone. Just after the first glimpse of the lake, a souvenir shop and food market on the left stand out like a sore thumb. Just beyond them is a coffee shop; the best view of the lake is from its balcony. The view embraces the northern circumference of the lake and its small islands, which are the peaks of smaller volcanoes that pop up in the lake's middle.

⑪ The road from the coffee shop descends to the lake and follows the shore to **Toyako Onsen,** at the southwestern edge of the lake. This spa town is the chief holiday center for this part of the Shikotsu-Toya Park and, consequently, is loaded with hotels, inns, and souvenir shops. The hotels are open all year, but the busiest time is the summer (June through August), when Japanese families come by the droves for trout fishing, hiking, boating, visiting Nakanoshima island (in the center of the lake), and, of course, taking the curative waters of the hot springs.

Indeed, Toyako Onsen is famous for its curative waters, but the geographical wonder is **Showa Shinzan,** Japan's newest volcano, born in July 1945. Showa Shinzan surprised everyone, but no one more than the farmer who witnessed the volcano's creation from his potato patch. The volcano grew 8 inches a day for seven months and then erupted to form its peak of 1,312 feet. By this time the farmer had had enough. He gave up potatoes and became a civil servant, and a small museum took his place at the base of the volcano and chronicles both Showa Shinzan's development and the volcanic activity of the entire area.

Perhaps not to be outdone, one mountain over from Showa Shinzan, **Mt. Usu,** erupted in 1978. It did so with flair, sending out 200 tremors an hour before blowing its top. This advance notice allowed local residents to flee and photographers to set up their cameras. Their photographs are shown amid sound effects of thunder and lightning at the **Abuta Kazan Kagaku-kan Museum,** located at the foot of Mt. Usu. The presentation is dramatically realistic and better seen after, rather than before, taking the cable car to the top of Mt. Usu for the superb views of Lake Toya.

From Toyako Onsen, the road continues around the lake through Sobetsu Onsen, a quieter version of Toyako Onsen. Here the road splits: One branch continues around the lake; the other (closed in the winter) heads east to clamber over the mountains to **Noboribetsu.** This east road is the one to take. The 90-minute trip climbs up **Orofure Pass** (3,051 feet) and offers tremendous views of soaring mountains, hidden valleys, and, in the distance, Lake Toya, Mt. Yokei, Lake Kuttara, and the Pacific Ocean. The Donan Bus Line goes between Toyako

Onsen and Noboribetsu Onsen along this road and stops at Orofure Pass to let passengers enjoy the view.

(Do not confuse Noboribetsu Onsen with Noboribetsu, a city on the coast that is 20 minutes away by road from its namesake spa town. Noboribetsu is an ugly industrial city at which the JR trains stop. From the station, a shuttle bus runs up to Noboribetsu Onsen. Indeed, the whole coastal area from Date to Tomakomai is an industrial eyesore, made worse by a sagging regional economy.)

Noboribetsu Onsen ⓬ **Noboribetsu Onsen** is the most famous spa in Hokkaido, perhaps even in all of Japan. Its 11 types of hot-spring waters are said to cure ailments ranging from rheumatism to diabetes. Most hotels have their own baths, and the grandest of them all are the baths at the **Dai-ichi Takimoto-Kan Hotel.** The hotel is a monstrosity with 365 rooms, video game halls, buffet dining rooms, and evening cabarets, but its baths are the best. The 12 pools in each area (men's and women's) have seven different waters at varying temperatures. Signs above each pool are in Japanese, so which minerals are in the waters and what they do to one's body remain mysteries to most foreigners. The solution is just to try them. Even for non-hot-spring fanatics, these baths are worth the ¥2,000 nonresident fee to attend, if only for the view beyond the bathhouses' plate-glass window: it looks upon the steaming, volcanic gases of Jigokudani (*see below*). On the floor beneath the baths is a swimming pool with a slide for those who like their water straight. The baths are open to nonresidents only from 9 to 3, though once in you can stay as long as you can take it.

The other famous sight of Noboribetsu Onsen is **Jigokudani** (The Valley of Hell), a couple hundred yards from the village. It is a volcanic crater, though it looks like a bow-shape valley; it has a diameter of 1,476 feet and lots of seething, boiling mud. Boiling water spurts out of thousands of holes, sounding like the heartbeat of earth itself, though, because of its strong sulfur smell, others have described it differently. Apparently, the Dante-like inferno is a popular place for suicides. Entire families have been known to make their last leaps from here.

Other nearby places for families are the **Bear Ranch** and **Ukara-no-Sato,** a commercial replica of an Ainu village. Both are located on the slopes of Mt. Shirohei, and access is via the cable car from Noboribetsu Onsen. The few elderly Ainu who perform a dance or two every couple of hours at Ukara-no-Sato look bored to tears. The bears, all 150 of them, are tame and lethargic. The ranch and the five replica Ainu houses are solely for the tourists, but, perhaps because of its location and because the bears are not in minuscule cages, the area is less depressing than the Ainu village at Shiraoi (*see below*). *Admission (including gondola): ¥2,100. Open 6AM–8 PM in the summer; 9–4:30 in the winter.*

Three miles south of Noboribetsu Onsen is **Date Jidai-mura,** a reconstructed Edo village named for the members of the Date clan who migrated here from Sendai after the fall of the Shogunate. The complex includes samurai houses and geisha pleasure palaces watched over by actors attired in traditional garb. A visit here is probably not worth the hefty fee. *Tel. 0143/83-3311. Admission: ¥500 parking, ¥2,000 to enter the grounds* *only, ¥3,500 to enter grounds and buildings. Open 9–7. Closed Nov.–Apr.*

The village of Noboribetsu Onsen is a tourist town, so expect masses of hotels and souvenir shops. However, though the modern hotel architecture could be far more aesthetic and in tune with its surroundings of mountains and forests, the village is not without charm. At least its main street still has cobblestones, and there is a stream that runs through the village. More important, the buildings do not block out the presence of the mountains.

The Ainu have been almost completely wiped out. Fewer than a hundred full-blooded Ainu are left, though no one knows exactly how many. First evicted from Honshu, they then lost their ancestral lands and heritage with the colonization of Hokkaido. One of the few remaining places in Hokkaido to see their culture (artificially) preserved is at the model village **Shiraoi,** 30 minutes by car (40 minutes by bus) on Route 36 toward Tomakomai.

⑬ Shiraoi has a feeling of finality. As if in a zoo, Ainu sit in their reconstructed grass houses with their heirlooms. They appear even more lethargic than at Ukara-no-Sato. Here, too, are bears, even more pitiful as they sit cramped in cages. Yet, despite the depression that sets in while visiting here, one should make the trip, perhaps for reasons of conscience and definitely for the **Ainu Folklore Museum.** The museum has one of the best collections of the Ainu crafts and artifacts that were once part of their daily lives. *Admission: ¥515. Open Apr.–Oct., 8–5:30; Nov.–Mar., 8:30–4:30. Closed Dec. 30–Jan. 4.*

⑭ Your last stop before returning to Sapporo should be **Lake Shikotsu.** To reach the lake, continue from Shiraoi to Tomakomai on the freeway and take a left up to Shikotsu Onsen (or by train to Tomakomai; then a 40-minute bus ride from Tomakomai Station).

Lake Shikotsu is the deepest lake in Hokkaido (outfathomed only by Honshu's Lake Tazawa as the deepest in all of Japan). Swimmers should remember that although the beach shelves gently for 33 feet, it drops suddenly to an eventual depth of 1,191 feet. The lake's shape is a classic caldera except for the two active volcanoes, which have risen to crumble its periphery on both the north and south shores. The southern volcano, Mt. Tarumae, has a bus service that chugs three-quarters of the way to its top, where you can walk 40 minutes to the summit for views embracing all of Lake Shikotsu. At the base of the northern volcano, Mt. Eniwa, is **Marukoma Onsen,** one of the very few spas left in Japan where mixed bathing is still in fashion in its *rotemburo* (outdoor thermal springs) along the lakeshore.

Rental boats are available for leisurely drifting around the lake, and sightseeing boats offer tours. *½-hr. trips halfway around the lake cost ¥840, and 1-hr.-and-40-min. trips around the lake cost ¥1,540.*

From Lake Shikotsu, the quickest route back to Sapporo (by car or bus) is via Chitose and up the expressway. You could also return to Tomakomai by bus and take the JR train back westward in the direction of Hakodate, or take the bus to Chitosekudo (Chitose Airport) and get the JR train to Sapporo.

Central Hokkaido, the Sea of Okhotsk, and the Northern Cape

The third excursion goes east from Sapporo to Daisetsuzan National Park, on to Akan National Park, and then to the Sea of Okhotsk on the east coast. From there the route quickly goes to Hokkaido's northernmost cape and to the islands of Rebun and Rishiri before returning to Sapporo.

Getting Around This journey may be accomplished by train and bus. However, because traveling between Daisetsuzan and Akan requires several bus changes, a rented car is more convenient and more enjoyable for this part of the excursion.

Even with a car, we do recommend taking the train to Asahikawa and renting a car from there. Also, it is a long drive north of Mombetsu along the coast of the Sea of Okhotsk to Hokkaido's north cape. Hence, we recommend returning the car to Asahikawa, or dropping it off at Mombetsu, for travels north to Wakkanai and Rebun and Rishiri islands. Then, either take the train back to Sapporo or fly.

Exploring The main gateway to Daisetsuzan National Park is **Asahikawa,**
15 Hokkaido's second largest city. Asahikawa is vast and sprawling, even though it was only in 1885 that the first pioneers established their base here. Now just under half a million people reside in an area of 225 square miles. The endless suburbs are depressing, but the center of town is small, easy to navigate, and friendly. Several international hotels, including the sparkling Palace Hotel, are in the center of downtown, close to the pedestrian shopping mall (the first such car-free mall in Japan) and the nightly scene of restaurants, izakayas, and bars.

Asahikawa's major attractions are the **Ainu Kinenkan** (memorial hall) and the **Ice Festival** in February. The Ainu Kinenkan is a reasonably good Ainu museum that includes a rather uninspired dance performance by a couple of elderly Ainu in traditional dress. If you have visited either Shiraoi or Akan, there is little reason to see more of the same here. (Admission: ¥310. Open 9:30–4:30; closed Mon.) The Ice Festival is a smaller version of Sapporo's Snow Festival (150 sculptures, compared with the 300 at Sapporo), but Asahikawa's has more of a country-fair feel.

There are several routes to take from Asahikawa into the Daisetsuzan National Park. However, only one road runs completely through the park. That is from north to south—Asahikawa to Sounkyo and through the park to Shikaoi; the road is closed south of Sounkyo in the winter, forcing travelers to turn east and leave the mountains for Kitami, in the plains. Other roads, mainly from the west, make stabs into the mountains here and there and then retreat.

16 On the west side of the park, the spa towns of **Asahida Onsen**
17 and **Shirogane Onsen** serve as hiking centers in the summer and ski resorts in the winter. Shirogane, located at 2,461 feet, has had especially good skiing since its mountain, Mt. Tokachi, erupted in 1962 to form a blanket of lava, making a superb ski bowl. Asahida, with Yukomambetsu Onsen close by, is where one can take a cable car part of the way up Mt. Tokachi (Hokkaido's highest mountain) and hike to the 7,513-foot summit. In the late spring, the slopes are blanketed with alpine flowers.

Daisetsuzan National Park

⑱

The geographical center of Hokkaido and the largest of Japan's national parks, **Daisetsuzan** contains the very essence of rugged Hokkaido: vast plains, soaring mountain peaks, hidden gorges, cascading waterfalls, forests, wildflowers, a spa resort, hiking trails, and wilderness. Daisetsuzan (Great Snow Mountains) refers to the park's five major peaks, all of them towering more than 6,500 feet. Their presence dominates the area and controls man's entry into the park.

⑲

For an excursion through the park, the first place to head for is **Sounkyo,** less than two hours southeast by car from Asahikawa. Alternatively, one can take the bus in front of Asahikawa's JR station, which goes directly to Sounkyo Onsen. If you are using a Japan Rail Pass, you can save some money by taking the JR train to Kamikawa Station and transfering onto the Dohuku Bus for the 30-minute run to Sounkyo.

Sounkyo (*kyo* means "gorge") is the park's most scenic attraction, a 15-mile ravine extending into the park from its northeast entrance. For a 5-mile stretch, sheer cliff walls rise on both sides of the canyon as the road winds up into the mountains. Halfway up is the Sounkyo Onsen spa resort. How the Japanese are able to abuse scenic splendors with their ugly resort hotels is beyond belief. But they do, and Sounkyo Onsen is yet another example. One hotel in particular, the Chyo Hotel, sticks out as an eyesore of concrete. Sitting on a bluff, the hotel dominates what otherwise would be a dramatic view of the gorge. Instead, guests of the hotel do have a magnificent view but also a view of other concrete hotels down the gorge. Still, you have no option but to stay in Sounkyo Onsen if you choose to stay in this area of the park. Drop by the **Sounkyo Tourist Information** (tel. 0165/85–3350) for maps. For assistance in finding lodging, contact the **Sounkyo Tourist Accommodation Office** (tel. 0165/82–1811). You can also try the small youth hostel (tel. 0165/85–3148.)

Resting precariously on the side of the gorge are a couple of grocery stores, some houses, and a couple of inns and restaurants, plus the inevitable souvenir shops that make up the village of Sounkyo. There is also the small **Sounkyo Museum** (tel. 0165/85–3476, open 9–7), which has exhibits on the formation of Mt. Daisetsuzan. Activities take place in the resort hotels, not in the village, and during the day most people are out on the trails hiking through the park. One popular trip is to use the combination of a seven-minute gondola, or ropeway, ride (cost: ¥650 one way) and a 15-minute ride on a chair lift (cost: ¥210 one way) from Sounkyo up Mt. Kurodake for panoramic views over the Daisetsuzan mountain range. For the best views, including one looking over Sounkyo, take the hour's walk to the very top. In July or August the mountain is bedecked in Alpine flowers. The other activity is to rent a bicycle from Sounkyo's bus terminal (cost: ¥1,200 a day) and pedal through the gorge. A bicycle has the advantage over a car because the road goes through dark tunnels, blocking out the views, whereas the bike path skirts along the edge of the gorge.

Two miles up the road from Sounkyo Onsen are two picturesque waterfalls, **Ryusei-no-taki** (Shooting Star) and **Ginga-no-taki** (Milky Way). Neither is dramatic, but because they are like twins, separated only by a protruding cliff face called Heavenly Castle Rock, they form a balanced beauty. The road continues past the falls, following the Ishikawa River through perpendic-

ular cliffs and fluted columns of rock until it reaches the
⑳ dammed-up **Lake Daisetsu.** The dam is a feat of engineering, its
walls constructed only of earth and rubble. In itself, the dam
has no particular visual merit, but the lake behind has islands
that appear to float and a surrounding backdrop of mountains
clad with conifers.

At the lake the road divides. The right fork goes south and
traverses the rough wilderness and least visited part of the
park. The road is unpaved in parts, and there are no public
buses. If you do not have a car, you must hitchhike as far as
Nukabira, where you can catch buses and trains. This route is
dramatic as it climbs up through **Mikuni Pass** (closed in winter)
and drops down to lush valleys and through small ghost towns.
In one such ghost town, **Mitsumata,** stop in at the only restaurant, where you will be enthusiastically welcomed with a dish
of *shika* (deer) soba noodles—noodles with deer meat. So fortified, it is an easy 11-mile run into **Nukabira** and civilization.
㉑ Nukabira is a quiet spa town close to **Lake Shikaribetsu,** the
park's only natural lake. In the winter, toward the end of December, the lake becomes frozen over and an igloo village is established on the ice, where several weddings are generally
performed with great ceremony. During March, the igloo village becomes the site of the local festival, the Shikaribetsu
Kotan Festival.

㉒ The left fork at Lake Daisetsu veers east to **Kitami** and Abashiri on the Sea of Okhotsk. The road is well paved, and buses
make frequent trips between Sounkyo Onsen and Kitami. As
spectacular as the route south, this road to Kitami climbs over
the forested mountains and breaks through the peaks at
Sekihoku Pass. However, the distance is short, and within 12
miles from the lake the road has left Daisetsuzan National Park
to descend among flat fields of peppermint that sparkle white
and purple in season.

The road continues to Kitami and Abashiri on Hokkaido's east
coast; however, south from Kitami is Akan National Park.

Akan National   **Akan National Park** rivals Shikotsu-Toya National Park for its
Park   scenic combination of lakes and mountains. And while the
㉓   mountains are not as high as those in Daisetsuzan, they are no
less imposing. In addition, Akan has three major lakes, each of
which has a unique character. And, crucial to the success of any
resort in Japan, the park has an abundance of thermal springs.

Getting Around   There is virtually no train service through the park except for
the JR Senmo Line from Kushiro to Shari and Abashiri. Trains
on this line stop at Teshikaga and Kawayu Onsen.

There are buses to Lake Akan from Kushiro and Kitami. There
is also a bus from Lake Akan to Abashiri through the Bihiro
Pass.

Coming from Sounkyo Onsen and arriving at Kitami, there is a
road (and bus service) heading south to the small town of
Tsubetsu, where it joins Route 240, entering Akan National
㉔ Park shortly before **Lake Akan.** From the southern part of
Daisetsuzan National Park at Nukabira, a road to Kamishihoro
continues to Ashiyoro, which connects with Route 241; this
runs directly to Akan. Bicycles may be rented at the Akan Bus
Terminal and at Akan View Hotel.

Exploring   Lake Akan in the western part is surrounded by primeval forest and the smoking volcanoes **Me-kan** and **O-kan** (Mr. and Mrs. Akan). The lake itself is famous for *marimo*—green balls of duckweed about 6 inches in diameter. Marimo are rare, and the only other areas they can be found are in Lake Yamanaka near Mt. Fuji, in Japan and in a few lakes in North America, Siberia, and Switzerland. These strange plants act much like submarines, absorbing oxygen from the water and then rising to the surface, where they exhale and sink. They also serve as weather forecasters, spending more time on the surface when the sun shines and settling on the bottom when inclement weather portends. Lake Akan is especially beautiful in the winter when it is frozen over and surrounded by snow-clad mountains. A popular sport at this time is skating between the *wakasagi* (smelt) fishermen. The wakasagi are hooked from ice holes and laid on the ice to immediately freeze. Their freshness makes them popular minced and eaten raw. Some eat them fried.

The town of **Akan-kohan** is the major resort area. This small village has expanded around the lake as new hotels are built. As is true in so much of Hokkaido, the hotels are not very attractive. The key is to obtain a room over the lake so that you are looking at nature's and not man's creation. The actual village center is fairly small and charming if you turn a blind eye to the souvenir shops with their endless rows of carved bears. The bears are great in number here because a small Ainu population lives in the village.

25 From Akan the road to **Teshikaga** is along the Akan Traverse. The distance is only 32 miles, but it has more than its share of scenery. The road winds past O-Akan, and at one point you can look over the drop-off to the right and its volcanic cone almost seems at eye level. It's not a road to be driven at night; not only are the views missed, but also the bears come out to play! The local bus between Akan and Teshikaga takes this road, and whether it is for the pleasure of the passengers or for the nerves of the driver, the bus stops for a rest at the Sokodail, an observational lookout.

26 Teshikaga is a small resort town with a few Japanese inns; the Mashu Hot Springs is nearby. **Lake Mashu** itself is a 20-minute drive (30 minutes by bus) from Teshikaga.

Lake Mashu is ringed by 656-foot-high rock walls. Curiously, no water has been found to either enter or leave the lake, so what goes on in its 695-foot depths is anybody's guess. Perhaps that mystery and the dark-blue water combine to exert a strange hypnotic effect and cause tourists to stare endlessly down from the cliffs into the lake. These cliff sides are incredibly steep and have few or no footholds. You may live longer if you forgo the pleasure of inspecting the water's clarity, said to be clear to a depth of 115 feet. Instead, appreciate the lake from its two observation spots on the west rim. You'll recognize them by the souvenir and food stands.

27 The road continues past Lake Mashu for nine miles to **Kawayu Onsen,** lined with relatively expensive hotels (with mostly Japanese-style rooms) for those who believe in its curative hot springs. Kawayu is not particularly attractive. However, just before Kawayu is **Io-san,** an active volcano that emits sulfurous steam from vents in two ravines. There is a car park and souvenir/grocery store just off the road. Buy a couple of fresh eggs from the store, then walk up to one of the saucepan-size pools and boil them.

28 The road from Kawayu goes around **Lake Kussharo,** where various hotels and campgrounds line the shore. Lake Kussharo (sometimes spelled Kutcharo) is Akan National Park's largest lake. Once it had nearly a perfect caldera shape, but other volcanoes have since sprung up and caused its shores to become flat and less dramatic. It is, however, an ideal area for camping and is popular with families who come for boating and paddling in the water. The lake is at its finest in the autumn, when the different shades of golds and greens on the trees extend from the lake shore into the higher mountain altitudes.

29 At the north end of the lake, the road climbs up **Bihoro Pass,** affording the last great view of Akan National Park's mountains and the green waters of Lake Kussharo below. At Bihoro the road swings west to Ashikawa or east to Ashibiri.

An alternative exit from Akan National Park is to return from the lake to Kawayu Hot Springs and continue two miles to a "T" junction and the Kawayu JR station. There, take either Route 391 northeast or the train to Abashiri. Or, you can make a side **30** trip south to **Kushiro,** either by train or car.

A word or two about Kushiro before discussing Abashiri and the Sea of Okhotsk: Kushiro is a port city of no great appeal, which used to be known for its rather seedy entertainment area for sailors and the tourists coming in off the Tokyo ferry. But the city is getting a new lease on life. Part of the old waterfront has been restored with 50 specialty shops, entertainment, and a terminal for sightseeing boats. Even the entertainment district has some revamped bars with traditional fireplaces where fish is cooked to order. Just to the north and west of Kushiro (30 **31** minutes by bus) is **Kushiro Great Marsh,** home to the red-crested crane (*tancho*). These birds were close to extinction four decades ago; they have slowly come back and now number about 400. The crane—long-legged, pointy-billed, with a white body trimmed in black and a scarlet cap on its head—is a symbol of long life and happiness. Although said to live a thousand years, the birds actually live about 80 and "marry" for life. Each March, the female lays two eggs. The husband and wife select one to nurture. Despite the fact that the birds have made something of a comeback under government protection, there are fears that not enough is being done to preserve their habitat. The Japanese are peculiarly reluctant to preserve nature, despite their avowed appreciation of it.

It is difficult to recommend a trip to see the cranes in the summer: The birds are shy and go deep into the swamps. Only a few are on view, and they are kept behind a fence. In the winter, when they come for food handouts, they are easier to spot.

Sea of Okhotsk north to Rebun and Rishiri Islands From Akan, the northeast coast is only two hours away. This coast has a feeling of being at the end of the world; it is located in the outer reaches of Japan, abutting the icy waters of the Sea of Okhotsk. The people make their living catching fish in the summer; in the winter, the sea is frozen, and survival depends on how successful the summer catch has been. The icy cold waters produce the sweetest shrimp you'll ever taste, and the hairy crab (best in May) may look ugly but its meat is so delicate that you forgive it. Except for the Shiretoko Peninsula, which the Ainu named the "World's End," the coastline is relatively flat, and the drama is in the isolation rather than the scenery. The major town on the coast, Abashiri, is not large, and the distances between points of interest become farther apart. However, all the points mentioned in this excursion can easily be reached by public transportation.

After a short detour to the Shiretoko Peninsula, the itinerary sketched below travels up the coast from Abashiri to Cape Soya, Hokkaido's (and Japan's) most northerly point, and crosses by ferry from Wakkanai to Rebun and Rishiri islands.

Getting There   **By Train.** On the JR railway system, a line connects Abashiri to Kushiro; the train passes through Akan National Park at Teshigawa and Kawayu. Traveling west from Abashiri, the JR train goes to Asahikawa and to Sapporo, some five hours away. North of Abashiri, trains go to Mombetsu and then swing inland, traveling up the north cape to Wakkanai. A short line also runs south from Abashiri, along the coast to Shari.

By Bus. A bus leaves Lake Akan and, with a transfer at Bihoro, goes to Abashiri.

Exploring
32   **Abashiri** is the main town on the Sea of Okhotsk, but it is quite small. In winter, ice floes jam up on its shores and stretch out to sea as far as the eye can see. A museum at **Mt. Tento** observes the ice floes and explains their role in nature. *Admission: ¥1,000. Open 8–6.*

Down the hill from Mt. Tento, toward Lake Abashiri, is the **Abashiri Prison Museum** (Abashiri Kangoku), which recalls the days when convict labor was used to develop the region. Although it's in a separate location, the prison museum is now part of the Municipal museum, and the two are covered by a single admission ticket. The **Municipal Museum** houses a good collection of Ainu artifacts and anthropological findings taken from the nearby Moyoro Shell Mound that are believed to be relics from aboriginal people who predate the Ainu. It is located across the railroad tracks to the south of downtown and near Katsuradai Station. *Admission: ¥1,000. Open 8:30–5.*

Another museum is the **Oroke Kinenkan,** which opened in 1978 to keep alive the heritage of a small tribe, the Oroke, nomadic reindeer herders who, in dwindling numbers, live on Sakhalin Island. And, just south of Abashiri (five minutes on the JR Semmo Line—disembark at Hamakoshimuzu Station), swans come down from Siberia in the winter to hole up at Tofutsu Lagoon. In summertime (July and August), between the lagoon and the Sea of Okhotsk, the main attraction is the **Natural Flower Gardens.** This is where the locals take their afternoon promenades.

33   If you continue traveling south of Abashiri on the Kanno Line train beyond Hamakoshimuzu, you will reach **Shari.** Shari is the end of the line and the jumping-off point for the **Shiretoko Peninsula.** Not many tourists make this trip except for a few Japanese seeking to go off the beaten track. To get there by public transport (summer only), take a 55-minute bus ride from Shari
34   to **Utoro.** There is a sightseeing boat out of Utoro that goes out to the cape. As the boat skirts the shore and rounds the cape's tip, the views are impressive, with 600-foot cliffs coming straight out of the sea and rugged mountains inland. You can also drive along the north shore to **Kamuiwakka Onsen** under

Mt. Io. Along the shore are hot-water pools (*rotemburo*). They are free; just take your clothes off and hop in.

Returning to Abashiri and going north, the traveler finds that the road runs along the coast of the Sea of Okhotsk to **Mombetsu.** (The train takes an inland route to Mombetsu.) Small summer resort hotels dot the coast, especially along the shores of Lake Saroma, a seawater lagoon almost locked in by two sand pits. However, all you can look at here are the sea to the right and distant mountains to the left.

Mombetsu is a small port whose main industry is fishing the Sea of Okhotsk in the summer. In the winter the sea freezes, and Mombetsu is bitterly cold and surrounded by ice floes. Yet, ironically, Mombetsu receives the most tourists in the winter. They come to see the ice floes and board a special boat, the *Gerinko Go*, which acts as an icebreaker, moving through the floes. *Reservations and tickets, tel. 01582/4–8000. Cost: ¥2,000.*

The **Okhotsk Sea Ice Museum** opened in 1991 as a multi-functional facility to promote understanding of ice floes. Its main feature is the Astrovision Hall, where spectacular views of sea ice are projected on a 360° dome re-creating the experience of flying over the Okhotsk Sea when the ice floes are most impressive. There is also a low temperature simulation room, where visitors, clad in Eskimo-type clothing, experience the severe cold and wander around blocks of sea ice. *Admission: ¥1,000. Open 9–5.*

Mombetsu also has a small and attractive museum, with examples of Hokkaido's flora and fauna, some stone arrowheads, ancient pottery, and relics from Japan's 1905 war with Russia. *Admission free. Open 10:30–5:30 (4:30 in winter).*

That's it, aside from a small, friendly entertainment section, a few shops on the main street, and a couple of hotels. But Mombetsu is the last settlement fit to be called a town until Wakkanai, 190 miles to the north, the ferry port for Rebun and Rishiri islands.

If you want to head straight back to Sapporo from Mombetsu, a new, well-paved highway cuts through the wooded mountain range to Asahikawa, a journey that takes a little over three hours by car or bus. Then, from Asahikawa, the train makes the 90-minute run to Sapporo.

The journey north from Mombetsu to Wakkanai is long and tiring, passing through the occasional fishing village, but with usually only rocky promontories to interrupt the flat coastline. Thirty-two miles before reaching **Cape Soya,** the mountains move out toward the sea. Out across the cold sea stands the Soviet Union's Sakhalin Island. Cape Soya is at the northernmost limits of Japan; just offshore is a little island with a wind-whipped monument marking the end of Japan's territory. (A public bus makes the hour-long run up from Wakkanai to Cape Soya six times a day.) Then, shortly thereafter and to the west, there is the first glimpse of Rishiri Island and its volcanic cone standing on the horizon. But first, one must enter the town of Wakkanai.

Wakkanai is a working-class town that subsists on farming the scrubland and fishing the cold waters for Alaskan pollack and Atka Mackerel when the sea is not packed with ice floes. The area seems like it's at the top of the world. Wakkanai is an isolated outpost of man. In the winter, the nights are long, and in the summer there is a feeling of poetic solitude that comes from the eerie quality of the northern lights. From Wakkanai Park, on a ridge to the west of the city, is a commanding view of Sakhalin, an island taken over by the Russians at the end of World War II. Several monuments in this park are dedicated to the days when Sakhalin was part of Japan. One commemorates nine female telephone operators who committed suicide at their post office in Maoka (on Sakhalin) when the island changed hands. Few visitors come to Wakkanai other than to wait for one of the three ferries that daily make the 2½-hour crossing to both **Rebun Island** and **Rishiri Island.** (Higashi-Nihon Ferry, tel. 0162/23–3780; fare: ¥2.060. By the way, there is also a ferry between **Kafuka** on Rebun Island and **Oshidomari** and **Kutsugata** on Rishiri Island (fare: ¥920).

Rebun is the older island, created by an upward thrust of the earth's crust. The island is long and fairly skinny, running from north to south. Along the east coast are numerous small fishing villages where men bring their catch, usually *nukaboke* (a foot-long fish), to smoke in an old metal drum, while women rake in the edible yellowish-green seaweed (*kombu*) from the shore. On the west coast, cliffs stave off the waves coming in from the Japan Sea. Inland during the short summer months is a spectacle of wild alpine flowers, 300 species in all, blanketing the mountain meadows. In Momoiwa, the wildflowers are in such profusion in mid-June that one fears to walk, for each step seems to crush a dozen delicate flowers, including the white-pointed usuyo-kiso, a flower found only on Rebun.

Rishiri is the result of a submarine volcano whose cone now protrudes 5,640 feet out of the water. The scenery is wilder than on Rebun, and, though a larger island, Rishiri has fewer inhabitants. The ruggedness of the terrain makes it harder to support life, and it's less suitable for hiking than is Rebun. To see this island, it is better to take one of the regularly scheduled buses, which make a complete circle of the island in two hours. There are six a day, both clockwise and counterclockwise. Get off at any of the several tourist stops along the way, and take the hiking routes laid out to the major scenic spots. With the tree line at about 3,000 feet, views are alpine panoramas of wildflowers, a cone-shape mountain, and wide expanses of sea. Tokyo and the industry of Honshu are not part of this Japan. These two islands remain beautiful refuges from modern industrialism.

From Oshidomari, the ferry to Wakkanai takes just over two hours. From there the train takes six hours to return to Sapporo, 210 miles away. There are also flights directly back to Sapporo (Chito), and there is an overnight ferry (about ¥8,000 for second class, ¥13,000 for a private first-class cabin) from Kutsugata (Rishiri) and Kafuka (Rebun) to Otaru, which is 25 miles from Sapporo. For reservations and schedules, call the Otaru office, tel. 0134/22–0830.

Dining and Lodging

Dining

Western food is served in all the major Sapporo hotels. Invariably, it is French-accented Continental cuisine and always fairly expensive. Sapporo also has a number of ethnic restaurants, from Italian to Russian to Indian, and there are even American fast-food chains. In the hinterlands, Western food is less common. However, almost all the large resort hotels offer a Western menu.

The joy of Hokkaido, however, is its regional food. We strongly recommend that you eat out whenever possible at local Japanese restaurants. Most restaurants that are reasonably priced will have a visual display of their menu in the window. On this basis, you can decide what you want before you enter. If you cannot order in Japanese and no English is spoken, lead the waiter to the window display and point.

Hokkaido is known for its seafood. **Salmon** (*akiaji*), **squid** (*ika*), **sea urchin** (*uni*), **herring** (*nishin*), and **shellfish** are abundant, but the real treat are fat, sweet scallops (*kaibashira*) collected from Wakkanai. Ramen (a Chinese-noodle soup) is the staple, and it is extremely popular and inexpensive.

The other great favorite is **kegani** (*hairy crabs*). Supposedly, it is forbidden to catch them, but not to eat them—the local people enjoy them too much for that rule to be in effect!

Genghis khan (also spelled *jingisukan*) are thin strips of mutton cooked in an iron skillet. Then, added to the sizzling mutton are seasoned vegetables—usually onions, green peppers, and cabbage.

A 3% federal consumer tax is added to all restaurant bills. Another 3% local tax is added if the bill exceeds ¥7,500. Tipping is not the custom. At more expensive restaurants, a 10%–15% service charge is also added to the bill.

Category	Cost *
Very Expensive	over ¥6,000
Expensive	¥4,000–¥6,000
Moderate	¥2,000–¥4,000
Inexpensive	under 2,000

Cost is per person without tax, service, or drinks

Lodging

With one or two exceptions, accommodations in Hokkaido consist of modern, characterless hotels built for Japanese tour groups. Large, unattractively furnished sitting areas and spacious lobbies are the norm. Usually the redeeming factor is the view. Invariably, hotel prices correlate with the views offered and with the size of the public areas and guest rooms.

Outside Sapporo and Hokkaido's industrial and/or commercial cities, hotels quote prices on a per-person basis with two meals, exclusive of service and tax. If you do not want dinner at your hotel, it is usually possible to renegotiate the price. The hotel categories below reflect the cost of a double room with private bath and no meals. Bear in mind, then, that except for city hotels, you will be expected to take breakfast and dinner at the hotel and that will be the rate quoted unless you specify otherwise. On the average, the food charges are 50%, per person, of the room cost. So, for example, if the double room is in the expensive category (¥15,000–¥20,000), then add ¥15,000 to ¥20,000 for two meals for two people.

A 3% federal consumer tax is added to all hotel bills. Another 3% local tax is added if the bill exceeds ¥15,000. At most hotels, a 10%–15% service charge is added to the total bill. Tipping is not necessary.

Category	Cost *
Very Expensive	over ¥20,000
Expensive	¥15,000–¥20,000
Moderate	¥10,000–¥15,000
Inexpensive	under ¥10,000

Cost is for double room, without tax or service

The most highly recommended restaurants and accommodations are indicated by a star ★.

Akan

Lodging   **Hotel Yamoura.** At the south end of the village and still on the lake front, the Yamoura is smaller than the area's other resort hotels. Three-quarters of the rooms are Japanese style, and these are the better ones—they look onto the lake. The manager is friendly; though he speaks no English, he is very enthusiastic toward foreigners who stay at his hotel. *Akan-kohan, Akan 085, tel. 0154/67–2311. 70 rooms. Facilities: Continental and Japanese restaurants, thermal baths, boat rentals. AE, V. Expensive.*

★ **New Akan Hotel.** In Japanese eyes, this establishment is the most prestigious in the area, but, despite its ideal location on Lake Akan, it tends toward sterility and vastness. A recent improvement is the addition of the Annex Crystal of 72 rooms (half Japanese and half Western-style); this section is less crowded with groups. *Akan-kohan, Akan 085, tel. 0154/67–2121, fax 0154/67–3339. 296 rooms. Facilities: Continental and Japanese dining, thermal baths, shops, boat rentals. AE, DC, MC, V. Expensive.*

★ **Hotel Parkuin.** The owners of this small hotel are really friendly, and the father is proud of his daughter's English (which is very limited). Because the hotel is not on the lake (it's just off the main road that skirts the village), request a room on the top floor to get a view of the lake and mountains. There are Japanese- and Western-style rooms; the Japanese restaurant, which attracts a local clientele, is especially good with its grilled fish. *Akan-kohan, Akan 085, tel. 0154/67–3211. 34 rooms. AE, MC, V. Inexpensive.*

Asahikawa

Dining **Claire France.** At the Palace Hotel, this is the best restaurant in town for French cuisine. Its rooftop setting is attractive and formal, though the views are only of the tops of other nearby buildings. *6-6 Chome, Asahikawa 070, tel. 0166/25–8811. Reservations advised. Jacket and tie required. AE, DC, MC, V. Lunch, dinner. Expensive.*

★ **Izakaya Yakara.** This bustling and cheerful bar is one floor up in a two-story building (next to a parking lot) and half a block south of the movie house on the main street. The chefs work in an open cooking area that allows non-Japanese speaking diners to see and point to the kind of food that takes their fancy. The main dishes are meats and fish grilled over charcoal. Guests can sit either at a counter or on tatami matting. *Tel. 0166/23–8228. No reservations. Dress: informal. V. Dinner 6–10. Moderate.*

Lodging **Palace Hotel.** The Palace, Asahikawa's newest hotel, opened in
★ 1987. Decorated with mock marble, the public spaces are brightly lit and airy, with potted plants separating the registration area from the lounge. Use the Polestar lounge on the 15th floor for a skyline view. The Claire France restaurant is on the same floor. The Palace is located downtown, one block from the New Hokkai. Some English is spoken. *6-6 Chome, Asahikawa 070, tel. 0166/25–8811, fax 0116/25–8200. 265 rooms (mostly Western-style). Facilities: Japanese and French restaurants, coffee/tea lounge. AE, DC, MC, V. Expensive.*

Toyo Hotel. Opposite the Palace Hotel on the main street, this small hotel has recently refurbished its rooms with white-and-gray decor. The Toyo is used to serving Japanese guests but is friendly and helpful to Westerners. No English spoken. *7-chome, Shichijo-dori, Asahikawa 070, tel. 0166/22–7575, fax 0116/23–1733. 107 rooms (mostly Western-style). Facilities: Japanese restaurant. AE, DC, MC, V. Moderate.*

Chitose

Lodging **Hotel Nikko Chitose.** This is the best hotel in the Chitose area if you wish to be near Sapporo airport, about 2 miles away. It is owned by Japan Airlines and is used by its flight crews. *4-4-4 Honcho, Chitose-shi 066, tel. 0123/22–1121, fax 0123/22–1153. 203 rooms, mostly Western-style. Facilities: Continental and Japanese restaurants. AE, DC, MC, V. Expensive.*

Hakodate

Lodging **Harborview Hotel.** Next to the Hakodate JR station and near buses to destinations within town, this hotel is very conveniently located. It maintains a fresh, cheerful ambience and a friendly staff. There is a pleasant coffee/tea lounge and a sociable bar in the lobby. Guest rooms are standard Western style, furnished in light blue or peach—not particularly attractive but comfortable enough for an overnight. *14–10 Wakamsatsu-cho, Hakodate 040, tel. 0138/22–0111, fax 0138/23–0154. 190 Western rooms. Facilities: Japanese and Western restaurants, coffee shop, bar, banquet rooms. AE, DC, MC, V. Moderate.*

Hakodate Ryokan. This small house with tatami rooms is located 10 minutes by foot from the JR station. *28-7 Omoricho, Hakodate 040, tel. 0138/26–1255, fax 0138/26–1256. 15 rooms, 4* with bath. *Facilities: Japanese and Continental breakfasts only. No credit cards. Inexpensive.*

Pension Kokian. The reason for selecting this lodging is its central, waterfront location, close to the historical sights. On the next street are several cafés and bars. The small tatami rooms are nothing special, with smudged walls and cracked plaster. The shared toilet facilities are basic, and for your bath you are told to hop on a tram for the 15-minute ride to the public baths at Yashigashira Onsen. Better than the accommodations is the restaurant, which has been spruced up so that even locals come in to dine. *13-2 Suchikocho, Hakodate 040, tel. 0138/26–5753, fax 0138/22–2710. 15 rooms. Facilities: restaurant; 2 meals included in price. No credit cards. Inexpensive.*

Kushiro

Lodging **Kushiro Pacific Hotel.** This hotel is recommended mainly for its central location (five minutes by taxi from the train station). The staff is efficient, some English is spoken, and the rather small rooms are clean. *2-6 Sakaecho, Kushiro 085, tel. 0154/24–8811, fax 0154/23–9192. 132 rooms, mostly Western style. Facilities: Continental and Japanese food served in the restaurant. AE, MC, V. Moderate.*

Lake Shikotsu

Lodging **Marukoma Onsen Ryokan.** Neither the building nor its interior furnishings have any aesthetic value, but the lobby, lounges, and restaurant face the northwest shore of Lake Shikotsu. The tatami-style guest rooms have plain, modern, light-wood furnishings. If you have a room facing the lake and mountain, the view is splendid. Service is attentive and tolerant of foreigners, and dinner—served in your room—is above average. However, the real benefit of this ryokan is that besides the indoor thermal pool facing the water, there is a public *rotemburo* (outside thermal pool) on the lake shore, within yards of the hotel. *Poropnai, Bangaichi, Chitose-shi 066-02, tel. 0123/25–2341. 60 Japanese-style rooms. Facilities: coffee shop, bar, game room, thermal pool and private beach on lakefront. AE, DC, MC, V. Moderate.*

Mombetsu Area

Dining The entertainment area is located three streets up from the Harbor View Hotel (*see* Lodging, *below*). Though the area is small, there are plenty of bars that serve food and one or two modest discotheques (try the **New Jazz Club**). There are fewer restaurants than bars. While many of the restaurants have visual displays in their windows to indicate prices and the type of food served, the bars do not. Count on about ¥5,000 per person if you go into one of the bars that have hostesses with whom to talk, though that will be in Japanese, not English. Prices can climb steeply, so establish the costs before you gulp too much whiskey.

Lodging **Harbor View Hotel.** This is the best Western-style hotel in
★ town. Even though the Harbor View is modest, it is clean and comfortable. Request a room overlooking the harbor. The woman who owns the hotel is extremely helpful and speaks fluent English, a rarity in Mombetsu. *Mombetsu 094, tel. 01582/*

4–6171. 32 Western-style rooms. Facilities: small restaurant with Japanese and Western menu. V. Moderate.

★ **Hotel Koen.** Located 30 miles south of Mombetsu on Rte. 238, this small hotel is steps away from the beach. It attracts the Japanese going to the sea in the summer and making snowmobile trips in the winter. This establishment has simple, clean accommodations and a cafeteria-style restaurant that serves marvelous fresh shrimp (¥ 1,000 per plate) and delicious hairy crabs. At least, stop here for lunch. *Toppushi, Sahomacho, Tokoru-gun 093, tel. 01587/2–3117. 40 rooms. Facilities: Japanese cuisine served in cafeteria-style restaurant, boat rentals, snowmobiling. V. Moderate.*

Togiya Ryokan. This ryokan is an extremely friendly, old-fashioned inn. It's not elegant, but it has the warmth of rural Japan. The inn is located on a small street, one block up from the harbor road and two blocks east of the station. No English is spoken, but mama-san does wonders with your use of a dictionary. Good Japanese family fare (fish—raw and grilled) is served in your room. *Mombetsu 094, tel. 01582/3–3048. 15 rooms, none with private bath, but good, deep, Japanese baths are prepared for you. Facilities: Japanese food served in your room. No credit cards. Moderate.*

Noboribetsu Onsen

Lodging **Dai-ichi Takimotokan.** This huge, famous spa hotel may have as many as 1,200 guests at one time. They come to enjoy its thermal pools, the best and most famous throughout Japan. The hotel is very expensive, yet it has zero ambience. It is like a giant youth hostel and, invariably, fully booked. Service is efficiently impersonal, and you must hike from your bedroom to the lobby and to the thermal baths. The hotel's new extension has only increased the traffic to and from the baths. A vast dining room, the Food Plaza, serves average Japanese and Western food and features nightclub variety acts. *55 Noboribetsu-Onsen, Noboribetsu 059–05, tel. 0143/84–2111, fax 0143/84–2202. 401 rooms. Facilities: electronic game room, shops, thermal baths (nonguests pay ¥2,000 to use the baths). AE, DC, MC, V. Very Expensive.*

Noboribetsu Grand Hotel. This is another huge hotel with large, barren public rooms. Since it is at the bottom of the village and off to the side, its modern ugliness is well hidden. *154 Noboribetsu-Onsen, Noboribetsu 059–05, tel. 0143/84–2101, fax 0143/84–2543. 350 rooms, mostly Japanese-style. Facilities: Japanese restaurant, thermal baths, shops. AE, DC, MC, V. Expensive.*

★ **Akiyoshi Hotel.** This is a friendly, hospitable, modern ryokan in the center of the village. Antiques and paintings are judiciously placed to give a balance between traditional hospitality and modern amenities. If you enjoy sleeping on tatami with a futon, this is recommended as the most personable hotel in town. *Noboribetsu-Onsen, Noboribetsu 059–05, tel. 0143/84–2261, fax 0143/84–2263. 50 Japanese-style rooms. Facilities: Japanese food served either in the room or in the restaurant, thermal bath. AE, V. Moderate–Expensive.*

★ **Ryokan Hanaya.** A member of the Japanese Inn Group, this small inn is located less than 10 minutes on foot from the center of Noboribetsu. The young owners, Mr. and Mrs. Imai, speak English, and they keep their inn clean and fresh. Each of the tatami rooms has cushions with backs, making it easier for

Westerners to sit cross-legged. Each also has an alcove with a writing table, two chairs, a house telephone, minibar, and coin-operated TV. Breakfast, either Western or Japanese, and dinner are served on request in your room. The common baths, one for men and another for women, have two pools. One is fed by a sulphur mineral spring what gushes water at 45° C and is supposedly good for muscle tension, backaches, rheumatism, and skin diseases; the other is filled with mineral-less water to soak off the sulphur. Each faces a picture window looking onto the mountainside. *134 Noboribetsuonsenmachi, Noboribetsu 059-05, tel. 0143/84–2521, fax 0143/84–2240. (Coming from JR Noboribetsu Station, take the bus to Noboribetsu Onsen and get off at the Hanaya-mae bus stop.) 18 rooms without bath. Facilities: Breakfast and dinner in room on request. AE, DC, MC, V. Inexpensive.*

Otaru

Lodging   **Otaru International Hotel.** Above a shopping arcade, this modern hotel in town is reached by an escalator from the main street. The lobby area is rather bare and uncomfortable, but the guest rooms are cheerful, though small. *3-9-1 Inaho, Otaru 047, tel. 0134/33–2161, fax 0134/33–7744. 76 rooms, mostly Western style. Facilities: Chinese, Japanese, and Continental restaurants. AE, MC, V. Moderate.*

Shikutsu Ryokan. This is a popular but slightly overrated ryokan. The furnishings are worn, and the staff does not seem to be overjoyed at having foreigners stay. *2-15 Inaho 3-chome, Otaru 047 (located just outside Otaru and toward the aquarium), tel. 0134/22–5276. 20 rooms, 10 with private bath. Facilities: only Japanese food is offered. No credit cards. Moderate.*

Sapporo

Dining   Continental food is served in all the major hotels in either a formal dining room and/or coffee shop. Invariably, the formal dining room looks to French cuisine for inspiration, and the food is always expensive. Most large hotels, aside from their Japanese restaurants, have a Chinese restaurant. Most of the restaurants, whatever their culinary origin, use visual displays for their menus, so, even if you do not speak Japanese, ordering at a local Japanese restaurant is easy. The greatest concentration of restaurants is in the entertainment district of Susukino. Hokkaido is known for its *ramen,* a Chinese noodle served in broth. There are more than 1,000 ramen shops in Sapporo, but do try to make it to **Ramen Yokocho,** located in a small alley that runs perpendicular to, and starts one block south of, Susukino Avenue. In the same area there are as many as three dozen tiny shops with counter service. The current favorite is **Hikoma,** easy to find because of the line outside waiting for a seat.

Ambrosia Room. On the penthouse floor of the Keio Plaza Hotel, this restaurant serves ambitious French fare by an extremely attentive and personable staff. Perhaps more memorable than the cooking, though, is the view over the botanical gardens. *Keio Plaza Hotel, 7-2 Nishi, Kita 5, Chuo-ku, Sapporo 060 (downtown), tel. 011/271–0111. Reservations suggested. Jacket and tie required. AE, DC, MC, V. Lunch noon–3, dinner 6–10. Very Expensive.*

Big Jug. In the Grand Hotel, this casual beer hall–type

brasserie is good for lunch, with a limited Continental menu
and an opportunity to talk. It's popular with businessmen.
*Sapporo Grand Hotel, 4 Nishi, Kita 1, Chuo-ku (downtown),
tel. 011/261–3311. Reservations not necessary. Jacket and tie
required. AE, DC, MC, V. Lunch noon–3, dinner 6–10. Expensive.*

★ **Yamatoya.** Excellent sushi and sashimi is served here, with
counter service on the left and tatami seating on the right. *3
Nishi, Kita 2, Chuo-ku (downtown), tel. 011/251–5667 (located
across the street from the JAL office). No reservations. Jacket
and tie required. V. Open 11–10. Closed Sun. Expensive.*

★ **Izakaya Karumaya.** Downstairs in Plaza 109 (on the south side
of the main east–west street in Susukino), this local bar has the
best yakitori in town. The elegant atmosphere makes it popular with Japanese and foreigners. (There is an English-language menu.) Aside from yakitori, Karumaya also serves oden
as one of its specialties. *4 Minamo, 5 Nishi Chuo-ku
(Susukino), tel. 011/512–9157. No reservations. Dress: informal. V. Open 5 PM–2 AM. Moderate.*

Sapporo Beer Brewery. *Genghis khan* (mutton) is popular here,
though other Japanese dishes are offered. You'll find a festive
atmosphere in either the garden or the cavernous halls of the
old brewery (east of the station). *Nishi 6, Kita 9, Higashi-ku,
tel. 011/742–1531. No reservations. Dress: informal. AE, MC,
V. Open 11:30–9. Moderate.*

Sasa Sushi. This small restaurant has a wide variety of sushi
and is extremely popular with the local businessmen. Sit at the
counter and you'll usually strike up a conversation with fellow
patrons. *2 Nishi, Kita 2, Chuo-ku (downtown), tel. 011/222–
2897 (close to the Hokkaido Tourist Office). No reservations.
Dress: casual but neat. Open 11–10. Closed Sun. V. Moderate.*

Shioya. In the Plaza 109 building, this popular restaurant
serves grilled fish, but the side orders of sashimi and yakitori
are also delicious. Seating is either at the counter or at tables.
It's a casual place where talking to fellow diners is a likely possibility. No English is spoken, but sign language suffices, and
the prices are not too high. *4 Minamo, 5 Nishi Chou-ku
(Susukino), tel. 011/512–1241. No reservations. Dress: informal. AE, V. Moderate.*

Silo. This has a countrylike decor and a menu to match. The res-
taurant serves only Hokkaido foods, including bear and deer.
Some English is spoken. *5 Minamo, 3 Nishi, Chuo-ku in the
Hokusen Bldg. (Susukino), tel. 011/531–5837. No reserva-
tions. Dress: informal. No credit cards. Dinner 5–11. Closed
Sun. Moderate.*

Aginokoken. Uptown and across from the Grand Hotel,
Aginokoken is one of the more well-known ramen shops. You
enter from the street level (there's a large ramen bowl statue
outside) and go downstairs into the cellar restaurant. Choose
either the counter or a table, which you might share with other
diners if the restaurant is crowded. Though there are one or
two other items available, ramen is the specialty, and the
steaming bowl of noodles will only set you back ¥600–¥1,200.
*3 Nishi, Kita 1, Sanwa Ginko (Bank) Building, tel. 011/232–
8171. No reservations. Dress: informal. No credit cards. Open
11–9. Inexpensive.*

Yoyotei. A genghis khan dinner is offered in case you cannot
make it to the Sapporo Beer Brewery. Young waitresses in Ba-
varian dresses and a large open space combine to re-create a
German beer hall. *5 Minamo, 4 Nishi, Chuo-ku, on the 5th floor*

of the Matsuoka Bldg. (Susukino), tel. 011/241–8831. No reservations. Dress: informal. No credit cards. Open 4–10. Inexpensive.

Lodging
ANA Zennikku Hotel. In the heart of the business center, three blocks from the JR station, this is Sapporo's tallest high-rise hotel (26 floors). Shops and a coffee/pastry restaurant are on the ground floor, and up the escalator is an open lobby area with lounges and bars. The rooms are spacious and brightly decorated. Good views are available from the Sky Restaurant and Sky Lounge. The hotel is convenient for ANA passengers, because it runs buses to and from Chitose Airport. *1 Nishi, Kita 3, Chuo-ku, Sapporo 060, tel. 011/221–4411, fax 011/222–7624. 470 rooms, mostly Western style. Facilities: French and Japanese restaurants on the penthouse floors. AE, DC, MC, V. Very Expensive.*

★ **Grand Hotel.** This is Sapporo's oldest established Western hotel, centrally located on the main commercial street. Built in 1934 and renovated in 1984, the Grand is in the tradition of a great European hotel. It has a range of restaurants—Japanese, Chinese, French, and a pub (The Big Jug), popular for business lunches. The service is first-rate. The rooms in the new annex have a fresher, more modern tone than those in the older wing. The hotel's numerous facilities, from a cake and coffee shop to elegant restaurants, create a more lively atmosphere than you may expect from Sapporo's oldest hotel. *4 Nishi, Kita 1, Chuo-ku, Sapporo 060, tel. 011/261–3311, fax 011/222–5164. 585 rooms, mostly Western style. Facilities: Japanese, Chinese, and French restaurants, shopping arcade. AE, DC, MC, V. Very Expensive.*

Keio Plaza Hotel. A five-minute walk to the right of the JR station, the Keio is a large, modern hotel with a vast, open-plan lobby. Since it stands between the botanical gardens and the Hokkaido University campus, the views from the guest rooms on the upper floors are the best in town. The rooms are very spacious for a Japanese hotel. If you are not staying here, the views may be enjoyed from the Ambrosia (French) and Miyama (Japanese) restaurants on the hotel's 22nd floor. The 24-hour Jurin coffee shop, one of the few all-night restaurants in town, can be a welcome respite for the insomniac suffering from jet lag. The enthusiastic and helpful staff will always find someone to help out in English, if required. *7-2 Nishi, Kita 5, Chuo-ku, Sapporo 060, tel. 011/271–0111, fax 011/271–7943. 525 rooms, mostly Western style. Facilities: Several Japanese restaurants, as well as French, Mediterranean, and Chinese restaurants, 24-hr. coffee shop, health club facilities, car rental, and tour desk. AE, DC, MC, V. Very Expensive.*

Sapporo Renaissance Hotel. This upscale Ramada hotel, which opened in late 1991, has slightly larger rooms than other high-priced hotels in town for the same price. Its drawback is its location, a short taxi ride from most places you'll want to visit—five minutes to Susskino, 10 minutes to the JR Station. The hotel's lobby area and public facilities are rarely crowded, and the fitness club, with a large swimming pool and baths, is excellent (although guests not staying on the Renaissance Club floor must pay ¥3,000 to use the club). Guest rooms are indistinguishable from those at other modern hotels; they have light color schemes and cheap-looking furniture. The hotel's one touch of humor is the mural painted on the arched ceiling of the reception lobby depicting the Japanese islands supported by

Western cherubs and Roman-looking gods. Many of the staff speak English. *1-1, Toyohira 4-jo 1-chome, Toyohira-ku, Sapporo 062, tel. 011/821–1111, fax 011/842–6191. 321 Western-style rooms, 2 Japanese-style suites. Facilities: 6 restaurants, 2 bars, business center, fitness center with indoor pool and sauna, shops, banquet rooms. AE, DC, MC, V. Very Expensive.*

Hotel Alpha Sapporo. This hotel has the best location for tourists who want to walk to the shopping and downtown area of the city and be close to the evening action in Susukino. The service is excellent and the decor of warm rust-browns and reds makes it an inviting place to return after a day of sightseeing. Smaller than most of the other top hotels, the hotel's staff soon knows you by name. Guest rooms tend to be a little ordinary, but the rooms are larger than most standard hotel rooms in Japan. The French restaurant, La Couronne, imports many of its ingredients from France and serves them in an elegant wood-paneled dining room. *Nishi 5, Minami 1, Chuo-ko, Sapporo 060, tel. 011/221–2333, fax 011/221–0819. 146 rooms. Facilities: 4 restaurants, indoor pool, beauty parlor. AE, DC, MC, V. Expensive.*

Hotel Arthur. Located south of Susskino and at the top of Nakajima Park, this hotel opened in 1989, and although the guest room carpeting needs to be replaced, the hotel has been well maintained. The rooms are reasonably large for Japan, and the dark-stained furniture gives them a European feel. Bathrooms have a hand-held shower, and the toilet is in a separate room that adjoins the alcove dressing area. The spacious lobby area has an open lounge where meals are served looking through huge windows onto the park. On the second floor are Japanese and European restaurants. The staff's English is limited, but their willingness to help foreign guests is not. *S 10, W 6, Chuo-ku, Sapporo 064, tel. 011/561–1000, fax 011/521–5522. 229 Western-style rooms. Facilities: 3 restaurants, sauna, beauty salon, gift shop. AE, DC, MC, V. Moderate–Expensive.*

★ **Fujiya Santus Hotel.** Although more than 10 years old the Fujiya Santus has kept up a fresh appearance. The staff is wonderfully friendly, and the smallness of the hotel adds to the personal warmth. The price is at the low end of this category, too, which makes it a good value. *7 Nishi, Kita 3, Chuo-ku, Sapporo 060 (located next to the botanical gardens, which is pleasant, but requires a 10-min. walk to downtown and the JR station), tel. 011/271–3344, fax 011/241–4182. 40 rooms, 32 Western style. Facilities: restaurant. V. Moderate.*

Nakamuraya. This ryokan near the Botanical Park has a 90-year-old history—ancient for Sapporo—though the current building is more recent. The six-tatami sized rooms seem larger because of the spacious cupboards, built-in minibar, and wide window shelf. Most rooms have private bathrooms, albeit tiny ones. The staff is diffident with foreign guests, but warms up after you've managed a few words in Japanese. The large communal bath is most appreciated in winter. When making reservations, explain that you saw a listing in the Japanese Inn Group brochure; otherwise you may be charged a higher rate. The Japanese dinner (¥3,000) is expansive with a selection of fresh seafood from Hokkaido's waters. *7 Nishi, Kita 3, Chuo-ku, Sapporo 060, tel. 011/241–2111, fax 011/241–2118. 32 rooms, mostly Japanese style. Facilities: Japanese restaurant. AE. Moderate.*

★ **Hotel Public.** The best and swankiest (lots of marble) business hotel in town, the Public has a friendly staff and Western-size beds, instead of the normal narrow ones found in business hotels. The Public also has a reasonable restaurant. *1 Minamo, 15 Nishi, Chuo-ku, Sapporo 060, tel. 011/644–7711. 120 Western-style rooms. Facilities: Japanese and Continental restaurants on the 2nd floor, typing service. AE, MC, V. Inexpensive.*

Sounkyo Onsen

Note: Rates tend to be 20% lower during the winter season. The **Tourist Office Hotel Association** (tel. 01658/2–1811) can help you find accommodations.

Lodging **Chyohotel.** Perched on a bluff halfway up the side of the gorge, this hotel has the best views (and, because of this, spoils some of the natural beauty). Its corner window in the huge foyer lounge looks straight down the gorge; however, the hotel itself is an ugly and mammoth building, cold and sterile in the modern Japanese style. While rooms that face the gorge may merit the hotel's price, a room at the back looks onto a parking lot, another ugly building, and cliff walls. *Sounkyo-Onsen, tel. 01658/5–3241. 275 rooms, mostly Japanese style. Facilities: thermal baths, shops, electronic game room. AE, DC, MC, V. Expensive.*

★ **Mount View Hotel.** This hotel has the nicest design around and an air of freshness to it. Built as a modern interpretation of an alpine inn, the decor is in cheerful, warm pastels. Unfortunately, as a recent newcomer to Sounkyo, it is situated down by the road and has limited views. Nevertheless it has taste, which the other hotels lack. *Sounkyo-Onsen, tel. 01658/5–3011. 40 rooms. Facilities: thermal baths. V. Expensive.*

Kumoi. This small new ryokan offers simple but clean tatami rooms. *Sounkyo-Onsen, tel. 01658/5–3553. 22 rooms, 6 with private bath. Facilities: Continental breakfast on request, thermal bath. AE. Moderate.*

Pension Yukara. This small inn is better priced than many in Sounkyo-Onsen and the owners are hospitable to foreigners. There's air-conditioning in the summer and hot springs to soak in year-round. *Sounkyo 078, tel. 0165/85–3216. (Reservations may be made through the Welcome Inn association.) 3 Japanese and 8 Western rooms without bath. Facilities: dining room, thermal baths. MC, V. Inexpensive.*

Toyako Onsen

Lodging **Toya Park Hotel.** This is a sister hotel to the Toya Park Sun Palace, but it's smaller and more personal, though not quite as deluxe. The manager enjoys speaking English. Located at the head of the town and on a slight bluff, it has an unrestricted view of the town. However, only the Japanese-style guest rooms face the lake. *Toyako-Onsen, tel. 01427/5–2445, fax 01427/5–3918. 167 rooms, about half Western-style, half Japanese-style. Facilities: Continental and Japanese restaurants, thermal baths, tennis courts, electronic game room. AE, DC, MC, V. Moderate.*

Nakanoshima. This is a small hotel with a restaurant 2 miles farther around the lake and going west from Toyako Onsen. No English is spoken, but the owners are happy to use sign language. *Sobetsu-Onsen, tel. 01427/5–2283. 30 rooms, mostly Japanese style. No credit cards. Inexpensive.*

English-Japanese Tourist Vocabulary

Basics 基本的表現

Pronunciation key: a-ah, e-hey, i-we, o-so, u-true, g-go, kyu-cue. In Japanese, all syllables receive equal stress.

Yes/No	hai/i-e	はい／いいえ
Please	o-ne-gai shi-ma-su	お願いします
Thank you (very much)	(do-mo)a-ri-ga-to go-zai-ma-su	（どうも）ありがとうございます
You're welcome	do i-ta-shi-mash-te	どういたしまして
Excuse me	su-mi-ma-sen.	すみません
Sorry	go-men na-sai	ごめんなさい
Good morning	o-ha-yo go-zai-ma-su	お早うございます
Good day/afternoon	kon-ni-chi-wa	こんにちは
Good evening	kom-ban-wa	こんばんは
Good night	o-ya-su-mi na-sai	おやすみなさい
Goodbye	sa-yo-na-ra	さようなら
Mr./Mrs./Miss	-san	一さん
Pleased to meet you	ha-ji-me-mash-te	はじめまして
How do you do?	do-zo yo-rosh-ku	どうぞよろしく

Numbers 数

The first reading is used for reading numbers, as in telephone numbers, and the second is often used for counting things.

1	i-chi / hi-to-tsu	一／一つ	14	ju-yon	十四
2	ni / fu-ta-tsu	二／二つ	15	ju-go	十五
3	san / mit-tsu	三／三つ	16	ju-ro-ku	十六
4	shi / yot-tsu	四／四つ	17	ju-shi-chi	十七
5	go / i-tsu-tsu	五／五つ	18	ju-ha-chi	十八
6	ro-ku / mut-tsu	六／六つ	19	ju-kyu	十九
7	na-na / na-na-tsu	七／七つ	20	ni-ju	二十
8	ha-chi / yat-tsu	八／八つ	21	ni-ju-i-chi	二十一
9	kyu / kokonotsu	九／九つ	30	san-ju	三十
10	ju / to	十／十	40	yon-ju	四十
11	ju-i-chi	十一	50	go-ju	五十
12	ju-ni	十二	60	ro-ku-ju	六十
13	ju-san	十三	70	na-na-ju	七十

80	ha-chi-ju	八十	1000	sen	千
90	kyu-ju	九十	10,000	i-chi-man	一万
100	hya-ku	百	100,000	ju-man	十万

Days of the Week 曜日

Sunday	ni-chi-yo-bi	日曜日
Monday	ge-tsu-yo-bi	月曜日
Tuesday	ka-yo-bi	火曜日
Wednesday	su-i-yo-bi	水曜日
Thursday	mo-ku-yo-bi	木曜日
Friday	kin-yo-bi	金曜日
Saturday	do-yo-bi	土曜日

Months 月

January	i-chi-ga-tsu	一月	July	shi-chi-ga-tsu	七月
February	ni-ga-tsu	二月	August	ha-chi-ga-tsu	八月
March	san-ga-tsu	三月	September	ku-ga-tsu	九月
April	shi-ga-tsu	四月	October	ju-ga-tsu	十月
May	go-ga-tsu	五月	November	ju-i-chi-ga-tsu	十一月
June	ro-ku-ga-tsu	六月	December	ju-ni-ga-tsu	十二月

Useful Expressions, Questions, and Answers よく使われる表現

Do you speak English?	ei-go ga wa-ka-ri-ma-ska	英語がわかりますか。
I don't speak Japanese.	ni-hon-go ga wa-ka-ri-ma-sen	日本語がわかりません。
I don't understand.	wa-ka-ri-ma-sen	わかりません。
I understand.	wa-ka-ri-mash-ta	わかりました。
I don't know.	shi-ri-ma-sen	知りません。
I'm American/British.	wa-ta-shi wa a-me-ri-ka/ i-gi-ri-su jin desu	私はアメリカ／イギリス人です。
What's your name?	o-na-mae wa nan deska	お名前は何ですか。
My name is . . .	. . . to mo-shi-ma-su	……と申します。
What time is it?	i-ma nan-ji deska	今何時ですか。
How?	do yat-te	どうやって。
When?	i-tsu	いつ。
Yesterday/today/ tomorrow	ki-no/kyo/ash-ta	きのう／きょう／あした
This morning	kesa	けさ
This afternoon	kyo no go-go	きょうの午後
Tonight	kom-ban	こんばん

Excuse me, what?	su-mi-ma-sen, nan de-ska	すみません、何ですか。
What is this/that?	ko-re/so-re wa nan de-ska	これ／それは何ですか。
Why?	na-ze de-ska	なぜですか。
Who?	dare desu ka	だれですか。
I am lost.	mi-chi ni ma-yo-i-mash-ta	道に迷いました。
Where is . . .	. . . wa do-ko de-ska	……はどこですか。
the train station?	e-ki	駅
the subway station?	chi-ka-te-tsu-no-eki	地下鉄の駅
the bus stop?	ba-su tei	バス停
the taxi stand?	tak-shi-i no-ri-ba	タクシー乗り場
the airport?	ku-ko	空港
the post office?	yu-bin-kyo-ku	郵便局
the bank?	gin-ko	銀行
the . . . hotel?	. . . ho-te-ru	…..ホテル
the elevator?	e-re-be-ta	エレベーター
Where are the restrooms?	toi-re wa do-ko de-ska	トイレはどこですか。
Here/there/over there	ko-ko/so-ko/a-so-ko	ここ／そこ／あそこ
Left/right	hi-da-ri/mi-gi	左／右
Straight ahead	mas-su-gu	まっすぐ
Is it near/far?	chi-kai/to-i de-ska	近い／遠いですか。
Are there any rooms?	he-ya ga a-ri-ma-ska	部屋がありますか。
I'd like . . .	. . . ga ho-shi-i no desu ga	….がほしいのですが。
a newspaper	shim-bun	新聞
a stamp	kit-te	切手
the key	ka-gi	鍵
I'd like to buy . . .	. . . o kai-tai no de-ske do	……を買いたいのですけど。
a ticket to . . .	. . . ma-de no kip-pu	……までの切符
a map	chi-zu	地図
How much is it?	i-ku-ra de-ska	いくらですか。
It's expensive/cheap.	ta-kai/ya-su-i de-su ne	高い／安いですね。
A little/a lot	sko-shi/tak-san	少し／たくさん
More/less	mot-to o-ku/sku-na-ku	もっと多く／少なく
Enough/too much	ju-bun/o-su-gi-ru	十分／多すぎる
I'd like to exchange . . .	. . . ryo-gae shi-te i-ta-da-ke-ma-ska.	…….両替して頂けますか。
dollars to yen	do-ru o en ni	ドルを円に
pounds to yen	pon-do o en ni	ポンドを円に
How do you say . . . in Japanese?	ni-hon-go de . . . wa do i-i-ma-ska	日本語で……はどう言いますか。
I am ill/sick.	wa-ta-shi wa byo-ki de-su	私は病気です。
Please call a doctor.	i-sha o yon-de ku-da-sai	医者を呼んで下さい。
Please call the police.	kei-sa-tsu o yon-de ku-da-sai	警察を呼んで下さい。
Help!	tas-ke-te	助けて！

Restaurants レストラン

Basics and Useful Expressions よく使われる表現

A bottle of . . .	. . . ip-pon	.....一本
A glass/cup of . . .	. . . ip-pai	.....一杯
Ashtray	hai-za-ra	灰皿
Plate	sa-ra	皿
Bill/check	kan-jo	かんじょう
Bread	pan	パン
Breakfast	cho-sho-ku	朝食
Butter	ba-ta	バター
Cheers!	kam-pai	乾杯！
Chopsticks	ha-shi	箸
Cocktail	kak-te-ru	カクテル
Dinner	yu-sho-ku	夕食
Excuse me!	su-mi-ma-sen	すみません
Fork	fo-ku	フォーク
I am diabetic.	wa-ta-shi wa to-nyo-byo de-su	私は糖尿病です。
I am dieting.	dai-et-to chu de-su	ダイエット中です。
I am a vegetarian.	sai-sho-ku shu-gi-sha de-su	菜食主義者です。
I cannot eat . . .	. . . wa ta-be-ra-re-ma-sen	......は食べられません。
I'd like to order.	chu-mon o shi-tai desu	注文をしたいです。
I'd like . . .	. . . o o-ne-gai-shi-ma-su	......をお願いします。
I'm hungry.	o-na-ka ga su-i-te i-ma-su	お腹が空いています。
I'm thirsty.	no-do ga ka-wai-te i-ma-su	喉が渇いています。
It's good/bad.	oi-shi-i/ma-zu-i de-su	おいしい／まずいです。
Knife	nai-fu	ナイフ
Lunch	chu-sho-ku	昼食
Menu	men-yu	メニュー
Napkin	nap-kin	ナプキン
Pepper	ko-sho	こしょう
Please give me . . .	. . . o ku-da-sai.	......を下さい。
Salt	shi-o	塩
Set menu	tei-sho-ku	定食
Spoon	su-pun	スプーン
Sugar	sa-to	砂糖
Wine list	wain ris-to	ワインリスト
What do you recommend?	o-su-su-me ryo-ri wa nan de-ska	お勧め料理は何ですか。

Meat Dishes 肉料理

焼き肉	yakiniku	Thinly sliced beef and liver are marinated then barbecued over an open fire at the table.

すき焼き	sukiyaki	Thinly sliced beef, green onions, mushrooms, thin noodles, and cubes of tofu are simmered in a large iron pan in front of you. These ingredients are cooked in a mixture of soy sauce, mirin (cooking wine), and a little sugar. You are given a saucer of raw egg to cool the sukiyaki morsels before eating. Using chopsticks, you help yourself to anything on your side of the pan and dip it into the egg and then eat. Best enjoyed in a group.
しゃぶしゃぶ	shabu-shabu	Extremely thin slices of beef are plunged for an instant into boiling water flavored with soup stock and then dipped into a thin sauce and eaten.
肉じゃが	niku-jaga	Beef and potatoes stewed together with soy sauce.
ステーキ	suteki	steak
ハンバーグ	hambagu	Hamburger pattie served with sauce.
トンカツ	tonkatsu	Breaded deep fried pork cutlets.
しょうが焼	shoga-yaki	Pork cooked with ginger.
酢豚	subuta	Sweet and sour pork, originally a Chinese dish.
からあげ	kara-age	fried chicken
焼き鳥	yakitori	Pieces of chicken, white meat, liver, skin, etc. threaded on skewers with green onions and marinated in sweet soy sauce and grilled.
親子どんぶり	oyako-domburi	Literally, "mother and child bowl"—chicken and egg in broth over rice.
他人どんぶり	tanin-domburi	Literally, "strangers in a bowl"—similar to oyako domburi, but with beef instead of chicken.
ロール・キャベツ	roru kyabetsu	Rolled cabbage; beef or pork rolled in cabbage and cooked.
はやしライス	hayashi raisu	Beef flavored with tomato and soy sauce with onions and peas over rice.
カレーライス	kare-raisu	Curried rice. A thick curry gravy typically containing beef is poured over white rice.
カツカレー	katsu-kare	Curried rice with tonkatsu.
お好み焼き	okonomiyaki	Sometimes called a Japanese pancake, this is made from a batter of flour, egg, cabbage, and meat or seafood, grilled then covered with green onions and a special sauce.
シューマイ	shumai	Shrimp or pork wrapped in a light dough and steamed.
ギョーザ	gyoza	Pork spiced with ginger and garlic in a Chinese wrapper and fried or steamed.

Seafood Dishes 魚貝類料理

焼き魚	yakizakana	broiled fish
塩焼	shio yaki	Fish sprinkled with salt and broiled until crisp.
さんま	samma	saury pike
いわし	iwashi	sardines
しゃけ	shake	salmon
照り焼き	teriyaki	Fish basted in soy sauce and broiled.
ぶり	buri	yellowtail
煮魚	nizakana	stewed fish
さばのみそ煮	saba no miso ni	Mackerel stewed with soy-bean paste.
揚げ魚	agezakana	fried fish
かれいフライ	kare furai	fried halibut
刺身	sashimi	Very fresh raw fish. Served sliced thin on a bed of white radish with a saucer of soy sauce and horseradish. Eaten by dipping fish into soy sauce mixed with horseradish.
まぐろ	maguro	tuna
あまえび	amaebi	sweet shrimp
いか	ika	squid
たこ	tako	octopus
あじ	aji	horse mackerel
さわら	sawara	Spanish mackerel
しめさば	shimesaba	Mackerel marinated in vinegar.
かつおたたき	katsuo no tataki	Bonito cooked just slightly on the surface. Eaten with cut green onions and thin soy sauce.
どじょうの柳川なべ	dojo no yanagawa nabe	Loach cooked with burdock root and egg in an earthen dish. Considered a delicacy.
うな重	una-ju	Eel marinated in a slightly sweet soy sauce is charcoal-broiled and served over rice. Considered a delicacy.
天重	ten-ju	Deep fried prawns served over rice with sauce.
海老フライ	ebi furai	Deep fried breaded prawns.
あさりの酒蒸し	asari no sakamushi	Clams steamed with rice wine.

Sushi 寿司

寿司	sushi	Basically, sushi is rice, fish, and vegetables. The rice is delicately seasoned with vinegar, salt, and sugar. There are basically three types of sushi: nigiri, chirashi, and maki.

にぎり寿司	nigiri zushi	The rice is formed into a bite-sized cake and topped with various raw or cooked fish. The various types are usually named after the fish, but not all are fish. Nigiri zushi is eaten by picking up the cakes with chopsticks or the fingers, dipping the fish side in soy sauce, and eating.
まぐろ	maguro	tuna
とろ	toro	fatty tuna
たい	tai	red snapper
さば	saba	mackerel
こはだ	kohada	gizzard shad
さけ	sake	salmon
はまち	hamachi	yellowtail
ひらめ	hirame	flounder
あじ	aji	horse mackerel
たこ	tako	octopus
あなご	anago	sea eel
えび	ebi	shrimp
甘えび	ama-ebi	sweet shrimp
いか	ika	squid
みる貝	miru-gai	giant clam
あおやぎ	aoyagi	round clam
卵	tamago	egg
かずのこ	kazunoko	herring roe
かに	kani	crab
ほたて貝	hotate-gai	scallop
うに	uni	sea urchin
いくら	ikura	salmon roe
ちらしずし	chirashi sushi	In chirashi sushi, a variety of seafood is arranged on the top of the rice and served in a bowl.
巻き寿司	maki sushi	Raw fish and vegetables or other morsels are rolled in sushi rice and wrapped in dried seaweed. Some popular varieties are listed here.
鉄火巻	tekka-maki	tuna roll
かっぱ巻	kappa-maki	cucumber roll
新香巻	shinko-maki	shinko roll (shinko is a type of pickle)
カリフォルニア巻	kariforunia-maki	California roll, containing crabmeat and avocado. This was invented in the U.S. but was re-exported to Japan and is gaining popularity there.
うに	uni	Sea urchin on rice wrapped with seaweed.

| いくら | ikura | Salmon roe on rice wrapped with seaweed. |
| 太巻 | futomaki | Big roll with egg and pickled vegetables. |

Vegetable Dishes 野菜料理

おでん	oden	Often sold by street vendors at festivals and in parks, etc., this is vegetables, octopus, or egg in a thick batter and boiled.
天ぷら	tempura	Vegetables, shrimp, or fish deep fried in a light batter. Eaten by dipping into a thin sauce containing grated white radish.
野菜サラダ	yasai sarada	vegetable salad
大学いも	daigaku imo	fried yams in a sweet syrup
野菜いため	yasai itame	"stir-fried" vegetables
きんぴらごぼう	kimpira gobo	Carrots and burdock root, fried with soy sauce.
煮もの	nimono	stewed vegetables
かぼちゃ	kabocha	pumpkin
さといも	satoimo	taro root
たけのこ	takenoko	bamboo shoots
ごぼう	gobo	burdock root
れんこん	renkon	lotus root
酢のもの	sumono	Vegetables seasoned with vinegar.
きゅうり	kyuri	cucumber
和えもの	aemono	Vegetables and fish mixed with miso or vinegar.
ねぎ	tamanegi	onions
おひたし	ohitashi	Boiled vegetables with soy sauce and dried shaved bonito or sesame seeds.
ほうれん草	horenso	spinach
漬物	tsukemono	Japanese pickles. Made from white radish, eggplant or other vegetables. Considered essential to the Japanese meal.

Egg Dishes 卵料理

ベーコン・エッグ	bekon-eggu	bacon and eggs
ハム・エッグ	hamu-eggu	ham and eggs
スクランブルエッグ	sukuramburu eggu	scrambled eggs
ゆで卵	yude tamago	boiled eggs
目玉焼	medama-yaki	fried eggs, sunny-side up
オムレツ	omuretsu	omelet
オムライス	omuraisu	Omelet with rice inside, often eaten with ketchup.
茶わんむし	chawan mushi	Vegetables, shrimp, etc., steamed in egg custard.

Tofu Dishes 豆腐料理

Tofu, also called bean curd, is a white, high-protein food with the consistency of soft gelatin.

冷やっこ	hiya-yakko	Cold tofu with soy sauce and grated ginger.
湯どうふ	yudofu	boiled tofu
あげだしどうふ	agedashi dofu	Lightly fried plain tofu dipped in soy sauce and grated ginger.
マーボーどうふ	mabo dofu	Tofu and ground pork in a spicy red sauce. Originally a Chinese dish.
とうふの田楽	tofu no dengaku	Tofu broiled on skewers and flavored with miso.

Rice Dishes ごはん料理

ごはん	gohan	steamed white rice
おにぎり	onigiri	Triangular balls of rice with fish or vegetables inside and wrapped in a type of seaweed.
おかゆ	okayu	rice porridge
チャーハン	chahan	Fried rice; includes vegetables and pork.
ちまき	chimaki	A type of onigiri made with sweet rice.
パン	pan	Bread, but usually rolls with a meal.

Soups 汁もの

みそ汁	miso shiru	Miso soup. A thin broth containing tofu, mushrooms, or other morsels in a soup flavored with miso or soy-bean paste. The morsels are taken out of the bowl and the soup is drunk straight from the bowl without a spoon.
すいもの	suimono	Soy sauce flavored soup, often including fish and tofu.
とん汁	tonjiru	Pork soup with vegetables.

Noodles 麺類

うどん	udon	Wide flour noodles in broth. Can be lunch in a light broth or a full dinner called "nabeyaki udon" when meat, chicken, egg, and vegetables are added.
そば	soba	Buckwheat noodles. Served in a broth like udon or, during the summer, cold on a bamboo mesh and called "zaru soba."
ラーメン	ramen	Chinese noodles in broth, often with "chashu" or roast pork. Broth is soy sauce or miso flavored.
そう麺	somen	Very thin noodles, usually served cold with a tsuyu or thin sauce. Eaten during the summer.
ひやむぎ	hiyamugi	Similar to somen, but made from wheat.

| やきそば | yakisoba | Noodles fried with beef and cabbage, garnished with pickled ginger and flavored with Worcestershire sauce. |
| スパゲッティ | supagetti | Spaghetti. There are many interesting variations on this dish, notably spaghetti in soup, often with seafood. |

Fruit 果物

アーモンド	amondo	almonds
あんず	anzu	apricot
バナナ	banana	banana
ぶどう	budo	grapes
グレープフルーツ	gurepufurutsu	grapefruit
干しぶどう	hoshibudo	raisins
いちご	ichigo	strawberries
いちじく	ichijiku	figs
かき	kaki	persimmons
キーウイ	kiiui	kiwi
ココナツ	kokonatsu	coconut
くり	kuri	chestnuts
くるみ	kurumi	walnuts
マンゴ	mango	mango
メロン	meron	melon
みかん	mikan	tangerine (mandarin orange)
桃	momo	peach
梨	nashi	pear
オレンジ	orenji	orange
パイナップル	painappuru	pineapple
パパイヤ	papaiya	papaya
ピーナッツ	piinattsu	peanuts
プルーン	purun	prunes
レモン	remon	lemon
りんご	ringo	apple
さくらんぼ	sakurambo	cherry
西瓜	suika	watermelon

Dessert デザート類

アイスクリーム	aisukuriimu	ice cream
プリン	purin	caramel pudding
クレープ	kurepu	crêpes
ケーキ	keki	cake
シャーベット	shabetto	sherbet
アップルパイ	appuru pai	apple pie

ようかん	yokan	sweet bean paste jelly
コーヒーゼリ	kohii zeri	coffee-flavored gelatin
和菓子	wagashi	Japanese sweets

Drinks 飲物

Alcoholic 酒類

ビール	biiru	beer
生ビール	nama biiru	draft beer
カクテル	kakuteru	cocktail
ウィスキー	uisukii	whisky
スコッチ	sukotchi	scotch
バーボン	babon	bourbon
日本酒（酒） あつかん ひや	nihonshu (sake) atsukan hiya	Sake, a wine brewed from rice. warmed sake cold sake
焼酎	shochu	Spirit distilled from potatoes.
チューハイ	chuhai	Shochu mixed with soda water and flavored with lemon juice or other flavors.
ワイン 赤 白 ロゼ	wain aka shiro roze	wine red white rose
シャンペン	shampen	champagne
ブランデー	burande	brandy

Non-alcholic その他の飲物

コーヒー	kohii	coffee
アイスコーヒー	aisu kohii	iced coffee
日本茶	nihon cha	Japanese green tea
紅茶	kocha	tea
レモンティー	remon tii	tea with lemon
ミルクティー	miruku tii	tea with milk
アイスティー	aisu tii	iced tea
ウーロン茶	uron cha	oolong tea
ジャスミン茶	jasumin cha	jasmine tea
牛乳／ミルク	gyunyu/miruku	milk
ココア	kokoa	hot chocolate
レモンスカッシュ	remon sukasshu	carbonated lemon soft drink
ミルクセーキ	miruku seki	milk shake
ジュース	jusu	juice, but can also mean any soft drink
レモネード	remonedo	lemonade

Index

Personal Itinerary

Departure *Date*

Time

Transportation

Arrival *Date* *Time*

Departure *Date* *Time*

Transportation

Accommodations

Arrival *Date* *Time*

Departure *Date* *Time*

Transportation

Accommodations

Arrival *Date* *Time*

Departure *Date* *Time*

Transportation

Accommodations

Personal Itinerary

Arrival *Date* _____ *Time* _____

Departure *Date* _____ *Time* _____

Transportation _____

_____

_____

Accommodations _____

_____

_____

Arrival *Date* _____ *Time* _____

Departure *Date* _____ *Time* _____

Transportation _____

_____

_____

Accommodations _____

_____

_____

Arrival *Date* _____ *Time* _____

Departure *Date* _____ *Time* _____

Transportation _____

_____

_____

Accommodations _____

_____

_____

Arrival *Date* _____ *Time* _____

Departure *Date* _____ *Time* _____

Transportation _____

_____

_____

Accommodations _____

_____

_____

Addresses

Name	*Name*
Address	*Address*
Telephone	*Telephone*
Name	*Name*
Address	*Address*
Telephone	*Telephone*
Name	*Name*
Address	*Address*
Telephone	*Telephone*
Name	*Name*
Address	*Address*
Telephone	*Telephone*
Name	*Name*
Address	*Address*
Telephone	*Telephone*
Name	*Name*
Address	*Address*
Telephone	*Telephone*
Name	*Name*
Address	*Address*
Telephone	*Telephone*
Name	*Name*
Address	*Address*
Telephone	*Telephone*

Fodor's Travel Guides

Available at bookstores everywhere, or call 1–800–533–6478, 24 hours a day.

U.S. Guides

Alaska

Arizona

Boston

California

Cape Cod, Martha's Vineyard, Nantucket

The Carolinas & the Georgia Coast

Chicago

Colorado

Florida

Hawaii

Las Vegas, Reno, Tahoe

Los Angeles

Maine, Vermont, New Hampshire

Maui

Miami & the Keys

New England

New Orleans

New York City

Pacific North Coast

Philadelphia & the Pennsylvania Dutch Country

The Rockies

San Diego

San Francisco

Santa Fe, Taos, Albuquerque

Seattle & Vancouver

The South

The U.S. & British Virgin Islands

The Upper Great Lakes Region

USA

Vacations in New York State

Vacations on the Jersey Shore

Virginia & Maryland

Waikiki

Walt Disney World and the Orlando Area

Washington, D.C.

Foreign Guides

Acapulco, Ixtapa, Zihuatanejo

Australia & New Zealand

Austria

The Bahamas

Baja & Mexico's Pacific Coast Resorts

Barbados

Berlin

Bermuda

Brazil

Brittany & Normandy

Budapest

Canada

Cancun, Cozumel, Yucatan Peninsula

Caribbean

China

Costa Rica, Belize, Guatemala

The Czech Republic & Slovakia

Eastern Europe

Egypt

Euro Disney

Europe

Europe's Great Cities

Florence & Tuscany

France

Germany

Great Britain

Greece

The Himalayan Countries

Hong Kong

India

Ireland

Israel

Italy

Japan

Kenya & Tanzania

Korea

London

Madrid & Barcelona

Mexico

Montreal & Quebec City

Morocco

Moscow & St. Petersburg

The Netherlands, Belgium & Luxembourg

New Zealand

Norway

Nova Scotia, Prince Edward Island & New Brunswick

Paris

Portugal

Provence & the Riviera

Rome

Russia & the Baltic Countries

Scandinavia

Scotland

Singapore

South America

Southeast Asia

Spain

Sweden

Switzerland

Thailand

Tokyo

Toronto

Turkey

Vienna & the Danube Valley

Yugoslavia

Special Series

Fodor's Affordables

Caribbean

Europe

Florida

France

Germany

Great Britain

London

Italy

Paris

**Fodor's Bed &
Breakfast and
Country Inns Guides**

Canada's Great
Country Inns

California

Cottages, B&Bs and
Country Inns of
England and Wales

Mid-Atlantic Region

New England

The Pacific
Northwest

The South

The Southwest

The Upper Great
Lakes Region

The West Coast

The Berkeley Guides

California

Central America

Eastern Europe

France

Germany

Great Britain &
Ireland

Mexico

Pacific Northwest &
Alaska

San Francisco

**Fodor's Exploring
Guides**

Australia

Britain

California

The Caribbean

Florida

France

Germany

Ireland

Italy

London

New York City

Paris

Rome

Singapore & Malaysia

Spain

Thailand

Fodor's Flashmaps

New York

Washington, D.C.

Fodor's Pocket Guides

Bahamas

Barbados

Jamaica

London

New York City

Paris

Puerto Rico

San Francisco

Washington, D.C.

Fodor's Sports

Cycling

Hiking

Running

Sailing

The Insider's Guide
to the Best Canadian
Skiing

Skiing in the USA
& Canada

**Fodor's Three-In-Ones
(guidebook, language
cassette, and phrase
book)**

France

Germany

Italy

Mexico

Spain

**Fodor's
Special-Interest
Guides**

Accessible USA

Cruises and Ports
of Call

Euro Disney

Halliday's New
England Food
Explorer

Healthy Escapes

London Companion

Shadow Traffic's New
York Shortcuts and
Traffic Tips

Sunday in New York

Walt Disney World
and the Orlando Area

Walt Disney World
for Adults

**Fodor's Touring
Guides**

Touring Europe

Touring USA:
Eastern Edition

**Fodor's Vacation
Planners**

Great American
Vacations

National Parks
of the East

National Parks
of the West

**The Wall Street
Journal Guides to
Business Travel**

Europe

International Cities

Pacific Rim

USA & Canada

WHEREVER YOU TRAVEL, *H*ELP IS NEVER FAR AWAY.

From planning your trip to providing travel assistance along the way, American Express® Travel Service Offices* are always there to help.

Japan

FUKUOKA
1-3 Shimo-Kawabata-Cho
Hakata-Ku
(92) 272-2111

KYOTO
52 Daikoku-Cho, Sanjo Sagaru
Kawaramachi Dori, Nakagyo-Ku
(75) 212-3677

NAGOYA
Nagoya Hirokoji Bldg., First Floor
2-3-1 Sakae Naka-Ku
(52) 204-2246

OSAKA
Ushu,Honmachi Bldg.
3-1-6 Honmachi, Chuo-Ku
(6) 264-6300

SAPPORO
Onose Bldg., First Floor
Nishi 3-Chome, Kita 3-Jou
(11) 251-0057

TOKYO
Yurakucho-Denki Bldg.
1-7-1 Yurakucho, Chiyoda-Ku
(3) 3214-0280

American Express Tower
4-30-16 Ogikubo, Suginami-Ku
(3) 3220-6010

Shinjuku Gomeikan Bldg., First Floor
3-3-9 Shinjuku, Shinjuku-Ku
(3) 3352-1555

Toranomon Mitsui Bldg.
3-8-1 Kasumigaseki, Chiyoda-Ku
(3) 3504-3004

OKINAWA

Okinawa Tourist Service
2-3 Matsuo 1-Chome, Naha City
(98) 862-1111

Okinawa Tourist Service
241 Aza-Yamazato, Okinawa City
(98) 933-1152

thinks much about his own rights and is always ready to assert them. But he does not think so much about the rights of others."[36]

The Male Ego

The bumps, ogles, and blares of anarchic individualism assaulted those who worked, shopped, and strolled downtown. The fights for wall space, a vending spot, or a piece of government property were constant and often nasty. Yet quarrels rarely provoked fisticuffs among the upper classes, who had too much to lose by acting rashly. The occasional duel was a calmer and more civilized affair. Justo Sierra served as a witness to one such battle on the *campo de honor* (field of honor), when, after an exchange of harsh words in public, two dueling writers shot at each other; one never wrote again.[37]

The middle and working classes of Santa María and Guerrero were less opposed to settling differences with their fists. And spontaneous violence was often the only tool of negotiation in the eastern barrios, where "each street," wrote politician and criminologist Miguel Macedo, "is completely filled with a veritable swarm of ragged men, women, and children who get easily stirred up by jests and gibes, and where hurt feelings often turn into bloody calamities among this multitude that gives not a thought to tomorrow and takes liberty as a license for disorder." Minor disagreements, observed Macedo, often triggered violent reactions:

> The fights that result in so many of the serious injuries and deaths that occur in Mexico are caused by trivial incidents, usually accidental and spontaneous, and rarely a result of long-standing problems. A mishap in the street, a difference of opinion, an impolitic word or a strange look — these cause the fights that take so many of the lives . . . of our lower classes. The crime happens rapidly, without antecedents, and explodes just as easily on a friend as on a stranger.[38]

There were plenty of irksome if potentially harmless mishaps in the streets of Mexico City that the twitchy male ego turned into violent confrontations. Being a man in Mexico, even an upper-class one, meant having to prove oneself continually. Manhood was twisted into machismo, Juan Tablada remembers, at an early age: "Manhood and masculinity were virtually synonymous with depravity and rule breaking. Before your first cigarette, drink, or woman, your older friends, who had proudly done it all before, invariably said 'Do it! Or you're no man!' And fearing the epithets of 'faggot,' 'pussy,' and 'wimp,' the neophyte had to endure the physical and moral nausea that tobacco, alcohol, and the crude manners of a whore might cause in an adolescent."[39]

These were the lessons that prepared boys for a world in which a man did not tolerate furtive looks or ambiguous words. *Ser muy hombre*, to be a real man, was a "hallowed phrase." It meant never back down, or *rajarse*, as Mexicans still say. A real man did not yield on the streets, unless he wanted to make a special show of his power through chivalry; once cornered, he would fight to the finish; and if jailed, he would admit no wrong. The idea, wrote Macedo, was to impose oneself on others "at whatever cost, even by taking someone's life, which you respect just as you do your own — that is, scarcely at all." This meant fighting without purpose and killing without reason: a shoemaker stabs his journeyman because he refuses to work at night, a man in a *pulquería* kills another for looking at him the wrong way, a customer shoots a clerk for giving him incorrect change.[40] Individualism without privacy, egos without restraint. Here was the combination that made Mexico City so dangerous.

The pugnacity of the male, according to Samuel Ramos, was a consequence of his deep-seated mistrust.[41] It was mistrust of a man's enemies, his friends, and his women. Criminologist Julio Guerrero sought to explain why "the inherited Spanish jealousies" had only worsened throughout the nineteenth century, and how "infidelity had become a motive for the injured man to seek a vengeance sanctioned by custom if not by law — a bloody vengeance carried out by his own hand." Between independence and Díaz's first presidency, Mexico was in a chronic state of civil war and suffered two foreign invasions. For almost three generations the meanings of "honor" had been defined largely by generals, robbers, and tyrants. Because every man shared his ordeals, and military and political secrets, with his woman, her adultery was a double betrayal: "it not only stained her man's honor, but let into the home a possible enemy."[42] And that could be deadly, for a treacherous act or a costly error committed by a soldier, a fellow thief, or a political ally was avenged by first taking the perpetrator's life, and then by confiscating his wife, mistress, or daughters.

Betrayal and mistrust, therefore, were the twin themes of the nineteenth century. Virtually every independence hero was betrayed to the firing squad. After defeating the French in 1867, and having discredited the Conservatives as accomplices, the Liberals then turned on each other with untold acts of calumny and treachery. And President Porfirio Díaz, perhaps fearing betrayal himself, intentionally ruined the reputation of Manuel González, his closest military comrade, political advisor, and apparent best friend.[43]

Most men suspected that every other was on the hunt, and that their main quarry was women. Even refined aristocrats "admired" young ladies with provocative stares and suggestive words, which their elders saw as a debased and rude form of chivalry.[44] Yet the older generation's gallantry also combined the same indulgence of women, at least in the courting stages, with a severe distrust of men. Tablada, for example, tells a story of a young man who, one misty day at the beginning of Díaz's rule, stopped his horse beneath a woman's balcony on a downtown street. She threw down a rope, to which he fastened a bottle of cognac. Hearing the laughs of neighbors, she shut her balcony door after securing the gift. "Tipping back his huge flopping sombrero, the rider faced down the nearest group of men, staring at them long and hard, before spurring his horse and galloping away. Yet the laughs were not mocking, but sympathetic. Mexico still indulged such dare-devilry, perhaps because our society had yet to perfect civilized urban protocol."[45]

Gallantry continued throughout Díaz's rule. If a man's sense of honor (which in Mexico was a public affair, not a personal concern) was called into question, or given a chance to shine, he would challenge another man's right to his woman. "Our race," wrote Rubén Campos, "makes a fetish of gallantry":

If a woman asks a Mexican man, whom she barely knows, for favor and protection, he will give it even at the cost of his life. If a woman (young and beautiful, of course), asks for the protection of an unknown against even her own lord and master, the Mexican (young and fearless, of course), readies himself for the task and pathetically calls the offending man to account, all the while being careful to do so politely. We Mexicans handle these situations as if we were living in the Middle Ages; we use the same high-sounding and courteous, if provocative, words of the old knighted gentlemen. Even a mellow old man will always rush to the side of a woman. Only the old-timer might play Odysseus instead of Ajax.[46]

The question of paternity—of the man himself, of his children, and of his grandchildren—was of course a difficult one. Even for a wealthy male who was able to keep strict control of his woman, there was no greater torment than his thinking that a rival, perhaps only through an oblique look, was insinuating cuckoldry or questioning his paternity. The entire mestizo race, after all, was founded on the taking of Indians by the conquering Spaniards. During colonial times the racial prerogatives afforded to Spanish officials and creole landlords generally allowed them to take Indian or mestizo women as they pleased. During much of the nineteenth century, when soldiers were away from their wives, lovers, and daughters for long stretches, rape and pillage were the unwritten laws of the land. And throughout the Porfiriato rural landowners had certain rights to the women who lived on their haciendas and in surrounding villages. Even in the capital city, economic clout implied a kind of coercive sexual power. Mestizo and Indian servants were often sexual targets in the middle- and upper-class homes they cleaned. The constant suspicion of infidelity and the gnawing doubts about paternity seem reasonable given the high rates of illegitimate births, the fact that only 15 percent of children born out of wedlock were recognized by both father and mother, and the many novels that featured fornication and adultery among aristocrats, the middle classes, and the eastern poor.[47]

There was a particularly savage form of control that was related, if only distantly, to the male's general behavior toward women. Many men turned on the city's vagabond dogs, who were apparently treated with "extraordinary cruelty."[48] Ángel del Campo wrote a popular story about one of those dogs, which has since become famous:

> He was a street dog, skinny, with straight and pointy ears, lively eyes, a sharp snout, bristly hair, thin paws and a droopy tail. He had the look of an Indian dog—the look of a wolf; he got his name, Pinto, because he was dirty yellow with black stains. . . . What did he get to eat? If he waited at the front door of a restaurant, they went at him with the charcoal tongs. If he went to a butcher shop, they kicked him. If he found a bone, a more famished yet stronger dog snatched it from him. . . . He might follow someone home, but that person, when he got to his house, would kick him or shut the door in his snout. . . . One morning a man called out to him and threw him a piece of meat. At last there was someone who would save him from his hunger. Pinto never felt better as he sniffed the fresh meat and then wolfed it down. Suddenly a shooting pain leaped through his veins, his insides were exploding, he stumbled and fell. He had been poisoned! The trash cart was his coffin, the dump his cemetery.[49]

Deadly Rituals

"The ruthless display of bloody carcasses in the butcher shop . . . the news-display of the most gruesome pictures of any murder or accident, the permitting of beggars on the street with the most loathsome malformations and diseases; the repulsive sanguinary images of the crucified Christ—all express a secret passion for the horrible." That was the view of journalist Carleton Beals, an American; but the Mexican Julio Guerrero also saw in such displays the same inveterate fetish with death: "the bloody and bellicose ways of the savage," he wrote, "are still at large."[50]

Whether or not that is true, it is a fact that their violent history had sown deep mistrust among Mexicans while giving them a penchant for the images of gore, savagery, and death. Consider the main historical phases that preceded Díaz's reign. Tenochtitlan's largest monuments were built for Huitzilopochtli, the god of war, who compelled the Aztecs to conquer other tribes—not for resources, territory, or laborers, but for captives to be slaughtered in his honor. The Spaniards defeated the Indian empire with horses, smallpox, and the spite of tens of thousands of disaffected Aztec vassals. They then built a colonial government that, while far less savage than the Aztec state, tyrannized its orphaned subjects for three centuries. Mestizos fighting for independence cried, "Long live the Virgin of Guadalupe! Death to the Bad Government! Death to the Spanish!"[51] Once free, those Mexicans fought among themselves for most of another century, a period of chaos, wrote a daily in 1886, that had left its mark on the Mexican character: "Owing to the cruel and bitter history of the last sixty or so years, Mexico is an unhappy and miserable country that does not deserve a place among civilized nations."[52]

Díaz managed to expel the last foreign intruders, quell the conflicts between factions of the upper classes, wipe out the bandits who plagued the countryside, and restrain the violence of the state. But he could not void the cruelty in his country's past: "The source of our crime and violence" wrote Guerrero in 1901, "is innate."[53] Just when it looked as if the violence had been tamed, or at least confined to personal disputes, the revolution that turned Díaz out in 1911 saw a million Mexicans dead in less than a decade. Like the bloody cry of independence in 1810, or the clergy's banner of "Long Live Religion! Death to Tolerance!" at the 1857 constitutional convention, the call for revolution was a negative one. Don Ramón, in D. H. Lawrence's *The Plumed Serpent*, says, "Whenever a Mexican cries *Viva!* he ends up with *Muera!* When he says *Viva!* he really means *Death for Somebody or Other!* If I think of all the Mexican revolutions, I see a skeleton walking ahead of a great number of people, waving a black banner with *Viva la Muerte!* written in large white letters. *Long Live Death!*"[54]

Death meant funerals, and funerals were public spectacles. The first part of a service, especially among the lower classes, was the old custom of the *velorio*, the laying of the deceased on a table, surrounding him or her with candles, and inviting kin, friends, and acquaintances to observe the body and pay their respects to its soul over the course of several days. These solemn occasions, observed Guerrero, "would frequently degenerate into bloody bacchanals that occur around the deceased in the yellow, hazy candle-light."[55] Even so, the event was attended with great solemnity, and even the poor tried to scrape up enough money to paste posters on neighborhood walls, print advertisements in the newspapers, or send personal invitations

> in big, black-bordered envelopes [that] are usually decorated with a picture of a tomb. The information is conveyed in faultless Spanish, that Señor Don Jesús Santa María Hidalgo died yesterday at noon, and that his bereaved wife, who mourns under the name of 'Doña María José Concepción de los Ángeles Narro Henriandos y Hidalgo,' together with his family, desire you to honor them by participating in the ceremonies of burial, and in supplicating the Mother of God and the Redeemer of the world to grant the soul of the dead husband a speedy release from the pains of Purgatory, and eternal bliss in Paradise.[56]

Most bodies were buried in Dolores Cemetery, which was just south of Chapultepec Park; the rich were interred in outlying graveyards like Tepeyac, around Guadalupe, or in the Spanish burial ground just beyond the nearby town of Tacuba. Coffins went to their appointed cemeteries in open hearses that prominently displayed their flower-strewn and canopied contents as they moved slowly through the city. The wealthy often indulged in a black hearse, which was plumed, draped, and liveried, and often hired an additional car or two for friends. The middle and lower classes rented plainer, mule-drawn versions of the same. The poor leased handsome coffins and cheap hearses, and transferred the body from its temporary casket to a basic pine box before depositing it in the grave. Only *pelados*, who were generally Indians, did not take their last trip in a hearse. They were laid out in humble coffins and carried on the shoulders of friends. Just before a coffin was lowered into the earth, the nearest relative unfastened it—the coffin was never screwed down, but secured by a lock whose key was held by the chief mourner—so that the manager of the cemetery could look inside and satisfy himself that it contained the right corpse. Friends would also identify the body, after which the casket was relocked. When the coffin had been finally laid to rest, the key was given back to the chief mourner.[57]

The city's dead were mourned collectively on the Día de los Muertos (Day of the Dead). Women burned smoky candles around framed prints of the Virgin of Guadalupe. Children played with toy figurines of devils and hearses. Cakes and breads were shaped as skulls, given ghoulish eyes of maraschino cherries, and painted with eerie, syrupy grins. Indians peddled candy coffins in the Zócalo.[58] And mourning picnickers, wrote a newspaper, jammed Dolores Cemetery:

> All Souls' Day is given over the common herd, to honor their dead . . . The custom in Mexico on All Souls' Day (Nov. 2) is to go to the cemetery and deposit wreaths and candles on and about the graves of the dead. The lower classes then retire to the grave of someone else's dead, and then, seated upon the headstone or even upon the mound, enjoy a big meal of "pan de los muertos" [dead man's bread] and other good things, typical dishes like mole de guajolote [turkey with mole sauce], etc. This appropriation of other graves as lunching places often leads to grave disputes with the offended representatives of the family, and bloody battles are rather the rule than the exception in the cemeteries on All Souls' Day.[59]

Mexicans took every opportunity to consecrate the darker side of life. Even the ascension of Jesus was celebrated primarily as a public execution of the man who betrayed him. During Holy Week churches were shrouded, shops and stores were closed, people refused to work, and only pedestrian traffic was allowed in the city.[60] Not a church bell rang between Thursday and Saturday's Hallelujah Mass. Accustomed to hearing the bells as indicators of time, as preventers of evil, and as signs of regularity, the people filled the silence with the sounds of *matracas*, rattles that were whirled to strike a cogged wheel against a narrow projecting strip. Tens of thousands of handheld *matracas*, and some huge ones that were placed in church towers, kept up a relentless racket. Other people celebrated with various kinds of brightly painted and filigreed noisemakers, some of which boasted silver figures of *matadores* (bullfighters), *tlachiqueros*, and *aguadores*.[61]

All week long street vendors lined the Zócalo and even Alameda Park to sell figurines of the traitor by the thousands. Indians from surrounding villages and local mestizo artisans made Judas figures "according to their own ideas of ugliness. . . . Some had the faces of animals, others had merely grotesque human features, while others had bat-like wings, and horns, and hoofs; but all were ugly as sin, which is what they represented." Each was a human form — "dudes, ruffians, ass-headed beings, devils" — and often a caricature of some living person, like a politician or a policeman, or a parody of a common physical attribute, like the drinker's bulbous nose. Many wore a top hat that signified "authority." The Judas figures were generally made of cardboard frames anywhere from three or four inches to eight or ten feet in height, and they had a fuse attached to the mustache or the finger-tips that ran, with strong explosives attached along the line, completely around the body.[62]

Judases had been burned and exploded regulary since the 1850s. They were banned from the Plateros strip by 1900, however, and never made it to the neighborhoods along Reforma. But almost everywhere else, throughout Díaz's tenure, Holy Saturday was devoted to the humiliation and murder of the renegade.

Revenge for an act of betrayal: it answered a need deep in Mexican history. Tens of thousands of children carried around explosive figurines, and hundreds of effigies commissioned by local shopkeepers and *pulqueros* were hung by wire across streets or lifted up on poles. Judas was usually portrayed "with folded hands, arms akimbo, with legs in running posture and in every conceivable attitude. Some of them," continued an observer, "bear suggestive mottoes such as 'I am a scion of the Devil' and 'Let me give up the Ghost.' Each person must destroy a Judas." Most people did just that, on Saturday morning, as the church bells pealed for the first time in two days. On Tacuba Street, just northwest of the Zócalo, "stretched on wires on strings from one house to the other were bright-colored, hideous figures, representing the maldito [accursed one] dangling in grotesque attitudes against the blue sky. On various street corners he is being burned in effigy. Firecrackers are exploding . . . bells are ringing from every belfry. Grief is noisy in the tropics." Noisy, and frantic, too. As the Judases exploded, many participants "were wrought up to a pitch of religious frenzy, and if an arm or a leg was thrown off intact they seized and tore it with their teeth, as if it were in truth a part of the misguided traitor of centuries ago." Because many effigies were filled with meat, soap, bread, candy, and sometimes coins, people scrambled madly after them, risking injury from the explosions, and each other.[63]

The rich had their fun with Judas, too. The government and the church conspired in the late 1890s to outlaw Judas burnings from the downtown, but not before some of the wealthy had a few good years of exploding their own effigies. Members of the Jockey Club used to hang and detonate Judases that were holding bags of centavos or had coins pasted on their clothing. They laughed from the balcony as the mob rushed for the coins, and then tossed down more to incite further trampling, shoving, and punching. Each year the crowd grew larger, the disorder escalated, and the number of injuries increased from the explosions and the ensuing rush for money. In 1893, the men of the Jockey Club pulled off their greatest stunt. They sent up an aerostat whose balloon was covered with coins and whose gondola carried four Judas figures: a mulatto, a singer, a beggar, and a butter salesman mounted on a pig; each was covered in coins. The balloon was floated over San Francisco Street above the heads of the crowd, which was described as "rabid, soulless, and maddened." When the church bells rang out the hallelujah, the Judases exploded their contents onto the streets, and the frenzied crowd rushed for the scattered coins. The clubmen, a city paper reported, "burst out in laughter and enjoyed to the fullest this savage and brutal fight that resulted in bruises, breaks, sprains, and punctured eyes."[64]

Man and Bull

Like the exploding Judases, bullfights transformed daily violence into a public spectacle. Díaz made the fights legal in 1886. For years they had been outlawed in the capital, to help soften Mexico's notorious image among the English and Americans who were being wooed as investors, and to appease those who felt, like President Díaz's wife, Carmen, that the slaying of animals in public arenas was bad for the national character. The liberal papers fulminated against the spectacles, and the church thought the fights offended not only Catholics, but all honorable people. But those same periodicals, even the ones read almost exclusively by middle- and upper-class Catholics, regularly covered bullfighting at home and in Spain. In one of the ceaseless congressional debates about the fate of bulls and men in Mexico, a congressman argued that "bullfights awaken savage instincts; and Mexicans, with so little respect for authority, only learn more contempt for it at these events." His colleague retorted by repeating the police chief's line that the fights were good because, "with five policemen I can watch five thousand *pelados*," and added that the fights diminished violence because the people who attended them had less time to commit crimes. "Was bullfighting a national custom?" another politician asked rhetorically. "In no way. We Mexicans have descended from the Aztecs, and they had no bulls."[65] Whatever Díaz thought about the fights, he legalized them in the mid-1880s, when, as William Beezely writes, "he had realigned political power, garnered a national and international reputation, and stood ready for recognition as the father of his country—who would mediate, orchestrate, reward, and punish. This new patriarch was ready for a return to ritual displays of paternalism."[66]

After 1886, partisans of the sport no longer had to leave the city to see the fights. The capital had six plazas by 1888, all but one of them on the west side. Most of these wooden rings were dilapidated or had been razed by 1899, when the more modern Plaza México was opened, and all of them were gone by 1907, when the huge Gran Plaza de Toros was erected in the southwestern barrio of Condesa. The Gran Plaza held twenty thousand spectators and was the largest structure in the world devoted solely to bull-baiting. The public spent more money in these arenas than in all the city's theaters, museums, circuses, and parks combined.[67] Everyone talked about the matches, especially during the winter fight season, and about the *toreros*, mostly Spaniards, who happened to be in town. Store shelves were full of bullfighting memorabilia, wooden bulls were favorite toys, and matadors were kids' heroes.[68]

The bullfighters were generally from the lower classes and, with few exceptions, like the Spaniard Luis Mazzantini, they were excluded from high society. They dressed in Andalusian style, hung out in bars, and often got into trouble.[69] In the 1880s and 1890s only one Mexican, Ponciano Díaz, was as popular, if not quite as good, as Spaniards like Mazzantini, Diego "Four Fingers" Prieto, and Cayetano Leal. But in 1907, nineteen-year-old Rodolfo Gaona arrived in the capital with his daring group of young Indian matadors. Gaona immediately became a national hero. He was Mexico's one true *maestro de la tauromaquia* (master bullfighter). In the 1890s aficionados would recite, out of national pride,

> I don't care for Mazzantini
> nor for Four Fingers
> who I want is Ponciano,
> the king of the fighters.

By the end of the Porfiriato they could legitimately claim that the Mexican Gaona was the greatest *torero* in Mexico.[70]

"In the fights," said the newspaper *El Imparcial*, "all are worthy of praise — the bull, the horses, the matadors. There is only one contemptible thing: the public." Lower-class taurophiles were in the pawnshops on Saturday trying to get ticket money for Sunday, when caravans of trams and carriages took off from the Zócalo in the early afternoon and unloaded their excited passengers at the west-side rings. Fans from the eastern barrios milled around the stadium — whistling, clanking cowbells, and telling lewd jokes. The lower classes filed into the arena and headed for their seats *de sol* (in the sun), which cost less than half as much as those *de sombra* (in the shade). The sunny side was a sea of men wearing conoidal straw sombreros and soft leather hats. Their shaded superiors across the way were dressed in the black, best-day suits of employees, clerks, and factory hands, sometimes accompanied by powdered women in white dresses. The upper classes looked down on it all from their shady reserved sections.[71]

Women were never taken to the sunny side, where hats were plucked off heads and sent skimming over the crowd, food was hurled at uncovered heads, and fists were thrown at impertinent faces. "The sunny side," wrote a newspaper, "from the front rows up to the roof terrace, is a colossal mass of agitated and unpredictable people, who must disgust even themselves."[72] Those seated in the lower rows of the shady side were also boisterous, for they had a chance to catch a *torero*'s hat or cloak, "to impart an impressive thwack to the bull should he leap the barrier and course through the passageway," or "pelt an inept or clumsy *torero* with oranges." But it was the sunbaked mob that got especially agitated over canceled matches, sluggish bulls, and clumsy matadors. An unruly crowd once demanded that the fighters who had canceled that day be "barbecued." Botched performances brought a hail of oranges, bottles, and even seats that were ripped up and heaved into the ring. On one occasion the crowd was upset about what they thought were costly tickets and a poor show. They threw the regular stuff, tried to burn down the stadium, and withdrew, yelling, "¡Viva Ponciano! ¡Muera Mazzantini!" Spaniards still dominated the business, so it was easy for hooligans to justify their actions by saying, "I love my country."[73]

But they all came for the show. It was man pitted against nature, a display of the key masculine virtues of Mexican society: never back down; conquer and, in this case, kill your enemy with composure, courtesy, and flair. As the crowd grew restless, the "president"—on special occasions Díaz himself, but usually a city councilman or his designated replacement—would take his seat and give the signal to start.[74] One of the city's military bands would strike up a tune to announce the procession of the *cuadrilla*, the bullfighting team. Two mounted officers dressed in black breeches would emerge from a gate beneath the president's box. After each cantered around in a semicircle on either side of the ring, they met back at the center, saluted the president, and disappeared. They reappeared together at the head of the *cuadrilla*, which was led by four to six matadors. Each wore his special hat, draped his cape over the left shoulder of a thickly embroidered jacket that covered a white shirt and tie, and sported tight, knickerslike pants that gave way to white stockings and low-cut black shoes. In sequence followed the *banderilleros*, whose job it was to stick darts in the bull's shoulders, the mounted *picadores*, who prodded and wounded the bull with thrusts of their iron-tipped pikes, and a small corps of ring attendants. Upon reaching the center of the ring they all saluted the president by doffing their caps, and the procession broke away.

As the bull entered the ring through a narrow passageway, a thin dagger with fluttering ribbons was thrust between his shoulders. Irritated, the bull snorted up a small cloud of dust from the sanded arena and trotted uncomfortably around the ring. In rode two mounted men, the *picadores*, with their feet firmly planted in large, boxed stirrups. They watched as the matador entered to taunt the bull with his cape. After the animal took several harmless passes, the great fighter left the ring to the *picadores*. Their nags, blindfolded and emaciated, did not pass their last days in tall pasture, but were served up as bullbait. One of the *picadores* advanced toward the bull and pierced his shoulder with his lance. The bull, as if stung by a great wasp, charged and rammed his horns into the horse's underside, spilling out blood and entrails onto the reddening sand. Several *banderilleros* now jumped into the ring. Aided by auxiliary fighters who distracted the bull with their capes, they took turns running upon the bull, and high on their toes with posteriors taut, their arms described long arcs as they plunged pairs of barbed darts deep into the bull's neck. His fury piqued, the bull charged the dying nag that was dragging itself out of the arena. The *picador* saw the bull rushing upon him, dismounted, and ran, leaving the horse to a deep thrust of the bull's horns. The bull furiously worked his horns up and down, ground the horse's twisted neck and head into the sand, and emptied out its body.

The roaring crowd was now as riled as the bull. The bull backed away and was distracted as attendants removed the mess. The grand matador, at a signal from the president, waved everyone out of the ring. He patiently maneuvered the bull with his cape so that he could deliver the final blow, a deep thrust of a long-bladed dirk into the animal's neck. If the job was done gracefully, the crowd applauded earnestly, and the president awarded the matador with an ear, or the tail.[75]

CHAPTER 5

Appearance & Reality

Díaz's dictatorship was characterized . . . above all, by respect for
legal forms, which were zealously observed to keep alive the idea that
Mexico's laws, if not obeyed, were respected.
— *Emilio Rabasa*, La evolución histórica de México

On 16 September 1910, Porfirio Díaz presided over his
country's centennial celebration of independence. At no time since the city
fell into Spanish hands was it so spectacular. The municipal and national
governments had spent ten years and huge sums of money rebuilding the
downtown. They paved the streets, renovated the municipal palace, and
razed colonial hospitals to make way for theaters, ministries, and post offices.
In the weeks before the celebration, the city council prohibited all construction, put uniforms on street sweepers and trash haulers, and asked everyone — at least those in the western parts of the city — to tidy their houses,
put out flowers, and hang flags. Just as foreign dignitaries began to arrive,
the police swept *pelados* off the downtown streets and kept them out of the
west side's parks and plazas. The special day was full of parades, speeches,
and banquets. There were handshakes, backslaps, and kind words for all.
Mexico was now an adult in the family of nations, and old rivalries and conflicts were forgiven, if not forgotten. Spain returned the military uniform of
independence hero José María Morelos, who was shot by the Spaniards in
1815. "Long live your great president," exhorted the Spanish ambassador;
"Long live Spain, our great mother," answered Díaz, with a catch in his
throat. The French returned the keys to the city, which had been in Paris
since 1863. And the Americans honored the *niños héroes*, the young cadets
who died during the U.S. occupation of 1847, and paid this tribute to *el presidente:* "As Rome had Augustus, and England its Isabel and Victoria, Mexico

has Porfirio Díaz. All is well in Mexico. Under Porfirio Díaz a nation has been created."[1]

But all was not well in Mexico. Eight months later the president was sailing for France, forced out by the early rumblings of a revolution that would last for seven years, kill one in ten Mexicans, and so devastate the nation that another decade was required to regain a semblance of the "Order, Peace, and Progress" that the dictator had imposed on Mexico for thirty-five years. Díaz's regime, like his capital bedizened for the celebration, confirmed the old idea that once models or styles in politics, music, architecture — or in cities — have realized their potential, they soon degenerate. That no one could see this in a country where the disparities between the wealthy few and the destitute masses were grotesque, where the job of personally holding together such a large and rapidly changing nation was beyond even Díaz's extraordinary political skills, and where resentment of the capital's oppressive power in the provinces had reached dangerous levels was no surprise. Mexicans, no less than people anywhere else, were adept at blinding themselves to unpleasantness. But they expanded that natural, human impulse into an axiom of their culture: in Mexico, nothing was as it seemed.

The discrepancy between the apparent and the real seemed so large to Charles Flandrau, an American whose brother owned a coffee farm in eastern Mexico, that he took the phrase "¡No hay reglas fijas!" ("There are no fixed rules!") as an epitome of Díaz's republic.[2] The erratic investment practices of businessmen and the unpredictable work habits of laborers, a dictator who regularly fixed and then elaborately celebrated his own elections, a people with a weak commitment to punctuality — these gave Flandrau the impression that the behavior of Mexicans was confused, even anarchic.

Yet there were plenty of rules in Mexico City, probably more than in Flandrau's home state of Minnesota, though the American had trouble deciphering them. He thought rules and laws were to be understood literally and observed strictly. But in Mexico City, most of the rules that were followed were unwritten, and most that were written went unheeded. The unwritten rules worked to establish boundaries and secure trust. The written rules, from election statutes to hygienic codes, were always bent and often broken: "We have good laws," wrote a journalist, "but they aren't worth anything."[3] Yet lawbreaking, and the corruption that substituted for law enforcement, adhered to strict procedures of their own. In this way the law did function, if indirectly, by forcing those who twisted it to somehow create the appearance of legality, which became more important than lawfulness itself.

What fooled Flandrau, then, was that the idea in Mexico was to *appear* to be following rules. All of Díaz's elections were rigged, and all but his first broke a constitutional amendment that prohibited re-election, the very reform he fought his way into power to enact. But his electoral victories were given the semblance of legality by amendments to his amendments, and they were given legitimacy in the eyes of the people by the pageantry of power. As with rules, so with feelings: what mattered was to give the appearance of the right sentiment at the proper time. Díaz's Mexico was already famous for its courtesy. Yet the warmth and vulnerability apparently tendered by politeness actually functioned to establish distance. And the servility of poor workers and peasants masked a seething enmity for those who lorded over them.

Mexicans lived in the gaps between the spoken word and its real meaning, between the written law and its practical application, between the form of politics and the substance of statecraft, between a fawning deference to superiors and a deep resentment of authority. The world of Mexicans was oblique, emotional, and personalist. To outsiders this appeared as a lack of fixity and sincerity. But living in the gaps between one's words and true feelings helped Mexicans deflect and negotiate the mistrust and the violent encounters that lurked around every corner. And inhabiting the space between law and reality was inevitable in a divided society that tried to adopt the legal codes of Europe and the United States.

But when those gaps got squeezed a little too hard, or for too long, the apparent and the real rubbed against each other. By the end of Díaz's reign there were many among the wealthy who were no longer content with the mere façade of democracy. For more than a generation they had yielded power to a dictator in return for the stability, security, and prosperity he gave them. Now they wanted that power for themselves, and democracy was the way to get it. When Díaz told an American journalist in 1908 that he would soon offer free and fair elections, some of the wealthy, for the first time, took his word literally. And when Díaz was openly challenged by disgruntled factions of the upper classes, masses of poor country folk, who for so long had tolerated the abuses of rapacious landlords and crooked politicos, finally had an outlet for their immemorial grievances.

Words, Gestures, and Meanings

The greatest void in Mexican life lay between what was said and what was meant. "The lie," wrote Esquivel Obregón, "is the evil that has tainted all of our social life . . . and may destroy Mexico." By lying he didn't mean the manipulative act of knowingly telling a falsehood, but the Mexican custom of tailoring the truth to accommodate the audience and the circumstances at hand. To Esquivel and many others, this kind of fibbing illustrated the inability of most Mexicans to deal directly with their world, a problem that may have arisen in the sixteenth century. "The Spaniards are so haughty and cruel" wrote a Spanish judge in 1565, "that the Indians are afraid to say anything that will displease them." Like most everything else in Mexico, equivocation took a poetic form. The Mexican, wrote Flandrau, has a "genius for stringing words upon a flashing chain of shrugs and smiles—of presenting you with a verbal rosary which later you find yourself unable to tell."[4]

Visitors saw one particular form of prevarication so often that they called Mexico "the land of *no hay*"—pronounced "no eye" and meaning "there aren't any."[5] Imagine a scene in which you ask for bananas in a small neighborhood store. "No hay," says the woman. But as you lean across the counter to look over the piles of fruits and vegetables on the floor, you see a large branch of ripe bananas. "What about those?" you ask. "Oh, you want ripe bananas? All right." Make the necessary adjustments of venue, goods, and persons, and you will have a scenario that happened every day to almost everyone who shopped in Mexico City.

When Juvenal asked, "What can I do in Rome? I never learned how to lie," he was noting the traits of cleverness and deception that are integral to urban life. Merchants in Mexico City were certainly employing those kinds of smarts—to get a better price, to manipulate a desire, to generate goodwill by pretending to offer a customer the last bit of the product that he was sure to intimate he was saving for himself. But the real reason behind *no hay* was *pena*, or the fear of it. *Pena* means shame or embarrassment, but it combines the private guilt of Catholicism, the public humiliation of Puritanism, and the fear once inspired by Huitzilopochtli, the Aztec god of war. The desire to dodge *pena* affected every interaction among Mexicans, down to retail sales. The seller, for instance, might have had bananas, sombreros, or train tickets to Puebla, but not green bananas for frying, or pointy sombreros, or first-class tickets. So he said, "No hay." The customer took the cue to provide more information—that any type of sombrero would do, or only a second-class ticket was wanted. In this way the seller could offer his wares with some surety that the shopper would buy them. He thereby avoided rejection and even disapproval, which could generate conflict. The fear of *pena* got everyone to do their best to avoid any controversy, even one as slight as the refusal to buy a retailer's wares, that might bring public shame.

Every country has its own forms of politeness, but in Mexico the unwritten rules of courtesy could have filled volumes. To break those rules was to disrupt. "'No es costumbre,' a lady will tell you disdainfully, if you diverge a fraction from their most trivial social law." What the outsider saw as rigid politeness actually served as a protective coating. It did so by appearing to offer freely and publicly what was most private and hallowed. People introduced themselves with "Para servirle," "At your service." The offer was misleading because no Mexican humbled himself before an equal, never mind an underling. When first receiving a new acquaintance at home, the owner invariably issued as a welcome, "Ya tomó Usted posesión de su casa"—"You have now taken possession of your house." In reply to the question, "Where do you live?" a Mexican said, "Su casa de Usted, No. 10, a la Calle Tacuba," meaning "Your house, the house where you are welcome, is number 10 on Tacuba Street." The phrase "Mi casa está muy a su disposición," "My house is entirely at your disposal," was a common addendum to either of the above, and letters were often headed "de la casa de Usted," "from your house." Visitors often took these phrases literally, though one longtime guest knew better: "in truth the recipient of such offers would alone deceive himself should he suppose that the Mexican proposed to make him a gift of his house."[6]

It may, in fact, have been easier to get into elite circles and wealthy houses in Europe and North America than in Mexico City, where the very design of a house, like the peasant hut surrounded by cacti or agave, was meant to shield the family from society. Colonial palaces had small, usually grilled, windows, a large wooden door, and an imposing façade. The mansions along Reforma were often set back, fenced off, and fortresslike. "The windows of these mansions were always closed," wrote a contemporary, "and the doors were opened only for carriages and servants." Even the small adobe houses of the eastern slums offered but a tiny window and a heavy door to the street. Those who did get into a middle- or upper-class house never made it beyond the front living room. The *sala*, as it was called, was cold, stilted, and virtually identical from one house to the next. Except for a marble-top table placed directly beneath the chandelier, all of the furniture—typically a large sofa or two, chairs made of Austrian bentwood with rattan seats and backs, and some small tables loaded with gimcracks—was pushed up against the walls.[7]

While chatting over tea in the *sala*, a guest would invariably "just adore" the host's clothing or jewelry, or praise a wall hanging. The owner of the esteemed good then offered it immediately, but rhetorically, of course, to the admirer. "One admires a watch or a cabinet. 'It is yours,' is the prompt reply, which means nothing, it is only a figure of speech like 'I hope you are quite well.'" One's personal possessions, like the house, were freely offered up in speech. But they were as jealously guarded as the privacy of the rich dames who drove in closed carriages, even in balmy and sunny weather, and refused to leave them while shopping.[8]

Middle- and upper-class men greeted each other with a back-patting embrace that went on long enough for everyone around them to indulge in all sorts of endearing epithets. Their ladies met by kissing, the children kissed the hands of their parents, and a well-bred child said to a grownup of distinction, "I kiss your hands." If friends met five times a day, the ceremony was gone through as often. A difficult point in Mexican etiquette was that of seating a party in a restaurant or a theater. The men vied with each other, in a contest of courtesy and power that might last an entire minute, to be the last to enter and take a seat.[9] Mere acquaintances poured it on especially thick. A guest meets the hostess of an evening party:

> "Honoured madam, I feel most happy in offering myself, without novelty, to your service! I hope you are excellently well!"
>
> "At your disposal, Colonel," was the reply, "as are also my husband and my house."
>
> "Madam," continued the officer, "your most humble, dutiful servant!"
>
> "Sir, I am rejoiced!"
>
> "Madam, I have the supreme honour to kiss your feet!" (advancing a step and bowing).
>
> "Sir, I have the honour to kiss your hand!"
>
> "Madam, I have the pleasure in being your servant, and that of this honourable company."
>
> "Colonel, we are all at your service!"[10]

The flattery, the politeness, and the rhetorical gift-giving all assured potential enemies that everything was well, at least for now. The French confidently interpreted the apparently warm welcome they received upon entering the capital as occupiers. "All the 'Vivas,'" wrote a local French paper, "seemed to come from the heart." But the ousted Mexican president, Benito Juárez, knew better: "These people of Mexico [City] are so strange. For anyone who does not know them and who is foolish, their ovations and flatteries are intoxicating, they sweep him off his feet and destroy him." Another type of courtesy took the form of a truly kind gesture. Mexicans accompanied a friend for part of the journey when that person was leaving the city in a carriage. Friends and family members were met at the train station. A gentleman walked companions, siblings, or in-laws to the nearest tram stop after having dined together. This prolonging of physical proximity was a way of shielding a small circle of intimates and loved ones from a hostile world.[11]

Mexicans customized their inherited taste for Spanish formality by exaggerating it. As with etiquette, so with romance. The gallantry that had defined relations between the sexes in colonial Mexico only intensified throughout the nineteenth century. The male's courtship ritual was not called "howling wolf," but "playing the bear." It was "so named from the restless walking to and fro of the love-stricken youth in front of the window of his inamorata, in a manner not unlike a captive bear in a cage. The same method pursued in the United States," continued the observer, "would either result in a man being sent to the lunatic asylum as suffering from a 'brain storm' or to a workhouse." If the man stalked with all the subtlety of a hungry grizzly, he had been enticed coyly: "it is self-evident that a young Mejicana, true to the traditions of her Castilian forebears, can make as much havoc with her languishing dark eyes, and the softly fluttering fan which supplements them, as any other girl arrayed in the full rational outfit of courtship." The little tricks that she played with her fan and handkerchief, and especially with her eyes, were key because conversing publicly with unknown men or mere acquaintances, especially for middle- and upper-class girls, was outlawed or strictly monitored. Once on confidential terms, however, and while walking ten yards in front of a chaperon, or sitting in the corner of the *sala*, or talking through the bars of her window, the flowery language of romance took over. These kinds of phrases were strung together and dangled as enticements and assurances:

Child of my soul!
Do you love me?
I adore you, I idolize you!
I would die for you!
I love you more than my own life!
I think only of you!
I'd kill myself for you!
Don't ever forget me!
You'll always be mine!
You'll be my only love!
Don't deceive me![12]

The bear put his new possession in a cage of her own. The sweet words, the declarations of love, and the oaths of fidelity too often turned into a familiar story of neglect, resentment, and resignation. Esther Maqueo, a character in a novel called *¡Castigo!* (Punishment!), says this about upper-class women: "The young girls of our community are sentenced to marry without love; they have no opportunity to choose; they have to wait until they are sought and never know what they will draw from the precarious lottery of matrimony. The girl who through daily contact and habit manages to secure the affection of her husband does not ask for more. Love is a luxury that the women of our class cannot enjoy." The young matron was typically relegated, immediately upon her marriage, to the status of her mother and grandmother. Her responsibility was to her home and husband, and if she belonged to the upper classes she was seldom seen again at social affairs unless seated with her husband or a chaperon. Among the lower classes, where marriage was far less common, the scenario was often courtship, love, and abandonment.[13]

The ideal of female virtue, among men at any rate, was the woman who endured her troubles with resignation. Endurance was a useful trait, because most men — if the novels, essays, memoirs, and travel books written about the city are at all accurate — cheated on their legal and common-law wives as part of an ongoing need to confirm their manliness in a society that constantly demanded proof. An article in the Law of Family Relations, which was adopted after the Revolution and removed many legal restrictions on women, reflected the reality of adultery. The article provided that, while adultery by the wife was always grounds for divorce, adultery by the husband was so only if the fornication took place in the conjugal home, if the wife suffered a public scandal or insult, and if the man paid for the living quarters of his mistress.[14]

Perhaps the most common form of infidelity was to have sexual relations, as many men did at one time or another, with prostitutes. Lower- and middle-class boys were often brought by older brothers, friends, or uncles for an early sexual education. The wealthy used the trade as well. Men with "famous last names and London suits" were paramours of the prostitute Santa, and hookers "flaunted their Parisian dresses and Boston shoes" in theaters and restaurants. There certainly were plenty of them. In 1900 over 10,000 women were registered with the Health and Police Departments as "public women." Good women were "private" in that they were sheltered in the home and chaperoned outside it. Luis Lara y Pardo, in his 1908 *La prostitución en México*, calculated that 120 of every 1,000 women between the ages of fifteen and thirty were registered prostitutes. Thousands more worked clandestinely in the streets and provided sexual services while working as domestic servants. The fact of prostitution was made evident each afternoon, when groups of "public women" made their weekly trip to the government doctor to be examined. "There is surely," wrote Lara y Pardo, "nothing more indecorous, cynical, and contrary to the spirit of the regulation [of mandated exams] than this daily procession of hundreds of women to the doctor." Nothing, that is, except how Health Department officials ranked those women in categories of "pretty," "average," and "ugly." [15]

What was unique to Mexico City was not that romance soured, or that men cheated on their wives, or that prostitution was big business. It was that the relations between the sexes were defined by the same mistrust, flattery, and fatalism that split other parts of Mexican life into one world of appearances, and another of facts. Cajolery was a man's major mode of ingratiation. The literal words, like those offering the family jewelry, were often distinct from their intended meaning. Yet many women lived in the gap between the visions of love and fidelity they acquired as children and later heard during courtship, and the wreckage of thwarted dreams and broken promises that was strewn all around them. The men lived with other contradictions. Every man dreaded being made a cuckold. But men in Mexico did not develop the respect for each other's marriages that might have eased their own fears. They lived anxious lives of mutual mistrust in which each did to others what he did not want done to himself. They also lived with the paradox of deriving private pleasure through illicit relations with "bad" women while publicly lauding the female virtues of chastity, duty, and resignation and fully expecting that their mothers, wives, and daughters would live up to them. The emotional glue that held all this together was guilt. One had only to feel remorse in a permissive Catholicism to be forgiven, and then carry on as before. But guilt often turned to blame — of the particular woman a man may have cheated with, and of women in general. It also intensified the inherited "Spanish jealousies" that Guerrero complained about.[16] For might not a man's wife or daughter be susceptible to the very temptations that he himself offered to other women?

Posing

The rituals of courtesy and courting required Mexicans to perfect the "unconscious habit of quietly or violently 'composing' themselves at every moment of their lives into some kind of a frameable picture." The composing was so natural in real life—"Not even the Parisian face," wrote another visitor, "is so flexible in expression, so fit for archness, so graphic to the mood"—that in the theater the illusion of acting was unnecessary. The prompter was only partially hidden behind his hood in the middle of the stage, and he was clearly heard giving the lines before they were voiced by the player. D. H. Lawrence searched in vain for something solid and central in the Mexican personality. Yet when he peered beyond the masks, deep into the Mexican's eyes, he saw only "a raging black hole, like the middle of a maelstrom."[17]

No Mexican better composed himself than Porfirio Díaz. How consciously he cast himself into some kind of frameable picture is hard to know. But pose he did. El Presidente was famous for his ability to shed tears. When a distinguished visitor praised his work, Díaz cried; when the Committee of the Friends of General Díaz came round to inform him that all of Mexico demanded his re-election, he wept; when he went into the streets on his birthday to shake hands with the people, tears streamed down his cheeks. Yet Benito Juárez feared those tears. "If we're not careful," he warned a friend, "Porfirio could kill us while crying." Díaz was equally famous for the impenetrable mask he wore when bidding for power or calling an opponent's bluff, a guise that earned him the nickname La Esfinge, the Sphinx. James Creelman saw the first of those sides in "the sense of nervous challenge" that issued from Díaz's "sensitive, spread nostrils," and the other in his "wide-open, fearless, dark eyes." Creelman's description hints at two sides of Díaz's personality that mirrored dueling elements of his country's mestizo character: the obsidian stare of the Indian's "fearless, dark eyes," and the "nervous" and "sensitive" nature of the more romantic Spaniard. Together they gave off an "intense, magnetic something"—the vague, Sphinx-like image that Díaz used to command his people. Yet as much as Díaz tried to impose upon himself what his biographer Carleton Beals called "an iron unity," that front was often cracked by the "anarchic nature" of the mestizo, whose personality was "a tense interplay, a see-saw between moodiness and violence, social squeamishness and anarchy, egoism and hectic pursuit of foreign gods." Díaz was all of these. He could weep while delivering a speech, then stoically order the murder of an opponent; he hid behind the façade of legality, but brooked no challenge to his rule; he waved the Mexican flag but let foreigners pilfer his country.[18]

The daily posing was a response to the hostility that infused Mexican life. Interaction among members of society was about negotiating what politician Miguel Macedo called the raw facts of "commanding and obeying, being served and serving." And because the Mexican wanted to defy authority, but seldom dared to, he acquired what Sierra called "the habit of dissembling and the habit of flattery."[19] Deference, sycophancy, and inflated respect for titles were merely masks for resentment in a society where real political power was not given by the law, but was taken by the man. Colonial magistrates, foreign invaders, Mexican *caudillos*, and now a mestizo dictator had made a history that was too hot and too personal to allow Mexicans to view authority with a healthy balance of respect and skepticism.

When Andrés Molina complained about the Mexicans' weak idea of *patria* (homeland), he meant that his countrymen did not satisfy their individual wants in ways that benefited society as a whole. Every Mexican enthusiastically shouted ¡Viva México! on Independence Day. But the rich refused to pay taxes, rarely gave money to charity, and did not privately build museums, universities, or libraries. And wealthy landlords, many of whom worked at high levels in the government, regularly ignored the city's sanitation and building codes and leased out filthy apartments in decrepit tenements. Each person treated public space as if it belonged to him or her alone and saw public institutions as bank accounts to be drawn on, but not invested in. And Mexicans seemed to feel remorse only when their behavior was exposed publicly — that is, when they felt the sting of *pena* and not when they examined their own actions and felt bad about them. The Mexican, wrote a foreigner, "only cringes when he fancies that he has done wrong and is about to be punished." From lying and adultery to corruption and murder, it was not the deed itself but detection that was the disgrace.[20]

The masks and formulas were also the product of an "inferiority complex," according to Samuel Ramos, which made the Mexican "run from himself and hide in a fanciful world."[21] After enduring three centuries of colonialism and two foreign invasions in the nineteenth century, modern Mexico grew up in the shadows of Europe and America. "We Mexicans," wrote José López-Portillo y Rojas,

> are quick to copy anything that comes from outside, and not only clothing and styles but ideas and systems, and we think we can get ahead by parodying foreign ways. In just the field of letters — I don't need to offer examples from legislation, politics, and tastes — everyone knows that, with a few honorable exceptions, our literature has been a sad parody of continental, especially French, writing. Proof of this is that though we are a young country our literature is already ridiculously decadent.[22]

This copycat behavior, of course, *was* modern culture in Mexico City. Mexico was not an economic powerhouse or a hub of cultural progress. It was a place that hitched its wagon to the economic and cultural engines of Europe and America and quite naturally tried to follow the leaders. When architect Rivas Palacios submitted his designs for a new Legislative Palace, the unfinished shell of which stands today as the Monument to the Revolution (which interrupted its construction), he decked them out with French and English logos and symbols so the jury would not suspect that either design was too national in character. "A word in Washington," lamented a city paper, "resonates in Mexico like an order. We cannot think about our own destiny without thinking about the United States, always the prime and inevitable factor in our own calculations." A sumptuous "Garden Party" was held in 1907 to honor Elihu Root, the visiting U.S. secretary of state. The party, wrote its official historians, "was in no way an effort of vain ostentation and splendor, but rather a highly important event that was carefully staged so that our illustrious visitors could judge the degree of culture attained by our upper and middle classes." In 1884, the Jockey Club celebrated the birthday of Porfirio Díaz by hosting a *charreada*, a traditional display of horsemanship, at its Peralvillo racecourse. Despite the *charreada*'s apparent success, it was the club's last. Its members buckled under the ridicule of a Parisian visitor who derided everything about it, from the costumes to the horses.[23]

Most upper-class Mexicans knew that their servants and drivers were not up to regal standards, that the shops on San Francisco Street were not those of the first-rate Parisian boulevards, and that the city had a difficult time doing the finer things in life with grace. And some surely noted the hypocrisy, as Manuel Gómez Morín remembered it, in

> the spectacle of the good and silly señores of the Jockey Club playing *auteuil* in the hippodrome, dressed in their gray frockcoats ordered from London or the Belle Jardiniere, sporting sideburns and speaking bad English, bad French, and bad Spanish, while their country estates were worked with feudal technology and enslaved peons. That was the time when those men outlawed the peasant's white cotton trousers in the city, but thought nothing of it on his hacienda: there all was well.[24]

The gap between the backward economic base of wealthy Mexicans and their continental styles of consumption, and the difference between how those styles were lived in Europe and how they were copied in Mexico City, had somehow to be bridged in thought. What emerged was a cultural schizophrenia. Self-doubt and self-loathing were hidden beneath pomposity and grandiosity. The towering independence monument was the biggest in the land, and emancipation day the grandest of the year, yet freedom from Spain only set Mexicans against each other for sixty years. And when they did finally make the modern state that brought them such great progress, it was at the cost of economic dependence and cultural subservience. Mexicans took pride in their indigenous heritage by putting Cuauhtémoc on Reforma; but one heroic Aztec, who served as an emblem of Mexican nationalism because he had defended his city against intruders, belied the everyday reality of the downtrodden Indian. The Fine Arts Palace, and the new Legislative Palace, were to be as big and fine as any in the world, even if imported opera companies would fill the great stage and "legislation" was just another name for executive decrees. When statues, buildings, and official celebrations fell short, bombast took over. We Mexicans "get drunk on pretentious oratory," says a character in González Peña's novel *La fuga de la quimera;* "we live in the realm of the ideal and care little for the real, the concrete. That is why we like the bright, smiling lie more than the blunt truth." And when sheer bluster failed to comfort, mythmaking tried its hand. Mexicans, wrote Moisés Sáenz, saw their history as an "epopoeia," their wars as the "deeds of heroes," and their leader, Porfirio Díaz, as "a superman, a role model for rulers." The lower classes acquired a sense of inferiority less from comparisons made with Europe and America through travel, reading, or hearsay than from being lorded over by their superiors, who supplemented the antique distinctions of race and caste with modern ones of class and culture. The elite Mexican, declared Ramos, "imitates the forms of European civilization to feel equal to the European, and thus prove himself superior to the uncivilized Mexican masses."[25]

One of Mexico's great problems, said the reviewers of a book on the port city of Veracruz, is that Mexicans don't know who they are. "We have a grandiose idea about the richness of our land and people," they continued, "yet no real idea of how to exploit that wealth. Perhaps we exaggerate our potential but we certainly are not, as many think, inept and inferior and incapable of producing a great, progressive culture. Our sense of inferiority does us enormous harm. . . . It paralyzes us, and in a way is a kind of self-fulfilling prophecy."[26]

The Charade of Legality

In his inaugural address to the Scientific and Artistic Convention at the 1910 centennial celebration of independence, Jorge Vera Estañol described how Mexico's liberal constitution was made for "an advanced moral and intellectual culture, which helps explain that frequent contrast between the real and the apparent in Mexico, and the forsaking of the roots of an institution for a reverence of its form." Díaz exploited that contrast to create what López-Portillo y Rojas called a "special system for governing," an authoritarian state that used mock elections and plenty of pageantry to "give the appearance of a constitutional government and generate a great respect for the idea of law."[27]

But to have gained even the *appearance* of lawfulness, if only as respect for the *idea* of law, was an exceptional achievement, for Díaz ruled Mexico with an authority as absolute as an Aztec king's. Díaz's system was democratic, but in form only. There were regular elections and three nominally independent branches of government, but there was no real competition for access to the machinery of state through fair voting, or any genuine checks and balances between the president, the congress, and the courts. The Aztecs, in contrast, spread power among the king, the priests, and aristocratic advisors. Mexico's military generals, like the capital's police chiefs, were named by Díaz, and each of them was either a friend of the president or had proved his loyalty. The Aztec king had to contend with a separate warrior caste. Díaz picked Supreme Court judges by hand, removed them at will, and rebuffed efforts to create an independent judicial system. "Sad it is to confess," said a magistrate, "the court does not respect its own decisions [but exercises] a loose and capricious versatility that results in the discrediting of all its judgments and the most complete uncertainty among its litigants." Aztec judges enjoyed esteem, life tenure, and considerable autonomy from the king.[28]

The dictator also named "elected" officials, even for remote parts of the country. He made Luis Pombo a congressman. "I hope one day to know the people of Colotlán" wrote Pombo — to his new constituency. Not once was the legislature constituted through a real vote. Senators and deputies were all Díaz's friends and acquaintances, or people recommended to him by confidants. Díaz wrote up the election lists with his minister of government, and then, in a show of impartiality, he refused to hold audiences with his candidates until the minister announced that "the popular will has mandated their victories." Many of the victors were Díaz's former military or political companions, and though most were old and ineffective, all were loyal. Some were younger aristocrats who were recommended by influential backers and naturally did exactly as they were told. A select few were talented advisors who were given congressional seats and control over special commissions.[29]

Most of his political minions may have been friends and acquaintances, but Díaz placed a higher premium on loyalty and subservience than he did on fraternity. He often turned on friends he thought had become too independent or powerful, and he forgave enemies who could be useful. "In politics," Díaz had learned, "there is no room for either love or hate." There was room only for Don Pérfido, as some called him, and those who gained by doing his bidding.[30]

Because Díaz carefully checked the progress of his friends, and either vanquished or converted his enemies, he kept an extraordinary amount of control in his own hands. "In this country you can't do anything without the direct and immediate influence of the man who has been running Mexico for more than twenty years." That was a daily paper's optimistic response in 1900 to the city's new mayor and future governor, Guillermo Landa y Escandón, who was on excellent terms with Díaz. After fighting for two decades against the dictator's sham democracy, the paper had finally yielded to the truth: government in Mexico was not about the quality of its laws, their enforcement, or even whether or not they were obeyed at all. Mexican politics was about the exercise of personal power. It was not the position that mattered, but the individual who filled it. Díaz picked the men who directed his government, and those men, not the machinery of state, ran Mexico. Mexico's "progress, credit, and peace," consequently, "all depend on Porfirio Díaz. But Díaz is mortal, and our progress, our credit, and our peace will die with him." Francisco Bulnes was right. When Díaz fell, Mexico fell with him.[31]

Díaz was like most of his people: he was a mestizo, he was from the countryside, and he knew how to work with his hands, ride a horse, and shoot a gun. And though his younger, educated, and more-refined wife, Carmen, taught him not to spit, slurp, or pick his teeth, she could not remove provincialisms from his speech or get him to spell correctly or write grammatically. As a roughhewn soldier in president's clothing, Díaz was a perfect match for his countrymen. The dictator revered the forms of democracy, but not the right of his people to vote freely, voice an opinion candidly, or get a fair hearing before the law. The typical Mexican valued the formulas that helped him negotiate his fractious city, but he only grudgingly respected another person's right to his wealth, or his personal privacy, or even his space on the sidewalk. Government worked by personally tying judges, governors, and councilmen into a political clique around El Presidente; it did not coordinate activities between and respect the jurisdiction of courts, state governments, and city councils. Mexicans trusted and feared the power of real live men and loved the formal ceremonies of state that glorified them; abstractions like justice or representation, or institutions like the Supreme Court or the legislature, as such, had little meaning for most of them.

If the conduct of the state replicated the behavior of its people, it also reflected the pattern of its recent history. The French Revolution had Danton and Robespierre, yet is remembered for its novel demand for "Liberty, Equality, and Fraternity." The American Revolution had Paul Revere and the Boston Tea Party, but is celebrated for its Declaration of Independence. It is not, however, the principle of sovereignty that Mexicans honor on 16 September. The great monument on Reforma was erected "to the Heroes of Independence," to the individuals, that is, who fought the battles. Mexicans had good reason for seeing their history as the actions of individual men, rather than the playing out of some larger theme like freedom or democracy. They fought for independence *against* Spanish colonialism, but *for* what? Political freedom did not quickly translate into clear visions, tangible liberties, or prosperity. For two bloody generations *caudillos* fought among themselves to see who could gain a military advantage, build a personal following, and then form a government. Power was too anarchic for institutions, and too personal for principles. There were only men with forces strong enough to coax temporary loyalties, and slogans vague enough to accommodate contradictory beliefs. Even the differences between Liberals and Conservatives, who apparently fought over issues of church and state, were typically of personality, not politics. It was Díaz who finally imposed his will on Mexico and fashioned its divided peoples into a nation. While plotting to take power, he issued this clarion call: "My plan is to offer no revolutionary plan, only generalities, without compromising the future."[32]

The themes of form over substance, and of personal clout over institutional authority, were also played out in the drama of city government. Mexico City was ostensibly run by an elected council led by a mayor. Yet each councillor owed his position to Díaz, who prepared the lists of candidates. If the vote of the designees in the electoral college did not establish the official candidate as the winner, as happened occasionally in the early years, the count was simply changed. Such minor kinks had been worked out of the system by the mid-1880s. "Everyone knows," wrote a frustrated *El Tiempo*, which often put two exclamation points after the word *election*, "that the *appointments*, improperly called *elections*, are fixed and decided in the offices of the ministries, the governor, and ultimately in the office of the Grand Elector himself." There was no campaigning or competition. Voting was simply the "verification of the official list."[33] After one such verification, in 1884, *El Monitor Republicano* reported that "people are still indignant about last Sunday's city elections. . . . The so-called electoral college scoffed at the will of the electorate. The old style of gaining power through the barrel of a gun would be better than this cynical, brazen, and annoying joke that the government papers call respect for the will of the majority."[34]

If elections were a farce, so too were the words "Liberty and Constitution," which preceded the governor's signature on every city document. It was a strange motto for a city that had no political autonomy, and that served as the capital of a nation whose president mocked in practice the laws he revered in the abstract. But this was a city, remember, that according to one Mexican writer had a habit of "foresaking the roots of an institution for a reverence of its form."[35]

Municipal elections tried to hide the fact that the mayor and his city council were "docile instruments that basically carry out the will of the highest power in the land." The capital was run by a governor who was appointed by Díaz. The council rubber-stamped the governor's initiatives, had two of its members represent the city as lawyers, and produced annual reports about budgets and projects. Over the years, as the governor's office and federal ministries seized control of the city's courts, jails, and schools, took over its police, health, and public works departments, and assumed the task of writing its budgets, the annual reports became as perfunctory as the duties of the councilmen.[36]

The governor and his men, who so easily dispensed with the mayor and the city council, had even less time for journalists who masqueraded as city planners. This was another gap between form and substance: the city's upper classes and its high officials valued newspapers as signs of progress and as sources of information, yet hated them when they acted as public watchdogs. *El Tiempo*, Catholic and conservative yet a big believer in public accountability, often prefaced its suggestions to the city council and its governor with something like "even though our voice, like those of the other papers, won't even be heard." Sometimes it took an even more plaintive tone, exhorting "'no more slogans and no more official coercion,' the people ought to say, 'we demand a city government that, instead of mocking and ignoring us, respects us, because in your hands we place our honor and security, even our dignity.'" The papers had plenty to criticize. *El Tiempo* was not wrong when it complained that a few "honest" if "fraudulently elected" councilmen could not get the government to show "any interest in the welfare of the city." The city government couldn't even pick up trash regularly, account for its spending, or coordinate street paving with the laying of sewer mains. The inefficiency was made worse by grotesque imbalances in spending. The downtown and the west side got most of the money, and thus the paved streets, the sewer lines, and the parks; the east got nothing. When the issue was not east versus west, it was what the money was spent on. Journalists often asked bitter rhetorical questions about the city's spending strategies: "Does the city government think that firecrackers, streamers, and public events are enough to hide from visitors the decaying and asphyxiating mountains of trash, the lakes of filth, and the centers of infection that assault one's eyes, damage one's sense of smell, upset one's stomach, stain one's clothes, and bring about death?"[37] The papers' criticisms and suggestions were at times acknowledged, but never heeded. The city government fought the sniping of the papers with an official publication—*Municipio Libre* (The Free City).

If administrative inefficiencies and preferential spending did not literally defraud the public, the graft skimmed off by a cabal of insiders did. The Ministries of Health, Government, Treasury, and Public Works operated out of the National Palace to fix elections, devise budgets, and award contracts for sewers, tramways, street paving, and other public works. The heads of these ministries, along with city councilmen, regularly used their inside knowledge to speculate in property that the city was about to buy up or improve. They also collected fees or stock for negotiating the cumbersome bureaucracy for American transport and construction firms. The most powerful among them got rich by providing foreign capitalists with access to the Treasury and Public Works Departments, and to Díaz himself. The same two dozen or so councilmen, governors, and ministry officials were on the boards of the foreign firms that did business in Mexico City, and they held stock in local construction, cement, and real estate companies.[38] These activities, like those of Tammany Hall, were hard to track. Without a free press or reform parties it was impossible even to bring them to the public's attention.

The law in Mexico was inflicted on those without the power to avoid it. Because a strict application of virtually any law would have shown almost everyone to be in noncompliance, there were endless possibilities for bureaucrats, politicians, and the police to charge money *not* to enforce the rules. A conspicuous example was the condition of tenements in the eastern part of the city. They were owned by landlords who lived in the west and who violated almost every sanitation and building regulation on the books because they had the influence and the money to keep city officials from enforcing the codes. The owners of brothels, *pulquerías,* and gaming dens paid officials and policemen not to enforce ordinances that curbed hours, prohibited rear entrances, limited the number of drinks, and stipulated hygienic conditions. Average citizens faced a crueler form of extortion. Policemen collected fees from the poor who did not want to spend a day in jail for being charged with *raterismo* (even if, as was often the case, they were found innocent by the governor the next day), and from those who could not afford to get licenses for a market stall or pay a daily fee for selling without a permit.[39]

Street cops were motivated to shake down the citizens they were supposed to protect since they themselves were being robbed by their superiors. Chiefs fined policemen for minor infractions and kept the money. They also forced the men to honor the saint's days of their superiors — the interior secretary, the governor, the inspector general, his secretaries, and the chiefs of the foot and mounted police forces — by handing over a full day's pay. Gendarmes and their officers would also collaborate in corruption. One trick was for the commissary to order a new prisoner, who was in for only a few days on a minor infraction, to hand his money or valuables over to the precinct station's repository. The policemen who escorted the prisoner to a holding cell then told him that the chief planned to ship him off to the Valle Nacional. The gendarme offered to let the prisoner escape for an article of clothing. So the prisoner was freed, the cop got a piece of clothing to pawn, and the commissary kept the money, the watch, or the jewelry. To ensure that the men had not pawned their revolvers and uniforms, and that their officers were not padding payrolls, the entire force passed in review once a month in the Zócalo before the inspector general, the governor, and treasury officials.[40]

Respect for the law, Aeschylus knew, includes an element of fear:

Should the city, should the man
rear a heart that nowhere goes
in fear, how shall such a one
any more respect the right?

But Mexicans did not respect the law as much as they feared that it would be applied to them. Rules were enforced on a case-by-case and usually personal basis. If you were powerful, then you could generally avoid the law. If you were not, then the law could be visited upon you at any time, usually as a means of extortion, and even out of spite. The secret police, complained a pro-Díaz newspaper, carried out "despicable vendettas," accused their

enemies as "known thieves," and denounced women who would not con-
cede favors to them as "clandestine prostitutes." The sad result, lamented *El
Tiempo*, was that, "when laws are not followed, and government does not
enforce them, both the law and the government lose their credentials, fail to
inspire confidence, and instead provoke anxiety."[41]

The Justifiers

"The abstract theories of democracy and the practical, effective application of them," said Díaz, "are often necessarily different."[42] The gaps between the forms of democracy and their underlying substance, such as that
between an elected city council and the reality of a municipal dictatorship,
were papered over with celebrations of rigged elections and a façade of con-
stitutionalism. Díaz and his cronies knew how to modify the imported institutions of modern life to fit Mexican reality, and how to hold aloft ideals
(elections, law, justice) that they corrupted in practice.

Díaz felt that his people were incapable of handling the kind of democracy that had grown up in the United States and in parts of Europe. He wrote
the following, in 1891, to a governor who was intent on instituting popular
juries:

> No matter how favorable our opinion might be of our homeland, we are
> still not convinced that its sons and daughters, who only recently have
> become engaged in the defense of the independence and the institutions
> of the country, have developed sufficient moral and intellectual capacity
> to pronounce, in an oral hearing, upon the circumstances of a crime and
> apply the law correctly and with due consideration . . . While we are
> preparing this kind of solid and indispensable base, it would be unwise
> and even dangerous to impose obligations knowing that they won't be
> fulfilled.[43]

For the same reasons, Díaz agreed with advisor Miguel Macedo that free
municipal elections, like the ones held in Mexico City in 1876, elected only
leaders who were "incompetent and heterogeneous." The elections were
nullified and the executive branch took over the task of designating municipal officials, a practice that Macedo would later conclude was "superior to
truly popular elections; it has contributed in great measure to the public
good, allowing city government . . . to be run by honest, intelligent, and ad-
ministratively talented men, though they lack popularity among the illiterate masses who form the majority of the population."[44] Honest they proba-

bly were not; intelligent they might have been; but unpopular, that they certainly were. Yet if Díaz felt that his country was not ready for the substance of democracy, he did want its trappings, if only to show the world that Mexico was progressive and prove to his people that their laws, if not obeyed, were respected.

A dozen or so talented individuals, known collectively as the *científicos*, or the "scientists," helped Díaz fit abstract theories of democracy to Mexican reality. These men had become the country's political elite by the late 1880s. In contrast to other Latin American countries, where the wealthy either held power themselves or selected politicians to run the state for them, Mexico's government was manned by a small group of intellectuals who were answerable to Díaz alone, unknown outside the capital, and allowed to profit from their administrative duties. Díaz fought his way into power and gave "Order, Peace, and Progress" to a divided and weak ruling class, which was happy to hand the state over to him in exchange for business opportunities and a measure of control over their own regional politics.[45]

In the early years, the *científicos* worked as lawyers for various ministries, as advisors on commissions that examined ideas for government financing and administration, and as reviewers of codes that dealt with commerce, banks, and railroads. They gained experience and influence throughout the 1880s, and made a real bid for power in the early 1890s by trying to use their organization, the Liberal Union, to establish political parties in Mexico. They failed, and from then on were drawn directly into Díaz's regime as ministers of finance, education, public works, and government, as key senators and deputies, and as heads of newspapers. They met regularly to keep informed of business activities and political developments, and many were members of the Bancaria, a big business clearinghouse that issued contracts for the construction of buildings, sewers, streets, and rails. The profits from those contracts were divided among the *científicos* and their small circle of friends. They soon acquired a reputation among the populace as a thieving cabal, or what was known in Mexico as a *carro completo* — a full railcar with no room for anyone else.[46]

The philosophy of the *científicos* was built around attacks on doctrinaire liberalism, calls for constitutional reform, and justifications for strong government as a counter to anarchy. The interplay of these ideas can be seen in the most dramatic intellectual battle fought in Díaz's Mexico, the struggle over the 1857 Constitution. The *científicos* regarded it as imported, artificial, and ineffectual. The emphasis on universal suffrage, individual liberties, the rights of man, federalism, and a weak executive was regarded by Justo Sierra and his colleagues as exaggerated, arbitrary, and disruptive dogma based on faith rather than on a scientific analysis of the Mexican reality. From early on, in their "liberal-conservative" journal *La Libertad* — liberal because they wanted progress, conservative because they wanted order — the *científicos* made a frank appeal for authoritarian government: "Rights! Society now rejects them. What it wants is bread, . . . a little less of rights in exchange for a little more of security, order, and peace. We have already enacted innumerable rights, which produce only distress and malaise in society. Now let us try a little tyranny, but honorable tyranny, and see what results it brings."[47]

We esteem liberty, wrote Telésforo García, "but following the road marked by science, we do not love it independent of its results." Even *El Tiempo* agreed that "there is no liberty without authority." Of the *científicos*, only Justo Sierra, in 1900, began to worry publicly about the permanence of dictatorship. He was reluctant to back another re-election; but in the end he did anyway.[48]

The *científicos* fashioned Díaz's political façade and had their own image manipulated for public consumption. Religious newspapers like *El País*, *El Tiempo*, and *La Voz* were allowed to fight against what they saw as the *científicos'* atheism, secularism, and materialism. Francisco Bulnes, himself a key *científico* and a powerful member of Congress, mounted calculated attacks meant to distance the *científicos* from Díaz. All the while, Rafael Reyes Spíndola, an avowed *científico* and editor of the subsidized newspapers *El Mundo*, *El Mundo Ilustrado*, and *El Imparcial*, was responsible for making the *científicos* acceptable to the public by suppressing, spreading, or coloring news of them.[49]

Like the *científicos*, most of the press was bought and paid for. A character in Emilio Rabasa's *El cuarto poder* tells a new writer about the job: "The paper is for the government, though I wish it were for the opposition, because then it would be more interesting and easier. But that's all right. Our job is to defend the government, applaud its policies and activities, and when you don't understand something, like the public debt, which is boring and complicated, just write in general terms and say that the benefits of the law are obvious, and that it shows the clear thinking, deep understanding, and patriotic feelings of whichever ministry it happens to be."[50]

The few owners and editors who could not be bought, like Filomena Mata, Daniel Cabrera, and Victoriano Agüeros, were jailed. Not once did the Supreme Court issue a writ of habeas corpus on their behalf.[51] *Salas de distinción* — privileged cells — were maintained for the "educated class," even though they were illegal according to the penal code, which stipulated a separate jail for political prisoners. It was the warden's prerogative to determine which of his prisoners qualified as members of that class. The chosen few embellished their private quarters with furniture and sometimes were permitted to entertain private guests. The *departamento de distinción* ("the privileged section") was jokingly called the *departamento de la prensa* ("the press section"). Despite the conveniences, the opposition press complained that political prisoners were mistreated by common criminals.[52] Cabrera said, in 1892, after leaving Belem prison, "Each day the independent press is restrained further. When one journalist is released from Belem, another takes his place. They try to fan the flames of terror, and no matter how much moral or physical courage the journalist has, it becomes impossible to maintain a position of honest opposition . . . In spite of all the power and comfort that the forces of Tuxtepec [i.e., Díaz] now enjoy, they continue to hit what is now a tiny group of independent journalists with an iron fist."[53]

The press, like the city council, the national legislature, and the presidency itself, was "no more than a mere fantasy, an unreal entity, a decorative body." It served, López-Portillo y Rojas concluded, "only to give the appearance that such an institution actually existed." The men of government and journalism "shined not by generating insights into the nation's problems, or by having original ideas," grumbled historian José Valadés, "but by perfecting the art of speech making." Díaz knew that Mexico needed legislatures, courts, and newspapers to show off its progress and to occupy its talented and ambitious men. He knew how to provide the forms of those institutions while removing their substance. And he knew how to quiet the crowing of politicians, intellectuals, and journalists, whom he called *profundistas* (deep thinkers): "What that cock needs," he used to say, "is a little corn."[54]

But in the end, when Díaz ran short on corn and the reality of dictatorship rubbed too closely against the theory of republicanism, those cocks would crow again — this time for Revolution.

NOTES

CHAPTER 1: CITY & NATION

1. Altamirano and Alamán cited in Enrique Krauze, *Siglo de caudillos: biografía política de México (1810–1910)*, 83, 177.

2. *El Tiempo*, 15 September 1883; see also 18 September 1883.

3. On symbols see J. Lafaye, *Quetzalcóatl y Guadalupe*; Eric Wolf, "The Virgin of Guadalupe: A Mexican National Symbol"; Rachel Phillips, "Mansa/Malinche: Masks and Shadows." On the national psychology see Emilio Uranga, *Análisis del ser de México*; Samuel Ramos, *El perfil del hombre y la cultura en México*; José Vasconcelos, *La raza cósmica*. On nationalism see Frederick Turner, *The Dynamic of Mexican Nationalism*.

4. Eric Wolf, *Europe and the People without History*, 385–389.

5. Justo Sierra, *La evolución política del pueblo mexicano*, 44.

6. Octavio Paz, *El laberinto de la soledad*, 86.

7. Arthur Schopenhauer, *Complete Essays of Schopenhauer*, 66.

CHAPTER 2: EAST & WEST

1. Adolfo Dollero, *México al día*, 15–16; T. Philip Terry, *Terry's Mexico*, 267, 293; E. H. Blichfeldt, *A Mexican Journey*, 114, 119–122, 128; Edith O'Shaughnessy, *Diplomatic Days*, 167; Fanny Gooch, *Face to Face with the Mexicans*, 80; Martin Ballou, *Aztec Land*, 136, 162–163.

2. Terry, *Terry's Mexico*, 292; *El Tiempo*, 21 September 1910; Guillermo Tovar de Teresa, *La ciudad de los palacios: crónica de un patrimonio perdido*, 40–41, 46.

3. Gustavo Casasola, *Biografía ilustrada del General Porfirio Díaz*, 71, 134–135.

4. *The Mexican Herald*, 18 October 1908; Salvador Novo, *México*, 49.

5. Terry, *Terry's Mexico*, 294; Dollero, *México al día*, 15; *El Tiempo*, 28 October 1883; *Siglo Diez y Nueve*, 17 March 1896; *El Mundo*, 23 January 1898.

6. *El Tiempo*, 18 January 1887; Terry, *Terry's Mexico*, 295–296.

7. Blichfeldt, *A Mexican Journey*, 128–129; Terry, *Terry's Mexico*, 297, 294; *El Tiempo*, 17 July 1886; Stanton Davis Kirkham, *Mexican Trails*, 7, 21; Mexico, *Guía general descriptiva de la República mexicana*; Mexico, Consejo Superior de Gobierno de Distrito, "Informes del Administración de Rastros y Mercados, 1903–1914"; *El Tiempo*, 22 July 1886; Terry, *Terry's Mexico*, 267, 293; Federico Gamboa, *Santa*, 97; Wallace Thompson, *The Mexican Mind: A Study of National Psychology*, 79; Genaro García, *Crónica oficial de las fiestas del Primer Centenario de la Independencia de México*, 129–132, 150–153; Carlos González Peña, *La chiquilla*, 231, 241–242; *El Tiempo*, 18 September 1883, 17 June 1886, 18 September 1887, 18 September 1906; Mexico, Secretaría del Ayuntamiento Constitucional de México, "Plaza Mayor, 1908"; Mexico, *Guía general descriptiva*.

8. Miguel Macedo, *La criminalidad de México*, 7.

9. Jonathan Kandell, *La Capital*, 326–352; Manuel Payno, *Los bandidos de Río Frío*; Guillermo Prieto, *Memorias de mis tiempos, 1828–1853*; Krauze, *Siglo de caudillos*.

10. Jan Bazant, *Los bienes de la iglesia en México*, 103–124; Kandell, *La Capital*, 298, 328–352; Alfonso Vásquez Mellado, *La ciudad de los palacios*, 199–201.

11. Edward Gibbon, *The History of the Decline and Fall of the Roman Empire*, vol. 1, 172.

12. Charles Lummis, *The Awakening of a Nation*, 5; Mexico, *Estadísticas económicas del porfiriato: comercio exterior de México, 1877–1911*, 78; Fernando Rosenzweig, "El desarrollo económico de México de 1877 a 1911."

13. Diego López Rosado, *Los servicios públicos de la Ciudad de México*, 190–191; Mexico, *Discurso por el C. Gral. Manuel González Cosío*, 39.

14. Emile Ruhland, *Directorio general de la Ciudad de México* (1890), 33–173; John Lear, "Workers, Vecinos and Citizens: The Revolution in Mexico City, 1909–1917," 107–108; Miguel Macedo, *Mi barrio*, 26–50.

15. Emile Ruhland, *Directorio general de la Ciudad de México* (1897), 49–292, 305–345, 360; Gooch, *Face to Face*, 86; William Curtis, *The Capitals of Spanish America*, 36–37; Nevin Winter, *Mexico and Her People Today*, 50; Ballou, *Aztec Land*, 129; Sanborn Map Company, *Insurance Maps of City of Mexico*; *El Tiempo*, 29 May 1906.

16. G. Garza Villarreal, *El proceso de industrialización en la Ciudad de México*, 127–132; Kandell, *La Capital*, 371, 383; López Rosado, *Los servicios públicos*, 201; Mexico, Dirección General de Estadística, *Estadísticas sociales del porfiriato*, 63; Lear, "Workers, Vecinos and Citizens," 64, 83; Bulnes, cited in Moisés González Navarro, *La vida social: el porfiriato. Historia moderna de México*, 388; Rodney Anderson, *Outcasts in Their Own Land: Mexican Industrial Workers, 1906–1911*, 20; Ruhland, *Directorio (1897)*, 342–355; Inés Herrera Canales, "La circulación," 444–447, 461; Charles E. Goad, *Map of Mexico City*; Laura Elena Castillo Méndez, *Historia del comercio en la Ciudad de México*, 50–51; Mexico, Dirección General de Estadística, *Anuario estadístico de la República mexicana 1896*, 233–243; idem, *Anuario estadístico de la República mexicana 1902*, 68–72; idem, *Anuario estadístico de la República mexicana 1907*, 61–84; Stephen Haber, *Industry and Underdevelopment: The Industrialization of Mexico, 1890–1940*, 64–65.

17. Walter McCaleb, *Present and Past Banking in Mexico*, 135–137; Colegio de México, *Fuerza de trabajo*, 179–180, 187–188; Francisco Bárbara Lavalle, *Los bancos mexicanos hasta 1910*, 10–15, 29–33, 63–68.

18. Colegio de México, *Fuerza de trabajo*, 170; Goad, *Map of Mexico City*; Jesús Galindo y Villa, *Reseña histórico-descriptiva de la Ciudad de México*, 131–133; Ruhland, *Directorio (1897)*, 305–315, 323–324, 419–420; Curtis, *The Capitals of Spanish America*, 39; Winter, *Mexico and Her People*, 55; Castillo Méndez, *Historia del comercio en la Ciudad de México*, 50–51; Manuel Torres Torija, "Ciudad de México," 64–66.

19. Mexico, *Ministerio de Hacienda, Mexican Year Book*, 518, 519; López Rosado, *Los servicios públicos*, 191; Fred Powell, *The Railroads of Mexico*, 1–6; Moreno Toscano, *Ciudad de México: ensayo de construcción*, 207–212; Gustavo Aguilar, *Los presupuestos mexicanos*, 173; Marcello Carmagnani, "El liberalismo, los impuestos in-

ternos y el Estado Federal Mexicano, 1857–1911"; Mexico, Consejo Superior de Gobierno de Distrito, *Memoria 1907;* Jesús Galindo y Villa, *La Ciudad de México,* 131; Castillo Méndez, *Historia del comercio en la Ciudad de México,* 53; Haber, *Industry and Underdevelopment,* 81; Lummis, *The Awakening of a Nation,* 39–40; Limantour as cited in Mario Contreras and Jesús Tamayo, *México en el siglo XX, 1900–1913,* 171.

20. See also José Juan Tablada, *La feria de la vida (memorias),* 144, 152, 200; Gustavo Casasola, *Seis siglos de historia gráfica de México,* vol. 3, 1198–1199, 1385–1386; Thomas Brocklehurst, *Mexico To-day: Country with a Great Future,* 25.

21. Ballou, *Aztec Land,* 134.

22. Winter, *Mexico and Her People,* 57.

23. Terry, *Terry's Mexico,* 258–260.

24. Gamboa, *Santa,* 214; *El Tiempo,* 6 January 1906; Percy F. Martin, *Mexico of the Twentieth Century,* 185–186; Wallace Gillpatrick, *The Man Who Likes Mexico,* 106–108; Tablada, *La feria de la vida,* 90–91; Charles Flandrau, *Viva Mexico!,* 290; Curtis, *The Capitals of Spanish America,* 37–38; Terry, *Terry's Mexico,* 258–260; *Siglo Diez y Nueve,* 6 April 1888.

25. *El Tiempo,* 18 September 1883; José María Marroquín, *La Ciudad de México,* vol. 2, 108–114.

26. Luis Reyes de la Maza, *Cien años de teatro en México,* 116–119; John Dizikes, *Opera in America: A Cultural History,* 225.

27. "Prólogo," in Manuel Gutiérrez Nájera, *Poesías completas,* vol. 1, 7–8.

28. Gutiérrez Nájera, *Poesías completas.*

29. Luis Urbina, *La vida literaria de México,* 219–223; Boyd Carter, *En torno a Gutiérrez Nájera,* 205–243; Gutiérrez Nájera, *Poesías completas.*

30. Manuel Gutierréz Nájera, *Cuentos completos,* 154–160.

31. Gutiérrez Nájera, in Urbina, *La vida literaria,* 231–233.

32. López Rosado, *Los servicios públicos,* 202–208; Mexico, Secretaría del Ayuntamiento Constitucional, "Obras públicas, 1901."

33. Novo, *México,* 257–281.

34. Tablada, *La feria de la vida,* 153; Luis Salazar, *La arquitectura y la arqueología;* see also Torres Torija, "Ciudad de México," 61–62, 75–77.

35. *El Mundo Ilustrado,* 7 August 1898; see also Torres Torija, "Ciudad de México," 75–77.

36. Henry James, *The American Scene,* 164.

37. Fanny Calderón de la Barca, *Life in Mexico during a Residence of Two Years in That Country,* 59; Paula Kollonitz, *The Court of Mexico,* 151–152; Salvador Novo, *La Ciudad de México en 1873,* 83; see also Marroquín, *La Ciudad de México* (1900), vol. 1, 269; Leonardo Pasquel, *La alameda central,* 37; *El Tiempo,* 25 July 1884, 6 August 1886.

38. Ramón Beteta, *Járano,* 25; Kirkham, *Mexican Trails,* 7; Federico Gamboa, *Suprema ley,* 66; Terry, *Terry's Mexico,* 326–327; Blichfeldt, *A Mexican Journey,* 137; José Valadés, *El porfirismo: el nacimiento,* 183; Dollero, *México al día,* 90–91; González Peña, *La chiquilla,* 26.

39. Flandrau, *Viva Mexico!,* 293; see also O'Shaughnessy, *Diplomatic Days,* 113.

40. Mexico, Ministerio de Gobernación, *Inauguración del monumento a Juárez.*

41. Martin, *Mexico of the Twentieth Century*, 184–185; Terry, *Terry's México*, 372, 376–377; Brocklehurst, *Mexico To-day*, 74; Albert Gray, *México As It Is*, 57–58; José María Marroquín, *La Ciudad de México* (1903), vol. 3, 642–655.

42. Terry, *Terry's Mexico*, 376–377; Galindo y Villa, *Reseña histórico-descriptiva de la Ciudad de México*, 119–120.

43. Cited in Krauze, *Siglo de caudillos*, 192.

44. Novo, *México*, 290, 292.

45. *El Tiempo*, 21 September 1883.

46. Sierra, *La evolución política*, 82.

47. Marroquín, *La Ciudad de México* (1903), vol. 3, 647–648; Gustavo Baz, *Un año en México*, 133–140; *El Tiempo*, 16 March 1884, 7 December 1886; *Siglo Diez y Nueve*, 20 August 1887, 22 August 1887.

48. Paz, *El laberinto*, 34; Marroquín, *La Ciudad de México* (1903), vol. 3, 653.

49. Antonio Rivas Mercado, *Inauguración del monumento a la independencia*; John Lynch, *The Spanish American Revolutions, 1808–1826*, 306–319; Krauze, *Siglo de caudillos*, 51–94.

50. Marroquín, *La Ciudad de México* (1903), vol. 3, 650–655.

51. Juan Bribiesca, *Memoria documentada*, 198; Terry, *Terry's Mexico*, 380–381; Dollero, *México al día*, 92–93; Ballou, *Aztec Land*, 132–133; Gillpatrick, *The Man Who Likes Mexico*, 106–107; Carlos Pacheco, *Map of the City of Mexico*; Manuel Marroquín y Rivera, *Proyecto de abastecimiento y distribución de agua potable*; "Plano de la Ciudad de México," 1910, in Terry, *Terry's Mexico*.

52. Manuel Rivera Cambas, *México pintoresco, artístico y monumental*, 62; Moreno Toscano, *Ciudad de México*, 191; Manuel Ceballos Ramírez, "La encíclica rerum novarum y los trabajadores católicos en la Ciudad de México (1891–1913)"; *El Tiempo*, 17 July 1886; María Dolores Morales, *Investigaciones sobre la historia de la Ciudad de México*, 1; Mexico, Consejo Superior de Gobierno de Distrito, "Inspectores sanitarios de las cuarteles de la capital," 87–101; González Navarro, *La vida social*, 99.

53. Vicente Martín Hernández, *Arquitectura doméstica de la Ciudad de México (1890–1925)*, 52–53, 104, 121–122.

54. Julio Guerrero, *La génesis del crimen en México*, 171–173.

55. González Navarro, *La vida social*, 394; Susan Bryan, "Teatro popular y sociedad durante el porfiriato"; Ricardo Castillo, *Teatro nacional*; *Siglo Diez y Nueve*, 13 July 1887; *El Tiempo*, 27 April 1886; Manuel Gutiérrez Nájera, "Un público o una piara?" in *Obras IV*, 340–342; idem, "Las tandas del principal," "El empresario Navarrete y las tandas," and "Teatro de títeres" in *Obras III*, 302–315; González Peña, *La chiquilla*, 58–59.

56. Guerrero, *La génesis del crimen*, 172; see also 171–173; González Navarro, *La vida social*, 395; Hernández, *Arquitectura doméstica*, 42–48; Fernando Benítez, *La Ciudad de México*, vol. 2, 301.

57. José Cossio, "Algunas noticias sobre las colonias de esta capital," 12–21, 27–29; María Dolores Morales, "Francisco Somero y el primer fraccionamiento de la Ciudad de México, 1840–1889."

58. Jorge H. Jiménez Muñoz, *La traza del poder*, 25–35, 66–102; María del Carmen Collado, *La burguesía mexicana: el emporio Braniff y su participación política*,

69–75; Morales, *Investigaciones sobre la historia de la Ciudad de México*, 17, 27; María Dolores Morales, "La expansión de la ciudad de México en el siglo XIX: el caso de los fraccionamientos."

59. Dollero, *México al día*, 21; Cossio, "Algunas noticias," 17–18, 27–29; López Rosado, *Los servicios públicos*, 195–197; Lear, "Workers, Vecinos and Citizens," 82, 87, 90, 110–111.

60. Martin, *Mexico of the Twentieth Century*, 189; Lummis, *The Awakening of a Nation*, 68; Carlos González Peña, *La fuga de la quimera*, 86; García, *Crónica oficial*, 3–41; Casasola, *Seis siglos*, 1035–1036; Flandrau, *Viva México!*, 137; Hernández, *Arquitectura doméstica*, 126–132, 152, 157–160, 174–178; O'Shaughnessy, *Diplomatic Days*, 282–283.

61. *El Mundo Ilustrado*, 27 November 1898, 4 December 1898, 11 December 1898, 18 December 1898.

62. Lear, "Workers, Vecinos and Citizens," 83; Kandell, *La Capital*, 370.

63. Rosa King, *Tempest over Mexico*, 37, 39.

64. *El Tiempo*, 17 July 1886; Ruhland, *Directorio (1897)*, 391; Macedo, *Mi barrio*, 26–50; Terry, *Terry's Mexico*, 261–262, 343–350; Adriana López Monjardín, *Hacia la ciudad del capital, 1790–1870*, 138–141, 158–182; Mexico, Dirección General de Estadística, *Estadísticas sociales del porfiriato*, 69; Lear, "Workers, Vecinos and Citizens," 38–39.

65. Mexico, *Discurso por el C. Pedro Rincón Gallardo* (1884), 47–48; *El Tiempo*, 8 March 1883, 10 March 1883, 6 October 1883, 9 October 1883, 16 October 1886, 27 November 1888. See also *Siglo Diez y Nueve*, 29 June 1887; Pacheco, *Map of the City of Mexico*; Ralph Roeder, *Hacia el México moderno: Porfirio Díaz*, vol. 1, 197.

66. Marroquín y Rivera, *Proyecto de abastecimiento*; *El Mundo Ilustrado*, 29 October 1899.

67. Mexico, *Discurso (1884)*, 47–48; González Navarro, *La vida social*, 87–101; Mexico, Consejo Superior de Gobierno de Distrito, "Salubridad e higiene, 1903–1907"; idem, "Inspectores sanitarios de las cuarteles de la capital"; *La Gaceta*, 25 April 1900.

68. Her statue was dedicated in 1900 with a poem by Gutiérrez Nájera. See *El Tiempo*, 6 February 1900; Manuel Gutiérrez Nájera, "A La Corregidora," in José Emilio Pacheco, *Antología del modernismo (1884–1921)*, vol. 1, 26–27.

69. Terry, *Terry's Mexico*, 261; Ruhland, *Directorio (1897)*, 396–397; Marroquín, *La Ciudad de México* (1900), vol. 2, 314, 319, 320; Mexico, *Discurso por el C. Gral. Manuel González Cosío* (1891), 22.

70. Lear, "Workers, Vecinos and Citizens," 48, 59–76; Frederick Shaw, "The Artisan in Mexico City, 1824–1853"; Payno, *Los bandidos de Río Frío*, 11, 42–43; Moreno Toscano, *Ciudad de México*, 191; Cossio, "Algunas noticias," 16; Morales, *Investigaciones sobre la historia de la Ciudad de México*, 1–59; Hernández, *Arquitectura doméstica*, 37–41; González Peña, *La chiquilla*, passim.

71. *El Tiempo*, 17 February 1886; Ruhland, *Directorio (1897)*, 342–345, 355–366, 416–422; Hernández, *Arquitectura doméstica*, 40.

72. Cited in López Rosado, *Los servicios públicos*, 213; see also Mexico, Consejo Superior de Gobierno de Distrito, "Rastros y Mercados, 1903–1914."

73. Ruhland, *Directorio (1897)*, 355–368; *Gil Blas*, 21 October 1896.

74. Ángel de Campo, *La rumba*, 185–189, 209–212.

75. *El Tiempo*, 1 May 1886. Quotation in Rivera Cambas, *México pintoresco (1880)*, vol. 2, 93; see also 95 and Mexico, Ministerio de Hacienda, *Mexican Year Book*, 569–570.

76. Terry, *Terry's Mexico*, 358; see also Ruhland, *Directorio (1897)*, 357, 417.

77. Rivera Cambas, *México pintoresco (1880)*, vol. 2, 90; Mexico, Consejo Superior de Gobierno de Distrito, "Rastros y Mercados, 1903–1914."

78. Rivera Cambas, *México pintoresco (1880)*, vol. 2, 145–147, 176–178, 242; Mexico, Consejo Superior de Gobierno de Distrito, "Inspectores sanitarios," 28–48; Emilio Rabasa, *El cuarto poder*, 33–38; Salvador Quevedo y Zubieta, *La camada*, 72; *El Tiempo*, 26 January 1910.

79. *El Tiempo*, 2 February 1884; Mexico, Consejo Superior de Gobierno de Distrito, "Inspectores sanitarios," 28–48; Lear, "Workers, Vecinos and Citizens," 87, 90; Mexico, Consejo Superior de Gobierno de Distrito, "Rastros y Mercados, 1903–1914"; Mexico, *Boletín Oficial del Consejo Superior de Gobierno de Distrito*; Mexico, Consejo Superior de Gobierno de Distrito, "Policía, 1903–1910."

80. Calderón de la Barca, *Life in Mexico*, 113.

81. Rivera Cambas, *México pintoresco (1882)*, vol. 2, 184; *Siglo Diez y Nueve*, 13 December 1892.

82. F. Hoeck, *The Mexico City Guide*, 178; Mexico, *Discurso (1891)*, 21; Gamboa, *Suprema ley*, 167; José Romero, *Guía de la ciudad de México y demás municipalidades del Distrito Federal*, 110.

83. *El Imparcial*, 9 April 1902; see also González Navarro, *La vida social*, 99–101.

84. Quotation from Mexico, Consejo Superior de Gobierno de Distrito, "Colonias," 519–520; see also Moreno Toscano, *Ciudad de México*, 220–224; *El Imparcial*, 9 April 1902; Jiménez Muñoz, *La traza del poder*, 22–24; *El Tiempo*, 14 September 1886.

85. Terry, *Terry's Mexico*, 257; Cossio, "Algunas noticias," 23; *El Tiempo*, 26 January 1910; Laurence Rohlfes, "Police and Penal Correction in Mexico City, 1876–1911: A Study of Order and Progress in Porfirian Mexico," 88; Dollero, *México al día*, 25–28.

86. Mexico, Consejo Superior de Gobierno de Distrito, "Inspectores sanitarios," 19–27; *El Tiempo*, 30 September 1900; Cossio, "Algunas noticias," 24–27; Rivera Cambas, *México pintoresco (1880)*, vol. 2, 90; Dollero, *México al día*, 18; Valadés, *El porfirismo*, 112.

87. Novo, *La Ciudad de México en 1873*, 83–84; González Navarro, *La vida social*, 99–101; Mexico, *Discurso (1884)*, 44–46; Moreno Toscano, *Ciudad de México*, 200; Rabasa, *El cuarto poder*, 14; Rivera Cambas, *México pintoresco (1882)*, vol. 2, 241; Lear, "Workers, Vecinos and Citizens," 134.

88. Terry, *Terry's Mexico*, 247; Brocklehurst, *Mexico To-Day*, 78; Hoeck, *The Mexico City Guide*, 168–169; Rivera Cambas, *México pintoresco (1882)*, vol. 2, 377, 378.

89. United States, *Report on Industry and Commerce in Mexico*, 3–8, 14–18, 74–75; Hoeck, *The Mexico Guide*, 169, 173, 175; Moisés González Navarro, *Las huelgas textiles en el porfiriato*, 245–267; Mexico, Dirección General de Estadística, *Anuario es-*

tadístico 1896, 233–243; idem, *Anuario estadístico 1902*, 68–72; idem, *Anuario estadístico 1907*, 61–84; Haber, *Industry and Underdevelopment*, 27–39, 48–49, 67–69; Mexico, Ministerio de Hacienda, *Mexican Year Book*, 524–543.

CHAPTER 3: PEASANTS & PROVINCIALS

1. Martín Luis Guzmán, *The Eagle and the Serpent*, 3–4.
2. Mexico, *Discurso por el C. Pedro Rincón Gallardo* (1886), 43; idem, *Discurso* (1884), 55; idem, *Discurso* (1891), 6–11; *El Tiempo*, 14 February 1887, 24 August 1883; *Siglo Veinte y Uno*, 27 November 1887, 12 July 1887; Alberto Pani, *Hygiene in Mexico: A Study of Sanitary and Educational Problems*, 7, 33, 60–61; Nicolás Islas y Bustamante, *Cuadros de mortalidad*; González Navarro, *La vida social*, 14, 43–52, 101–102.
3. Mexico, *Memoria que el Ayuntamiento Constitucional de 1879 presente a sus comitentes*, 25–34; idem, *Discurso* (1884), 45–46; idem, *Discurso* (1886), 41; López Rosado, *Los servicios públicos*, 186.
4. Quotation from Moisés González Navarro, "México en una laguna," 506–508, 512; see also idem, *La vida social*, 118–122. Editorial from *El Tiempo*, 11 October 1887; see also Mexico, *Memoria que el Ayuntamiento Constitucional de 1879*, 37–38; González Navarro, "México en una laguna," 506, 508, 512.
5. *El Tiempo*, 4 July 1883, 12 July 1883, 8 August 1886, 28 July 1887, 14 October 1887, 21 June 1888; *El Monitor Republicano*, 31 July 1887; *Siglo Diez y Nueve*, 1 August 1887, 26 July 1888, 4 July 1888; Mexico, Ayuntamiento Constitucional de México, "Inundaciones, 1880–1903"; *El Tiempo*, 11 October 1887, 17 June 1886, 29 August 1885, 14 March 1886; *Siglo Diez y Nueve*, 12 July 1887; González Navarro, "México en una laguna," 506–508, 512.
6. *El Tiempo*, 6 February 1886; González Navarro, "México en una laguna," 515.
7. López Rosado, *Los servicios públicos*, 198–199; Mexico, Ministerio de Hacienda, *Mexican Yearbook*, 567; González Navarro, "México en una laguna," 511.
8. Kandell, *La Capital*, 371–372; *El Imparcial* from González Navarro, "México en una laguna," 517, 521; López Rosado, *Los servicios públicos*, 197–200; *El Tiempo*, 18 March 1900, 21 March 1900.
9. Peñafiel cited in González Navarro, *La vida social*, 93, 76; see also Quevedo y Zubieta, *La camada*, 54; *La República*, 22 April 1880; Manuel Marroquín y Rivera, *Memoria descriptiva de la Obras de Provisión de Aguas Potables*, 3; López Rosado, *Los servicios públicos*, 217–223; Mexico, Junta Directiva del Saneamiento de la Ciudad de México, #4720; Mexico, Consejo Superior de Gobierno de Distrito, "Salubridad e higiene, 1903–1907"; *Siglo Diez y Nueve*, 29 June 1887; González Navarro, "México en una laguna," 518–520; *El Tiempo*, 23 February 1906.
10. Mary Blake and Margaret Sullivan, *Mexico: Picturesque, Political, Progressive*, 87; *El Tiempo*, 12 March 1885, 17 July 1886; *Siglo Diez y Nueve*, 10 January 1888; *El Tiempo*, 31 May 1886; *El Monitor Republicano*, 6 October 1882; Mexico, Consejo Superior de Gobierno de Distrito, "Informe de la Comisión de Obras Públicas y de Ríos y Acequias"; *Siglo Diez y Nueve*, 26 June 1888, 12 July 1888, 19 July 1888; *El*

Tiempo, 22 July 1886; Mexico, Junta Directiva del Saneamiento de la Ciudad de México, #4720; Mexico, Consejo Superior de Gobierno de Distrito, "Salubridad e higiene, 1903–1907"; *Siglo Diez y Nueve*, 14 February 1893.

11. Marroquín y Rivera, *Memoria descriptiva de las Obras de Provisión de Aguas Potables*, 3; López Rosado, *Los servicios públicos*, 219–222; González Navarro, "México en una laguna," 519, 520.

12. López Rosado, *Los servicios públicos*, 188.

13. *El Tiempo*, 11 October 1888, 3 August 1883, 27 November 1888; 30 August 1885, 19 February 1887, 24 February 1887; López Rosado, *Los servicios públicos*, 241; *El Imparcial*, 9 April 1902; John Kenneth Turner, *Barbarous Mexico*, 97–99.

14. *Gil Blas*, 21 October 1896.

15. Guerrero, *La génesis del crimen*, 137–138; *El Tiempo*, 20 June 1886, 4 June 1895, 23 Janaury 1910; Mexico, Consejo Superior de Gobierno de Distrito, "Rastros y Mercados, 1903–1914"; idem, "Policía, 1903–1910"; Mexico, *Boletín Oficial del Consejo Superior de Gobierno de Distrito*; Mexico, Secretaría de Gobierno de Distrito Federal, "Limpia, 1909–1911."

16. López Rosado, *Los servicios públicos*, 241; Ramón Beteta, *La mendicidad en México*, 96–97; González Navarro, *La vida social*, 85; Turner, *Barbarous Mexico*, 97–99.

17. Beteta, *La mendicidad en México*, 83–96; Rómulo Velasco Ceballos, *Las loterías*, 114–116, 120–123.

18. López Rosado, *Los servicios públicos*, 221; Pani, *Hygiene in Mexico*, 115–116.

19. Calderón de la Barca, *Life in Mexico*, 295–296; Flandrau, *Viva Mexico!*, 282; *El Tiempo*, 3 October 1883; *Siglo Diez y Nueve*, 23 November 1887; *El Imparcial*, 6 August 1895.

20. Pani, *Hygiene in Mexico*, 33, original emphasis.

21. Quevedo y Zubieta, *La camada*, 54.

22. González Navarro, *La vida social*, 90; Benítez, *La Ciudad de México*, 301; Mexico, Dirección General de Estadística, *Estadísticas sociales del porfiriato*, 125; Pani, *Hygiene in Mexico*, 34; *El Tiempo*, 3 October 1883, 14 February 1906; *Siglo Diez y Nueve*, 29 June 1887; *Siglo Diez y Nueve*, 14 February 1906, 22 November 1887; *El Tiempo*, 22 April 1884, 16 March 1886.

23. Pani, *Hygiene in Mexico*, 61; Flandrau, *Viva Mexico!*, 182; Mexico, Consejo Superior de Gobierno de Distrito, "Policía, 1903–1910."

24. González Navarro, *La vida social*, 72–82; Francisco Bulnes, *El verdadero Díaz y la Revolución*, 140–141; Valadés, *El porfirismo: el nacimiento*, 172; Juan Felipe Leal and Mario Huacuja Roundtree, *Economía y sistema de haciendas en México: la hacienda pulquera*, 80–99, 103.

25. Valadés, *El porfirismo: el nacimiento*, 172; Leal and Roundtree, *Economía y sistema de haciendas*, 89–99, 103; Brocklehurst, *Mexico To-day*, 65; Winter, *Mexico and Her People*, 65; Terry, *Terry's Mexico*, lxxxiii–lxxxiv.

26. Mexico, *Memoria (José Ceballos, Gobernador)*, 84; Leal and Roundtree, *Economía y sistemas de haciendas*, 103–104, 113–127; Rivera Cambas, *México pintoresco* (1882), vol. 2, 90–92; González Navarro, *La vida social*, 73–74.

27. Terry, *Terry's Mexico*, lxxxiv; Flandrau, *Viva Mexico!*, 267; Winter, *Mexico and Her People*, 64–65; Rivera Cambas, *México pintoresco* (1882), vol. 2, 90–92; *El Tiempo*, 13 May 1885, 27 May 1885, 13 August 1885, 4 January 1886, 17 May 1890; Mexico, Consejo Superior de Gobierno del Distrito, "Pulquerías, 1907"; Blake and Sullivan, *Mexico*, 94.

28. Anita Brenner, *The Wind That Swept Mexico*, plate 10; last quotation from Terry, *Terry's Mexico*, lxxxiv.

29. Rivera Cambas, *México pintoresco* (1882), vol. 2, 91.

30. Winter, *Mexico and Her People*, 65–66.

31. Terry, *Terry's Mexico*, lxxxiv.

32. *El Tiempo*, 12 July 1890, 20 August 1890, 24 March 1888, 12 September 1889, 4 May 1900; Rivera Cambas, *México pintoresco* (1882), vol. 2, 91–92; González Navarro, *La vida social*, 72–77, 398.

33. Trinidad Sánchez Santos, *La ciudad de dolor*, 93; González Navarro, *La vida social*, 77, 416; *El Tiempo*, 26 July 1883, 27 July 1883, 28 July 1883, 11 August 1883, 17 March 1886, 20 August 1887, 15 February 1890, 13 November 1900; Carlos Roumagnac, *Los criminales en México*, 47.

34. Anderson, *Outcasts in Their Own Land*, 94; Carmen Reyna, "El trabajo en las panaderías"; *El Tiempo*, 26 July 1883, 31 May 1886.

35. *El Tiempo*, 17 May 1886, 31 August 1883, 9 August 1883; González Navarro, *La vida social*, 72–75; Beteta, *Járano*, 25–31; J. R. Flippin, *Sketches from the Mountains of Mexico*, 266–268; Sánchez Santos, *La ciudad de dolor*, 9, 62.

36. Julio Sesto, *El México de Porfirio Díaz*, 231–232; Samuel Ramos, *El perfil del hombre y la cultura en México*, 77.

37. Quotations in this and next paragraph from Guerrero, *La génesis del crimen*, 158–168; see also *El Tiempo*, 28 September 1883, 2 April 1887, 23 June 1887, 8 November 1887, 15 November 1887, 31 January 1890, 19 July 1906, 7 March 1910; 29 March 1910; *Siglo Diez y Nueve*, 3 September 1888, 10 September 1888.

38. Sesto, *El México de Porfirio Díaz*, 231–232; Blichfeldt, *A Mexican Journey*, 114–115; Terry, *Terry's Mexico*, liii.

39. *El Tiempo*, 22 September 1900, 28 March 1900, 19 April 1900; see also Mexico, *Discurso* (1884), 53; Guerrero, *La génesis del crimen*, 320–321; D. H. Lawrence, *The Plumed Serpent (Quetzalcoatl)*, 15.

40. O. L. "Holy Week in Mexico," 522–524; James Creelman, "President Díaz: Hero of the Americas," 238; O'Shaughnessy, *Diplomatic Days*, 167; Rafael Delgado, *Los parientes ricos*, 188; *El Tiempo*, 2 February 1884; González Navarro, *La vida social*, 463–470.

41. Cited in William Beezley, *Judas at the Jockey Club*, 99–100.

42. Gonzalo de Murga, "Atisbos sociológicos. El fraccionamiento de tierras. Las habitaciones baratas," 486; Rohlfes, "Police and Penal Correction in Mexico City," 154–156; González Navarro, *La vida social*, 397; Vicente Morales and Manuel Cabellero, *El Señor Root en México*.

43. Beezley, *Judas at the Jockey Club*, 112; Anderson, *Outcasts in Their Own Land*, 280–281; González Navarro, *La vida social*, 92, 396–397.

44. José López-Portillo y Rojas, *La parcela*, 1–2, 5; González Peña, *La fuga*, 152–153; Antonio García Cubas, *El libro de mis recuerdos*, 241; Brocklehurst, *Mexico To-day*, 25–29; Flandrau, *Viva Mexico!*, 133, 280–285.

45. Cited in Ramos, *El perfil del hombre*, 30.

46. Flandrau, *Viva Mexico!*, 283.

47. Bryan, "Teatro popular," 153.

48. Reyes de la Maza, *Cien años de teatro en México*, 131–132.

49. Flandrau, *Viva Mexico!*, 43; Delgado, *Los parientes ricos*, 44–45.

50. Sierra, as cited in Charles Hale, *The Transformation of Liberalism in Late Nineteenth Century Mexico*, 236; José Yves Limantour, *Discurso pronunciado en la ceremonia de clausura del Concurso Científico Nacional*, 4, 14; *El Tiempo*, 29 April 1885, 10 June 1886, 11 June 1886, 10 July 1890, 18 August 1900; *Siglo Diez y Nueve*, 24 February 1893. Final quotation from González Navarro, *La vida social*, 170; see also 163–172.

51. González Navarro, "México en una laguna," 509; *El Tiempo*, 12 July 1895.

52. Juan Gómez-Quiñones, "Social Change and Intellectual Discontent: The Growth of Mexican Nationalism, 1890–1911," 187; Mexico, *Discurso* (1884), 50.

53. Ralph Roeder in Enrique Krauze, *Porfirio Díaz: místico de la autoridad*, 87.

54. Quevedo y Zubieta, *La camada*, 35; González Peña, *La fuga*, 99.

55. Justo Sierra, *The Political Evolution of the Mexican People*, 62.

56. Alexander von Humboldt, *Political Essay on the Kingdom of New Spain*, 87–88.

57. Ibid.

58. Sierra, *La evolución política*, 98.

59. Gómez-Quiñones, "Social Change and Intellectual Discontent," 158; Anderson, *Outcasts in Their Own Land*, 259.

60. Sierra, *The Political Evolution of the Mexican People*, 87.

61. Ibid., 348, 92.

62. Ramos, *El perfil del hombre*, 38; see also M. Romero, *Geographical and Statistical Notes on Mexico*, 80; Moisés Sáenz and Herbert Priestly, *Some Mexican Problems*, 59; O'Shaughnessy, *Diplomatic Days*, 70, 270; Evelyn Waugh, *Robbery under Law: The Mexican Object-Lesson*, 33.

63. D. Jesús Díaz de León, "Concepto del indianismo en México," 22–23; Sierra, *La evolución política*, 93–98; Ramos, *El perfil del hombre*, 38–49; Sáenz and Priestly, *Some Mexican Problems*, 57; Andrés Molina Enríquez, *Los grandes problemas nacionales*, 42, 262–263, 331.

CHAPTER 4: DEATH & DISORDER

1. Rivera as cited in Frances Toor, *Monografía: las obras de José Guadalupe Posada*, iii–iv.

2. Ron Tyler (ed.), *Posada's Mexico*, 3–10; López-Portillo y Rojas, *La parcela*, 6; Roberto Berdecio and Stanley Appelbaum, *Posada's Popular Mexican Prints*, vii–xx.

3. Agustín Yáñez, *Al filo del agua*, 14.

4. Bertram Wolfe, *The Fabulous Life of Diego Rivera*, 33–35; Tyler, *Posada's Mexico*, 7, 9; Rubén M. Campos, *El folklore literario de México*, 372–373.

5. Molina Enríquez, *Los grandes problemas nacionales*, 262–263, 42, 331.

6. Cited in José Valadés, *El porfirismo: historia de un régimen, el crecimiento*, vol. 2, 34–35.

7. Payno, *Los bandidos de Río Frío*, 371–434; Paul Vanderwood, *Disorder and Progress: Bandits, Police, and Mexican Development*, 67.

8. From 1878, cited in Valadés, *El porfirismo: el nacimiento*, 133–134.

9. Alicia Hernández Chávez, "Origen y ocaso del ejército porfiriano"; Vanderwood, *Disorder and Progress*, 58, 70.

10. Krauze, *Porfirio Díaz*, 33.

11. Merle Simmons, "Porfirio Díaz in Mexico's Historical Ballads," 4–5.

12. Vanderwood, *Disorder and Progress*, 53, 107–108, 114.

13. Creelman, "President Díaz," 244.

14. Vanderwood, *Disorder and Progress*, 124, 135–136; see also *El Tiempo*, 6 May 1890.

15. Cited in Macedo, *La criminalidad*, 5–8.

16. *El Tiempo*, 17 May 1890, 11 August 1883, 20 August 1887, 27 August 1887, 1 May 1890, 19 February 1895; *El Mundo*, 21 January 1898, 23 January 1898; *La Gaceta Comercial*, 23 May 1900; Rivera Cambas, *México pintoresco* (1882), vol. 2, 146–147; *El Mundo*, 1 January 1898; González Peña, *La fuga*, 2; González Navarro, *La vida social*, 390–393; Guerrero, *La génesis del crimen*, 168–170; *El Tiempo*, 17 July 1889.

17. Rohlfes, "Police and Penal Correction in Mexico City," 155–156, 235–236, 258; Guererro, *La génesis del crimen*, 136–137; Turner, *Barbarous Mexico*, 54–55; *El Tiempo*, 25 March 1895, 23 May 1906; Francisco Bulnes, *The Whole Truth about Mexico*, 49–50.

18. Flippin, *Sketches*, 267; González Navarro, *La vida social*, 416–420; Roumagnac, *Los criminales en México*, 47–50; *El Tiempo*, 26 July 1883, 27 July 1883, 11 August 1883, 17 March 1886, 20 August 1887, 7 June 1889, 15 February 1890, 13 November 1900; Rohlfes, "Police and Penal Correction in Mexico City," 161–163; Turner, *Barbarous Mexico*, 71–72.

19. Rohlfes, "Police and Penal Correction in Mexico City," 30–32.

20. *El Tiempo*, 11 September 1884, 4 August 1884, 16 October 1884, 25 September 1885, 16 September 1886, 4 August 1887; *El Mundo*, 16 January 1889; Pedro Santini, "La policía de la Ciudad de México durante el porfiriato"; Turner, *Barbarous Mexico*, 96.

21. *El Hijo del Ahuizote*, 6 May 1894.

22. Brocklehurst, *Mexico To-Day*, 19; Turner, *Barbarous Mexico*, 125–126.

23. Rohlfes, "Police and Penal Correction in Mexico City," 77–78, 117–118.

24. Ibid., 210. See also Dollero, *México al día*, 19; de Campo, *La rumba*, 296–297; Rohlfes, "Police and Penal Correction in Mexico City," 210, 211, 212.

25. Terry, *Terry's Mexico*, 369; *El Tiempo*, 21 December 1888; *The Mexican Herald*, 8 October 1908, 13 October 1908; Roumagnac, *Los criminales en México*, passim;

El Tiempo, 22 August 1883; *El Monitor Republicano,* 21 December 1887; *Municipio Libre,* 17 May 1881; Rohlfes, "Police and Penal Correction in Mexico City," 204, 210–217, 324.

26. *El Nacional,* 13 February 1895.

27. *El Mundo,* 16 January 1898, 23 January 1898.

28. *El Tiempo,* 28 September 1883, 13 November 1900, 23 June 1900, 14 July 1900.

29. *El Tiempo,* 2 July 1883, 4 May 1887, 19 February 1887, 1 December 1887, 6 January 1906; *El Nacional,* 13 February 1895; Terry, *Terry's Mexico,* 259.

30. Vásquez Mellado, *La ciudad de los palacios,* 263–264; *Siglo Diez y Nueve,* 6 May 1888; Mary Barton, *Impressions of Mexico,* 14.

31. Heriberto Frías, *Los piratas del boulevard,* 9; González Peña, *La chiquilla,* 237; Gooch, *Face to Face,* 160; Valadés, *El porfirismo: el nacimiento,* 177.

32. *El Tiempo,* 12 April 1887, 22 October 1900.

33. Bulnes, *The Whole Truth about Mexico,* 149–150.

34. Aristotle, *Politics,* 114.

35. Friedrich Katz, "The Liberal Republic and the Porfiriato, 1867–1910"; Juan Felipe Leal, *La burguesía y el estado mexicano;* Daniel Cosío Villegas, *El porfiriato, vida económica: historia moderna de México;* Jiménez Muñoz, *La traza del poder,* 66–102.

36. Creelman, "President Díaz," 241.

37. In Valadés, *El porfirismo: el nacimiento,* 173.

38. Macedo, *La criminalidad,* 10–11; see also Flandrau, *Viva Mexico!,* 68; Carleton Beals, *Porfirio Díaz: Dictator of Mexico,* 197; Moisés Sáenz, *México íntegro,* 44; John Reed, *Insurgent Mexico,* 159–161; Sierra, *La evolución política,* 128.

39. Tablada, *La feria de la vida,* 93–94.

40. González Navarro, *La vida social,* 421–425; Guerrero, *La génesis del crimen,* 248–255; Macedo, *La criminalidad,* 10–11; *El Tiempo,* 27 August 1887.

41. Ramos, *El perfil del hombre,* 84–91; see also Kollonitz, *The Court of Mexico,* 167; Molina Enríquez, *Los grandes problemas nacionales,* 262–263, 37, 42.

42. Guerrero, *La génesis del crimen,* 124–128; R. H. Mason, *Pictures of Life in Mexico,* vol. 1, 49.

43. Beals, *Porfirio Díaz,* 246–250; Hubert Bancroft, *History of Mexico,* 327–331, 363, 406, 418–419; Laurens Ballard Perry, *Juárez and Díaz,* 56–187.

44. Campos, *El folklore literario de México,* 615–619; Valadés, *El porfirismo: el crecimiento,* vol. 1, 177.

45. Tablada, *La feria de la vida,* 251–252.

46. Campos, *El folklore literario de México,* 618–619.

47. Mexico, *Boletín Mensual de Estadística del Distrito Federal;* Dollero, *México al día,* 20; Carleton Beals, *Mexico: An Interpretation,* 153; Luis Lara y Pardo, *La prostitución en México,* 25; Guerrero, *La génesis del crimen,* 341–344; González Peña, *La fuga;* De Campo, *La rumba;* Delgado, *Los parientes ricos;* Quevedo y Zubieta, *La camada;* Rabasa, *El cuarto poder;* Federico Gamboa, *Suprema ley;* González Peña, *La chiquilla,* 225–254.

48. *El Tiempo,* 17 April 1887, 4 June 1895, 23 January 1910; E. Tweedie, *Mexico As I Saw It,* 205; Barton, *Impressions of Mexico,* 29–30.

49. Ángel de Campo, "El pinto," 35.

50. Beals, *Mexico*, 201; Guerrero, *La génesis del crimen*, 63, 248–249, quotation on 249.

51. Krauze, *Siglo de caudillos*, 31; Bancroft, *History of Mexico*, 283.

52. *El Tiempo*, 5 January 1886.

53. Guerrero, *La génesis del crimen*, 248–249.

54. Lawrence, *The Plumed Serpent*, 40.

55. Guerrero, *La génesis del crimen*, 167–168.

56. Curtis, *The Capitals of Spanish America*, 34.

57. Martin, *Mexico of the Twentieth Century*, 234; Gooch, *Face to Face*, 89–90; Tweedie, *Mexico As I Saw It*, 214; O'Shaughnessy, *Diplomatic Days*, 91.

58. O'Shaughnessy, *Diplomatic Days*, 141.

59. *The Mexican Herald*, 1 November 1908.

60. Beezley, *Judas at the Jockey Club*, 99–100.

61. Frederick Starr, *Catalogue of a Collection of Objects Illustrating the Folklore of Mexico*, 80–82.

62. O. L., "Holy Week in Mexico," 524–525; Beezley, *Judas at the Jockey Club*, 101; Starr, *Catalogue of a Collection of Objects*, 80–82.

63. José Núñez y Domínguez, "Los Judas en México," 94–95; Dollero, *México al día*, 89–90; Beezley, *Judas at the Jockey Club*, 93–107; Winter, *Mexico and Her People*, 233–234; O'Shaughnessy, *Diplomatic Days*, 249; O. L., "Holy Week in Mexico," 526; Starr, *Catalogue of a Collection of Objects*, 81–82.

64. Beezley, *Judas at the Jockey Club*, 108–111.

65. González Navarro, *La vida social*, 727–729.

66. Beezley, *Judas and the Jockey Club*, 17.

67. González Navarro, *La vida social*, 728–731; Terry, *Terry's Mexico*, xcvii; Casasola, *Seis siglos*, vol. 3, 1010–1012.

68. González Navarro, *La vida social*, 741.

69. *El Tiempo*, 27 September 1895.

70. Casasola, *Seis siglos*, vol. 3, 1012–1017; González Navarro, *La vida social*, 735, 737, 739.

71. Cited in González Navarro, *La vida social*, 727–744.

72. *Siglo XIX*, 16 January 1888.

73. Terry, *Terry's Mexico*, xcviii; Lawrence, *The Plumed Serpent*, 3–4; Baz, *Un año en México*, 46–47; *El Tiempo*, 25 December 1885, 30 August 1887, 3 December 1889.

74. Mexico, Ayuntamiento Constitucional, *Reglamento para corridas de toros*, article 4, 4.

75. Casasola, *Seis siglos*, vol. 3, 1010–1018; Terry, *Terry's Mexico*, xcvii–c; Lawrence, *The Plumed Serpent*, 1–19.

CHAPTER 5: APPEARANCE & REALITY

1. *El Tiempo*, 11 January 1910, 21 March 1910, 13 April 1910; Krauze, *Siglo de caudillos*, 26–28; García, *Crónica oficial*.

2. Flandrau, *Viva Mexico!*, 20.

3. *El Tiempo*, 13 May 1885.

4. T. Esquivel Obregón, "La influencia de España y Estados Unidos sobre México," 37, 95; Sierra, *La evolución política*, 128, 389; Francisco González Pineda, *El mexicano*, 27–71; Thompson, *The Mexican Mind*, 36; Tweedie, *Mexico As I Saw It*, 150; Beals, *Mexico*, 212; Ramos, *El perfil del hombre*, 96; Flippin, *Sketches*, 21; Alonzo de Zorita, *Life and Labor in Ancient Mexico: The "Brief and Summary Relation of the Lords of New Spain,"* 138; Flandrau, *Viva Mexico!*, 120–121.

5. D. H. Lawrence, *Mornings in Mexico*, 38–40; see also Winter, *Mexico and Her People*, 220.

6. Elizabeth Visere McCary, *An American Girl in Mexico*, 32; Winter, *Mexico and Her People*, 213–214; Mason, *Pictures of Life in Mexico*, 48; Guerrero, *La génesis del crimen*, 177–182; Martin, *Mexico of the Twentieth Century*, 192–193, 212; Terry, *Terry's Mexico*, lxiii–lxiiv; Tweedie, *Mexico As I Saw It*, 147; Calderón de la Barca, *Life In Mexico*, 256–257; Gooch, *Face to Face*, 97.

7. Winter, *Mexico and Her People*, 164–165; Gooch, *Face to Face*, 94, 107–109; Thompson, *The Mexican Mind*, 66; José Valadés cited in E. Krauze and Fausto Zerón-Medina, *Porfirio: el poder*, 47; Flandrau, *Viva Mexico!*, 136–138; Hernández, *Arquitectura doméstica*, 157–179.

8. Tweedie, *Mexico As I Saw It*, 147; Gooch, *Face to Face*, 94–98; Winter, *Mexico and Her People*, 162.

9. Flippin, *Sketches*, 285–287; Terry, *Terry's Mexico*, lxiii; Brocklehurst, *Mexico To-day*, 198; Gooch, *Face to Face*, 96–99.

10. Cited in Kandell, *La Capital*, 309–310; see also Gooch, *Face to Face*, 161.

11. Cited in Kandell, *La Capital*, 307–310, 343; see also Winter, *Mexico and Her People*, 213–214.

12. Guerrero, *La génesis del crimen*, 124–128; Tablada, *La feria de la vida*, 251–279; Winter, *Mexico and Her People*, 167–170; Flippin, *Sketches*, 280–284; Beals, *Mexico*, 148; Blake and Sullivan, *Mexico*, 61; Gooch, *Face to Face*, 115, 153–154; Thompson, *The Mexican Mind*, 67–69; Delgado, *Los parientes ricos*, passim.

13. Félix Palavicini, *¡Castigo!*, 222; González Peña, *La fuga*; Delgado, *Los parientes ricos*; Beals, *Mexico*, 190–193; Brocklehurst, *Mexico To-Day*, 201; Winter, *Mexico and Her People*, 164–170, 210–211; Thompson, *The Mexican Mind*, 67–69; Gooch, *Face to Face*, 118–119.

14. Guerrero, *La génesis del crimen*, 341–344; Tablada, *La feria de la vida*, 93–94; Mexico, *Boletín Mensual de Estadística del Distrito Federal*; Dollero, *México al día*, 20; Gooch, *Face to Face*, 183–184; de Campo, *La rumba*; Quevedo y Zubieta, *La camada*; Rabasa, *El cuarto poder*; Gamboa, *Suprema ley*; González Peña, *La chiquilla*; Lara y Pardo, *La prostitución en México*; Gamboa *Santa*; Ernest Gruening, *Mexico and Its Heritage*, 627–628.

15. Guerrero, *La génesis del crimen*, 341–344; Beals, *Mexico*, 193; Gamboa, *Santa*, 108–111; González Peña, *La chiquilla*, 245; Reyes de la Maza, *Cien años de teatro en México*, 131–132; Benítez, *La Ciudad de México*, 320; *El Mundo*, 9 January 1898; Gonzalo de Murga, "Atisbos sociológicos," 486; Lara y Pardo, *La prostitución en México*, 20–25, 32, 72–73; Mexico, Consejo Superior de Gobierno de Distrito,

"Proyecto de reglamento de la inscripción sanitaria de mujeres públicas de la Ciudad de México; Policía, 1903–1910."

16. Guerrero, *La génesis del crimen*, 125.

17. Flandrau, *Viva Mexico!*, 29, 285; Lummis, *The Awakening of a Nation*, 178; Gooch, *Face to Face*, 43–57; Thompson, *The Mexican Mind*, 94; Lawrence, *The Plumed Serpent*, 78, 40.

18. Turner, *Barbarous Mexico*, 273; Lummis, *The Awakening of a Nation*, 113; Gillpatrick, *The Man Who Likes Mexico*, 118; Krauze, *Porfirio Díaz*, 75, 65; Creelman, "President Díaz," 232; Beals, *Porfirio Díaz*, 197, 325; Sierra, *La evolución política*, 389.

19. Macedo, *La criminalidad*, 7; Sierra, *La evolución política*, 128; see also Beals, *Mexico*, 202.

20. Molina Enríquez, *Los grandes problemas nacionales*, 292–340; Sáenz and Priestly, *Some Mexican Problems*, 57; *El Tiempo*, 25 July 1883, 11 October 1888; *Siglo Diez y Nueve*, 20 September 1888, 30 September 1888; Vásquez Mellado, *La ciudad de los palacios*, 232; González Navarro, *La vida social*, 495–500; Martin, *Mexico of the Twentieth Century*, 212–213; Flippin, *Sketches*, 21; Moisés Saenz, *México íntegro*, 44; Flandrau, *Viva Mexico!*, 73–76.

21. Ramos, *El perfil del hombre*, 48, 76, 96; see also Molina Enríquez, *Los grandes problemas nacionales*, 292–340; Sáenz and Priestly, *Some Mexican Problems*, 73–76.

22. López-Portillo y Rojas, *La parcela*, 5.

23. Hernández, *Arquitectura doméstica*, 152; *El Tiempo*, 16 September 1885, 23 January 1884; Morales and Caballero, *El Señor Root en México*, 61, 80, 107; Gene Yeager, "Porfirian Commercial Propaganda: Mexico in the World of Industrial Expositions"; Beezley, *Judas at the Jockey Club*, 7.

24. Cited in Krauze, *Porfirio Díaz*, 118–119.

25. Morales and Caballero, *El Señor Root en México*, 90–91; Torres Torija, "Ciudad de México," 61–62, 75–77; González Peña, *La fuga*, 130; Sáenz, *México íntegro*, 240; Ramos, *El perfil del hombre*, 76.

26. *La Gaceta Comercial*, 10 April 1900.

27. Jorge Vera Estañol, "Discurso inaugural," 5; José López-Portillo y Rojas, *Elevación y caída de Porfirio Díaz*, 351.

28. Rohlfes, "Police and Penal Correction in Mexico City," 51; Beals, *Porfirio Díaz*, 289–291; López-Portillo y Rojas, *Elevación y caída*, 259–260; William Prescott, *History of the Conquest of Mexico*, 45–47.

29. José Valadés, *El porfirismo: historia de un régimen, el crecimiento*, vol. 1, 23–24, 34–36; Beals, *Porfirio Díaz*, 289; Krauze, *Porfirio Díaz*, 43–45; López-Portillo y Rojas, *Elevación y caída*, 327.

30. Emilio Rabasa, *La evolución histórica de México*, 101; Krauze, *Porfirio Díaz*, 35–37, 89–90.

31. *El Tiempo*, 4 January 1900; Vera Estañol, "Discurso inaugural," 5; Sierra, *La evolución política*, 396; Bulnes as cited in Krauze, *Porfirio Díaz*, 93.

32. Cited in Beals, *Porfirio Díaz*, 181.

33. Miguel Macedo, "El municipio," vol. 1, 684; *El Tiempo*, 1 February 1884,

6 December 1884, 17 December 1884, 23 December 1884, 22 December 1885, 21 December 1887, 10 March 1888, 17 July 1890, 19 July 1890.

34. Cited in Ricardo García Granado, *Historia de México*, vol. 1, 231–232.

35. Mexico, Consejo Superior de Gobierno de Distrito, "Policía, 1903–1910"; idem, "Salubridad e higiene, 1903–1907"; idem, *Memoria 1907*; Vera Estañol, "Discurso inaugural," 5.

36. *El Tiempo*, 17 June 1886, 27 October 1900; Macedo, "El municipio," 684–688.

37. *El Tiempo*, 13 July 1883, 8 November 1884, 30 July 1887, 5 February 1895, 4 January 1900, 21 July 1883, 3 August 1883, 30 August 1883, 30 August 1884, 17 December 1884, 23 December 1884, 21 January 1886, 30 July 1887, 5 February 1895, 4 January 1900, 10 August 1887, 27 May 1889, 25 January 1884, 4 December 1886, 26 August 1891, 1 February 1884.

38. B. W. Aston, "The Public Career of Don José Ives Limantour," 54, 65–66; Luis Lara y Pardo, *De Porfirio Díaz a Francisco Madero*, 38–52; Salvador Quevedo y Zubieta, *El General González y su gobierno en México*, passim; Jiménez Muñoz, *La traza del poder*, 23–44, 63–65, 78–86, appendix; Beals, *Porfirio Díaz*, 328–338.

39. *Siglo Diez y Nueve*, 20 September 1888, 30 September 1888; *El Tiempo*, 18 July 1884, 26 July 1884; *Diario del Hogar*, 30 August 1885; Gruening, *Mexico and Its Heritage*, 55; Rohlfes, "Police and Penal Correction in Mexico City," 57, 136–137, 151; Héctor Díaz Zermeno, "La escuela nacional"; Mexico, Consejo Superior de Gobierno de Distrito, "Rastros y Mercados, 1903–1914."

40. Rohlfes, "Police and Penal Correction in Mexico City," 127–128; Guerrero, *La génesis del crimen*, 381.

41. Aeschylus, "The Eumenides," 153; as reported by *La Patria de México* and cited in Rohlfes, "Police and Penal Correction in Mexico City," 68; *El Tiempo*, 11 January 1884.

42. Creelman, "President Díaz," 235.

43. Cited in Roeder, *Hacia el México moderno*, vol. 2, 24–25.

44. Macedo, "El municipio," 686.

45. Rabasa, *La evolución histórica de México*, 114–115; Beals, *Porfirio Díaz*, 315–342; Bulnes, *El verdadero Díaz y la Revolución*, 164–169; Alan Knight, *The Mexican Revolution*, 1–36.

46. López-Portillo y Rojas, *Elevación y caída*, 262; William Raat, "Positivism in Díaz's Mexico, 1876–1910: An Essay in Intellectual History," 26, 198–199; Aston, "The Public Career," 54, 65–66; Beals, *Porfirio Díaz*, 328–337; Hale, *The Transformation of Liberalism*, 137; Jiménez Muñoz, *La traza del poder*, 23–44, 63–65, 78–86, appendix; Leopoldo Zea, *Apogeo y decadencia del positivismo en México*, 210; López-Portillo y Rojas, *Elevación y caída*, 273–275.

47. Cited in Hale, *The Transformation of Liberalism*, 34.

48. Ibid., 27; *El Tiempo*, 10 August 1883, 16 January 1884; see also Zea, *Apogeo y decadencia del positivismo*, 96–97, 213; Sierra, *La evolución política*, 383–399; Krauze, *Porfirio Díaz*, 89–90.

49. Ceballos Ramírez, "La encíclica," 17, 27; Raat, "Positivism in Díaz's Mexico," 96, 242; Aston, "The Public Career," 66; Beals, *Porfirio Díaz*, 337–338.

50. Rabasa, *El cuarto poder*, 23.

51. *El Tiempo*, 14 March 1886, 19 March 1886, 27 July 1887, 9 July 1895; Beals, *Porfirio Díaz*, 295.

52. Rohlfes, "Police and Penal Correction in Mexico City," 207.

53. Cited in Roeder, *Hacia el México moderno: Porfirio Díaz*, vol. 2, 38–39.

54. López-Portillo y Rojas, *Elevación y caída,* 330; Valadés, *El porfirismo*, vol. 1, 35–36; Krauze, *Porfirio Díaz*, 51.

BIBLIOGRAPHY

PRIMARY SOURCES

Newspapers
El Tiempo, 1883–1910.
Siglo Diez y Nueve, 1887–1900.

Archives
Archivo General de la Nación, Mexico City
Archivo Histórico del ex-Ayuntamiento, Mexico City
Bancroft Library, University of California–Berkeley
Hermeroteca Nacional, Mexico City

SECONDARY SOURCES

Aeschylus. "The Eumenides." In David Greene and Richmond Lattimore, eds., *The Complete Greek Tragedies: Aeschylus*. Chicago: University of Chicago Press, 1992.
Aguilar, Gustavo. *Los presupuestos mexicanos*. Mexico City, 1940.
Anderson, Rodney. *Outcasts in Their Own Land: Mexican Industrial Workers, 1906–1911*. DeKalb: Northern Illinois University Press, 1976.
Aristotle. *Politics*. London: Penguin, 1981.
Aston, B. W. "The Public Career of Don José Ives Limantour." Ph.D. dissertation, Texas Tech University, 1972.
Ballou, Martin. *Aztec Land*. Boston: Houghton Mifflin, 1890.
Bancroft, Hubert. *History of Mexico*. New York: Bancroft Co., 1914.
Bárbara Lavalle, Francisco. *Los bancos mexicanos hasta 1910*. Mexico City: Siglo XX, 1919.
Barton, Mary. *Impressions of Mexico*. London: Methuen, 1911.
Baz, Gustavo. *Un año en México*. Mexico City: Dublán, 1887.
Bazant, Jan. *Los bienes de la iglesia en México*. Mexico City: Colegio de México, 1971.
Beals, Carleton. *Mexico: An Interpretation*. New York: B. W. Huebsch, 1923.
——— . *Porfirio Díaz: Dictator of Mexico*. London: Lippincott, 1932.
Beezley, William. *Judas at the Jockey Club*. Lincoln: University of Nebraska Press, 1987.
Benítez, Fernando. *La Ciudad de México*. 3 vols. Mexico City: Salvat, 1981.
Berdecio, Roberto, and Stanley Appelbaum. *Posada's Popular Mexican Prints*. Toronto: Dover, 1972.
Beteta, Ramón. *Járano*. Mexico City: Fondo de Cultura Económica, 1966 [1920].
——— . *La mendicidad en México*. Mexico City: 1930.
Blake, Mary, and Margaret Sullivan. *Mexico: Picturesque, Political, Progressive*. Boston: Lee and Shepard, 1888.
Blichfeldt, E. H. *A Mexican Journey*. New York: Cromwell, 1912.

Brenner, Anita. *The Wind That Swept Mexico*. Austin: University of Texas Press, 1971.

Bribiesca, Juan. *Memoria documentada*. Mexico City, 1898.

Brocklehurst, Thomas. *Mexico To-day: Country with a Great Future*. London: John Murray, 1883.

Bryan, Susan. "Teatro popular y sociedad durante el porfiriato." *Historia Mexicana* 33, no. 129 (1983): 131–169.

Bulnes, Francisco. *El verdadero Díaz y la Revolución*. Mexico City: Editorial Rosebero Gómez de la Fuente, 1920.

———. *The Whole Truth about Mexico*. New York, 1916.

Calderón de la Barca, Fanny. *Life in Mexico during a Residence of Two Years in That Country*. New York: E. P. Dutton, 1937 [1843].

Campos, Rubén M. *El folklore literario de México*. Mexico City: Talleres Gráficos de la Nación, 1921.

Cardoso, C. F. S. *Formación y desarrollo de la burguesía en México, siglo XIX*. Mexico City: Siglo XXI, 1978.

Carmagnani, Marcello. "El liberalismo, los impuestos internos y el estado federal mexicano, 1857–1911." *Historia Mexicana* 38, no. 3 (1989): 471–496.

Carter, Boyd. *En torno a Gutiérrez Nájera*. Mexico City: Ediciones Botas, 1960.

Casasola, Gustavo. *Biografía ilustrada del General Porfirio Díaz*. Mexico City: Ediciones G. C., 1970.

———. *Historia gráfica de la Revolución mexicana*. 5 vols. Mexico City, 1967.

———. *Seis siglos de historia gráfica de México*. 3 vols. Mexico City, 1966.

Castillo, Ricardo. *Teatro nacional*. Mexico City: Editorial Mundial, 1912.

Castillo Méndez, Laura Elena. *Historia del comercio en la Ciudad de México*. Mexico City: Colección Popular, 1973.

Ceballos Ramírez, Manuel. "La encíclica rerum novarum y los trabajadores católicos en la Ciudad de México (1891–1913)." *Historia Mexicana* 33, no. 1 (1983): 3–38.

Colegio de México. *Fuerza de trabajo*. Mexico City, 1956.

Contreras, Mario, and Jesús Tamayo. *México en el siglo XX, 1900–1913*. Mexico City: UNAM, 1975.

Cosío Villegas, Daniel. *El porfiriato, vida económica: historia moderna de México*. Mexico City: Editorial Hermes, 1957.

Cossio, José. "Algunas noticias sobre las colonias de esta capital." *Boletín de la Sociedad Mexicana de Geografía y Estadística* 47, no. 1 (September 1937): 5–41.

Creelman, James. "President Díaz: Hero of the Americas." *Pearson's Magazine* 19, no. 3 (March 1908).

Curtis, William. *The Capitals of Spanish America*. New York: Harper and Brothers, 1888.

de Campo, Ángel. "El pinto." In *Ocios y apuntes*, 35–42. Mexico City: Porrúa, 1993 [1890].

———. *La rumba*. Mexico City: Porrúa, 1958 [1891].

del Carmen Collado, María. *La burguesía mexicana: el emporio Braniff y su participación política*. Mexico City: Siglo XXI, 1987.

Delgado, Rafael. *Los parientes ricos*. Mexico City: Porrúa, 1988 [1902].

de Murga, Gonzalo. "Atisbos sociológicos. El fraccionamiento de tierras. Las habitaciones baratas." *Boletín de la Sociedad de Geografía y Estadística de la República Mexicana,* quinta época, vol. 6 (1913).

de Zorita, Alonzo. *Life and Labor in Ancient Mexico: The "Brief and Summary Relation of the Lords of New Spain."* New Brunswick: Rutgers University Press, 1963.

Díaz de León, D. Jesús. "Concepto del indianismo en México." *Concurso Científico y Artístico del Centenario.* Mexico City: La Viuda de F. Díaz de León, 1911.

Díaz Zermeno, Héctor. "La Escuela Nacional Primaria en la Ciudad de México — 1876–1910." *Historia Mexicana* 28 (1979): 59–90.

Dizikes, John. *Opera in America: A Cultural History.* New Haven: Yale University Press, 1993.

Dollero, Adolfo. *México al día.* Mexico City, 1911.

Esquivel Obregón, T. "La influencia de España y Estados Unidos sobre México." Madrid: Casa Editorial Calleja, 1918.

Flandrau, Charles. *Viva Mexico!* London: Eland Books, 1982 [1908].

Flippin, J. R. *Sketches from the Mountains of Mexico.* Cincinnati, 1889.

Frías, Heriberto. *Los piratas del boulevard.* Mexico City, n.d.

Galindo y Villa, Jesús. *La Ciudad de México.* Mexico City, 1901.

———. *Reseña histórico-descriptiva de la Ciudad de México.* Mexico City: Imprenta Díaz de León, 1901.

Gamboa, Federico. *Santa.* Mexico City: Ediciones Botas, 1960 [1903].

———. *Suprema ley.* Mexico City: Editorial Hispano, 1920 [1896].

García, Genaro. *Crónica oficial de las fiestas del primer centenario de la independencia de México.* Mexico City: Talleres Gráficos de la Nación, 1911.

García Cubas, Antonio. *El libro de mis recuerdos.* Mexico City, 1904.

García Granado, Ricardo. *Historia de México.* 2 vols. Mexico City: Editorial Jus, 1956.

Garza Villarreal, G. *El proceso de industrialización en la Ciudad de México.* Mexico City: Colegio de México, 1985.

Gibbon, Edward. *The History of the Decline and Fall of the Roman Empire.* 3 vols. New York: Heritage Press, 1946 [1776].

Gillpatrick, Wallace. *The Man Who Likes Mexico.* New York: Century, 1911.

Goad, Charles E. *Map of Mexico City.* London, 1897.

Gómez-Quiñones, Juan. "Social Change and Intellectual Discontent: The Growth of Mexican Nationalism, 1890–1911." Ph.D. dissertation, UCLA, 1972.

González Navarro, Moisés. *Las huelgas textiles en el porfiriato.* Puebla: Editorial Cajica, 1970.

———. "México en una laguna." *Historia Mexicana* 4, no. 4 (1955): 506–522.

———. *La pobreza en México.* Mexico City: Colegio de México, 1985.

———. *La vida social: el porfiriato. Historia moderna de México.* Mexico City: Editorial Hermes, 1957.

González Peña, Carlos. *La chiquilla.* Valencia: Sempere, 1906.

———. *La fuga de la quimera.* Madrid: Editorial-América, 1915.

González Pineda, Francisco. *El mexicano.* Mexico City: Pax-Mexicana, 1961.

Gooch, Fanny. *Face to Face with the Mexicans.* Carbondale: Southern Illinois University Press, 1966 [1887].

Gray, Albert. *Mexico As It Is*. New York: Dutton, 1869.

Gruening, Ernest. *Mexico and Its Heritage*. New York: Century, 1928.

Guerrero, Julio. *La génesis del crimen en México*. Mexico City: Librería de la Viuda de Ch. Bouret, 1901.

Gutiérrez Nájera, Manuel. "A la corregidora." In José Emilio Pacheco, ed., *Antología del modernismo (1884–1921)*, 26–27. Mexico City: UNAM, 1970.

———. *Cuentos completos*. Mexico City: Fondo de Cultura Económica, 1958.

———. *Obras III*. Mexico City: UNAM, 1974.

———. *Obras IV*. Mexico City: UNAM, 1984.

———. *Poesías completas*. Mexico City: Porrúa, 1953.

Guzmán, Martín Luis. *The Eagle and the Serpent*. New York: Knopf, 1930.

Haber, Stephen. *Industry and Underdevelopment: The Industrialization of Mexico, 1890–1940*. Stanford: Stanford University Press, 1989.

Hale, Charles. *The Transformation of Liberalism in Late Nineteenth Century Mexico*. Princeton: Princeton University Press, 1989.

Hernández, Vicente. *Arquitectura doméstica de la Ciudad de México (1890–1925)*. Mexico City: UNAM, 1981.

Hernández Chávez, Alicia. "Origen y ocaso del ejército porfiriano." *Historia Mexicana* 19, no. 1 (1989): 256–296.

Herrera Canales, Inés. "La circulación." In Ciro Cardoso, ed., *México en el Siglo XIX*, 437–464. Mexico City: Nueva Imagen, 1990.

Hoeck, F. *The Mexico City Guide*. Mexico City, 1894.

Islas y Bustamante, Nicolás. *Cuadros de mortalidad*. Mexico City, 1892.

James, Henry. *The American Scene*. New York: Harper and Brothers, 1907.

Jiménez Muñoz, Jorge H. *La traza del poder*. Mexico City: Codex, 1993.

Kandell, Jonathan. *La Capital*. New York: Random House, 1988.

Katz, Friedrich. "The Liberal Republic and the Porfiriato, 1867–1910." In Leslie Bethell, ed., *Mexico since Independence*, 49–124. Cambridge: Cambridge University Press, 1991.

King, Rosa. *Tempest over Mexico*. Boston: Little, Brown, 1935.

Kirkham, Stanton Davis. *Mexican Trails*. New York: Knickerbocker Press, 1911.

Knight, Alan. *The Mexican Revolution*. Lincoln: University of Nebraska Press, 1986.

Kollonitz, Paula. *The Court of Mexico*. London: Saunders, Otley, 1867.

Krauze, Enrique. *Porfirio Díaz: místico de la autoridad*. Mexico City: Fondo de Cultura Económica, 1987.

———. *Siglo de caudillos: Biografía política de México (1810–1910)*. Mexico City: TusQuets, 1994.

Krauze, Enrique, and Fausto Zerón-Medina. *Porfirio: el poder*. Mexico City: Clio, 1993.

Lafaye, J. *Quetzalcóatl y Guadalupe*. Mexico City: Fondo de Cultura Económica, 1977.

Lara y Pardo, Luis. *De Porfirio Díaz a Francisco Madero*. New York: Polyglot, 1912.

———. *La prostitución en México*. Mexico City, 1908.

Lawrence, D. H. *Mornings in Mexico*. New York: Knopf, 1927.

———. *The Plumed Serpent (Quetzalcoatl)*. Cambridge: Cambridge University Press, 1987 [1926].

Leal, Juan Felipe. *La burguesía y el estado mexicano.* Mexico City: El Caballito, 1972.

Leal, Juan Felipe, and Mario Huacuja Roundtree. *Economía y sistema de haciendas en México: la hacienda pulquera.* Mexico City: ERA, 1978.

Lear, John. "Workers, Vecinos and Citizens: The Revolution in Mexico City, 1909–1917." Ph.D. dissertation, University of California–Berkeley, 1993.

Limantour, José Yves. *Discurso pronunciado en la ceremonia de clausura del Concurso Científico Nacional.* Mexico City: Tipografía de la Oficina Impresora del Timbre, 1901.

López Monjardín, Adriana. *Hacia la ciudad del capital, 1790–1870.* Mexico City: INAH, 1985.

López-Portillo y Rojas, José. *Elevación y caída de Porfirio Díaz.* Mexico City: Lib. Española, 1921.

———. *La parcela.* Mexico City: Porrúa, 1961 [1898].

López Rosado, Diego. *Los servicios públicos de la Ciudad de México.* Mexico City: Porrúa, 1976.

Lummis, Charles. *The Awakening of a Nation.* New York: Harper and Brothers, 1898.

Lynch, John. *The Spanish American Revolutions, 1808–1826.* New York: Norton, 1986.

Macedo, Miguel. *La criminalidad en México.* Mexico City: Oficina Tipografía de la Secretaría de Fomento, 1897.

———. *Mi barrio.* Mexico City, 1930.

———. "El municipio." In Justo Sierra, ed., *México, su evolución social,* 665–690. Mexico City: J. Ballesca, 1901.

Marroquín, José María. *La Ciudad de México.* Mexico City, 1900, vols. 1, 2.

———. *La Ciudad de México.* Mexico City, 1903, vol. 3.

Marroquín y Rivera, Manuel. *Memoria descriptiva de las Obras de Provisión de Aguas Potables.* Mexico City: Muller y Hnos., 1914.

———. *Proyecto de abastecimiento y distribución de agua potable.* Mexico City, 1901.

Martin, Percy. *Mexico of the Twentieth Century.* London: Edward Arnold, 1907.

Mason, R. H. *Pictures of Life in Mexico.* 2 vols. London: Smith and Elder, 1851.

McCaleb, Walter. *Present and Past Banking in Mexico.* New York: Harper and Brothers, 1920.

McCary, Elizabeth Visere. *An American Girl in Mexico.* New York: Dodd, Mead, 1904.

Mexico. *Boletín mensual de Estadística del Distrito Federal.* Mexico City, 1901–1913.

———. *Boletín oficial del Consejo Superior de Gobierno de Distrito,* vol. 19, no. 45 (1912).

———. *Discurso por el C. Gral. Manuel González Cosío.* Mexico City, 1889.

———. *Discurso por el C. Gral. Manuel González Cosío.* Mexico City, 1891.

———. *Discurso por el C. Pedro Rincón Gallardo.* Mexico City, 1884.

———. *Discurso por el C. Pedro Rincón Gallardo.* Mexico City, 1886.

———. *Estadísticas económicas del porfiriato: Comercio exterior de México, 1877–1911.* Mexico City, 1960.

———. *Estadísticas sociales del porfiriato.* Mexico City, 1956.

———. *Guía general descriptiva de la República mexicana.* Mexico City, 1899.

———. *Memoria (José Ceballos, Gobernador).* Mexico City: Ed. Dublán, 1888.

————. *Memoria que el Ayuntamiento Constitucional de 1879 presente a sus comitentes.* Mexico City, 1880.

Mexico. Ayuntamiento Constitucional. "Inundaciones, 1880–1903." No. 2275 in Archivo Histórico del ex-Ayuntamiento, Mexico City.

————. *Reglamento para corridas de toros.* Mexico City: F. Díaz de León, 1888.

Mexico. Consejo Superior de Gobierno de Distrito. "Inspectores sanitarios de los cuarteles de la capital." In Mexico, *Memoria, 1907.* Mexico City, 1908.

————. *Memoria, 1907.* Mexico City, 1908.

————. "Policía 1903–1910." No. 617 in the Archivo Histórico del ex-Ayuntamiento, Mexico City.

————. "Salubridad e higiene, 1903–1907." In the Archivo Histórico del ex-Ayuntamiento, Mexico City.

Mexico. Consejo Superior de Gobierno de Distrito. "Colonias." Nos. 519–520 in the Archivo Histórico del ex-Ayuntamiento, Mexico City.

————. "Informe de la Comisión de Obras Públicas y de Ríos y Acequias."

————. "Informes de la Administración de Rastros y Mercados, 1903–1914." No. 608 in the Archivo Histórico del ex-Ayuntamiento, Mexico City.

————. "Proyecto de reglamento de la inscripción sanitaria de mujeres públicas de la Ciudad de México; Policía, 1903–1910." No. 617 in the Archivo Histórico del ex-Ayuntamiento, Mexico City.

————. "Pulquerías, 1901." No. 1769 in the Archivo Histórico del ex-Ayuntamiento, Mexico City.

Mexico. Dirección General de Estadística. *Anuario estadístico de la República mexicana 1896.* Mexico City, 1897.

————. *Anuario estadístico de la República mexicana 1902.* Mexico City, 1903.

————. *Anuario estadístico de la República mexicana 1907.* Mexico City, 1912.

————. *Estadísticas sociales del porfiriato.* Mexico City, 1956.

Mexico. Gobierno de Distrito Federal. "Limpia 1909–1911." No. 1723 in the Archivo Histórico del ex-Ayuntamiento, Mexico City.

Mexico. Junta Directiva del Saneamiento de la Ciudad de México. No. 4720 in the Archivo Histórico del ex-Ayuntamiento, Mexico City.

Mexico. Ministerio de Gobernación. *Inauguración del monumento a Juárez.* Mexico City, 1910.

Mexico. Ministerio de Hacienda. *Mexican Year Book.* London: McCorquodale, 1908.

Mexico. Secretaría del Ayuntamiento Constitucional. "Obras públicas, 1901." No. 1504a in the Archivo Histórico del ex-Ayuntamiento, Mexico City.

————. "Plaza Mayor, 1908." In the Archivo Histórico del ex-Ayuntamiento, Mexico City.

Molina Enríquez, Andrés. *Los grandes problemas nacionales.* Mexico City: Carranza, 1909.

Morales, María Dolores. "La expansión de la ciudad de México en el siglo XIX: el caso de los fraccionamientos." In Alejandra Moreno Toscano, ed., *Ciudad de México: ensayo de construcción,* 191–198. Mexico City: UNAM, 1978.

———. "Francisco Somero y el primer fraccionamiento de la Ciudad de México, 1840–1889." In Ciro Cardoso, ed., *Formación y desarrollo de la burguesía en México, siglo XIX*, 188–230. Mexico City: Siglo XXI, 1978.

———. *Investigaciones sobre la historia de la Ciudad de México*. Mexico City: UNAM, 1978.

Morales, Vicente, and Manuel Caballero. *El Señor Root en México*. Mexico City: Talleres de Imprenta 'Artes y Letras,' 1908.

Moreno Toscano, Alejandra. *Ciudad de México: ensayo de construcción*. Mexico City: UNAM, 1978.

Novo, Salvador. *La Ciudad de México en 1873*. Mexico City: Porrúa, 1973.

———. *México*. Barcelona: Ediciones Destino, 1968.

Núñez y Domínguez, José. "Los Judas en México." *Mexican Folkways* 5, no. 2 (1929): 90–104.

O. L. "Holy Week in Mexico." *Lippincott's Magazine* 57 (1896): 522–526.

O'Shaughnessy, Edith. *Diplomatic Days*. New York: Harper and Brothers, 1911.

Pacheco, Carlos. *Map of the City of Mexico*. Mexico City: Ministry of Public Works, 1885.

Pacheco, José Emilio. *Antología del modernismo (1884–1921)*. 2 vols. Mexico City: UNAM, 1970.

Palavicini, Félix. *¡Castigo!* Mexico City, 1926.

Pani, Alberto. *Hygiene in Mexico: A Study of Sanitary and Educational Problems*. New York: G. P. Putnam's Sons, 1917.

Pasquel, Leonardo. *La alameda central*. Mexico City, 1980.

Payno, Manuel. *Los bandidos de Río Frío*. Mexico City: Porrúa, 1991 [1891].

Paz, Octavio. *El laberinto de la soledad*. Mexico City: Fondo de Cultura Económica, 1993 [1950].

Perry, Laurens Ballard. *Juárez and Díaz*. DeKalb: Northern Illinois University Press, 1978.

Phillips, Rachel. "Mansa/Malinche: Masks and Shadows." In Beth Miller, ed., *Women in Hispanic Literature: Icons and Fallen Idols*. Berkeley & Los Angeles: University of California Press, 1983.

Powell, Fred. *The Railroads of Mexico*. Boston: Stratford, 1921.

Prescott, William. *History of the Conquest of Mexico*. New York: A. L. Burt, [1843].

Prieto, Guillermo. *Memorias de mis tiempos, 1828–1853*. Mexico City: Editorial Patria, 1970.

Quevedo y Zubieta, Salvador. *La camada*. Mexico City: Librería Bouret, 1912.

———. *El General González y su gobierno en México*. Mexico City, 1884.

Raat, William. "Positivism in Díaz's Mexico, 1876–1910: An Essay in Intellectual History." Ph.D. dissertation, University of Utah, 1967.

Rabasa, Emilio. *El cuarto poder*. Mexico City: Porrúa, 1982 [1888].

———. *La evolución histórica de México*. Mexico City: Porrúa, 1956 [1921].

Ramos, Samuel. *El perfil del hombre y la cultura en México*. Mexico City: Editorial Pedro Robredo, 1938 [1934].

Reed, John. *Insurgent Mexico*. New York: International Publishers, 1988.

Reyes de la Maza, Luis. *Cien años de teatro en México*. Mexico City: Sep/Setentas, 1972.

Reyna, Carmen. "El trabajo en las panaderías." *Historia Mexicana* 31, no. 3 (1982): 431–448.

Rivas Mercado, Antonio. *Inauguración del monumento a la independencia*. Mexico City, 1910.

Rivera Cambas, Manuel. *México pintoresco, artístico y monumental*. 2 vols. Mexico City: Imprenta de la Reforma, 1880.

——. *México pintoresco, artístico y monumental*. 2 vols. Mexico City: Imprenta de la Reforma, 1882.

Roeder, Ralph. *Hacia el México moderno: Porfirio Díaz*. 2 vols. Mexico City: Fondo de Cultura Económica, 1973.

Rohlfes, Laurence. "Police and Penal Correction in Mexico City, 1876–1911: A Study of Order and Progress in Porfirian Mexico." Ph.D. dissertation, Tulane University, 1983.

Romero, José. *Guía de la Ciudad de México y demás municipalidades del Distrito Federal*. Mexico City: Porrúa, 1910.

——. *Guía general descriptiva de la República mexicana*. Mexico City, 1899.

Romero, M. *Geographical and Statistical Notes on Mexico*. Washington, D.C., 1898.

Rosenzweig, Fernando. "El desarrollo económico de México de 1877 a 1911." *Trimestre Económico* 32, nos. 3–4 (1965): 405–454.

Roumagnac, Carlos. *Los criminales en México*. Mexico City: Tipografía "El Fénix," 1905.

Ruhland, Emile. *Directorio general de la Ciudad de México*. Mexico City: J. F. Jens, 1890.

——. *Directorio general de la Ciudad de México*. Mexico City: J. F. Jens, 1897.

Sáenz, Moisés. *México íntegro*. Mexico City: Imprenta Torres Aguirre, 1939.

Sáenz, Moisés, and Herbert Priestly. *Some Mexican Problems*. Chicago: University of Chicago Press, 1926.

Salazar, Luis. *La arquitectura y la arqueología*. Mexico City, 1897.

Sanborn Map Company. *Insurance Maps of City of Mexico*. New York, 1905.

Sánchez Santos, Trinidad. *La ciudad de dolor*. Mexico City, 1903.

Santini, Pedro. "La policía de la Ciudad de México durante el porfiriato." *Historia Mexicana* 33, no. 1 (1983): 97–129.

Schopenhauer, Arthur. *Complete Essays of Schopenhauer*. New York: Wiley, 1942.

Sesto, Julio. *El México de Porfirio Díaz*. Valencia: Sempere, 1910.

Shaw, Frederick. "The Artisan in Mexico City, 1824–1853." In Elsa Frost et al., eds., *El trabajo y los trabajadores en la historia de México*, 399–418. Mexico City: Colegio de México, 1979.

Sierra, Justo. *La evolución política del pueblo mexicano*. Mexico City: UNAM, 1957 [1901].

——. *The Political Evolution of the Mexican People*. Austin: University of Texas Press, 1969 [1901].

Simmons, Merle. "Porfirio Díaz in Mexico's Historical Ballads." *New Mexico Historical Review* 31, no. 1 (1956): 1–23.

Starr, Frederick. *Catalogue of a Collection of Objects Illustrating the Folklore of Mexico.* Mexico City: Kraus, 1967 [1898].

Tablada, José Juan. *La feria de la vida (memorias).* Mexico City: Ediciones Botas, 1937.

Terry, T. Philip. *Terry's Mexico.* London, 1911.

Thompson, Wallace. *The Mexican Mind: A Study of National Psychology.* Boston: Little and Brown, 1922.

Toor, Frances. *Monografía: las obras de José Guadalupe Posada.* Mexico City, 1930.

Torres Torija, Manuel. "Ciudad de México." In Francisco Trentini, *El florecimiento de México.* Mexico City: Bouligny and Schmidt, 1906.

Tovar de Teresa, Guillermo. *La ciudad de los palacios: crónica de un patrimonio perdido.* Mexico City: Fundación Cultural Televisa, 1992.

Trentini, Francisco. *El florecimiento de México.* Mexico City: Bouligny and Schmidt, 1906.

Turner, Frederick. *The Dynamic of Mexican Nationalism.* Chapel Hill: University of North Carolina Press, 1968.

Turner, John Kenneth. *Barbarous Mexico.* Austin: University of Texas Press, 1990 [1910].

Tweedie, E. *Mexico As I Saw It.* London: Hurst and Blackett, 1901.

Tyler, Ron, ed. *Posada's Mexico.* Washington, D.C.: Library of Congress, 1979.

United States. *Report on Industry and Commerce in Mexico.* Washington, D.C., 1918.

Uranga, Emilio. *Análisis del ser de México.* Mexico City: Porrúa, 1952.

Urbina, Luis. *La vida literaria de México.* Madrid: Imprenta Sáenz Hermanos, 1917.

Valadés, José. *El porfirismo: Historia de un régimen, el crecimiento.* Vol. 1. Mexico City: Editorial Patria, 1948.

———. *El porfirismo: Historia de un régimen, el crecimiento.* Vol. 2. Mexico City: UNAM, 1987.

———. *El porfirismo: El nacimiento.* Mexico City: Porrúa, 1941.

Vanderwood, Paul. *Disorder and Progress: Bandits, Police, and Mexican Development.* Lincoln: University of Nebraska Press, 1981.

Vasconcelos, José. *La raza cósmica.* Barcelona, 1925.

Vásquez Mellado, Alfonso. *La ciudad de los palacios.* Mexico City: Editorial Diana, 1991.

Velasco Ceballos, Rómulo. *Las loterías.* Mexico City, 1934.

Vera Estañol, Jorge. "Discurso inaugural." In *Concurso Científico y Artístico del Centenario.* Mexico City, 1911.

von Humboldt, Alexander. *Political Essay on the Kingdom of New Spain.* Norman: University of Oklahoma Press, 1988 [1808].

Waugh, Evelyn. *Robbery under Law: The Mexican Object-Lesson.* London: Catholic Book Club, 1940.

Winter, Nevin. *Mexico and Her People Today.* Boston: L. C. Page, 1907.

Wolf, Eric. *Europe and the People without History.* Berkeley & Los Angeles: University of California Press, 1982.

———. "The Virgin of Guadalupe: A Mexican National Symbol." *Journal of American Folklore* 71 (1958): 34–39.

Wolfe, Bertram. *The Fabulous Life of Diego Rivera.* Chelsea, Mich.: Scarborough House, 1990.

Yáñez, Augustín. *Al filo del agua.* Mexico City: Porrúa, 1955.

Yeager, Gene. "Porfirian Commercial Propaganda: Mexico in the World of Industrial Expositions." *The Americas* 34, no. 2 (1977): 230–243.

Zea, Leopoldo. *Apogeo y decadencia del positivismo en México.* Mexico City: Colegio de México, 1964.

INDEX